DATE DUE

ESSENTIAL SUPREME COURT DECISIONS

Summaries of Leading Cases in U.S. Constitutional Law

Fifteenth Edition

JOHN R. VILE

ROWMAN & LITTLEFIELD PUBLISHERS, INC.
Lanham • Boulder • New York • Toronto • Plymouth, UK

Published by Rowman & Littlefield Publishers, Inc.
A wholly owned subsidary of The Rowman & Littlefield Publishing Group, Inc.
4501 Forbes Boulevard, Suite 200, Lanham, Maryland 20706
www.rowmanlittlefield.com

Estover Road, Plymouth PL6 7PY, United Kingdom

British Library Cataloguing in Publication Information Available

Library of Congress Cataloging-in-Publication Data

Vile, John R.
    Essential Supreme Court decisions : summaries of leading cases in U.S. constitutional
law / John R. Vile. — 15th ed.
        p. cm.
    Rev. ed. of: Summaries of leading cases on the Constitution / Joseph F. Menez and
John R. Vile. 14th ed. 2004.
    Includes bibliographical references and index.
    ISBN 978-1-4422-0384-6 (cloth : alk. paper) — ISBN 978-1-4422-0385-3 (pbk. : alk.
paper) — ISBN 978-1-4422-0386-0 (electronic)
    1. Constitutional law—United States—Digests. I. Menez, Joseph Francis, 1917–
Summaries of leading cases on the Constitution. II. Title.
    KF4547.4.V55 2010
    342.7300264—dc22   2010008375

Printed in the United States of America

Contents

Preface to the Fifteenth Edition   xxi

Acknowledgments   xxv

This Is Our Supreme Court   xxvii

1 Article I: The Legislative Branch   **1**
Powers   2
  Commerce   2
    Gibbons v. Ogden (1824)   2
    Brown v. Maryland (1827)   3
    Cooley v. Board of Wardens (1851)   4
    United States v. E. C. Knight Co. (1895)   5
    In re Debs (1895)   6
    Champion v. Ames (1903)   7
    The Shreveport Case (1914)   8
    Hammer v. Dagenhart (1918)   9
    Stafford v. Wallace (1922)   10
    Ashwander v. Tennessee Valley Authority (1936)   11
    Kentucky Whip and Collar Co. v. Illinois
      Central R.R. Co. (1937)   12
    West Coast Hotel Co. v. Parrish (1937)   13
    [*United States v. Carolene Products*
      Company (1938)]*
    [*United States v. F. W. Darby Lumber Co.* (1941)]
    Wickard v. Filburn (1942)   14

---

* Brackets denote related cases found in other chapters of this book.

United States v. Southeastern Underwriters
    Association (1944)   15
Heart of Atlanta Motel, Inc. v. United States (1964)   16
United States v. Lopez (1995)   17
Jones v. United States (2000)   18
[*United States v. Morrison* (2000)]
Gonzales v. Raich (2005)   19

Delegation of Powers   21
J.W. Hampton, Jr. & Co. v. United States (1928)   21
Panama Refining Co. v. Ryan (1935)   22
Schechter Poultry Corp. v. United States (1935)   23
United States v. Curtiss-Wright Export Corp. (1936)   24
Yakus v. United States (1944)   25
Mistretta v. United States (1989)   26

Implied Powers   28
McCulloch v. Maryland (1819)   28
McGrain v. Daugherty (1927)   29
Watkins v. United States (1957)   29
Barenblatt v. United States (1959)   30

Taxing/Spending and Regulatory Powers   31
Hylton v. United States (1796)   31
Veazie Bank v. Fenno (1869)   32
Collector v. Day (1871)   33
Legal Tender Cases (1871)   34
Pollock v. Farmers' Loan and Trust Co. (1895) 35
Northern Securities Co. v. United States (1904)   37
McCray v. United States (1904)   38
South Carolina v. United States (1905) 38
Swift and Co. v. United States (1905)   39
Standard Oil Co. of New Jersey v. United States
    (1910)   40
Bailey v. Drexel Furniture Co. (1922)   41
United States v. Butler (1936)   42
Steward Machine Co. v. Davis (1937)   42
*National Labor Relations Board v. Jones & Laughlin
    Steel Corporation* (1937)   43
Helvering v. Davis (1937)   45
Graves v. New York ex rel. O'Keefe (1939)   45
Mulford v. Smith (1939)   47

National Labor Relations Board v. Yeshiva University
(1980)   48
NCAA v. Board of Regents of University of Oklahoma
(1984)   48
South Dakota v. Dole (1987)   49
Eldred v. Ashcroft (2003)   50

Privileges and Terms of Members   51
Powell v. McCormack (1969)   51
Gravel v. United States (1972)   52
U.S. Term Limits, Inc. v. Thornton (1995)   53

2   Article II: The Executive Branch   57
Powers   58
Martin v. Mott (1827)   58
Ex parte Merryman (1861)   59
Mississippi v. Johnson (1867)   60
In re Neagle (1890)   61
Myers v. United States (1926)   62
Ex parte Grossman (1925)   63
Rathbun, Humphrey's Executor v. United States (1935)   64
Youngstown Sheet & Tube Co. v. Sawyer (1952)   65
Dames and Moore v. Regan (1981)   66
Haig v. Agee (1981)   67

Privileges and Limitations   68
United States v. Nixon (1974)   68
Nixon v. Fitzgerald (1982)   69
Clinton v. Jones (1997)   70

3   Articles I and II: Distinct Yet Overlapping Powers   73
Separation of Powers Issues   74
United States v. Lovett (1946)   74
Immigration and Naturalization Service v.
    Chadha (1983)   75
Bowsher v. Snyar (1986)   77
Morrison v. Olson (1988)   78
Clinton v. City of New York (1998)   79

Treaties and Executive Agreements   80
Head Money Cases (1884)   80
Missouri v. Holland (1920)   81

United States v. Belmont (1937)   82
Goldwater v. Carter (1979)   83

War-Making Powers   84
The Prize Cases (1863)   84
Ex parte Milligan (1866)   85
Selective Draft Law Cases (1918)   86
Hamilton v. Kentucky Distilleries &
    Warehouse Co. (1919)   87
Ex parte Quirin (1942)   88
Korematsu v. United States (1944)   89
Duncan v. Kahanamoku (1946)   90
Woods v. Cloyd W. Miller Co. (1948)   90
Johnson v. Eisentrager (1950)   91
[*Youngstown Sheet & Tube Co. v. Sawyer* (1952)]
Rostker v. Goldberg (1981)   93
Hamdi v. Rumsfeld (2004)   93
Rasul v. Bush (2004)   95
Hamdan v. Rumsfeld (2006)   97
Boudmediene v. Bush (2008)   100

4   Article III: The Judicial Branch   103
Judicial Jurisdiction and Standing   105
Marbury v. Madison (1803)   105
Martin v. Hunter's Lessee (1816)   106
Cohens v. Virginia (1821)   107
Eakin v. Raub (1825)   108
Ableman v. Booth (1859)   109
Ex parte McCardle (1869)   110
Commonwealth of Massachussetts v. Mellon (Frothingham
    v. Mellon) (1923)   111
Erie Railroad Co. v. Tompkins (1938)   112
Cooper v. Aaron (1958)   113
Flast v. Cohen (1968)   114
Stone v. Powell (1976)   115
Missouri v. Jenkins (1990)   116
Elk Grove v. Newdow (2004)   118

Political Questions Doctrine   119
Luther v. Borden (1849)   119
Muskrat v. United States (1911)   120
[*Coleman v. Miller* (1939)]

Baker v. Carr (1962)   121
|*Powell v. McCormack* (1969)|
Nixon v. United States (1993)   123

5 Articles IV and VI: Federalism   **125**
Eleventh Amendment and Sovereign Immunity of States   127
Hans v. Louisiana (1890)   127
Monaco v. Mississippi (1934)   128
Alden v. Maine (1999)   128
Kimel v. Florida Board of Regents (2000)   130
*University of Alabama Board of Trustees v.
Garrett* (2001)   131
*Lapides v. Board of Regents of University of
Georgia* (2002)   132
*Federal Maritime Commission v. South Carolina State
Ports Authority* (2002)   133

Federal Preemption   134
Southern Pacific Co. v. Arizona (1945)   134
Pennsylvania v. Nelson (1956)   135
Sprietsman v. Mercury Marine (2002)   136

Judicial Jurisdiction over States   137
Chisholm v. Georgia (1793)   137
|*Cohens v. Virginia* (1821)|
Cherokee Nation v. Georgia (1831)   138
Worcester v. Georgia (1832)   139
Puerto Rico v. Branstad (1987)   140

Limits on the States   141
|*McCulloch v. Maryland* (1819)|
Leisy v. Hardin (1890)   141
Virginia v. Tennessee (1893)   142
Edwards v. California (1941)   143
*Camps Newfound/Owatonna v. Town of
Harrison* (1997)   143
Crosby v. National Foreign Trade Council (2000)   145
Cook v. Gralike (2001)   146
Smith v. Doe (2003)   147
|*Gonzales v. Raich* (2005)|

Limits on Federal Regulation of States   148
New York v. United States (1992)   148

[*United States v. Lopez* (1995)]
Printz v. United States, Mack v. United States
   (1997)   150
United States v. Morrison (2000)   151

Status of the States   153
   Texas v. White (1869)   153
   [*Slaughterhouse Cases* (1873)]
   Coyle v. Smith (1911)   154
   Ziffrin v. Reeves (1939)   155

Tenth Amendment and State Police Powers   156
   United States v. F. W. Darby Lumber Co. (1941)   156
   National League of Cities v. Usery (1976)   157
   Equal Employment Opportunity Commission v. Wyoming
      (1983)   158
   Garcia v. San Antonio Metropolitan Transit
      Authority (1985)   159

**6   Articles V and VII: Constitutional Amending Process and
      Ratification of the Constitution**   **161**
The Amending Process   162
   Hollingsworth v. Virginia (1798)   162
   National Prohibition Cases (1920)   163
   Hawke v. Smith (1920)   164
   Dillon v. Gloss (1921)   165
   Coleman v. Miller (1939)   166

7   Property Rights   **169**
Contract Clause (Article 1, Section 10)   171
   Calder v. Bull (1798)   171
   Fletcher v. Peck (1810)   171
   Trustees of Dartmouth College v. Woodward (1819)   172
   Charles River Bridge Co. v. Warren River Bridge
      (1837)   173
   Stone v. Mississippi (1880)   174
   Home Building and Loan Association v. Blaisdell
      (1934)   175
   United States Trust Co. v. New Jersey (1977)   176

Due Process (Economic) and Freedom of Contract (Fifth and
   Fourteenth Amendments)   177
   Slaughterhouse Cases (1873)   177
   Munn v. Illinois (1877)   178

Santa Clara County v. Southern Pacific Railroad Company
(1886) 180
Holden v. Hardy (1898) 180
Lochner v. New Yok (1905) 181
Muller v. Oregon (1908) 182
Bunting v. Oregon (1917) 183
Adkins v. Children's Hospital (1923) 184
Nebbia v. New York (1934) 185
Morehead v. New York ex rel. Tipaldo (1936) 186
[*West Coast Hotel Co. v. Parrish* (1937)]
*Lincoln Federal Labor Union No. 19129 v. Northwestern
Iron and Metal Co.* (1949) 187
Giboney v. Empire Storage & Ice Co. (1949) 188
BMW of North America, Inc. v. Gore (1996) 189
State Farm Mutual Auto Insurance Company v. Campbell
(2003) 190

Takings Clause (Fifth Amendment) 192
Village of Euclid, Ohio, v. Ambler Realty Co. (1926) 192
Hawaii Housing Authority v. Midkiff (1984) 192
Dolan v. City of Tigard (1994) 193
Kelo v. City of New London (2005) 194

8 The Bill of Rights and Its Application to the States **197**
Incorporation 200
Barron v. Baltimore (1833) 200
Gitlow v. New York (1925) 200
Palko v. Connecticut (1937) 201
United States v. Carolene Products Co. (1938) 202
Adamson v. California (1947) 204
Rochin v. California (1952) 205
[*Griswold v. Connecticut* (1965)]
[*Duncan v. Louisiana* (1968)]

9 First Amendment: Religious Rights **207**
Establishment Clause 209
*Everson v. Board of Education of Ewing
Township* (1947) 209
*Illinois ex rel. McCollum v. Board of Education,
Champaign County, Illinois* (1948) 210
Zorach v. Clauson (1952) 211
Engel et al. v. Vitale et al. (1962) 212
Abington School District v. Schempp (1963) 213

Lemon v. Kurtzman (1971)   214
Wisconsin v. Yoder (1972)   216
Stone v. Graham (1980)   217
Widmar v. Vincent (1981)   217
Marsh v. Chambers (1983)   219
Wallace v. Jaffree (1985)   220
Edwards v. Aguillard (1987)   221
Lee v. Weisman (1992)   222
Zobrest v. Catalina Foothills School District (1993)   223
Agostini v. Felton (1997)   224
Santa Fe School District v. Doe (2000)   225
Good News Club v. Milford Central School (2001)   226
Zelman v. Simmons-Harris (2002)   228
[Elk Grove v. Newdow (2004)]
Van Orden v. Perry (2005   229
McCreary County v. American Civil Liberties Union
    (2005)   230

Free Exercise Clause   232
Reynolds v. United States (1879)   232
Cantwell v. Connecticut (1940)   233
Murdock v. Pennsylvania (1943)   234
Marsh v. Alabama (1946)   234
Welsh v. United States (1970)   236
United States v. Lee (1982)   237
Goldman v. Weinberger (1986)   238
*Employment Division, Department of Human Resources
    of Oregon v. Smith* (1990)   239
Church of Lukumi Babalu Aye v. City of Hialeah
    (1993)   240
Rosenberger v. University of Virginia (1995)   241
[City of Boerne v. Flores (1997)]
Board of Regents v. Southworth (2000)   243
Gonzales v. Centro Espirita (2006)   244

10   First Amendment: Political Rights   247
Association [Implied], Assembly, and Petition   249
DeJonge v. Oregon (1937)   249
Hague v. Congress of Industrial Organizations
    (1939)   250
United Public Workers of America v. Mitchell (1947)   251
NAACP v. Alabama (1958)   252

Branti v. Finkel (1980)   252
Board of Directors of Rotary International v. Rotary Club of Duarte (1987)   253
Frisby v. Schultz (1988)   255
Hurley v. Irish-American Gay, Lesbian and Bisexual Group of Boston (1995)   256
Boy Scouts of America v. Dale (2000)   257
Rumsfeld v. Forum (2006)   258

Press   259
Abrams v. United States (1919)   259
Near v. Minnesota ex rel. Olson (1931)   260
Grosjean v. American Press Co. (1936)   261
Bridges v. California (1941)   261
Martin v. City of Struthers, Ohio (1943)   262
New York Times Company v. Sullivan (1964)   263
New York Times Company v. United States (1971)   265
Branzburg v. Hayes (1972)   265
Nebraska Press Association v. Stuart (1976)   266
Herbert v. Lando (1979)   267
Gannett Co. v. DePasquale (1979)   268
Richmond Newspapers, Inc. v. Commonwealth of Virginia (1980)   269
Chandler and Granger v. Florida (1981)   270
Hustler *Magazine v. Falwell* (1988)   271

Speech   272
Campaign-Related   272
Buckley v. Valeo (1976)   272
Elrod v. Burns (1976)   273
Republican Party of Minnesota v. White (2002)   274
Citizens United v. Federal Election Commission (2010)   276

Commercial Speech   279
Virginia State Board of Pharmacy v. Virginia Citizens Consumer Council, Inc. (1976)   279
First National Bank of Boston v. Bellotti (1978)   280
44 Liquormart, Inc. v. Rhode Island (1996)   281

Obscenity   282
Burstyn v. Wilson (1952)   282
Roth v. United States (1957)   282

Ginzburg v. United States (1966)   283
Miller v. California (1973)   284
New York v. Ferber (1982)   285
Reno v. American Civil Liberties Union (1997)   286
National Endowment for the Arts v. Finley (1998)   287
Ashcroft v. The Free Speech Coalition (2002)   288
Ashcroft v. American Civil Liberties Union (2004) 289

Subversive Speech   291
Schenck v. United States (1919)   291
|*Gitlow v. New York* (1925)|
American Communications Association v. Douds
   (1950)   292
Dennis v. United States (1951)   292
Keyishian v. Board of Regents (1967)   293
Brandenburg v. Ohio (1969)   294

Symbolic Speech or Speech and Conduct   295
Cox v. New Hampshire (1941)   295
West Virginia State Board of Education v. Barnette
   (1943)   296
Tinker v. Des Moines (1969)   297
Lynch v. Donnelly (1984)   298
Texas v. Johnson (1989)   299
Erie v. Pap's A.M. (2000)   300
Virginia v. Black (2003)   302

Time, Place, and Manner Restrictions on Speech   303
Kovacs v. Cooper (1949)   303
Feiner v. New York (1951)   304
Federal Communications Commission v. Pacifica
   Foundation (1978)   305
Snepp v. United States (1980)   306
Bethel School District No. 403 v. Fraser (1986)   307
Hazelwood School District v. Kuhlmeier (1988)   308
Morse v. Frederick (2007) 309
Garcetti v. Ceballos (2006) 310

11   Second, Third, and Fourth Amendments   **313**
Gun Control   315
District of Columbia v. Heller (2008)   315

Electronic Surveillance   317
Olmstead v. United States (1928)   317

Katz v. United States (1967)   318
United States v. United States District Court (1972)   319

Other Search and Seizure   320
Weeks v. United States (1914)   320
Mapp v. Ohio (1961)   321
Terry v. Ohio (1968)   322
Chimel v. California (1969)   323
Zurcher v. the Stanford Daily (1978)   323
Marshall v. Barlow's, Inc. (1978)   324
United States v. Ross (1982)   325
United States v. Leon (1984)   326
Nix v. Williams (1984)   328
New Jersey v. T.L.O. (1985)   329
California v. Ciraolo (1986)   330
California v. Greenwood (1988)   331
Knowles v. Iowa (1998)   332
*Board of Education of Independent School District No. 92
of Pottawatomie County v. Earls* (2002)   332
[*Lawrence v. Texas* (2003)]
Thorton v. United States (2004)   333
Safford Unified School District # 1 v. Redding (2009)   335

12   Fifth, Sixth, Seventh, and Eighth Amendments   **337**
Double Jeopardy and Right to Confrontation   339
United States v. Lanza (1922)   339
[*Palko v. Connecticut* (1937)]
Coy v. Iowa (1988)   340
Sattazahn v. Pennsylvania (2003)   341

Due Process   342
[*Adkins v. Children's Hospital* (1923)]
Tumey v. Ohio (1927)   342
Bolling v. Sharpe (1954)   343
O'Connor v. Donaldson (1975)   344
Bordenkircher v. Hayes (1978)   345
DeShaney v. Winnebago Social Services (1989)   345
Scheidler v. National Organization for Women (2003)   346
Caperton v. A.T. Massey Coal Co., Inc. (2009)   347

Juries   348
Hurtado v. California (1884)   348
Norris v. Alabama (1935)   349

Duncan v. Louisiana (1968)   350
Burch v. Louisiana (1979)   351
Duren v. Missouri (1979)   352
Batson v. Kentucky (1986)   353

Right to Counsel   354
Powell v. Alabama (1932)   354
Chambers v. Florida (1940)   355
Gideon v. Wainwright (1963)   356
Escobedo v. Illinois (1964)   357
Miranda v. Arizona (1966)   358
Argersinger v. Hamlin (1972)   359
Dickerson v. United States (2000)   359

Self-Incrimination and Immunity   360
[*Adamson v. California* (1947)]
Ullmann v. United States (1956)   360
Murphy v. Waterfront Commission of New York Harbor
   (1964)   362
Malloy v. Hogan (1964)   362
Schmerber v. California (1966)   363
Marchetti v. United States (1968)   364

Cruel and Unusual Punishment   365
State of Louisiana ex rel. Francis v. Resweber (1947)   365
Gregg v. Georgia (1976)   366
McCleskey v. Kemp (1987)   367
Thompson v. Oklahoma (1988)   368
Payne v. Tennessee (1991)   370
Atkins v. Virginia (2002)   371
Ring v. Arizona (2002)   372
Ewing v. California (2003)   373
Baze v. Rees (2008)   374

**13   Ninth Amendment, Right to Privacy, and Other
    Unenumerated Rights**   **377**
The Right to Privacy and Other Unenumerated Rights   378
Meyer v. Nebraska (1923)   378
*Pierce v. Society of Sisters of the Holy Names of Jesus and
    Mary* (1925)   379
Buck v. Bell (1927)   380
Griswold v. Connecticut (1965)   381
Shapiro v. Thompson (1969)   382

Roe v. Wade (1973) 383
Zablocki v. Redhail (1978) 384
Harris v. McRae (1980) 385
Bowers v. Hardwick (1986) 386
Planned Parenthood of Southeastern Pennsylvania v. Casey (1992) 387
Vacco v. Quill, Washington v. Glucksberg (1997) 389
Lawrence v. Texas (2003) 390
Gonzales v. Carhart (2007) 392

14 Thirteenth and Fourteenth Amendments **395**
Due Process (Economic) and Freedom of Contract 398
Enforcement Powers 398
Katzenbach v. Morgan (1966) 398
South Carolina v. Katzenbach (1966) 399
City of Boerne v. Flores (1997) 400

Equal Protection and Privileges and Immunities 401
African Americans and Racial Classifications 401
Scott v. Sandford (1857) 401
[*Slaughterhouse Cases* (1873)]
The Civil Rights Cases (1883) 403
Plessy v. Ferguson (1896) 404
Missouri ex rel. Gaines v. Canada (1938) 405
Screws v. United States (1945) 406
Shelley v. Kraemer (1948) 407
Sweatt v. Painter (1950) 408
McLaurin v. Oklahoma State Regents (1950) 409
[*Bolling v. Sharpe* (1954)]
Brown v. Board of Education of Topeka (1954) 409
Brown v. Board of Education II (1955) 410
Loving v. Virginia (1967) 411
Jones v. Alfred H. Mayer Co. (1968) 412
Swann v. Charlotte-Mecklenburg Board of Education (1971) 413
Moose Lodge No. 107 v. Irvis (1972) 413
Milliken v. Bradley (1974) 414
Regents of the University of California v. Bakke (1978) 415
United Steel Workers of America v. Weber, Kaiser Aluminum v. Weber, United States v. Weber (1979) 416

Fullilove v. Klutznick (1980)   417
Adarand Constructors, Inc., v. Pena (1995)   418
Gratz v. Bollinger (2003)   420
Grutter v. Bollinger (2003)   422
Ricci v. DeStefano (2009)   424
Protection, Privileges, and Immunities: Aliens   425
United States v. Wong Kim Ark (1898)   425
Truax v. Raich (1915)   426
Girouard v. United States (1946)   427
Oyama v. California (1948)   428
Takahashi v. Fish & Game Commission (1948)   429
Foley v. Connelie (1978)   430
Plyler v. Doe (1982)   430
Protection, Privileges, and Immunities: Sexual Classifications   432
Reed v. Reed (1971)   432
Frontiero v. Richardson (1973)   432
Michael M. v. Superior Court of Sonoma County
   (1981)   434
Hishon v. King & Spalding (1984)   435
United States v. Virginia (1996)   436
Protection, Privileges, and Immunities: Various Other
Classifications   437
San Antonio Independent School District v. Rodriguez
   (1973)   437
Cleburne v. Cleburne Living Center (1985)   437
Meritor Savings Bank v. Vinson (1986)   439
Gregory v. Ashcroft (1991)   440
Romer v. Evans (1996)   441
Miller v. Albright (1998)   442
Connecticut Department of Public Safety v. John Doe
   (2003)   444
[*Lawrence v. Texas* (2003)]

15 Voting Rights   **445**
Voting Rights   446
Ex parte Yarbrough (1884)   446
Guinn v. United States (1915)   447
Nixon v. Condon (1932)   448
United States v. Classic (1941)   449
Smith v. Allwright (1944)   449
Gomillion v. Lightfoot (1960)   451

Wesberry v. Sanders (1964)   451
Reynolds v. Sims (1964)   452
Oregon v. Mitchell (1970)   453
Dunn v. Blumstein (1972)   454
Shaw v. Reno (1993)   455
Bush v. Vera (1996)   456
Bush v. Gore (2000)   457
Crawford v. Marion County (2008)   460
Northwest Austin Municipal Utility District Number One v.
   Holder (2009)   461

Members of the Supreme Court of the United States, 1789–2010   463

The Constitution of the United States   467

Glossary of Legal Terms   487

Alphabetical List of Cases Briefed   501

Chronological List of Cases by Chief Justice   ·   511

Index   521

About the Author   535

PREFACE TO THE FIFTEENTH EDITION

More than fifty years and fourteen previous editions of continuous use have established the value of this volume. This value is tied to the gravity of the subject it treats. American constitutional law is as important and exciting as the dream of constitutional government. In addition to its intellectual appeal, constitutional law has practical consequences. Because the United States has a written constitution enforceable in courts, citizens find that guarantees of political participation and basic rights are realities rather than mere aspirations.

Like many important subjects, the study of constitutional law can be difficult. Undergraduates in political science and history often find constitutional law to be among the more demanding studies that they encounter within the social sciences. Similarly, law students generally find classes on constitutional law to be at least as challenging as classes on torts or contracts.

There are a variety of reasons for this. Although cases involving civil rights and liberties are often quite engaging and contemporary, cases involving judicial review and jurisdiction, separation of powers, federalism, congressional powers under the commerce and taxing clauses, and the like (typically the staple of first semester courses on U.S. constitutional law) may seem quite arcane. Moreover, the Supreme Court has a long history, and important cases frequently originate from earlier centuries. Such cases often focus on technical questions about issues that are not exactly in today's headlines or that are not generally understood. Few students who begin constitutional law understand, for example, that most rights in the first ten amendments are applied to the states not directly, but via the due process clause of the Fourteenth Amendment (see chapter 8 on the Bill of Rights and its application to the states). In addition to changes that have occurred in political circumstances and ordinary terminology during such time periods, cases often come complete with their own language of "legalese," as recognized by the inclusion of a glossary of legal terms at the end of this volume.

Constitutional law is usually taught in classes in political science, history, and law. In classes in political science and law, students typically use a "casebook" that contains excerpts of key cases grouped according to topic. Law professors sometimes supplement such casebooks with "hornbooks," or commentaries that are often as massive as the volumes they purport to explain. In classes in constitutional law, professors expect students to read cases before coming to class, be prepared to discuss them, and leave with an understanding not only of what individual cases say but how they relate to one another. History classes are more likely to take a secondary text on constitutional developments as a point of departure, but such texts will often be supplemented by readings from key cases.

Professors in all these disciplines are likely to encourage students to "brief" cases prior to class and may even require the submission of such written briefs as part of the class grade. As the terminology suggests, a "brief" provides a skeletal outline of key aspects of a case. Professors vary in the elements they want in a brief, but this book provides those elements that professors most typically request. At a minimum, professors will generally want the name of the case followed by identification of the justice or justices writing decisions, a discussion of the most important facts of the case, the central question(s) the case poses, the opinion at which the Court arrived, its reasons for coming to this decision, and notes on major concurring and dissenting opinions. Identifying the central question in each case, the Court's answer to this question, and its reasons for it are especially important with the reasoning generally the largest part of a brief.

How long should a brief be? Briefs that are too long leave students preparing for an exam or paper with materials little shorter, and thus of little more help, than the cases reviewed. By contrast, briefs that are too short are likely to leave students struggling to remember the basic facts and issues in the cases. The length of briefs will thus typically vary with the length and complexity of individual cases.

With more than fifty years of use, this book has proven itself as a useful tool for conscientious students of the U.S. Constitution and its history, but, like other tools, it can be abused. It has been said that the ultimate touchstone of constitutionality is not what the Court or any other institution has said about it, but the Constitution itself. So too, the ultimate source for Supreme Court opinions should be the decisions themselves and not what this author or anyone else has to say about them. Students who use this book as a substitute for reading and briefing cases on their own, and for grappling with the original language and reasoning in opinions, will probably find that they will do better than those who read neither. But students who rely solely on this book will be profoundly disadvantaged when compared with those who conscientiously begin by reading and briefing cases, attending classes, participating in class discussions and studying groups, and using this book and similar aids to check and further their understandings of such decisions.

This book is a useful guide for how to brief cases and generally points students in the right direction as to the meaning of key cases. However, wise students will quickly discover that cases often stand for more than one principle and that they might thus appear in some casebooks to illustrate issues other than the ones they illustrate here. Because it is arranged both topically and chronologically within chapters, this book will also help students to understand how cases they read fit into larger historical contexts. There is no unanimously agreed upon canon of the most important Supreme Court cases, and no two casebooks compiled by different authors will likely cover an identical list of cases. Thus, although students will undoubtedly find that many cases in their casebooks are not briefed here, they are likely to find that many cases are briefed here that are not in their books. They will thus have the opportunity to put their readings within larger contexts by reading summaries of other cases contemporary to the ones they are assigned.

In short, this book is a supplement to, and not a substitute for, reading Supreme Court decisions and scholarly commentaries on them. It can point the way to understanding court decisions, but it cannot serve in place of close reading and intellectual grappling with such cases. Briefs contained here provide skeletal outlines of the way that justices have thought, but students will need to read cases closely to understand the Court's reasoning in depth.

I began teaching just over thirty years ago, when this book, rather than I, was in mid-age. By that point it was already a widely available resource much prized by students. I am pleased to be able to continue my own teaching by continuing to update such a worthy study aid and honored that the publishers have asked me to guide this volume into its second fifty years. I have extensively revised this edition to cover important cases since the publication of the last edition, to delete cases that appeared to be of little practical usefulness, and to add significant materials on concurring and dissenting opinions to earlier cases. I hope that the volume continues to prove to be of help to those who seek better understanding of the U.S. Constitution and the Supreme Court decisions that explicate it.

John R. Vile
Middle Tennessee State University

Acknowledgments

I am grateful to acknowledge my debt to the two previous scholars who authored the earlier editions of this volume, to those they have previously acknowledged as helping them, and to those who helped me bring this revised and expanded volume to press. The last reorganization for the last edition was the most extensive that has been done since this book was first published in 1954, but I remain grateful that I did not need to begin this book from scratch but was able to build upon the firm foundation that Professors Paul C. Bartholomew and Joseph F. Menez had already laid. I believe this book remains unique in its format, and, I hope, in its accessibility to students of U.S. constitutional law and history. As I revised and updated this book, I felt as though I was treading in huge footprints. I have aspired to maintaining both the high scholarly standards and the readability and accessibility to students of the original versions and trust that this new volume will bring continuing pride to the families of those who wrote them.

Naturally, I am grateful to Rowman & Littlefield for approaching me about revising this book. I am especially grateful to my editors, Jon Sisk and Darcy Evans, and production editor Lynda Phung. I owe special thanks to my student aide, Dawn Johnson, whose work was unflagging and whose computer and editing skills were essential. She spent countless hours separating cases into individual computer files, recombining them into new chapters, reformatting files, adding new cases, and editing my own prose. It was especially useful to have an undergraduate's perspective on what features of the existing book were most helpful and which could be most improved. I have queried numerous other students about how this book could be reorganized and improved. I continue to value my contacts with undergraduates in the classroom, and much of my confidence in the value of this book stems from the experiences that I have had in teaching undergraduate courses in constitutional law.

I also appreciate the work of my secretary Pam Davis in troubleshooting various computer glitches and other matters that I encountered when writing this book.

I continue to be awed by the way that computers have made cases increasingly accessible to scholars, and I am especially grateful to have been at an institution that has made access to Supreme Court cases available from my home and office. Middle Tennessee State University has continued to provide a supportive environment for me, and I will always be grateful for its service as my academic home. Since writing the last edition of this book, I have moved from my perch as chair of the Department of Political Science to a new position as dean of the University Honors College, and I am grateful that this job continues to allow me time to continue my research and writing.

I am pleased to dedicate this book to the two daughters who have brought such joy and pride to my wife and me.

THIS IS OUR SUPREME COURT

Chief Justice Charles Evans Hughes once observed that "We are under a Constitution, but the Constitution is what the judges say it is." The chief justice was stretching a point, of course, because as Alexander Hamilton noted in *The Federalist*, the Court has neither the power of the purse nor the sword but only judgment. A good deal of its power depends on congressional grants, it must convince the executive to enforce its decisions, and when it lags or outstrips public opinion, it finds little support. The people have demonstrated that they retain ultimate power when on four occasions they have amended the Constitution to "recall" a previous Supreme Court opinion (see the Eleventh, Fourteenth, Sixteenth, and Twenty-sixth Amendments)! Judicial activists would like to push the Court forward in an ever-widening circle of cases, but as Justice John Marshall Harlan II wrote: "The Constitution is not a panacea for every blot upon the public welfare."

Of the three branches, the judicial branch is easily the most prestigious and most traditional. Alexis de Tocqueville, the very perceptive Frenchman who came to this country and in 1835 published his magisterial *Democracy in America*, noted:

> If I were asked where I place the American aristocracy, I should reply without hesitation . . . that it occupies the judicial bench and bar. . . . Scarcely any political question arises in the United States that is not resolved, sooner or later, into a judicial question.

Unlike the presidency and Congress, the "political branches," the Supreme Court is barely visible. Its proceedings are not televised, the justices do not hold press conferences and rarely appear on television, they generally avoid the Washington social scene, and they rarely engage in public debate. And yet, the

Court remains in the center of issues. As Justice Oliver Wendell Holmes once wrote: "We are very quiet there, but it is the quiet of a storm center."

Created under Article III of the Constitution, the Supreme Court heads a co-equal branch of government that is independent of the other two "political [or elected] branches." At least since Chief Justice John Marshall's historic decision in *Marbury v. Madison* (1803), the Court has exercised the power, known as judicial review (and better grounded in general constitutional principles than in specific constitutional mandates), to declare acts of Congress or actions of governmental officials brought in cases before it to be unconstitutional and therefore void—it had previously exercised a similar power over state legislation. The Court also exercises the power of statutory interpretation, deciding on the meaning of disputed laws. Whereas only constitutional amendments or changes in judicial interpretation can overturn judicial interpretations of the Constitution, Congress can rewrite legislation that it believes the Court has misinterpreted.

The Court has nine members, a number set by statute in 1869. President Franklin D. Roosevelt attempted to "pack" the Court in 1937 when it was opposing his New Deal programs, and his failure to receive congressional approval for this proposal does not bode well for future alterations of the number of justices. Once all-male and all-white, as of 2010, two African Americans, three women, several Jews, an individual of Italian ancestry, and another of Latino ancestry have now occupied seats on the Court, and more minority appointments seem destined to follow. Although the members are lawyers and are increasingly drawn from the ranks of former judges, in contrast to the presidency and the Congress, the Constitution lays down no qualifications. Without exception, however, the justices have been active in public life. "This is a select company," said Chief Justice Warren Burger, "not because we are all-knowing, but because we were selected and we are here." Justice Louis D. Brandeis commented that "the reason the public thinks so much of the justices is that they are the only people who do their own work," a sentiment somewhat called into question by the increasing reliance of justices on their clerks, typically newly minted J.D.s from the nation's most prestigious law schools.

The president nominates all federal judges, including Supreme Court justices, and they are confirmed with the "advice and consent" of the Senate, which takes its role seriously enough to have rejected close to a fourth of the nominees to this body. In order to assure their relative independence, the Constitution guarantees that their salaries may not be lowered during their service, and they serve "during good behavior." Justices thus exit the court only through death, resignation, retirement, or (in a possibility never yet successful for a Supreme Court justice) after impeachment by the U.S. House of

Representatives and removal by a two-thirds majority vote of the Senate. Judicial nominations are often hotly contested along ideological lines (witness Robert Bork's unsuccessful fight in the Reagan administration and Clarence Thomas's barely successful efforts in the George H. W. Bush administration), and there is a good deal of journalistic and scholarly scorekeeping once justices reach the bench. Justices are often defined as "liberal," "conservative," or "centrist," or as belonging to this or that "bloc" or "camp." But neither the justices themselves nor careful Court-watchers see the membership so neatly categorized. There is a certain amount of unconscious yielding on lesser matters but no real sacrifice of principle. Although some justices share views and often vote together, there are no "blocs" in the sense of a number of persons who act in concert or as a unit. Even when one may guess how a justice might vote on the closest issues, said Justice Lewis F. Powell, "advance predictions are hazardous, even for those who serve together." Although Article III of the U.S. Constitution vests the Supreme Court with a limited number of cases of "original jurisdiction," in which it is the first and last court to hear a case, the Court is primarily an appellate court, reviewing decisions of lower federal courts and, because the United States has a federal system of government, from state courts, typically the state supreme court. The Court must thus wait for cases to come to it. Quoting Justice Oliver Wendell Holmes Jr., Justice William O. Douglas once observed that "Being a judge is like being an oyster: You've got to wait for the food to come washing up to your mouth with the high tide. And you watch many of the best mussels float by." Litigants file petitions or "writs" for the Court to review, the most common of which is called a writ of certiorari. The Court now receives close to 9,000 such writs a year and has almost complete discretion over which it chooses to hear. Clerks largely do the work of scanning through petitions for writs of certiorari to decide which cases have merit. The Court operates by a "rule of four" in which it only accepts cases that four or more justices agree to hear. When the Court decides not to accept a case, it leaves the lower court's decision in place, but this does not necessarily mean that the Court would have come to the same decision. The Court often waits until it thinks a case is "ripe" for review, and it often prefers to have several lower court rulings in place before it undertakes its own review; indeed, one of the Supreme Court's key functions is to reconcile practices in conflicting jurisdictions below it.

When Earl Warren was chief justice, the Court issued decisions in close to two hundred cases a year, but under the leadership of the subsequent three chiefs, the Court has more than cut this number in half. This, of course, is the public work of the Court. Since the Constitution provides for only one Supreme Court, this precludes the Court from separating into panels, chambers, or sections. Moreover, except in rare cases of court vacancies or when justices recuse themselves or find themselves unable to participate because of illness, every justice passes on each case. The Court neither contains nor encourages the specialist; what the Court seeks and gets is the generalist. But justices, whose offices have been compared to nine private law firms, are fiercely individualist and independent, and thus individualist opinions now predominate over institutional opinions for the Court

Completed in 1935, the four-story Supreme Court building, measuring nearly 400 by 300 feet, is located east of the Capitol, which it faces across a wide plaza. The doors to the main entrance are sliding leaves of bronze, each weighing six and one-half tons. Eight relief panels trace the growth of law from ancient Greece and Rome to the young United States. Finished at a cost of $9,000,000, it is an imposing marble edifice dedicated to preserving the Union as one of laws and not of men. Exhibiting twenty-four massive columns and containing marble from Spain, the courtroom was deliberately made small—it measures 82 by 91 feet with a coffered ceiling 44 feet high— so that the audience would not have an impact upon the judicial proceedings. Chief Justice Rehnquist, once asked if justices were able to insulate themselves from public opinion, replied: "No, and it would probably be unwise to try. We read newspapers and magazines, we watch news and television, we talk to our friends about current events. No judge worthy of his salt would ever cast his vote in a particular case simply because he thought the majority of the public wanted him to vote that way."

In addition to the section set off for the bar and the raised area where the nine justices sit, there are benches made available for the general public. Of the 300 seats, 112 are allotted to the press, the justices' families, and members of the bar. The remaining 188 seats are available to the public on a first-come-first-served basis. On days in which very important cases are being argued, some seats in the public area are rotated every three minutes to accommodate the tourists. Close to the Court benches, there are special areas: members of the press are seated in red benches on the left side of the courtroom, the red benches on the right are for guests, the black chairs in front of the benches are for officers of the Court, or distinguished dignitaries. There is even a seat for the president if he desires to visit the Court. The Court does not permit any writing, whispering, sketching, taping, or photographing, although the Court does make audiotapes, which individuals may subsequently buy, of arguments in individual cases. In an unusual move, the Court made audiotapes of the arguments in the historic *Bush v. Gore* decision in December 2000 (effectively halting the election count in the state of Florida and thus sealing George W. Bush as the winner of the state's electoral votes) almost immediately after the arguments were made. Students may now access tapes of oral arguments at http://oyez.nwu.edu.

By statute a "term" begins in October and by custom ends the following July for "vacation." When justices are not in Washington, petitions follow them even in diplomatic pouches. On very rare occasions there is a special sitting of the Court, when it can extend its term, as in the Pentagon Papers case (1971) and the Nixon Tapes ruling (1974), and reassembles as in the case of the Nazi saboteurs (1942) and the Rosenberg espionage trial (1953). The Court is in session two weeks and in recess for two weeks. When the Court is "on" it hears oral arguments; when it is "off" it is deciding petitions, researching cases, and writing opinions. Six justices must participate in each decision, and cases are decided by a majority. In the event of a tie vote, the decision of the lower court is sustained although the case may be reargued.

At 10:00 A.M. Monday through Wednesday, the Court pages part the beautiful drapes allowing the justices, who have previously met and shaken hands all around, to enter the courtroom. The clerk cries out:

> Oyez, oyez, oyez! All persons having business before the honorable, the Supreme Court of the United States, are admonished to draw near and give their attention, for the Court is now sitting. God save the United States and this honorable Court.

The Court hears two cases before noon and, following an hour's recess, it hears two cases until it adjourns at three. Punctuality is the rule for the Court and for its litigants. The advocate's time—typically, one-half hour—is monitored by the Court Marshal. When the white light flashes at the advocate's lectern, there are five minutes left. At the red light the chief justice, promptly but firmly, says "Thank you, ... The case is submitted." Once when former President Grover Cleveland addressed the Court, he looked up at the clock and remarked that, despite the closing time, he would take only a couple of minutes to complete his argument. Melville Fuller, who was appointed chief justice by Cleveland, remarked with great courtesy: "Mr. Cleveland, we will hear you tomorrow." On another occasion, Chief Justice Charles Evan Hughes (known for being able to cut counsel off in the middle of the word "if"), when asked how much time was left, responded: "14 seconds." Solicitor Stanley Reed, who subsequently became a justice, once fainted before the Court.

Unlike the days of the Court "Greats"—attorneys Daniel Webster, Henry Clay, and John C. Calhoun—when arguing a case before the Supreme Court was a major event that brought out in attendance Washington's social set, what counts today is merit, not reputation. In cases of great public import, the one-hour-per-case limit has been increased as in the three hours for *United States v. Nixon* (1974) and two hours for *Bowsher v. Synar* (1986). The scant one-half hour provided the advocate is frequently dissipated by questions from the bench. The "Felix Problem"—called after Justice Felix Frankfurter, a former law professor who consumed a good deal of an advocate's allotted time—treated counsels as students taking an examination; a colleague once noticed that his musings in conference were typically 50 minutes long, the length of a standard Harvard lecture. Justices Antonin Scalia and Ruth Bader Ginsburg are the most loquacious members of the current court, with Justice Clarence Thomas speaking from the bench so rarely that occasions, as in cases involving cross-burning and affirmative action, when he does so become cause for journalistic comment. The Court looks with disfavor on any oral argument that is read from a prepared text and requires an advocate to answer any question that is asked. Once when a lawyer said he was coming to a point, Justice James McReynolds snapped: "You're there already!" Justice Thurgood Marshall told a lawyer who did return to his question to forget it; he was no longer interested.

The most frequent lawyer before the Court is the solicitor general of the United States, who has his own office in the Supreme Court building. The solicitor's principal function is to decide what cases the government will or will not appeal. He is often called the ninth-and-a-half member because he has an advantage that an attorney appearing less often does not possess. He not only argues on behalf of the government, he also decides which cases to bring to the Court, and which to appeal. The solicitor general, to illustrate the extent of his visibility, participates in about half of the Court's entire docket and perhaps two-thirds of all argued cases. Robert Jackson, a former solicitor general, relates that he made three arguments in every case:

> First came the one that I planned—as I thought, logical, coherent, complete. Second was the one actually presented—interrupted, incoherent, disjointed, disappointing. The third was the utterly devastating argument that I thought of after going to bed that night.

However hazardous and traumatic the exchange between the justices and the advocate, it can be significant, as Chief Justice Charles Evans Hughes once commented: "I suppose . . . that the impressions that a judge has at the close of a full oral argument accords with the convictions which control his final vote."

When the Court is in recess studying appeals, petitions, and writing opinions, conferences are held on Wednesday afternoons and all day Friday. The justices are called to conference by a buzzer that rings in the several chambers five minutes before the hour. The oak-paneled conference room is lined with books containing lower court and Supreme Court opinions. There is a portrait of the fourth and arguably the greatest chief justice, John Marshall. Each justice's chair is different and bears a nameplate. Justices are seated according to seniority. The main law library has more than 500,000 volumes in a variety of formats and a staff of twenty-five to serve the justices. Each justice has an agenda of the cases to be discussed and, in addition, a movable cart containing all the materials he might need in discussion.

There are no clerks, stenographers, pages, or even a tape recorder visible. There is absolute secrecy and confidentiality. If it is necessary to get material outside the conference chamber or answer the door, the most recently appointed justice acts as a "doorkeeper." Justice Tom Clark was the junior justice for five years and was fond of relating that he "was the highest paid doorkeeper in the world." Like chiefs before him, Chief Justice John G. Roberts, Jr. opens a session by giving the judicial history of the case and putting the precise question before the justices. Beginning with the most senior down to the most junior, the justices state their views, but some justices have noted that they and their colleagues more frequently report their position than engage in genuine dialogue. Still, discussions can be heated. If the chief justice perceives that nothing more can be said on the issue, the chief will call for a vote. The chief justice is considered to be *primus inter pares*, or first among equals. Good chiefs are expected to exercise both good "task" leadership, to help expedite the work of the Court, and good "social" leadership, to preserve relative harmony in a collective setting.

The chief has the tactical advantage of opening discussion of the cases and setting the tone of the discussion. If the chief justice votes with the majority, the chief has still another advantage. The chief can write the opinion or assign it to someone else (if the chief is in the minority, this privilege goes to the ranking dissenter). This gives the chief a special opportunity for leadership. Assignments are not made at the conference but formally in writing several days later. If the decision is considered a "landmark" one, the chief justice often writes the opinion, thus throwing the weight of the Court behind it; chiefs sometimes work very hard at getting unanimity in important cases, as was perhaps best exemplified in Chief Justice Earl Warren's successful efforts in *Brown v. Board of Education* (1954) overturning the doctrine of "separate but equal" in race relations. The chief might assign the opinion to the justice whose position is closest to his own on the issue, or the chief justice might recognize the "realities of external politics" and select a justice whose views will carry more weight.

Almost every chief justice has assigned a "conservative" opinion to a "liberal" judge, as when Justice Hugo Black wrote the opinion for the famous Japanese internment case, *Korematsu v. United States* (1944), and a "liberal" opinion to a "conservative" judge, as when Justice Tom Clark was assigned *Abington School District v. Schempp* (1963), which dealt with prayer and Bible reading in schools.

Writing an opinion is laborious as well as artful. Rufus Choate once observed: "You cannot drop the Greek alphabet and pick up the *Iliad*." At this point a legal battle is likely to occur all over again if one or more of the majority justices disputes the terminology, the content, the style, or the structure of the decision. Occasionally, the judge who wrote the opinion will not backtrack on his or her style or statements—what Justice Oliver Wendell Holmes called "pulling out all the plums and leaving all the dough"—thus provoking his or her supporters to write concurring opinions, that agree with the result but not with the reasoning of a holding. In a memo to Justice Felix Frankfurter, Justice Harlan Fiske Stone wrote: "If you wish to write, placing the case on the ground which I think tenable and desirable, I shall cheerfully join you. If not, I will add a few observations myself."

The political effect of concurring opinions, however, is to weaken the majority opinion. Not only is the force and singleness of the majority opinion lost, but its message can be scattered by dicta, that is, interesting but extraneous material. The use of individual opinions now predominates over institutional opinions for the Court. Moreover, a justice might write a dozen drafts of an opinion, circulate them for approval, and then see them disintegrate. As Justice Lewis Powell put it: "The drafting of an opinion is a process, not an event. . . . What really dismays a justice is to circulate a draft opinion, and receive no word at all except perhaps a cryptic note or two saying: 'I will wait circulation of the dissent.'" In some cases, a powerful dissent has succeeded in changing a majority into a minority opinion. After reading such a dissent, Chief Justice William H. Taft wrote his colleagues: "I think we made a mistake in this case," and wrote a new and contrary opinion that carried the Court.

Although the dissent is an appeal to what Chief Justice Charles Evans Hughes called "the brooding spirit of the law, to the intelligence of a future day," still, it is not the controlling law. It attempts to undermine the Court's reasoning and discredit its results. Justice Robert Jackson noted that a dissent was a confession of a "failure to convince the writer's colleagues, and the true test of a judge is his influence in leading, not in opposing, his court." Especially when they represent the view of a single justice who is not forced to compromise his/her views in order to muster the votes of other justices, dissents may be more sharply worded, and thus more memorable, than majority opinions.

When the majority and minority opinions are ready, they are printed in the Supreme Court's special, high-security printing room. Copies for distribution by the Public Information Office are made available to the public. Camera-ready copies of the "Bench Opinions" are sent to the Government Printing Office (GPO).

In the city where even serious leaks are almost a daily occurrence, it is the glory of the Court's personnel that advance knowledge of an opinion is rarely known. The final opinions, being public knowledge, go across town to the Government Printing Office and are first issued as "advance sheets" (small-size paperbacks) and later as bound volumes.

There is no particular pattern for delivering oral opinions. At one time—from 1867 to 1965—opinions were always "reserved" for Monday, jocularly called judgment day. Chief Justice Warren Burger altered this practice largely to avoid or reduce weekend pressures and high overtime payments to the Court's printers.

The reading of opinions can take different forms depending upon the length, the number of concurring and dissenting opinions, or the importance of a case. There is no prior announcement as to when the cases will be handed down. Each justice selects the style he likes. Some justices read the Court's prepared "syllabus" or digest that precedes the full opinion, some outline the decision themselves, sticking close to the text, and still others might simply indicate their vote and refer the listener to the text.

As the justices read the opinions, the ever-present pages circulate printed copies to distinguished visitors in the foreground of the Court. Meanwhile, a phone rings in the Information Office and printed copies are released to reporters gathered there. The case is finished. The justices have judged. New constitutional issues will absorb their energies, for as the great Chief Justice John Marshall declared: "We must never forget that it is a Constitution we are expounding."

FOR FURTHER READING

Abraham, Henry J. *The Judicial Process: An Introductory Analysis of the Court of the United States, England, and France.* 7th ed. New York: Oxford University Press, 1996. Arguably, the best comparative study of the judicial systems in the United States and in other major democracies.

Abraham, Henry J. *Justices, Presidents, and Senators: A History of the U.S. Supreme Court Appointments from Washington to Bush II.* 5th ed. Lanham, Md.: Rowman & Littlefield, 2007. A thorough review of judicial appointments from the beginning of the republic to the present.

Cushman, Clare, ed. *The Supreme Court Justices, Illustrated Biographies, 1789–1995.* 2nd ed. Washington, D.C.: Congressional Quarterly, 1995. Includes biographies and histories of all U.S. Supreme Court justices.

Hall, Kermit, ed. *The Oxford Companion to the Supreme Court of the United States.* 2nd ed. New York: Oxford University Press, 2005. A veritable gold mine of information on individual court decisions, Supreme Court justices, legal terms, and so on.

Maroon, Fred J. *The Supreme Court of the United States*. Text by Suzy Maroon. New York: Thomasson-Grant & Lickle, 1996. Details the architecture of the U.S. Supreme Court Building.

McCloskey, Robert. *The American Supreme Court*. Revised by Stanford Levinson. Chicago: University of Chicago Press, 2001. A short but accurate general overview of the role that the Supreme Court has played in U.S. history.

O'Brien, David M. *Storm Center: The Supreme Court in American Politics*. 8th ed. New York: W. W. Norton, 2008. An engaging look at the U.S. Supreme Court.

Perry, Barbara A. *The Priestly Tribe: The Supreme Court's Image in the American Mind*. Westport, Conn.: Praeger, 1999. Combines discussions of judicial lore with popular perceptions of the Court.

Schultz, David, Michelle Deardorff, and John R. Vile. *Contemporary Constitutional Law*. 2 vols. Volume I: *Institutions, Politics, and Process*; Volume II, *Civil Rights and Liberties*. New York: Oxford University Press, 2010. A recent casebook for undergraduate classes in American constitutional law.

Vile, John R. *A Companion to the United States Constitution and Its Amendments*. 5th ed. Westport, Conn.: Praeger, 2010. Analyzes provisions of the U.S. Constitution and major interpretations by the U.S. Supreme Court.

Vile, John R., ed. *Great American Judges: An Encyclopedia*. 2 vols. Santa Barbara, Calif.: ABC-CLIO, 2003. Provides biographies of notable U.S. Supreme Court justices and other judges who have served throughout U.S. history on state and federal courts. These volumes complement an earlier set entitled *Great American Lawyers: An Encyclopedia*, 2001, with a similar historical focus.

Chapter One

ARTICLE I: THE LEGISLATIVE BRANCH

Including the Sixteenth and Seventeenth Amendments

The Framers of the U.S. Constitution anticipated that, of the three branches of government, the members of the legislature would be closest to the people. The Framers underscored this status by devoting the first of the seven major divisions, called articles, of the Constitution to the legislative branch.

The early sections of this article delineate the qualifications and terms of members of Congress. The U.S. Congress, like the English Parliament, is divided into two houses (the principle of bicameralism), each of which is designed to act as a brake on the other. The Constitution apportions the lower house, or House of Representatives, according to state population (with slaves originally counted as three-fifths of a person), and its members serve for two-year terms. State legislatures originally appointed members of the Senate to six-year terms, but, under provisions of the Seventeenth Amendment, the people of the states now elect them.

The Supreme Court has decided a number of important cases relating to the privileges of members. In *Powell v. McCormack* (1969), for example, the Court ruled that Congress may not add to the constitutionally specified requirements for membership. In *Gravel v. United States* (1972), the Court ruled that congressional aides share in some aspects of congressional immunity, and in *U.S. Term Limits v. Thornton* (1995) it ruled that states cannot impose term limits on its members.

After describing how Congress was to be configured and how its members would be elected, Article I, Section 7 specified that proposed bills will become law only after being passed in identical form by both houses of Congress and signed by the president. If the president exercises a veto, two-thirds majorities in both houses can still adopt the law. Article I, Section 8 further enumerated, or listed, congressional powers. Today's Congress exercises far more powers than did the congress under the Articles of Confederation.

1

Article I, Section 9 limits the powers of Congress, and Article I, Section 10 further limits the powers of the states.

In *McCulloch v. Maryland* (1819) the Supreme Court affirmed that Congress could exercise certain implied powers in addition to those that were specifically enumerated. This decision largely rested on the last clause of Article I, Section 8, known as the "necessary and proper clause." Arguably, recent decisions, in *Immigration and Naturalization Service v. Chadha* (1983) and in *Clinton v. City of New York* (1998), respectively outlawing the "legislative veto" and the "item veto," (and briefed under "Separation of Powers Issues" in chapter 3 on "Overlapping Powers") have further reinforced the specific lawmaking procedures outlined in Article I, Section 7.

Although Congress exercises a variety of powers, most laws are based on a few general grants of power. Among the most important are the clauses granting Congress authority over commerce between the states and with foreign nations and Indian tribes, the clause granting it power to tax and spend on behalf of the general welfare (the ever-important "power of the purse" that was enhanced when the Sixteenth Amendment overturned a contrary Supreme Court decision and provided for a federal income tax), and, as mentioned above, the clause granting it power to make all laws "necessary and proper" for carrying out its other powers. In an age of almost constant foreign threats, the congressional power to declare war, treated in a subsequent chapter, is also a major power.

Although the power is not unlimited, the power to conduct congressional investigations is among the powers recognized as necessary and proper for carrying out other congressional powers. The Court has allowed Congress to delegate some powers to other agencies and branches, but typically only when Congress sets forth "intelligible principles" to guide such discretion.

Subsequent amendments, most notably the Fourteenth (discussed in later chapters), have granted Congress additional powers. Congress thus remains one of the world's most powerful legislative bodies, a tribute to the Framers' vision of representative government. The system of elections and the courts continues to ensure that its powers are kept within constitutional boundaries.

POWERS

Commerce

Gibbons v. Ogden, 9 Wheaton (22 U.S.) 1; 6 L. Ed. 23 (1824)

Facts—The state of New York gave exclusive navigation rights to all water within the jurisdiction of the state of New York to R. R. Livingston and R.

Fulton, who assigned Ogden the right to operate between New York City and New Jersey ports. Gibbons owned two steamships running between New York and Elizabethtown, which were licensed under act of Congress. Ogden gained an injunction against Gibbons, who appealed.

Question—Can a state grant exclusive rights to navigate its waters?

Decision—No.

Reasons[*]—*C.J. Marshall* (6–0). Congressional power to regulate commerce is unlimited except as prescribed by the Constitution. Commerce is more than traffic; it is intercourse, thus including navigation, and it is regulated by prescribing rules for carrying on that intercourse. Regulating power over commerce between states does not stop at the jurisdictional lines of states, and may be exercised within a state, but it does not extend to commerce wholly within a state. When the state law and federal law conflict on this subject, federal law must be supreme. Thus the act of the state of New York was unconstitutional. Any matter that affects interstate commerce is within the power of Congress.

Note—This case, argued for Gibbons by Daniel Webster, is almost always the starting point for discussions of the commerce power and is noteworthy because it was the first one ever to go to the Court under the commerce clause. Marshall defined commerce very broadly and received popular acclaim for striking down a monopoly. The commerce clause has become one of the primary bases for the expansion of congressional powers.

ﻌﻬ

Brown v. Maryland, 12 Wheaton (25 U.S.) 419; 6 L. Ed. 678 (1827)

Facts—A Maryland law required all importers of foreign goods to have a license issued by the state. The indictment in this case charged Brown with having imported and sold some foreign goods without having a license to do so.

Question—Can the legislature of a state constitutionally require the importer of foreign goods to take out a license from the state before he shall be permitted to sell the goods imported?

---

[*] Quoted passages in the "reasons" in the briefs throughout this book are taken from the opinions of each case cited.

Decision—No.

Reasons—*C.J. Marshall* (6–1). The powers remaining with the states as a result of the Constitution may be so exercised as to come in conflict with those vested in Congress. When this happens, that which is not supreme must yield to that which is supreme. It results necessarily from this principle that the taxing power of the states must have some limits. The Maryland statute authorizing a tax on imports interfered with the federal government's control of commerce with foreign countries. Although not denying the right of a state to tax property within the state, state taxing of imports would derange the measures of Congress to regulate commerce, and affect materially the purpose for which that power was given. "It is sufficient for the present to say, generally, that when the importer has so acted upon the thing imported, that it has become incorporated and mixed up with the mass of property in the country, it has, perhaps, lost its distinctive character as an import, and has become subject to the taxing power of the state; but while remaining the property of the importer, in his warehouse, in the original form or package in which it was imported, a tax upon it is too plainly a duty on imports to escape the prohibition in the Constitution." The Court held the action of Maryland also to be contrary to the provision in the Constitution expressly forbidding states to tax imports.

Note—The "original package" case, Brown covers commerce from abroad to the states, as *Leisy v. Hardin*, 135 U.S. 100 (1890) covers commerce among the American states.

∽১ৡ

Cooley v. The Board of Wardens of the Port of Philadelphia, 12 Howard (53 U.S.) 299; 13 L. Ed. 996 (1851)

Facts—The Board of Wardens of the port of Philadelphia, acting under a statute of the state of Pennsylvania that established an elaborate system of regulations regarding pilots in the port including monetary penalties for failure to comply with the regulations, attempted to enforce the regulations. Cooley violated the regulations and when tried alleged that they were unconstitutional.

Question—Does congressional power to regulate interstate commerce preclude all state pilotage regulations?

Decision—No.

Reasons—*J. Curtis* (6–2). The grant of power to regulate commerce does not contain any terms that expressly exclude the states from exercising any authority over this subject matter. Although Congress has the power to regulate pilots, its legislation manifests an intention to allow states to regulate in this area. Curtis observed that "the power to regulate commerce, embraces a vast field, containing not only many, but exceedingly various subjects, quite unlike in their nature; some imperatively demanding a single uniform rule, operating equally on the commerce of the United States in every port; and some, like the subject now in question, as imperatively demanding that diversity, which alone can meet the local necessities of navigation."

J. McLean and *J. Wayne* dissented.

Note—The Court adopted a "selective exclusiveness doctrine" in which Congress would regulate commerce that was national and uniform, and the states would regulate such matters that were considered to be local.

United States v. E. C. Knight Co., 156 U.S. 1; 15 S. Ct. 249; 39 L. Ed. 325 (1895)

Facts—The government charged that the E. C. Knight Company, with four others, had contracted with the American Sugar Refining Company for the purchase by the latter of the stocks and properties of these corporations, and for the issuance of stock in the American Sugar Refining Company. It charged that this transaction was intended to bring about control of the price of sugar in the United States, together with a monopoly of the manufacture and sale of refined sugar in this country, in violation of the Sherman Antitrust Act (1890).

Question—May Congress prevent the intrastate purchase of refining companies in order to prevent a monopoly in interstate commerce?

Decision—No.

Reasons—*C.J. Fuller* (8–1). The power to control manufacturing involves in a certain sense the control of its disposition, but only in a secondary sense. The exercise of that power brings the operation of commerce into play, but only indirectly. The regulation of commerce applies to subjects of commerce, not to those of internal police. The fact that an article is manufactured with an intent of export to another state does not of itself make such an article an item of interstate commerce. It becomes so when it begins its journey in interstate commerce. The act of 1890 did not attempt to deal with monopolies as such, but with conspiracies to monopolize trade among the several states. In the case at hand, the object was private gain from manufacture of the commodity, not control of interstate or foreign commerce. There was nothing in the proofs to indicate any intention to restrain trade or commerce.

   J. Harlan authored a vigorous dissent indicating that he thought monopolies did obstruct interstate commerce and further arguing that this was a national problem that only the national government could adequately handle.

Note—*E. C. Knight* was reversed in *National Labor Review Board v. Jones and Laughlin Steel Corp.* (1937). *Knight* was the first big interpretation of the Sherman Antitrust Act. The practical effect of Knight was a legal "no man's land"—the doctrine of "dual federalism" that was seemingly erased in *United States v. F.W. Darby Lumber Co.*, 312 U.S. 100 (1941). but which has reemerged in more recent cases dealing with the relationship between state and federal powers.

In re Debs, 158 U.S. 564; 15 S. Ct. 900; 39 L. Ed. 1092 (1895)

Facts—Eugene V. Debs and associates, officers of the American Railway Union, had instituted a strike against the Pullman Company of Chicago. To enforce their demands they picketed the railway cars of that company and would not allow them to either enter or leave Chicago. In doing this they stopped interstate commerce and also the cars carrying U.S. mail. The federal court granted an injunction against the union picketing, and when Debs and the other officers of the union resisted, they were convicted of contempt.

Question—Is the federal government able to prevent a forcible obstruction of interstate commerce and of the mails?

Decision—Yes.

Reasons—*J. Brewer* (9–0). "The entire strength of the nation may be used to enforce in any part of the land the full and free exercise of all national powers and the security of all rights entrusted by the Constitution to its care. The strong arm of the national government may be put forth to brush away all obstructions to the freedom of interstate commerce or the transportation of the mails. If the emergency arises, the army of the nation, and all its militia, are at the service of the nation to compel obedience to its laws." Brewer further observed: "It is obvious from these decisions that while it is not the province of the government to interfere in any mere matter of private controversy between individuals, or to use its great powers to enforce the rights of one against another, yet, whenever the wrongs complained of are such as affect the public at large, and are in respect of matters which by the Constitution are entrusted to the care of the nation, and concerning which the nation owes the duty to all the citizens of securing to them their common rights, then the mere fact that the government has no pecuniary interest in the controversy is not sufficient to exclude it from the courts, or prevent it from taking measures therein to fully discharge those constitutional duties."

Note—Governor John Altgeld of Illinois strongly protested the introduction of troops to break up the strike, as did, years later, Governor Orval Faubus of Arkansas when President Dwight Eisenhower sent troops to Little Rock to control violence and assist in school integration—see *Cooper v. Aaron* (1958). When President John Kennedy dispatched federal troops to Mississippi to force the state university to admit James Meredith, a black student, Governor Ross Barnett protested vehemently.

∝≫

Champion v. Ames (The Lottery Case), 188 U.S. 321; 23 S. Ct. 321; 47 L. Ed. 492 (1903)

Facts—Congress passed legislation in 1895 to suppress lottery traffic through national and interstate commerce and the postal service. The regulation provided a prison term for each violation. Charles Champion was arrested for violating the act and claimed that the act was unconstitutional since the law at issue was a prohibition rather than a mere regulation.

Question—Did Congress exceed its power in passing the legislation in question?

Decision—No.

Reasons—*J. Harlan* (5–4). Congress by the act did not assume to interfere with traffic or commerce in lottery tickets carried on exclusively within the limits of any state, but had in view only commerce of that kind among the several states. As a state may, for the purpose of guarding the morals of its own people, forbid all sales of lottery tickets within its limits, so Congress, for the purpose of guarding the people of the United States against the "widespread pestilence of lotteries" and to protect the commerce that concerns all the states, may prohibit the carrying of lottery tickets from one state to another. Congress alone has the power to occupy by legislation the whole field of interstate commerce. If the carrying of lottery tickets from one state to another be interstate commerce, and if Congress is of the opinion that an effective regulation for the suppression of lotteries, carried on through such commerce, is to make it a criminal offense to cause lottery tickets to be carried from one state to another, the Court knew of no authority to hold that the means was not appropriate. The Court held "that lottery tickets are subject to traffic among those who choose to sell or buy them; that the carriage of such tickets by independent carriers from one state to another is therefore interstate commerce; that under its power to regulate commerce among the several states Congress—subject to the limitations imposed by the Constitution upon the exercise of the powers granted—has plenary authority over such commerce, and may prohibit the carriage of such tickets from state to state; and that legislation to that end, and of that character, is not inconsistent with any limitation or restriction imposed upon the exercise of the powers granted to Congress."

Dissenting justices led by *C.J. Fuller* argued that lottery tickets were not legally items of commerce, that they were not inherently harmful, and that Congress was interfering with police powers legitimately vested in the states.

Note—This case demonstrates how Congress can use its power under the commerce clause to exercise some federal "police powers."

⚜

The Shreveport Case (Houston, E. & W. Texas Ry. Co. v. United States), 234 U.S. 342; 34 S. Ct. 833; 58 L. Ed. 1341 (1914)

Facts—This case involved the power of Congress and its agent, the Interstate Commerce Commission, to control railroad rates between points within the same state. The commission had fixed rates between the city of Shreveport, Louisiana, and certain points in eastern Texas for which Shreveport is the natural trade center. Motivated by a natural desire to keep Texas trade safe for the Texans, the government of that state had endeavored to fix the rates between the eastern Texas points and such cities as Dallas and Houston so low that these eastern points would trade with the Texas cities even though they were farther away than was Shreveport. At this point the ICC ordered the intra-Texas rates raised to the same level as the interstate Texas-Louisiana rates.

Question—May Congress regulate local and intrastate commerce when such commerce impinges on interstate commerce?

Decision—Yes.

Reasons—*J. Hughes* (7–2). The Supreme Court upheld the right of the federal government to regulate the local or intrastate commerce in this case on the theory that it had such a close and substantial relation to interstate commerce that the satisfactory control of one required the simultaneous and identical control of the other. "Congress, in the exercise of its paramount power, may prevent the common instrumentalities of interstate and intrastate commercial intercourse from being used in their intrastate operations to the injury of interstate commerce. This is not to say that Congress possesses the authority to regulate the internal commerce of a state, as such, but that it does possess the power to foster and protect interstate commerce, and to take all measures necessary or appropriate to that end, although intrastate transactions or interstate carriers may thereby be controlled."

Dissenting *J. Lurton* and *J. Pitney* did not explain the reason for their dissent.

⚜

Hammer v. Dagenhart, 247 U.S. 251; 38 S. Ct. 529; 62 L. Ed. 1101 (1918)

Facts—In 1916 the Keating-Owen Act was passed. This provided that commodities produced under conditions in factories where children under fourteen years of age were employed or in mines where children under sixteen years of age were employed should be excluded from shipment in interstate or foreign commerce. Hours of employment were also specified for children between fourteen and sixteen years of age. Dagenhart, the father of two children, one under fourteen and the other between fourteen and sixteen, both of whom were employed in a mill in North Carolina, brought suit to enjoin Hammer, U.S. District Attorney, from enforcing the law against the employment of his two children. He got this injunction and Hammer took an appeal to the Supreme Court. The penalties connected with the act made it financially impossible to employ children under the age of sixteen because any establishment producing goods with the aid of under-aged children could not ship its products in interstate commerce until thirty days after cessation of the practice.

Question—Can Congress exclude from interstate commerce all goods manufactured by child labor?

Decision—No.

Reasons—*J. Day* (5–4). The making of goods and the mining of products is not commerce, and the fact that those things go afterwards into interstate commerce does not make them in their production interstate commerce per se. Congress has the power to regulate and deny to interstate commerce such products as impure foods, liquors, drugs, and others having possible harmful effects. However, there is nothing harmful, in themselves, in goods produced by child labor; therefore, this power does not apply. Child labor may be regulated only under the police power of the states, and therefore, Congress may not violate this state right. Thus the act "not only transcends the authority delegated to Congress over commerce, but also exerts a power as to a purely local matter to which the federal authority does not extend."

J. Holmes argued in dissent that the law adopted by Congress fell under its authority to regulate commerce and that prohibition is no less prohibition "when applied to things now thought evil." Although seeking to exclude his own judgments on such matters, Holmes opined that there was far greater consensus on the evil of "premature and excessive child labor" than on regulation of alcohol and other goods the legality of which the Court had upheld in prior cases.

Note—*United States v. Darby*, 312 U.S. 100 (1941), which upheld the Fair Labor Standards Act of 1938, reversed *Hammer*.

๛

Stafford v. Wallace, 258 U.S. 495; 42 S. Ct. 397; 66 L. Ed. 735 (1922)

Facts—Stafford and Company, engaged in the buying and selling of livestock, brought suit against Secretary of Agriculture H. C. Wallace to prohibit him from enforcing the Packers and Stockyards Act of 1921, which they contended was unconstitutional. The act provided for federal authority to supervise the business of the commission men and of the livestock dealers in the great stockyards of the country. Congress passed the act because, after extensive investigation, it found that the nation's "Big Five" meatpackers were engaged in a conspiracy in violation of antitrust laws to control the business of the purchase of livestock, their preparation for use in meat products, and the distribution and sale thereof in this country and abroad.

Question—Did Congress have the authority under the commerce clause to supervise the activities of the meatpackers?

Decision—Yes.

Reasons—*C.J. Taft* (7–1). Congress was exercising its established authority over interstate commerce. The stockyards are not a place of rest or final destination. Thousands of head of livestock arrive daily by carload and must be promptly sold and disposed of and moved out to give place to the constantly flowing traffic that presses behind. The stockyards are but a throat through which the current flows, and the transactions that occur therein are only incident to this current from the West to the East, and from one state to another. Such transactions cannot be separated from the movement to which they contribute, and necessarily take on its character. The commission men are essential in making the sales without which the flow of the current would be obstructed, and this, whether they are made to packers or dealers. The dealers are essential to the sales to the stock farmers and feeders. The sales are not in this aspect merely local transactions. They create a local change of title, but they do not stop the flow; they merely change the private interests in the subject of the current, not interfering with, but on the contrary, being indispensable to its continuity. The origin of the livestock is in the West, its ultimate destination known to, and intended by all engaged in the business is in the Middle West and East, either as meat products or stock for feeding and fattening. The stockyards and the sales are necessary factors in the middle of this current of commerce.

J. McReynolds did not explain the reason for his dissent. *J. Day* took no part in the decision.

Note—This case demonstrates that activities that closely affect the "stream of commerce" may be made subject to federal regulation even though the activities take place wholly within a state. *Stafford* follows logically from *Shreveport*, which allowed Congress to regulate intrastate railroad rates when necessary for effective regulation of interstate rates.

⌖

Ashwander v. Tennessee Valley Authority, 297 U.S. 288; 56 S. Ct. 466; 80 L. Ed. 688 (1936)

Facts—The TVA, an agency of the federal government, entered into a contract with the Alabama Power Company, providing for the purchase by the TVA, among other items, of certain transmission lines and real property. Also included in the contract were the interchange of hydroelectric energy and the sale by the TVA to the power company of the surplus power from the Wilson Dam. The plaintiffs, who held preferred stock in the power company, were unable to get results in protesting the contract to the power company. Therefore, they sought a decree restraining these activities as repugnant to the Constitution. The district court issued a decree annulling the contract and the Circuit Court of Appeals reversed.

Question—Is the contract of the TVA with the Alabama Power Company beyond the constitutional power of the federal government?

Decision—No.

Reasons—*C.J. Hughes* (8–1). The Court first considered the constitutional authority for the construction of the Wilson Dam, which was supported on the grounds that it was constructed under the exercise of war and commerce powers, that is, for the purpose of national defense and the improvement of navigation. Secondly, the Court considered the constitutional authority to dispose of electric energy generated at the Wilson Dam. Here it held that the authority to dispose of property constitutionally acquired by the United States is expressly granted to Congress by Section 3 of Article 4 of the Constitution. This section provides: "The Congress shall have power to dispose of and make all needful rules and regulations respecting the territory or other property belonging to the United States; and nothing in this Constitution shall be so construed as to prejudice any claims of the United States, or of any particular state."

J. McReynolds argued in dissent that the national government was improperly exercising powers that were not entrusted to it by the U.S. Constitution.

Note—*J. Brandeis's* concurrence set out the "Ashwander Rules," announcing various maxims of self-restraint that the Supreme Court will generally follow before declaring congressional legislation to be unconstitutional.

Kentucky Whip and Collar Co. v. Illinois Central R.R. Co., 299 U.S. 334; 57 S. Ct. 277; 81 L. Ed. 270 (1937)

Facts—The Ashurst-Sumners Act of 1935 made it unlawful to ship in interstate commerce goods made by convict labor into any state where the goods are intended to be received, possessed, sold, or used in violation of its laws. Packages containing convict-made goods must be plainly labeled so as to show the names and addresses of shipper and consignee, the nature of the contents, and the name and location of the penal or reformatory institution where the article was produced. The petitioner manufactured in Kentucky, with convict labor, horse collars, harness, and strap goods that were marketed in various states. The Illinois Central received twenty-five separate shipments, for transportation in interstate commerce, none of which was labeled as required. The respondent refused to accept the shipments, and the petitioner brought suit for a mandatory injunction to compel shipment.

Question—Does Congress have the power to prohibit in interstate commerce useful and harmless articles made by convict labor?

Decision—Yes.

Reasons—*C. J. Hughes* (8–0). The congressional power to regulate commerce is complete in itself, acknowledging no other limitations than those the Constitution prescribes. The question here is whether this statute goes beyond the authority to "regulate." The power to prohibit interstate transportation has been upheld in many cases. In fact, in the exercise of its control over interstate commerce, Congress may have the quality of police regulations. In so regulating, Congress may shape its policy to aid valid state laws in the protection of persons and property. Therefore, Congress may prevent transportation in interstate commerce of articles in which the state has the constitutional authority to forbid traffic in its internal commerce. The Ashurst-Sumners Act has substantially the same provisions as the Webb-Kenyon Act. The subject matter is different, the effects are different, but the principle is the same. Where the subject of commerce is one on which the power of a state may be constitutionally exerted, Congress may prevent interstate commerce from being used to frustrate the state policy. Labels are but a reasonable provision for carrying out the purposes of the act.

West Coast Hotel Co. v. Parrish, 300 U.S. 379; 57 S. Ct. 578; 81 L. Ed. 703 (1937)

Facts—Washington State laws prohibited wages below a living wage and conditions of labor detrimental to the health and morals of women and minors. Such wages were established by the state's Industrial Welfare Commission composed of members of management, labor, and the government. Elsie Parrish brought suit to recover the difference between her wages and those established by the Industrial Welfare Commission over a period of years during which the West Coast Hotel Company had employed her.

Question—Is the statute regulating minimum wages for women and children contrary to the due process clause of the Fourteenth Amendment?

Decision—No.

Reasons—*C.J. Hughes* (5–4). The principle controlling the decision—the Fourteenth Amendment—was not in doubt. Those attacking minimum wage regulation alleged that they were being deprived of freedom of contract. "What is this freedom? The Constitution does not speak of freedom of contract. It speaks of liberty and prohibits the deprivation of liberty without due process of law. In prohibiting that deprivation, the Constitution does not recognize an absolute, an uncontrollable liberty. Liberty in each of its phases has its history and connotation. But the liberty safeguarded is liberty in a social organization that requires the protection of law against the evils that menace the health, safety, morals and welfare of the people. Liberty under the Constitution is thus necessarily subject to the restraints of due process, and regulation which is reasonable in relation to its subject and is adopted in the interests of the community is due process."

The minimum wage requirement of the state of Washington did not seem to the Court to have gone beyond the boundary of its broad protective power. The wage was fixed after full consideration by representatives of employers, employees, and the public. No one was forced to pay anything; it simply forbade employment at rates fixed below the minimum requirement for health and right living. This, the Court held, was a valid exercise of state police power, and it was the conclusion of the Court that "the case of *Adkins v. Children's Hospital* should be, and it is overruled." (This decision also had the effect of reversing *Morehead v. New York ex rel. Tipaldo*.)

In dissent, *J. Sutherland* argued for continuing adherence to precedents regarding freedom of contract and objected to the majority's apparent consideration of economic exigencies rather than what Sutherland regarded as constitutional commands.

Wickard v. Filburn, 317 U.S. 111; 63 S. Ct. 82; 87 L. Ed. 122 (1942)

Facts—Filburn owned and operated a small farm in Montgomery County, Ohio, maintaining a herd of dairy cattle, selling milk, raising poultry, and selling poultry and eggs. He was accustomed to raising a small acreage of winter wheat, of which a portion was sold, part fed to poultry and livestock, part used for making flour for home consumption, and the rest kept for seeding the following year. In 1940, according to the Second Agricultural Adjustment Act, he was given a wheat acreage of 11.1 acres and a normal yield of 20.1 bushels of wheat an acre. He sowed, however, 23 acres, and harvested from his excess acreage 239 bushels, which was subject to a penalty of 49 cents a bushel, or $117.11 in all. Filburn claimed that he did not produce excess wheat for the purpose of marketing but for his own consumption on his farm. He refused to pay the penalty, or to store the excess according to regulations.

Question—Does Congress possess the power under the commerce clause of the Constitution to regulate the production and consumption of wheat destined for personal use on the farm?

Decision—Yes.

Reasons—*J. Jackson* (9–0). Marketing, according to the act, included, in addition to the conventional meaning, whatever might be consumed on the premises. Questions of federal power cannot be sidestepped by calling such activities indirect. Whether the appellant's activity was local or whether it was regarded as commerce or not, if it exerted a substantial economic effect on interstate commerce, such activity could be regulated by Congress. The consumption of homegrown wheat is the most variable factor in the disappearance of the wheat crop. Even though the appellant's contribution to the demand for wheat may have been trivial, it did not remove him from the field of federal regulation. His contribution, together with others in similar circumstances, had a substantial influence on price and market conditions. Therefore, homegrown wheat competes with commercially grown wheat in commerce. The stimulation of commerce is a regulatory function clearly within the power of Congress.

United States v. Southeastern Underwriters Association 322 U.S. 533; 64 S. Ct. 1162; 88 L. Ed. 1440 (1944)

Facts—The Southeastern Underwriters Association represented private stock companies that sold fire insurance in six southeastern states. They were indicted in a federal District Court for violating the Sherman Antitrust Act by fixing and maintaining arbitrary and noncompetitive premium rates, and by monopolizing the trade and commerce in fire insurance in and among the same states. They contended that selling insurance was not commerce and did not come under the interstate commerce regulations.

Question—Do fire insurance transactions that stretch across state lines constitute "commerce among the several states" subject to congressional regulation?

Decision—Yes.

Reasons—*J. Black* (4–3). The basic responsibility in interpreting the commerce clause is to make certain that the power to govern intercourse among the states remains where the Constitution placed it. That power is vested in

Congress, to be exercised for the national welfare as Congress shall deem necessary. No commercial enterprise of any kind that conducts its activities across state lines is wholly beyond the regulatory power of Congress under the commerce clause. The insurance business is no exception.

Note—Southeastern reversed the long-standing precedent, *Paul v. Virginia*, 8 Wallace (75 U.S.) 168 (1869). Congress reacted by passing the McCarran Act permitting the states to continue to regulate insurance, and it was upheld in *Prudential Insurance Company v. Benjamin*, 328 U.S. 408 (1946). The results of the McCarran Act make it appear that the issue in *Southeastern* had never been decided.

Heart of Atlanta Motel, Inc. v. United States, 379 U.S. 241; 85 S. Ct. 348; 13 L. Ed. 2d 258 (1964)

Facts—The owner of a large motel in Atlanta, Georgia, which restricted its clientele to white persons, brought suit for a declaratory judgment and for an injunction to restrain enforcement of Title II of the Civil Rights Act of 1964, which outlawed distinguishing on the basis of race, color, religion, or national origin in making available public accommodations.

Question—Does Congress have the power to outlaw racial discrimination in public accommodations under its power to regulate interstate commerce?

Decision—Yes.

Reasons—*J. Clark* (9–0). The power of Congress over interstate commerce includes the power to regulate local incidents and activities in both the states of origin and destination of the commerce that might have a substantial and harmful effect on that commerce. The Court concluded that "the action of the Congress in the adoption of the act as applied here to a motel which concededly serves interstate travelers is within the power granted it by the Commerce Clause of the Constitution as interpreted by this Court for 140 years."

In a concurring opinion, *J. Douglas* argued that the Court should place greater reliance on congressional powers to enforce civil rights through Section 5 of the Fourteenth Amendment rather than focusing on the commerce clause.

Note—This decision evaded the limitations imposed in the *Civil Rights Cases*, 109 U.S. 3 (1883) by focusing on federal powers under the commerce clause rather than on the Fourteenth Amendment, which reached only state actions. The Court applied the doctrine from *Heart of Atlanta Motel* in a companion case, *Katzenbach v. McClung*, 379 U.S. 294 (1964), involving a restaurant that purchased much of its food through interstate commerce.

◦⤙⨤

United States v. Lopez, 514 U.S. 549; 115 S. Ct. 1624; 131 L. Ed. 2d 626 (1995)

Facts—A twelfth-grade student was convicted of violating the Gun-Free School Zones Act of 1990 for knowingly possessing a firearm at a school. Lopez appealed his conviction in a U.S. District Court to the U.S. Fifth Circuit Court, which found that the act exceeded federal powers to regulate interstate commerce.

Question—Does the Gun-Free School Zones Act of 1990 exceed congressional powers under the commerce clause?

Decision—Yes.

Reasons—*C.J. Rehnquist* (5–4). Starting with "first principles," Rehnquist noted that "The Constitution creates a Federal Government of enumerated powers." One such power was that of regulating interstate and foreign commerce. Initially devoted chiefly to limiting state legislation discriminating against such commerce, interpretations of the clause have since been widened to allow greater federal regulation of commercial activities. Such activities may be divided into three broad areas—regulations of the "channels of interstate commerce," the "instrumentalities" of such commerce, and activities "having a substantial relation to interstate commerce." Since the first two are involved in this case, the Court must examine the third. The statute at issue "is a criminal statute that by its terms has nothing to do with 'commerce' or any sort of economic enterprise, however broadly one might define those terms," and Congress made no attempt to assess such a relationship on a case-by-case basis or to establish a commercial nexus in this area of policy. To find such a nexus would be to invest Congress with "a plenary police power that would authorize enactment of every type of legislation." To uphold this law, the Court "would have to pile inference upon inference in a manner that would bid fair to convert congressional authority under the Commerce Clause to a general police power of the sort retained by the States."

　J. Kennedy's concurring opinion expressed some concern over the Court's past history in this area but concluded that the Court's decision was necessary to preserve federalism and the powers reserved to the states. *J. Thomas's* concurrence called for a reexamination of the "substantial effects" test, which he believed has invested Congress with excessive power. *J. Stevens's* dissent argued that commerce depends on education and that guns threaten such education.

J. Souter's dissent argued for deference to rationally based legislative judgments as to what affects commerce. *J. Breyer* argued that power to regulate commerce included the power to regulate local activities that affect interstate commerce, that Congress can consider the cumulate effects of gun possession, and that courts are obligated to defer to congressional judgments as to such effects. He believed that Congress could reasonably have found a rational basis for connecting gun violence in schools with disruptions of interstate commerce. Souter believed this decision was inconsistent with past precedents, that it rested on a false distinction between commercial and non-commercial activities, and that it threatened "legal uncertainty in an area of law that, until this case, seemed reasonably well settled."

Jones v. United States, 529 U.S. 848; 120 S. Ct. 1904; 146 L. Ed. 2d 902 (2000)

Facts—A section of the Organized Crime Control Act of 1970 made it a federal crime to damage a building "used in interstate or foreign commerce." Dewey Jones threw a Molotov cocktail through his cousin's house, not injuring him, but causing extensive damage. He was convicted in a U.S. District Court in Indiana for violating the federal law, a decision affirmed by the Seventh Circuit Court of Appeals.

Question—Does the Organized Crime Control Act of 1970 cover damage to property used as a private residence?

Decision—No, such property does not fall under congressional regulation of interstate commerce.

Reasons—*J. Ginsburg* (9–0). Ginsburg noted that the language of the federal statute applied to structures "used in" commercial activities. This house was a private residence, and the government's attempts to tie the property to commercial use are weak. It is not sufficient that its owner used the house as collateral to secure a loan, that he had an out-of-state insurance policy, or that he used out-of-state natural gas. The house was used as a private residence and not as part of a "trade or business." The precedent in *United States. v. Lopez* (1995) was thus relevant. To utilize the government's construction in this case would be to obliterate the words "used in." Where possible, the Court should construe legislation so as not to displace matters of criminal law upon which states had already legislated.

J. Stevens's concurrence likewise argued that congressional laws should not be used to preempt state laws, where such an intention was not expressly stated. *J. Thomas's* concurrence reserved judgment as to whether the law in question could be constitutionally applied "to all buildings used for commercial activities."

☙

Gonzales v. Raich, 545 U.S. 1; 125 S. Ct. 2195; 162 L. Ed. 2d 1 (2005)

Facts—Angel Raich and Diane Monson are California residents who had permission on the state's Compassionate Use Act to use marijuana prescribed by medical doctors for a variety of ailments for which other medications had failed. Federal agents destroyed six cannabis plants that Monson cultivated, and she and Raich (who relied on two caregivers to provide her with the drug) sought to enjoin further federal enforcement of the law against them. The Ninth Circuit Court of Appeals reversed a district court and issued a preliminary injunction.

Question—Does Congress have power under the commerce clause and the necessary and proper clause to prohibit the local cultivation and use of marijuana that is undertaken in compliance with California law?

Decision—Yes

Reasons—*J. Stevens* (6–3). Efforts by the national government to regulate marijuana date back to 1937 but were increased after the declaration of a "war on drugs" in 1970 and Congress's adoption of the Comprehensive Drug Abuse Prevention and Control Act, or Controlled Substance Act (CSA). This act created "a closed regulatory system making it unlawful to manufacture, distribute, dispense, or possess any controlled substance except in a manner authorized by the CSA." Under this scheme, marijuana was classified as a Schedule I drug, because of its "high potential for abuse, lack of any accepted medical use, and absence of any accepted safety for use in medically supervised treatment." Raich and Monson question whether this power extends to "the intrastate manufacture and possession of marijuana for medical purposes pursuant to California law." The court has recognized congressional power to regulate the channels and instrumentalities of commerce and "activities that substantially affect interstate commerce." *Wickard v. Filburn* (1942) extended this control to wheat that was grown for home consumption. As in *Wickard*, Congress has concluded that local use could substantially affect commerce as a whole. Moreover, it is not the Court's responsibility to decide whether this judgment is correct but only to ascertain "whether a 'rational basis' exists for so concluding." The CSA was adopted as part of "a comprehensive framework for regulating the production, distribution, and possession" of drugs. The activities at issue are "quintessentially economic," economic being defined as "the production, distribution, and consumption of commodities." Medical exemptions "would undermine the orderly enforcement of the entire regulatory scheme." Under the supremacy clause "state action cannot circumscribe Congress' plenary commerce power." Exemptions are likely to "increase the supply of marijuana in the California market," and will provide opportunities for unscrupulous physicians and others to evade federal law.

J. Scalia, concurring, further emphasized the role of the necessary and proper clause in interpreting federal powers under the commerce clause. He viewed California's regulations as reasonably adapted to this end, in a matter involving economic activities. Drugs are "fungible commodities," which need to be regulated as a whole, and federal regulation does not violate state sovereignty.

J. O'Connor, dissenting. The Court needs to enforce limits on the commerce clause "to protect historic spheres of state sovereignty from excessive federal encroachment." Federalism "promotes innovation" and allows states to serve as laboratories. Under police powers, states have been permitted "to define criminal law and to protect the health, safety, and welfare of their citizens." This case is not materially distinguishable from *United States v. Lopez* (1995) and *United States v. Morrison* (2000). Granting Congress power to enact such a broad regulatory scheme "is tantamount to removing meaningful limits on the Commerce Clause." The Court needs "to identify a mode of analysis that allows Congress to regulate more than nothing . . . and less than everything." Here it can do so by recognizing the distinction between "medical and nonmedical" drug uses. The activities at issue here are neither commercial, nor were the drugs within "the stream of commerce." Congress asserted a connection between such uses and commerce in general but made no efforts to prove it as it did in the case of *Wickard v. Filburn*: "There is simply no evidence that homegrown medicinal marijuana users constitute, in the aggregate, a sizable enough class to have a discernable, let alone substantial, impact on the national illicit drug market—or otherwise to threaten the CSA regime." CSA's declarations are too vague and are not specific to marijuana and do not take account of the fact that California had adopted an identification card system for qualified patients.

J. Thomas, dissenting. If Congress can regulate intrastate goods that have never been bought or sold, "then it can regulate virtually anything—and the

Federal Government is no longer one of limited and enumerated powers."
As the Founders understood it, "Commerce, or trade, stood in contrast to
productive activities like manufacturing and agriculture." Here the respondents are part of "a distinct and separable subclass (local growers and users
of state-authorized, medical marijuana) that does not undermine the CSA's
interstate ban." Any seepage of medical marijuana into the illicit drug market
is likely to have little effect on the market as a whole. Congress is encroach-
ing on state police powers. The "substantial effects" test "is a 'rootless and
malleable standard' at odds with the constitutional design." "[T]he majority's
view—that because *some* of the CSA's applications are constitutional, they
must *all* be constitutional—undermines its reliance on the substantial effects
test." "The majority's rush to embrace federal power 'is especially unfortunate given the importance of showing respect for the sovereign States that
comprise our Federal Union.'"

Delegation of Powers

*J.W. Hampton, Jr. & Co. v. United States, 276 U.S. 394; 48 S. Ct. 348; 72
L. Ed. 624 (1928)*

Facts—J.W. Hampton, Jr. and Company imported some goods at a New
York port and was assessed a rate higher than fixed by statute. The collector
of the port assessed the increase under authority of a proclamation by the
president. The basis of the tariff was an act of Congress setting up a Tariff
Commission under the executive branch of the government. The act gave the
president the power to fix and change duties on imports after investigation by
the commission and notice given to all parties interested to produce evidence.
This was the so-called flexible tariff provision. The law provided that the
increase or decrease of the tariff duties should not exceed 50 percent of the
rate set by Congress. The Hampton Company contended that the act gave the
president the power to legislate and therefore was unconstitutional.

Question—Does the act allowing the president to alter specified tariffs invoke improper delegation of legislative power?

Decision—No.

Reasons—*C.J. Taft* (9–0). The Court held that the true distinction is between
the delegation of power to make the law, which necessarily involves a discretion as to what it shall be, and conferring an authority or discretion as to its

execution, to be exercised under and in pursuance of the law. The first cannot be done; the second, as was the case here, is valid.

The Court referred to the reasoning in *Field v. Clark*, 143 U.S. 649 (1892), to substantiate the point that Congress did not delegate legislative powers to the president, because nothing involving the contents of the law was left to the president's determination. The legislative power was performed when Congress passed an act setting up the Tariff Commission as a part of the executive branch, placing the power to execute the law in the hands of the president, and setting down the general rules of action under which both the commission and the president should proceed.

"What the president was required to do was merely in execution of the act of Congress. It was not the making of law. He was the mere agent of the lawmaking department to ascertain and declare the event upon which its expressed will was to take effect."

The Court also upheld the protection features of the tariff act as a proper exercise of its power over foreign commerce, as well as on the basis of action by the First Congress, which was composed, in part, of Framers of the Constitution.

❧

Panama Refining Co. v. Ryan, 293 U.S. 388; 55 S. Ct. 241; 79 L. Ed. 446 (1935)

Facts—Section 9 (c) of the National Industrial Recovery Act (NIRA) had given the president the power to forbid the transportation in interstate commerce of oil produced or withdrawn from storage in violation of state law. The Panama Refining Company, as owner of an oil refining plant in Texas, sued to restrain the defendants, who were federal officials, from enforcing regulations from the Department of Interior based on the National Industrial Recovery Act, on the grounds that Section 9 (c) of the act was unconstitutional.

Question—Does Section 9 (c) of the National Industrial Recovery Act unconstitutionally delegate legislative power to the president?

Decision—Yes.

Reasons—*C.J. Hughes* (8–1). The statute did not contain any definition of the circumstances or conditions in which the transportation was to be permitted or prohibited. In other words, the power of the president was purely discretionary. He was not merely filling in the details of a legislative policy, since no legislative policy was outlined to guide or control him. While very broad powers of administrative regulation may be delegated to the president, a legislative statement of policy must be sufficiently definite to prevent the exercise upon his part of pure discretion. Section 9 (c) of the NIRA in essence delegates the power to legislate to the president and is therefore unconstitutional and void.

Note—This is known as the "Hot Oil Case" in reference to oil produced or withdrawn from storage in violation of state law. It was the first New Deal statute declared void as an unconstitutional delegation of power. The well-known maxim *delegata potestas non potest delegari* (delegated power cannot be redelegated) is the basis of the decision. Delegated power to the president in foreign affairs has escaped Court censure, as in *United States v. Curtiss-Wright Export Corp.*, 299 U.S. 304 (1936), but is still denied to the states, as decided in *Knickerbocker Ice Co. v. Stewart*, 253 U.S. 149 (1920).

Schechter Poultry Corp. v. United States, 295 U.S. 495; 55 S. Ct. 837; 79 L. Ed. 1570 (1935)

Facts—The A.L.A. Schechter Poultry Corp. was convicted in the U.S. District Court for the Eastern District of New York on an indictment charging violations of what was known as the "Live Poultry Code," established by executive order under the National Industrial Recovery Act (NIRA). The Circuit Court of Appeals sustained the conviction in the district court on sixteen counts for violation of the code, but reversed the conviction on two counts that charged violation of requirements as to minimum wages and maximum hours of labor, as these were not deemed to be within the congressional power of regulation. The NIRA provided for the setting up of codes that would establish certain standards that were to be upheld under force of civil and criminal action. If an industry did not set up its own code, it would be up to the president to impose a code upon it. Schechter was a poultry dealer in New York City and disregarded the code. When tried, he was found guilty on eighteen counts. He then took the case to the Supreme Court.

Question—(a) Was the act an illegal delegation of legislative powers? (b) Was the poultry in this case considered within the domain of the interstate commerce power of Congress?

Decision—(a) Yes; (b) No.

Reasons—*C.J. Hughes* (9–0). (a) The act set no standard or rules of conduct to be followed. It was too broad a declaration, leaving the president too much room for discretion. The act left virtually untouched the field of policy. The president in approving a code could impose his own conditions. It was an unconstitutional delegation of legislative power. The Constitution provides that "all legislative powers herein granted shall be vested in a Congress of the United States, which shall consist of a Senate and House of Representatives," and the Congress is authorized "to make all laws which shall be necessary and proper for carrying into execution" its general powers. The Congress is not permitted to abdicate or to transfer to others the essential legislative functions with which it is thus vested.

(b) Although the poultry came from various states, when it arrived in New York it remained there and was processed. Congress could regulate it until it reached New York; after that it was intrastate commerce and as such Congress could not control it.

J. Cardozo wrote a notable concurring opinion in which he focused on what he considered to be untrammeled delegation of congressional legislative powers.

☙

United States v. Curtiss-Wright Export Corp., 299 U.S. 304; 57 S. Ct. 216; 81 L. Ed. 255 (1936)

Facts—Curtiss-Wright Export Corp. sold armaments to Bolivia, a country then engaged in armed conflict in the Chaco region in South America The company was charged with violating the joint resolution of Congress empowering the president to forbid the sale of any articles of war to countries engaged in armed conflict if this prohibition of sale would promote peace between the combatants. The president issued such a proclamation and made violation of it punishable as a crime.

Question—Is this joint resolution of Congress an illegal delegation of legislative power to the president?

Decision—No.

Reasons—*J. Sutherland* (7–1). "It is important to bear in mind that we are here dealing not alone with an authority vested in the president by an exertion of legislative power; but with such an authority plus the very delicate, plenary and exclusive power of the president as the sole organ of the federal government in the field of international relations—a power which does not require as a basis for its exercise an act of Congress, but which, of course, like every other governmental power, must be exercised in subordination to the applicable provisions of the Constitution. It is quite apparent that if, in the maintenance of our international relations, embarrassment—perhaps serious embarrassment—is to be avoided and success for our aims achieved, congressional legislation which is to be made effective through negotiation and inquiry within the international field must often accord to the president a degree of discretion and freedom from statutory restriction which would not be admissible were domestic affairs alone involved. . . .

"Practically every volume of the United States Statutes contains one or more acts or joint resolutions of Congress authorizing action by the President in respect of subjects affecting foreign relations which either leave the exercise of the power to his unrestricted judgment, or provide a standard far more general than that which has always been considered requisite with regard to domestic affairs. . . . A legislative practice such as we have here, evidenced not by only occasional instances, but marked by the movement of a steady stream for a century and a half of time, goes a long way in the direction of proving the presence of unassailable ground for the constitutionality of the practice, to be found in the origin and history of the power involved, or in its nature, or in both combined. . . ."

Note—*Curtiss-Wright* is often linked to *Missouri v. Holland*, 252 U.S. 416 (1920) in terms of foreign policy and treaty powers. A good deal of *Curtiss-Wright* is expansive and dicta, but, except for the inherent power doctrine, more clearly noted in *In re Neagle*, 135 U.S. 1 (1890) and modified in *Youngstown Sheet and Tube Co. v. Sawyer*, 343 U.S. 579 (1952), the Court has not repudiated its language. The War Powers Act of 1973 is still another attempt to contain *Curtiss-Wright*. Article 1, Section 8 clearly sets out Congress's delegated powers. Congress can use or not use its powers but cannot violate the axiom *delegata potestas non potest delegari*—delegated power cannot be redelegated. But a delegated power is possible in which Congress sets up the objective and then authorizes an administration or commission to carry it out and allows an administrator to determine and act when certain conditions exist.

Yakus v. United States, 321 U.S. 414; 64 S. Ct. 660; 88 L. Ed. 834 (1944)

Facts—The petitioner was tried and convicted for willfully selling wholesale cuts of beef at prices above the maximum prices prescribed by the price regulations set down by the federal price administrator under the authority of the Emergency Price Control Act of January 30, 1942, as amended by the Inflation Control Act of October 2, 1942.

Question—Do the acts in question involve an unconstitutional delegation to the price administrator of the legislative power of Congress to control prices?

Decision—No.

Reasons—*C.J. Stone* (6–3). "The essentials of the legislative function are the determination of the legislative policy and its formulation and promulgation as a defined and binding rule of conduct—here the rule, with penal sanctions, that prices shall not be greater than those fixed by maximum price regulations which conform to standards and will tend to further the policy which Congress has established. These essentials are preserved when Congress has specified the basic conditions of fact upon whose existence or occurrence, ascertained from relevant data by a designated administrative agency, it directs that its statutory command shall be effective. It is no objection that the determination of facts and the inferences to be drawn from them in the light of the statutory standards and declaration of policy call for the exercise of judgment, and for the formulation of subsidiary administrative policy within the prescribed statutory framework. . . . The standards prescribed by the present Act, with the aid of the 'statement of the considerations' required to be made by the administrator, are sufficiently definite and precise to enable Congress, the courts, and the public to ascertain whether the administrator, in fixing the designated prices, has conformed to those standards. Hence we are unable to find in them an unauthorized delegation of legislative power."

Mistretta v. United States, 488 U.S. 361; 109 S. Ct. 647; 102 L. Ed. 2d 714 (1989)

Facts—The Sentencing Reform Act of 1984 created a Sentencing Commission consisting of seven members appointed by the president, and including three federal judges. Indicted for a cocaine sale, Mistretta challenged the commission as a violation of separation of powers and an excessive delegation of legislative powers. A U.S. District Court in Missouri rejected this plea that both parties appealed to the U.S. Supreme Court before judgment by the Eighth Circuit Court of Appeals.

Questions—(a) Does the law creating the Sentencing Commission delegate impermissible legislative power? (b) Does the establishment of the Sentencing Commission violate the doctrine of separation of powers?

Decisions—(a) No; (b) No.

Reasons—*J. Blackmun* (8–1). The Sentencing Commission was created after concerns were expressed about wide disparities in sentencing and the uncertainties that these disparities created. The commission was designed to devise such guidelines. The nondelegation doctrine was not designed to prevent Congress "from obtaining the assistance of its coordinate Branches." The doctrine does not prohibit all delegation but simply provides that in making delegations, the legislature should provide "an intelligible principle to which the person or body authorized to [exercise the delegate authority] is directed to conform." In this case the Congress directed the commission to consider seven factors related to offense categories and even more detailed guidance as to the characteristics of an offender. As to separation of powers, the Constitution does not mandate complete separation but was designed to prevent excessive accumulation of power within a single branch. Concerns over the Sentencing Commission constitute "'more smoke than fire.'" The institution is "a peculiar institution within the framework of our Government," but it is not illegal. There is no obstacle to placing such a commission within the judicial branch. The commission "is not a court" but "an independent agency in every relevant sense." Placing the commission within the judicial branch has not increased the power of this branch. Although the Constitution contains an "incompatability clause" prohibiting legislators from holding joint offices, there is "no comparable restriction" for judges who have performed extrajudicial functions throughout American history. Such appointments do not therefore violate the separation of powers. Judges on the commission serve voluntarily, and their service on the commission does not diminish their authority as judges. Although they may be removed from the commission under certain limited circumstances, they may not be removed from their judicial positions.

J. Scalia's dissent argued that the "guidelines" developed by the commission "have the force and effect of laws." Moreover, this "lawmaking function" is "completely divorced from any responsibility for execution of the law or adjudication of private rights under the law." Because the commission's power is unaccountable, it is undemocratic. The Sentencing Commission does not so much commingle branches as create "a new Branch altogether, a sort of junior varsity Congress." "And in the long run the improvisation of a constitutional structure on the basis of currently perceived utility will be disastrous."

Implied Powers

McCulloch v. Maryland, 4 Wheaton (17 U.S.) 316; 4 L. Ed. 579 (1819)

Facts—Although the U.S. Constitution made no direct mention of the subject, Congress incorporated the Bank of the United States, a branch of which it established in Baltimore. The state of Maryland required all banks not chartered by the state to pay a tax on each issuance of bank notes. McCulloch, the cashier of the Baltimore branch of the Bank of the United States, issued notes without complying with the state law. Action was brought on the part of Maryland to recover the penalties.

Questions—(a) Does Congress have the power to incorporate a bank? (b) May the state of Maryland tax a branch of the U.S. Bank located in Maryland?

Decisions—(a) Yes; (b) No.

Reasons—*C.J. Marshall* (7–0). The Constitution empowers the government to lay and collect taxes; to borrow money; to regulate commerce; to declare and conduct war; and to raise and support armies and navies. The Constitution also grants Congress the power "to make all laws which shall be necessary and proper for carrying into execution" the expressed powers in the Constitution. This provision is included within the powers of Congress and does not limit Congress to choosing those means that are "absolutely" necessary. By incorporating a bank, Congress is creating the means to attain the goals of the powers entrusted to them. The Tenth Amendment does not include the limitation "expressly" before the word "reserved," and thereby does not bar the congressional exercise of implied powers.

The Constitution and the laws made in pursuance thereof are supreme and cannot be controlled by the various states. If the state of Maryland could regulate the laws of the federal government, then the Constitution and federal laws would soon lose their significance. "Let the end be legitimate, let it be within the scope of the Constitution, and all means which are appropriate, which are plainly adapted to that end, which are not prohibited, but consist with the letter and spirit of the Constitution, are constitutional." When Maryland taxed the operations of the federal government, it acted upon institutions created by people over whom it claimed no control. The power to tax involves the power to destroy. Because such a tax could be used to destroy an institution vitally necessary to carry out the operations of the national government, it is unconstitutional and void.

Note—*McCulloch* proclaimed the doctrine of implied congressional powers and of federal supremacy. In the *Legal Tender Cases*, 12 Wallace 457 (1871), and in

Juilliard v. Greenman, 110 U.S. 421 (1884), *McCulloch* was supplemented by the development of the doctrine of "resulting" (or resultant) powers.

❧

McGrain v. Daugherty, 273 U.S. 135; 47 S. Ct. 319; 71 L. Ed. 580 (1927)

Facts—The Senate decided to investigate the activities of Harry M. Daugherty, former attorney general of the United States. It subpoenaed Mally S. Daugherty, a brother of the former attorney general, to appear before the committee that was conducting the hearings. He refused, the Senate issued a warrant to compel him to appear and testify, and the Senate sent McGrain, its deputy sergeant-at-arms, to arrest him. Daugherty applied for and received a writ of habeas corpus to discharge him from custody on the ground that the Senate exceeded its powers under the Constitution.

Question—May Congress compel a private individual to appear before it or one of its committees and give testimony?

Decision—Yes.

Reasons—*J. Van Devanter* (8–0). The power to legislate carries with it by necessary implication information needed in the rightful exercise of that power and to employ compulsory process for that purpose. Although it was investigating the former attorney general, and the resolution that brought the committee into existence had not in turn avowed its intent to aid legislation, the subject was such that the information received could be of valuable help in enacting further laws.

❧

Watkins v. United States, 354 U.S. 178; 77 S. Ct. 1173; 1 L. Ed. 2d 1273 (1957)

Facts—John T. Watkins, a labor union organizer, appeared as a witness in compliance with a subpoena issued by a subcommittee of the Committee on Un-American Activities of the House of Representatives. Although Watkins indicated he would answer questions about his relations with the Communist Party and questions concerning his acquaintance with current members, he refused to answer those questions involving persons whom he believed had separated from the party on the ground that these were not relevant to the work of this committee. He was indicted and convicted for contempt of

Congress under a statute making criminal refusal to answer "any questions pertinent to the question under inquiry."

Question—May a witness at a congressional committee hearing properly refuse to answer questions on the basis of their lack of pertinency?

Decision—Yes.

Reasons—*C.J. Warren* (6–1). Although the power of Congress to conduct investigations is inherent in the legislative process and is a broad power, the inquiry "must be related to and in furtherance of a legitimate task of the Congress." The Bill of Rights is applicable to investigations as to all forms of governmental actions, so the First Amendment freedoms of speech, press, religion, and political belief and association must not be abridged. Further, the First Amendment may be invoked against infringement of the protected freedoms by law or by lawmaking. There is a freedom not to speak. "Protected freedoms should not be placed in danger in the absence of a clear determination by the House or the Senate that a particular inquiry is justified by a specific legislative need." This requires that the instructions to an investigating committee spell out that group's jurisdiction and purpose with sufficient particularity. "There is no congressional power to expose for the sake of exposure." In this instance, none of the several sources—the authorizing resolution, the remarks of the chairman, or the remarks of members of the committee—was adequate to convey sufficient information as to the pertinency of the questions. Watkins was thus "not accorded a fair opportunity to determine whether he was within his rights in refusing to answer, and his conviction is necessarily invalid under the Due Process Clause of the Fifth Amendment."

J. Clark argued in dissent that the requirements the Court was imposing on congressional investigations were both "unnecessary and unworkable."

Note—Although there were some factual differences between the two cases, the Supreme Court arguably retreated from this opinion, which stirred strong sentiment against the Court, in *Barenblatt v. United States*.

❧

Barenblatt v. United States, 360 U.S. 109; 79 S. Ct. 1081; 3 L. Ed. 2d 1114 (1959)

Facts—Barenblatt, a one-time college professor, was called as a witness before a subcommittee of the House Committee on Un-American Activities, which was investigating communist infiltration in education. After refusing on First Amendment grounds to testify to his own or anyone else's possible associations with the Communist Party, Barenblatt was convicted of contempt in a U.S. District Court, a conviction later reaffirmed, after first being vacated, by the Court of Appeals for the District of Columbia.

Issue—Was Barenblatt obligated to respond to committee questions about possible connections to the Communist Party?

Decision—Yes.

Reasons—*J. Harlan* (5–4). The power of Congress to investigate is broad but not unlimited. In *Watkins v. United States*, the Court questioned the vagueness of Rule XI that provided authorization for committee investigations into alleged un-American activities, but the Court did not invalidate all committee authority. Its authority covers investigations into education. Barenblatt questioned the pertinency of the committee's questions, but he did not raise this claim, except obliquely, at his hearing, and he refused to testify to matters, including his association with the Communist Party, that were clearly pertinent. Barenblatt resisted testifying on the basis that such testimony interfered with his First Amendment rights of speech and association. However, the committee has wide legislative authority to investigate threats to national security, and the Court recognized that the Communist Party differs from others in that it is controlled from abroad and professes revolutionary ideology. Barenblatt claimed that the committee was conducting its investigation for the purpose of "exposure," but it is not up to the Court to question the motives of Congress.

   J. Black's dissent argued that the investigation violated rights to speech and association, that the committee's search for "un-American activities" was vague, and that rights of freedom of speech and association should not be balanced away. The Constitution protects "the right to err politically," and individuals should not be penalized for what they believe and for associating with individuals of their choice. The primary purpose of the committee was the impermissible one of subjecting Barenblatt to "humiliation and public shame." *J. Brennan's* dissent classified the committee's purpose of "exposure purely for the sake of exposure."

⁊

Taxing/Spending and Regulatory Powers

Hylton v. United States, 3 Dallas (3 U.S.) 171; 1 L. Ed. 556 (1796)

Facts—This was a case brought from the circuit court in Virginia challenging the 1794 congressional law imposing a tax on carriages. It was stipulated that Hylton had 125 such vehicles (undoubtedly a ploy to establish a sufficient monetary amount to give standing in a federal court), which he refused to pay the tax on. The Circuit Court was equally divided on the constitutionality of the tax.

Question—Was the congressional tax on carriages constitutional?

Decision—Yes.

Reasons—(3–1, with *J. Wilson* having expressed his support for the tax while riding circuit). Each justice expressed his view separately.

J. Chase argued that the constitutionality of the tax centered on the distinction between direct and indirect taxes. Article I, Section 2 provides that direct taxes should be apportioned among the states by population whereas Article I, Section 8 provides that other "taxes, duties, imposts, and excises" must be laid uniformly. Chase believed the carriage tax was a duty that was constitutional as long as it was, like this tax, laid uniformly. Chase further registered his belief "that the direct taxes contemplated by the Constitution are only two, to wit, a capitation, or poll tax, simply, without regard to property, profession or any other circumstances; and a tax on LAND." He further noted that "it is unnecessary, at this time, to determine whether this court, constitutionally possesses the power to declare an act of Congress void, on the ground of its being made contrary to, and in violation of, the Constitution."

J. Patterson agreed citing the requirement for uniformity of direct taxes as the Framers' way of protecting the Southern states that had slaves and "extensive tracts" of "thinly settled" and "not very productive" land. He considered taxes on "consumable commodities" to be indirect taxes, subject only to the requirement for uniformity.

J. Iredell agreed stating that "As all direct taxes must be apportioned, it is evident that the Constitution contemplated none as direct but such as could be apportioned." Such direct taxes would include "a land or a poll tax." *J. Cushing* dissented without citing his reasons.

Note—The Constitution did not define direct or indirect taxes. The Supreme Court's decision in *Pollock v. Farmers' Loan & Trust Co.* (1895) later invalidated the national income tax as an improper direct tax, but the Sixteenth Amendment subsequently overturned that decision.

❧

Veazie Bank v. Fenno, 8 Wallace (75 U.S.) 533; 19 L. Ed. 482 (1869)

Facts—In 1866, Congress passed an act imposing a tax of 10 percent on notes of private persons, state banks, and state banking associations. The Veazie Bank paid the tax under protest, alleging Congress had no power to pass such an act. This was a suit by the bank against the collector, Fenno, for reimbursement.

Question—Is this an unauthorized use of the taxing power of Congress?

Decision—No.

Reasons—*C.J. Chase* (5–2). Congress had just undertaken to provide for a uniform currency for the country. To protect the newly established national bank from undue competition from the state banks, Congress was using its power indirectly when it could have used a direct method. Congress had to protect the newly established bank notes and restrain the notes of the state banks as money. Under its power to regulate the circulation of coin, it was able to do this. "It cannot be doubted that under the Constitution the power to provide a circulation of coin is given to Congress. And it is settled by the uniform practice of the government and by repeated decisions, that Congress may, constitutionally authorize the emission of bills of credit. . . . Having thus, in the exercise of undisputed constitutional powers, undertaken to provide a currency for the whole country, it cannot be questioned that Congress may, constitutionally, secure the benefits of it to the people by appropriate legislation. To this end, Congress has denied the quality of legal tender to foreign coins, and has provided by law against the imposition of counterfeit and base coin on the community. To the same end, Congress may restrain, by suitable enactments, the circulation as money of any notes not issued under its own authority. Without this power, indeed, its attempts to secure a sound and uniform currency for the country must be futile."

   J. Nelson, dissenting, argued that states had power under the Tenth Amendment to create banks and that national taxation of such entities gave the national government undue control over such institutions.

Collector v. Day (Buffington v. Day), 11 Wallace (78 U.S.) 113; 20 L. Ed. 122 (1871)

Facts—Judge Day of the Probate Court for Barnstable County, Massachusetts, brought a suit against Buffington, collector of internal revenue, to recover federal income tax assessments upon his salary during the years 1866 and 1867, as judge of the Court of Probate and Insolvency, Barnstable County, Mass. Judge Day, having paid the tax under protest, brought suit to recover the amount paid and obtained judgment. The collector then sued for a writ of error.

Question—Can Congress constitutionally impose a tax upon the salary of a judicial officer of a state?

Decision—No.

Reasons—*J. Nelson* (8–1). The work that a judge does is a vital function of the state. It is one of the reserved rights of the state coupled with the passing of laws and the administration of them. The federal government has only the delegated power that the states gave it, and since this is a part that the states reserved for themselves, these governmental actions are not properly subject to the taxing power of Congress.

The means and instrumentalities employed for carrying on the operations of state governments should not be liable to be crippled or defeated by the taxing power of another government. One of these means and instrumentalities is the judicial department of the state, and in its establishment the states are independent of the general government.

Although there is no express provision in the Constitution that prohibits the general government from taxing the means and instrumentalities of the states, the exemption rests upon necessary implication and is upheld by the law of self-preservation.

J. Bradley argued in dissent that the national government should have the same power to tax salaries of state officials as it had of taxing salaries of its own.

Note—In *Graves et al., Tax Commissioners v. New York ex rel. O'Keefe*, 306 U.S. 466 (1939), the Supreme Court reversed this decision. It decided that nondiscriminatory state taxation of the salaries of federal officials was not the same as direct taxation of that government.

☙⚚

Legal Tender Cases (Knox v. Lee; Parker v. Davis), 12 Wallace (78 U.S.) 457; 20 L. Ed. 287 (1871)

Facts—Congress provided for the issuance of paper money and made such money legal tender for the payment of private debts. Knox had purchased a number of sheep that had been confiscated under the Confederacy in Texas during the Civil War. Lee, after the war, brought suit to recover the value of the sheep and won. The payment was to be made in U.S. Treasury certificates called "greenbacks," which were of less value than gold or silver. When Knox was about to pay the debt in greenbacks, Lee appealed the case to secure payment in gold or silver. In the second case, Davis asked for a writ of specific performance to compel Parker to transfer real estate upon payment of a set sum of money that Davis had previously offered to pay in legal tender notes.

Question—Does Congress have the power to make the Treasury notes legal tender applicable to both previous and subsequent contracts?

Decision—Yes.

Reasons—*J. Strong* (5–4). "And here it is to be observed it is not indispensable to the existence of any power claimed for the federal government that it can be found specified in the words of the Constitution, or clearly and directly traceable to some one of the specified powers. Its existence may be deduced fairly from more than one of the substantive powers expressly defined, or from them all combined. . . . And it is of importance to observe that Congress has often exercised, without question, powers that are not expressly given nor ancillary to any single enumerated power. Powers thus exercised are what are called by Judge Story, in his Commentaries on the Constitution, resulting powers, arising from the aggregate powers of the government."

The statute here was passed as a war measure to obtain credit for the equipment of armies and the employment of money to an extent beyond the capacity of all ordinary sources of supply. If nothing else would have supplied the necessities of the Treasury, these acts would be valid. To say that some other means might have been chosen is mere conjecture, and if it be conceded, it proves nothing more than that Congress had the choice of means for a legitimate end, each appropriate and adapted to that end. The Court could not say that Congress ought to have adopted one rather than the other.

C.J. Chase authored a dissent arguing for reaffirmation of an earlier decision in *Hepburn v. Griswold*. Chase did not believe the actions of the government were necessary and proper, believing them to be in violation of contract rights.

Note—This case reverses the first legal tender case, *Hepburn v. Griswold*, 8 Wallace 603 (1870), one of the earliest uses of substantive due process. The legal tender cases were tinged by politics and charges of Court-packing by President Grant.

❧

Pollock v. Farmers' Loan and Trust Co., 158 U.S. 601; 15 S. Ct. 912; 39 L. Ed. 1108 (1895)

Facts—Charles Pollock, a citizen of the state of Massachusetts, filed a bill on behalf of himself and all other stockholders of the company against the

Farmers' Loan and Trust Company, a corporation of the state of New York. The bill alleged that the defendant claimed authority under the provisions of the act of August 1894 (a statute providing for the imposition of a tax on incomes in excess of $4,000 received by individuals, associations, or corporations) to pay to the United States a tax of 2 percent on the net profits of money in question including income derived from real estate and bonds of municipal corporations owned by it. Moreover, the bill alleged that such a tax was unconstitutional, in that the income from stocks and bonds of the states of the United States, counties, and municipalities therein is not subject to taxation.

Question—Is this a direct tax? Did any partial unconstitutionality of the 1894 income tax law render it void in its entirety?

Decision—Yes (to both questions).

Reasons—*C.J. Fuller* (5–4). "If the revenue derived from municipal bonds cannot be taxed because the source cannot be, the same rule applies to revenue from any other source not subject to the tax; and the lack of power to levy any but an apportioned tax on real estate and personal property equally exists as to the revenue therefrom."

The same statute may be in part constitutional and unconstitutional, and if the parts are wholly independent of each other, that which is constitutional may stand and that which is unconstitutional will be rejected. If they depend on each other for the outcome or purpose of the legislation, then both parts or all of the statute is unconstitutional.

The income from realty formed a vital part of this scheme for taxation. If that were to be stricken out and also all income from invested property, the largest part of the anticipated revenue would be eliminated, and this would leave the burden of the tax to be borne by the professions, trades, and labor. Thus, what was intended as a tax on capital would have remained in substance a tax on occupations and labor. This was not the intention of Congress and the whole law had to be declared unconstitutional.

J. Harlan, *J. Brown*, *J. Jackson*, and *J. White* all authored dissents arguing that the constitutional prohibition of "direct taxes" was limited, that this decision conflicted with precedents, and that the people should consider using the amending process, as they eventually did, to overturn this decision.

Note—During the Civil War, Congress had levied an income tax to finance the war, which the Court upheld in *Springer v. United States,* 102 U.S. 586 (1881). *Pollock* reversed this view and the Sixteenth Amendment, in turn, reversed *Pollock.*

Northern Securities Co. v. United States, 193 U.S. 197; 24 S. Ct. 436; 48 L. Ed. 679 (1904)

Facts—The Northern Pacific and Great Northern Railroad Companies purchased most of the stock of the Burlington Railroad. The first two companies ran parallel lines and the Burlington was a connecting line. The Northern Pacific and Great Northern entered into a combination to form a New Jersey corporation, called the Northern Securities Company. This company held three-fourths of the stock of the two companies. The United States charged them with violating antitrust laws.

Question—Does this railroad combination restrain trade among the several states and therefore violate the antitrust laws?

Decision—Yes.

Reasons—*J. Harlan* (5–4). This combination was, within the meaning of the act, a "trust," but, even if not, it was a combination in restraint of interstate and international commerce and that was enough to bring it under the condemnation of the act. The mere existence of such a combination and the power acquired by the holding company as its trustee constituted a menace to, and a restraint upon, that freedom of commerce which Congress intended to recognize and protect, and which the public was entitled to have protected. Even if the state allowed consolidation, it would not follow that the stockholders of two or more state railroad corporations, having competing lines and engaged in interstate commerce, could lawfully combine and form a distinct corporation to hold the stock of the constituent corporations, and by destroying competition between them in violation of the act, restrain commerce among the states and with foreign nations.

 J. White and *J. Holmes* authored dissents. White questioned whether Congress had authority to regulate stock ownership. In his dissent, Holmes uttered his famous statement that "Great cases like hard cases make bad law" and questioned not only congressional powers but the Court's interpretation of the congressional statute.

Note—In reacting to Holmes's dissent, President Theodore Roosevelt, who appointed Holmes as a liberal only to see him vote as a conservative, stormed, "I could carve out of a banana a judge with more backbone than that."

McCray v. United States, 195 U.S. 27; 24 S. Ct. 769; 49 L. Ed. 78 (1904)

Facts—McCray was sued by the United States for a statutory penalty of $50. He purchased for resale a fifty-pound package of oleomargarine artificially colored to look like butter, to which were affixed internal revenue stamps for uncolored oleomargarine rather than for artificially-colored oleo.

Question—Was the tax upon the colored oleomargarine an unconstitutional attempt to use the federal taxing power to regulate a matter reserved to the states?

Decision—No.

Reasons—*J. White* (6–3). "Undoubtedly, in determining whether a particular act is within a granted power, its scope and effect are to be considered. Applying this rule to the acts assailed, it is self-evident that on their face they levy an excise tax. That being their necessary scope and operation, it follows that the acts are within the grant of power." The Supreme Court refused to go behind the appearance of a revenue act and inquire into the motives of indirect regulation that might have inspired Congress. This legislation helped prevent fraud by preventing the marketing of oleomargarine colored to look like butter.

The dissenting justices did not author an opinion.

South Carolina v. United States, 199 U.S. 437; 26 S. Ct. 110; 50 L. Ed. 261 (1905)

Facts—South Carolina was the sole dispenser of wholesale and retail liquor within the state. All profits went to the state treasury. Prior to 1901, the state paid the U.S. tax, but on April 14, 1901 the state authorities refused further payments.

Question—Should this state agency be granted immunity from taxation by the federal government because it was exercising the sovereign power of a state?

Decision—No.

Reasons—*J. Brewer* (6–3). "The necessity of regulation may induce the states to the possession of other fields such as tobacco and other objects of internal revenue tax. But "if one state finds it thus profitable, other states may follow, and the whole body of internal revenue tax be thus stricken down." The national government would be crippled. If all the states exercised such power, the efficiency of the national government could be destroyed. The exemption of state agencies and instrumentalities from national taxation is limited to those which are strictly governmental in character and does not extend to those which are used by the state in the carrying on of ordinary business. Thus "whenever a state engages in business which is of a private nature, that business is not withdrawn from the taxing power of the nation."

J. White, dissenting, argued that the doctrine advanced in this case would allow both state and federal governments to destroy one another.

Swift and Co. v. United States, 196 U.S. 375; 25 S. Ct. 276; 49 L. Ed. 518 (1905)

Facts—The government charged a number of corporations, firms, and individuals of different states, dealing in fresh meat throughout the United States with colluding not to bid against each other in the livestock markets or the different states, to bid up prices to induce cattlemen to send their stock to the yards, to fix selling prices, and to restrict shipments of meat, to establish a uniform rule of credit to dealers, to keep a blacklist, to make uniform and improper charges for cartage, and to get less than lawful rates from the railroads.

Question—Is this an illegal monopoly in violation of the Sherman Antitrust Act?

Decision—Yes.

Reasons—*J. Holmes* (9–0). Although the combination alleged embraces restraint and monopoly of trade within a single state, its effect upon commerce among the states was not accidental. The combination intended to monopolize interstate commerce protected from restraint by the Sherman Act of 1890, since the meat shipments and sales involved were between citizens of diverse states.

"It is said that this charge was too vague and that it does not set forth a case of commerce among the states. Taking up the latter objection first, commerce among the states is not a technical legal conception, but a practical one, drawn from the course of business. When cattle are sent for sale from a place in one state, with the expectation that they will end their transit, after purchase, in another, and when in effect they do so, with only the interruption necessary to find a purchaser at the stock yards, and when this is a typical, constantly recurring course, the current thus existing is a current of commerce among the states, and the purchase of the cattle is a part and incident of such commerce. . . . It is immaterial if the section also embraces domestic transactions.

"It should be added that the cattle in the stock yard are not at rest."

❦

Standard Oil Co. of New Jersey v. United States, 221 U.S. 1; 31 S. Ct. 502; 55 L. Ed. 619 (1910)

Facts—John D. Rockefeller and associates were convicted of violating the Sherman Antitrust Act. The specific charge of violation involved a combining of the stocks of a number of companies in the hands of Standard Oil of New Jersey. The decree of the lower court enjoined the company from voting the stocks or exerting control over the various subsidiary companies, some thirty-seven in number. These companies, in turn, were ordered not to pay dividends to Standard Oil Co. of New Jersey or to cooperate in any way in making effective the combination. With this background the case went to the Supreme Court.

Question—Did this combination of oil companies violate the Sherman Antitrust Act?

Decision—Yes.

Reasons—*C.J. White* (9–0). This was a combination that would result in the control of interstate and foreign commerce by this group rather than the only one authorized to do so, the Congress of the United States. Hence this was an illegal operation, and it had to be abolished. The Court proceeded to set forth what has come to be known as the "rule of reason." This, briefly, simply provides that the restraint of trade outlawed by the Sherman Act is not to apply to every contract or combination in restraint of trade, but only to those that do so unreasonably. "Undoubtedly, the words 'to monopolize' and 'monopolize,' as used in the section, reach every act bringing about the prohibited results. The ambiguity, if any, is involved in determining what is intended by monopolize. But this ambiguity is readily dispelled in the light of the previous history of the law of restraint of trade to which we have referred and the indication which it gives of the practical evolution by which monopoly and the acts which produce the same result as monopoly, that is, an undue restraint of the course of trade, all came to be spoken of as, and to be indeed synonymous with, restraint of trade. . . . It becomes obvious that the criteria to be resorted to in any given case for the purpose of ascertaining whether violations of the section have been committed is the rule of reason guided by the established law and by the plain duty to enforce the prohibitions of the act, and thus the public policy which its restrictions were obviously enacted to observe."

Note—The "rule of reason" in Standard Oil came to mean only monopolies on restraints of trade that were "unreasonably" so. This doctrine, added to the view that manufacturing trusts were not involved in interstate commerce, greatly weakened the Sherman Act. Congress reinforced it in 1914 with the Clayton Act and the Federal Trade Commission Act. See *Northern Securities* (1904).

Bailey v. Drexel Furniture Co., 259 U.S. 20; 42 S. Ct. 449; 66 L. Ed. 817 (1922)

Facts—Congress passed the Child Labor Tax Law of 1919 requiring that those employing children under the age of fourteen must pay a tax amounting to 10 percent of their net profits. Bailey, collector of internal revenue, assessed a tax on the Drexel Furniture Company, which hired a boy under the age of fourteen. The company paid the tax under protest. It contended that the Child Labor Tax Law violated the states' powers under the Tenth Amendment.

Question—Did Congress exercise constitutional power in passing the Child Labor Tax Law?

Decision—No.

Reasons—*C.J. Taft* (8–1). The Court was of the opinion that the tax required in the Child Labor Tax Law was passed by Congress for the purpose of enforcing police power legislation. Although the Child Labor Law did not declare the employment of children illegal, the same purpose was accomplished by imposing the tax. The Court did not deny the power of Congress to tax. The tax in this law, however, seemed to accomplish the purpose of a penalty for not obeying the employment standards set down by Congress. The employment standard within a state is clearly a state power. Therefore, the Court ruled that the power to tax by Congress must be reasonably adapted to the collecting of a tax and not solely to the achievement of some other purpose plainly within the power of the states.

   J. Clark dissented without filing a written opinion.

Note—*Bailey* and *Hammer v. Dagenhart* (1918), decided under the influence of "dual federalism," were reversed in *United States v. Darby* (1941).

United States v. Butler, 297 U.S. 1; 56 S. Ct. 312; 80 L. Ed. 477 (1936)

Facts—In accordance with the Agricultural Adjustment Act of 1933, the secretary of agriculture ordered the payment of crop reduction benefits on cotton. To meet these, processing taxes were levied on the processors. The act provided also for the levying of taxes upon existing stocks of floor goods that would have been subject to processing taxes had the law been effective earlier. The receiver for a Massachusetts cotton mill, the Hoosac Mills Corporation, attacked the constitutionality of these processing and floor taxes.

Question—Is this processing tax on agricultural products a proper exercise of the federal taxing power?

Decision—No.

Reasons—*J. Roberts* (6–3). The act invaded the rights reserved to the states. It was a statutory plan to regulate and control agricultural production that was beyond the power delegated to the federal government. "Resort to the taxing power to effectuate an end which is not legitimate, not within the scope of the constitution, is obviously inadmissible."

The tax was based on the general welfare clause of the Constitution. This limits rather than enlarges the power to tax. The law took money from one group for the benefit of another group. This was not a tax.

The act was not optional; it forced the farmer to comply with it under threat of financial ruin. Congress cannot invade state jurisdiction to compel individual action. "At best it is a scheme for purchasing with federal funds submission to federal regulation of a subject reserved to the states."

J. Stone's dissent emphasized the need for judicial self-restraint and for limiting itself to a review of the constitutionality rather than the wisdom of legislation.

Note— In *Mulford v. Smith*, 307 U.S. 38 (1939), the Court practically, if not formally, overruled *Butler*.

⁖

Steward Machine Co. v. Davis, 301 U.S. 548; 57 S. Ct. 883; 81 L. Ed. 1279 (1937)

Facts—The petitioner, an Alabama corporation, paid a tax in compliance with the Social Security Act. It filed claim for refund to recover the payment ($46.14), asserting a conflict between the statute and the Constitution. Funds realized are used to aid the states in the administration of their unemployment compensation laws.

Question—Is the tax a valid exercise of federal power?

Decision—Yes.

Reasons—*J. Cardozo* (5–4). Stewart Machine Co. contended that it is not lawful to tax a right, and that, as such, employment is not open to taxation. However, employment is a business relation, and business is a legitimate object of the taxing power.

Stewart Machine Co. further claimed that the tax was based on an ulterior motive that was essentially contrary to the Tenth Amendment. However, neither the taxpayer nor the state was coerced in this matter. The taxpayer fulfilled the mandate of his local legislature. The state chose to administer unemployment relief under laws of its own making. Nor did the statute call for the state to surrender powers essential to its quasi-sovereign existence. The state did not bind itself to keep the law in force. The state might repeal the statute. *J. McReynolds, J. Sutherland,* and *J. Butler,* dissenting, argued that the federal power exercised in this case contravened the Tenth Amendment, with its reservation of certain powers to the states.

❧

National Labor Relations Board v. Jones & Laughlin Steel Corporation, 301 U.S. 1; 57 S. Ct. 615; 81 L. Ed. 893 (1937)

Facts—In a proceeding under the National Labor Relations Act of 1935, the National Labor Relations Board found that the Jones & Laughlin Steel Corporation had violated the act by engaging in unfair labor practices. The unfair labor practices included discriminating against the members of the union with regard to hiring and tenure of employment and coercing and intimidating its employees. The National Labor Relations Board tried to enforce the provisions of the act, and the corporation failed to comply. The Circuit Court of Appeals refused to enforce the order of the board, holding that the order lay beyond the range of federal power.

Question—Can Congress regulate labor relations under its interstate commerce power?

Decision—Yes.

Reasons—*C.J. Hughes* (5–4). "The fundamental principle is that the power to regulate commerce is the power to enact 'all appropriate legislation' for its protection or advancement; . . . to adopt measures 'to promote its growth and insure its safety' . . . 'to foster, protect, control and restrain.' . . . That power is plenary and may be exerted to protect interstate commerce 'no matter what the source of the dangers which threaten it.' . . . Although activities may be intrastate in character when separately considered, if they have such a close and substantial relation to interstate commerce that their control is essential or appropriate to protect that commerce from burdens and obstructions, Congress cannot be denied the power to exercise that control. . . . The fact remains that the stoppage of those operations by industrial strife would have a most serious effect upon interstate commerce. In view of respondent's far-flung activities, it is idle to say that the effect would be indirect or remote. It is obvious that it would be immediate and might be catastrophic. We are asked to shut our eyes to the plainest facts of our national life and to deal with the question of direct and indirect effects in an intellectual vacuum."

The cardinal principle of statutory construction is to save and not to destroy. The Court has repeatedly held that as between two possible interpretations of a statute, by one of which it would be unconstitutional and by the other valid, its plain duty is to adopt that which will save the act. The main purpose of the act was to obstruct interference with the flow of interstate commerce.

The steel industry is one of the great basic industries of the United States, affecting interstate commerce at every point. The steel strike of 1919–1920 had far-reaching consequences. The fact that there appeared to have been no major disturbance in this case, did not dispose of the possibilities of the future. Congress had constitutional authority to safeguard the right of the employees to self-organization and freedom in the choice of representatives for collective bargaining.

J. McReynolds authored a dissent in a companion case, pointing to the Court's departure from well-established precedents that distinguished between regulations of production and of subsequent commerce and between the regulation of industries that have a direct effect and those that have only an indirect effect on interstate commerce.

Note—*Jones & Laughlin Steel* and *West Coast Hotel v. Parrish* (1937) pointed to a shift to a more governmentally regulated industrial economy. The underpinnings of *Carter v. Carter Coal Co.*, 298 U.S. 238 (1936), were reversed.

Helvering v. Davis, 301 U.S. 619; 57 S. Ct. 904; 81 L. Ed. 1307 (1937)

Facts—George P. Davis, a shareholder of the Edison Illuminating Company of Boston, brought suits to restrain the corporation from making the payments and deductions called for by the Social Security Act under Titles VIII and II. The District Court held that the tax on employees was not the issue, and that the tax on employers was constitutional. The Court of Appeals reversed the decision, holding that Title II was an invasion of powers reserved by the Tenth Amendment to the states, or to the people. The tax on employers was considered invalid for the additional reason that it was not the type of excise understood when the Constitution was adopted.

Question—Does the tax imposed upon employers invade powers reserved to the states by the Tenth Amendment?

Decision— No.

Reasons—*J. Cardozo* (7–2). Under the Constitution, Congress can spend money for the general welfare; however, difficulties are left when the power is conceded. The line must be drawn between one welfare and another: general and particular. There is a middle ground. The discretion is not confided to the courts. The discretion belongs to the Congress, unless the choice is clearly wrong. The spreading from state to state of unemployment is an ill not particular but general, which may be checked, if Congress so determines, by the resources of the nation. The ill is all one, or at least not greatly different, whether men are thrown out of work because there is no longer work to do or because the disabilities of age make them incapable of doing it. Consequently, when money is spent to promote the general welfare, the concept of welfare is shaped by Congress and not by the states.

   J. McReynolds and *J. Butler* issued a single sentence indicating their view that this tax violated the Tenth Amendment.

Note—*Helvering* was handed down the same day as *Charles C. Steward Machine Co. v. Davis*, 301 U.S. 548 (1937), and greatly relied on it.

Graves v. New York ex rel. O'Keefe, 306 U.S. 466; 59 S. Ct. 595; 83 L. Ed. 927 (1939)

Facts—The Home Owners' Loan Corporation (HOLC), a federal government corporation, employed O'Keefe, a resident of New York. He contended that as a federal employee, his salary was exempted from state income tax. The HOLC, as designed by Congress, was completely a federal government project, but the act nowhere evinced any congressional purpose to grant immunity from state taxation of employee salaries. In his income tax return, O'Keefe included his salary as subject to the New York state income tax and sought a tax refund on the basis of his federal employment.

Question—Does a state tax upon the salary of an employee of the federal government impose an unconstitutional burden upon that government?

Decision—No.

Reasons—*J. Stone* (7–2). The Court ruled that the state income tax is a nondiscriminatory tax on income applied to salaries at a specified rate. It is not in form or substance a tax upon the Home Owners' Loan Corporation or its property or income, nor did the corporation or the government pay the tax from its funds. It was laid directly on the income of the respondent that he received as compensation for his services. These funds were his private funds and not the funds of the government. The only possible basis for implying a constitutional immunity from state income tax of the salary of an employee of the national government or of a governmental agency is that the economic burden of the tax is in some way passed on so as to impose a burden on the national government. Private funds received as compensation for services to the federal government constitute in no way a burden on the federal government when such funds are taxed by the state.

Tax immunity evolves from the premise that there is an implied immunity between the state and federal taxing powers as a limitation to prevent interference each by the other in the exercise of that power where the other government's activities are concerned. There is no implied restriction, therefore, no burden, on the federal government because the theory that a tax on income is legally a tax on its source is not tenable. The tax here is nondiscriminatory. Any burden that would exist here is one that the Constitution presupposes in a system of dual governments, such as our federal system, and cannot be held to be within the implied taxing restrictions of the state. If such an immunity were implied it would impose too greatly on the taxing power confirmed to the state.

J. Butler argued in dissent that since the Home Owners' Loan Corporation was a U.S. entity not subject to state tax, then neither should the salaries of its employees be subject to this tax.

Note—*Graves* overruled *Dobbins v. Erie County*, 16 Peters 435 (1842) and *Collector v. Day*, 11 Wallace 113 (1871). Since *McCulloch v. Maryland*, 4

Wheaton 316 (1819), the Court moved from reciprocal immunity to reciprocal taxation, subject, though, to the "supremacy clause" of the Constitution (Article VI, Clause 2).

Mulford v. Smith, 307 U.S. 38; 59 S. Ct. 648; 83 L. Ed.1092 (1939)

Facts—The Agriculture Act of 1938, based upon the commerce power of the Constitution, regulated the marketing of various farm products. Congress set detailed limits in the act and left it to the secretary of agriculture to put the act into effect. The purpose of the act was "to regulate interstate and foreign commerce in cotton, wheat, corn, tobacco, and rice to the extent necessary to provide an orderly, adequate, and balanced flow of such commodities in interstate and foreign commerce through storage of reserve supplies, loans, marketing, quotas, assisting farmers to obtain, in so far as practicable, parity prices for such commodities and parity of income, and assisting consumers to obtain an adequate and steady supply of such commodities at fair prices." The appellants brought suit under the portion of the act dealing with marketing quotas for flue-cured tobacco.

Question—(a) Is the act beyond the powers delegated to Congress? (b) Does it result in an unconstitutional delegation of legislative power to the secretary of agriculture? (c) Does it deprive farmers of their property without due process of law?

Decision—(a) No; (b) No; (c) No.

Reasons—*J. Roberts* (7–2). (a) The tobacco produced was for interstate commerce. The law did not limit the amount of the crop grown, but limited only what might be sold. It was a regulation of commerce granted to Congress in the Constitution. "The motive of Congress in exerting the power is irrelevant to the validity of the legislation."

(b) There was no improper delegation of legislative power since definite standards were set down in the act both in the fixing of quotas and in their allotment among states and farms.

(c) The act dealt only with the marketing and not with the growing of crops. The farmers could hold over their tobacco until a late year if they saw fit.

J. Butler, in dissent, cited *United States v. Butler* to support his view that this law was an improper interference with state powers under the Tenth Amendment.

*National Labor Relations Board v. Yeshiva University, 444 U.S. 672; 100
S. Ct. 856; 63 L. Ed 2d 115 (1980)*

Facts—Yeshiva, a private university in New York City, conducted a wide variety of arts and sciences programs at its undergraduate and graduate schools.
The University Faculty Association (union) filed a petition with the NLRB
seeking certification as bargaining agent for the full-time faculty members
at ten of the thirteen schools. The university opposed the petition contending that all of its faculty members were managerial or supervisory personnel
and are not considered employees within the meaning of the National Labor
Relations Act.

Question—Are the full-time faculty members of Yeshiva University excluded from the categories of employees entitled to collectively bargain under
the National Labor Relations Act?

Decision—Yes.

Reasons—*J. Powell* (5–4). "There is no evidence that Congress has considered whether a university faculty may organize for collective bargaining
under the act. The act was intended to accommodate the type of management
employee relations that prevail in the pyramidal hierarchies of private industry. The authority [of Yeshiva University's faculty] is absolute. They decide
what courses will be offered, when they will be scheduled, and to whom
they will be taught. They debate and determine teaching methods, grading
policies, and matriculation standards. . . . It is difficult to imagine decisions
more managerial than these. In arguing that a faculty member exercising
independent judgment acts primarily in his own interest and therefore does
not represent the interest of his employer, the board assumes that the professional interests of the faculty and the interests of the institution are distinct,
separable entities with which a faculty member could not simultaneously be
aligned, we perceive no justification for this. The faculty's professional interests . . . cannot be separated from those of the institution."
     J. Brennan, dissenting, argued that the NLRB was better suited to balance
the respective interests involved in this case than was the Supreme Court.

*NCAA v. Board of Regents of University of Oklahoma, 468 U.S. 85; 104 S.
Ct. 2948; 82 L. Ed. 2d 70 (1984)*

Facts—In 1981 the National Collegiate Athletic Association (NCAA) adopted
a plan for televising football games of member institutions. The plan proposed
to reduce the adverse effect of live television upon game attendance by limiting

the total number of football games and the number that any one college may televise. The NCAA had separate agreements with ABC and CBS that allowed each network to telecast the live "exposures." The College Football Association (CFA) wanted·a voice in the formulation of television policy and contracted with NBC. The NCAA threatened to retaliate against any member that complied with the CFA-NBC contract. The District Court said NCAA had violated the Sherman Act. The Court of Appeals affirmed the decision.

Question—Does the telecasting plan of NCAA violate the Sherman Antitrust Act?

Decision—Yes.

Reasons—*J. Stevens* (7–2). "[T]he challenged practices of the NCAA constitute a restraint of trade in the sense that they limit members' freedom to negotiate and enter into their own television contracts." Because it places a ceiling on the number of games member institutions may televise, "the horizontal agreement places an artificial limit on the quantity of televised football that is available to broadcasters and consumers . . . the challenged practices create a limitation on output; our cases have held that such limitations are unreasonable restraints of trade." "Under the Sherman Act the criterion to be used in judging the validity of a restraint on trade is its impact on competition . . . because it restrains price and output, the NCAA's television plan has a significant potential for anticompetitive effects." The Court found that by "fixing a price for television rights to all games, the NCAA creates a price structure that is unresponsive to viewer demand and unrelated to the prices that would prevail in a competitive market." In addition, the NCAA's plan would foreclose many telecasts that would occur in a competitive market. The judgment of the Court of Appeals is affirmed.

J. White, a former professional football player, argued in dissent that as "an unincorporated, nonprofit educational institution," the NCAA should be treated differently than professional sports leagues.

꒚

South Dakota v. Dole, 483 U.S. 203; 107 S. Ct. 1793; 97 L. Ed. 2d 171 (1987)

Facts—Congress adopted the National Minimum Drinking Age Amendment of 1984 withholding a portion of federal highway construction funds to states that did not raise their minimum drinking age to 21. South Dakota, which permitted those 19 years of age and older to purchase beer with up to 3.2 percent alcohol, sought an injunction claiming that the law exceeded congressional powers under the spending clause (Article I, Section 8, Clause 1) and violated the Twenty-first Amendment, reserving state powers over alcohol. The U.S. District Court and the Eighth U.S. Circuit Court of Appeals rejected the state challenge.

Question—Does the National Minimum Drinking Age Amendment of 1984 exceed federal powers under the spending clause or the Twenty-first Amendment?

Decision—No.

Reasons—*C.J. Rehnquist* (7–1). Federal powers under the spending clause are limited. Such powers must meet four criteria. They must be exercised in pursuit of "the general welfare." Congress must state its intentions unambiguously. Congressional regulations must be related to the programs they finance, and such congressional stipulations must not violate specific constitutional prohibitions. Rehnquist found all four conditions to be present. Constitutional bars to direct regulation of activity, like the consumption of alcohol, are "less exacting than those on its authority to regulate indirectly." In this case, the federal inducement, 5 percent of highway construction funds otherwise available, offers "relatively mild encouragement to the States to enact higher minimum drinking ages" and is "a valid use of the spending power."

    J. Brennan and *J. O'Connor* authored dissents. Brennan's brief dissent argues that states retain power to regulate alcohol under the Twenty-first Amendment. O'Connor agrees with the criteria Rehnquist established for measuring exercises of the spending clause but did not find the establishment of a minimum drinking age to be "sufficiently related to interstate highway construction" (as opposed to safety) to justify the federal inducement offered in this case.

❧

Eldred v. Ashcroft, 537 U.S. 186; 123 S. Ct. 769; 154 L. Ed. 2d 683; 2003 U.S. LEXIS 751 (2003)

Facts—In the 1998 Copyright Term Extension Act (CTEA), sometimes known as the Sonny Bono Law (in honor of a former California congressman), Congress extended copyright protection from 50 to 70 years after an author's death. It applied this extension not only to future works but also to those already in existence. The District Court and the District of Columbia Circuit Court both upheld the law against charges that it violated the prohibition against copyrights in perpetuity or the First Amendment.

Question—Does the retroactive extension of copyright protection violate congressional powers in Article I, Section 8 to grant copyrights for "limited times" or the First Amendment?

Decision—No.

Reasons—*J. Ginsburg* (7–2). Article I, Section 8 grants Congress power "[t]o promote the Progress of Science . . . by securing [to Authors] for limited Times . . . the exclusive Right to their . . . Writings." Throughout its history, Congress has applied new copyright laws both to existing and future works. In this case such legislation served not only to equalize treatments of new and old copyrights but also to equalize U.S. practice with that of other nations. This was not a case where Congress was attempting to evade the "limited Times" requirement by "stringing together 'an unlimited number of "Limited Times."'" Judgment as to the appropriate time period for a copyright was primarily a legislative decision to which the judiciary should give deference. In contrast to patents, copyrights do not grant a monopoly on an idea but only on particular expressions of this idea; moreover, copyright law permits fair use. The Framers regarded limited grants of monopoly as consistent with First Amendment rights for which it further provided under the fair-use doctrine.

J. Stevens and *J. Breyer* authored dissents arguing that the extension of copyright to existing works was inconsistent with the promotion of scientific progress and qualifying the Court's interpretation of the historical record and of past precedents.

Note—This decision had the effect, among others, of extending Disney's claims to Mickey Mouse likenesses and to claims of film studios for old movies.

৵৶

PRIVILEGES AND TERMS OF MEMBERS

Powell v. McCormack, 395 U.S. 486; 89 S. Ct. 1944; 23 L. Ed. 2d 491 (1969)

Facts—Adam Clayton Powell Jr., a flamboyant African American, had been elected from the Eighteenth Congressional District of New York to serve in the U.S. House of Representatives of the Ninetieth Congress. When he was not permitted to take his seat, Powell brought suit in federal District Court. He contended that the House could exclude him only if it found that he failed to meet the requirements of age, citizenship, and residence as stated in Article I, Section 2 of the Constitution.

Question—Can the House or Representatives exclude a duly elected member for reason other than failure to meet the qualifications set forth in the Constitution?

Decision—No.

Reasons—*C.J. Warren* (8–1). Both the intentions of the Framers of the Constitution and the basic principles of our democratic system "persuade us that the Constitution does not vest in the Congress a discretionary power to deny membership by a majority vote." The Court noted further that the provisions of Article I, Section 5 empowering each House to judge the qualifications of its own members is at most a "textually demonstrable commitment" to Congress to judge only the age, citizenship, and residency qualifications expressly set forth in the Constitution. Congress had the power to expel (rather than exclude) Powell, but it would have to do so by an explicit vote of two-thirds or more of its members.

Gravel v. United States, 408 U.S. 606; 92 S. Ct. 2614; 33 L. Ed. 2d 583 (1972)

Facts—As chair of the Subcommittee on Building and Grounds of the Senate Public Works Committee, Senator Mike Gravel read portions of the classified Pentagon Papers at a hearing and placed the entire committee report into the public record. He and his assistant, Leonard S. Rodberg, later arranged with Beacon Press to publish the Pentagon Papers. They were subsequently subpoenaed to testify before a grand jury investigating the publication of such top-secret materials. The District Court held that the speech and debate clause protected the men from testifying before a jury but not the private publication of the documents. The First Circuit Court of Appeals did not think the senator or his aide were protected by the speech and debate clause for activities in connection with the private publication but found a common-law privilege "akin to the judicially created immunity of executive officers from liability for libel contained in a news release issued in the course of their normal duties."

Questions—(a) Does protection of members of Congress under the speech and debate clause extend to their aides? (b) Does the speech and debate clause protect members of Congress and their aides for publication of top-secret documents previously read into the congressional record?

Decisions—(a) Yes; (b) No.

Reasons—*J. White* (5–4). The protections of the speech and debate clause are broad and extend to aides who act as the "alter egos" of members of Congress and without whom they would find it difficult to function. The Court has long rejected "a literalistic approach in applying the privilege." This clause, however, does not immunize a member of Congress or his aides against grand jury inquiry into their arrangements to publish a top-secret document with a commercial press: "private publication by Senator Gravel through the cooperation of Beacon Press was in no way essential to the deliberations of the Senate; nor does questioning as to private publication threaten the integrity or independence of the Senate by impermissibly exposing its deliberations to executive influence." The Court thus rejected the appellate court's "judicially fashioned privilege so far as to immunize criminal conduct proscribed by an Act of Congress or to frustrate the grand jury's inquiry into whether publication of these classified documents violated a federal criminal statute." The immunity of the senator and his aide extend only to legislative acts.

J. Stewart argued in dissent that if members of Congress cannot guarantee confidentiality to their sources, they may dry up, and he denied that the interests of the executive overrode those of the legislature in this instance.

J. Douglas, dissenting, considered publication of the Pentagon Papers to be simply another means by which a member of Congress could inform the public about important matters of public policy. The First Amendment protected against inquiry into this role.

J. Brennan, dissenting, thought the Court was giving too narrow a reading to the speech and debate clause that did not give adequate attention to the "informing function" that members of Congress perform. He further argued that statements made by Thomas Jefferson and other Founding Fathers buttressed his views. Immunity from grand jury requirement was "essential to the performance of the informing function."

U.S. Term Limits, Inc. v. Thornton, 514 U.S. 779; 115 S. Ct. 1842; 131 L. Ed. 2d 881 (1995)

Facts—The Arkansas state constitution prohibited the names of otherwise eligible candidates from appearing on ballots for Congress if such individuals had served two previous terms in the U.S. Senate or three in the U.S. House. The Arkansas trial court and the state supreme court ruled that this restriction violated the qualifications clauses for members of Congress in Article I of the U.S. Constitution.

Question—Does a state requirement barring the names of congressional candidates who have served a designated number of terms from appearing on ballots for Congress violate Article I of the U.S. Constitution?

Decision—Yes.

Reasons—*J. Stevens* (5–4) argued that the qualifications for members outlined in Article I of the U.S. Constitution were designed to be exclusive, and it was irrelevant that Arkansas phrased its restriction as a "ballot access restriction rather than as an outright disqualification." Stevens relied strongly on *Powell v. McCormack* (1969), and the history that supported it. In that case, which invalidated a congressional attempt to exclude a duly elected member who met specified age, citizenship and residency requirements, the Court ruled that such qualifications were exclusive. Stevens further denied that the power to add to such qualifications was reserved to the states by the Tenth Amendment. He argued both that such a power was not within the original powers of the states to reserve and that the qualifications set forth in the Constitution were designed to be exclusive, thus divesting states of any such powers they might have possessed. The Framers intended to adopt a "uniform national system" of congressional qualifications and specified that the federal government would provide the salaries of such representatives. Debates over the Constitution and its subsequent ratification evinced no intention that the Framers intended for the states to add to constitutionally specified qualifications. The debates did evince the "egalitarian ideal—that election to the National Legislature should be open to all people of merit." Moreover, "the right to choose representatives belongs not to the States, but to the people." There is no evidence that states attempted to impose limits in early American history, and the Arkansas regulations cannot be considered part of a state's power to regulate the "Times, Places and Manner of Holding Elections," since they relate to substance rather than mere procedures. If people want to limit the terms of members of Congress, they must do so through an amendment to the U.S. Constitution.

J. Kennedy's concurrence noted that the Framers attempted to "split the atom of sovereignty." The right to select representatives is a right guaranteed by the federal Constitution and not a state right.

J. Thomas's dissent started with an evocation of "first principles," most notably the idea that, according to the Tenth Amendment, states had reserved those powers not delegated to the national government. The notion of popular sovereignty undergirding the Constitution tracks rather than erases state boundaries. Powers were reserved not simply by the states, but by the people, and "unless the Federal Constitution affirmatively prohibits an action by the States or the people, it raises no bar to such action." The qualifications clauses were intended to set "minimum eligibility requirements" for members of Congress, not to preclude additional state qualifications. Indeed, prior to the Seventeenth Amendment, state legislatures selected U.S. senators. "The fact that the Framers did not grant a qualification-setting power to Congress does not imply that they wanted to bar its exercise at the state level." Evidence from the Constitutional Convention and the ratification debates does not show that the Framers opposed the imposition of additional state qualifications but only that they were silent on the subject. Early practice shows that some states actually implemented additional qualifications, albeit not those at issue in this case. States can rightfully take notice of high election rates among incumbents and do something about them.

Chapter Two

ARTICLE II: THE EXECUTIVE BRANCH

Including the Twenty-Second Amendment

Article II of the Constitution sets forth the powers of the executive branch. In most contemporary parliamentary systems, the head of the government, generally designated as the prime minister, is head of the majority party or coalition in the legislative branch. By contrast, the Framers of the Constitution decided to invest executive powers in an individual with an electoral base independent of that of Congress.

This mechanism for selecting the president is called the Electoral College and usually, although not always (witness the 2000 election in which George W. Bush was selected over Al Gore, despite Gore's lead in the popular vote), results in the selection of the individual with the greatest number of popular votes. Electoral votes are distributed so that each state has a number of electors equal to its total number of U.S. representatives and senators, and all but two small states currently use a winner-take-all mechanism. Since there are 435 members of the House, 100 members of the Senate, and three votes allocated to the District of Columbia, it takes 270 electoral votes to gain a majority of the 538 votes in the Electoral College. In an increasingly democratic age, the electoral mechanism allows the president and the president's running mate to claim a national electoral mandate that no other such government officials can claim. Because the president and vice president are elected independently of Congress, the nation often has a system of "divided government" where members of one party occupy one branch and members of another party occupy majorities in one or both houses of the legislative branch.

The president must be thirty-five years of age and a natural-born citizen who has been in the United States for at least fourteen years. Under the terms of the Twenty-second Amendment, presidents are now limited to two four-year terms, or, in the case of vice presidents who take over during a president's term, no longer than ten years of total service.

The Constitution designates the president as the commander-in-chief of the military forces (thus exemplifying the principle of civilian control over the military), and the president is responsible for executing the laws. Because the United States does not have a monarch, the president serves as both Head of the Government and the symbolic Head of State. The president thus not only appoints (with senatorial consent) ambassadors, but he also receives them. The president also selects members of his cabinet and of the federal judiciary, again with Senate approval. The president wears many "hats," some designated in the Constitution and others not. Theodore Roosevelt often referred to the rhetorical power of the president as stemming from the "bully pulpit" that the presidency provided. Presidents are also regarded as leaders of the political party that brought them to power.

One of the president's main powers is the power to veto legislation. It takes a two-thirds vote of both houses of Congress to override such a veto. As the next chapter of this book demonstrates, the president and Congress generally share powers in the area of foreign affairs. While Congress is designated to "declare" war, the president most typically "wages" it in the role of commander-in-chief.

The Constitution does not specify who has power to fire members of the cabinet, but *Myers v. United States* (1926) vested broad powers in the president, later qualified for quasi-judicial and quasi-legislative agencies. *In re Neagle* (1890) recognized at least some inherent powers in the presidency.

In recent years, presidential privileges and prerogatives have become subjects of dispute. *United States v. Nixon* (1974) limited "executive privilege" to withhold certain documents, and *Clinton v. Jones* (1997) ruled that presidents could be sued in office for acts committed prior to assuming the presidency. By contrast, *Nixon v. Fitzgerald* (1982) had provided broad prohibitions against suits brought against the president in conjunction with official duties taken while in office.

Just as the judicial branch has the power to invalidate legislation it believes to be in conflict with the U.S. Constitution, so too it can void presidential actions that it believes supersede the powers of the executive office. On many occasions, however, the judicial branch affirms that the president's powers remain as broad as the Framers envisioned them to be.

POWERS

Martin v. Mott, 12 Wheaton (25 U.S.) 19; 6 L. Ed. 537 (1827)

Facts—In August 1814, the governor of the state of New York, in compliance with a request from the president of the United States, ordered certain companies of militia to assemble in the city of New York for the purpose of entering the service of the United States. The president acted in accordance with a federal statute empowering him to call the militia wherever there shall be danger of invasion. Mott, a private in one of the companies called, refused to comply with the order of the governor. In 1818 a court-martial fined him ninety-six dollars, and when he refused to pay, he was sentenced to twelve months' imprisonment. Martin, a deputy U.S. marshal, seized certain goods of Mott, which Mott sought to recover by action of replevin, designed for such occasions.

Question—Can the president, under the law, call forth the militia of the states when no invasion has taken place?

Decision—Yes.

Reasons—*J. Story* (7–0). One of the best means to repel invasion is to provide the necessary forces before the enemy has reached the soil. Who shall judge whether a state of emergency has arisen, if not the president? If any officer or inferior soldier were permitted to decide for himself, where would the case end? The power invested in the president for the faithful execution of his responsibility constitutes him the best judge of the facts. "Whenever a statute gives a discretionary power to any person, to be exercised by him, upon his own opinion of certain facts, it is a sound rule of construction, that the statute constitutes him the sole and exclusive judge of the existence of those facts. . . . It is no answer, that such a power may be abused, for there is no power which is not susceptible of abuse."

❦

Ex parte Merryman, 17 Fed. Cas. 9487 (1861)

Facts—A military officer acting on the authority of his commanding officer arrested the petitioner, a citizen of Baltimore. He was accused of treason against the United States. The chief justice of the United States, while on Circuit Court duty, issued a writ of habeas corpus directing the commanding officer to deliver the prisoner. The officer refused on the grounds that the president had authorized him to suspend the writ.

Question—Can the president suspend the writ of habeas corpus?

Decision—No.

Reasons—*C.J. Taney*, while on circuit duty. The Court held that the petitioner was entitled to be set free on the grounds that (1) the president, under the Constitution, cannot suspend the privilege of the writ of habeas corpus. Only Congress can exercise this power since the provision appears in the article of the Constitution dealing with Congress, and in a list of limitations on Congress. (2) A military officer cannot arrest a person not subject to the rules and articles of war, except in the aid of civil authority when the individual has committed an offense against the United States. In such a case the military officer must deliver the prisoner immediately to civil authority to be dealt with according to law.

Note—Congress subsequently passed an act allowing the president to lift the writ whenever, in his judgment, the public safety may require it, although it is unclear that he was "authorized" by the act or by the Constitution itself. In three instances Congress did suspend the writ: in 1871 in South Carolina involving the Ku Klux Klan; in 1905 in an injunction in the Philippines; and in World War II in Hawaii.

Mississippi v. Johnson, 4 Wallace (71 U.S.) 475; 18 L. Ed. 437 (1867)

Facts—This case involved a bill in equity by which the state of Mississippi sought to enjoin President Andrew Johnson and the general in command of the military district of Mississippi and Arkansas from enforcing the Reconstruction Acts of 1867.

Question—Can the judiciary issue an injunction to the president to forbid him from carrying into effect an act of Congress?

Decision—No.

Reasons—*C.J. Chase* (9–0). The Congress is the legislative department of the government. The president is the executive department. Neither can be restrained in its action by the judicial department, though the acts of both, when performed in proper cases, are subject to its cognizance. The impropriety of such interference, the Court held, could be clearly seen upon consideration of its possible consequences. If the injunction were granted, the Court would have no power to enforce it. If the president did not enforce the bill according to the wishes of this Court, he would be subject to impeachment by the Congress and the Court could not stop the proceedings. "It is true that a state may file an original bill in this Court. And it may be true, in some cases, that such a bill may be filed against the United States. But we are fully satisfied that this Court has no jurisdiction of a bill to enjoin the president in the performance of his official duties, and that no such bill ought to be received by us."

In re Neagle (Cunningham v. Neagle), 135 U.S. 1; 10 S. Ct. 658; 34 L. Ed. 55 (1890)

Facts—David Neagle was a deputy U.S. marshal traveling with Mr. Justice Field, who was holding Circuit Court. Terry, a former California supreme court justice with whom Field had previously served and against whom Field had later imposed a sentence, had threatened Field. Neagle was assigned by the attorney general to accompany and protect Field. Terry approached Field in what was considered to be a threatening fashion, whereupon Neagle shot and killed him. Neagle was arrested by local authorities for murder but was released on a writ of habeas corpus by the federal Circuit Court on the grounds that he was held for "an act done or omitted in pursuance of a law of the United States," within the meaning of the federal statute providing for the issuance of the writ in such cases. However, the law under which Neagle acted was an executive order of the president.

Question—Did the president have the right to assign someone to guard a Supreme Court justice absent a specific law making this authorization?

Decision—Yes.

Reasons—*J. Miller* (6–2). "It would be a great reproach to the system of government of the United States, declared to be within its sphere sovereign and supreme, if there is to be found within the domain of its powers no means of protecting the judges, in the conscientious and faithful discharge of their duties, from the malice and hatred of those upon whom their judgments may operate unfavorably. . . ." Just as a sheriff must keep the peace of the state and local laws of California, so Neagle, a deputy U.S. marshal, was bound to keep the peace in regard to the federal laws. The attack on Mr. Justice Field was the breaking of the peace of the United States and it was a duty of Neagle to keep that peace. "We cannot doubt the power of the president to take measures for the protection of a judge of one of the courts of the United States, who, while in the discharge of the duties of his office, is threatened with a personal attack which may probably result in his death. . . ."

Note—This case has been used to support the idea that the president has certain inherent powers that he can exercise in domestic affairs.

Myers v. United States, 272 U.S. 52; 47 S. Ct. 21; 71 L. Ed. 160 (1926)

Facts—Congress passed the Tenure of Office Act, which sought to prevent the president's removal of any official for whose appointment the concurrence of the Senate was required, without in turn obtaining senatorial approval for his dismissal. This formula was subsequently reenacted in a statute of 1876 pertaining to postmasters of the first three classes, concurrence of the Senate being stipulated as necessary for removal as well as appointment. In 1920, President Wilson removed Myers, the postmaster of Portland, Oregon, without obtaining or even requesting the consent of the Senate. Myers claimed that, under the terms of the 1876 statute, his removal was unlawful and sued for salary due him.

Question—Is the consent of the Senate required for the removal of an individual whom the president appointed with the advice and consent of that body?

Decision—No.

Reasons—*C.J. Taft* (6–3). Section 6 of the act of July 12, 1876, under which Myers was appointed provided that "Postmasters of the first, second and third classes shall be appointed and may be removed by the president by and with the consent of the Senate, and shall hold their offices for four years unless sooner removed or suspended according to law." Taft referred to Madison's opinion given in the House of Representatives during the First Congress on Tuesday, May 18, 1789. The vesting of the executive power in the president was essentially a grant of the power to execute the laws. But the president alone and unaided cannot execute the laws. He must execute them by the assistance of subordinates. The Court has since repeatedly affirmed this view. The further implication must be, in the absence of any express limitation respecting removals, that as the president's selection of administrative officers is essential to the execution of the laws by him, so is his power of removing those for whom he cannot continue to be responsible.

The power to prevent the removal of an officer who has served under the president is different from the authority to consent to or reject his appointment. When a nomination is made, it may be presumed that the Senate is, or may become, as well advised as to the fitness of the nominee as the president, but in the nature of things defects in ability or intelligence or loyalty in the administration of the laws of one who has served under the president are facts as to which the president or his trusted subordinates must be better informed than the Senate, and the power to remove him may therefore be regarded as confined, for very sound practical reasons, to the governmental authority that has administrative control. The power of removal is incident to the power of appointment, not to the power of advising and consenting to appointment, and when the grant of the executive power is enforced, by the express mandate to take care that the laws be faithfully executed, it emphasizes the necessity for including within the executive power as conferred the exclusive power of removal. All three branches of the government held such a view for more than seventy-four years (1789–1863). The Court concluded that, for the reasons given, it must therefore hold that the provision of the law of 1876 by which the unrestricted power of removal of first-class postmasters was denied to the president was in violation of the Constitution and invalid.

In dissents, *J. Holmes*, *J. Brandeis*, and *J. McReynolds* stressed that Congress had created the job in question and that Congress had the power to vest such appointments and removals in individuals other than the president, thus disputing the idea that removal was an inherent presidential power.

Note—*Rathbun, Humphrey's Executor v. United States*, 295 U.S. 602 (1935), sharply reduced the extent of *Myers* by limiting this power in the cases of appointments to quasi-legislative and quasi-judicial bodies. Similarly, in *Wiener v. United States*, 357 U.S. 349 (1958), the Court limited Eisenhower's removal power in the case of a member of a war claims commission.

☙

Ex parte Grossman, 267 U.S. 87; 45 S. Ct. 332; 169 L. Ed. 527 (1925)

Facts—Philip Grossman was sued for violating the National Prohibition Act. The District Court of Chicago granted an injunction against him. Two days later an information was filed against him that he had violated the temporary order, and he was arrested, tried, found guilty of contempt, and sentenced to one year and $1,000 fine. The president granted a pardon, on the condition that Grossman pay the fine. After he was released, he was sent by the court to the House of Correction to serve the sentence, despite the pardon.

Question—Does the president have power to pardon this type of offense?

Decision—Yes.

Reasons—*C.J. Taft* (9–0). Contempts are crimes even though no trial by jury is allowed, as they are infractions of the laws and are intended as efforts to defeat the operation of a court order. That which violates the dignity and authority of federal courts, such as an intentional effort to defeat their decrees, violates a law of the United States and so is an offense against the United States. "For civil contempts, the punishment is remedial and for the benefit of the complainant, and a pardon cannot stop it. For criminal contempts, the sentence is punitive in the public interest to vindicate the authority of the court and to deter other like derelictions. . . . The executive can reprieve or pardon all offenses after their commission, either before trial, during trial or after trial, by individuals, or by classes, conditionally or absolutely, and this without modification or regulation by Congress."

Note—The president's pardoning power is found in the Constitution (Article 2, Section 2, Clause 1): "The power flows from the Constitution alone . . . and . . . it cannot be modified, abridged, or diminished by the Congress." See *Schick v. Reed*, 419 U.S. 256 (1974). In 1977 President Carter issued a blanket pardon to Vietnam draft dodgers but not to servicemen who deserted. The U.S. District Court for the Western District of Michigan rejected a challenge of President Ford's pardon of Richard Nixon in *Murphy v. Ford*, 390 F.SUPP.1372 (1975).

Rathbun, Humphrey's Executor v. United States, 295 U.S. 602; 55 S. Ct. 869; 79 L. Ed. 1611 (1935)

Facts—On December 10, 1931, President Herbert Hoover nominated William E. Humphrey to succeed himself as a member of the Federal Trade Commission, and the Senate confirmed him. He was duly commissioned for a term of seven years, ending on September 25, 1938. On July 25, 1933 President Roosevelt asked the commissioner for his resignation, on the grounds that his administration could more effectively carry out his aims with his own personnel. Humphrey refused and was removed by the president on October 7, 1933. Samuel F. Rathbun, executor of the deceased Humphrey's estate, brought suit.

Question—(a) Do the provisions of the Federal Trade Commission Act stating that "any commissioner may be removed by the president for inefficiency, neglect of duty, or malfeasance in office" restrict the power of the president to remove a commissioner except for one or more of the causes named? (b) If so, is such a restriction valid under the Constitution?

Decision—(a) Yes; (b) Yes.

Reasons—*J. Sutherland* (9–0). In the act setting up the Federal Trade Commission the term of office was set at seven years because the exacting and difficult character of the work made it desirable for commissioners to acquire the expertise that comes from experience. Congress also intended to create a commission not subject to the government, nor under any political domination or control, but separate from any existing department. Congress considered the length and certainty of tenure to be a vital factor in setting up the commission, and therefore limited executive removal power to the causes mentioned. This case differs from *Myers v. United States*. However, Myers was a postmaster, exercising an executive function, subject to the control of the chief executive, which differs greatly from a commissioner having legislative and judicial power.

Congress has power to create such quasi-legislative or quasi-judicial agencies and the authority to fix the period of office and to forbid removal, except for specified causes. "We think it plain under the Constitution that illimitable power of removal is not possessed by the president in respect of offices of the character of those just named. The authority of Congress, in creating quasi-legislative or quasi-judicial agencies, to require them to act in discharge of their duties independently of executive control cannot well be doubted, and that authority includes, as an appropriate incident, power to fix the period during which they shall continue, and to forbid their removal except for cause in the meantime."

Youngstown Sheet & Tube Co. v. Sawyer, 343 U.S. 579; 72 S. Ct. 863; 96 L. Ed. 817 (1952)

Facts—In 1951 a dispute arose between the steel companies and their employees over terms and conditions in new collective bargaining agreements. Long-continued conferences failed to settle the dispute. The employees' representative, United Steel Workers of America, CIO, announced its intention to strike when the agreements expired on December 31. The Federal Mediation and Conciliation Service intervened, but unsuccessfully, and the president then referred the dispute to the Federal Wage Stabilization Board to investigate and make recommendations for fair and equitable terms of settlement. This failing, the union called for a nationwide strike to begin at 12:01 A.M., April 9. The indispensability of steel led President Truman to believe that the proposed strike would immediately jeopardize national defense (the United States was engaged in conflict in Korea), and he issued an executive order directing Secretary of Commerce Charles Sawyer to seize the steel mills and keep them running.

Question—Is the seizure order within the constitutional power of the president?

Decision—No.

Reasons—*J. Black* (6–3). The power of the president to issue such an order must stem from an act of Congress or from the Constitution itself. Only two statutes authorize seizure under certain conditions, but the government admitted these conditions were not met. Moreover, the Congress rejected an amendment to the Taft-Hartley Act authorizing governmental seizures in an emergency. Nor is there any provision in the Constitution that would warrant this seizure. As commander-in-chief of the Armed Forces, the president has no right to seize private property to keep labor disputes from stopping production. This was a matter of Congress only, not for military authorities. Neither does the Constitution permit the president to legislate—a function that belongs only to Congress, in good times or in bad times. "This seizure order cannot stand."

In a notable concurring opinion, *J. Jackson* distinguished among cases where a president was acting with the consent of Congress (and his powers were therefore at their maximum), where a president was acting in the absence of congressional authorization (a kind of twilight zone), and cases (where presidential powers were at their minimum) where the president was acting contrary to congressional specification. Since Congress had specifically rejected the idea of granting the president the power to seize industry, Jackson though this case fell within the latter category.

J. Vinson, J. Reed, and *J. Minton* thought that the majority opinion reduced the president's role to that of a congressional errand boy and would have deferred to the president's view that his intervention was necessary for national defense.

⊘↯

Dames and Moore v. Regan, 453 U.S. 654; 69 L. Ed. 2d 918; 101 S. Ct. 2972 (1981)

Facts—Pursuant to the International Economic Powers Act, President Carter declared a national emergency on November 14, 1979, and blocked the removal or transfer of all property and interests in property of the government of Iran that were subject to the jurisdiction of the United States. This was in retaliation—the Court calls it a "bargaining chip"—against the Iranian seizure of the American Embassy and the capture of U.S. diplomatic personnel as hostages. On January 19, 1981, the American hostages were released following an executive agreement—authorized by Congress—by President Carter and "ratified" by President Reagan, that obligated the United States to terminate all legal proceedings in U.S. courts involving Iran and to bring about the termination of such claims through arbitration in an Iran–U.S. Claims Tribunal. Dames and Moore, who had a nearly $1 million claim against Iran, contested the constitutionality of the agreement.

Question—Is the agreement concluded with Iran to terminate the hostage crisis in which claims between the two countries will be transferred from American courts to an Iran–U.S. Claims Tribunal constitutional?

Decision—Yes.

Reasons—*J. Rehnquist* (9–0). Our decision rests "on the narrowest possible ground capable of deciding the case . . . we attempt to lay down no general 'guidelines' covering other situations not involved here, and attempt to confine the opinion only to the very questions necessary to decision of the case." Moreover, ". . . decisions of the Court in this area have been rare, episodic, and afford little precedential value for subsequent cases." The president acted with the expressed authorization of Congress and thus his actions merit the strongest presumption and the widest latitude of judicial interpretation. "We think both the legislative history and cases interpreting the TWEA [Trading with the Enemy Act] fully sustain the broad authority of the executive when acting under this congressional grant of power." The statutes support a broad scope for executive action in circumstances under review. Though settlements have been made by treaty "there is also a long standing practice of settling such claims by executive agreement without the advice and consent of the Senate." Since 1952 the president has entered into at least ten binding settlements with foreign nations, including an $80 million settlement with the People's Republic of China. Nor has the president divested the federal courts of jurisdiction inasmuch as "those claims not within the jurisdiction of the claims tribunal will 'revive' and become judicially enforceable in United States Courts."

∽ঌৠ

Haig v. Agee, 453 U.S 280; 101 S. Ct. 2766; 69 L. Ed. 2d 640 (1981)

Facts—Agee, an American citizen and a former employee of the CIA, announced a campaign "to expose CIA officers and agents and to take measures necessary to drive them out of the countries where they are operating." Because Agee's activities abroad resulted in the identification of alleged undercover CIA agents and intelligence sources in foreign countries, Secretary of State Alexander Haig revoked Agee's passport, on the basis of a regulation authorizing him to revoke a passport where he determines that an American citizen's activities abroad causes or is likely to cause serious damage to the national security or the foreign policy of the United States. Agee contended that the revocation would violate a Fifth Amendment liberty interest in a right to travel and a First Amendment right to criticize government policies.

Question—May the president, acting through the secretary of state, revoke a passport on the ground that the citizen's activities abroad are causing or are likely to cause serious damage to the national security or foreign policy of the United States?

Decision—Yes.

Reasons—*C.J. Burger* (7–2). "The Passport Act does not in so many words confer upon the secretary a power to revoke a passport, nor, . . . does it expressly authorize denials of passport applications. Neither, however, does any statute expressly limit those powers. It is beyond dispute that the secretary has the power to deny a passport for reasons not specified in the statutes. The history of passport controls since the earliest days of the Republic shows congressional recognition of executive authority to withhold passports on the basis of substantial reasons of national security and foreign policy. It is 'obvious and unarguable' that no governmental interest is more compelling than the security of the nation. Protection of the foreign policy of the United States is a governmental interest of great importance, since foreign policy and national security considerations cannot neatly be compartmentalized. Agee . . . endangered the interests of countries other than the United States, thereby creating serious problems for American foreign relations and foreign policy. Restricting Agee's foreign travel, although perhaps not certain to prevent all of Agee's harmful activities, is the only avenue open to the government to limit these activities."

PRIVILEGES AND LIMITATIONS

United States v. Nixon, 418 U.S. 683; 94 S. Ct. 3090; 41 L. Ed. 2d 1039 (1974)

Facts—As a result of the break-in of the Democratic National Committee headquarters at the Watergate complex in Washington, D.C., the investigations and subsequent trial of a number of persons disclosed that President Nixon had taped an indefinite number of conversations in the Oval Office of the White House. Special Prosecutor Leon Jaworski had a subpoena *duces tecum* issued to President Nixon. This ordered the surrender of certain of the tapes and papers to federal District Judge John J. Sirica for his judgment as to what portions of the tapes were irrelevant and inadmissible. The president claimed that these materials were immune from subpoena under the theory of executive privilege.

Question—Can a federal court order the chief executive of the United States to surrender materials that the president wishes to withhold as a matter of executive privilege?

Decision—Yes.

Reasons—*C.J. Burger* (8–0, *J. Rehnquist* not participating). The Constitution does not contain any explicit reference to an executive privilege of confidentiality. However, the president shares not only in the generalized right to privacy that others have but also in his need for confidential advice. In a case like this involving a criminal trial, the needs of fair administration of justice had to be balanced against the importance of the president's need for confidentiality. While taking note of the doctrine of separation of powers, the Court observed that there is no unqualified presidential privilege of immunity from judicial process under all circumstances. To read the Art. II powers of the president as providing an absolute privilege as against a subpoena essential to enforcement of criminal statutes on no more than a generalized claim of the public interest in confidentiality of nonmilitary and nondiplomatic discussions would upset the constitutional balance of "a workable government" and gravely impair the role of the courts under Art. III.

Note—This landmark case resulted in the release of incriminating information about President Nixon's involvement in the cover-up of the Watergate Affair that eventually led to a vote by the House Judiciary Committee to impeach him and to Nixon's subsequent resignation before the full House took a vote or the Senate tried him. In a highly unpopular move, President Ford subsequently pardoned Nixon for any laws he might have broken.

❧

Nixon v. Fitzgerald, 457 U.S. 731; 102 S. Ct. 2690; 73 L. Ed. 2d 349 (1982)

Facts—Fitzgerald lost his job as a management analyst with the Air Force during the Nixon presidency after Fitzgerald was involved in a public hearing exposing cost overruns on a transport plane. After failing to appeal his dismissal within the statute of limitations, Fitzgerald amended his complaint as a civil suit against former President Nixon. The U.S. District Court failed to grant Nixon immunity, and the Court of Appeals for the District of Columbia Circuit agreed. Nixon and Fitzgerald came to a monetary settlement but left some $28,000 riding on the outcome of whether the courts would accept the idea of presidential immunity in this case.

Question—Does a U.S. president have absolute immunity for civil suits raised against him for actions taken in his official capacity as president?

Decision—Yes.

Reasons—*J. Powell* (5–4). Powell viewed immunity from civil suits in connection with official presidential actions to be related to the president's unique office, to the separation of powers, and to U.S. history. "The President's unique status under the Constitution distinguishes him from other executive officials." Such suits could divert the president's energies from his duties. The president's visibility would further make him "an easily identifiable target for suits for civil damages." Similarly, the doctrine of separation of powers required attention to possible intrusion on exercises of presidential authority, which cover matters involving a great deal of discretionary responsibility. Exempting presidents from civil suits for actions they take while in office will still leave the remedy of impeachment as well as scrutiny by the press and oversight by Congress.

C.J. *Burger's* concurrence put further focus on separation of powers, arguing that the decision allowed the president to act "free from risk of control, interference, or intimidation by other branches," and, particularly, from "undue judicial scrutiny."

J. *White's* dissent argued that the immunity granted in this case was too broad and threatened the idea of a government of laws. Although the speech and debate clause granted absolute immunity to members of Congress, the Constitution vested no such immunity in the President, and White's review of the historical record indicated that the Founders had not intended to grant such immunity. Although presidential immunity might not leave the nation defenseless, "it will leave future plaintiffs without a remedy, regardless of the substantiality of their claims." J. *Blackmun* also emphasized the president's accountability under the law and questioned the settlement to which Nixon and Fitzgerald had agreed, leading him to believe that the Court had improvidently granted standing in this case.

Clinton v. Jones, 520 U.S. 681; 117 S. Ct. 1636; 137 L. Ed. 2d 945 (1997)

Facts—Paula Corbin Jones brought suit against President Bill Clinton for "'abhorrent' sexual advances" that he allegedly made to her in a motel when he was governor of Arkansas and she was a state employee. The U.S. District Court judge permitted the process of discovery to proceed in the case but ruled that any trial would have to be postponed until after Clinton left office. The Eighth U.S. Circuit Court of Appeals ruled that the case could proceed.

Question—While in office, does a U.S. president have immunity from civil actions involving behavior prior to becoming president?

Decision—No.

Reasons—*J. Stevens* (9–0). In *Nixon v. Fitzgerald* (1982) the Court recognized absolute presidential immunity for civil damages arising from his official duties while in office. Suits against presidents for civil actions arising prior to their assumption of the presidency have been rare. Immunity for liability from official actions is designed to keep the president from being overly cautious in fulfilling his duties. The presidency was not designed, however, to be above the laws but to be amenable to them. The office of the president is unique, but the president remains subject to oversight by the other two branches. It seems unlikely that this suit would "occupy any substantial amount of the petitioner's time." The president's request for immunity from a suit while he is in office does not take account of Jones's interest in this case and could result in the loss of valuable evidence. Courts can manage the risk that subjecting presidents to lawsuits might result in "frivolous litigation," or if the problem becomes serious, Congress could respond by appropriate legislation.

J. Breyer's concurring opinion emphasized the extent to which the president needed authority "to control his own time and energy." He should be protected from judicial orders in civil cases "to the extent that those orders could significantly interfere with his efforts to carry out his ongoing public responsibilities." Believing that the majority may have underestimated the dangers that such cases might bring about in the future, courts might "have to develop administrative rules applicable to such cases (including postponement rules of the sort at issue in this case) in order to implement the basic constitutional directive."

Note—The investigation of this case led in part to uncovering Clinton's affair (and its concealment) with intern Monica Lewinsky that resulted in his impeachment by the U.S. House of Representatives. The U.S. Senate did not convict.

Chapter Three

ARTICLES I AND II:
DISTINCT YET OVERLAPPING POWERS

The framers of the U.S. Constitution believed deeply in the principles of separation of powers and checks and balances. The two principles were designed to work together. By dividing power among three separate branches, the framers hoped that each would check excesses of the other. Powers could not be cleanly divided among the branches, and the Constitution contains examples of overlapping powers among them. Madison explained in Federalist 51 that "the great security against a gradual concentration of the several powers in the same department consists in giving to those who administer each department the necessary constitutional means and personal motives to resist encroachments of the others."

Congress has attempted creatively to meet new challenges posed by modern times; the judicial branch has attempted to weigh each mechanism for meeting such challenges on its own grounds. Thus, in *Immigration and Naturalization Service v. Chadha* (1983), the Court struck down the legislative veto. By contrast, it upheld a federal sentencing commission and a special prosecutor law in *Mistretta v. United States* (1989) and *Morrison v. Olson* (1988).

The president is entrusted with the responsibility for negotiating treaties, but these have to be approved by the Senate. The Constitution does not specify which branch can terminate treaties, leaving another fruitful field for judicial adjudication as demonstrated by *Goldwater v. Carter* (1979). Executive agreements between the president and foreign governments, albeit often negotiated with congressional approval, sometimes replace formal treaties and receive occasional judicial oversight.

The Constitution divides war powers between the legislative and executive branches. The Constitution grants Congress the power to declare war, but it designates the president as commander-in-chief of the armed services. During times of war, the Court has often given fairly broad authority to the legislative

73

and executive branches, especially the latter. Thus, in *The Prize Cases* (1863), it approved Lincoln's blockade of southern ports; in *Korematsu v. United States* (1944), it approved the exclusion of Japanese Americans from designated military zones on the West Coast; and in *Rostker v. Goldberg* (1981), it approved a congressional decision to require males, but not females, to register for a possible draft. At other times, however, the courts have clipped presidential powers. Thus, in *Ex parte Milligan* (1866) the Court struck down a military trial of a civilian during the Civil War, and in *Youngstown Sheet & Tube Co. v. Sawyer* (1952) it struck down President Truman's seizure of U.S. steel mills in order to avoid a threatened strike.

Although the judicial branch often has to decide on the constitutionality of actions taken by the legislative and executive branches relative to war powers or to decide which, if either, branch has authority in a given area, courts rarely seek to impose their own views on matters pertaining to national security, and might not be successful if they tried. Often the legislative and executive branches appear to choose to leave the boundaries between them relatively muddy rather than to challenge them directly in Court.

The War Powers Resolution of 1973 was designed to clarify the president's powers to send troops absent declared war. It provided for consultation between the president and selected members of Congress, notification within forty-eight hours of new troop deployments and an explanation of the rationale for such deployments, and withdrawal of such troops within a sixty-day period (with the possibility of a thirty-day extension), if Congress did not give such approval. This law still remains to be interpreted by the U.S. Supreme Court despite the fact that it contains a legislative veto, a mechanism the Court declared to be unconstitutional in the Chadha case.

The chapter ends with a quartet of cases that explore the tension between congressional and presidential powers after the terrorist attacks of September 11, 2001. Although some of the issues are familiar, their application in new contexts shows their continuing relevance. In at least two decisions, the Court has refused to grant the president a "blank check" in handling these matters.

SEPARATION OF POWERS ISSUES

United States v. Lovett, 328 U.S. 303; 66 S. Ct. 1073; 90 L. Ed. 1252 (1946)

Facts—Lovett, Watson, and Dodd had been working for the government for several years, and the government agencies that had lawfully employed them were fully satisfied with their work and wished to keep them employed. In 1943 Congress passed the Urgent Deficiency Appropriation Act, which provided that no salary should be paid respondents unless they were reappointed to their jobs by the president with the advice and consent of the Senate. Notwithstanding the failure of the president to reappoint them, they continued at their jobs and sued for their salaries.

Question—Is this a bill of attainder, which the Constitution forbids?

Decision—Yes.

Reasons—*J. Black* (8–0). In *Cummings v. Missouri* the Court said, "A bill of attainder is a legislative act which inflicts punishment without a judicial trial." If the punishment be less than death, the act is termed a bill of pains and penalties, but both are included in the meaning of the Constitution. Congressman Dies mentioned Lovett, Watson, and Dodd along with thirty-six other named government employees as "irresponsible, unrepresentative, crackpot, radical bureaucrats" and affiliates of "communist front organizations." He urged that Congress refuse to appropriate money for their salaries. This in effect would force the governmental agencies to discharge them and stigmatize their reputations, which would seriously impair their chances to earn a living. This clearly punished the individuals without a judicial trial, which is forbidden by the Constitution.

Note—Relatively few bill of attainder cases have come before the Supreme Court. In the Test Oath Cases—*Cummings v. Missouri*, 4 Wallace 277 (1867) and *Ex parte Garland*, 4 Wallace 333 (1867)—the Court struck down bills of attainder, and more recently it declared a section of the Landrum-Griffin Labor Act (1959) void, in *United States v. Brown*, 381 U.S. 437 (1965). Instead of deciding Lovett as a bill of attainder case (the practical effect of which was to guarantee a job at public expense), it might have decided it on grounds that it violated the president's power of removal as set out in *Rathbun, Humphrey's Executor* (1935).

Immigration and Naturalization Service v. Chadha, 462 U.S. 919; 103 S. Ct. 2764; 77 L. Ed. 2d 317 (1983)

Facts—Chadha, an alien, had been lawfully admitted to the United States. His visa expired and the INS—under the Immigration and Nationality Act that authorized either house of Congress by resolution to invalidate the decision of the executive branch—ordered his expulsion, even though the attorney general, according to law, lifted the suspension. After the House vetoed the attorney general's decision, Chadha again appealed to the Board of Immigration Appeals, which now agreed with Chadha. The Court of Appeals said that the House was exceeding constitutional authority in ordering Chadha's deportation and violating the doctrine of separation of powers.

Question—Is a one-house congressional veto constitutional?

Decision—No.

Reasons—*C.J. Burger* (7–2). "We reject the view that Chadha lacks standing inasmuch that if the veto provision violates the Constitution and is severable, the deportation order will be cancelled. Congress suggests alternative relief—other avenues that might be open but "at most these other avenues are speculative." Congress's authority over aliens is not contested. What is "challenged . . . is whether Congress has chosen a constitutionally permissible means of implementing that power." Congress has plenary authority "in all cases in which it has substantive legislative jurisdiction . . . so long as the exercise of that authority does not offend some other constitutional restriction." Eleven presidents from Mr. Wilson through Mr. Reagan "have gone on record at some point to challenge congressional vetoes as unconstitutional."

The efficiency, convenience, or usefulness of a law or procedure will not save it if it offends the Constitution. Since the Constitutional Convention (1787), the operative mandate is that legislation must, before becoming law, go first to the president and that a presidential veto could not be overridden except by both houses of Congress (the principle of bicameralism). This power to veto legislation "was based on the profound conviction . . . that the powers conferred on Congress were . . . to be most carefully circumscribed." Except for a narrow exception, not germane here, the presentment clauses serve the important purpose of assuring that a "national perspective is grafted on the legislative process." The Court of Appeals is affirmed.

J. Powell, concurring, said that the decision should be based on the narrower ground that Congress was unconstitutionally trying to assume a judicial function.

J. White, dissenting, argued that the legislative veto was an important invention that should not be invalidated on the basis of a narrow view of separation of powers.

J. Rehnquist and *J. White* believed that the legislative veto was so integral to the law in question that invalidation of the former also required invalidation of the latter.

Note—*Chadha* is a major separation of powers case. Before attacking a thorny issue involving Congress, the Court—as it did in *Baker v. Carr* (1962) and *Powell v. McCormack* (1969)—quickly pointed out that this is a judicial and not a "political question."

৵৵

Bowsher v. Snyar, 478 U.S. 714; 106 S. Ct. 3181; 92 L. Ed. 2d 583 (1986)

Facts—The Balanced Budget and Emergency Deficit Control Act of 1985 (popularly known as the Gramm-Rudman-Hollings Act) put a cap on the amount of federal spending for the fiscal years 1986 through 1991. If in any fiscal year the budget rises beyond the prescribed maximum, by more than a specified sum, the act mandated across-the-board cuts in federal spending. The comptroller general had, as a consequence, the responsibility of preparing a report to the president indicating the projected revenues and reductions to reduce the deficit. The president will issue an order mandating these cuts. No sooner was the act signed when twelve congressmen contested its constitutionality. The District Court ruled, inter alia, that the comptroller's role in the deficit reduction process was constitutionally infirm under the doctrine of separation of powers. It went to the Supreme Court on direct appeal.

Question—"The question . . . is whether the assignment by Congress to the comptroller general . . . of certain functions under the Balanced Budget and Emergency Deficit Control Act of 1985 violates the doctrine of separation of powers."

Decision—Yes.

Reasons—*C.J. Burger* (7–2). "Even a cursory examination of the constitution reveals the influence of Montesquieu's thesis that checks and balances were the foundation of a structure of government that would protect liberty." No officer of the government can sit in Congress. The president is responsible not to the Congress, but to the people, subject only to impeachment proceedings, and even here the chief justice presides if it involves the president. This system to be sure, produces, at times, conflicts, confusion, and discordance "but it was deliberately so structured to assure full, vigorous and open debate." The fundamental necessity "of maintaining each of the three general departments of government entirely free . . . is hardly open to serious question." In *INS v. Chadha* (1983), we struck down a one-house "legislative veto provision." To permit an officer (comptroller general) supervised by Congress to execute the laws would be, in essence, to permit a congressional veto. It is urged that the comptroller general performs his duties independently of Congress. This view "does not bear close scrutiny." Although nominated by the president the comptroller general is removed not only by congressional impeachment but also by a joint resolution. The dissent is in error in believing the comptroller general is free of congressional influence. It is not enough to believe that judicial assessment turns on whether an officer exercising power is on good terms with Congress, for the fathers were dealing with structural protection against abuse of power." The judgment of the District Court is affirmed.

J. White argued in dissent that the majority was applying a "distressingly formalistic" view of separation of powers in this case. *J. Blackmun* argued in dissent that, if Congress attempted to remove the comptroller general, the Court could then declare that action to be unconstitutional.

☙

Morrison v. Olson, 487 U.S. 654; 108 S. Ct. 2597; 101 L. Ed. 2d 569 (1988)

Facts—The issue here is the constitutionality of the independent counsel provisions of the Ethics in Government Act of 1978. It began as a controversy between the House Judiciary Committee and the Environmental Protection Agency (EPA) with regard to producing certain documents. It was alleged that, along with two other officials, Edward Schmultz and Carol E. Dinkins, who withheld documents from the committee, Theodore B. Olson had given the judiciary committee false testimony. The special division (a special court created by the act) appointed Alexia Morrison as independent counsel with respect to Olson and gave her jurisdiction to investigate Olson's testimony or any other matter involving a violation of federal law. The Federal District Court upheld the act's constitutionality and ordered the executive officials in contempt for ignoring the subpoenas. The Court of Appeals reversed the ruling, holding that the act violated the appointments clause of the Constitution, the limitations of Article III, and the principle of separation of powers.

Question—Does the independent counsel provision of the Ethics in Government Act violate the Constitution's appointments clause, Article III, or the doctrine of separation of powers?

Decision—No.

Reasons—*C.J. Rehnquist* (7–1). As to the tenure of the independent counsel she may be removed (other than by impeachment and conviction) only by the attorney general and only for good cause; and by the special division "acting either on its own or on the suggestion of the attorney general." Moreover, the act provides for congressional oversight of the activities of independent counsels. The distinction between "inferior" and "principal" is not easy to determine but in our view the independent counsel "falls on the 'inferior officer' side of that line." She can be removed by the attorney general, has limited duties, can only operate within the scope of her jurisdiction, is a temporary appointment. The Court is aware that its judicial power is limited to "cases" or "controversies" and that, broadly stated, it will not assume nonjudicial duties and is sufficiently isolated to resist any kind of encroachment. We do not think the act deprives the president of control of the independent counsel or truncates his power to faithfully execute the law. "Time and again we have reaffirmed the importance in our constitutional scheme of the separation of governmental powers into the three coordinate branches." Nor do we believe this case involves an attempt by Congress "to increase its own powers at the expense of the executive branch . . . nor think that the act works in any judicial usurpation of properly executive functions." The decision of the Court of Appeals invalidating the Ethics in Government Act of 1974 is reversed.

J. Scalia authored a classic dissent arguing that this law violated separation of powers by effectively forcing a president to launch an investigation that he did not think was warranted by individuals that Scalia did not think were properly accountable to the executive branch.

Note—The special prosecutor law has been allowed to expire in the aftermath of what many observers thought were problems with the investigation of the Iran-Contra affair during the Reagan administration and Kenneth Starr's investigation of President Clinton that led to his impeachment.

◌৯৶

Clinton v. City of New York, 524 U.S. 417; 118 S. Ct. 2091; 141 L. Ed. 2d 393 (1998)

Facts—Congress adopted the Line Item Veto Act, which became effective in 1997. This act gave the president the powers to cancel "(1) any dollar amount of discretionary authority; (2) any item of new direct spending; or (3) any limited tax benefit" without vetoing the entire bill of which it was a part. After determining that such cancellation would reduce the federal debt and not harm or impair governmental functions or national interests, the president was obligated to send a special cancellation message to Congress within five days to be effective if Congress did not override such a veto by majority vote. The city of New York and health care providers appealed exercises of the Line Item Veto Act by President Clinton that would have cancelled a congressional waiver of monies it would otherwise have had to pay to the United States as derived from taxes on health care providers. Similarly, Idaho farmers' cooperatives challenged Clinton's veto of a tax benefit, which would have arguably made their purchase of new processing facilities less expensive. A U.S. District Court consolidated the cases, determined that at least one party had standing, and concluded that the Line Item Veto Act violated the presentment clause (all legislation must be presented to the president for his veto, subject to a two-thirds override by both houses of Congress). The U.S. Supreme Court expedited review of the case.

Questions—(a) Do the groups challenging the exercise of the president's veto have standing? (b) Is the Line Item Veto Act constitutional?

Decisions—(a) Yes; (b) No.

Reasons—*J. Stevens* (6–3). Both the city of New York and the Idaho farm cooperative stood to gain or lose depending on the constitutionality of the president's actions. New York stood to pay additional taxes, while, if the veto stood, the farmers' cooperative stood to lose a tax benefit that it would otherwise have gained in acquiring the processing facility. Both litigants accordingly had standing.

In reviewing the terms of the Line Item Veto Act, Stevens found that the law effectively enabled the president to repeal a section of legislation. The Court found that "There is no provision in the Constitution that authorizes the President to enact, to amend or to repeal statutes" (438). Unlike the veto specifically outlined within the Constitution, a line item veto occurs not "before the bill becomes law" but "after the bill becomes law" (439). This procedure bypassed the "'finely wrought' procedure that the framers designed" (440). Stevens distinguished such line item vetoes from mere "exercises of discretionary authority" (442) or the power either to decline to spend or implement tax provisions. Stevens concluded that "If the Line Item Veto Act were valid, it would authorize the President to create a different law—one whose text was not voted on by either House of Congress or presented to the President for signature" (448).

J. Scalia's dissent questioned the standing of the Idaho cooperative but argued that the Line Item Veto Act satisfied the requirements of the presentment clause. *J. Breyer's* dissent argued that the Line Item Veto Act violated neither "any specific textual command" nor "any implicit separation-of-powers principle" (469–70).

TREATIES AND EXECUTIVE AGREEMENTS

Head Money Cases (Edye v. Robertson), 112 U.S. 580; 5 S. Ct. 247; 28 L. Ed. 798 (1884)

Facts—In 1882 Congress passed an act providing that a duty of fifty cents should be collected for each and every passenger who was not a citizen of the United States, coming from a foreign port to a U.S. port. Individuals and steamship companies brought suit against the collector of customs at New York, W. H. Robertson, for the recovery of the sums of money collected. The act was challenged on the grounds that it violated numerous treaties of our government with friendly nations.

Question—Is this act void because of conflict with a treaty?

Decision—No.

Reasons—*J. Miller* (9–0). A treaty is a compact between independent nations, which depends for its enforcement upon the interest and honor of the governments that are parties to the treaty. Treaties that regulate the mutual rights of citizens and subjects of the contracting nations are in the same category as acts of Congress. When these rights are of such a nature as to be enforced by a court of justice, the court resorts to the treaty as it would to a statute. However, the Constitution gives a treaty no superiority over an act of Congress. "In short, we are of the opinion, that, so far as a treaty made by the United States with a foreign nation can become the subject of judicial cognizance in the courts of this country, it is subject to such acts as Congress may pass for its enforcement, modification or repeal."

❧

Missouri v. Holland, 252 U.S. 416; 40 S. Ct. 382; 64 L. Ed. 641 (1920)

Facts—The United States entered into a treaty with Great Britain to protect migratory birds. In the treaty was a provision that each of the contracting powers undertake to pass laws to forbid the killing, capturing, or selling of the birds except in accordance with certain regulations. Although the federal government had not pursued appeals in earlier cases in which courts had struck down federal regulations of wild game as violations of state power under the Tenth Amendment, Congress enacted legislation under the new treaty and Missouri brought suit, saying that the act and treaty violated its reserved powers under the Tenth Amendment.

Question—Do the treaty and statute interfere invalidly with the rights reserved to the states by the Tenth Amendment?

Decision—No.

Reasons—*J. Holmes* (7–2). Acts of Congress must be made in pursuance of the Constitution, but treaties are valid when made under the authority of the

United States. "We do not mean to imply that there are no qualifications to the treaty-making power; but they must be ascertained in a different way. It is obvious that there may be matters of the sharpest exigency for the national well-being that an act of Congress could not deal with but that a treaty followed by such an act could, and it is not lightly to be assumed that, in matters requiring national action, 'a power which must belong to and somewhere reside in every civilized government' is not to be found. . . . Here a national interest of very nearly the first magnitude is involved. It can be protected only by national action in concert with that of another power. The subject matter is only transitorily within the state and has no permanent habitat therein.

"If the treaty is valid there can be no dispute about the validity of the statute under Article I, Section 8, as a necessary and proper means to execute the powers of the government."

Note—Although subsequent Supreme Court decisions have made reservations to its reasoning, Missouri seemed to hold that Congress might do by treaty what is inadmissible by law. The Bricker Amendment, proposed in 1954 and defeated after a close vote, attacked this view. Had the amendment been adopted it would (a) have reduced a treaty to the status of a law, (b) brought the House into the treaty process, and (c) reversed *Missouri v. Holland.*

United States v. Belmont, 301 U.S. 324; 57 S. Ct. 758; L. Ed. 1134 (1937)

Facts—The United States brought suit against Belmont to recover money deposited in a New York bank. The USSR had confiscated this money when it had nationalized its industries, and, after the United States and the USSR had exchanged diplomatic recognition, the USSR had assigned its rights to money owed it by Russian nationals to the United States. The U.S. District and Circuit Courts had dismissed the complaint for failure to state a cause of action, arguing that recognition of such confiscation went against New York law.

Questions—(a) Does the United States have grounds for seeking this money? (b) Does U.S. or state law prevail in cases where diplomatic agreements appear contrary to state policies?

Decisions—(a) Yes; (b) U.S. law prevails in such circumstances.

Reasons—*J. Sutherland* (9–0). Every sovereign state must recognize the sovereignty of every other. Sovereignty is "not a judicial question, but one the determination of which by the political departments conclusively binds the courts." This agreement followed the exchange of ambassadors between the United States and the USSR. This recognition validated the acts of the Soviet government. Whereas the Constitution divides domestic powers between the state and national governments, "Governmental power over external affairs is not distributed, but is vested exclusively in the national government." Treaties require the advice and consent of the Senate but international compacts, individually called a "protocol, a modus vivendi, a postal convention" or "agreements like that now under consideration" do not. The supremacy of federal treaties applies also to such agreements: "As to such purposes the State of New York does not exist. Within the field of its powers, whatever the United States rightfully undertakes, it necessarily has warrant to consummate." The argument that the Soviet action constituted an unconstitutional taking under the Fifth and Fourteenth Amendments has no place because "our Constitution, laws and policies have no extraterritorial operation."

J. Stone, concurring, did not think that New York had a policy against recognition of what the Soviet Union had done, but he believed that "a state may refuse to give effect to a transfer, made elsewhere, of property which is within its own territorial limits, if the transfer is in conflict with its public policy." The United States might override such a policy through a treaty, but there had been no need to do so and it had not done so in this case.

Goldwater v. Carter, 444 U.S. 996; 100 S. Ct. 533; 62 L. Ed. 2d 428 (1979)

Facts—The U.S. Constitution requires Senate approval of treaties but is silent as to their termination. After the U.S. recognized the People's Republic of China, President Jimmy Carter terminated a treaty the United States had with Taiwan (the other nation, located on the island of Formosa, that claimed to represent the Chinese people). Senator Barry Goldwater and other members of the U.S. Congress questioned his authority to do so. The U.S. District Court dismissed the case, but the U.S. Court of Appeals for the District of Columbia ruled that the president had authority under his power to recognize foreign governments.

Question—Will the Court take cognizance of a case in which members of Congress challenge a presidential termination of a treaty without Senate approval?

Decision—Not in this case.

Reasons—(6–3). The Court issued a summary judgment to the U.S. District Court to vacate its judgment and dismiss the complaint.

J. Powell, concurring, believed the case was "not ripe for judicial review," because Congress had taken no official action regarding Carter's termination of the treaty. Powell did not, however, believe that such an issue was a nonjusticiable political question. He did not believe the Constitution had entrusted this issue to a coordinate branch of government; he believed that the judiciary could fashion standards to resolve this issue; and he saw little likelihood that the decision would embarrass another of the political branches.

J. Rehnquist, concurring (4 votes), believed the issue was "political" because "it involves the authority of the President in the conduct of our country's foreign relations and the extent to which the Senate or the Congress is authorized to negate the action of the President."

J. Blackmun, dissenting, wanted to schedule the case for oral argument and give it full consideration.

J. Brennan, dissenting, would affirm the Court of Appeals decision and side with the president on the basis that "the Constitution commits to the President alone the power to recognize, and withdraw recognition from, foreign regimes."

WAR-MAKING POWERS

The Prize Cases, 2 Black (67 U.S.) 635; 17 L. Ed. 459 (1863)

Facts—By proclamations of April 15, April 19, and April 27, 1861, President Lincoln established a blockade of southern ports. These cases were brought to recover damages suffered by ships carrying cargoes to the Confederate states during the blockade, which had been raided by public ships of the United States. The blockade was declared before Congress had a chance to assemble and take action on the matter.

Question—Did a state of war exist at the time this blockade was instituted that would justify it?

Decision—Yes.

Reasons—*J. Grier* (5–4). "Although a civil war is never publicly proclaimed, *eo nomine*, against insurgents, its actual existence is a fact in our domestic history that the Court is bound to notice and to know. By the Constitution, Congress alone can declare a national or foreign war. It cannot declare war against a state or any number of states, by virtue of any clause in the Constitution. The Constitution confers on the president the whole executive power. He must take care that the laws be faithfully executed. He is commander-in-chief of the army and navy of the United States, and of the militia of the several states when called into the service of the United States. He has no power to initiate or declare war, either against a foreign nation or a domestic state. But he is authorized to call out the militia and use the military and naval forces of the United States in case of invasion by foreign nations, and to suppress insurrection against the government of a state or of the United States.

"If a war be made by invasion by a foreign nation, the president is not only authorized but bound to resist force by force. He does not initiate the war, but is bound to accept the challenge without waiting for any special legislative authority. And whether the hostile party be a foreign invader or domestic states organized in rebellion, it is nonetheless a war, although the declaration of it be unilateral.

"The greatest of civil wars was not gradually developed by popular commotion, tumultuous assemblies, or local unorganized insurrections. However long may have been its previous conception, it nevertheless sprung forth suddenly from the parent brain, a Minerva in the full panoply of war. The president was bound to meet it in the shape it presented itself, without waiting for Congress to baptize it with a name; and no name given to it by him or them could change the fact. . . . Whether the president in fulfilling his duties, as commander-in-chief, in suppressing an insurrection, has met with such armed hostile resistance, and a civil war of such alarming proportions as will compel him to accord to them the character of belligerents, is a question to be decided by him, and this court must be governed by the decision and acts of the political department of the government to which this power was entrusted. 'He must determine what degree of force the crisis demands.' The proclamation of blockade is, itself, official and conclusive evidence to the court that a state of war existed which demanded and authorized a recourse to such a measure, under the circumstances peculiar to the case."

J. Nelson and three colleagues, focusing on the congressional power to declare war, argued that the president could not impose a blockade without prior congressional action.

ᴏꙸꙶ

Ex parte Milligan, 4 Wallace (71 U.S.) 2; 18 L. Ed. 281 (1866)

Facts—Milligan, who was not and had never been in the U.S. military, was tried, convicted, and sentenced to be hanged by a military commission established under presidential authority. The president approved the sentence. In a habeas corpus proceeding, Milligan contended the commission had no jurisdiction over him and that he was not accorded a jury trial. The Circuit Court asked the Supreme Court for an opinion.

Question—Did the military tribunal have any legal power and authority to try and to punish Milligan?

Decision—No.

Reasons—*J. Davis* (9–0). Every trial involves the exercise of judicial power. No part of the judicial power of the country was conferred on the military commission because the Constitution expressly vests it "in one supreme court and in such inferior courts as the Congress may from time to time ordain and establish." The military cannot justify action on the mandate of the president because he is controlled by law, and is duty-bound to execute, not make, the laws. In times of grave emergencies, the Constitution allows the government to make arrests without a writ of habeas corpus, but it goes no further. Martial law can be applied only when there is real necessity, such as during an invasion that would effectually close the courts and civil administration. However, as long as the civil courts are operating, as they were in this case, then the accused is entitled to a civil trial by jury. "The Constitution of the United States is a law for rulers and people, equally in war and in peace, and covers with the shield of its protection all classes of men, at all times, and under all circumstances. No doctrine involving more pernicious consequences was ever invented by the wit of men than that any of its provisions can be suspended during any of the great exigencies of government."

In a concurring opinion, *C.J. Chase* and three other justices argued that although Congress had not authorized military courts to try civilians in this case, it had the power to do so if it thought the civilian courts were unequal to the task.

✎

Selective Draft Law Cases (Arver v. United States), 245 U.S. 366; 38 S. Ct. 159; 62 L. Ed. 349 (1918)

Facts—On May 18, 1917, Congress provided that all male citizens between the ages of 21 and 30, with certain exceptions, should be subject to military service, and authorized the president to select from them a body of one million men. All persons made liable to service by the act were required to present themselves at a time appointed by the president for registration. The plaintiffs failed to present themselves as required and were prosecuted and convicted.

Question—Does Congress have constitutional authority to draft men to raise military forces?

Decision—Yes.

Reasons—*C.J. White* (9–0). The power of conscription is included in the constitutional power to raise armies. The power is not limited by the fact that other powers of Congress over state militia are narrower in scope than powers over the regular army. The Court stated that when the Constitution came to be formed, one of the recognized necessities for its adoption was the want of power in Congress to raise an army and the dependence upon the states for their quotas. In supplying the power it was manifestly intended to give Congress all and leave none to the states, since, besides the delegation to Congress of authority to raise armies, the Constitution prohibited the states, without the consent of Congress, from keeping troops in time of peace or engaging in war.

"Finally, as we are unable to conceive upon what theory the exaction by government from the citizen of the performance of his supreme and noble duty of contributing to the defense of the rights and honor of the nation, as the result of a war declared by the great representative body of the people, can be said to be the imposition of involuntary servitude in violation of the prohibition of the Thirteenth Amendment, we are constrained to the conclusion that the contention to that effect is refuted by its mere statement."

Hamilton v. Kentucky Distilleries & Warehouse Co., 251 U.S. 146; 40 S. Ct. 106; 64 L. Ed. 194 (1919)

Facts—On November 11, 1918, the armistice with Germany was signed. Ten days later, Congress passed and the president approved the War-Time Prohibition Act, which provided that alcoholic beverages held in bond should not be moved therefrom except for export. The purpose was to conserve the manpower of the nation and to increase the efficiency of war production. The Kentucky Distilleries contended that the act was invalid since hostilities had ceased. Furthermore, they held that the government could not enforce such an act since the Constitution reserved the police power to the states.

Question—Was the War-Time Prohibition Act valid?

Decision—Yes.

Reasons—*J. Brandeis* (9–0). The United States lacks general police power, and the Tenth Amendment reserved such power to the states. However, when the United States exerts any of the powers conferred upon it by the Constitution, no valid objection can be based upon the fact that such exercise may be attended by the same incidents that attend the exercise by a state of its police power, or that it may tend to accomplish a similar purpose. The power of wartime emergencies is not limited to victories in the field and the dispersion of the insurgent forces. It inherently carries with it the power to guard against the immediate renewal of the conflict and to remedy the evils that have arisen from its rise and progress. Since the security of the nation was involved, the government had to be given a wide latitude of discretion as to the limitations of war powers.

Ex parte Quirin, 317 U.S. 1; 63 S. Ct. 1; 87 L. Ed. 3 (1942)

Facts—The petitioners were all born in Germany. All lived in the United States and returned to Germany between 1933 and 1941, where they attended sabotage school. After completing this training, Quirin and two others boarded a submarine and proceeded to Amagansett Beach, N.Y. They landed on or about June 13, 1942, carrying a supply of explosives and wearing German infantry uniforms. They buried their uniforms and proceeded to New York City. The four remaining petitioners proceeded by submarine to Ponte Vedra Beach, Florida. These men were wearing caps of German marine infantry and carrying explosives. They buried uniform parts and proceeded to Jacksonville, Florida, and thence to various points in the United States. Agents of the FBI took all of them into custody. All had received instructions to destroy war industries and war facilities in the United States. The president of the United States by order of July 2, 1942, appointed a military commission and directed it to try the petitioners for offenses against the law of war and Articles of War, and prescribed regulations on trial and review of record of the trial and any decision handed down by the commission.

Question—Was trial by a military commission without jury legal?

Decision—Yes.

Reasons—*C.J. Stone* (8–0). The federal government must provide for the common defense. The president has the power to carry into effect all laws that Congress passes regarding the conduct of the war and all laws defining and punishing offenses against the law of nations. These men were nothing more than spies. They fall under this category by their actions. "It has not hitherto been challenged, and, so far as we are advised, it has never been suggested in the very extensive literature of the subject that an alien spy, in time of war, could not be tried by military tribunal without a jury.

"We conclude that the Fifth and Sixth Amendments did not restrict whatever authority was conferred by the Constitution to try offenses against the law of war by military commission, and that petitioners, charged with such an offense not required to be tried by jury at common law, were lawfully placed on trial by the Commission without a jury."

Korematsu v. United States, 323 U.S. 214; 65 S. Ct. 193; 89 L. Ed. 194 (1944)

Facts—Korematsu, an American citizen of Japanese ancestry, remained in California after the Commanding General of the Western Defense Command ordered it cleared of all persons of Japanese descent under Executive Order 34, itself based on Executive Order No. 9066 and on an act of Congress. He refused to leave and was convicted under the law.

Question—Was the executive order excluding Japanese Americans from areas of the West Coat a proper exercise of the war power?

Decision—Yes.

Reasons—*J. Black* (6–3). Although agreeing that racial classifications were suspect and should be subject to the highest judicial scrutiny, Black argued that "Korematsu was not excluded from the Military Area because of hostility to him or his race. He was excluded because we are at war with the Japanese Empire, because the properly constituted military authorities feared an invasion of our West Coast and felt constrained to take proper security measures, because they decided that the military urgency of the situation demanded that all citizens of Japanese ancestry be segregated from the West Coast temporarily, and finally, because Congress, reposing its confidence in this time of war in our military leaders—as inevitably it must—determined that they should have the power to do just this. There was evidence of disloyalty on the part of some, the military authorities considered that the need for action was great, and time was short. We cannot—by availing ourselves of the calm perspective of hindsight—now say that at that time these actions were unjustified."

In dissent, *J. Roberts*, *J. Jackson*, and *J. Murphy* distinguished this case from an earlier decision in *Hirabayashi v. United States*, 320 U.S. 81 (1943), which had permitted curfews for Japanese Americans. Murphy believed the military decision to exclude Japanese Americans from the West Coast had been based on racism while Jackson focused chiefly on the dangerousness of the precedent that he thought the Court was setting.

Note—The only question presented here was the right of the military to evacuate persons. Rather than martial law, the war power was used. The

Court refused to rule on the basic constitutional issues of the relocation, confinement, and segregation of Japanese Americans.

During the Reagan administration, Congress adopted legislation compensating the living victims of the exclusion and relocation orders. The U.S. Supreme Court subsequently refused to review and thus left in place lower court decisions overruling the original decision because it had been based on misleading information supplied by military authorities.

❦

Duncan v. Kahanamoku, 327 U.S. 304; 66 S. Ct. 606; 90 L. Ed. 688 (1946)

Facts—Immediately following the Pearl Harbor attack, Governor Poindexter of the Territory of Hawaii proclaimed martial law, suspended the writ of habeas corpus, closed the local courts, and turned over the powers of government to the commanding general of the U.S. Army in Hawaii. The president approved the measure, and the military ruled Hawaii until October 24, 1944, with minor relaxations. The procedure aroused much opposition, and suits were brought to test the validity of the convictions of civilians by the military courts. In February 1944, Duncan, a civilian shipfitter employed by the Navy, was convicted of assault for engaging in a brawl with two Marine sentries. He was tried by a military tribunal rather than by a civil court.

Question—Was the military government of Hawaii valid under the Hawaiian Organic Act?

Decision—No.

Reasons—*J. Black* (6–2). Civilians in Hawaii are entitled to their constitutional privilege of a fair trial. In 1900, when Congress passed the Hawaiian Organic Act, it never intended to overstep the boundaries of military and civilian power. Martial law was never intended, in the meaning of the act, to supersede the civilian courts, but only to come to the assistance of the government, and maintain the defense of the island.

❦

Woods v. Cloyd W. Miller Co., 333 U.S. 138; 68 S. Ct. 421; 92 L. Ed. 596 (1948)

Facts—The District Court for the Northern District of Ohio declared unconstitutional Title II of the Housing and Rent Act of 1947, which continued in force rent control provisions of previous legislation. The act became effective on July 1, 1947, and the following day the appellee demanded of its tenants 40 percent and 60 percent increases for rental accommodations in the Cleveland Defense–Rental Area, an admitted violation of the act.

Question—Does Congress's right to establish rent controls under its war powers extend beyond the cessation of hostilities?

Decision—Yes.

Reasons—*J. Douglas* (9–0). The war powers of Congress include the power "to remedy the evils which have arisen from its rise and progress." This power continues for the duration of the emergency and does not necessarily end with the cessation of hostilities. The deficit in housing caused by the heavy demobilization of veterans and the reduction of residential construction due to lack of materials during the period of hostilities still continued. Since the war effort contributed heavily to that deficit, Congress might retain controls, even after the cessation of hostilities.

War powers, used indiscriminately, may swallow up all the powers of Congress, as well as the Ninth and Tenth Amendments. Any power can be abused. Such was not, however, the case in this situation. Also, questions as to whether or not Congress has overstepped its war powers are open to judicial inquiry.

∽৯✦

Johnson v. Eisentrager, 339 U.S. 763, 70 S. Ct. 936; 94 L. Ed. 1255 (1950)

Facts—Eisentrager, and twenty other German nationals were convicted of war crimes by U.S. military tribunals in China (with the consent of the Chinese government) for having passed on intelligence about U.S. forces to Japan after Germany formally surrendered to the U.S. in 1945. They were repatriated to Germany where they applied for writs of habeas corpus from Landsberg Prison where they were within U.S. control. A U.S. District Court dismissed the writ, but the U.S. Court of Appeals for the District of Columbia granted it.

Issue—Do U.S. civil courts have jurisdiction over enemy aliens overseas?

Decision—No.

Reasons—*J. Jackson* (6–3). There are no instances where courts in the U.S. or elsewhere have granted writs to alien enemies not within their territorial jurisdiction. "Citizenship is a high privilege." U.S. courts have also extended rights to resident aliens, but control over enemy aliens has been deemed essential since the Alien Enemy Act of 1798, and such aliens have been "constitutionally subject to summary arrest, internment and deportation whenever a 'declared war' exists." Lawful resident aliens have sometimes been permitted to bring judicial actions, but "the nonresident enemy alien, especially one who has remained in the service of the enemy, does not have even this qualified access to our courts, for he neither has comparable claims upon our institutions nor could his use of them fail to be helpful to the enemy." These prisoners here are "actual enemies." To grant jurisdiction here, the Court would have to extend the writ "even though he (a) is an enemy alien; (b) has never been or resided in the United States; (c) was captured outside of our territory and there held in military custody as a prisoner of war; (d) was tried and convicted by a Military Commission sitting outside the United States; (e) for offenses against the laws of war committed outside the United States; (f) and is at all times imprisoned outside the United States." Habeas corpus requires the production of prisoners in court. This would be quite difficult for prisoners located in Germany. Neither *Ex parte Quirin*, involving German saboteurs, nor *In re Yamashita*, involving the trial of a Japanese general, requires such an outcome. The Fifth Amendment does not apply to all persons, "whatever their nationality, wherever they are located and whatever their offenses." Granting habeas corpus relief would "extend coverage of our Constitution to nonresident alien enemies denied to resident alien enemies." The power of military authorities to punish violations against the laws of war is well established. "Certainly it is not the function of the Judiciary to entertain private litigation—even by a citizen—which challenges the legality, the wisdom, or the propriety of the Commander-in-chief in sending our armed forces abroad or to any particular region."

J. Black, dissenting. Courts do have jurisdiction of this case. There is no evidence that the Germans were spies or that they did anything other than obey the orders of their Japanese superiors. *Ex parte Quirin* and *Yamashita v. United States* both establish that enemy aliens can have standing. It is dangerous to deprive the petitioners of habeas corpus "solely because they were convicted and imprisoned overseas." The Court has to give due deference to commanders in the field, but "When a foreign enemy surrenders, the situation changes markedly." The scope of military review is narrow, but it exists. "Conquest by the United States, unlike conquest by many other nations, does not mean tyranny."

Rostker v. Goldberg, 453 U.S. 57; 101 S. Ct. 1; 69 L. Ed. 2d 478 (1981)

Facts—The Military Selective Service Act authorized the president to require the registration for possible military service of males but not females. In 1980, President Jimmy Carter reactivated the registration process for both males and females, but Congress allocated only those funds necessary for the men. Three men brought suit claiming that the act's gender-based discrimination violated the due process clause of the Fifth Amendment to the Constitution.

Question—Does the Military Selective Service Act violate the Fifth Amendment?

Decision—No.

Reasons—*J. Rehnquist (6–3). "Congress is a co-equal branch of government whose* members take the same oath we do to uphold the Constitution. . . . This Court has consistently recognized Congress's 'broad constitutional power' to raise and regulate armies and navies." Just as Congress's scope of power in this area is broad, "the lack of competence on the part of the courts is marked." While the Court does not abdicate its responsibility to decide constitutional questions, "the Constitution itself requires such deference to congressional choice." This case "is quite different from several of the gender-based discrimination cases . . . and the decision to exempt women from registration was not the 'accidental byproduct of a traditional way of thinking about women.' The purpose of the registration, therefore, was to prepare for a draft of combat troops. Women as a group . . . unlike men as a group, are not eligible for combat. . . . Congress's decision to authorize the registration of only men, therefore, does not violate the due process clause."

J. White dissented on the basis that the record indicated that a need might develop for both combat and noncombat positions. *J. Marshall* argued that excluding women from a fundamental obligation of citizenship was inconsistent with the equal protection component of the Fifth Amendment.

≈⊱⊰

Hamdi v. Rumsfeld, 542 U.S. 507; 124 S. Ct. 2633; 159 L. Ed. 2d 578 (2004)

Facts—Yaser Esam Hamdi, who was born in Louisiana in 1980 but moved as a child with his family to Saudi Arabia, was captured by U.S. forces in Afghanistan and detained first at Guantanamo Bay, Cuba, and then at a brig in Charleston, South Carolina on charges of being an "enemy combatant." His father, Esam Fouad Hamdi, claimed that his son had gone to Afghanistan to do "relief work," and filed a writ of habeas corpus asking for counsel, for an end to his interrogations, for a declaration that his detention violated the Fifth and Fourteenth Amendments, for an evidential hearing, and for his relief. The district court ordered that counsel be provided, but the Fourth Circuit Court of Appeals overturned on the basis that this did not show proper deference to the government's security and intelligence interests.

Question—To what rights is an American citizen, detained as an "enemy combatant" entitled?

Decision—The right to know the charges against him, the right to a hearing, and the right to counsel.

Reasons—*J. O'Connor* (for 4 justices; 5–4 ruling). The Authorization for the Use of Military Force provided authority for the government to detain Hamdi. Such detention is an important incident of war that allows the nations to keep enemies off the battlefield and can include U.S. citizens. Such detention should last no longer than hostilities nor is indefinite detention authorized for the use of interrogation. Neither *Ex parte Milligan* (1866) nor *Ex parte Quirin* (1942) exempt U.S. citizens from detention, nor should the government be forced to detain them overseas. Absent suspension, which has not occurred in this case, the writ of habeas corpus remains available. Hamdi disputes the government's contention that he was an enemy combatant. Consistent with other due process cases, most notably *Matthews v. Eldridge* (1976), the Court must weigh the respective interests of Hamdi and the government. *Matthews* noted that "commitment for *any* purpose constitutes a significant deprivation of liberty that requires due process protection," especially when such detention may be erroneous. There are also weighty interests in "ensuring that those who have in fact fought with the enemy during a war do not return to battle against the United States." Practical difficulties could also accompany a full-blown trial. A proper balance requires "notice of the factual basis for his classification, and a fair opportunity to rebut the Government's factual assertions before a neutral decisionmaker." Given combat exigencies, the government can use hearsay and "the Constitution would not be offended by a presumption in favor of the Government's evidence, so long as that presumption remained a rebuttable one and fair opportunity for rebuttal were provided." "We have long . . . made clear that a state of war is not a blank check for the President when it comes to the rights of the Nation's citizens. The government's proposed 'some evidence' standard is inadequate." However, "There remains the possibility that the standards we have articulated could be met by an appropriately authorized and properly constituted military tribunal." As part of due process, Hamdi is entitled to the right of counsel.

J. Souter, concurring in part, dissenting in part, and concurring in judgment. Hamdi is entitled to habeas corpus relief. The Authorization of the Use of Military Force is inadequate to justify Hamdi's detention without affording him rights. The government might even be violating the Geneva Convention. Souter would prefer to remand the case to the Court of Appeals rather than resolving constitutional issues, but he concurs in the plurality judgment in order to give the decision practical effect.

J. Scalia, dissenting. Hamdi should be prosecuted for treason, or the government should release him. The writ of habeas corpus is the only common law writ mentioned in the U.S. Constitution. The Suspension Clause serves as "a safety valve." Absent use of this suspension, Hamdi is entitled to be released. Milligan limits the authority of military tribunals over U.S. citizens. *Quirin* differs from this case in that the petitioners there were "*admitted* enemy invaders." The Court has no business attempting to come up with alternate procedures "to Make Everything Come Out Right." It is up to Congress, not the Court, to decide whether the writ should be suspended.

J. Thomas, dissenting. "This detention falls squarely within the Federal Government's war powers, and we lack the expertise and capacity to second-guess that decision." National security is "the primary responsibility and purpose of the Federal Government," and the "unitary Executive" has chief authority in this area as "the sole organ of the nation in its external relations." This authority "carries with it broad discretion." Courts lack relevant information and expertise. "Although the President very well may have inherent authority to detain those arrayed against our troops, . . . we need not decide that question because Congress has authorized the President to do so." In the context of this case, "due process requires nothing more than a good-faith executive determination." Judicial intervention is more likely to lead to anarchy than to the vindication of rights. Thus, "the Government's detention of Hamdi as an enemy combatant does not violate the Constitution."

❦

Rasul v. Bush, 542 U.S. 466 (2004)

Facts—Two Australian citizens and twelve Kuwaiti citizens who were captured in Afghanistan were among about 640 non-American citizens who were being held at the American Naval Base in Guantanamo Bay, which the U.S. leased from Cuba. These aliens filed for writs of habeas corpus. Both U.S. district and the U.S. circuit courts denied the petitions, relying largely on the precedent in *Johnson v. Eisentrager* (1950) involving aliens that the U.S. held at a base in Germany.

Question—Does the habeas corpus statute confer "a right to judicial review of the legality of executive detention of aliens in a territory over which the United States exercises plenary and exclusive jurisdiction, but not 'ultimate sovereignty?'"

Decision—Yes

Reasons—*J. Stevens* (6–3). Congress has given jurisdiction to federal courts over habeas corpus since the Judiciary Act of 1789, but habeas corpus is itself "a writ antecedent to statute . . . . throwing its root deep into the genius of our common law." The writ has been used "in a wide variety of cases involving executive detention, in wartime as well as in times of peace." The petitioners in this case differ from those in *Eisentrager*. Notably, they "are not nationals of countries at war with the United States, and they deny that they have engaged in or plotted acts of aggression against the United States." They have not been charged with wrongdoing, or been given access to a tribunal. *Eisentrager* devoted little attention to statutory jurisdiction because it relied on a previous decision in *Ahrens v. Clark* (1948) that had limited such jurisdiction in the case of others. Subsequent decisions have, however, filled in this statutory gap. Most notably *Braden v. 30th Judicial Circuit Court of Ky* (1973), ruled that prisoners no longer needed to be within the exercise of district court jurisdiction to qualify for habeas corpus review. By treaty, the U.S. exercises "complete jurisdiction and control" over Guantanamo. Statutes draw no distinction between citizens and aliens for such purposes so "Aliens held at the base, no less than American citizens, are entitled to invoke the federal court's authority" under the law. Historically, the writ extended to any territory "under the subjection of the Crown." The Alien Tort Statute is another possible source of jurisdiction.

J. Kennedy, concurring. The decision needs to be understood in light of separation of powers. Although *Eisentrager* "indicates that there is a realm of political authority over military affairs where the judicial power may not enter," this case differs in that "Guantanamo Bay is in every practical respect a United States territory, and it is one far removed from hostilities." Moreover, the detainees are being kept there indefinitely.

J. Scalia, dissenting. This is a novel holding that contradicts *Johnson v. Eisentrager* and misconstrues *Ahrens v. Clark*. "Federal courts are courts of limited jurisdiction," and they do not have jurisdiction in this case. The Court "springs a trap on the Executive, subjecting Guantanamo Bay to the oversight of the federal courts even though it has never before been thought to be within their jurisdiction—and thus making it a foolish place to have housed alien wartime detainees." The U.S. cannot exercise complete jurisdiction without sovereignty, and English historical precedents limited jurisdiction "to British *subjects*." Departing from precedents is especially unjustified in cases affecting the nation's ability to make war. This is "judicial adventurism of the worst sort."

❦

Hamdan v. Rumsfeld, 548 U.S. 557; 126 S. Ct. 2749; 165 L. Ed. 2d 723 (2006)

Facts—Salim Ahmed Hamdan, a Yemeni national held in custody at the U.S. prison in Guantanamo Bay, Cuba, and alleged to have been a member of the Taliban who served as Osama bin Laden's personal driver, filed for a writ of habeas corpus against Secretary of Defense Donald Rumsfeld to challenge the executive's power of trial by military commission for offenses connected to terrorism. A U.S. district court granted him a writ of habeas corpus, which the District of Columbia Circuit Court reversed.

Questions—Was Hamdan entitled to a writ of habeas corpus? Was the military commission that was constituted to try him constitutional?

Decisions—Yes; No.

Reasons—*J. Stevens* (5–3, with *C.J. Roberts* recusing himself) thought the military commission lacked power to try Hamdan under the Uniform Code of Military Justice and the Geneva Conventions; 4 [of 8] justices did not think the offenses with which he was charged were offenses under the law of war that such a commission could try. In 2001, President Bush issued a comprehensive military order to govern the "Detention, Treatment, and Trial of Certain Non-Citizens in the War Against Terrorism," and on July 3, 2003, Bush announced his intention to try Hamdan and five other Guantanamo Bay detainees by military commission. Hamdan was charged with joining a criminal enterprise involving terrorism. A Combatant Status Review Tribunal (CSRT) had already decided that Hamdan was an "enemy combatant." The government filed a motion to dismiss his petition for habeas corpus on the basis of the Detainee Treatment Act of 2005 (DTA). It contends that the section entitled "Judicial Review of Detention of Enemy Combatants," was designed to withdraw jurisdiction even over pending cases, but Stevens believed that "ordinary principles of statutory construction suffice to rebut the Government's theory." He cited a "presumption against retroactivity" absent specific language that he found missing from part of this bill. The government further argues that the Court should await a final outcome of the military court proceedings before granting review, but Stevens rejects this argument, ruling that prior cases arguing for such abstention are not directly relevant. Most notably, the Court expedited review in the *Quirin* Case, involving German saboteurs. In thus reviewing the case, Stevens observes that "The military commission, neither mentioned in the Constitution nor created by statute, was born of military necessity." It is still unclear whether the President may convene such tribunals without congressional approval, but "we held in *Quirin* that Congress had, through Article of War 15, sanctioned the use of military commissions in such circumstances" [that is, in cases involving "offenders or offenses against the law of war"]. This did not provide authority to create such commissions in any circumstances. Military commissions have been used in three cases: as substitutes for civilian courts during times of martial law; "as part of a temporary military government over occupied enemy territory or territory regained from an enemy where civilian government cannot and does not function"; and "an 'incident to the conduct of war' when there is a need 'to seize and subject to disciplinary measures those enemies who in their attempt to thwart or impede our military effort have violated the law of war.'" *Quirin* is representative of the latter, although it also "represents the high-water mark of military power to try enemy combatants for war crimes." Colonel William Winthrop noted four preconditions of such tribunals. These involve offenses committed within a military commander's jurisdiction; during the war; involving violations of the laws of war; involving "violations of the laws and usages of war cognizable by military tribunals only" and breaches of orders or regulations not triable by court-martial. Hamdan, however, is being charged with offenses that began prior to the beginning of hostilities, and the offenses are not properly violations of the laws of war. Extending this power risks "concentrating in military hands a degree of adjudicative and punitive power in excess of that contemplated either by statute or by the Constitution." The charge of conspiracy is not an offense against the rule of war, nor is it recognized by either the Geneva or Hague Conventions. Nor did the Court address conspiracy when deciding the *Quirin* Case. Military commissions are limited to trying overt acts that occurred during the conflict rather than conspiracies that preceded it. In any event, the commission lacks the power to proceed in this case because the procedures that the government has established are inadequate. In permitting hearsay evidence and evidence secured through coercion and in refusing to open some proceedings to the defendant, the commission would deny Hamdan due process. Moreover, waiting until a verdict is rendered to review the verdict could provide inadequate relief. The proceedings of military commissions should conform "insofar as practicable" with those of courts-martial. Here the President's "practicability" determination "is insufficient to justify variances from the procedures governing courts-martial." Stevens further denied that *Johnson v. Eisentrager* (1950), an appeal by Germans held at a military base after World War II, stood for a different principle. Stevens emphasized that his decision does not prohibit the government from

detaining Hamdan "for the duration of active hostilities in order to prevent
. . . harm," but in meting out criminal punishment, "the Executive is bound to
comply with the rule of law that prevails in this jurisdiction."

J. Breyer, concurring. "Congress has not issued the Executive a 'blank
check.'" "Concentration of powers puts personal liberty in peril of arbitrary
action by officials." The procedures here must be compared to those involving court-martials. Hamdan has been in U.S. custody for an extended period,
presenting "no exigency requiring special speed or precluding careful consideration of evidence." Breyer pointed to a number of structural differences
between the military commission in this case and regular court-martials. Congress could change existing limits, but they remain until it does so. Breyer
would not, however, decide at this point whether an accused has to be present
at all stages of a trial, whether the Geneva Convention is binding, the validity
of the conspiracy charges against Hamdan, or other limitations that *J. Stevens*
believed were elements of the common law of war.

J. Scalia, dissenting. The Detainee Treatment Act unambiguously with-
draws habeas corpus jurisdiction from courts in this case and courts should
heed its "plain meaning," as they have done in previous cases. The Court's
use of legislative history is particularly egregious in that it elevates self-serving statements by partisans. The provision does not violate the Suspension
Clause because Congress provides collateral remedies. "Even if Congress had
not clearly and constitutionally eliminated jurisdiction over this case, neither
this Court nor the lower courts ought to exercise it." The political branches
should be exercising primary responsibility in this area.

J. Thomas, dissenting. The president's unitary character, and the decisive-
ness, secrecy, and dispatch with which he can operate give him primary
responsibility in this area, and his powers are strengthened where, as here, he
is acting with congressional authorization. This case falls under Winthrop's
criteria. The conflict at issue dates at least as far back as bin Laden's Declaration of Jihad in August 1996. Hamdan has been properly charged with "membership in a war-criminal enterprise and conspiracy to commit war crimes."
These have long been understood to be war offenses. The president is in a far
better position to judge "military necessity" than is the Court. The Court's
determination "that conspiracy to massacre innocent civilians does not violate the laws of war . . . is unsustainable." Nor do the proceedings violate the
Geneva Convention. The president can adjust proceedings to contingencies.
Hamdan's plea for review is not ripe. "But there is neither a statutory nor
historical requirement that military commissions conform to the structure and
practice of courts-marital. A military commission is a different tribunal, serving a different function, and thus operates pursuant to different procedures."
The procedures established in this case are fair, and that is sufficient.

J. Alito, dissenting. The military commission "is 'a regularly constituted court.'" It does not need to be identical to courts-martial. "It makes no sense to strike down the entire commission structure based on speculation that some evidence might be improperly admitted in some future case."

Note—A military commission eventually convicted Hamdan of one charge but not of conspiracy, and he was sent to Yemen after his release from Guantanamo.

∽✗

Boudmediene v. Bush, 553 U.S. 723 (2008)

Facts—Boumediene, Al Odah, and other foreign nationals who were captured by U.S. military forces in Afghanistan, Bosnia, and Gambia were being held at the U.S. base in Guantanamo, Cuba. They were tried by the Combatant Status Review Tribunals (CSRTs) to see if they were "enemy combatants." The deputy secretary of defense established these tribunals after the Court decided in *Hamdi v. Rumsfeld* (2004) that they were entitled to due process. *Rasul v. Bush* (2004) had further established that habeas corpus jurisdiction extended to Guantanamo. The Detainee Treatment Act of 2005 (DTA) had ruled that courts did not have habeas corpus jurisdiction over aliens detained at Guantanamo, and when the Court ruled in *Hamdan v. Rumsfeld* (2006) that this limitation did not apply to pending cases, Congress adopted new regulations MCA Section 7, limiting such jurisdiction.

Questions—Does MCA Section 7 deny federal courts jurisdiction to hear habeas corpus actions pending at the time of its enactment? If so, is this constitutional?

Decisions—Yes; no.

Reasons—*J. Kennedy* (5–4). The language of the statute makes it clear that Congress intends for the law to apply to pending cases. In determining whether this violates the Suspension Clause, the Court had to examine the effect of the petitioners' status as enemy combatants and their location at Guantanamo Bay. Kennedy observed that the writ of habeas corpus was one of the few liberties that the Constitution included prior to the adoption of the Bill of Rights, which he traced back to the Magna Carta and through the Petition of Rights (1627), and the Habeas Corpus Act of 1679. Article I, Section 9 of the Constitution specified that "The Privilege of the Writ of Habeas Corpus shall not be suspended, unless when in Cases of Rebellion or Invasion the public

Safety may require it." During ratification debates, Edmund Randolph called this "an 'exception' to the 'power given to Congress to regulate courts.'" Under common law, "a petitioner's status as an alien was not a categorical bar to habeas corpus relief," but the precise range of the writ is more difficult to determine. Petitioners thought the Court should note that English jurisdiction extended to the Channel Islands and India, and the government noted that it did not apply to Scotland and Hanover, but there were differences that made direct analogies difficult. Moreover, the historical record was simply not complete. The U.S. contends that Guantanamo is not within its sovereignty, but while this may be true of de jure sovereignty, it does not appear to be true of de facto sovereignty over an area where there are no rival courts. The Constitution recognized that the U.S. would acquire territories, and it extended protection to individuals who inhabited them in the Insular Cases. In *Reid v. Covert*, it further extended protection to American citizens abroad. In *Johnson v. Eisentrager* (1950), the Court had limited habeas corpus jurisdiction to enemy aliens at the Landsberg Prison in Germany, but the U.S. did not exercise the same sovereignty there that it did at Guantanamo. Ultimately, these cases established that "questions of extraterritoriality turn on objective factors and practical concerns, not formalism." The government's approach raises serious separation-of-powers concerns that cannot be contracted away. Here the petitioners are not U.S. citizens, but they dispute their status as enemy combatants. The CSRTs provide only limited review and "fall well short of the procedures and adversarial mechanisms that would eliminate the need for habeas corpus review." Detainees have a "personal representative" but not a lawyer to represent them. Confinement makes it difficult for detainees to present evidence. Moreover, there are differences between the status of the detainees here and those at the Landsberg Prison. Although the Court has never before held "that noncitizens detained by our Government in territory over which another country maintains *de jure* sovereignty have any rights under our Constitution," this conflict is now the longest in U.S. history and the U.S. clearly has de facto control over Guantanamo. "If the privilege of habeas corpus is to be denied to the detainees now before us, Congress must act in accordance with the requirements of the Suspension Clause." Congress has flexibility in interpreting habeas corpus procedures, but the process it has substituted here is inadequate. It has limited the authority of the Courts of Appeal simply to ascertaining whether CSRTs complied with procedures established by the secretary of defense. Moreover, the initial determination of enemy combatant status has been made by the executive rather than by a judicial process. Although the government argues that its procedures comply with the decision in *Hamdi*, that case did not deal specifically with the suspension of the writ. The "closed and accusatorial" nature of CRTS proceedings magnify the risk of error. The current mechanism offers inadequate redress for cases where new evidence emerges after initial CSRT hearings. Detainees need to have access to habeas corpus review by U.S. district courts, especially in cases where individuals have been detained for six years or more. Congress is free to channel such appeals to a specific district court.

J. Souter, concurring, thought that the Court had given a clear indication of its position in *Rasul v. Bush*. He further emphasized the length of time that the detainees had been in custody.

C.J. Roberts, dissenting, objected to the Court's substitution of its own "shapeless procedures" for those that Congress had already established. He further questioned whether the detainees had exhausted available remedies before coming to the Court. He believed the CRST procedures "meet the minimal due process requirements outlines in *Hamdi*," and that the Court should see how they work before invalidating them. The majority decision would simply add additional lawyers to an already cumbersome process. The Court should give greater deference to military habeas corpus proceedings than to others. The majority's concern about the discovery of new evidence can be met under existing procedures by remanding the case for a new determination. The majority has further failed to clarify exactly how the remedies it requires will differ from those in place. It has exiled the Great Writ "to a jurisdictionally quirky outpost, with no tangible benefit to anyone."

J. Scalia, dissenting. The writ of habeas corpus should not be extended to aliens abroad, and this decision is likely to have "disastrous consequences" on the war on terror. Enemy detainees are dangerous, and some who have been released have engaged in terrorist acts. The decision is contrary to that in *Johnson v. Eisentrager*, because the United States does not maintain sovereignty over Guantanamo. The decision is based on "an inflated notion of judicial supremacy," contrary to the original understanding of the Suspension Clause. "The Nation will live to regret what the Court has done today."

Chapter Four

ARTICLE III: THE JUDICIAL BRANCH

Many constitutional law textbooks begin with a chapter or chapters on judicial powers. They do so, not because the judicial article is listed first in the U.S. Constitution (it is third) but because their texts center on U.S. Supreme Court decisions. Readers specifically interested in the U.S. Supreme Court will want to consult not only this chapter but also the essay "This Is Our Supreme Court" at the beginning of this book. The Supreme Court is part of the broader judicial system outlined in Article III of the U.S. Constitution. Since Article III is the sketchiest of the first three "distributing articles," much of the judicial system has developed through customs and usages.

Because the United States is a federal system, that divides powers between the national and state governments, each state has its own court system. It is therefore more accurate to refer to fifty-one court systems than to one. Like the system of national courts described below, most state courts are arranged hierarchically, with three or four levels of courts. There are typically three or four such levels with lower trial courts reviewed by appellate courts. States all have an equivalent to the U.S. Supreme Court, but sometimes they use different terminology to describe such courts.

The only court specifically mentioned in the U.S. Constitution is the U.S. Supreme Court, housed in Washington, D.C. It is at the apex of a federal system currently composed of three primary layers. At the lowest rung are the U.S. District Courts, of which there are currently ninety-four. These are trial courts, or courts of "original jurisdiction." Above these are eleven numbered U.S. Courts of Appeal as well as a special Court for Appeals for the District of Columbia and another to hear specialized cases. Cases begin in the trial courts, and may then be appealed through the U.S. Courts of Appeal (or through state supreme courts or their equivalents) to the U.S. Supreme Court. For well over a century, the number of justices has been set at nine. These include eight associate justices and the chief justice. The chief justice heads conference deliberations and by custom has the power to write or assign opinions in which he or she is in the majority.

State judges may be appointed, elected, or filled by some combination of these two methods. By contrast, the president appoints all federal judges subject to the "advice and consent" of the U.S. Senate. All federal judges serve "during good behavior," meaning that they remain in office until they die, retire, or are impeached, convicted, and removed from office (although some lower federal judges have been so removed, no impeachment of a U.S. Supreme Court justice has ever resulted in such a conviction). Congress may raise, but not lower the salaries of judges during their tenure in office.

Judges straddle the line between law and politics. The confirmation battles of federal judges have become particularly bitter in recent years. Judges are invariably lawyers with devotion to legal principles and knowledge of precedents. As citizens they are aware of the opinions around them.

Judges exercise two primary powers—that of statutory interpretation and that of judicial review. The first power enables judges to decide on the meaning of laws. If legislatures believe they are mistaken, they may adopt new laws. The power that is more frequently emphasized in classes on American constitutional law and history is the power of judicial review. This power, first asserted over congressional laws in Chief Justice John Marshall's decision in *Marbury v. Madison* (1803), allows courts to strike down laws and or executive actions as unconstitutional. Such rulings may only be reversed by future court decisions or through the complicated process of constitutional amendment.

Almost all the cases heard by the U.S. Supreme Court are cases of appellate jurisdiction. It therefore concentrates on questions of law rather than of fact. Cases get to the U.S. Supreme Court through a series of petitions or writs, the most important of which is a writ of certiorari. The Supreme Court has almost complete discretion over which cases it chooses to hear. It currently operates according to a "rule of four" whereby it only hears cases that four of the nine justices vote to hear. Justices then review written briefs and schedule such cases for oral arguments. Justices subsequently vote on their decisions, which are assigned to individual justices and published. In addition to majority opinions filed on behalf of the courts, many cases also contain concurring and/or dissenting opinions. A concurrence signals that a justice or justices agree with the outcome but for somewhat different reasons. Dissenters try to persuade readers that the Court's decision is wrong.

In order to bring a case to Court, parties must establish "standing," that is, a concrete interest in the case. Courts must further decide that such cases are "justiciable," or capable of judicial resolution. The Court has developed numerous doctrines both to assert its own prerogatives and to protect itself from deciding cases that are not yet "ripe," that are "moot," or that may not be easily capable of judicial resolution.

One of the most elusive of these doctrines is the political questions doctrine. In such cases, the Court decides that one or both of the other two branches of government would more appropriately resolve the issue. This doctrine has never been fixed and continues to evolve over time. One of the most important of these decisions was in *Baker v. Carr* (1962), in which the Court outlined six essential questions that made cases "political" in nature. The term is arguably something of a misnomer since most Supreme Court decisions are at least partly "political" in nature, but it reemphasizes the tenuous line that the Court must walk between law and politics.

JUDICIAL JURISDICTION AND STANDING

Marbury v. Madison, 1 Cranch (5 U.S.) 137; 2 L. Ed. 60 (1803)

Facts—In compliance with the Judiciary Act of 1801, President John Adams signed a commission for William Marbury as a justice of the peace for the county of Washington, D.C. The seal of the United States was affixed to the commission, but it never reached Marbury. James Madison, the incoming secretary of state under Jefferson (a Democratic Republican rather than a Federalist) refused to deliver the commission. Marbury went directly to the U.S. Supreme Court for a writ of mandamus requiring Secretary of State Madison to deliver to Marbury his commission. The Judiciary Act of 1789 in Section 13 had provided that the Supreme Court could issue writs of mandamus.

Questions—(a) Has the applicant a right to the commission he demands? (b) If that right has been violated, do the laws of the United States afford him a remedy? (c) Is this remedy a mandamus issuing from the Supreme Court? (d) The question that Marshall does not state, but for which this decision is most famous, is can the Supreme Court void an act of national legislation that it considers to be unconstitutional?

Decisions—(a) Yes; (b) Yes; (c) No; (d) Yes.

Reasons—*C.J. Marshall* (5–0). By signing Marbury's commission, President Adams appointed him a justice of the peace. The seal of the United States affixed thereto by the secretary of state was conclusive testimony of the legitimacy of the signature, and of the completion of the appointment. That appointment, under its terms, conferred on Marbury a legal right to the office for the space of five years. Thus, Marbury had a right to the commission he demanded.

Where there is a legal right, there is also a legal remedy by suit, or action at law, whenever that right is invaded. Marbury had a legal right, and this right was obviously violated by Madison's refusal to deliver to him the commission. Thus a remedy under United States laws was due Marbury.

The Supreme Court of the United States had no power to issue a mandamus to the secretary of state since this would be an exercise of original jurisdiction not warranted by the Constitution. Congress had no power to enlarge the Supreme Court's original jurisdiction beyond the limited circumstances involving diplomatic personnel and disputes among the states described in Article III of the Constitution.

The people designed the Constitution as a written instrument designed to control government. The Constitution is "either a superior paramount law, unchangeable by ordinary means, or it is on a level with ordinary legislative acts [like the provision of the Judiciary Act in question]." Marshall argued that the Constitution was in the former category of fundamental law and that "It is emphatically the province and duty of the judicial department to say what the law is." When faced with a conflict between an unconstitutional law (as further examples, Marshall cited cases where a state lays a prohibited export tax, adopts a bill of attainder or ex post facto law, or flouts constitutional guidelines regarding convictions for treason) and the Constitution, the judges, who take an oath to uphold the Constitution, must enforce the more fundamental law. Otherwise, provisions of the Constitution could be flouted with impunity. Judges take an oath to uphold the U.S. Constitution: "Why does a judge swear to discharge his duties agreeably to the constitution of the United States, if that constitution forms no rule for his government? if it is closed upon him, and cannot be inspected by him?" Marshall also noted that the supremacy clause in Article VI of the Constitution makes "the constitution itself" the supreme law of the land.

Note—This is the first time the Court declared an act of Congress unconstitutional, and thus established the doctrine of judicial review. It was not until a half century later in *Dred Scott v. Sandford*, 19 Howard 393 (1857) that the Court was to do it again.

Martin v. Hunter's Lessee, 1 Wheaton (14 U.S.) 304; 4 L. Ed. 97 (1816)

Facts—In the case of *Fairfax's Devisee v. Hunter's Lessee*, 7 Cranch (11 U.S.) 603, the Court reversed the decision of the state court and sustained title to certain Virginia land previously held by Lord Fairfax, a citizen and inhabitant of Virginia until his death in 1781. He devised the land to Denny Fairfax (previously Denny Martin), a native-born British subject who resided in England until his death. The Court held that Denny Fairfax, although an alien enemy, whose property might have been confiscated, was in complete possession of the land at the time of the commencement of the suit in 1791 and up to the treaty of 1794. It was said to be clear "that the treaty of 1794 completely protects and confirms the title of Denny Fairfax, even admitting that the treaty of peace left him wholly unprovided for." Denny Fairfax died while the suit was still pending, and the Supreme Court vested title in his heirs. Hunter's lessee claimed title under the Commonwealth of Virginia.

Question—Does the appellate power of the United States extend to cases pending in the state courts?

Decision—Yes.

Reason—*J. Story* (6–0). Article III of the Constitution has given appellate jurisdiction to the Supreme Court in all cases under the Constitution where it has no original jurisdiction, subject, however, to such regulations and exceptions as Congress may prescribe. State judges in their official capacities are called on to decide cases, not according to the laws and constitution of their own state, but according to "the supreme law of the land"—the Constitution, laws, and treaties of the United States. Yet to all these cases, the judicial power of this Court is to extend according to the Constitution. It cannot extend by original jurisdiction, so it must extend to them by appellate jurisdiction or not at all.

A final motive, for the appellate power over the state tribunals, is the importance and necessity of uniformity of decisions throughout the United States. Different interpretations would result, and the laws, treaties, and the Constitution of the United States would never have the same construction or efficiency in any two states. For such an evil, the only remedy is the appellate jurisdiction of this Court.

Cohens v. Virginia, 6 Wheaton (19 U.S.) 264; 5 L. Ed. 257 (1821)

Facts—Congress passed a law in 1802 authorizing the District of Columbia to conduct lotteries. Acting under this authority, the city passed an ordinance creating a lottery. The state of Virginia had a law forbidding lotteries except as established by that state. P. J. and M. J. Cohen were arrested in Norfolk, Virginia, charged with selling tickets for the lottery. They were found guilty and fined $100. Then they appealed to the Supreme Court, to which Virginia did not object since the states desired to force the issue of the Supreme Court's authority over state actions.

Question—Is the jurisdiction of the Court excluded by the character of the parties, one of them a state and the other a citizen of that state?

Decision—No.

Reasons—*C.J. Marshall* (6–0). "Where, then, a state obtains a judgment against an individual, and the court, rendering such judgment, overrules a defense set up under the Constitutions or laws of the United States, the transfer of this record into the Supreme Court, for the sole purpose of inquiring whether the judgment violates the Constitution or laws of the United States can, with no propriety, we think, be denominated by a suit commenced or prosecuted against the state whose judgment is so far reexamined. Nothing is demanded from the state. No claim against it of any description is asserted or prosecuted. The party is not to be restored to the possession of anything. . . . Whether it be by writ of error or appeal, no claim is asserted, no demand is made by the original defendant; he only asserts the constitutional right to have his defense examined by that tribunal whose province it is to construe the Constitution and laws of the Union. It is, then, the opinion of the Court, that the defendant who removes a judgment rendered against him by a State court into this Court, for the purpose of reexamining the question, whether that judgment be in violation of the Constitution or laws of the United States, does not commence or prosecute a suit against the State, whatever may be its opinion where the effect of the writ may be to restore the party to the possession of a thing which he demands. . . ."

Note—In *Martin v. Hunter's Lessee*, 1 Wheaton 304 (1816), the Court held that the Constitution, in order to bring uniformity to U.S. jurisprudence, extended the appellate jurisdiction of the Supreme Court to cases in state courts that involved the Constitution, laws, and treaties of the United States. Cohens further established that when a state has obtained a judgment against an individual in a state court over a defense based on the Constitution or laws of the United States, the Supreme Court may review the decision.

☙

Eakin v. Raub, 12 Serg. & Rawle 330 (Pa. S. Ct.) (1825)

Facts—This otherwise insignificant Pennsylvania Supreme Court case, which dealt with the legitimacy of a state law designed to adjust the time that a person living abroad could make claims to unoccupied land, is often cited in constitutional law casebooks for Pennsylvania Justice John Bannister Gibson's dissenting opinion. Gibson challenged John Marshall's arguments in *Marbury v. Madison* (1803) for judicial invalidation of legislation that judges believe to be unconstitutional.

Question—Should judges have the power to declare acts passed by Congress to be unconstitutional?

Decision—No [Answer by the dissent].

Reason—*J. Gibson* (in dissent). The existence of a written constitution, per se, does not invest the judiciary with the power of judicial review. Absent "the impregnable ground of an express grant," which is missing from the U.S. and Pennsylvania constitutions, the judiciary should have no more right to review an act of legislation, other than to see if it was legitimately adopted, than the legislature would have to review acts of the judiciary. Marshall's opinion in *Marbury* thus took the doctrine of separation of powers too far. The legislative branch, whose members are elected by the people, better incorporates this sovereignty than does the judicial branch. The oath that judges take is not peculiar to them, and it is not intended to give judges the unspecified right of judicial review, but only to assure that they do their constitutionally mandated duties: it "is designed rather as a test of the political principles of the man, than to bind the officer in the discharge of his duty." The advantage of a written constitution stems not from the power that it invests in the judiciary but from its articulation of first principles that all can consult. If the people's representatives make a mistake in interpretation, they can change their minds or the people can replace them, but when the judiciary errs, a constitutional amendment or convention is required. Although rejecting judicial invalidation of federal laws, Gibson believed that the supremacy clause gave judges specific authority to invalidate state laws that they considered to be in violation of the U.S. Constitution.

❧

Ableman v. Booth, 21 Howard (62 U.S.) 506; 16 L. Ed. 169 (1859)

Facts—Ableman, a U.S. marshal, held Booth in custody, pending his trial in a District Court of the United States on the charge of having aided the escape of a fugitive slave from the custody of a deputy marshal in Milwaukee. The supreme court of Wisconsin issued a writ of habeas corpus.

Question—Can a state court grant a writ of habeas corpus to a prisoner arrested under the authority of the United States and in federal custody?

Decision—No.

Reasons—*C.J. Taney* (9–0). No state judge or court, after being judicially informed that the party is imprisoned under the authority of the United States, has the right to interfere with him, or to require him to be brought before them. And if the authority of the state, in the form of judicial process or otherwise, should attempt to control the marshal or other authorized officer or agent of the United States in any respect, in the custody of his prisoner, it would be his duty to resist it, and to call to his aid any force that might be necessary to maintain the authority of federal law against illegal interference. No judicial process, whatever form it may assume, can have any lawful authority outside the limits of the jurisdiction of the court or judge by whom it is issued; and an attempt to enforce it beyond these boundaries is nothing less than lawless violence.

Ex parte McCardle, 7 Wallace (74 U.S.) 506; 19 L. Ed. 264 (1869)

Facts—The Constitution assigns appellate jurisdiction to the Supreme Court with "such exceptions and under such regulations, as the Congress shall make." In February 1867 Congress passed an act granting the Supreme Court appellate jurisdiction in the matter of writs of habeas corpus in cases where persons were restrained in violation of the Constitution, or of any treaty or law of the United States. The military held McCardle in custody for trial before a military commission for the publication of incendiary and libelous articles in a newspaper that he edited. Before the judges acted upon his appeal, Congress repealed the act providing for the appellate jurisdiction.

Question—Does the Court have appellate jurisdiction in a case after the act pertaining to such jurisdiction has been repealed?

Decision—No.

Reasons—*C.J. Chase* (8–0). The Constitution grants appellate jurisdiction to the Court with exceptions and regulations by Congress. This does not imply that Congress grants appellate jurisdiction, but that it can make exceptions to that power. Therefore, the act of 1868 repealing the act of 1867 deprived the Court of jurisdiction in this case. When an act is repealed, it must be considered, except as to transactions past and closed, as if it never existed. The Court then had no choice but to decline jurisdiction of this case. This does not imply that the entire appellate jurisdiction of this Court over cases of habeas corpus was denied, but only appeals from the circuit courts under the act of 1867

Commonwealth of Massachusetts v. Mellon (Frothingham v. Mellon), 262 U.S. 447; 43 S. Ct. 597; 67 L. Ed. 1078 (1923)

Facts—The Maternity Act of November 23, 1921 provided for annual federal appropriations for states that cooperated to reduce maternal and infant mortality and protect the health of mothers and infants. The state of Massachusetts, in an original suit against the secretary of the treasury, Andrew Mellon, stated that the act of November 23, 1921, "The Maternity Act," was an unconstitutional attempt by the federal government to usurp reserved powers of the states as guaranteed by the Constitution in the Tenth Amendment.

Mrs. Frothingham appealed from a decision of the Circuit Court of Appeals of Washington, D.C., endeavoring to have the Supreme Court enjoin the enforcement of the act on the ground that the provisions of this act would take her property under the guise of taxation.

Questions—(a) Can the Supreme Court issue an enjoining order on a federal appropriation act in a suit brought by the state? (b) Can a taxpayer invoke the power of the court to enjoin a federal appropriation act on the ground that it is invalid because it imposes hardship?

Decisions—(a) No. Case dismissed; (b) No. Decision of lower court upheld.

Reasons—*J. Sutherland* (9–0). The state cannot institute judicial proceedings to protect citizens of the United States who are also its citizens from the operation of federal statutes. Further, the Supreme Court has no jurisdiction to enjoin the enforcement of an act of Congress, which is to become operative in any state only upon acceptance by it, on the grounds that Congress is legislating outside its power and into the reserved powers of the states. This is a political question and not judicial in character. "His [the taxpayer's] interest in the moneys of the treasury—partly realized from taxation and partly from other sources—is shared with millions of others, is comparatively minute and indeterminable, and the effect upon future taxation, of any payment out of the funds, so remote, fluctuating, and uncertain, that no basis is afforded for an appeal to the preventive powers of a court of equity." A party invoking judicial action to hold a law of appropriation unconstitutional must show direct injury sustained or threatened, not merely that the individual is suffering in an indefinite way with the general public.

Note—Although the *Mellon* principle is still strong, *Flast v. Cohen*, 392 U.S. 83 (1968), provides standing to taxpayers challenging some federal spending in violation of the establishment clause in the First Amendment.

৩৵

Erie Railroad Co. v. Tompkins, 304 U.S. 64; 58 S. Ct. 817; 82 L. Ed. 1188 (1938)

Facts—Tompkins, a citizen of Pennsylvania, was injured on a dark night by a passing freight train of the Erie Railroad Company while walking along its right of way at Hughestown in the state. He claimed that the accident occurred through negligence in the operation or maintenance of the train; that he was rightfully on the premises because he was on a commonly used footpath that ran for a short distance alongside the tracks; and that he was struck by something that looked like a door projecting from one of the moving cars. He brought an action in the federal court for southern New York, which had jurisdiction because the company is a corporation of that state. Erie insisted that its duty to Tompkins was no greater than that owed to a trespasser. It contended that its duty to Tompkins and hence its liability, should be determined in accordance with the Pennsylvania law: that under the law of Pennsylvania, as declared by the highest court, persons who use pathways along the railroad right of way are to be deemed trespassers; and that the railroad is not liable. Tompkins denied that any such rule had been established, and contended that since there was no statute of the state on the subject, the railroad's duty and liability were to be determined in federal courts as a matter of general law.

Question—Is the federal court bound by the alleged rule of Pennsylvania's common law as declared by the highest court of that state or free to exercise an independent judgment as to what the common law of the state is or should be?

Decision—In interpreting the common law, the federal court is bound by declaration of the highest state court on the state law.

Reasons—*J. Brandeis* (6–2). Except in matters governed by the federal Constitution or by acts of Congress, the substantive law to be applied in any case is the law of the state. And whether the law of the state shall be declared by its legislature in a statute or by its highest court in a decision is not a matter of federal concern. There is no federal general common law. Congress has no power to declare substitute rules of common law applicable in a state whether they be local in their nature or "general," be they commercial law or part of the law of torts. No clause of the Constitution purports to confer such a power upon the federal courts. So far as a state enforces common law, it does so on the basis of its own authority without regard to what it may have been in England or anywhere else. The authority and only authority is the state, and if that be so, the voice adopted by the state as its own should utter the last word.

Note—*Erie Railroad* overruled *Swift v. Tyson* (1842), which said there was a federal common law. This problem so plagued the federal courts for more than one hundred years that the Supreme Court grasped the Erie case to change the law.

Cooper v. Aaron, 358 U.S. 1; 78 S. Ct. 1401; 3 L. Ed. 2d 5 (1958)

Facts—After the Supreme Court decision in *Brown v. Board of Education* (1954) ruling that de jure racial segregation violated the equal protection clause of the Fourteenth Amendment, the school board and superintendent of schools in Little Rock, Arkansas, made plans to comply, beginning by desegregating grades 10 to 12. Arkansas governor Orval Faubus obstructed such plans by calling out the National Guard to stop nine African American students from entering the school. After the U.S. District Court issued an injunction against this action, the troops were withdrawn, but black children were later removed when unruly crowds formed outside the school, eventually leading President Eisenhower to dispatch federal troops to restore order. The school board subsequently asked for a delay of further desegregation efforts. A U.S. District Court granted this request, but the U.S. Eighth Circuit Court of Appeals reversed.

Questions—(a) Does a state have authority to defy orders of the U.S. courts? (b) Should the courts give the school board extra time to comply with court orders when other state actors generate opposition to its policies?

Decisions—(a) No; (b) No.

Reasons—*C.J. Warren* (9–0). In an unusual move, the Court listed the name of each justice at the beginning of the opinion. The Court ruled that "The constitutional rights of respondents are not to be sacrificed or yielded to the violence and disorder which have followed upon the actions of the Governor and Legislature." The equal protection clause of the Fourteenth Amendment forbids state-approved racial segregation. Article VI recognizes the U.S. Constitution "the 'supreme Law of the Land,' and it is the duty of the courts to uphold the law." In what many scholars consider to be one of the Court's broadest assertions of power, it asserted that "the federal judiciary is supreme in its exposition of the Law of the Constitution," and its decision in *Brown v. Board* is thus controlling. The Court further noted that its opinion in *Brown* had been unanimous and that the three justices who had been appointed since that decision also supported it.

J. *Frankfurter* authored a concurring opinion in which he argued that to yield to the actions the governor had precipitated would be "to enthrone official lawlessness and lawlessness if not checked is the precursor of anarchy."

༄

Flast v. Cohen, 392 U.S. 83; 88 S. Ct. 1942; 20 L. Ed. 2d 947 (1968)

Facts—Taxpayers in New York challenged the expenditures of federal funds under the Elementary and Secondary Education Act of 1965 as conflicting with the establishment clause of the First Amendment. A divided three-judge U.S. district court ruled that such a suit was barred under the Court's decision in *Frothingham v. Mellon* (1923).

Questions—(a) Are taxpayers, qua taxpayers, barred from bringing suit in federal courts? (b) If not, what standards govern such suits?

Decisions—(a) No; (b) Taxpayers may bring suit only under the taxing and spending clause of Article I, Section 8 and must show that the expenditures they question specifically exceed a specified constitutional mandate such as the establishment clause of the First Amendment.

Reasons—*C.J. Warren* (8–1). *Frothingham* had been ambiguous as to whether it was based on constitutional grounds or prudential considerations of judicial self-restraint. The "case and controversy" requirement involved complex issues of "justiciability" and "standing." Justiciability has traditionally prevented U.S. courts from issuing "advisory opinions." Standing is designed to assure that the parties before the Court have a personal stake in the outcome of its decision. Circumstances make it possible that individual taxpayers could have standing in some circumstances; thus *Frothingham* does not pose an absolute bar to such suits. To secure standing, a taxpayer must establish two nexuses. The taxpayer must first "establish a logical link between that [taxpayer] status and the type of legislative enactment attacked." Taxpayers are proper parties "to allege the unconstitutionality only of exercises of congressional power under the taxing and spending clause of Art. I, [sec.] 8" and not simply of "an incidental expenditure of tax funds in the administration of an essentially regulatory statute." Second, a "taxpayer must establish a nexus between that status and the precise nature of the constitutional infringement alleged." A taxpayer must thus demonstrate "that the challenged enactment exceeds specific constitutional limitations imposed upon the exercise of the congressional taxing and spending power and not simply that the enactment is generally beyond the powers delegated to Congress." In this case, the taxpayers were challenging a direct expenditure of federal funds, and the establishment clause of the First Amendment was specifically designed to limit the taxing and spending power. Thus, taxpayers did have the right to bring suit in this case.

J. Douglas's concurrence argued that the two nexuses that the Court established were not "durable," and he would have further opened up the judicial process so that "Taxpayers can be vigilant private attorneys general." *J. Stewart's* concurrence focused on the specific purpose of the establishment clause, and *J. Fortas* would specifically limit the Court's acceptance of taxpayer suits to such cases. *J. Harlan* dissented, rejecting both tests that the Court established as untenable and suggesting that the Court should only accept taxpayer suits when Congress specifically authorized them.

⌦

Stone v. Powell, 428 U.S. 465; 96 S. Ct. 3037; 49 L. Ed. 2d 1067 (1976)

Facts—Powell of California and Rice of Nebraska were both convicted in state courts of homicide. In both cases, these courts ruled that evidence in their cases should not be excluded under the exclusionary rule used to enforce the Fourth Amendment. Both subsequently appealed to federal courts, with the U.S. Ninth Circuit Court of Appeals siding with Powell against the state, and the Eighth Circuit siding with Rice. The prison wardens, named Stone and Wolff, appealed to the U.S. Supreme Court.

Question—In cases alleging violations of the Fourth Amendment, are defendants whose claims have been fully heard in state courts entitled to collateral habeas corpus review in federal courts of the admissibility of evidence?

Decision—No.

Reasons—*J. Powell* (6–3). Over the course of U.S. history, the power of federal courts to grant habeas corpus review has been continually expanded.

The exclusionary rule "was a judicially created means of effecting the rights secured by the Fourth Amendment." Although it is partly justified as a means of preserving judicial integrity, it has primarily been justified as a means of deterring illegal police conduct. It thus does not establish "a personal constitutional right," but has been limited to cases where it serves its deterrent rationale. The costs of applying the exclusionary rule through federal appeals could be substantial and the benefits minimal—"the additional contribution, if any, of the consideration of search-and-seizure claims of state prisoners on collateral review is small in relation to the costs." Thus, when state courts have "provided an opportunity for full and fair litigation of a Fourth Amendment claim, a state prisoner may not be granted federal habeas corpus relief on the ground that evidence obtained in an unconstitutional search or seizure was introduced at his trial."

C.J. Burger's concurrence expressed his continuing dissatisfaction with the costs of the exclusionary rule to the fact-finding process and argued that the application of the rule needed to be limited. *J. Brennan's* dissent argued that the Court's decision portended "substantial evisceration of federal habeas corpus jurisdiction." He did not think that all exclusionary rule considerations should evaporate after state review. In dissent, *J. White* agreed with Brennan that there was little reason to distinguish Fourth Amendment habeas corpus review from review in other cases, but also indicated that he would "join four or more other Justices in substantially limiting the reach of the exclusionary rule as presently administered under the Fourth Amendment in federal and state criminal trials." White was particularly concerned about the application of the rule to exclude evidence that police had obtained in "good faith," an area where the Court has subsequently made some exceptions; see, for example, *Arizona v. Evans*, 514 U.S. 1 (1995).

Note—In *Withrow v. Williams*, 507 U.S. 680 (1993), the Court, in a 5–4 decision written by *J. Souter*, distinguished this case from those involving review under the Sixth Amendment's right to counsel, which the Court believed was a personal constitutional right, and which it would therefore accept on collateral review.

❦

Missouri v. Jenkins, 495 U.S. 33; 110 S. Ct. 1651; 109 L. Ed. 2d 31 (1990)

Facts—A group of students in the Kansas City, Missouri, School District (KCMSD) filed suit against the city and the state for operating a racially segregated school system. The U.S. District Court agreed that violations had occurred and outlined expensive remedies involving, among other things, the construction of magnet schools. Although believing it had power to order the city to raise such taxes, the court initially settled instead for rolling back state laws prohibiting the city from raising such taxes. After dividing costs of improvements between the city and the state, the district court subsequently ordered KCMSD to raise local property taxes. Although acknowledging the lower court's power to order such increases, the U.S. Eighth Circuit Court of Appeals ruled that in the future the court should not directly levy such taxes but should "enjoy the operating of state laws" hindering such tax increases.

Questions—(a) Do courts have the power to order localities to raise taxes? (b) Were the judicial remedies ordered in this case excessive?

Decisions—(a) Unresolved; (b) Yes.

Reasons—*J. White* (9–0). After first deciding that the petition had been filed in a timely manner, White ruled that the Court did not need to decide whether judicially imposed taxes were unconstitutional under Article III (allocating judicial powers) or the Tenth Amendment (reserving powers to the states) because principles of comity, or mutual respect, should have governed the district court's decision in this case. Moreover, as the circuit court established, there was no need for the district court to order the tax increase since it had the alternative, which it eventually utilized, of enjoining state limitations on such tax increases. Although not deciding whether the district court order raising taxes was justified, White argued that "a court order directing a local government body to levy its own taxes is plainly a judicial act within the power of a federal court." In this case, the lower court clearly had authority to overturn state limits on taxation that would have thwarted the supremacy of federal law.

J. Kennedy's concurring opinion argued that "Today's casual embrace of taxation imposed by the unelected, life-tenured Federal Judiciary disregards fundamental precepts for the democratic control of public institutions." He believed that the plaintiffs and the KCMSD had entered into "a 'friendly adversary' relationship" designed to increase the local school budget. Kennedy objected to the circuit court's approval of the district court's past action in raising taxes and found little distinction between directly imposing the tax and ordering that the school district do so. Kennedy argued that "taxation is not a judicial function," susceptible to case and controversy requirements. Moreover, "A legislative vote taken under judicial compulsion blurs lines of accountability by making it appear that a decision was reached by elected representatives when the reality is otherwise." Kennedy argued that the majority's approval of lower court actions was imprudent.

Note—In a follow-up decision in *Missouri v. Jenkins*, 515 U.S. 70 (1995), the Supreme Court majority decided that the remedies imposed on the KC-MSD exceeded requirements under the equal protection clause of the Four-teenth Amendment and ruled that mandated spending requirements had been improperly apportioned to the state.

Elk Grove v. Newdow, 542 U.S. 1; 124 S. Ct. 2301; 159 L. Ed. 2d 98 (2004)

Facts—Michael A. Newdow, an avowed atheist, sued the Elk Grove Unified School District in California, where his daughter was enrolled in kinder-garten, because he objected to the daily pledge to the American flag, which includes the words "under God." A Magistrate Judge had concluded that the pledge did not violate the Constitution, but a divided Ninth Circuit Court of Appeals reversed.

Question—Does Newdow have standing to assert his daughter's interest in this case? Do the words "under God" in the pledge of allegiance constitute an improper establishment of religion in violation of the First and Fourteenth Amendments?

Decision—No; a majority does not address the second issue.

Reasons—*J. Stevens* (8–0 on the judgment; *J. Scalia*, who had made public statements affirming the pledge, did not participate). The pledge of allegiance to the flag dates back to the commemoration of the 400th anniversary of Columbus's discovery of America; Congress codified the pledge in 1942, and modified it in 1954 to include the words "under God."

After Michael Newdow filed the case, his estranged wife, Sandra Banning, who had exclusive legal custody of their daughter, asked to intervene on the basis that she and her daughter were Christians who had no objection to say-ing the pledge. In determining whether Newdow has standing, the Court must consider both constitutional and prudential issues. Generally, the Court leaves matters of domestic relations to the states, and California has determined that Banning has sole legal custody of the daughter. Instead of being the child's best friend, Newdow's own interests appear "not parallel" and indeed "potentially in conflict" with hers. Although the law allows Newdow to convey his own atheistic ideas to his child, he is claiming a very different "right to shield his daughter from influences to which she is exposed in school despite the terms of the custody order." Lacking such standing, the Court will not intervene.

C.J. Rehnquist, concurring. The Court has erected "a novel prudential standing principle in order to avoid reaching the merits of the constitutional claim," that its precedents do not support. It "should be governed by general principles, rather than ad hoc improvisations." Religious references pervade U.S. history. The pledges are voluntary and the words "under God" do not convert the pledge "into a 'religious exercise' of the sort described in *Lee* [*v. Weisman* (1992), involving prayer at school graduations]." "The phrase 'under God' is in no sense a prayer, nor an endorsement of any religion" but simply a recognition of the role of religion in U.S. history. To accept Newdow's case would be to give him a "heckler's veto."

J. O'Connor, concurring, would defer to the circuit court's decision that Newdow had standing, but does not believe reciting the pledge violates the establishment clause, which she interprets through the endorsement test. The words "under God" within the pledge serve "essentially secular purposes," like commemorating the role of religion in U.S. history, solemnizing public occasions, and the like. The appropriateness of this form of "ceremonial deism" can be established by the "history and ubiquity" of the clause, the "absence of worship or prayer" in the ceremony, its "absence of reference to particular religions," and its "highly circumscribed reference to God." Similarly, the recitation of the pledge does not violate the "coercion" test featured in *Lee v. Weisman.*

J. Thomas, concurring. Thomas believes that adherence to *Lee v. Weisman* would require elimination of the words "under God" in the pledge, but does not think that *Lee* was properly decided. The only kind of coercion that should worry the Court is that "accomplished 'by *force of law and threat of penalty*.'" Although the free exercise clause was designed to protect individual rights, the establishment clause was "a federalism provision intended to prevent Congress from interfering with state establishments." The establishment clause "probably prohibits Congress from establishing a national religion" or possibly from favoring particular religious faiths, but does not go further.

POLITICAL QUESTIONS DOCTRINE

Luther v. Borden, 7 Howard (48 U.S.) 1; 12 L. Ed. 581 (1849)

Facts—In 1841 the people of the state of Rhode Island were still using the old colonial charter with a few minor revisions, as their state constitution. This constitution strictly limited the right to vote. Led by a man named Dorr, the people at various mass meetings throughout the state instituted a new constitution whereby suffrage was greatly increased. The state government claimed that this was an insurrection and appealed to the president to declare martial law. Although then President Tyler pledged his support for the Charter Government, no federal forces were used. Members of the state militia led by Borden forced their way into the house of Luther, a Dorr adherent, who sued for trespass. Luther moved to Massachusetts in order to legalize a suit on the basis of diversity of citizenship.

Question—Can the Court decide as to the guaranty of a republican form of a state's government in accordance with Article IV, Section 4?

Decision—No.

Reasons—*C.J. Taney* (8–1). This is a purely political question and must be left in the hands of the political branches of the government to decide. Their decision moreover may not be questioned in a judicial tribunal. It would constitute a usurpation of power for the Supreme Court to attempt to decide the question. It the Court were to recognize the Dorr Government, actions of the Charter Government would be needlessly called into question. The enforcement of the guarantee of a republican form of government rests with the president or Congress. Congress makes such a decision when determining whether or not to seat a state's representatives. By law Congress designated the power to protect state governments to the president, and, in this case, the president had indicated his support for the Dorr Government. The visibility of the president's office helps keep such power from being abused.

❧

Muskrat v. United States, 219 U.S. 346; 31 S. Ct. 250; 55 L. Ed. 246 (1911)

Facts—An act of Congress authorized Muskrat and others to bring suit in the federal Court of Claims, with an appeal to the federal Supreme Court to determine the validity of certain acts of Congress that altered terms of certain prior allotments of Cherokee Indian lands.

Question—Can the Supreme Court judge the validity of an act of Congress as an abstract question rather than as an actual controversy or case?

Decision—No.

Reasons—*J. Day* (7–0). Congress is attempting to have the Court pass upon the validity of laws before they are properly brought to the Court. Federal judicial power extends only to "cases" and "controversies," defined by Marshall as suits "instituted according to the regular course of judicial procedure." This matter is not presented in such a "case" or "controversy." "The whole purpose of the law is to determine the constitutional validity of this class of legislation, in a suit not arising between parties concerning a property right necessarily involved in the decision in question, but in a proceeding against the government in its sovereign capacity, and concerning which the only judgment required is to settle the doubtful character of the legislation in question. . . . If such actions as are here attempted, to determine the validity of legislation, are sustained, the result will be that this court, instead of keeping within limits of judicial power, and deciding cases or controversies arising between opposing parties, as the Constitution intended it should, will be required to give opinions in the nature of advice concerning legislative action,—a function never conferred upon it by the Constitution."

Baker v. Carr, 369 U.S. 186; 82 S. Ct. 691; 7 L. Ed. 2d 663 (1962)

Facts—Voters brought this civil action alleging that the continuing apportionment of the Tennessee General Assembly by means of a 1901 statute debased the votes of the plaintiffs and denied them equal protection of the law under the Fourteenth Amendment. The constitution of Tennessee mandated a decennial reapportionment but all proposals for such since 1901 had failed to pass the General Assembly. In this period the relative standings of Tennessee counties in terms of qualified voters had changed significantly. The appellants asserted that the voters in certain counties have been placed in a position of constitutionally unjustified inequality vis-à-vis voters in irrationally favored counties. The appellants claimed injunctive and declaratory judgment relief. The plaintiffs alleged that any change in the apportionment that would be brought about by legislative action would be difficult or impossible.

Questions—(a) Do federal courts have jurisdiction of cases involving state legislative reapportionment? (b) Does the case state a justiciable cause of action?

Decisions—(a) Yes; (b) Yes.

Reasons—*J. Brennan* (6–2). This action arises under the Constitution according to Article III, Section 2 since the complaint alleges an apportionment that deprives the appellants of the equal protection of the laws in violation of the Fourteenth Amendment (previous cases involving "political questions" generally alleged that claims under the "republican form of government" clause in Article IV were nonjusticiable). The claim is not "so attenuated and unsubstantial as to be absolutely devoid of merit." Moreover, "the appellants do have standing to maintain this suit." Voters who allege facts showing disadvantage to themselves as individuals have standing to sue. Finally, the matter presented is justiciable. The mere fact that a suit seeks protection of a political right does not mean that it presents a nonjusticiable political question. The nonjusticiability of a political question is primarily a function of the separation of powers, the relationship between the judiciary and the coordinate branches of the federal government, and not the federal judiciary's relationship to the states. Brennan outlined six criteria for political questions:

[1] a textually demonstrable constitutional commitment of the issue to a coordinate political department; or [2] a lack of judicially discoverable and manageable standards for resolving it; or [3] the impossibility of deciding without an initial policy determination of a kind clearly for nonjudicial discretion; or [4] the impossibility of a court's undertaking independent resolution without expressing lack of the respect due coordinate branches of government; or [5] an unusual need for unquestioning adherence to a political decision already made; or [6] the potentiality of embarrassment from multifarious pronouncements by various departments on one question.

None of these criteria came into play in this particular case.

J. Douglas's concurrence focused on the fact that Tennessee was weighing the votes of some individuals more heavily than others. *J. Clark* could find no "rational basis" for Tennessee's apportionment system or any way for the voters to change it—the state had no initiative or referendum mechanism. *J. Stewart* wanted to keep the focus on the Court's jurisdiction and the justiciability of the subject matter.

In separate and stinging dissents, *J. Frankfurter* and *J. Harlan* warned about intervening in such a "political thicket." Frankfurter argued that the decision unduly enthroned the judiciary, while Harlan could find no historical evidence that the Fourteenth Amendment was designed to have the meaning the majority had attributed to it.

Note—*Baker* is a seminal case. In reversing *Colegrove v. Green*, 328 U.S. 549 (1946) the Supreme Court opened the federal courts to challenges of apportionment of legislative districts.

Nixon v. United States, 506 U.S. 224; 113 S. Ct. 732; 122 L. Ed. 2d 1 (1993)

Facts—Walter L. Nixon Jr., a U.S. federal district judge, was sentenced to prison for making false statements to a jury, but he refused to resign from his position and continued to draw his salary. He was subsequently impeached by the U.S. House of Representatives and convicted by the Senate. The Senate utilized Impeachment Rule XI that allowed a committee to make preliminary findings, which it then submitted to the full Senate before its vote. Nixon challenged the Senate's authority to use a committee for fact-finding purposes, arguing that the entire Senate had failed its constitutional obligation to "try" all impeachments. Both the U.S. District Court and the Court of Appeals for the District of Columbia Circuit ruled that the issue was nonjusticiable.

Question—Do courts have authority to review procedures used by the U.S. Senate in trying impeachments?

Decision—No, this is a political question committed to the legislative branch.

Reasons—*C.J. Rehnquist* (9–0). The first sentence of Article I, Section 3, Clause 6 gives the Senate the "sole" power to try impeachments. The issue of what the word "try" means in the context of an impeachment trial is a nonjusticiable political question, since the trial of impeachments is specifically delegated to the U.S. Senate, and *Baker v. Carr* (1962) specified that there is a political question when "there is 'a textually demonstrable constitutional commitment of the issue to a coordinate political department.'" Nixon's claim that the word "sole" has no substantive meaning must be rejected. It has no less meaning than any other word in the Constitution, and the fact that the Committee of Style added it does not make it meaningless. The fact that the president cannot pardon someone who has been impeached is likewise irrelevant since it does not overturn a conviction but merely mitigates its punishment. There is no evidence that the Framers of the Constitution intended for the judiciary to review impeachment issues. Indeed, "impeachment was designed to be the only check on the Judicial Branch by the Legislature." Protection against abuse of the Senate's trial power is provided both by the division of the power of impeachment from that of its trial and by the requirement of a two-thirds supermajority vote. This case is unlike *Powell v. McCormack* (1969) in that "there is no separate provision of the Constitution that could be defeated by allowing the Senate final authority to determine the meaning of the word 'try' in the Impeachment Trial Clause."

J. Stevens's concurrence emphasized that "the Framers decided to assign the impeachment power to the Legislative Branch." *J. White's* concurrence argued that the majority decision gave too much discretion to the Senate, and he would not rule out any judicial role in any such decision: "In a truly balanced system, impeachments tried by the Senate would serve as a means of controlling the largely unaccountable Judiciary, even as judicial review would ensure that the Senate adhered to a minimal set of procedural standards in conducting impeachment trials." White thinks it odd that the judiciary professes to be unable to define the word "try," and finds that history demonstrates that the Framers were aware that legislators sometimes delegated fact-finding functions in such trials. *J. Souter's* concurrence would also leave open the possibility of judicial review in "different and unusual circumstances," as, for example, if the Senate were to rest the results of such a trial on a coin toss.

Note—*C.J. Rehnquist*, who had written a book on impeachments called *Grand Inquests*, later presided over the Senate trial of President Bill Clinton.

Chapter Five

ARTICLES IV AND VI: FEDERALISM

Including Article I, Section 10, and the Tenth, Eleventh, Seventeenth, Eighteenth, and Twenty-First Amendments

When the framers proposed to replace the Articles of Confederation with the U.S. Constitution, they invented a new form of government now known as federalism. It was a hybrid form of government, somewhere between what is called a unitary government and a confederal government. A unitary government, like that in England, with which the framers were familiar, did not have a system of states with indivisible boundaries. Rather, power flowed directly from the national government to the people. By contrast, the confederal form of government, under which the framers had previously operated, required that the national government operate through the states, which, in fact, had primacy in the system.

By contrast, the framers of the U.S. Constitution created a system dividing power between the national government and the states and allowing both governments to operate directly on the people. Subsequent federal systems have all had written constitutions that attempt, at least in broad terms, to outline the respective powers of the state and national governments.

Articles IV and VI of the Constitution address federal issues (in addition Article I, Section 10 announced various restrictions on state governments, including the contract clause, which is discussed in this book under property rights). Article IV outlined various obligations that states owe to one another, described rights of state and national citizenship, provided for the admission of new states, and guaranteed each state a "republican" form of government (a matter treated in the previous chapter under the issue of "political questions"). In addition to dealing with various other matters, Article VI provided for the supremacy of the federal Constitution and of laws and treaties made under its authority.

Federalism has been one of the most persistent and divisive issues in U.S. history. Now-discredited doctrines of state interposition (outlined in the Virginia and Kentucky Resolutions of 1798), nullification (outlined in the South Carolina Exposition and Protest), and secession eventually led to the U.S. Civil War in which President Lincoln fought to preserve the Union. After that conflict, the Supreme Court declared in *Texas v. White* (1869) that the nation consisted of "an indestructible Union of indestructible states."

The judicial branch of government frequently patrols the border of state and national rights, and early in U.S. history, the Court issued a number of important cases establishing its authority in this area. It has limited both the scope of state exercises of power that it thought undermined national powers as well as the scope of national powers that it thought undermined states' rights. At times, the Court has ruled that the federal powers over commerce preempt state powers even in the absence of specific legislation on the subject (through the so-called "dormant commerce clause"). At other times, the Court tries to assess whether Congress specifically attempted to preempt areas of state power in adopting legislation or not.

Both the Tenth and Eleventh Amendments address the issue of federalism—the first, adopted as part of the Bill of Rights, by reserving certain unspecified powers to the states and the people thereof and the second, adopted in reaction to the Supreme Court decision in *Chisholm v. Georgia* (1793), by limiting certain suits against the states. Although Justice Harlan Fiske Stone appeared to pronounce the Tenth Amendment dead in *United States v. Darby* (1941), it and the Eleventh Amendment have had something of a renaissance in recent years. A number of recent cases have declared that the Eleventh Amendment needs to be interpreted beyond its literal language to recognize the principle of state sovereign immunity and its corollary that states cannot be sued without their consent. There is continuing debate as to whether the Court should serve as the primary patrol of national/state boundaries or whether this function should be chiefly left to the political branches where states are represented and can arguably defend themselves.

By providing for the direct election of senators, the Seventeenth Amendment arguably also altered existing federal arrangements by making it less likely that U.S. senators would see themselves as spokespersons for state legislatures, as opposed to the individual citizens of the states or nation. Some view the Seventeenth Amendment as a fundamental alteration in the federal system, whereas others see the amendment as providing even greater impetus for courts to patrol the borders of state/national relations. Although rarely adjudicated, the Twenty-first Amendment, in repealing the national prohibition of alcohol established by the Eighteenth Amendment, specifically vested states with power to limit the importing of such beverages into their boundaries.

ELEVENTH AMENDMENT AND
SOVEREIGN IMMUNITY OF STATES

Hans v. Louisiana, 134 U.S. 1; 10 S. Ct. 504; 33 L. Ed. 842 (1890)

Facts—Hans, a citizen of Louisiana, brought a suit in a Circuit Court of the United States against the state in order to recover money invested in state bonds and the interest thereupon. Alleging that the state had violated its contract, Hans brought his case under the provision in Article III extending federal jurisdiction to all cases arising under the laws of the United States. Louisiana argued that it could not be sued by one of its citizens without its consent.

Question—Does the Eleventh Amendment preclude a state from being sued by one of its citizens without its consent?

Decision—Yes.

Reasons—*J. Bradley* (9–0). Judicial decisions interpreting the Eleventh Amendment have established that a state cannot be sued by a citizen of another state or by a foreign state, but the Eleventh Amendment does not specifically address whether a state can be sued by one of its own citizens. Although Article III did not originally preclude suits by citizens of other states against a state, the decision in *Chisholm v. Georgia* (1793) permitting such suits "created . . . a shock of surprise throughout the country" that led to the adoption of the Eleventh Amendment. In adopting the Eleventh Amendment, the nation returned to the pre-Chisholm understanding, argued in dissent by *J. Iredell*, that the nature of state sovereignty precluded a state from being sued without its own consent. This intention had been demonstrated by Alexander Hamilton in Federalist 84 and by James Madison and John Marshall in debates over ratification of the Constitution. It is inappropriate to cite the "letter" of the Eleventh Amendment to preclude its object and to recognize "the cognizance of suits and actions unknown to the law, and forbidden by the law." The grant of jurisdiction in Article III was not designed to sidestep the exception that sovereign states cannot be sued without their consent. The fact that Congress conferred concurrent jurisdiction on the states and the nation in certain cases indicated that Congress did not intend to invest federal courts with new jurisdiction but only with jurisdiction that was already recognized. It is not the Court's responsibility to examine "the reason or expediency of the rule which exempts a sovereign State from prosecution in a court of justice at the suit of individuals." "It is enough for us to declare its existence."

J. Harlan's concurrence noted his objection to some of the Court's comments about the Court's decision in *Chisholm v. Georgia.*

$\mathcal{\infty} \mathcal{Y}$

Monaco v. Mississippi, 292 U.S. 313; 54 S. Ct. 745; 78 L. Ed. 1282 (1934)

Facts—The principality of Monaco sought to bring suit in the Supreme Court against the state of Mississippi over the nonpayment of bonds issued by the state, and alleged to be absolute property of the principality. The bonds were issued in 1833, were due in 1861 and 1866, issued in 1838 and due in 1850, issued in 1838 and due in 1858. They were handed down in a family of the state, but since private citizens cannot sue a state, the bonds were given to Monaco, on the theory that, as a foreign country, it would be able to sue the state.

Question—Can the principality of Monaco sue the state of Mississippi without that state's consent?

Decision—No.

Reasons—*C.J. Hughes* (9–0). The Court ruled that the states of the Union retain the same immunity to suits by a foreign state that they enjoy with respect to suits by individuals whether citizens of the United States or subjects of a foreign power. The foreign state enjoys a similar immunity and without her consent cannot be sued by a state of the Union. The principle of the Eleventh Amendment applies to suits against a state by a foreign state.

$\mathcal{\infty} \mathcal{Y}$

Alden v. Maine, 527 U.S. 706; 119 S. Ct. 2240; 144 L. Ed. 2d 636 (1999)

Facts—Congress provided under the Fair Labor Standards Act (FLSA) for individuals to sue states in their own courts. State employees sued Maine. As the suit was pending, the Supreme Court ruled in *Seminole Tribe v. Florida,* 517 U.S. 44 (1996), that Congress could not authorize Indian tribes to sue unconsenting states in federal courts. The U.S. District Court and the U.S. First Circuit accordingly dismissed the employees' suit as did the Superior Court and the Supreme Judicial Courts of Maine.

Question—Can Congress subject unconsenting states to private suits for damages in their own courts without their consent?

Decision—Not in the present case.

Reasons—*J. Kennedy* (5–4). Although the Eleventh Amendment Immunity specifically refers to suits commenced by a state or by citizens of other states or nations, state sovereign immunity "neither derives from nor is limited by the terms of the Eleventh Amendment." Rather, such immunity is "a fundamental aspect of the sovereignty which the States enjoyed before the ratification of the Constitution, and which they retain today . . . except as altered by the plan of the Convention or certain constitutional amendments." The Tenth Amendment reinforced the role of the states in the original Constitution. That Constitution recognized state sovereignty as did such Framers as Alexander Hamilton, James Madison, and John Marshall when they argued on its behalf. *Chisholm v. Georgia* (1793) called this sovereignty into question, but it was quickly overturned. In so doing "Congress acted not to change but to restore the original constitutional design." Kennedy observed that subsequent holdings "reflect a settled doctrinal understanding . . . that sovereign immunity derives not from the Eleventh Amendment but from the structure of the original Constitution itself." Overreliance on the precise words of the Eleventh Amendment would be "to engage in the type of ahistorical literalism we have rejected in interpreting the scope of the States' sovereign immunity since the discredited decision in Chisholm." The supremacy clause applies only when Congress is acting within the constitutional design, which was written to protect state sovereignty. Decisions shielding states from suits in federal courts apply with even greater force when they apply to cases brought within states' own courts: "a congressional power to authorize private suits against nonconsenting States in their own courts would be even more offensive to state sovereignty than a power to authorize the suits in a federal forum." Such suits could threaten the fiscal integrity of states and would make the national government more powerful in state courts than in its own. Immunity does not apply in cases where states give their consent to be sued, in instances where states have specifically limited their sovereignty, or in cases where individuals sue municipalities or, in some cases, state officials. This case does not fit within any of these exceptions. "Congress has vast power but not all power. When Congress legislates in matters affecting the States, it may not treat these sovereign entities as mere prefectures or corporations."

J. Souter, dissenting, argued that the majority view was based on a "natural law" conception rather than on the Constitution itself. Souter did not think that the Framers thought that state sovereign immunity was unalterable. He further argued that both the ideas of sovereignty and sovereign immunity were in flux at the time of the American Founding. No states at that time declared sovereign immunity to be among their rights, and there was not unanimity among those who thought states would be sovereign. Souter disagreed with the majority's interpretation of *Chisholm v. Georgia*. He further declared that "The State of Maine is not sovereign with respect to the national objective of the FLSA." Souter likened this decision to *National League of Cities v. Usery*, 426 U.S. 833 (1976), which has since been discredited and overturned. As the Court indicated in *Garcia v. SAMTA*, 469 U.S. 528 (1985), states should rely for protection on the structure of the federal system rather than on the courts. The decision in this case contradicts the venerable constitutional rule that "where there is a right, there must be a remedy." Souter further likened this case to the Court's use of substantive due process in the discredited case of *Lochner v. New York* (1905).

※

Kimel v. Florida Board of Regents, 528 U.S. 62; 120 S. Ct. 631; 145 L. Ed. 2d 522 (2000)

Facts—The Age Discrimination in Employment Act of 1967 (ADEA) made discrimination in employment on the basis of age illegal. Employees of public universities and of the Florida Department of Corrections sued states under this act, and the states evoked immunity under the Eleventh Amendment. The U.S. Eleventh Circuit Court of Appeals overturned U.S. District Court decisions ruling that the ADEA's abrogation of such immunity was unconstitutional. The Eleventh Circuit's decision was in conflict with decisions in other circuits.

Questions—(a) Did the ADEA contain a clear statement of Congress's intent to abrogate Eleventh Amendment immunity? (b) If so, was this a proper exercise of congressional authority under the enforcement clause of the Fourteenth Amendment?

Decisions—(a) Yes; (b) No.

Reasons—*J. O'Connor* (7–2 as to a; 5–4 as to b). Congress had expanded the scope of the ADEA, originally adopted in 1967, on a number of occasions. Past decisions had established that Congress can only abrogate state immunity against suits by doing so in unmistakable language. The ADEA satisfies that requirement. In *EEOC v. Wyoming* (1983), the Court upheld ADEA as a valid exercise of congressional powers under the commerce clause, but the Court also needs to examine the relationship of this law to the Eleventh Amendment. The decision in *Seminole Tribe v. Florida* (1996) indicated that "Even when the Constitution vests in Congress complete lawmaking authority over a particular area, the Eleventh Amendment prevents congressional authorization of suits by private parties against unconsenting States." Valid exercises of congressional power under Section 5 (the enforcement clause) of the Fourteenth Amendment do allow for the abrogation of Eleventh Amendment immunity. *City of Boerne v. Flores* (1997) indicates, however, that although Congress can "enforce" the Fourteenth Amendment, it cannot decree its substance. "The ultimate interpretation and determination of the Fourteenth Amendment's substantive meaning remains the province of the Judicial Branch." Congressional interpretation must pass the tests of "congruence and proportionality." Prior court decisions have subjected age discrimination to relaxed standards of review (upholding state age classifications in relation to the termination of police officers, members of the foreign service, and state judges) that the ADEA has sought to evade. Congress did not make adequate findings to indicate that such comprehensive legislation was warranted. Individuals may be entitled to relief under state age discrimination statutes, but Congress may not redefine the Fourteenth Amendment to accomplish this objective.

J. Stevens accepted the majority's view that Congress had clearly expressed its intention, but he would have allowed Congress, rather than the judicial branch, to guard state interests, since states are represented in that body. If Congress has power to protect rights, such power must necessarily abrogate Eleventh Amendment restrictions. Stevens voiced his continuing opposition to the opinion in *Seminole Tribe v. Florida*.

J. Thomas argued that abrogation of state Eleventh Amendment immunity fell outside congressional enforcement powers and that Congress had not clearly made such an intention to abrogate this immunity in this case.

◦৯৶

University of Alabama Board of Trustees v. Garrett, 531 U.S. 356; 121 S. Ct. 955; 148 L. Ed. 2d 866 (2001)

Facts—Two Alabama state employees, a nurse and a security officer, sued the state under the Americans with Disabilities Act of 1990, alleging that they had been discriminated against because of physical disabilities, cancer in one case, and asthma and sleep apnea, in the other. The U.S. District Court ruled that the Eleventh Amendment barred such suits, but the U.S. Eleventh Circuit Court of Appeals reversed.

Questions—(a) May individuals sue states under the Americans with Disabilities Act? (b) Are such suits barred by the Eleventh Amendment?

Decisions—(a) No; (b) Yes.

Reasons—*C.J. Rehnquist* (5–4). Although the specific terms of the Eleventh Amendment do not limit suits by citizens from within the states, the amendment has been understood to stand for the principle that "nonconsenting States may not be sued by private individuals in federal courts." Congress may not abrogate this limitation under its Article I powers, although it might under the Fourteenth Amendment, adopted after the Eleventh Amendment. Section 5 of the Fourteenth Amendment grants Congress power to enforce its provisions, but legislation that moves beyond the specific guarantees of Section 1 of the amendment "must exhibit 'congruence and proportionality,'" between the injury to be prevented or remedied and the means adopted to that end." *Cleburne v. Cleburne Living Center, Inc.*, 473 U.S. 432 (1985), dealing with state treatment of the mentally retarded, judged state legislation of the disabled by a standard of rationality. Congressional investigation leading to the Americans with Disabilities Act did not demonstrate widespread state discrimination against the disabled. Allowing individuals to sue the states without their consent would thus violate the principles of "congruence and proportionality" that should mark federal enforcement of the Fourteenth Amendment under Section 5.

J. Kennedy's concurrence stressed that this case did not preclude suits brought against states by the national government but only suits brought by private individuals. *J. Breyer's* dissent focused on the evidence that Congress had mustered in demonstrating state denials of equal protection to the disabled and argued that the standard to which the majority was holding the states was too high for an elected body. He further observed that the rules the Court had established to protect the states "run counter to the very object of the Fourteenth Amendment."

❧

Lapides v. Board of Regents of University of Georgia, 535 U.S. 613; 122 S. Ct. 1640; 152 L. Ed. 2d 806 (2002)

Facts—Lapides, a professor in the Georgia State University system, brought suit in a Georgia state court against actions by university officials in placing allegations of sexual harassment in his personnel file. Both parties agreed to remove the case to a U.S. District Court, but, once there, Georgia argued that sovereign immunity granted by the Eleventh Amendment prohibited further proceedings. Although agreeing that the federal claims Lapides had filed against the individuals he was suing were barred by their qualified immunity, the U.S. District Court ruled that Georgia had waived its Eleventh Amendment claims when the state attorney general agreed to remove the case to a federal court. The U.S. Eleventh Circuit Court of Appeals agreed with the District Court.

Question—Does a state's removal of a lawsuit from a state to a federal court waive its Eleventh Amendment immunity?

Decision—Yes.

Reasons—*J. Breyer* (9–0). It would be anomalous, inconsistent, and unfair to allow a state both voluntarily "to invoke federal jurisdiction" and "to claim Eleventh Amendment immunity." The state attorney general's decision to seek remedy in a federal court thus constituted a voluntary waiver of its immunity. This still left the federal court free to remand the case back to state courts if it found that the present case raised issues only of state law.

⟡

Federal Maritime Commission v. South Carolina State Ports Authority,
535 U.S. 743; 122 S. Ct. 1864; 152 L. Ed. 2d 962 (2002)

Facts—The South Carolina State Ports Authority refused permission to berth a cruise ship, which provided for gambling, at its facilities. The Federal Maritime Commission (FMC) brought the ship's case to a U.S. District Court, which appointed an Administrative Law Judge to hear the case. The judge found that South Carolina was entitled to sovereign immunity. The FMC subsequently decided that the ruling applied only to judicial decisions and not those of administrative agencies. The U.S. Fourth Circuit Court of Appeals reversed the FMC ruling.

Question—Does state sovereign immunity preclude the Federal Maritime Commission from bringing action against South Carolina?

Decision—Yes.

Reasons—*J. Thomas* (5–4). "Dual sovereignty is a defining feature of our Nation's constitutional blueprint." The states did not surrender their immunity from private law suits. The contrary decision in *Chisholm v. Georgia* (1793) is now recognized as erroneous and was overturned by the Eleventh Amendment. Addressing only the specific provision that led to the *Chisholm* decision, "the Eleventh Amendment does not define the scope of the States' sovereign immunity; it is but one exemplification of that immunity." Such immunity thus "extends beyond the literal text of the Eleventh Amendment." The framers of the Constitution did not anticipate the growth of administrative agencies so the Court has to ascertain whether the privilege at issue was of a type "from which the framers would have thought the States possessed immunity when they agreed to enter the Union." Thomas found that the modern administrative hearing was "functionally comparable" to that held by a judge in a courtroom and that such proceedings are similar to judicial proceedings with rules like those in federal civil litigation. Sovereign immunity was designed to preserve state dignity, and such dignity is no more consistent with states being called before administrative bodies than before courts. Thomas further rejected arguments that commission proceedings are not protected by sovereignty immunity because the adjudications are not self-executing or because they do not pose a threat to a state's financial integrity. Thomas argued that sovereign immunity applied against suits, monetary or otherwise.

J. Stevens and *J. Breyer* authored dissents with Stevens focusing on the inadequacy of the Court's earlier decision in *Alden v. Maine* (1999). Although he also rejected the Court's reasoning in that case, *J. Souter* emphasized that independent agencies were neither legislative nor judicial in nature. He further argued that the majority decision "lacks any firm anchor in the Constitution's text," specifically noting that the Eleventh Amendment referred only to "the judicial power of the United States." Similarly, while the Tenth Amendment reserved nondelegated powers to the states, the Constitution specifically delegated Congress with power over interstate and foreign commerce.

ॐ

FEDERAL PREEMPTION (ALSO SEE CHAPTER 1, POWERS OF CONGRESS, COMMERCE)

Southern Pacific Co. v. Arizona, 325 U.S. 761; 65 S. Ct. 1515; 89 L. Ed. 1915 (1945)

Facts—The Arizona Train Limit Law required that any person or corporation operating within the state a railroad train with more than fourteen passenger cars or more than seventy freight cars would pay a penalty for each violation of the act.

Question—Does the state statute regulating the length of trains contravene the commerce clause of the federal Constitution?

Decision—Yes.

Reasons—*C.J. Stone* (7–2). The Court reasoned that the Arizona law, viewed as a safety measure, afforded at most slight and dubious advantage, if any, over unregulated train lengths, because it resulted in an increase in expense and in the number of trains and train operations and a consequent increase in train accidents of a character generally more severe than those due to slack action in long trains. Its effect on commerce was regulation without securing uniformity of the length of trains operated in interstate commerce. Thus it prevented the free flow of commerce by delaying it and by substantially increasing its cost and impairing its efficiency.

In dissent, *J. Black* argued that in the absence of congressional legislation regulating the subject, the Supreme Court should not second-guess state legislative judgments related to matters of safety.

Pennsylvania v. Nelson, 350 U.S. 497; 76 S. Ct. 477; 100 L. Ed. 640 (1956)

Facts—An acknowledged member of the Communist Party, Steve Nelson was convicted in Allegheny County, Pennsylvania, of violation of the Pennsylvania Sedition Act. He was sentenced to imprisonment and fine. While the Pennsylvania statute proscribes sedition against either the government of the United States or the Commonwealth of Pennsylvania, this case was concerned only with alleged sedition against the United States.

Question—Does the Smith Act of 1940, which prohibits the knowing advocacy of the overthrow of the government of the United States by force and violence, supersede the enforceability of the Pennsylvania Sedition Act?

Decision—Yes.

Reasons—*C.J. Warren* (6–3). The Court examined the various federal acts on the subject, including the Internal Security Act of 1950 and the Communist Control Act of 1954, as well as the Smith Act, and concluded that Congress had intended to occupy the entire field of sedition. These acts, taken as a whole, "evince a congressional plan which makes it reasonable to determine that no room has been left for the states to supplement it. . . . 'Sedition against the United States is not a local offense. It is a crime against the Nation.' . . . It is not only important but vital that such prosecutions should be exclusively within the control of the federal government." The Court went on to note that enforcement of state sedition statutes would present a serious danger of conflict with the administration of the federal program and would produce conflicting or incompatible court decisions.

"Since we find that Congress has occupied the field to the exclusion of parallel state legislation, that the dominant interest of the federal government precludes state intervention, and that administration of state acts would conflict with the operation of the federal plan, we are convinced that" the state statute cannot stand. "Without compelling indication to the contrary, we will not assume that Congress intended to permit the possibility of double punishment."

J. Reed, dissenting, denied that Congress had attempted to preclude state sedition regulations and even cited a provision of the U.S. Code that provided for state jurisdiction in such cases.

⊘⅍

Sprietsman v. Mercury Marine, 537 U.S. 51; 123 S. Ct. 518; 154 L. Ed. 2d 466 (2002)

Facts—Sprietsman's wife was killed in a boating accident on a lake between Tennessee and Kentucky. He sued Mercury Marine, the manufacturer of the outboard motor on the boat, for not installing a propeller guard. The trial and intermediate courts found that the Federal Boat Safety Act (FBSA) of 1971 specifically prohibited such actions. The state supreme court affirmed on the basis that such preemption was implied.

Question—Did the Federal Boat Safety Act of 1971 preempt suits against propeller manufacturers under state tort law?

Decision—No.

Reasons—*J. Stevens* (9–0). Congress adopted the FBSA to regulate the safety of recreational boats by establishing minimum standards. In enacting the law, Congress specified that "Compliance with this chapter or standards, regulations, or orders prescribed under this chapter does not relieve a person from liability at common law or under State law," a position the secretary of transportation had reaffirmed. After extensive study, the Coast Guard decided not to require propeller guards, but it did not prohibit states from adopting such requirements. Sometimes federal legislation manifests an intent to occupy a field completely or parties find it impossible to meet both state and federal laws, but neither situations applies here. The Transportation Department's decision not to require propellers "left the law applicable to propeller guards exactly the same as it had been before the subcommittee began its investigation." Neither the solicitor general who argued the case before the Supreme Court nor the Coast Guard thought that federal law was designed to preempt state laws. Uniformity of regulation can be important, but this consideration is not "unyielding." In this case, "absent a contrary decision by the Coast

Guard, the concern with uniformity does not justify the displacement of state common-law remedies that compensate accident victims and their families."

JUDICIAL JURISDICTION OVER STATES

Chisholm v. Georgia, 2 Dallas (2 U.S.) 419 (1793)

Facts—A South Carolina citizen who was the executor of the estate of a merchant who had sold goods during the Revolutionary War to Georgia, for which he had not been compensated, brought suit against the state. Georgia refused to appear in court, claiming that it possessed the power of sovereign immunity.

Question—Can a state be sued in federal courts without its consent?

Decision—Yes.

Reasons—(4–1). Seriatim opinion.

J. *Iredell*, dissenting, looked to English precedents under which a sovereign could not be sued without the sovereign's consent. Although on the surface Article III might appear to invest the courts with jurisdiction, such jurisdiction can apply "only to such controversies in which a State can be a party." States, like other sovereigns, can be persuaded, but not compelled, to come to court. Moreover, even if the Constitution vested authority for such suits, such authority would not be effective in the absence of congressional legislation, which is not present in this case.

J. *Blair* argued that the U.S. Constitution should be "the only fountain" from which the Court should draw in settling this issue. Article III specifically permits a suit between a state and citizens of another state and does not distinguish cases in which a state is a defendant from those in which it is a plaintiff: "when a State, by adopting the Constitution, has agreed to be amenable to the judicial power of the United States, she has, in that respect, given up her right of sovereignty."

J. *Wilson* noted that the U.S. Constitution does not specifically use the word "sovereign." States are artificial persons who, like other persons, should be held accountable. Residents of the United States "are citizens" not "subjects." "Supreme Power resides in the body of the people," and, for purposes of the Union, Georgia can no longer claim its sovereignty. The poorest peasant is equal to the king. The U.S. Constitution not only could have vested jurisdiction over the state of Georgia, but it has actually done so. Having such jurisdiction, it may exercise it.

J. Cushing noted that the letter of Article III vests jurisdiction in the federal courts between states and citizens of other states. Such jurisdiction is necessary to protect the "rights of individuals." "If the Constitution is found inconvenient in practice in this or any other particular, it is well that a regular mode is pointed out for amendment."

C.J. Jay argued that sovereignty passed directly from the English monarch to the people of the United States. Both "the design" and "the letter and express declaration" of the Constitution vest sovereignty in federal courts in this case. Such a policy is "wise," "honest," and "useful," obviating "occasions of quarrels between States on account of the claims of their respective citizens."

Note—The Eleventh Amendment subsequently overturned this decision.

Cherokee Nation v. Georgia, 30 U.S. 1; 8 L. Ed. 25; U.S. LEXIS 337 (1831)

Facts—The Cherokee nation filed a suit enjoining Georgia from enforcing laws that parceled out Indian lands and otherwise interfered with their rights.

Questions—(a) Is an Indian tribe a state or a foreign nation that can bring a suit in Court? (b) Will the Court issue an injunction against Georgia?

Decisions—(a) No; (b) No.

Reasons—*C.J. Marshall* (4–2). Under the U.S. Constitution, Indian tribes did not constitute either a domestic state or a foreign nation. They could best be described as "domestic dependent nations" in the relation of a ward to a guardian. The tribe could thus not bring a case before the Court under Article III. Moreover, the request by the Cherokee nation "savours too much of the exercise of political power to be within the proper province of the judicial department." Thus, "[I]f it be true that the Cherokee nation have rights, this is not the tribunal in which those rights are to be asserted."

J. Johnson and *J. Baldwin* concurred, and *J. Thompson* dissented. Johnson agreed that the Cherokee tribe was neither a state nor a foreign nation. Baldwin thought that Marshall's opinion attempted to give the tribe a status it did not have under the Constitution. Thompson believed that the Indians could be considered as a foreign state over which the Court had competence and that they were entitled to relief under treaties and other agreements to which they were parties.

 ❧

Worcester v. Georgia, 31 U.S. 515; 8 L. Ed. 483 (1832)

Facts—Georgia adopted a law under which it sentenced a Vermont missionary to the Cherokees to four years in prison for residing within the Cherokee Territory without a license from the governor.

Questions—(a) Was the record of the case properly before the Supreme Court? (b) Can the Court take cognizance of a case involving an appeal of a state prosecution? (c) Are treaties with Native American tribes a matter for state or national authorities?

Decisions—(a) Yes; (b) Yes; (c) National.

Reasons—*C.J. Marshall* (5–1). (a) A case is considered to be before the Court when signed by the clerk, and this case was so certified.

(b-c) The Judiciary Act does not give the Court discretion over the cases it will accept. These include matters involving federal treaties. When Europeans came to America, they found the continent inhabited "by a distinct people divided into separate nations, independent of each other and of the rest of the world, having institutions of their own, and governing themselves by their own laws." The European nations, including Great Britain, who claimed each area, entered into treaties with the Indians and oversaw trade with them, keeping other European nations at bay in the process. This power later passed to the United Colonies and to the new nation under the U.S. Constitution. The United States has entered into a number of treaties with the Cherokees: "This relation was that of a nation claiming and receiving the protection of one more powerful: not that of individuals abandoning their national character, and submitting as subjects to the laws of a master." Treaties have recognized the territory of the Cherokees, and state laws repugnant to such treaties, including the law in question, are void.

J. McLean, concurring, agreed that the Court had properly accepted this case. He argued that it was just as important for the federal courts to review criminal cases originating in the states as to review civil cases. He further emphasized the role of the national government in managing relations with Native Americans through its power over commerce. The Native Americans "have always been admitted to possess many of the attributes of sovereignty."

As long as Native Americans retain their identity as tribes, the national government governs relations with them.

J. Baldwin, dissenting, did not think this case had been properly certified before the Court.

Note—Although the Marshall Court attempted to protect the rights of the Cherokees, the Court did not have the sympathy either of the state government, which refused to honor its decision, or of President Andrew Jackson. This decision was followed by the tragic Trail of Tears in which thousands of Cherokees were relocated to Oklahoma, many dying along the way.

~~~

Puerto Rico v. Branstad, 483 U.S. 219; 107 S. Ct. 2802; 97 L. Ed. 2d 187 (1987)

Facts—Ronald Calder struck two persons with his automobile. Army Villalba was killed and her husband, who had quarreled with respondent Calder earlier, was deliberately run over. On bail, Calder was charged with murder and attempted murder. He fled to Iowa. The governor of Puerto Rico requested Calder's extradition and was refused. Puerto Rico sought a mandamus in the district court holding that Iowa violated the extradition clause and the Federal Extradition Act. Resting on *Kentucky v. Dennison* (1861), the District Court held that the federal courts had no power to order a governor to fulfill the state's obligation under the extradition clause (Art. 4, Sec. 2). The Court of Appeals affirmed. Supreme Court granted certiorari.

Question—May a court order a state governor to extradite a criminal?

Decision—Yes.

Reasons—*J. Marshall* (8–0). *Dennison*, like today's *Branstad* case, involves extradition. It was much related to secession, a threatening civil war, and free and slavery states. Representatives of the Deep South withdrew from Congress and Justice Campbell resigned from the Supreme Court. "The Court firmly rejected the position taken by Dennison and the governors of other free states that the extradition clause requires only the delivery of fugitives charged with acts which would be criminal by the law of the asylum state." Despite the Court's belief that the extradition clause was absolutist, the Court concluded that "the words 'it shall be the duty' were not used as mandatory and compulsory, but as declaratory of the moral duty" created by the Constitution. Thus for over 125 years *Kentucky v. Dennison* has stood for two propositions, first that the extradition clause creates a mandatory duty to deliver up fugitives "on demand" and, second, that the federal courts cannot compel performance of this ministerial duty. We hold that the commands of the extradition clause "are mandatory, and afford no discretion to the executive officers or courts of the asylum state." The fundamental premise of *Dennison* that in all circumstances the states and the federal government must be viewed as coequal sovereigns "is not representative of the law today." *Kentucky v. Dennison* is the product of another time and hence the Court of Appeals is reversed.

LIMITS ON THE STATES

Leisy v. Hardin, 135 U.S. 100; 10 S. Ct. 681; 34 L. Ed. 128 (1890)

Facts—Leisy, a brewer of Peoria, Illinois, brought an action to recover a quantity of barrels and cases of beer that had been seized in a proceeding on behalf of the state, for violating the Iowa statute prohibiting the sale of intoxicating liquors in the state. The beer in question was shipped from Illinois and sold in the original packages.

Question—Can a state prohibit articles of commerce from being imported into the state, in the absence of legislation on the part of Congress?

Decision—No.

Reasons—*C.J. Fuller* (6–3). The power of Congress to regulate commerce is unlimited, except for those restrictions specified in the Constitution. If Congress does not regulate concerning certain phases of interstate commerce, that commerce shall be free and unhampered. Beer, therefore, may be brought into the state and sold, after which time it becomes mingled in the common mass of property of the state, and subject to its control. The right to sell any article brought into a state is an inseparable incident to the right to import the article.

Note—The original package doctrine regarding foreign imports, *Brown v. Maryland*, 12 Wheaton 419 (1827) was carried over and covered interstate commerce in *Leisy*. In *Leisy*, though, the Court invited Congress to enact legislation giving the states some power to regulate articles involved in interstate commerce, which it did in 1890 in the Wilson Act, subsequently validated in *In re Rahrer*, 140 U.S. 545 (1891).

Virginia v. Tennessee, 148 U.S. 503; 13 S. Ct. 728; 37 L. Ed. 537 (1893)

Facts—Virginia brought this suit to establish the true boundary line between herself and Tennessee. In 1801, commissioners, appointed with the approval of both states, established a boundary, and subsequently in 1803 both legislatures approved the boundary. Since that date, both states have adhered to the boundary, which Congress recognized in districting for judicial, revenue, and federal election purposes. Virginia sought to have the agreement declared null and void as having been entered into without the consent of Congress. The Constitution provides that "no state shall, without the consent of Congress . . . enter into any agreement or compact with another state, or with a foreign power. . . ."

Question—Does the Constitution prohibit states without the consent of Congress from appointing commissioners to run and mark the boundary line between them?

Decision—No.

Reasons—*J. Field* (8–0). What the Constitution implied by "agreement or compact" was any compact or agreement that endangered the power of the federal government, such as a war alliance or increasing the political power in the states. The Court further noted that the clause in the Constitution did not state when Congress should approve of a compact or agreement. The approval by Congress of the compact entered into between the states upon their ratification of the action of their commissioners is fairly implied from its subsequent legislation and proceedings. The exercise of jurisdiction by Congress over the country as a part of Tennessee on one side, and as a part of Virginia on the other, for a long succession of years, without question or dispute from any quarter, is as conclusive proof of assent to it by that body as can usually be obtained from its most formal proceedings.

"Looking at the clause in which the terms 'compact' or 'agreement' appear, it is evident that the prohibition is directed to the formation of any combination tending to the increase of political power in the states, which may encroach upon or interfere with the just supremacy of the United States."

Note—Article I, Section 10, Clause 1 prohibits a state from entering into treaties or to form an alliance or confederation. This limitation is absolute and unconstitutional. The prohibition in Clause 3 that a state cannot enter into an agreement or compact without the permission of Congress is less strict. Thus in *New Hampshire v. Maine* (426 U.S. 363,1976), locating a boundary between them did not require congressional consent nor according to *United States Steel Corp. v. Multistate Tax Commissioners* (434 U.S. 452, 1978) was consent necessary when twenty-one states set up an administrative unit to collect taxes. Disputes over compacts or agreements are subject to the Court's original jurisdiction.

Edwards v. California, 314 U.S. 160; 62 S. Ct. 164; 86 L. Ed. 119 (1941)

Facts—Edwards was a citizen of the United States and a resident of California. He left Marysville, California, for Spur, Texas, with the intention of bringing his wife's brother, Frank Duncan, to Marysville. Duncan was a resident of Texas. Edwards knew that Duncan was employed by the Work Projects Administration and that he was indigent. They traveled in Edwards's car. Duncan had about $20 when he left Texas and nothing when he arrived in California. He lived unemployed with Edwards for ten days, then received assistance from the Farm Security Administration. The District Court decided that Edwards violated the Welfare and Institutions Code of California by knowingly bringing a nonresident indigent person into the state.

Question—Is this law banning persons from knowingly bringing an individual into the state a valid exercise of the police power of the state of California?

Decision—No.

Reasons—*J. Byrnes* (9–0). The California statute concerning the entry of indigent persons violated the commerce clause of the federal Constitution. The passage of persons from state to state constitutes interstate commerce within the provisions of Article I, Section 8 of the Constitution delegating to Congress the authority to regulate interstate commerce, and the California law imposed an unconstitutional burden on such commerce. The concurring opinion noted that the right to move freely from state to state is an incident of national citizenship protected by the privileges and immunities clause of the Fourteenth Amendment against state interference.

Camps Newfound/Owatonna v. Town of Harrison, 520 U.S. 564; 117 S. Ct. 1590; 137 L. Ed. 2d 852 (1997)

Facts—Owatonna is a nonprofit corporation that operates a summer camp in Harrison, Maine, for the benefit of children of the Christian Science faith;

95 percent of its campers, who pay tuition of about $400 a week, are from out of state. The camp paid over $20,000 in real estate taxes from 1989 to 1991, but Maine did not assess such taxes on operations of similar organizations designed to benefit state citizens. The Maine Superior Court ruled that the law drew an impermissible distinction between organizations that served individuals in-state as opposed to out-of-state, but the Maine Supreme Judicial Court had reversed on the basis that Maine was effectively purchasing services of those who served its citizens.

Question—Does a Maine tax that treats organizations differently according to whether they primarily serve in-state or out-of-state residents violate the dormant commerce clause?

Decision—Yes.

Reasons—*J. Stevens* (5–4). A primary impetus for the U.S. Constitution was the conflict of commercial regulations. Precedents have established that the commerce clause "even without implementing legislation by Congress is a limitation upon the power of the States" [this is the meaning of the term, the "dormant" commerce clause]. Just as Maine could not tax a camp more heavily because its campers came from out of state, so too, it cannot give special exemptions. The camp "is unquestionably engaged in commerce, not only as a purchaser . . . but also as a provider of goods and services." In this respect, it is similar to hotels that serve out-of-state guests. The camp's nonprofit status does not affect its relationship to commerce. A central purpose of the Court's "negative Commerce Clause jurisprudence" is to prevent "this sort of 'economic Balkanization'" and "economic isolationism." Moreover, "That the tax discrimination comes in the form of a deprivation of a generally available tax benefit, rather than a specific penalty on the activity itself, is of no moment." The tax results in increased fees for the individual served, serving as "an export tariff that targets out-of-state consumers by taxing the businesses that principally serve them." The town's argument that this exemption is "either a legitimate discriminatory subsidy of only those charities that choose to focus their activities on local concerns, or alternatively a governmental 'purchase' of charitable services falling within the narrow exception to the dormant Commerce Clause for States in the role as 'market participants,'" is "unpersuasive" and contrary to precedents.

J. Scalia, dissenting, argued that "The Court's negative-commerce-clause jurisprudence has drifted far from its moorings." The desire to create a national market has needlessly usurped state police powers; "the provision at issue here is a narrow tax exemption, designed merely to compensate or subsidize those organizations that contribute to the public fisc by dispensing public benefits the State might otherwise provide." Any effect on interstate commerce is indirect. "States have restricted public assistance to their own bona fide residents since colonial times." While the results in this case "may well be in accord with the parable of the Good Samaritan, . . . they have nothing to do with the Commerce Clause."

J. Thomas, dissenting. A real estate tax is "the quintessential asset that does not move in interstate commerce." The Court's negative commerce clause decisions had become overly broad. Attention should be directed away from the dormant commerce clause and toward the import-export clause in Article I, Section 10, which prohibits states from laying "Imposts or Duties" on the same. Instead of focusing on negative commerce clause decisions, the Court should be most concerned with cases, when state law conflicts with federal law or when Congress has preempted a field through extensive legislation. The import-export clause can be interpreted to apply to goods from other states as well as from other countries. The tax at issue does not violate the prohibition on imports and exports, and should accordingly remain in place.

Crosby v. National Foreign Trade Council, 530 U.S. 363; 120 S. Ct. 2288; 147 L. Ed. 2d 352 (2000)

Facts—Massachusetts adopted a law limiting its agencies from purchasing goods or services from companies doing business with Burma (Myanmar). Soon thereafter, Congress passed a law, subsequently implemented by an executive order, vesting the president with broad powers to impose sanctions on Burma. Working through the Trade Council, companies challenged these laws as being in conflict with, and preempted by, national actions.

Question—Does the Massachusetts legislation limiting trade with Burma conflict with actions of the Congress and the president?

Decision—Yes.

Reasons—*J. Souter* (9–0). Congress may preempt state law either directly or through implication. Congress intended to "provide the President with flexible and effective authority over economic sanctions against Burma," with which the Massachusetts legislation conflicted. Congress further intended to limit such sanctions "to a specific range," which was superseded by the Massachusetts legislation. The Massachusetts legislation further interfered with the nation's attempt to develop a "comprehensive, multilateral strategy to bring democracy to and improve human rights practices and the quality of life in Burma." In so doing, the law undermined the president's capacity for effective diplomacy, as demonstrated by foreign complaints against the Massachusetts law and by testimony from executive officials about the adverse effects of the state laws.

In concurrence, *J. Scalia* argued that the intention of the federal legislation was clear on its face and he would thus have disregarded testimony by its sponsors and others who introduced or ratified it.

❦

Cook v. Gralike, 531 U.S. 510; 121 S. Ct. 1029; 149 L. Ed. 2d 44 (2001)

Facts—After the U.S. Supreme Court decision in *U.S. Term Limits, Inc. v. Thornton* (1995), Missouri adopted a constitutional amendment instructing each member of Congress from the state to support an amendment to the U.S. Constitution limiting House of Representatives members to three terms and Senate members to two. The Missouri amendment further provided that ballots would specifically designate incumbents who disregarded such instructions or candidates who failed to support the amendment. A nonincumbent candidate, Don Gralike, sought an injunction prohibiting Missouri's secretary of state from enforcing the provision. The U.S. District Court granted summary judgment, arguing that the Missouri provision violated the qualifications clause of Article I of the U.S. Constitution and First Amendment rights of free speech. The U.S. Eighth Circuit Court affirmed the District Court decision. Although Gralike withdrew from the election, Harmon, a nonincumbent Republican candidate intervened as the appellee.

Question—Does the Tenth Amendment reserve power to a state to designate candidates opposed to term limits?

Decision—No, such designations are limited by the election clause (Article I, 4, cl. 1) and are not valid time, place, or manner restrictions.

Reasons—J. *Stevens* (9–0). The court rejected Missouri's claim that it could give binding instructions to its congressional representatives. Although Missouri showed that some states once issued instructions to their congressional delegates, it failed to show that such instructions were legally binding. Indeed, evidence shows that the right to issue such binding instructions was specifically rejected when the wording of the First Amendment was formulated. Although states have power to regulate the "Times, Places and Manner of holding Elections for Senators and Representatives," subject to congressional regulations, Missouri's efforts went beyond "procedural regulations" and were designed to favor or disfavor classes of candidates.

J. Kennedy's concurring opinion further stressed that Missouri was impermissibly attempting to intrude upon the relationship between the people and their congressional representatives. *J. Thomas* denied that states were limited to powers designated to them by the Constitution but noted that Missouri had not argued this point. *C.J. Rehnquist's* concurrence focused on what he believed to be the First Amendment rights of candidates to run for office without having their names "accompanied by pejorative language requested by the State."

⌇

Smith v. Doe, 538 U.S. 84; 123 S. Ct. 1140; 155 L. Ed. 2d 164 (2003)

Facts—The Alaska Sex Offender Registration Act required a sex offender or child kidnapper to register with the state; nonaggravated offenders had to provide this basis on a yearly basis and aggravated offenders quarterly. The information was placed on the Internet. Two sex offenders who had been released from prison and completed rehabilitative programs challenged this law as an illegal ex post facto law, which Article I, Section 10 of the U.S. Constitution prohibited. The U.S. District Court granted summary judgment for the state, but the U.S. Ninth Circuit struck the law down as a punitive ex post facto law.

Question—Is the Alaska Sex Offender Registration Act, which requires filing of information by former sex offenders and posts this information on the Internet, an unconstitutional ex post facto law?

Decision—No.

Reasons—*J. Kennedy* (6–3). The requirements of the Alaska Sex Offender Registration Act are retroactive. If the law's primary purpose was punitive, then it would be an ex post facto law, but if its purpose were "civil and nonpunitive," it could still have a punitive effect. Alaska expressed as its primary purpose the interest in protecting the public safety, and the codification of the notification provisions of the law appears to confirm this. The seven factors outlined in *Kennedy v. Mendoza-Martinez*, 372 U.S. 144 (1963) provide a useful framework for deciding the effects of a law. The Court finds differences between this law and early "shaming punishments," or banishments. Here names are not posted for the purpose of public ridicule; indeed, the information posted on the Internet is already available in criminal records. Moreover, this law does not impose physical restraints on offenders or limit the activities in which they may engage. Individuals are not required to register in person, and they may move about as they want. The state did not choose to tailor the time that an individual must continue reporting to individual offenses or to judgments of continuing dangerousness, but sex offenders have been shown to have high rates of recidivism, and individuals desiring information of sex offenders must take positive steps to get it, making the notification system a "passive one." The Court does not need to decide "whether the legislature has made the best choice possible to address the problem it seeks to remedy" but "whether the regulatory means chosen are reasonable in light of the nonpunitive objectives."

J. Thomas, concurring, argued that the Court should limit its review to whether making information available is punitive and not to a choice of the means used, namely posting on the Internet.

J. Souter, concurring, argued that it was not easy to separate the criminal and civil consequences of this law, but thought that, given the relative "equipoise" presented, "What tips the scale for me is the presumption of constitutionality normally accorded a State's law."

J. Stevens, dissenting, believed that the law imposed significant affirmative obligations on sex offenders that brought about "a severe stigma on every person to whom they apply." Three facts pointed to the punitive nature of the laws—they (1) constitute a severe deprivation of the offender's liberty, (2) are imposed on everyone who is convicted of a relevant criminal offense, and (3) are imposed only on those criminals."

J. Ginsburg, dissenting, likened the law to shunning and believed that it was excessive "in relation to its nonpunitive purpose." She noted that in the case at hand it was applied to an individual who had remarried, established a business, had been awarded custody of a minor daughter, and whom a court had determined to have been rehabilitated.

Note—In a companion case, *Connecticut Department of Public Safety v. John Doe* (2003), the Court rejected a challenge to so-called "Megan's laws."

LIMITS ON FEDERAL REGULATION OF STATES

New York v. United States, 505 U.S. 144; 112 S. Ct. 2408; 120 L. Ed. 2d 120 (1992)

Facts—In the Low-Level Radioactive Waste Policy Amendments Act of 1985, Congress provided for the disposal of radioactive wastes by enacting three provisions. First, it offered monetary incentives, by allowing states to add surcharges to states that build their own waste disposal sites. Second, it permitted states to deny access to other states that did not create such sites. Third, it provided that states that did not develop such sites would have to "take title" to their radioactive wastes.

Question—Are these federally mandated provisions of the Low-Level Radioactive Waste Policy Amendment Act of 1985 constitutional?

Decision—The provisions offering monetary incentives and denying access to noncomplying states were constitutional, but the "take title" provisions constituted an exercise of power not delegated to Congress.

Reasons—*J. O'Connor* (6–3). The American federal government is one of limited powers. The fact that congressional powers are enumerated is a "mirror image" of the fact that powers not delegated to Congress are reserved to the states under the Tenth Amendment: "the Tenth Amendment confirms that the power of the Federal Government is subject to limits that may, in a given instance, reserve power to the States." Existing constitutional provisions, including the commerce clause, the general welfare clause, the necessary and proper clause, and the supremacy clause, allow for the expansion of the role of the federal government. Such clauses do not allow Congress to "commandeer the legislative processes of the States by directly compelling them to enact and enforce a federal regulatory program." To the contrary, the Framers of the Constitution devised a system where the national government would operate directly on individuals rather than on the states. Congress can use its spending power to "attach conditions on the receipt of federal funds." It may also offer the states the option of regulating an activity or having it preempted by federal powers under the commerce clause. By contrast, when the federal government attempts to "compel" state action, "the accountability of both state and federal officials is diminished." The provisions of the Waste Policy Amendments that offer incentives to the states are appropriate exercises of power under the spending clause. Similarly the provisions denying state access to waste sites is an appropriate exercise of congressional authority under the commerce clause. By contrast, the "take title" provision of the act "has crossed the line distinguishing encouragement from coercion." Such "commandeering" of state officials is "inconsistent with the Constitution's division of authority between federal and state governments." O'Connor argued that "Where a federal interest is sufficiently strong to cause Congress to legislate, it must do so directly; it may not conscript state governments as its agents." The states' original consent to this regulatory scheme is irrelevant. Federalism was designed "for the protection of individuals" as well as states. It is important to recognize that "States are not mere political subdivisions of the United States. State governments are neither regional offices nor administrative agencies of the Federal Government." Thus, "The Federal Government may not compel the States to enact or administer a federal regulatory program."

J. White's dissent argued that "the Court has mischaracterized the essential inquiry, misanalyzed the inquiry it has chosen to undertake, and undervalued the effect the seriousness of this public policy problem should have on the constitutionality of the take title provision." White viewed the legislation as a model example of "cooperative federalism" in action and argued that states should be stopped from questioning the constitutionality of a provision they have previously utilized. White believed the anti-commandeering provision is built from dicta in earlier cases, and cited an earlier case to say that any limitation designed to protect states as states "is one of process rather than one of result." *J. Stevens's* dissent likewise questioned the majority's view that the federal government could not issue directives to state governments.

Printz v. United States, Mack v. United States, 521 U.S. 898; S. Ct. 2365; 138 L. Ed. 2d 914 (1997)

Facts—The 1993 Brady Handgun Violence Prevention Act modified the Gun Control Act of 1968 by providing for a national system of criminal background checks for individuals interested in purchasing handguns. Until a national database could be established, the chief law enforcement officials (CLEOs) within a given area were directed to conduct such checks and report back within five days. Two sheriffs asserted that such direction was unconstitutional. District Courts in Montana and Arizona agreed, but the Ninth Circuit Court of Appeals reversed.

Question—Is the provision of the 1993 Brady Handgun Violence Prevention Act mandating state law enforcement officials to conduct background checks constitutional?

Decision—No, such a mandate exceeds federal powers.

Reasons—*J. Scalia* (5–4). Since no constitutional provision directly addressed the question posed by this case, Scalia attempted to answer the issue by examining the "historical understanding and practice," "the structure of the Constitution," and "the jurisprudence of this Court." He found that federal attempts to commandeer state officials were fairly unprecedented until recent years. Early practices indicated that states judges were sometimes expected to enforce federal laws, but do not appear to demonstrate directions to state executive officials. As to structure, the U.S. Constitution "established a system of 'dual sovereignty,'" in which the state and national governments acted on individual citizens rather than directly upon one another. This federal system was designed to protect liberty and is not undermined by the necessary and proper clause, since interference with state sovereignty would not be "proper." Prior precedents, most notably *New York v. United States*, 505 U.S. 144 (1992), limiting federal "take possession" mandates requiring states that have not otherwise complied with federal regulations to take title to radioactive wastes, further pose barriers to federal mandates to state officials. Having thus struck down the federal mandate, Scalia refused to decide whether the provision in question was severable from the rest of the law since no litigants had properly brought this issue before the Court.

J. O'Connor's concurrence argued that the provision of the Brady Act violated the Tenth Amendment. *J. Thomas's* concurrence cited both the Tenth Amendment and the Second Amendment |which he acknowledged had not been relied upon in this case|, which might be read to give "a personal right to keep and bear arms." *J. Stevens's* dissent attempted a point-by-point refutation of Scalia's views. Stevens justified the federal regulation as an exercise of its powers under the commerce and necessary and proper clauses. He argued that "when Congress exercises the powers delegated to it by the Constitution, it may impose affirmative obligations on executive and judicial officers of state and local governments as well as ordinary citizens." He further discounted the Court's interpretation of judicial precedents. *J. Souter's* dissent relied largely on language in the Federalist Papers. *J. Breyer's* dissent pointed to practices in foreign federal governments that tended to support the right of the national government to seek implementation of its laws through state constituent authorities.

<hr />

United States v. Morrison, 529 U.S. 598; 120 S. Ct. 1740; 146 L. Ed. 2d 658 (2000)

Facts—Christy Brzonkala, a student enrolled at Virginia Tech, brought suit against two male students for rape under a provision of the Violence Against Women Act of 1994, after the college provided ineffective redress. The U.S. District Court dismissed the complaint, deciding Congress had inadequate power to enact the law. The U.S. Fourth Circuit Court of Appeals first reversed the District Court, then held an en banc hearing and affirmed the decision.

Question—Does the commerce clause in Article I, Section 8 or Section 5 of the Fourteenth Amendment provide Congress with powers to provide civil remedies in cases involving violence against women?

Decision—No.

Reasons—*C.J. Rehnquist* (5–4). Congressional legislation needs to be based on one or more enumerated powers. In *United States v. Lopez* (1995), the Supreme Court ruled that congressional powers to regulate interstate and foreign commerce needed to be tied to the channels or instrumentalities of commerce or should have a "substantial relation" to such commerce. Such ties were lacking in this case. Laws dealing with gender-motivated acts of violence are not directed toward economic activity. Unlike *Lopez*, in this case Congress attempted to document economic impact, but such a decision "is ultimately a judicial rather than a legislative question, and can be settled finally only by this Court." If Congress were allowed to regulate such violence on the basis that it affected commerce, there is little that Congress could not regulate. Such regulation would obliterate the distinction "between what is truly national and what is truly local," and would interfere with state police powers over the subject. As to Section 5 of the Fourteenth Amendment, The *Civil Rights Cases* (1883) and other precedents establish that this amendment was designed to remedy state, rather than private, action. "If the allegations here are true, no civilized system of justice could fail to provide her [Brzonkala] a remedy for the conduct of respondent Morrison. But under our federal system that remedy must be provided by the Commonwealth of Virginia, and not by the United States."

J. Thomas's concurring opinion expressed continuing opposition to the Court's use of the "substantial effects" test in matters involving commerce, believing that this standard gave Congress excessive power.

J. Souter's dissent argued that aggregate acts of violence against women had a substantial effect on commerce that sanctioned congressional power in this case, and he cited congressional findings to that effect. He regarded congressional powers over commerce, combined with its powers under the necessary and proper clause, to be plenary and believed the Court was unwisely returning to earlier overly formalistic tests for ascertaining when congressional exercises of power were warranted.

J. Breyer's dissent pointed to the difficulty of drawing lines between economic and noneconomic activity and to the aggregated effect of diverse activities. He would apply minimal judicial review to cases where Congress asserted ties to commerce.

STATUS OF THE STATES

Texas v. White, 1 Wallace (74 U.S.) 700; 19 L. Ed. 227; 1868 U.S. LEXIS 1056 (1869)

Facts—Texas received certain interest-bearing bonds from the United States in 1850 for settlement of boundary claims. The Confederate government of Texas subsequently sold some of these bonds to White and others during the Civil War. The Reconstruction government of Texas then sought to restrain those bondholders from receiving payment from the national government and was asking for the bonds to be surrendered back to the state. Since this dispute involved a suit initiated by a state against citizens of another state, it appeared before the U.S. Supreme Court as a case of original jurisdiction.

Questions—(a) Is Texas still a state capable of pursuing a suit in a federal court? (b) If so, did Texas divest itself of its bonds when it attempted to transfer them to White and others in exchange for certain supplies?

Decisions—(a) Yes; (b) No.

Reasons—*C.J. Chase* (5–3). The term "state" describes political and geographical entities. It can refer to "people, territory, and government." Texas became a state in 1845, although it subsequently participated in the Civil War, after which the president appointed a provisional governor, who Congress subsequently replaced with another. The Union of States was designed to be "perpetual." Moreover, "the preservation of the States, and the maintenance of their governments, are as much within the design and care of the Constitution as the preservation of the Union and the maintenance of the National government. The Constitution, in all its provisions, looks to an indestructible Union, composed of indestructible States." Texas's attempt to secede was therefore null, although the state's rights were suspended during its rebellion, after which the president and Congress had the power to reconstruct it. Those representing this new government represent the state. When Texas attempted to sell its bonds, it was in rebellion and was seeking to further this rebellion. The rebel authorities therefore had no power to divest the state of the bonds. Although the U.S. government apparently redeemed some bonds, it made it clear during the Civil War that it did not regard Texas's transaction as legal, and subsequent purchasers knew about this ambiguity and took the corresponding risks.

J. Grier argued in dissent that although Texas remained a state as "a legal fiction," it ceased to be so "as a political fact." Even if so considered, however, Texas had no right to repudiate its former contracts. In attempting to do so, Texas is claiming that, although it is now a state, it was not one when it entered into the contract, thus assuming the role of a chameleon, assuming "the color of the object to which she adheres." *J. Swayne* also denied Texas's right to bring suit in this case.

Coyle v. Smith, 221 U.S. 559; 31 S. Ct. 688; 55 L. Ed. 853 (1911)

Facts—When Oklahoma was admitted as a state in 1907, Congress provided that the capital should be located at Guthrie until the year 1913. In 1910 the Oklahoma legislature provided for the removal of the capital to Oklahoma City.

Questions—(a) May Congress, under penalty of denying admission, impose limitations on a new state at the time of admission? (b) Will those limitations be binding after admission as a state?

Decisions—(a) Yes; (b) No.

Reasons—*J. Lurton* (7–2). (a) "The constitutional provisions concerning the admission of new states is not a mandate, but a power to be exercised with discretion." Therefore, Congress, in the exercise of this discretion, may impose conditions that a state-to-be must meet before Congress grants approval to its admission.

(b) Any restraints imposed by Congress on a new state before its admission can be ignored with impunity by that state after admission except such as have some bases in the Constitution. Congress has no power to limit the rights of a state. The constitutional duty of guaranteeing to each state a republican form of government does not allow Congress to place limits on them that would deprive them of equality with other states. The constitutional power of admission of states is based on the assumption that the new states will be on a par with other states. This is a union of equal states. If Congress could lay down binding conditions, as the one involved in this case on an incoming state, then the United States would include states unequal in power. When a state enters the Union, it at once becomes "entitled to and possessed of all the rights of dominion and sovereignty which belonged to the original states. She was admitted, and could be admitted, only on the same footing with them."

A clear distinction should be drawn between a matter involving political inequality of a new state (as here, and which is not binding after admission) and a matter involving a quid pro quo contractual relation (which is binding after admission).

Ziffrin v. Reeves, 308 U.S. 132; 60 S. Ct. 103; 84 L. Ed. 128 (1939)

Facts—Appellant, an Indiana corporation, had, since 1933, been receiving whisky from distillers in Kentucky for direct carriage to consignees in Chicago. It had permission under the Federal Motor Carriers Act of 1935 to operate as a contract carrier, and claimed the right to transport whisky in spite of the prohibitions of the Kentucky Alcoholic Beverages Control Law of 1938. It now sought to restrain the state from enforcing the contraband and penal provisions of the law. The Kentucky law forbade the carriage of intoxicating liquors by carriers other than licensed common carriers, and forbade distillers to deliver to an unauthorized carrier. Constant state control was exercised over the manufacture, sale, transportation, and possession of whisky. The corporation was denied a common carrier's certificate and transportation license by Kentucky. The corporation claimed that the law was unconstitutional because it was repugnant to the commerce, due process, and equal protection clauses.

Question—Is the Kentucky law limiting the transportation of intoxicants unconstitutional?

Decision—No.

Reasons—*J. McReynolds* (8–0). The Twenty-first Amendment allows a state to legislate concerning intoxicating liquor brought from without, unfettered by the commerce clause. Without doubt a state may absolutely prohibit the manufacture of intoxicants, their transportation, sale, or possession, irrespective of when or where produced or obtained or the use to which they are put. Further, a state may adopt measures reasonably appropriate to effectuate these inhibitions and exercise full police authority in respect of them. Under its police power, the state of Kentucky can permit the manufacture and sale of liquors only under certain conditions and regulate the way in which they are sold. In this way they cannot properly be regarded as an article of commerce.

The record shows no violation of the equal protection clause. A licensed common carrier is under stricter control than an ordinary contract carrier and may be entrusted with privileges forbidden to the latter.

The Motor Carrier Act of 1935 is said to secure the appellant the right claimed, but the Court could find nothing there that undertakes to destroy state power to protect her people against the evils of intoxicants or to sanction the receipt of articles declared contraband. The act has no such purpose or effect.

TENTH AMENDMENT AND STATE POLICE POWERS

United States v. F. W. Darby Lumber Co., 312 U.S. 100; 61 S. Ct. 451; 85 L. Ed. 609 (1941)

Facts—The appellee was engaged, in the state of Georgia, in the business of acquiring raw materials, which he manufactured into finished lumber with the intention of shipping it in interstate commerce to customers outside the state. Numerous counts charged the appellee with the shipment of lumber in interstate commerce from Georgia to points outside the state and that he employed workmen at less than the prescribed minimum wage or more than the prescribed maximum hours without payment of any wage for overtime. Another count charged the appellee with failure to keep records showing the hours worked each day a week by his employees, as required by the regulation of the administrator. The appellee sought to sustain the decision on the grounds that the prohibition of Congress was unauthorized by the commerce clause, and was prohibited by the Fifth Amendment.

Question—Does the congressional prohibition of the shipment in interstate commerce of lumber manufactured by employees whose wages are less than a prescribed minimum or whose weekly hours are greater than a prescribed maximum interfere with the powers reserved to the states?

Decision—No.

Reasons—*J. Stone* (9–0). The manufacture of goods in itself is not a matter of interstate commerce, but the shipment of such articles is. It was contended that the regulations of Congress in the matter of wages and hours belong properly to the states. However, the power of Congress to regulate interstate commerce is complete in itself, with no other limitations except those prescribed in the Constitution. Stone interprets the Tenth Amendment, reserving nondelegated powers to the states, as but a "truism" with little real teeth. The motive and purpose of the act in question was to keep interstate commerce from being an instrument in the distribution of goods produced under substandard conditions, as such competition would be injurious to interstate commerce. This was a matter of legislative judgment perfectly within the bounds of congressional power, and over which the courts are given no control. Congress has the power to regulate not only commerce between the states, but such intrastate activities that so affect interstate commerce as to make their regulation means to a legitimate end. As regards the congressional policy of excluding from interstate commerce all goods manufactured under substandard conditions, the enforcement of wages and hours, even though intrastate, is a valid means of protection, and therefore, within the reach of the commerce power.

Note—*Darby* reversed *Hammer v. Dagenhart*, 247 U.S. 251 (1918). In upholding the Fair Labor Standards Act of 1938, *Darby*, in effect, ruled that the unratified Child Labor Amendment, proposed by Congress in 1924, was unneeded. *Darby* closed the era of laissez-faire in which the Court restricted the economic powers of Congress. It returned to John Marshall's view of a broad, almost unlimited, commerce power.

~~~

National League of Cities v. Usery, 426 U.S. 833; 96 S. Ct. 2465; 49 L. Ed. 2d 245 (1976)

Facts—The Fair Labor Standards Act was amended in 1974 to extend its minimum wage and maximum hour provisions to most state and local employees. Cities and states brought suit against the secretary of labor for declaratory and injunctive relief, but were turned down by a three-judge U.S. District Court, partly on the basis that the Supreme Court had approved such federal regulations in *Maryland v. Wirtz*, 392 U.S. 183 (1968).

Question—Does the application of federal minimum wage and maximum hour provisions of the Fair Labor Standards Act to the state and local governments violate their rights under the Tenth Amendment to make key decisions affecting their citizens?

Decision—Yes.

Reasons—*J. Rehnquist* (5–4). The time has come to limit *Maryland v. Wirtz*. Although the commerce clause gives plenary authority to Congress, this authority is limited by specific constitutional restraints. The states have a vital role to play in the federal system, and the Tenth Amendment indicates that states should accordingly be treated differently than mere private citizens. Citing *Coyle v. Smith*, 221 U.S. 559 (1911), Rehnquist argued that: "We have repeatedly recognized that there are attributes of sovereignty attaching to every state government which may not be impaired by Congress, not because Congress may lack an affirmative grant of legislative authority to reach the matter, but because the Constitution prohibits it from exercising the authority in that manner." Federal wage and hour provisions can result not only in significant financial costs to the states but can also substantially interfere with the manner in which states choose to do their business. They will "significantly alter or displace the States' abilities to structure employer-employee relationships in such areas as fire prevention, police protection, sanitation, public health, and parks and recreation," all functions traditionally exercised by the states: "insofar as the challenged amendments operate to directly displace the States' freedom to structure integral operations in areas of traditional governmental functions, they are not within the authority granted Congress."

J. Blackmun's concurring opinion, interpreted the decision not as a flat prohibition on federal regulations affecting states but as the exercise of "a balancing approach." *J. Brennan*, joined by *J. White* and *J. Marshall*, dissented. The dissenters viewed the Court's decision as a "patent usurpation of the role reserved for the political process." They further said that the majority's reliance on the Tenth Amendment "must astound scholars of the Constitution" and remind them of the days that the Court used this and other constitutional provisions to invalidate federal programs. States are protected in the federal system through their representation within Congress. Moreover, they received lots of grants that more than compensate them for the costs of adhering to federal regulations. In his dissent, *J. Stevens* indicated that he thought that it was unwise for the federal government to act in the manner in which it did but not unconstitutional for it to do so.

Note—The Supreme Court overturned this decision in *Garcia v. San Antonio Metropolitan Transit Authority* (1985), deciding that it could not adequately distinguish the exercise of traditional from nontraditional state functions.

৵৵

Equal Employment Opportunity Commission v. Wyoming, 460 U.S. 226; 103 S. Ct. 1054; 75 L. Ed. 2d 18 (1983)

Facts—A supervisor for a state game and fish department was dismissed on reaching the age of 55. With the approval of his employer he could have been retained. He claimed that the dismissal violated the Age Discrimination in Employment Act (ADEA). The U.S. District Court ruled that congressional powers were limited by the Tenth Amendment.

Question—Did Congress have power to extend the ADEA to state and local government employees?

Decision—Yes.

Reasons—*J. Brennan* (5–4). Efforts in Congress to prohibit arbitrary age discrimination date back at least to the 1950s and surfaced in floor debates in what became Title VII of the Civil Rights Act of 1964. Protection from age discrimination was subsequently raised to age seventy in 1978. Originally the Age Discrimination in Employment Act (passed in 1967) did not apply to the federal government, to the states, their political subdivisions, or to employers with fewer than twenty-five employees. In 1974 Congress amended the act to include federal, state, and local governments, and employers with fewer than twenty employees. The appellees have not claimed that Congress exceeded the reach of the commerce power in enacting the ADEA but as to the Wyoming state game warden, the act "is precluded by virtue of external constraints imposed on Congress's commerce powers by the Tenth Amendment." The principle of state immunity articulated in the *National League of Cities v. Usery* (1976) is not meant to create a sacred province of state autonomy but to ensure the unique benefits of a federal system in which the states enjoy a "separate and independent existence." The state still assesses the fitness of a game warden and dismisses those wardens who appear unfit. "We conclude that the degree of federal intrusion in this case is sufficiently less serious than it was in *National League of Cities* so as to make it unnecessary for us to override Congress's express choice to extend its regulatory authority to the states."

Note—*J. Stevens*, in his concurring opinion, stressed that the commerce clause was the Framers' response to the central problem under the Constitution, and that *National League of Cities v. Usery* (1976) was wrongly decided in the spirit of the discredited Articles of Confederation and ought to be reversed. Two years later in *Garcia v. San Antonio* (1985) the Court reversed *Usery*. In a strong dissent in *EEOC v. Wyoming* (1983), *J. Powell* argued that (1) the Constitution does not mandate how a state should select its employees, (2) Stevens's view set no limitation on the ability of Congress to override state sovereignty, and (3) Congress has not equally placed restrictions on itself in the exercise of its own sovereign powers.

☙

Garcia v. San Antonio Metropolitan Transit Authority, 469 U.S. 528; 105 S. Ct. 1005; 83 L. Ed. 2d 1016 (1985)

Facts—The San Antonio Metropolitan Transit Authority (SAMTA) is a public mass transit authority. The Department of Labor held that SAMTA's operations are not immune from the minimum wage and overtime requirements of the Fair Labor Standards Act (FLSA) under *National League of Cities v. Usery* (1976). It was held that the commerce clause does not empower Congress to enforce such requirements against the states in an area of "traditional governmental function." The District Court held that a mass transit system is a traditional governmental function and under the *Usery* decision is exempt from the obligations imposed by the FLSA.

Question—May Congress regulate the wages of state transit employees under its commerce power without violating the powers reserved to the states under the Tenth Amendment?

Decision—Yes.

Reasons—*J. Blackmun* (5–4). The attempt to draw "the boundaries of state regulatory immunity in terms of traditional governmental function" is not only unworkable, but it also collides with federalist principles. This being so, the case of *National League of Cities* accordingly is overruled. During the pendency of *Garcia* "the Court ruled that a community rail service provided by the state-owned Long Island Rail Road did not constitute a 'traditional governmental function' and hence did not enjoy constitutional immunity. . . ." It long has been settled that Congress's authority "under the Commerce Clause extends to intrastate economic activities that affect interstate Commerce." Although the Court has difficulty drawing the line on what is or is not a governmental function—the only case to address this problem is *Long Island*—still "we simultaneously disavow 'a static historical view of state functions generally immune from federal regulation.'" Any rule of state immunity that looks to the "traditional," "integral," or "necessary" nature of governmental functions inevitably invites an unelected federal judiciary to make decisions about which state policies it favors and which ones it dislikes. The judgment of the district court is reversed. The majority argued that state interests were adequately protected by state representation in Congress and in the electoral college

    J. Powell and *J. O'Connor* authored vigorous dissents. Powell argued that "The States' role in our system of government is a matter of constitutional law, not of legislative grace." O'Connor evoked the "spirit" of the Tenth Amendment.

Chapter Six

Articles V and VII: Constitutional Amending Process and Ratification of the Constitution

Article V of the U.S. Constitution provided for an amending process by which the document could be changed short of force, and Article VII provided that the new Constitution would go into effect when ratified by nine of the existing thirteen states (applying, however, only to those states that ratified). The new amending process was much easier to exercise than the system under the Articles of Confederation, which required unanimous consent of the states, and which Article VII chose to bypass, but it is still difficult. As of 2010, only twenty-seven amendments have been adopted.

Article V outlines two methods for proposing amendments and two for ratifying them. An unutilized mechanism allows two-thirds of the states to call a convention to propose amendments. Otherwise two-thirds majorities in both houses of Congress must propose such amendments. Amendments are ratified by three-fourths of the states. Since Rhode Island did not send delegates to the Constitutional Convention and only twelve states attended, this is equivalent to the nine states required by Article VII for the original Constitution to go into effect. States ratify amendments at congressional specification either through their existing state legislatures or, as in the solitary case of the Twenty-first Amendment repealing national alcoholic prohibition, through special conventions called within each state.

The only remaining "entrenchment clause" in Article V reinforces the system of federalism, described in the previous chapter. It provides that no state can be deprived of its equal representation in the Senate without its consent and thus reiterates the importance of the Connecticut Compromise which apportioned the House by population and granted states equal representation in the Senate.

For many years, the Supreme Court issued decisions relative to the amending process beginning with *Hollingsworth v. Virginia* (1798), where it decided that a president's signature was unnecessary to legitimize an amendment. Similarly, early in the twentieth century, it affirmed the constitutionality of a number of contested amendments, and it ruled in *Dillon v. Gloss* (1921) that ratification of amendments should occur close enough to proposal as to reflect a contemporary consensus.

In *Coleman v. Miller* (1939), the Supreme Court decided that issues like the contemporaneousness of amending ratifications were "political questions" for Congress, rather than the Court, to resolve. In 1992, Congress exercised this power by accepting state ratifications of the Twenty-seventh Amendment limiting the timing of congressional pay raises that had been originally proposed more than two hundred years earlier with the original Bill of Rights.

In part because of its brevity, Article V did not address a number of important issues. These include whether states may rescind ratifications of amendments prior to the time they receive the required majorities, whether Congress can extend the time for ratification of amendments as it attempted to do in the case of the Equal Rights Amendment, and the length of time that state applications for a constitutional convention remain valid. This issue is, in turn, related to the much disputed question as to whether the states must call a general convention or whether they can call a convention to deal with a single issue.

The role of constitutional amendments in reversing Supreme Court decisions is important. The Eleventh Amendment reversed the Supreme Court decision in *Chisholm v. Georgia* (1793), the Fourteenth Amendment overturned *Scott v. Sandford* (1857), the Sixteenth Amendment reversed the decision in *Pollock v. Farmers' Loan & Trust Co.* (1895), and the Twenty-sixth Amendment modified the Supreme Court decision in *Oregon v. Mitchell* (1970). Ironically, once such amendments are tacked on to the Constitution, the Supreme Court then has to decide what such amendments mean! Were it not for the judicial branch, or a similar system, that often adopts constitutional interpretations to new circumstances, it is likely that the constitutional amending process would be exercised far more frequently than it is now. The line between interpreting and amending the Constitution remains a fine one.

THE AMENDING PROCESS

Hollingsworth v. Virginia, 3 Dallas (3 U.S.) 378; 1 L. Ed. 644 (1798)

Facts—After the Court's decision in *Chisholm v. Georgia* (1793), Congress proposed the Eleventh Amendment providing that no state could be sued by citizens of another state, or by citizens or subjects of a foreign state.

Question—Does an amendment to the U.S. Constitution require the president's signature?

Decision—No.

Reasons—*J. Chase* (unanimous). There is no necessity for an amendment to be shown to the president. The constitutional requirement of presidential signature applies only to ordinary legislation. The action of Congress in proposing an amendment is a constituent rather than legislative act.

⁂

National Prohibition Cases (Rhode Island v. Palmer), 253 U.S. 350; 40 S. Ct. 486; 64 L. Ed. 946 (1920)

Facts—The National Prohibition Cases consisted of seven cases questioning the constitutionality and legality of the Eighteenth Amendment and asking the lower courts for a restraining order against the Volstead Act enforcing that amendment.

Question—Is the Eighteenth Amendment providing for national alcoholic prohibition within the power to amend specified in Article V?

Decision—Yes.

Reasons—*J. Van Devanter* (7–2). The power to amend the Constitution was reserved by Article V. The Court noted the following points:

"1. The adoption by both Houses of Congress, each by a two-thirds vote, of a joint resolution proposing an amendment to the Constitution, sufficiently shows that the proposal was deemed necessary by all who voted for it. An express declaration that they regarded it as necessary is not essential. None of the resolutions whereby prior amendments were proposed contained such a declaration.
2. The two-thirds vote in each House, which is required in proposing an amendment is a vote of two-thirds of the members present—assuming the presence of a quorum—and not a vote of two-thirds of the entire membership, present and absent. . . .
3. The referendum provisions of state constitutions and statutes cannot be applied, consistently with the Constitution of the United States, in the ratification or rejection of amendments to it. . . .
4. The prohibition of manufacture, sale, transportation, importation, and exportation of intoxicating liquors for beverage purposes, as embodied in the Eighteenth Amendment, is within the power to amend reserved by Article Five of the Constitution.

5. That amendment, by lawful proposal and ratification, has become a part of the Constitution, and must be respected and given effect the same as other provisions of that instrument."

According to the Constitution, this amendment had been legally proposed by a two-thirds vote of the members present in each house, assuming the presence of a quorum, and ratified by a majority of the legislatures in three-fourths of the states. Incorporated into that amendment was the provision "that Congress and the several states shall have concurrent power to enforce this article by appropriate legislation." This Section Two of the amendment therefore authorized the Volstead Act. The words "concurrent power," giving concurrent power to Congress and the states to enforce that amendment, do not mean a joint power or require that legislation thereunder by Congress, to be effective, shall be approved or sanctioned by the several states or any of them, and is in no wise dependent on or affected by action, or inaction, on the part of the states or any of them.

∽⅋

Hawke v. Smith, 253 U.S. 221; 40 S. Ct. 495; 64 L. Ed. 871 (1920)

Facts—Hawke, a citizen of Ohio, sought to enjoin the secretary of state of Ohio from spending public money in preparing and printing ballots for a popular referendum on the ratification that the General Assembly had made of the proposed Eighteenth Amendment to the federal Constitution. The petition was sustained, and this judgment was affirmed by the Court of Appeals and Supreme Court of Ohio.

Question—Is the provision of the Ohio Constitution, extending the referendum to the ratification by the General Assembly of proposed amendments to the federal Constitution, in conflict with Article V of the Constitution of the United States?

Decision—Yes.

Reasons—*J. Day* (9–0). Article V of the federal Constitution says that "The Congress, whenever two-thirds of both Houses shall deem it necessary, shall propose Amendments to this Constitution, or, on the application of the legislatures of two-thirds of the several states, shall call a convention for proposing amendments, which, in either case, shall be valid . . . when ratified by the legislatures of three-fourths of the several states, or by conventions in three-fourths thereof. . . ." Article V is for the purpose of establishing an orderly manner in which changes in the Constitution can be accomplished. Ratification by a state of a constitutional amendment is not an act of legislation in the proper sense of the word. It is but an expression of the assent of the state to a proposed amendment. The power to legislate in the enactment of the laws of a state is derived from the people of the state, but the power to ratify a proposed amendment to the Constitution has its source in the federal Constitution. The act of ratification by the state derives its authority from the federal Constitution, to which the states and its people alike assent. The method of ratification is left to the choice of Congress. The determination of ratification is the exercise of a national power specifically granted by the Constitution. The language of Article V is plain. It is not the function of courts or legislative bodies, national or state, to alter methods that the Constitution has fixed.

Dillon v. Gloss, 256 U.S. 368; 41 S. Ct. 513; 65 L. Ed. 994 (1921)

Facts—Dillon was taken into custody under the National Prohibition Act of October 28, 1919 for transporting intoxicating liquor. He petitioned the court and sought to be discharged on a writ of habeas corpus from the court on grounds: (1) that the Eighteenth Amendment was invalid because the congressional resolution proposing the amendment declared that it should be inoperative unless ratified within seven years, and (2) that the act which he was charged with violating, and under which he was arrested, had not gone into effect at the time of the asserted violation nor at the time of the arrest. The Eighteenth Amendment was ratified January 16, 1919, but the secretary of state had not proclaimed its ratification until January 29, 1919. Dillon committed the violation on January 17, 1920. By the terms of the act it was to have gone into effect one year after being ratified. Dillon asserted it should have gone into effect one year after being proclaimed by the secretary of state, which would have been January 29, 1920.

Questions—(a) Can Congress set a reasonable time limit on the ratification of an amendment? (b) On what date does the ratification take effect?

Decisions—(a) Yes; (b) The day the last required state ratifies the amendment is the date the amendment becomes part of the Constitution.

Reasons—*J. Van Devanter* (9–0). (a) Article V discloses that it is intended to invest Congress with a wide range of power in proposing amendments. That the Constitution contains no express provision on the time limit for ratification is not in itself controlling, for with the Constitution, as with a statute or other written instruments, what is reasonably implied is as much a part of it as what is expressed. Proposal and ratification are but necessary steps in a single endeavor. There is a fair implication that ratification must be sufficiently contemporaneous in the required number of states to reflect the will of the people in all sections at relatively the same period, and hence that ratification must be within some reasonable time after the proposal.

The court held that Article V impliedly gives Congress a wide range of power in proposing amendments, and therefore a time limit of seven years for ratification is a reasonable use of this power.

(b) The Court held that the amendment takes effect the day the last state ratifies it, which is not necessarily the date when the secretary of state proclaims the amendment.

❦

Coleman v. Miller, 307 U.S. 433; 59 S. Ct. 972; 83 L. Ed. 1385 (1939)

Facts—In June 1924 Congress proposed the Child Labor Amendment. In January 1925 the legislature of Kansas adopted a resolution rejecting the proposed amendment, and sent a certified copy to the secretary of state of the United States. In January 1937 a resolution was introduced in the senate of Kansas ratifying the proposed amendment. There were forty senators, twenty in favor, and twenty rejecting it. The lieutenant governor, who presided over the Senate, cast his vote in favor of the resolution, which a majority of the members of the House of Representatives later adopted. Opponents challenged the right of the lieutenant governor to cast the deciding vote. They also challenged the vitality of the amendment, stating that a reasonable amount of time for ratification had elapsed.

Questions—(a) Can a state whose legislature has formally rejected a federal amendment later ratify it? (b) Do proposed amendments die of old age, if they remain before the states for too long a time?

Decisions—(a) The question of ratification in the light of previous rejection, or attempted withdrawal, should be regarded as a political question, with ultimate authority for its decision residing in Congress. (b) Congress, likewise, has the final say in the determination of whether or not an amendment has lost its vitality before the required ratifications.

Reasons—*C.J. Hughes* (7–2). The Court upheld, without considering the merits, the decision of the state supreme court that the lieutenant governor had the authority to break the tie.

Article V of the Constitution says nothing of rejection, but only of ratification. The power to ratify is conferred upon a state by the Constitution and persists even if previously rejected.

The political departments of the government dealt with previous rejection and attempted withdrawal in the adoption of the Fourteenth Amendment. Both were considered ineffectual in the presence of an actual ratification. This is a political question pertaining to the political departments, with final authority for the matter in the hands of Congress.

An amendment is not open for ratification for all time, since amendments are prompted by necessity. However, if Congress does not set a limit, as it did in the Eighteenth Amendment, the Court may not decide what constitutes a reasonable time. No criteria for a judicial determination of any kind of time limit exist in the Constitution.

Congress has the power under Article V to fix a reasonable time limit. If the time is not fixed in advance, it is open for determination at the time of promulgating the adoption of the amendment. This decision of Congress would not be subject to review by the Court. These questions are essentially political and are not justiciable.

Chapter Seven

PROPERTY RIGHTS

Contract Clause, Article I, Section 10;
Due Process Clause, Fifth and Fourteenth
Amendments; and Takings Clause, Fifth Amendment

John Locke, the English philosopher often most closely associated with the doctrine of classical liberalism on which the U.S. government was founded, put great emphasis on property rights, as did many of the American Framers. The United States continues to be as closely identified with a modified system of free enterprise, or capitalism, as it is with its form of democratic-republican government.

There are relatively few mentions of property rights within the U.S. Constitution. These include the prohibition in Article I, Section 10 prohibiting states from "impairing the obligation of contracts," the provision in the Fifth Amendment prohibiting the taking of property without just compensation, and the provisions in the Fifth and Fourteenth Amendments prohibiting the taking of "life, liberty, or property" without due process of law. These provisions have proved to be especially important during certain parts of U.S. history.

After the Court before him had decided in *Calder v. Bull* (1798) that the ex post facto clause applied only to criminal and not to civil matters, Chief Justice John Marshall broadly interpreted the contract clause during his tenure in office. In *Fletcher v. Peck* (1810), he extended this clause to include contracts to which state governments were parties, and in *Dartmouth College v. Woodward* (1819) he even extended this clause to include contracts entered into prior to the U.S. Constitution. Chief Justice Taney took a less restrictive view of the contract clause in *Charles River Bridge Co. v. Warren River Bridge* (1837) when he interpreted contracts so that any ambiguity benefited the state, and, at a time when the Court subsequently generally protected property rights via the due process clauses, the contracts clause fell into relative disuse and was almost nullified in *Home Building & Loan Association v. Blaisdell* (1934) before being partially revived in *United States Trust Company v. New Jersey* (1977) to deal with cases in which the state was attempting to modify a contract to which it was a party.

The primary purpose of the Fourteenth Amendment had been to secure the rights of former slaves and the Supreme Court rejected early attempts in the *Slaughterhouse Cases* (1873) and in *Munn v. Illinois* (1877) to apply this amendment to protect substantive economic rights. In *Santa Clara County v. Southern Pacific Railroad Co.* (1886), however, the Court declared that it considered corporations to be persons protected by the Fourteenth Amendment, and it was soon using this amendment more for the protection of property rights than for the protection of African Americans. Critics chided the Court for reading its own economic theories into the Constitution under the guise of substantive due process. The U.S. Supreme Court's decision in *Lochner v. New York* (1905) striking down a New York law regulating the hours of bakers marks the high point of such judicial intervention (and judicial activism). This activism continued through the early New Deal, during which time the Supreme Court invalidated a number of programs designed to regulate the economy. In 1937, in what some called "the switch in time that saved nine" because it is believed to have been in part a reaction to President Franklin D. Roosevelt's threat to "pack" the Supreme Court, the Court largely retreated from the idea that "liberty of contract" was absolute. The Court has subsequently proved to be fairly deferential to state and federal economic regulations, typically subjecting such legislation to its lowest level of scrutiny at the same time it has reviewed classifications dealing with race, gender, and fundamental rights with greater scrutiny. It is too early to tell whether recent decisions in *BMW of North America v. Gore* (1996) and *State Farm Insurance v. Campbell* (2003), both of which have used the due process clause to limit punitive damage awards, are responses to one specific issue or whether they represent a revival of substantive due process jurisprudence.

In recent years, there has been something of a revival of the "takings clause" of the Fifth Amendment. Although it does not use the specific words, this clause implicitly recognizes the government's right of eminent domain, that is, the right to take private property for public uses. It does so, however, while specifying that when the government engages in such taking, it must provide "just compensation." *Hawaii Housing Authority v. Midkiff* (1984) and *Kelo v. City of New London* (2005), demonstrate that the Court is generally willing to accept a broad interpretation of public purposes, but other recent cases demonstrate that the Court is insistent that government must pay when it takes private property for such public uses.

Other provisions of the Constitution involving congressional control over the coining of money, its power to tax and spend, and its power to regulate interstate and foreign commerce also relate to property rights. So does the Sixteenth Amendment permitting the income tax.

CONTRACT CLAUSE (ARTICLE 1, SECTION 10)

Calder v. Bull, 3 Dallas (3 U.S.) 386; 1 L. Ed. 648 (1798)

Facts—A dispute arose between Calder and his wife on one side and Bull and his wife on the other side concerning a right to property left by N. Morrison, a physician, in his will of March 1793. The Probate Court of Hartford rejected the will in question, and decided in favor of Calder and his wife. As a result of a law enacted in 1795 by the state legislature, a new hearing of the case, which was not allowed according to the old law, took place. This time the will involved in this case was approved, thus transferring the right of the property from Calder to Bull.

Question—Was this Connecticut statute permitting reconsideration of a will, a reconsideration previously not allowed by law, an ex post facto law?

Decision—No.

Reasons—*J. Chase* (4–0). Chase defined the term ex post facto law as contained in Article I, Section 10 of the Constitution as:

1. Every law that makes criminal an action done before the passing of the law and which was innocent when done, and punishes such an action.
2. Every law that aggravates a crime, or makes it greater than it was, when committed.
3. Every law that changes punishment, and inflicts a greater punishment, than the law annexed to the crime when committed.
4. Every law that alters the legal rules of evidence, and receives less or different testimony than the law required at the time of the commission of the offense, in order to convict the offender.

Thus a distinction must be made between retrospective laws and ex post facto laws. Likewise, ex post facto laws do not affect contracts, but only criminal or penal statutes.

❧

Fletcher v. Peck, 6 Cranch (10 U.S.) 87; 3 L. Ed. 162 (1810)

Facts—John Peck deeded to Robert Fletcher lands in the state of Georgia, which had been bought from the state of Georgia. The contract was executed in the form of a bill passed through the Georgia legislature in 1795, but it appears that most members had accepted bribes. The next legislature accordingly rescinded the act and took possession of the land. Fletcher sued Peck to regain the purchase price.

Question—Can one state legislature rescind an earlier state legislative grant of land that was an executed contract?

Decision—No.

Reasons—*C.J. Marshall* (5–0). A valid contract was executed. The state of Georgia was restrained either by general principles that are common to our free institutions or by particular provisions of the Constitution of the United States, from passing a law whereby the estate of the plaintiff in the premises so purchased could be constitutionally and legally impaired and rendered null and void. "One legislature is competent to repeal any act which a former legislature was competent to pass; and that one legislature cannot abridge the powers of a succeeding legislature." However, "if an act be done under a law, a succeeding legislature cannot undo it. . . . When, then, a law is in its nature a contract, when absolute rights have vested under that contract, a repeal of the law cannot divest those rights; and the act of annulling them, if legitimate, is rendered so by a power applicable to the case of every individual in the community."

Note—*Peck*, an unpopular decision, was the first case in which the Court held a state law contrary to the Constitution.

Trustees of Dartmouth College v. Woodward, 4 Wheaton (17 U.S.) 518; 4 L. Ed. 629 (1819)

Facts—In 1769 the English Crown chartered Dartmouth College. Later, in 1816, the state legislature of New Hampshire passed a law completely reorganizing the government of the college and changing the name to Dartmouth University. The old trustees of the college brought an action of trover (used in cases where a party is alleged to be wrongfully using the goods of another) against Woodward, who was secretary and treasurer of the college and had joined in the new university movement. He held the seal, records, and account books. The state decided against the old college trustees.

Question—(a) Does the Constitution protect a grant from the Crown, which preceded the Constitution, from state impairment? (b) Does the state act of 1816 impair the original charter, as contended by the old college trustees?

Decision—(a) Yes; (b) Yes.

Reasons—*C.J. Marshall* (5–1).

"This is plainly a contract to which the donors, the trustees, and the crown (to whose rights and obligations New Hampshire succeeds) were the original parties. It is a contract made on a valuable consideration. It is a contract for the security and disposition of property. . . . It is then a contract within the letter of the Constitution, and within its spirit also."

Corporations are designed to achieve a form of immortality for those who create them, and future donations may well depend on donors' beliefs that their money will continue to be directed where they want it to go. Dartmouth College was not a state institution but a private eleemosynary (charitable) institution.

The act of 1816 by the New Hampshire legislature gave the college a public and civil status, increased the number of trustees, and, therefore impaired the operations of the college as originally intended by the founders. The founders sought the charter in good faith, thus making a legally binding contract. Under the act of 1816, the charter as originally intended no longer existed. Thus the New Hampshire legislature violated the Constitution of the United States, and the act of 1816 was void.

Note—*Dartmouth* not only endorsed the sanctity of contracts for the college but also for business and corporate interests. Daniel Webster argued for the college from which he had graduated, by saying "It is, sir, . . . a small college, and yet there are those that love it."

❧

Charles River Bridge Co. v. Warren River Bridge, 11 Peters (36 U.S.) 420; 9 L. Ed. 773 (1837)

Facts—The Charles River Bridge Company brought action to stop the construction of the Warren River Bridge on the ground that the act authorizing its construction impaired the obligation of the contract between the Charles River Bridge Company and Massachusetts. The defendant received permission to erect another bridge of similar span within a few rods of the original bridge and was to give it to the state when paid for. The contention was that an original grant of ferry privileges to Harvard College in 1650 and a charter of 1785 incorporating the Proprietors of the Charles River Bridge (to which were transferred the rights of the college under the grant of 1650) constituted a contract whereby the plaintiffs were vested with an exclusive right to maintain a bridge "in that line of travel." Thus the Charles River Bridge Company implied that the privileges originally granted to Harvard College were transferred to them by means of the charter of 1785.

Question—Does the state grant of a charter to the Warren River Bridge Company violate its earlier charter with the Charles River Bridge Company?

Decision—No.

Reasons—*C.J. Taney* (5–2).

"If a contract on that subject can be gathered from the charter, it must be by implication, and cannot be found in the words used. . . . In charters of this description, no rights are taken from the public, or given to the corporation, beyond those which the words of the charter, by their natural and proper construction, purport to convey."

Implied privileges could prove to be unfavorable to the public and to the rights of the community; therefore it has always been the general operation of the Court to rule in favor of the public where an ambiguity exists in a contract between private enterprises and the public. Taney argued that his interpretation was more likely to promote progress as new forms of transportation superseded older ones, with which they would sometimes come into conflict. *J. Story* argued in dissent that the original monopoly granted to Harvard College remained implicit in the grant to the Charles River Bridge Company.

Note—Scholars often use this case to illustrate the change in the Court between the chief justiceships of John Marshall and Roger Taney. Whereas Marshall had stressed property rights, Taney was more interested in the rights of the majority.

Stone v. Mississippi, 101 U.S. 814; 25 L. Ed. 1079 (1880)

Facts—The legislature of Mississippi passed an act, approved February 16, 1867, entitled "An act incorporating the Mississippi Agricultural and Manufacturing Aid Society." Actually it was nothing but a lottery enterprise. The constitution of the state, adopted in convention May 15, 1868, and ratified by the people December 1, 1869, forbade the legislature to authorize any lottery. Criminal suit was brought against the lottery "society," which argued that it was operating under its charter.

Question—Did this state constitutional prohibition impair the obligation of contract?

Decision—No.

Reasons—*C.J. Waite* (8–0). Whether the contract existed depended on the authority of the legislature to bind the state and people of the state in this way in this case. A legislature cannot bargain away the police power of a state, which pertains to all matters affecting public health or morals. In their Constitution the people have expressed their wishes in this matter, so that no legislature can, by chartering a lottery company, defeat their wishes. The contracts protected by the Constitution are property rights, not governmental rights. Lotteries are a form of gambling, which can disturb a well-ordered community. The right to suppress them is governmental, and may be invoked at will. An arrangement like this "is a permit, good as against existing laws, but subject to future legislative and constitutional control or withdrawal."

Note—In general the contract clause cannot circumscribe the police power of the state. The general welfare takes precedence over the rights of individuals. Therefore, proper state legislation affecting contracts between individuals is valid. The contract clause has lost some of its force today in as much as what formerly was covered by it is now covered by the due process clause. In *United States Trust Company v. New Jersey*, 431 U.S. 1 (1977) the Court said the contract clause was "not a dead letter" but neither is it in fighting shape.

❧

Home Building and Loan Association v. Blaisdell, 290 U.S. 398; 54 S. Ct. 231; 78 L. Ed. 413 (1934)

Facts—The Home Building and Loan Association held a mortgage on the land of Blaisdell, which by reason of default, was foreclosed. Blaisdell appealed to the supreme court of Minnesota, which affirmed his claim on the grounds that "The Minnesota Mortgage Moratorium Law" provided that a party who is unable to pay or retire a mortgage at the date of redemption can, by petitioning the court, be granted a moratorium from foreclosure sales. The Home Building and Loan Association appealed to the Supreme Court of the United States.

Question—(a) Is the act contrary to the due process and equal protection clauses of the Fourteenth Amendment? (b) Does it violate the contract clause of the Constitution?

Decisions—(a) No; (b) No.

Reasons—*C.J. Hughes* (5–4). A law impairs the obligations of a contract when the law renders them invalid or releases or extinguishes them. Here the integrity of the mortgage indebtedness was not impaired; interest continued to run, the mortgagor was to pay the rental value of the premises as ascertained in judicial proceedings. The obligation remained.

Also, not only are existing laws read into contracts in order to fix obligations as between the parties, but the reservation of essential attributes of sovereign power is also read into contracts as a postulate of the legal order. This power—called the police power—is paramount to any right under contracts between individuals. "An emergency existed in Minnesota which furnished a proper occasion for the exercise of the reserved power of the state to protect the vital interests of the community."

In dissent, *J. Sutherland* emphasized his view that the Constitution did not change in times of emergency and that it should be interpreted without reference to the economic depression then in existence.

⊙⅗⅄

United States Trust Co. v. New Jersey, 431 U.S. 1; 97 S. Ct. 1505; 52 L. Ed. 2d 92 (1977)

Facts—New York and New Jersey entered into a covenant in 1962 agreeing that so long as bonds remained unpaid and outstanding, the Port Authority would not use bonds or resources for other than pledged purposes. In 1973, the states modified this agreement, which they then repealed in 1974, in order to direct funding to public transportation, partly in light of the emerging energy crisis. The New Jersey Superior Court and the New Jersey Supreme Court upheld this change.

Question—Did New Jersey's and New York's modification of an earlier covenant violate the contract clause in Article I, Section 10 of the Constitution?

Decision—Yes.

Reasons—*J. Blackmun* (4–3, two justices not participating). After a long review of the history of the Port Authority, Blackmun noted that the terms of the covenant it entered in 1962 were "self-evident." Despite such terms, the states attempted to repeal the covenant. Although the contract clause was important early in the nation's history, its use as a means of protecting property has largely been superseded by the Fourteenth Amendment. *Home Building and Loan Association v. Blaisdell*, 290 U.S. 398 (1934) and *El Paso v. Simmons*, 379 U.S. 497 (1965) are typical of modern cases on the clause which is no longer applied rigidly. Still, "Whether or not the protection of contract rights comports with current views of wise public policy, the Contract Clause remains part of our written Constitution." The trial court found a technical impairment of the contract clause in this case, but, as long as the clause is interpreted in light of state police powers, this is but a "preliminary step" in determining whether such an impairment is reasonable. The contract clause limits state modifications of private contracts, but it also limits modifications of its own. Past decisions have established that states cannot use the contract clause to surrender essential attributes of their sovereignty. In this case, the states' limitations were "purely financial," and did not compromise state powers. Alterations of contracts require greater scrutiny when "the State's self-interest is at stake." Although the states cite the need for mass transportation, energy conservation, and environmental concerns, total repeal of the contract was not needed to achieve these goals, which would have reasonably been foreseen when the contract was executed. The contract clause prohibits such repeal.

C.J. Burger, concurring, argued that a state could repeal a contract it entered only if it showed this to be "essential to the achievement of an important state purpose."

J. Brennan argued in dissent that "by creating a constitutional safe haven for property rights embodied in a contract, the decision substantially distorts modern constitutional jurisprudence governing regulation of private economic interests." He contended that the majority decision unduly limited the power of modern elected officials to represent their constituents. He further argued that the majority decision was in conflict with "judicial restraint." He believed that the financial welfare of bondholders could be adequately protected both "by the political processes and the bond market place itself."

⁂

DUE PROCESS (ECONOMIC) AND FREEDOM OF CONTRACT (FIFTH AND FOURTEENTH AMENDMENTS)

Slaughterhouse Cases, 16 Wallace (83 U.S.) 36; 21 L. Ed. 394 (1873)

Facts—These cases arose under a measure that the Louisiana legislature enacted in 1869. The act, motivated by genuine health concerns and by political corruption, regulated the business of slaughtering livestock in New Orleans. It required that such activities for the city and for a vast surrounding area should be restricted to a small section below the city of New Orleans, and provided that the slaughtering should be done in the houses of one corporation. This virtually granted a monopoly, even though the corporation was required to permit other butchers to have access to their facilities on payment of a reasonable fee.

Question—Did Louisiana's regulation of the butchers of New Orleans deny rights under the Thirteenth and Fourteenth Amendments?

Decision—No.

Reasons—*J. Miller* (5–4). The three post–Civil War amendments (the Thirteenth through Fifteenth) disclosed a unity of purpose: the achievement of the freedom of the slave race, the security and firm establishment of that freedom, and the protection of the new freedmen and citizens from oppression by their former owners. The Court held that the rights of others were not impaired because these amendments did not speak of the rights of citizens of the states. The Court drew a sharp distinction between the rights that were derived from state citizenship and those that were derived from citizenship of the United States. The Court held that citizens derived most civil rights from state citizenship rather than from national privileges and immunities, which the Court interpreted as being quite limited in scope. The majority believed that a more expansive view of the language of the Fourteenth Amendment, and especially the privileges and immunities clause, would be unjustified absent more specific constitutional language.

Dissenting justices argued for an expansive view of the Fourteenth Amendment, and especially the privileges and immunities clause. They argued that if the majority view of the amendment were accepted, the Fourteenth Amendment "was a vain and idle enactment, which accomplished nothing and most unnecessarily excited Congress and the people on its passage" (*J. Field's* language). The dissenters were, however, more interested in establishing economic rights than they were in expanding the rights of newly freed slaves.

Note—The *Slaughterhouse Cases* were decided only five years after the ratification of the Fourteenth Amendment (1868) and were the first interpretation of the amendment. The Court's narrow restriction of the privileges and immunities clause continues to this day.

⊘⅞

Munn v. Illinois, 94 U.S. 113; 24 L. Ed. 77 (1877)

Facts—Ira Y. Munn, et al., were grain warehousemen in Chicago, Illinois, and were sued by Illinois for transacting business without a state license in violation of a state statute that provided a maximum of charges for the storage of grain in a warehouse. The defendants admitted the facts charged, but alleged that the statute requiring said license was unconstitutional for attempting to fix that maximum rate of storage, on the ground that it was repugnant to the Constitution, which confers upon Congress the power to regulate commerce with foreign states and among the several states.

Question—Can the General Assembly of Illinois, under the limitations upon the legislative powers of the states imposed by the Constitution, fix by law regulations for the storage of grain in warehouses at Chicago and other places in the state?

Decision—Yes.

Reasons—*C.J. Waite* (7–2). The Court reasoned that it has always been an established principle that where members of the public have a definite and positive interest in a business, they have a right to regulate the operations of that business. The Court held that such was the case here, and it did not matter that these plaintiffs had built their warehouses and established their business before the regulations complained of were adopted. What they did was from the beginning always subject to possible regulations promoting the common good. They entered upon their business and provided themselves with the means to carry it on, subject to this condition. If they did not wish to submit themselves to such interference, they should not have clothed the public with an interest in their concerns. "Property does become clothed with a public interest when used in a manner to make it of public consequence, and affect the community at large. When, therefore, one devotes his property to a use in which the public has an interest, he, in effect, grants to the public an interest in the use, and must submit to be controlled by the public for the common good, to the extent of the interest he has thus created. He may withdraw his grant by discontinuing the use; but so long as he maintains the use, he must submit to the control. We know that this is a power which may be abused; but that is no argument against its existence. For protection against abuses by legislatures the people must resort to the polls, not to the courts."

In a strong dissenting opinion, *J. Field* argued that declaring a business to be in the public interest did not make it so, especially in the absence of any state-granted right or privilege. He thought the regulation was a restriction of property rights in violation of due process rights (what would become known as substantive due process) of the Fourteenth Amendment.

Santa Clara County v. Southern Pacific Railroad Company, 118 U.S. 394; 6 S. Ct. 1132; 30 L. Ed. 118 (1886)

Facts—California brought action against the Southern Pacific and other railroad companies for taxes and interest on taxes assessed on their property within the state. A U.S. Circuit Court had voided these taxes.

Significantly, as a relatively early interpretation of the Fourteenth Amendment, this case focused on the protection of property rights rather than on discrimination based on race. In the briefs, counsel for the railroads argued that "Corporations are persons within the meaning of the Fourteenth Amendment to the Constitution of the United States." According to Court records, prior to the oral argument, *C.J. Waite* announced that the Court would not consider the question "whether the provision in the Fourteenth Amendment to the Constitution which forbade a state to deny to any person within its jurisdiction the equal protection of the Constitution, applied to these corporations. We are all of the opinion that it does."

Question—(a) Are corporations considered to be persons under the Fourteenth Amendment? (b) Did California's taxation of railroad property violate the equal protection of law under the Fourteenth Amendment?

Decision—(a) Yes; (b) Yes.

Reasons—*J. Harlan* (9–0). The Court argued that the commission that assessed taxes on the railroad grouped such property with surrounding fences and other property that the commission had no legal authority to assess. The assessments were not separable and therefore constituted a denial of equal protection of the laws. The railroads were not liable for the taxes.

Holden v. Hardy, 169 U.S. 366; 18 S. Ct. 383; 42 L. Ed. 780 (1898)

Facts—Utah enacted an eight-hour day for workmen in underground mines, smelters, and similar places for the reduction of ore and metals, except in the event of an emergency. Violation of the statute was made a misdemeanor. Plaintiff in error was convicted of employing men contrary to the terms of the statute. He challenged the validity of the statute upon the ground of an alleged violation of the Fourteenth Amendment, in that it abridged the privileges or immunities of citizens of the United States, deprived both the employer and the laborer of his property without due process of law, and denied to them the equal protection of the laws.

Question—Is the Utah law regulating the hours of work for miners and similar dangerous occupations constitutional?

Decision—Yes.

Reasons—*J. Brown* (7–2). The Court reasoned that the act was a valid exercise of the police power of the state. The enactment did not profess to limit the hours of all workmen, but merely those who are employed in underground mines, or in the smelting, reduction, or refining of ores and metals. These employments, when too long pursued, the legislature has judged to be detrimental to the health of the employees, and so long as there are reasonable grounds for believing that this is so, its decision upon this subject cannot be set aside by the federal courts.

    J. Brewer and *J. Peckham* dissented without writing a formal opinion.

Note—Despite *Holden* and *Muller v. Oregon* (1908), upholding a ten-hour workday law applying to women in industry, and *Munn v. Illinois*, 94 U.S. 113 (1877), fixing rates in Chicago grain elevators, the Court generally followed the principles of substantive due process well into the 1930s.

⁂

Lochner v. New York, 198 U.S. 45; 25 S. Ct. 539; 49 L. Ed. 937 (1905)

Facts—A New York statute forbade any employee in a bakery of confectionery establishment to be permitted to work over sixty hours in any one week, or an average of over ten hours a day. Lochner was convicted in Utica of requiring and permitting an employee to work more than sixty hours in one week.

Question—Does this statute regulating the hours of bakers violate the Fourteenth Amendment?

Decision—Yes.

Reasons—*J. Peckham* (5–4). The right of an individual to make a contract with regard to his labor is part of the liberty of the individual protected by the Fourteenth Amendment. The right to purchase or sell labor is also part of this liberty, unless there are circumstances that exclude the right. Against these rights we have the police powers of the states, which under certain conditions may impose restrictions on the exercise of those rights. At times it is of great importance to determine which shall prevail—the right of the individual to labor for such a time as he may choose, or the right of the state to prevent an individual from laboring beyond a certain time prescribed by the state.

If this is a valid exercise of state police power, it involves the question of health. The Court held that there was no reasonable foundation for holding that this statute was necessary to safeguard the public health, or the health of bakers in general. The trade of a baker, while not the healthiest of occupations, does not affect health to such a degree that the legislature is warranted in interfering. At that rate, no trade or occupation would be able to escape acts of the legislature restricting the hours of labor.

The statute in question, the Court held, was an illegal interference in the rights of individuals, both employers and employees, for reasons entirely arbitrary. The Court was of the opinion that the only purpose of the act was to regulate the hours of labor in an occupation that is not dangerous in any degree to morals, nor in any substantial way injurious to health. This freedom to contract in relation to employment cannot be interfered with except by violating the Constitution.

J. Holmes and *J. Harlan* authored dissents arguing that the Court had extended the doctrine of freedom of contract too far. In a reference to a contemporary sociologist who was frequently cited by advocates of laissez-faire economics, Holmes observed that "the Fourteenth Amendment does not enact Mr. Herbert Spencer's Social Statics."

Note—Critics of judicial activism, and of substantive due process, often cite this case as a cautionary tale about such activism.

༄྅

Muller v. Oregon, 208 U.S. 412; 28 S. Ct. 324; 52 L. Ed. 551 (1908)

Facts—An Oregon statute made illegal the employment of women in any mechanical establishment, factory, or laundry for more than ten hours during the day. Muller was convicted and fined for violating this statute in his laundry.

Question—Is the Oregon statute constitutional?

Decision—Yes.

Reasons—*J. Brewer* (9–0). In *Lochner v. New York* (1905), the Court held that a law prohibiting a man from working more than ten hours a day was an unreasonable and arbitrary interference with his liberty to contract in relation to labor. A woman's physical well-being "becomes an object of public interest and care in order to preserve the strength and vigor of the race" and thus justifies the "special legislation restricting or qualifying the conditions under which she should be permitted to toil." The two sexes differ. This difference justifies a difference in legislation.

Note—In *Muller* Louis D. Brandeis, counsel for Oregon and a future Supreme Court justice, introduced what came to be known as the "Brandeis Brief"—a brief-preparing style that emphasized economics and sociology rather than precedent.

Bunting v. Oregon, 243 U.S. 426; 37 S. Ct. 435; 61 L. Ed. 830 (1917)

Facts—A statute of Oregon required that any person employed in a mill, factory, or manufacturing establishment should not work more than ten hours a day, except for necessary repairs, or in an emergency. However, an additional three hours could be spent, but with payment of time and one-half for the overtime period. Bunting employed a man named Hammersly for thirteen hours one day, with no payment for overtime.

Question—Does this statute limiting the hours of work violate the Fourteenth Amendment?

Decision—No.

Reasons—*J. McKenna* (5–3). The Court held that this was a valid extension of state police power. The state found that it was injurious to men to work longer than ten hours in the types of establishments mentioned. This was not a wage law (which would have been in violation of the state constitution), since no attempt was made to fix standard wages, which were left to the contracting parties. The provision for overtime was simply for the purpose of giving an additional reason for not working overtime. This was adequate reasoning for the legislative judgment in this case.

"But we need not cast about for reasons for the legislative judgment. We are not required to be sure of the precise reasons for its exercise, or be convinced of the wisdom of its exercise. It is enough for our decision if the legislation under review was passed in the exercise of an admitted power of government."

The dissenters did not write an opinion.

Adkins v. Children's Hospital, 261 U.S. 525; 43 S. Ct. 394; 67 L. Ed. 785 (1923)

Facts—The Minimum Wage Act of 1918 provided for the creation in the District of Columbia of a Minimum Wage Board. The board was authorized to investigate and ascertain the wages of women and minors and to set up standard minimum wages, which employers were forbidden to lower. The Children's Hospital employed several women at less than the minimum wage fixed by the board. Through the action of the Minimum Wage Board, these women lost their jobs. They were satisfied with their pay and working conditions. The women brought suit seeking to enjoin the enforcement of the minimum wage law and to permit the taking of whatever jobs they desired.

Question—Does the Minimum Wage Act violate the due process clause of the Fifth Amendment?

Decision—Yes.

Reasons—*J. Sutherland* (5–3). The right to contract about one's affairs is part of the liberty of the individual protected by the Fifth Amendment. There is no such thing as absolute freedom of contract, but freedom is the rule and restraint is the exception. The statute in question is simply a price-fixing law forbidding two parties to contract in respect to the price for which one shall render service to the other.

In distinguishing this decision from others allowing for the regulation of the hours of employment, Sutherland distinguished between "incidents of employment having no necessary effect upon the heart of the contract, that is, the amount of wages to be paid and received."

The price fixed by the board has no relation to the capacity and earning power of the employee, the number of hours worked, the character of the place or the circumstances or surroundings involved, but is based solely on the presumption of what is necessary to provide a living for a woman and preserve her health and morals.

The law considers the necessities of one party only. It ignores the necessities of the employer by not considering whether the employee is capable of earning the sum. If the police power of a state may justify the fixing of a minimum wage, it may later be invoked to justify a maximum wage, which is power widened to a dangerous degree. To uphold individual freedom is not to strike down the common good, but to further it by the prevention of arbitrary restraint upon the liberty of its members.

C.J. Taft and *J. Holmes* authored dissents. Taft saw the legislation as a way of preventing the evils of "the sweating system." Holmes further questioned the "dogma" of "freedom of contract."

Note—The Supreme Court reversed *Adkins* in *West Coast Hotel Co. v. Parrish* (1937).

⌖

Nebbia v. New York, 291 U.S. 502; 54 S. Ct. 505; 78 L. Ed. 940 (1934)

Facts—Nebbia, the proprietor of a grocery store in Rochester, New York, was convicted of violating an order of the New York Milk Control Board fixing the selling price of milk by selling two quarts of milk and a loaf of bread for 18¢, whereas the board had fixed the price of a quart of milk at 9¢. The New York Court of Appeals rejected Nebbia's argument that the order and the statute authorizing the order contravene the equal protection and due process clauses of the Fourteenth Amendment.

Question—Does a state violate the Fourteenth Amendment when it fixes the minimum and maximum prices of articles such as milk?

Decision—No.

Reasons—*J. Roberts* (5–4). The milk industry in New York has been the subject of long-standing and drastic regulation in the public interest. Unrestricted competition in this industry aggravated existing evils, and the normal law of supply and demand was inadequate to correct maladjustments detrimental to the community. An inquiry disclosed the trade practices that resulted in retail price-cutting, which reduced the income of the farmer below the cost of production. In light of this, the price fixing of the control board appeared not to be unreasonable, arbitrary, or without relation to the purpose of preventing ruthless competition from destroying the wholesale price structure on which the farmer depends for his livelihood and the community for an assured supply of milk.

The milk industry is of vital public interest since milk is a basic food in our diet, and the legislature of New York, realizing this, passed this law to safeguard the public interest. The Constitution does not secure to anyone the liberty to conduct his business in such a fashion as to inflict injury upon the public at large or a substantial group of the public.

"The phrase 'affected with a public interest' can, in the nature of things, mean no more than that an industry, for adequate reason, is subject to control for the public good. . . . So far as the requirement of due process is concerned, and in the absence of other constitutional restriction, a state is free to adopt whatever economic policy may reasonably be deemed to promote public welfare, and to enforce that policy by legislation adapted to its purpose. If the laws passed are seen to have a reasonable relation to a proper legislative purpose, and are neither arbitrary nor discriminatory, the requirements of due process are satisfied. . . . Times without number we have said that the Legislature is primarily the judge of the necessity of such an enactment, that every possible presumption is in favor of its validity, and that though the court may hold views inconsistent with the wisdom of the law, it may not be annulled unless palpably in excess of legislative power."

In dissent, *J. McReynolds* described this law as an arbitrary interference with due process and feared that the emergency rationale was being used to undermine long-standing constitutional rights.

Morehead v. New York ex rel. Tipaldo, 298 U.S. 587; 56 S. Ct. 918; 80 L. Ed. 1347 (1936)

Facts—Tipaldo was sent to jail upon the charge that, as manager of a laundry, he failed to obey the mandatory order of the state industrial commissioner of New York, prescribing minimum wages for women employees. Some of the employees were receiving less than the minimum wages established by the state industrial commissioner.

Question—Can a state fix minimum wages for women?

Decision—No.

Reasons—*J. Butler* (5–4). It was claimed that this case differed from the *Adkins* case in which such legislation was declared unconstitutional, in that here the minimum wage was prescribed in cases where the given wage was less than the fair and reasonable value of the services rendered and insufficient to meet the minimum cost of living necessary for health. This did not, however, change the principle of the case, namely, the exercise of legislative power to fix wages. The act left employers and men employees free to agree upon wages, but deprived employers and adult women of the same freedom. Likewise, women were restrained by the minimum wage in competition with men and were arbitrarily deprived of employment and a fair chance to find work. State legislation fixing wages for women is repugnant to the due process clause of the Fourteenth Amendment.

C.J. Hughes and *J. Stone* authored dissents both questioning the majority's continuing emphasis on freedom of contract in the face of possible exploitation of employees.

Note—Morehead was reversed by *West Coast Hotel Co. v. Parrish* (1937), a year later, when Justice Roberts switched positions, "the switch in time that saved nine," and took the starch out of President Roosevelt's "court packing" attempt to increase the number of justices to fifteen and appoint new judges who were more sympathetic to his policies.

಄ৡ

Lincoln Federal Labor Union No. 19129, American Federation of Labor, et al., v. Northwestern Iron and Metal Co., et al., 335 U.S. 525; 69 S. Ct. 251; 93 L. Ed. 212 (1949)

Facts—North Carolina made it unlawful for an employer to refuse employment to or to discharge anyone because of membership or nonmembership in a labor union, or for a labor organization and an employer to enter into a contract for a closed or union shop. An employer and officers of a labor union were convicted of a misdemeanor for entering into such a contract.

Question—Do these right-to-work laws violate rights guaranteed employers, unions, and their members by the U.S. Constitution?

Decision—No.

Reasons—*J. Black* (9–0). Neither the due process clause nor the equal protection clause prohibits the states from outlawing closed or union shop agreements. The constitutional right of workers to assemble to discuss and formulate plans for the furthering of their own interest in jobs cannot be construed as a constitutional guarantee that none shall get and hold jobs except those who join in such plans. Where conduct affects the interest of others and the general public, the legality of that conduct must be measured by whether the conduct conforms to valid laws.

The liberty of contracts protected by the Fourteenth Amendment is not unqualified. Due process does not forbid a state to pass laws designed to safeguard the opportunity of nonunion members to get and hold jobs, free from discrimination because they are not members of a union. The Court rejected the earlier due process philosophy of the cases and returned to the even earlier philosophy that the states have the power to legislate against what are found to be injurious practices in their internal commercial and business affairs, so long as their laws do not run afoul of some specific federal constitutional prohibition or some valid federal law. "Under this constitutional doctrine the due process clause is no longer to be so broadly construed that the Congress and state legislatures are put in a strait jacket when they attempt to suppress business and industrial conditions which they regard as offensive to the public welfare. Just as we have held that the due process clause erects no obstacle to block legislative protection of union members, we now hold that legislative protection can be afforded non-union workers."

Note—In a decision involving labor and food stamps, the Court held that Congress could withhold food stamps from a household of strikers without violating the First and Fifth Amendments *Lyng v. International Union, United Automobile, Aerospace, and Agricultural Implement Workers of America*, 485 U.S. 360 (1988). In still another important decision affecting labor, the Court held that a union is not permitted to solicit and extract dues from nonunion members for activities not related to labor-management bargaining *Communication Workers v. Beck*, 487 U.S. 735 (1988).

❧

Giboney v. Empire Storage & Ice Co., 336 U.S. 490; 69 S. Ct. 684; 93 L. Ed. 834 (1949)

Facts—The ice peddlers union of Kansas City, Missouri, sought to unionize all ice vendors in the city through an agreement with the ice wholesalers to refuse the sale of ice to nonunion peddlers. All but the Empire Ice Company agreed. The union proceeded to set up picket lines around the Empire Company's place of business and threatened union members with the loss of their cards if they crossed the picket line. The avowed purpose of the picketing was to compel the Empire Company to stop selling ice to nonunion peddlers. A Missouri statute prohibited competing dealers and their aiders and abettors from combining to restrain the freedom of trade.

Question—Does Missouri have paramount constitutional power over a labor union to regulate and govern the manner in which certain trade practices shall be carried on within the state of Missouri?

Decision—Yes.

Reasons—*J. Black* (9–0). The Court ruled that the Missouri statute regulated trade one way, and the union adopted a program to regulate trade another way. The state had provided for enforcement of its statutory rule by imposing civil and criminal sanctions. The union had provided for enforcement of its rule by sanctions against union members who crossed picket lines. The purpose of the statute was to prevent trust combinations such as the union sought to compel the Empire Company to enter. The constitutional power to prevent such combinations by a state is beyond question.

"The conditions developed in industry may be such that those engaged in it cannot continue their struggle without danger to the community. But it is not for judges to determine whether such conditions exist, nor is it their function to set the limits of permissible contest and to declare the duties which the new situation demands. This is the function of the legislature which, while limiting individual and group rights of aggression and defense, may substitute processes of justice for the more primitive method of trial by combat."

The state's power to govern in this field is paramount, and nothing in the constitutional guarantees of speech or press compels a state to apply or not to apply its antitrade restraint law to groups of workers, businessmen, or others.

BMW of North America, Inc. v. Gore, 517 U.S. 559; 116 S. Ct. 1589; 134 L. Ed. 2d 809 (1996)

Facts—Nine months after purchasing a new BMW car for just over $40,000, Dr. Ira Gore Jr. discovered that the car had been repainted. BMW had not revealed this to him or the dealer because it had a policy not to disclose damage in manufacturing or shipping that amounted to less than 3 percent of the car's value, and the cost of repainting the car had been just over $600. Gore received a judgment from an Alabama jury for $4,000 in compensatory damages (its estimate of the discount that the dealer would have had to give in order to sell the car if its damage had been revealed), and $4 million in punitive damages, an amount the Alabama Supreme Court later reduced to $2 million.

Question—Is the punitive damage award in this case so excessive as to constitute a denial of due process rights under the Fifth and Fourteenth Amendments?

Decision—Yes.

Reasons—*J. Stevens* (5–4). A state may utilize punitive damages to punish unlawful conduct and deter its repetition. Awards need not be uniform from state to state, and no state has the power to impose its own views on the subject on others. To the extent the original $4 million award was calculated on the basis of the total number of damaged cars sold throughout the United States, the Alabama Supreme Court correctly invalidated it. Due process requires fair notice. In this case, the Alabama award, even when reduced, exceeded three guideposts, namely, "the degree of reprehensibility of the nondisclosure; the disparity between the harm or potential harm suffered by Dr. Gore and his punitive damages award; and the difference between this remedy and the civil penalties authorized or imposed in comparable cases." As to reprehensibility, the damages suffered were "purely economic in nature," and were not treated severely in other states. Even the reduced award amounted to a 500 to 1 ratio between compensatory and punitive damages, whereas other cases appeared to range from 4 to 1 to 10 to 1. Comparable maximum fines for such behavior ranged from $5,000 to $10,000. Although unwilling to draw "a bright line marking the limits of a constitutionally acceptable punitive damages award," this case clearly "transcends the constitutional limit."

J. Breyer's concurrence classified the judgment in this case as an example of "arbitrary coercion" and argued that Alabama had not in fact followed rules designed to channel such arbitrary discretion.

J. Scalia's dissent viewed this decision as a resurrection of "substantive due process" that improperly intruded into state powers without giving states adequate guidance.

J. Ginsburg's dissent classified the majority decision as presenting "only a vague concept of substantive due process, a 'raised eyebrow' test." Ginsburg further questioned the wisdom of the U.S. Supreme Court attempting to patrol such an area on its own.

∾৵⋕

State Farm Mutual Auto Insurance Company v. Campbell, 538 U.S. 408 123 S. Ct. 1513; 155 L. Ed. 2d 585

Facts—Curtis Campbell was driving in Cache County, Utah, when Curtis decided to pass six vans. Todd Ospital, approaching from the other direction, swerved off the road to avoid a crash and was killed while disabling Robert Shusher. Although Campbell's fault was generally acknowledged, his insurance company, State Farm, contested the $50,000 judgments sought by Ospital's estate and Shusher. A jury subsequently returned a verdict of over $185,000, but State Farm refused to cover more than $50,000, even though the company had previously told Campbell that he would not be liable for money if the case were lost at trial. State Farm was pursuing a policy to keep its claims down. Slusher, Ospital, and Campbell subsequently pursued a bad faith claim against State Farm. Over time a jury awarded $2.6 million in compensatory damages and $145 million in punitive damages. The trial court reduced these awards to $1 million and $25 million, but the Utah Supreme Court reinstated them, and the case was appealed to the U.S. Supreme Court.

Question—Did the $145 million punitive damage award in this case violate the due process clause of the Fourteenth Amendment?

Decision—Yes.

Reasons—*J. Kennedy* (6–3). Compensatory damages and punitive damages serve differing functions. The first is designed to repay concrete losses, but the second serves broader functions. "The Due Process Clause of the Fourteenth Amendment prohibits the imposition of grossly excessive or arbitrary punishments on a tortfeasor." Excessive punitive damages "pose an acute danger of arbitrary deprivation of property." Kennedy applied the standards of *BMW of North America, Inc., v. Gore*, 517 U.S. 559 (1996), and concluded that the punitive damages were excessive. The case required courts to look first at "the degree of reprehensibility of the defendant's conduct." Although "State Farm's handling of the claims against the Campbells merits no praise," this case was used not simply to punish the company for what it did in this case but "to expose, and punish, the perceived deficiencies of State Farm's operations throughout the country." Moreover, in some states, this conduct was not even illegal. "The courts awarded punitive damages to punish and deter conduct that bore no relation to the Campbells' harm." In *BMW v. Gore*, the Court was reluctant "to identify constitutional limits on the ratio between harm, or potential harm, to the plaintiff and the punitive damages award," but "in practice, few awards exceeding a single-digit ratio between punitive and compensatory damages, to a significant degree, will satisfy due process." In this case, State Farm's actions resulted in no physical injuries, and the award was both unreasonable and disproportionate. *BMW v. Gore* suggested that the Court should examine any disparities between punitive damages and "civil penalties authorized or imposed in comparable cases." Had State Farm been convicted of fraud, the maximum penalty would have been $10,000. "The punitive award of $145 million, therefore, was neither reasonable nor proportionate to the wrong committed, and it was an irrational and arbitrary deprivation of the property of the defendant."

J. Scalia, dissenting, argued that the due process clause "provides no substantive protections against 'excessive' or 'unreasonable' awards of punitive damages," and that because "*BMW v. Gore* is insusceptible of principled application," he did not regard it as binding precedent

J. Thomas, dissenting, also denied that the Constitution was designed to constrain the size of punitive damage awards. This was "territory traditionally within the States' domain." Although the issue might be an appropriate subject for legislative action, there is plenty of evidence in this case to suggest that State Farm's behavior was highly reprehensible and there was no reason that the state of Utah should have to exclude evidence of out-of-state actions in coming to its conclusions.

TAKINGS CLAUSE (FIFTH AMENDMENT)

Village of Euclid, Ohio, v. Ambler Realty Co., 272 U.S. 365; 47 S. Ct. 114; 71 L. Ed. 303 (1926)

Facts—Appellee owned land within Euclid, Ohio. The village of Euclid passed a zoning law restricting the use of land to residential purposes. The Ambler Realty Company was holding it for industrial use because of its location and the resultant much higher value of the land than if used for residential lots.

Question—Did the zoning ordinance take the company's property without due process of law contrary to the Fourteenth Amendment?

Decision—No.

Reasons—*J. Sutherland* (6–3). The zoning ordinance is a valid exercise of the state's police power under which the state has the authority to abate a nuisance. Actually a nuisance may be merely a right thing in a wrong place. Noise, traffic, fire hazards, and the general desirability of an area for "residential" purposes, including the rearing of children, certainly come under the power of the state and its agencies to care for the public safety, health, morals, and general welfare. Concern for the common good may properly override an individual's property rights.

The dissenting justices did not author an opinion in this case.

Note—*Ambler* is often remembered for Sutherland's sassy remark: "A nuisance may merely be a right thing in the wrong place, like a pig in the parlor instead of the barnyard." In *City of Renton v. Playtime Theatres,* 475 U.S. 41 (1986) the Court upheld a zoning law prohibiting an adult movie house from locating within 1,000 feet of a park, school, or residential home.

❧

Hawaii Housing Authority v. Midkiff, 467 U.S. 229; 104 S. Ct. 2321; 81 L. Ed. 2d 186 (1984)

Facts—In Hawaii 40 percent of the land was owned by state and national governments, and seventy-two private landowners held title to 47 percent of the remaining land. This system dated back to Hawaii's feudal land tenure system in which land was controlled by chiefs and sub-chiefs and resulted in high land prices. Owners of land did not want to sell in part because of adverse tax consequences. In part to allay such consequences, Hawaii adopted the Land Reform Act of 1967 enabling the state to use its power of eminent domain to buy property where sufficient numbers of tenants indicated their desire to buy. After purchasing the property, the state would then sell it back to the former lessees. The U.S. District Court upheld most provisions of the law, but the U.S. Ninth Circuit Court of Appeals, with one judge dissenting, ruled that the law violated the public use provision of the Fifth Amendment.

Question—Does the Hawaii Land Reform Act of 1967 violate the public use provision of the takings clause of the Fifth Amendment as applied to the states by the Fourteenth?

Decision—No.

Reasons—*J. O'Connor* (8–0). After deciding that federal courts had not abused their discretion by intervening in this case, O'Connor cited *Berman v. Parker*, 348 U.S. 26 (1954), upholding the District of Columbia Redevelopment [slum-clearance] Act of 1945, as indicating that "The 'public use' requirement is . . . coterminous with the scope of a sovereign's police powers," and that the role of courts in overseeing such powers should be minimal. Although Hawaii was selling land it had condemned to private individuals, it was doing so in an attempt to remedy the problems of land oligopoly traceable to Hawaii's feudal origins. Successful or not, the law clearly fell within the ambit of state police powers. The public use requirement does not require "that condemned property by put into use for the general public," but only that the state's purpose be on behalf of the general public.

❦

Dolan v. City of Tigard, 512 U.S. 374; 114 S. Ct. 2309; 129 L. Ed. 304 (1994)

Facts—The city of Tigard, Oregon, conditioned its approval of a building permit to expand a plumbing and electric supply store on Dolan's willingness to give land adjoining a creek to the city for a public greenway and for the construction of a bicycle path. The Land Use Board of Appeals, the Oregon Court of Appeals, and the Oregon Supreme Court all upheld these conditions.

Question—Do these conditions violate the takings clause of the Fifth Amendment as applied to the states by the Fourteenth?

Decision—Yes.

Reasons—*C.J. Rehnquist* (5–4). The takings clause prohibits the taking of private property without just compensation. Requiring public access denies an individual a critical element of property rights, namely, the right to exclude others. Court decisions have long recognized the authority of states and localities to engage in land-use planning. Previous cases, however, have involved legislative classifications of "entire areas of the city" and did not require those being regulated to give their land to the government. At issue is whether there is an "essential nexus" between a legitimate state interest and the condition it imposes. In *Nollan v. California Coastal Commission*, 483 U.S. 825 (1987), the Court found such a nexus to be lacking. Here there is a connection between the city's desire to control flooding and its restriction on Dolan, but the Court must still examine "whether the degree of the exactions demanded by the city's permit conditions bears the required relationship to the projected impact of petitioner's proposed development." State cases have developed a number of tests to classify this relationship. After reviewing them, Rehnquist settled on a requirement that there be a "rough proportionality" between state objectives and state actions. Keeping an open flood plain is related to increases in potential water run-off from new construction, but the state gives no reason that a public greenway can better accomplish this objective than a private one, which would preserve the owner's right to exclude others. Similarly, the city showed minimal relationship between its objectives and the establishment of a bicycle path.

J. Stevens, dissenting, agreed that a state may not attach "arbitrary conditions" to building permits, but he denied that past decisions mandated "rough proportionality," especially in cases involving the regulation of businesses. Moreover, "The Court's narrow focus on one strand in the property owner's bundle of rights is particularly misguided in a case involving the development of commercial property." State regulations of such businesses should bear "a strong presumption of constitutional validity." The Court should not abandon this standard, especially in cases, like this, where the landowner is given a benefit. The Court is unnecessarily resurrecting "the doctrine of substantive due process."

J. Souter, dissenting, also denied the relevance of the *Nollan* precedent in a case involving commercial development.

※

Kelo v. City of New London, 545 U.S. 469, 125 S. Ct. 2655; 162 L. Ed. 2d 439 (2005)

Facts—The City of New London, Connecticut, approved a development plan to revitalize its downtown and waterfront areas. It created a private nonprofit entity, the New London Development Corporation (NLDC), which subsequently sought to use the power of eminent domain to take private houses, including those of Susetto Kelo, who had lived in her house since 1997, and Wilhelmina Dery and her husband Charles, who had lived in their house for more than 60 years. These and other homes and properties were well-kept. A Connecticut Superior Court allowed some of the takings and disallowed others, but the Connecticut Supreme Court upheld them all.

Question—Consistent with the takings clause of the Fifth Amendment (applied to the states by the Fourteenth), can a city allow a private entity to use the power of eminent domain to condemn well-kept private houses to further economic development?

Decision—Yes, a takings meets the "public use" requirement if it serves a "public purpose."

Reasons—*J. Stevens* (5–4). "The sovereign may not take the property of A for the sole purpose of transferring it to another private party B, even though A is paid just compensation . . . [but] a State may transfer property from one private party to another if future 'use by the public' is the purpose of the taking." A public purpose needs to be genuine, but the Court has long "rejected any literal requirement that condemned property be put into use for the general public." Instead, it has "embraced the broader and more natural interpretation of public use as 'public purpose.'" *Berman v. Parker* (1954) allowed the condemnation of an unblighted store as part of a larger redevelopment plan; similarly, *Hawaii Housing Authority v. Midkiff* (1984), allowed the compensated transfer of property from one set of individuals to another in order to combat a land oligopoly. *Ruckelshaus v. Monsanto Co.* (1984), applied similar principles to the use of dates for pesticide applications. New London had carefully formulated a comprehensive plan designed to increase jobs and tax revenues. Moreover, "Promoting economic development is a traditional and long-accepted function of government." This differs from a "one-to-one transfer of property" designed to benefit one party over another. Nor is it the Court's business to decide whether there is a "reasonable certainty" that the plan's benefits will actually materialize. States are, however, free to establish stricter standards than those required by the federal constitution.

J. Kennedy, concurring. The Court should apply rational-basis review, which does not mean that it should defer to obvious cases where the takings clause is used to benefit one party over another.

J. O'Connor, dissenting. The NLDC "is not elected by popular vote, and its directors and employees are privately appointed." The Fifth Amendment requires both "public use" and "just compensation." Cases transferring "private property to public ownership" (as for roads, hospitals, and military bases), and "private property to private parties," like railroads serving as "common carriers" are relatively unproblematic, but this case is different. O'Connor would hold that "economic development takings" are unconstitutional. Although agreeing with *Berman* and *Midkiff*, this case goes much further and is not the result of direct legislative action. Although the majority opinion suggests that courts can oversee such takings, it provides no details as to how they should do so. Moreover, requiring that such takings only be used for upgrades is inadequate. "The specter of condemnation hangs over all property. Nothing is to prevent the State from replacing any Motel 6 with a Ritz-Carlton, any home with a shopping mall, or any farm with a factory." Instead "nearly all real property is susceptible to condemnation on the Court's theory."

J. Thomas, dissenting. The Court should return to the "original meaning" of the takings clause, which requires "public use" rather than simple "public purpose." Public use was meant to give narrower scope than was the "general Welfare" clause. The common law provided nuisance laws to take care of cases involving uses of land that "adversely impacted the public welfare." The public use clause "embodied the Framers' understanding that property is a natural, fundamental right." This case differs from Mill Acts, allowing for compensated flooding of upstream lands by grist mills, which were common carriers or "quasi-public entities." The majority's understanding of "public use" is "boundlessly broad and deferential" and "not susceptible of principled application." This understanding largely emerged from dictum in early cases that was inconsistent with the language of the Fifth Amendment, to which the Court should return. In the meantime, "Though citizens are safe from the government in their homes, the homes themselves are not." Moreover, "The question whether the State can take property using the power of eminent domain is . . . distinct from the question whether it can regulate property pursuant to the police power." *Berman* resulted in the displacement of many minority communities. "When faced with a clash of constitutional principle and a line of unreasoned cases wholly divorced from the text, history, and structure of our founding document, we should not hesitate to resolve the tension in favor of the Constitution's original meaning."

Note: As of 2010, a sour economy had stymied the projected building boom in New London (Kelo's home site was in a vacant lot), and numerous states had adopted provisions to provide greater protections for private property than those that the Supreme Court had found in this case.

Chapter Eight

THE BILL OF RIGHTS AND ITS APPLICATION TO THE STATES

The Constitution of 1787 embedded some limitations on government designed to protect individual rights—for example, some of the property and procedural rights within Article I, Section 9, limiting the powers of Congress, and Article I, Section 10, limiting the powers of the states. For the most part, however, the Framers of the U.S. Constitution attempted to protect individual rights through balancing government structures and through specifically enumerating the rights that units of this government would have. The latter task became particularly problematic when, as in *McCulloch v. Maryland* (1819), the Court later recognized the existence of implied powers. Most framers anticipated a strengthened national government with relatively narrow purposes and would have found it difficult to imagine a national government with the breadth of powers that the present one now exercises. Accordingly, the framers did not devote much attention at the Philadelphia Convention of 1787 to drafting up specific limits on the new government.

As soon as the convention reported its recommendations to the people, the nation split into two camps. Federalists favored the new document, and Antifederalists opposed it. Although many Antifederalists were far more motivated by fears that the new national government would usurp existing state powers, Antifederalists found that many people feared the new government because it was not, like most state constitutions, limited by a bill of rights. Initially Federalists responded that a bill of rights was unnecessary. Some even argued (in the historic series of essays collected as *The Federalist*, for example) that such a list might prove dangerous because it would imply that the new government could do anything other than that which was not specifically prohibited. As Antifederalists began to propose either calling another constitutional convention or ratifying the new constitution conditionally upon insertion of a bill of rights, leading Federalists garnered support by agreeing to push for a bill of rights through Article V amending processes after ratification of the document. A number of leading Federalists eventually concluded that a properly written bill of rights was unlikely to do harm, and might even be useful.

Thomas Jefferson, who was then serving as a U.S. ambassador to France, was among those who sought to persuade his friend James Madison of the benefits of a bill of rights. Among the arguments that Jefferson initially mustered and that Madison subsequently introduced in Congress in arguing for this bill, was that such a bill of rights would educate the people as to which liberties were most important and that the guarantees within such a bill of rights would be enforceable in courts.

Madison subsequently compiled the suggestions that he had received from the states and combined them with provisions within existing constitutions to propose what, after being modified by Congress, became a series of twelve amendments. The first two, which dealt with representation in Congress and with the timing of congressional pay raises were not initially ratified (the second would become the Twenty-seventh Amendment when belatedly ratified in 1992), but the remaining ten became known as the Bill of Rights.

Madison had hoped to embed new amendments within the text of the U.S. Constitution, but Congressman Roger Sherman argued that they should instead be attached to the end of the document. Madison conceded this procedural point in part to gain approval for his substantive amendments. Arguably, this actually gave greater prominence to these amendments than they might otherwise have had.

Today Americans are as likely to celebrate the guarantees in the Bill of Rights as they are to laud any other provisions of the document. As the following chapters will show, these include vital political rights like freedom of speech, press, and peaceable assembly, protections for the rights of individuals accused of crimes or on trial for them, and other protections that Americans today regard as being of the very essence of constitutional government.

Initially applied only to the national government, the Supreme Court eventually applied most provisions of the Bill of Rights to the states via the due process clause of the Fourteenth Amendment. In one of his last important decisions, *Barron v. Baltimore* (1833), Chief Justice John Marshall had explained that the Bill of Rights had been adopted in reaction to fears of the exercise of national powers, not the exercise of the powers of the states. His argument was bolstered by the fact that the opening words of the First Amendment say "Congress [a branch of the national government] shall make no law" and that the Constitution specifically referred to the states in sections (like Article I, Section 10), where it attempted to limit them. Marshall's view prevailed until the ratification of the Fourteenth Amendment in 1868.

Some of the leading congressional proponents of this amendment hoped and thought that the amendment would overturn the decision in *Barron v. Baltimore* and apply provisions of the Bill of Rights to the states, but by a wide majority, the post–Civil War Court rejected this view, which Justice John Marshall Harlan I had so forcefully advocated.

In *Gitlow v. New York* (1925), however, the Supreme Court decided that the free speech guarantee of the First Amendment applied to the states, and it began to add additional rights in later cases. In *Palko v. Connecticut* (1937), a case involving double jeopardy, Justice Benjamin Cardozo elaborated the view of "selective incorporation." Rejecting the idea that the due process clause of the Fourteenth Amendment applied all the provisions of the Bill of Rights to the states (a view known as "total incorporation"), he argued that the clause applied those provisions of the Bill of Rights to the states that are "implicit in a scheme of ordered liberty." In *Adamson v. California* (1947) the justices outlined a whole array of opinions. Justice Felix Frankfurter espoused the view that the Fourteenth Amendment required fundamental fairness, and that this could not simply be ascertained by deciding whether or not a right was listed in the Bill of Rights. Justice Hugo Black outlined the view of "total incorporation," earlier held by John Marshall Harlan I. Black, like Harlan, believed the leading authors of the Fourteenth Amendment intended to overturn *Barron v. Baltimore* and apply all the provisions of the Bill of Rights to the states. Still other justices argued that the due process clause was intended to protect important rights whether they are in the Bill of Rights or not. Such views are sometimes designated as "selective incorporation plus" or "total incorporation plus," and they are perhaps best encapsulated in contemporary opinions finding an unstated "right to privacy" within the document.

At present, courts have applied the right of privacy and all but a handful of the provisions of the Bill of Rights to both state and national governments. Throughout the remainder of this book, briefs will often note that a particular provision of the Constitution within the Bill of Rights is being applied to the states not directly but via the due process clause of the Fourteenth Amendment. This is a continuing reminder that, in a federal system, restraints that apply to one level of government may not apply to another unless specifically recognized as doing so.

This chapter includes a brief of *United States v. Carolene Products* (1938). Like most casebooks, the brief will cover footnote four, in which Justice Harlan Fiske Stone noted that the Court would be less likely to apply the rational basis test, with its presumption of constitutionality, to legislation that did not involve ordinary regulatory legislation. The first exception Stone noted was that involving specific provisions of the Bill of Rights, either directly or as applied to the states in the Fourteenth Amendment. The historic footnote, which has ever since served as the basis of a judicial "double standard," reiterates the importance of the Bill of Rights in modern jurisprudence.

INCORPORATION

Barron v. Baltimore, 7 Peters (32 U.S.) 243; 8 L. Ed. 672 (1833)

Facts—The city of Baltimore in paving its streets diverted several streams from their natural course, with the result that they made deposits of sand and gravel near Barron's Wharf, which rendered the water shallow and prevented the approach of vessels, rendering the wharf practically useless. Barron alleged that the city's action violated the clause in the Fifth Amendment that forbids taking private property for public use without just compensation. He contended that this amendment, being a guarantee of individual liberty, ought to restrain the states, as well as the national government.

Question—Does the Fifth Amendment restrain the states as well as the national government?

Decision—No, the provisions of the Bill of Rights, of which the Fifth Amendment is a part, are designed to limit the national government rather than the state governments.

Reasons—*C.J. Marshall* (7–0). The people of the United States established the Constitution for their own government, not for the government of the individual states. The powers they conferred on that government were to be exercised by that government. Likewise, the limitations on that power, if expressed in general terms, are necessarily applicable only to that government. The Fifth Amendment contains certain restrictions obviously restraining the exercise of power by the federal government. Since the Constitution is a document framed for the government of all, it does not pertain to the states unless directly mentioned.

❧

Gitlow v. New York, 268 U.S. 652; 45 S. Ct. 625; 69 L. Ed. 1138 (1925)

Facts—Benjamin Gitlow, a socialist, was convicted in New York courts for violating the state's criminal anarchy laws by publishing and circulating pamphlets and leaflets detrimental to the government. These publications advocated overthrowing organized government by violent and other unlawful means.

Questions—(a) Does the freedom of speech guaranteed by the First Amendment of the U.S. Constitution apply to the states? (b) Does the New York State Criminal Anarchy statute contravene the due process clause of the Fourteenth Amendment?

Decisions—(a) Yes; (b) No.

Reasons—*J. Sanford* (7–2). The freedom of speech in the First Amendment should also protect against state abridgements of freedom of speech: "For present purposes we may and do assume that freedom of speech and the press—which are protected by the First Amendment from abridgment by Congress—are among the fundamental personal rights and 'liberties' protected by the due process clause of the Fourteenth Amendment from impairment by the states."

There is, however, no absolute right to speak or publish, without responsibility, whatever one may choose. A state in the exercise of its police power may punish those who abuse this freedom by utterances inimical to the public welfare. Utterances such as the statute prohibited, by their very nature, involve danger to the public peace and to the security of the state. The statute was not arbitrary or unreasonable.

J. Holmes argued that "every idea is an incitement" and that the speech involved in this case did not pose a "clear and present danger" to the state and should not therefore be prohibited.

Note—In *Gitlow* the Supreme Court began applying individual provisions of the Bill of Rights to the states as well as to the national government. Over the course of time, almost all of these provisions have been so applied through a process known as "selective incorporation." Under this doctrine, the due process clause of the Fourteenth Amendment has been used to apply those provisions in the Bill of Rights regarded to be fundamental.

Palko v. Connecticut, 302 U.S. 319; 58 S. Ct. 149; 82 L. Ed. 288 (1937)

Facts—Palka (the reporter spelled the name incorrectly) was indicted in Connecticut for murder in the first degree. A jury found him guilty of murder in the second degree and sentenced him to life imprisonment. The state appealed this verdict, and the Supreme Court of Errors for Connecticut ordered a new trial. The basis for this order was the discovery that there had been error of law to the prejudice of the state in the lower court. At the second trial additional evidence was admitted and additional instructions given to the jury. A verdict of first degree murder was returned and Palko was sentenced to death. He appealed the legality of this procedure under the due process clause of the Fourteenth Amendment, claiming double jeopardy.

Question—Does the new trial and subsequent sentence to death, deprive the appellant of due process under the Fourteenth Amendment?

Decision—No.

Reasons—*J. Cardozo* (8–1). Cardozo noted that previous cases had applied some provisions of the Bill of Rights to the states and refused to apply others calling for some sort of rationalizing principle. Cardozo concluded that the due process clause of the Fourteenth Amendment applied to the states only those provisions of the Bill of Rights (Amendments I to VIII) that are "of the very essence of a scheme of ordered liberty." These provisions are those that involve principles of justice "so rooted in the traditions and conscience of our people as to be ranked as fundamental."

The Court noted further that there could be no valid charge of double jeopardy and no deprivation of due process unless the first trial had been without error. Since there was error in the conduct of the first trial and the second trial was requested by the state to rectify the errors of the first trial, and to further the purposes of justice, there was no deprivation of due process involved.

J. Butler dissented without writing an opinion.

Note—*Palko* remains one of the clearest articulations of the principle of "selective incorporation," the idea that the due process clause of the Fourteenth Amendment does not apply all the provisions of the Bill of Rights to the states but only those rights listed there that are most fundamental. While continuing to adhere to this general principle, over time the Court has recognized an increased number of such rights as so fundamental.

✵

United States v. Carolene Products Co., 304 U.S. 144; 58 S. Ct. 778; 82 L. Ed. 123 (1938)

Facts—In March 1923 Congress passed the "Filled Milk Act," which prohibited the shipment in interstate commerce of skimmed milk compounded with any fat or oil other than milk fat, so as to resemble milk or cream. The appellee was indicted in southern Illinois for shipping in interstate commerce certain packages of a filled milk compound.

Question—Does this regulation exceed the power of Congress over interstate commerce, and thus deprive individuals of property without due process of law?

Decision—No.

Reasons—*J. Stone* (6–1). The statute describes filled milk as an adulterated article of food, injurious to health, and a fraud upon the public. "Even in the absence of such aids the existence of facts supporting the legislative judgment is to be presumed, for regulatory legislation affecting ordinary commercial transactions is not to be pronounced unconstitutional unless in the light of the facts made known or generally assumed it is of such a character as to preclude the assumption that it rests upon some rational basis within the knowledge and experience of the legislators." In this case, it is at least debatable whether commerce in filled milk should be left unregulated, partially restricted, or entirely prohibited. That was a decision for Congress, and as such, the prohibition of shipment in interstate commerce of this product was a constitutional exercise of the power to regulate interstate commerce. Congressional power to regulate commerce is the power to prescribe the rules by which commerce is to be governed. This extends to the prohibition of shipments in such commerce. This power is complete and unlimited, except as limited by the Constitution. Congress is free to exclude from interstate commerce articles whose use in states may be injurious to public health, morals, or welfare, or that contravene the policy of the state of their destination.

Note—*Carolene Products* contains the now-famous footnote four of *Justice Harlan Fiske Stone*. This footnote set up a double standard of adjudication presuming that economic legislation would be presumed constitutional unless on its face it obviously was not, while subjecting other types of legislation to greater judicial scrutiny. Legislation requiring such exacting scrutiny included that violating a specific provision of the Bill of Rights and/or the Fourteenth Amendment, legislation related to political processes (especially where democratic channels were blocked), and legislation directed against religious, racial, or other "discrete and insular minorities" who might not be able to protect themselves through majoritarian political processes.

Adamson v. California, 332 U.S. 46; 67 S. Ct. 1672; 91 L. Ed. 1903 (1947)

Facts—Adamson was convicted, without recommendation for mercy, by a jury in the superior court of the state of California of murder in the first degree. The state supreme court affirmed his life sentence.

Citing the Fifth and Fourteenth Amendments, Adamson challenged the provisions of California law that permitted the court and counsel to comment on, and the court and jury to consider, a defendant's failure to explain or deny evidence.

Questions—(a) Do the provisions of the California state constitution and its penal law abridge the guarantee against self-incrimination and of due process? (b) Do all the guarantees in the Bill of Rights apply to the states as well as to the national government?

Decisions—(a) No; (b) No.

Reasons—*J. Reed* (5–4). The Fourteenth Amendment does not make this clause of the Fifth Amendment effective as a protection against state action. The clause in the Bill of Rights is for the protection of the individual from the federal government, and its provisions are not applicable to the states. As a matter of fact, the Fourteenth Amendment forbids a state from abridging privileges of citizens of the United States, leaving the state free, so to speak, to abridge, within the limits of due process, the privileges and immunities of state citizenship.

The Fourteenth Amendment undoubtedly guarantees a right to a fair trial. However, the due process clause does not include all the rights of the federal Bill of Rights under its protection. The purpose of due process is not to protect the accused against a proper conviction, but against an unfair conviction. The Court held that the state may control such a situation as this, where the defendant remains silent, with its own ideas of efficient administration of criminal justice.

J. Frankfurter's concurring opinion argued that the California procedure did not violate fundamental rules of fairness. *J. Black's* ringing dissent, based on his review of the congressional debates on the Fourteenth Amendment, argued for total incorporation of the Bill of Rights. *J. Murphy* went even further in suggesting that the Fourteenth Amendment carried over all the provisions of the Bill of Rights to the states without necessarily being limited to them—the view often designated as "total incorporation plus."

Note—*Malloy v. Hogan*, 378 U.S. 1 (1964) and *Murphy v. New York Waterfront Commission*, 378 U.S. 52 (1964) reversed *Adamson*. *Griffin v. Califor-*

nia, 380 U.S. 609 (1965), along with reversing *Twining v. New Jersey*, 211 U.S. 78 (1908), also reversed *Adamson*.

❧

Rochin v. California, 342 U.S. 165; 72 S. Ct. 204; 96 L. Ed. 183 (1952)

Facts—Police with information that Rochin might be selling narcotics went to his house, entered an open outside door, forced open the door to his bedroom where he was in bed with his common-law wife, spied two capsules on his nightstand, attempted unsuccessfully to keep Rochin from swallowing them, and subsequently took him to a hospital and had an emetic administered that caused him to vomit them up. On the basis of this evidence, a California superior court convicted Rochin of possessing morphine, a decision affirmed by the district court of appeals and the supreme court of California.

Question—Did police conduct in this case violate due process of law as guaranteed by the Fourteenth Amendment?

Decision—Yes.

Reasons—*J. Frankfurter* (8–0). States largely control the administration of justice but the Supreme Court has a responsibility to oversee such conduct. The standards used to determine what constitutes due process of law "are not authoritatively formulated anywhere as though they were specifics." Such determinations, however, need not be arbitrary. Judges do not simply impose their personal views when determining what due process is but derive their conclusions from the wide body of law, and specifically from Anglo-American jurisprudence. In this case, the conduct in question "shocks the conscience." Frankfurter explained: "Illegally breaking into the privacy of the petitioner, the struggle to open his mouth and remove what was there, the forcible extractions of his stomach's contents . . . is bound to offend even hardened sensibilities. They are methods too close to the rack and the screw to permit of constitutional differentiation." When conducting investigations, states are bound to "respect certain decencies of civilized conduct." As in the case of coerced confessions, the methods in this case, "offend the community's sense of fair play and decency" and "afford brutality the cloak of law."

    J. Black, concurring, accused the majority of formulating too nebulous a standard. He reiterated his argument in *Adamson v. California*, that the Court should simply apply the Fifth Amendment guarantee against self-incrimination to this case. In a separate concurrence, *J. Douglas* also advocated voiding this conviction "because of the command of the Fifth Amendment."

Chapter Nine

FIRST AMENDMENT: RELIGIOUS RIGHTS

The First Amendment is one of the most revered and important provisions of the U.S. Constitution. Originally the third of twelve proposals advanced in reaction to calls for a bill of rights, this amendment became the first when the first two proposals failed to be ratified (one of them later became the Twenty-seventh Amendment when it was belatedly ratified in 1992).

Like most other amendments within the Bill of Rights, the First Amendment contains multiple guarantees. These include provisions for religious freedom, for freedom of speech and of the press, and for peaceable assembly and petition. Over time, the Supreme Court has decided that each of these guarantees is a limit on both state and national governments. This chapter treats the two opening clauses dealing with religion, and the next chapter covers the political rights that this amendment guarantees.

The two provisions of the First Amendment that deal with religion are respectively the establishment clause and the free exercise clause. In prohibiting Congress from adopting a law respecting the "establishment of religion," the first clause clearly prohibits the establishment of a national church. Many justices and scholars, however, have argued that it should be interpreted more broadly.

The establishment clause is often linked to the idea, attributed to Roger Williams (who feared state corruption of the church) and later to Thomas Jefferson (who feared church corruption of the state), of a wall of separation between church and state. Justices with such a view argued for strict separation of church and state. Others believe it is proper to accommodate religion as long as one specific religion is not favored over others. Some justices believe the clause calls for government "neutrality," but this idea is not always easy to translate into practice.

The Supreme Court expanded on earlier principles to formulate the Lemon Test in the case of *Lemon v. Kurtzman* (1971). This three-part test requires that valid laws on the subject have a clear "secular purpose," have the "primary effect" of neither advancing nor inhibiting religion, and avoid "excessive entanglement" between church and state. Justices have criticized each of the three prongs of the Lemon Test. Moreover, on occasion the Court ignores the Lemon Test and looks instead to historical practice.

The Supreme Court has struck down most religious exercises in public schools such as prayer, Bible reading, and other devotional exercises as a violation of the establishment clause that makes nonbelievers appear to be outsiders. As a consequence, religious believers sometimes feel that their beliefs have been marginalized, and much like Roman Catholics in the nineteenth century (who faced a distinctly Protestant curriculum in public schools), many Protestant groups have begun to form their own schools.

The Court has had to decide whether programs of governmental aid to religious institutions conflict with the establishment clause. In *Everson v. Board of Education of Ewing Township* (1947), the Court majority used strong language in which it said that no governmental aid should go to parochial schools but then approved of monies to provide transportation for parents of children going to parochial schools. Similarly, a number of recent cases have suggested that governmental aid should not be denied to students in need of special assistance simply because they attend parochial schools. Dissenting justices fear that any such assistance signals the evils the American Founders hoped to prevent and fear that debates over such aid will enter into political discourse. The twin decisions in *Van Orden v. Perry* and *McCreary County v. ACLU* (2005) show how such controversies sometimes center on religious displays on public property.

The second clause dealing with religion, the free exercise clause, provides broad guarantees for citizens seeking to practice their faith but has never been understood to provide for absolute freedom of religion. In an early case, *Reynolds v. United States* (1879), the Supreme Court distinguished religious belief, which is absolute, from religiously motivated conduct, in this case bigamy, which is not.

Scholars and justices continue to debate just how much freedom the free exercise clause is designed to allow. Despite a prior precedent in *Sherbert v. Verner* (1963), which had ruled that the state must show a "compelling interest" in denying unemployment benefits to individuals who refused to accept a job that required them to work on their Sabbath, in *Employment Division v. Smith* (1990), the Supreme Court decided that the clause did not require states to exempt individuals from generally applicable laws on the basis of religious faith. When Congress subsequently attempted to see that such laws were not adopted absent a "compelling state interest," the Court decided in *Boerne v. Flores* (1997) that Congress was improperly attempting to reinterpret the Fourteenth Amendment, thus raising the question of the degree to which constitutional interpretation is the prerogative of the judicial branch and the degree to which interpretation may be shared with the legislative branch.

Establishment and free exercise cases often overlap with one another and with other clauses in the First Amendment and elsewhere in the Constitution. In *West Virginia Board of Education v. Barnette* (1943), treated in chapter 10, dealing with symbolic speech, the Court thus had to decide whether compulsory flag salutes that conflicted with minority religious views were constitutional (it reversed an earlier decision and declared that such salutes could not be compelled). Similarly, in *Rosenberger v. Rector and Visitors of the University of Virginia* (1995), the Court had to decide whether denial of student funds to a religious group was a proper attempt to avoid establishment or (as it decided) an impermissible content-based viewpoint discrimination in violation of freedom of speech. Recent years have seen renewed attention to the possibility of governmental funding of "faith-based initiatives," which will undoubtedly find their way into courts.

The Constitution has made a unique contribution to church/state relations. The lines established by the First Amendment are nonetheless imprecise, and the debate continues between those who support almost complete separation of church and state and those who are more comfortable with greater accommodation, between those who elevate free exercise rights over other rights and those who believe that such rights give no special status to those who are challenging generally applicable laws that are not specifically aimed at religious minorities.

ESTABLISHMENT CLAUSE

Everson v. Board of Education of Ewing Township, 330 U.S. 1; 67 S. Ct. 504; 91 L. Ed. 711 (1947)

Facts—A New Jersey statute authorized local school districts to make rules and contracts for the transportation of children to schools. In this case, Ewing Township provided reimbursement to taxpayers using the public bus system in the township to transport their children. The reimbursement was also made to the parents of Catholic school children going to and from parochial schools. The appellant, a taxpayer, challenged the right of the board to reimburse parents of parochial school students.

Question—Does this statute providing reimbursement for parents who send their children to parochial schools violate the establishment clause of the First Amendment as applied to the states by the Fourteenth?

Decision—No.

Reasons—*J. Black* (5–4). The transportation of children to their schools is in the same category as the provision of police protection near school crossings, the availability of fire protection, sanitary sewer facilities, public highways, and sidewalks. To cut off these facilities would make it far more difficult for the parochial schools to operate. This was not the intention of the First Amendment. Under the amendment state power can no more handicap religions than favor them. Here the children attending Catholic schools were receiving no more than the benefits of public welfare legislation and therefore the New Jersey statute was not unconstitutional. It did not run contrary to the concept of separation of church and state.

J. *Black* said that "The 'establishment of religion' clause means at least this: Neither a state nor the Federal Government can set up a church, neither can pass laws which aid one religion, aid all religions, or prefer one religion over another. Neither can force nor influence a person to go to or remain away from church against his will or force him to profess a belief or disbelief in any religion. No person can be punished for entertaining or professing religious beliefs or disbeliefs, for church attendance or non-attendance. No tax in any amount large or small, can be levied to support any religious activities or institutions, whatever they may be called, or whatever form they may adopt to teach or practice religion. . . . In the words of Thomas Jefferson, the clause against establishment of religion by law was intended to erect 'a wall of separation between church and state.'"

In dissent, *J. Jackson* and *J. Rutledge* accused the majority of refusing to apply the implications of its own reasoning.

Note—*Justice Black's* famous "wall between church and state" (actually a Jeffersonian metaphor that was in turn borrowed from Roger Williams) surfaced for the first time in a court decision. Critics believe that the metaphor has sown confusion rather than leading to clarification. Contrary to popular belief, the metaphor is not found within the text of the U.S. Constitution.

Illinois ex rel. McCollum v. Board of Education, Champaign County, Illinois, 333 U.S. 203; 68 S. Ct. 461; 92 L. Ed. 648 (1948)

Facts—Public schools in Champaign County, Illinois, allowed religious teachers to provide weekly in-house religious instruction. School authorities provided a period of thirty or forty-five minutes taken from the time of the regular school day. If the children did not attend the religious instruction, they were given something else to do in this time. The school board did not pay the instructors, and the children were required to have parental consent to attend these classes.

Question—Does this use of the school building and school time violate the First and Fourteenth Amendments?

Decision—Yes.

Reasons—*J. Black* (8–1). There was a close cooperation between the secular and religious authorities in promoting religious education. Classes were conducted in the regular classrooms of the school building. The operation of the state's compulsory education system assisted in and was integrated with the program of religious education carried on by the separate sects. Pupils compelled by law to attend school for a secular education were released in part from their duty if they went to these religious classes. This was beyond all question a utilization of the tax-supported public system to aid religious groups to spread their faith, and it fell squarely under the ban of the First Amendment (as made applicable to the states by the Fourteenth Amendment).

In dissent, *J. Reed* pointed to past examples of church/state accommodation and argued that Illinois had not crossed the line of permissibility in this case.

Zorach v. Clauson, 343 U.S. 306; 72 S. Ct. 679; 96 L. Ed. 954 (1952)

Facts—New York City arranged a program permitting its public schools to release students during the school day so that they might go to religious centers for religious instruction or devotional exercises. A student was released on the written request of his parents. The churches made a weekly list of the children released from the public school, but who had not reported for religious instruction. This "released time" program involved neither the use of the public school classrooms nor the expenditure of any public funds. All costs were paid by the religious organizations.

Question—Does the New York City statute permitting release time violate the First Amendment, which, by reason of the Fourteenth Amendment, prohibits the states from establishing religion or prohibiting its free exercise?

Decision—No.

Reasons—*J. Douglas* (6–3). There was no issue concerned here with the prohibition of the "free exercise" of religion. No one was forced to attend the religious instruction, nor was the religious training brought into the classrooms of the public schools.

The First Amendment does reflect the philosophy of separation of church and state, but does not say that in every and all respects there must be separation. It rather defines ways in which there shall be no dependency, one on the other. This is only common sense.

The concept of separation of church and state would have to be pressed to extreme views to condemn the present law on a constitutional basis. We are a religious people with a belief in a Supreme Being. Our government shows no partiality to any one group, but lets each flourish. The state follows the best of our traditions when it schedules its events so as to encourage religious instruction. The government may not finance religious instruction. The government may not finance religious groups, undertake religious instruction, blend secular and sectarian education, nor use secular institutions to force some religion on any person. However, there is no constitutional requirement for government to be hostile to religion. The *McCollum* case cannot be expanded to cover this case, unless separation of church and state means that public institutions cannot accommodate the religious needs of the people. "We cannot read into the Bill of Rights such a philosophy of hostility to religion."

J. Black, *J. Frankfurter*, and *J. Jackson* all authored dissents questioning the majority's distinction between this case and *McCollum* and arguing that the state was using its power of coercion to advance religion.

Engel et al. v. Vitale et al., 370 U.S. 421; 82 S. Ct. 1261; 8 L. Ed. 2d 601 (1962)

Facts—The New York State Board of Regents had recommended, and the local school board had directed the school district's principal, that the following prayer be said aloud by each class in the presence of the teacher at the beginning of each school day: "Almighty God, we acknowledge our dependence upon Thee, and we beg Thy blessings upon us, our parents, our teachers, and our country." The parents of ten pupils challenged the use of the prayer.

Question—Does the use of the state-imposed prayer violate the establishment clause of the First Amendment made applicable to the states by the Fourteenth Amendment?

Decision—Yes.

Reasons—*J. Black* (6–1). Using the public school system to encourage recitation of the prayer is inconsistent with the establishment clause since this is a religious activity and governmental officials composed the prayer as a part of a governmental program to further religious beliefs. The fact that the prayer may be denominationally neutral and the fact that its observance on the part of the students is voluntary cannot change the application of the establishment clause. The establishment clause is violated by the enactment of laws that establish an official religion regardless of whether those laws coerce nonobserving individuals or not. It is an historical fact that governmentally established religions and religious persecutions go hand in hand. "When the power, prestige, and financial support of government is placed behind a particular religious belief, the indirect coercive pressure upon religious minorities to conform to the prevailing officially-approved religion is plain."

Under the First Amendment's "prohibition against governmental establishment of religion, as reinforced by the provisions of the Fourteenth Amendment, government in this country, be it state or federal, is without power to prescribe by law any particular form of prayer which is to be used as an official prayer in carrying on any program of governmentally-sponsored religious activity."

J. Stewart's dissent viewed the action of the school board as an attempt to allow the majority of school children who wanted to do so to share in the nation's spiritual heritage.

৩৶

Abington School District v. Schempp, 374 U.S. 203; 83 S. Ct. 1560; 10 L. Ed. 2d 844 (1963)

Facts—Pennsylvania by statute required that at least ten verses from the Bible should be read, without comment, at the opening of each public school on each school day. Any child could be excused from attending the Bible reading upon written request of his parent or guardian. The Schempp family, members of the Unitarian church, brought suit to enjoin enforcement of the statute. In a companion case (*Murray v. Curlett*) Mrs. Murray and her son, professed atheists, brought similar action against a similar situation in Baltimore, which also permitted recitation of the Lord's Prayer.

Question—Does the requirement of Bible reading and/or recitation of the Lord's Prayer in public schools violate the establishment clause of the First Amendment made applicable to the states by the Fourteenth Amendment?

Decision—Yes.

Reasons—*J. Clark* (8–1). The establishment clause withdrew all legislative power respecting religious belief or the expression thereof. "The test may be stated as follows: What are the purpose and the primary effect of the enactment? If either is the advancement of inhibition of religion then the enactment exceeds the scope of legislative power as circumscribed by the Constitution . . . in both cases the laws require religious exercises and such exercises are being conducted in direct violation of the rights of the appellees and petitioners. Nor are these required exercises mitigated by the fact that individual students may absent themselves upon parental request, for that fact furnishes no defense to a claim of unconstitutionality under the establishment clause."

J. Stewart argued in dissent that the Court had adopted an unnecessarily narrow view of the separation of church and state that in fact interfered with the free exercise of religion.

Note—*Murray v. Curlett*, 374 U.S. 203 (1963) reached the same conclusion as *Abington*. The Court has continued its balancing act, as seen in *Stone v. Graham*, 449 U.S. 39 (1980), in which the Court banned posting the Ten Commandments in classrooms, and *Widmar v. Vincent*, 454 U.S. 263 (1981), which opened up state university classrooms on First Amendment grounds for student religious groups.

Lemon v. Kurtzman, 403 U.S. 602; 91 S. Ct. 2105; 29 L. Ed. 2d 745 (1971)

Facts—Rhode Island and Pennsylvania established programs designed to provide state aid to parochial elementary and secondary schools. Pennsylvania reimbursed schools for the cost of teachers' salaries, texts, and materials used in teaching secular subjects. Rhode Island paid teachers of such subjects a supplement of up to 15 percent of their salaries. In both cases, the states attempted to see that money was given only for instruction related to secular subjects. A three-judge U.S. District Court had held that the Rhode Island law violated the establishment clause whereas a similar court had upheld the Pennsylvania law.

Questions—(a) Do the state programs in question violate the establishment clause of the First Amendment as applied to the states by the Fourteenth? (b) What is the appropriate test to be applied in such cases?

Decisions—(a) Yes; (b) The Court will examine establishment clause cases under a three-pronged test (that came to be known as the Lemon Test) under which it will examine whether a law has a secular purpose, whether the primary effect of the law is to advance or inhibit religion, and whether the law fosters excessive entanglement between church and state.

Reasons—*C.J. Burger* (7–1). Reviewing cases since *Everson v. Board of Education* (1947), involving reimbursement of bus transportation for parents of children attending parochial schools, the Court cited *Walz v. Tax Commission* (1970), the case upholding tax exemptions of religious property, to argue that the establishment clause was designed to avoid the evils of "sponsorship, financial support, and active involvement of the sovereign in religious activity." The Court believed these goals could in turn be translated into three tests. They required that a statute "must have a secular legislative purpose . . . its principal or primary effect must be one that neither advances nor inhibits religion . . . [and] the statute must not foster 'an excessive government entanglement with religion.'" The laws at issue have a clear secular purpose, but the regulations imposed to guarantee that teachers do not foster religion foster excessive entanglement between church and state. The religious atmosphere of parochial schools in both states is pervasive. Although the state can ascertain the content of secular textbooks relatively easily, teachers cannot be so easily overseen. Even when teachers act in good faith, there is the possibility that they will impermissibly foster religion. Moreover, continuing questions about state aid to parochial schools were likely to lead to undesirable political divisiveness.

J. Douglas's concurrence also focused on the entanglement raised by "the surveillance or supervision of the States." *J. Brennan* agreed with the Court's decision in these cases but disagreed with the aid that the Court sanctioned in a companion case, *Tilton v. Richardson*, 403 U.S. 672 (1971) for construction of buildings at religious colleges and universities. He also focused on the danger of any state subsidies to parochial schools. *J. White*, who agreed with the decision in *Tilton*, but not the decision in *Lemon*, pointed to the dual roles of parochial schools in performing "religious and secular functions." White argued that the Court's finding of entanglement was contrary to the testimony of the teachers and to its treatment of college and university professors in *Tilton*. He found that the decision presented "an insoluble paradox: The State cannot finance secular instruction it if permits religion to be taught in the same classroom; but if it exacts a promise that religion not be so taught—a promise the school and its teachers are quite willing and on this record able to give—and enforces it, it is then entangled in the 'no entanglement' aspect of the Court's Establishment Clause jurisprudence."

Note—The three-pronged Lemon Test continues to be highly controversial. The Court does not apply the test to all establishment clause cases.

Wisconsin v. Yoder, 406 U.S. 205; 92 S. Ct. 1526; 32 L. Ed. 2d 15 (1972)

Facts—Suit was brought by Wisconsin against members of the Amish church to force them to abide by the state's compulsory school attendance law, which required children to attend public or private school until the age of sixteen. The Amish parents refused to send their children to school beyond the eighth grade. Their objection to higher education generally is that the values it teaches are in marked variance with the Amish values and way of life. They agree that elementary education is necessary since their children must have the basic skills "in order to read the Bible, to be good farmers and citizens and to be able to deal with non-Amish people when necessary in the course of daily affairs."

Question—Does the Wisconsin compulsory attendance law as applied to Amish families infringe on the free exercise clause of the First Amendment?

Decision—Yes.

Reasons—*C.J. Burger* (6–1). However strong a state's interest in universal compulsory education, it is by no means absolute to the exclusion or subordination of all other interests. The traditional way of life of the Amish is not merely a matter of personal preference but one of deep religious conviction, shared by an organized group, and intimately related to daily living. "A way of life that is odd or even erratic but interferes with no rights or interests of others is not to be condemned because it is different." The First and Fourteenth Amendments prevent the state from enforcing this law in the case of the Amish.

    J. Douglas, in a partial dissent, argued that the wishes of the children, as well as those of the parents, should be consulted before the Court rendered a decision in this case.

Note—The Court has long noted a distinction between religious beliefs and acts. Thus, Mormons were penalized for practicing polygamy, *Reynolds v. United States* 98 U.S. 145 (1897); Jehovah's Witnesses for allowing their children in violation of child welfare law to distribute religious tracts at night, *Prince v. Massachusetts*, 321 U.S. 158 (1944); and Jewish merchants had to adhere to a Sunday closing law, *Braunfeld v. Brown*, 366 U.S. 599 (1961). Is the Court "establishing" a particular religion in Wisconsin in making an exception for the Amish? In *United States v. Lee*, 455 U.S. 252 (1982), the Court held that while an individual Amish is exempt from Social Security taxes, his employees are not. Although concurring, *J. Stevens* noted that the attempt to distinguish *Lee* from *Yoder* was "unconvincing."

Stone v. Graham, 449 U.S. 39; 101 S. Ct. 690; 66 L. Ed. 2d 199 (1980)

Facts—A Kentucky statute required that a copy of the Ten Commandments be posted on the wall of each public school classroom in the state. The copies were to be purchased by private contributors.

Question—Does the Kentucky statute requiring posting of the Ten Commandments in school classrooms violate the establishment and free exercise clauses of the First Amendment?

Decision—Yes.

Reasons—*Per Curiam* (5–4). This Court has already announced a three-part test for determining whether a challenged state statute is permissible under the First Amendment: "First, the statute must have a secular legislative purpose; second, its principal or primary effect must be one that neither advances nor inhibits religion . . . ; finally, the statute must not foster 'an excessive government entanglement with religion.' If a statute violates any of these three principles, it must be struck down under the establishment clause. . . . The pre-eminent purpose for posting the Ten Commandments on schoolroom walls is plainly religious in nature. The Ten Commandments is undeniably a sacred text . . . and no legislative recitation of a supposed secular purpose can blind us to that fact. . . . It does not matter that the posted copies of the Ten Commandments are financed by voluntary private contributions for the mere posting of the copies under the auspices of the legislature provides the 'official support of the state . . . Government' that the establishment clause prohibits."

 J. Rehnquist, dissenting, stressed that posting the Ten Commandments could be justified as serving a secular legislative purpose.

Widmar v. Vincent, 454 U.S. 263; 102 S. Ct. 269; 70 L. Ed. 2d 440 (1981)

Facts—The University of Missouri at Kansas City, a state university, generally opened its facilities for the activities of registered student groups. Although a registered religious group named Cornerstone originally sought and received permission to conduct its meetings in university facilities, the university subsequently informed the organization that Cornerstone's meetings could no longer be held in university buildings. The exclusion was based on a regulation adopted by the Board of Curators that prohibited the use of university buildings or grounds "for purposes of religious worship or religious teaching." Members of Cornerstone alleged that the university's discrimination against religious activity and discussion violated their rights of free exercise of religion, equal protection, and freedom of speech under the First and Fourteenth Amendments to the Constitution.

Question—Can a state university, which makes its facilities generally available for the activities of registered student groups, close its facilities to a registered group desiring to use the facilities for religious worship and religious discussion?

Decision—No.

Reasons—*J. Powell* (8–1). "With respect to persons entitled to be there, our cases leave no doubt that the First Amendment rights of speech and association extend to the campuses of state universities." It is possible—perhaps even foreseeable—that religious groups will benefit from access to university facilities. "But this court has explained that a religious organization's enjoyment of merely 'incidental' benefits does not violate the prohibition against the 'primary advancement' of religion. . . . We are satisfied that any religious benefits of an open forum at UMKC would be 'incidental' within the meaning of our cases . . . an open forum in a public university does not confer any imprimatur of state approval on religious sects or practices. . . . The forum is available to a broad class of non-religious as well as religious speakers; there are over 100 recognized student groups at UMKC. The provision of benefits to so broad a spectrum of groups is an important index of secular effect. . . . In the absence of empirical evidence that religious groups will dominate UMKC's open forum, . . . the advancement of religion would not be the forum's 'primary effect.' . . . The basis for our decision is narrow. Having created a forum generally open to student groups, the university seeks to enforce a content-based exclusion of religious speech. Its exclusionary policy violates the fundamental principle that a state regulation of speech should be content-neutral, and the university is unable to justify this violation under applicable constitutional standards."

J. White argued in dissent that although a state institution should have the right to accommodate religion, it should not be constitutionally required to do so and that there was "room for state policies that may incidentally burden religion."

Marsh v. Chambers, 463 U.S. 783; 103 S. Ct. 3330; 77 L. Ed. 2d 1019 (1983)

Facts—Chambers, a taxpayer and Nebraska legislator, called into question the long-standing practice of the state legislature to pay a chaplain to begin each session with prayer. The U.S. District Court held that the prayers were not unconstitutional, but state payment to a chaplain was. The U.S. Eighth Circuit applied the three-part test in *Lemon v. Kurtzman*, 403 U.S. 602 (971) and declared both practices unconstitutional.

Question—Does Nebraska's practice of opening its sessions with prayers by a paid chaplain violate the establishment clause of the First Amendment as applied to the states by the Fourteenth?

Decision—No.

Reasons—*C.J. Burger* (6–3). The practice of opening legislative sessions with prayers "is deeply embedded in the history and tradition of this country," and has long coexisted with the principle of disestablishment of religion. The practice dates back to the Continental Congress, and the Congress at the time the Bill of Rights was proposed (a Congress that consisted of many individuals who had been present at the Constitutional Convention), and has been followed in most states. Such prayers do not constitute an establishment but are "simply a tolerable acknowledgment of beliefs widely held among the people of this country." The compensation of chaplains is also a long-standing practice.

J. Brennan, dissenting, would have overturned the practice on the basis of the three-part Lemon Test. Brennan argued that the law had no secular purpose, had the primary effect of advancing religion, and fostered excessive entanglement between church and state and led to political divisiveness. The practice was contrary to four purposes of the establishment clause, namely, the guarantee of individual right to conscience, keeping the state from interfering with the autonomy of political life, preventing "the trivialization and degradation of religion by too close an attachment to the organs of government," and reducing political battles. He thought the practice violated "the imperatives of separation and neutrality." He argued against historical analysis in part because of his view that "the Constitution is not a static document whose meaning on every detail is fixed for all time by the life experience of the Framers."

J. Stevens dissented on the basis that he thought the religious beliefs expressed by chaplains would "tend to reflect the faith of the majority of the lawmakers' constituents," making it unlikely that leaders of minority faiths would be so chosen.

Note—This is an example in which the majority relied on historical practice and essentially ignored the Lemon Test.

$\sim\!\!\!\downarrow$

Wallace v. Jaffree, 472 U.S. 38; 105 S. Ct. 2479; 86 L. Ed. 2d 29 (1985)

Facts—Ismael Jaffree filed a complaint on behalf of his minor children against the Mobile County School Board, various school officials, and several teachers. He sought a declaratory judgment and an injunction restraining the defendants from allowing regular religious services or other forms of religious expression. An Alabama statute permitted one minute of silence for "meditation or voluntary prayer" each day in the public schools. A U.S. District Court found the statute permissible on the grounds that a state could establish a state religion if it chose, and the Court of Appeals reversed the decision.

Question—Does a state statute that the state has amended to permit a moment of silence for "meditation and voluntary prayer" violate the establishment clause?

Decision—Yes.

Reasons—*J. Stevens* (6–3). The Court's affirmance of the Court of Appeals' reversal "makes it unnecessary to comment at length on the district court's remarkable conclusion that the federal constitution imposes no obstacle to Alabama's establishment of a state religion." It is firmly embedded in our constitutional jurisprudence "that the several states have no greater power to restrain the individual freedoms protected by the First Amendment than does the Congress." Here, as in *West Virginia v. Barnette*, "we are faced with a state measure which forces an individual, as part of his daily life . . . to be an instrument for fostering public adherence to an ideological point of view he finds unacceptable." The Court has concluded that the First Amendment embraces "the right to select any religious faith or none at all." *Lemon v. Kurtzman* (403 U.S. 602) held that in construing the establishment clause a statute (1) must have a secular legislative purpose, (2) must neither advance nor inhibit the practice of religion, and (3) must not foster an excessive government entanglement with religion. The second and third criteria will not be considered "if a statute does not have a clearly secular purpose." The Alabama statute has none.

    J. O'Connor, in a concurring opinion, indicated that moment of silence laws were not per se unconstitutional but could become so when specifically designed to aid religion.

J. White, *J. Burger*, and *J. Rehnquist* wrote dissents. They did not think the addition of language specifically permitting prayer constituted an undue establishment of religion.

Edwards v. Aguillard, 482 U.S. 578; 107 S. Ct. 2573; 96 L. Ed. 2d 510 (1987)

Facts—A Louisiana act forbade the teaching of the theory of evolution unless accompanied by a discussion of "creation science." The act did not require the teaching of one or the other, but if either was taught, the other must be also. School boards were forbidden to discriminate against anyone who chose to be a creation scientist or to teach creationism. The statute was challenged as a violation of the establishment clause of the First Amendment and the constitution of Louisiana. The Louisiana Supreme Court upheld the statute, but the U.S. District Court and the U.S. Fifth Circuit declared it invalid.

Question—Does the Louisiana statute requiring public schools that teach evolution also to teach "creation science" violate the First Amendment's establishment clause?

Decision—Yes.

Reasons—*J. Brennan* (7–2). The three-part test established in *Lemon v. Kurtzman* (1971) requires a law to have a secular purpose, to avoid advancing or inhibiting religion, and to avoid excessive entanglement of government with religion.

If the law were enacted for the purpose of endorsing religion, "no consideration of the second or third criteria (of *Lemon*) is necessary." It is clear "that requiring schools to teach creation science with evolution does not advance academic freedom." There can be no legitimate state interest in protecting particular religions from scientific views distasteful to them. "The preeminent purpose of Louisiana legislature was clearly to advance the religious viewpoint." The Louisiana act violates the First Amendment and seeks "to employ the symbolic and financial support of government to achieve a religious purpose."

J. Scalia's dissent argued for greater deference to the state and to its judgment that the legislation at issue had a legitimate secular legislative purpose.

Lee v. Weisman, 505 U.S. 577; 112 S. Ct. 2649; 120 L. Ed. 2d 467 (1992)

Facts—A public school principal in Providence, Rhode Island, invited a rabbi to deliver prayers at a middle school graduation exercise. The U.S. District Court, while it did not enjoin the prayers at this graduation, subsequently granted an injunction sought by the parent of a school-age child against such future prayers, arguing that they had the primary effect of advancing religion, prohibited by the second prong of the Lemon Test. The U.S. First Circuit Court of Appeals affirmed the lower court's decision that the practice violated the establishment clause of the First Amendment.

Question—Do school officials violate the establishment clause when they invite members of the clergy to give prayers at public school graduations?

Decision—Yes.

Reasons—*J. Kennedy* (5–4). Controlling precedents indicate that the action of the school here was unconstitutional. The action of the principal in inviting a member of the clergy to deliver a prayer at a graduation constituted state promotion of religious activity at a ceremony that, although technically not compulsory, was "in a fair and real sense obligatory." The Constitution protects speech by "ensuring its full expression," but it protects worship by prohibiting state sponsorship. Here students were psychologically coerced into standing during a prayer that some disapproved apparently because it was thought that the majority favored such an exercise. This exercise was fundamentally different from the practice of allowing a chaplain to begin a state legislative session in prayer, which the Court approved in *Marsh v. Chambers*, 463 U.S. 783 (1983), because the psychological pressures were far greater in the context of school graduations.

J. Blackmun's concurrence sought to demonstrate that this decision was in accord with earlier Supreme Court precedents. He argued that "The mixing of government and religion can be a threat to free government, even if no one is forced to participate." *J. Souter's* concurrence argued that the establishment clause was designed to prohibit governmental practices that favored religion in general and not simply those that preferred one denomination to another. He also argued that it was unnecessary to show that a governmental act relative to religion was coercive to show that it was unconstitutional.

J. Scalia's dissent accused the majority of ignoring the history both of general public recognitions of religion and of school graduations in particular. He further objected to the Court's reliance on the doctrine of "psychological coercion." He did not think that voluntarily standing for a prayer could be interpreted as anything other than respect for the views of others. He further denied that the principal, who had issued a two-page pamphlet to the rabbi describing how to make public prayers inclusive, had in any real way "directed" what the rabbi would say. Scalia argued that there was no real threat of religious coercion absent any threat of "penalty or discipline." He further expressed his dismay with the Lemon Test, but argued that even it had greater validity than the majority's "psycho-coercion test."

Zobrest v. Catalina Foothills School District, 509 U.S. 1; 113 S. Ct. 2462; 125 L. Ed. 2d 1 (1993)

Facts—The parents of James Zobrest, a deaf student, applied to a public school district for an interpreter to accompany their son to classes at a Roman Catholic high school. Both the U.S. District Court and the U.S. Ninth Circuit Court found that such aid violated the establishment clause of the First Amendment, as applied to the states by the Fourteenth, by impermissibly entangling church and state.

Question— Does a state violate the establishment clause when it provides an interpreter for a deaf student in a parochial school?

Decision— No.

Reasons—*C.J. Rehnquist* (5–4). Agreeing that courts should not decide on the constitutionality of an act when such a question could be avoided by reference to other issues of statutory construction, Rehnquist noted that such other issues had not been properly raised in the lower court decisions. The majority considered the provision of an interpreter to be a benefit neutrally applied whether parents sent their children to public or private schools, as in the provision of tax deductions approved in *Mueller v. Allen* (1983) and services for the blind in *Witters v. Washington Department of Services for the Blind* (1986). The mere physical presence of a state employee on sectarian school premises was irrelevant since this presence was not designed to relieve the school of costs it would otherwise incur and since the task of an interpreter, who was simply there to translate what others were saying, was quite different from that of a teacher [Editor's note: This distinction may no longer be especially relevant in the aftermath of *Agostini v. Felton* (1997)].

J. Blackmun and *J. O'Connor* authored dissents. Blackmun argued both that the Court should seek to address statutory issues before deciding on constitutional matters and that this was the first decision in which the Court unwisely "has authorized a public employee to participate directly in religious indoctrination." O'Connor wanted the case remanded for consideration of statutory issues.

✑

Agostini v. Felton, 521 U.S. 203; 117 S. Ct. 1997; 138 L. Ed. 2d 391 (1997)

Facts—Title I of the Elementary and Secondary Education Act of 1965 was designed to provide full educational opportunity to all school students regardless of economic background. In *Aguilar v. Felton*, 473 U.S. 402 (1985), citing concerns about the establishment clause of the First Amendment, the Supreme Court prohibited public school teachers from entering parochial schools to provide remedial education, and such programs were subsequently conducted, at considerable additional costs, at off-campus sites. Parents from New York City came to Court under Federal Rule of Civil Procedure 60(b)(5) seeking relief from this earlier decision, claiming that factual circumstances and judicial precedents have changed such as to invalidate the decision in *Aguilar v. Felton*. Both the U.S. District Court and the U.S. Second Court of Appeals refused to overrule *Aguilar*.

Questions—(a) Is *Aguilar v. Felton* still good precedent? (b) Does a state violate the Firth and Fourteenth Amendments when it provides remedial education by public school teachers in sectarian facilities?

Decisions—(a) No; (b) No.

Reasons—*J. O'Connor* (5–4). The considerable additional costs of providing remedial education outside parochial schools were known when Aguilar was decided and are thus irrelevant. Similarly, statements by five justices in *Board of Education of Kiryas Joel Village School District. v. Grumet* (1994) questioning A*guilar* addressed issues not directly before the Court in that case and are not therefore dispositive. However, establishment clause decisions since *Aguilar* and a companion case *School District of Grand Rapids v. Ball*, 473 U.S. 373 (1985) have undermined those decisions, which were based on the idea that the presence of teachers in parochial schools would impermissibly advance religion through intentional or unintentional involvement of teachers in advancing religious beliefs, through creating a symbol of church/state union, or through impermissible financing of religious belief and on the belief that monitoring to prevent the preceding would lead to excessive entanglement between church and state. The Court abandoned these assumptions in *Zobrest v. Catalina Foothills School District* (1993), where it permitted a deaf student to bring a sign language interpreter to a parochial school, and in *Witters v. Washington Department of Services for the Blind* (1986), where it permitted a blind student to study at a Christian college. The Court did not believe it was reasonable to assume that public school teachers will depart from their assigned duties simply because they enter a parochial school. *Witters* has undermined the notion that the presence of public employees on parochial school property will create an improper symbolic union, and no governmental funds are directly allocated to parochial schools under Title I programs. The Court found no evidence that the administrative cooperation involved in administering this program would lead to impermissible entanglement between church and state. The Court further noted that the doctrine of stare decisis, or adherence to precedent, was "not an inexorable command" and had less relevance in constitutional decisions, where the only alternative to judicial reconsideration was a constitutional amendment, than in others.

In dissent, *J. Souter* supported the continuing validity of *Aguilar*, arguing that a clear line of division was needed between secular and parochial school instruction. Souter argued that the precedent in Zobrest was especially unconvincing in this case since the interpreter acted more like a hearing aid than a teacher. *J. Ginsburg's* dissent advanced her view that Federal Rules of Procedure did not properly permit a hearing in this case.

Santa Fe School District v. Doe, 530 U.S. 290; 120 S. Ct. 2266; 147 L. Ed. 2d 295 (2000)

Facts—Two sets of students and parents brought suit against the Santa Fe School District in Texas for policies related to student prayers at football games. These revised policies permitted students to decide by election whether or not to have such prayers and, if so, to elect a student to deliver them. The District Court upheld this provision as long as the invocations were required to be "nonsectarian and nonproselytizing." The U.S. Fifth Circuit Court of Appeals decided that, even after being so modified, the provisions for such prayers violated the establishment clause of the First Amendment.

Question—Do student-led, student-initiated invocations broadcast at public school football games violate the establishment clause of the First Amendment as applied to the states by the Fourteenth?

Decision—Yes.

Reasons—*J. Stevens* (6–3). Although the Supreme Court's decision in *Lee v. Weisman* (1992) dealt with school graduations, it was applicable here. The majoritarian process utilized to decide whether to have invocations and who will deliver them was the result of a school decision to allow prayers to be delivered. The fact that one of the purposes of such prayers was to solemnize the event, suggested that the school was endorsing religious expression. This message of endorsement would be enhanced by the fact that the invocations would be delivered at regularly scheduled events on school property. Such endorsement would convey the impression that believers are "insiders" and others are "outsiders." In addition to those students who attend games because they believe extracurricular activities are an integral part of their school experience, team members, cheerleaders, band members, and others may have little choice but to attend and be subjected to what they find to be "a personally offensive religious ritual." The school has evinced an unconstitutional purpose of facilitating prayer. The district's "governmental electoral mechanism . . . turns the school into a forum for religious debate . . . [and] empowers the student body majority with the authority to subject students of minority views to constitutionally improper messages."

C.J. Rehnquist's dissent claimed that the "tone" of the majority opinion "bristles with hostility to all things religious in public life." The Court's decision was premature in enjoining a policy that the school had yet to put into practice. Rehnquist pointed out that the school district had cited a number of secular purposes including that of solemnizing sporting events, promoting good sportsmanship and safety, and establishing an appropriate environment for the activity. In contrast to *Lee v. Weisman*, Rehnquist believed that the speech here was not school-created, but student-created, and a form of "private speech" not enjoined by the establishment clause.

❦

Good News Club v. Milford Central School, 533 U.S. 98; 121 S. Ct. 2093; 150 L. Ed. 2d 151 (2001)

Facts—Milford Central School barred the Good News Club, an evangelical Christian organization, from using its facilities after hours. A U.S. District Court and the U.S. Second Circuit Court of Appeals upheld the policy.

Questions—(a) Does Milford's exclusion of the Good News Club violate freedom of speech? (b) If so, does the establishment clause still require this exclusion?

Decisions—(a) Yes; (b) No.

Reasons—*J. Thomas* (5–3). The U.S. Circuit Courts had been split as to "whether speech can be excluded from a limited public forum on the basis of the religious nature of the speech." The Court should follow its decisions in *Lamb's Chapel v. Center Moriches Union Free School District*, 508 U.S. 384 (1993) and *Rosenberger v. Rector and Visitors of University of Virginia*, 515 U.S. 810 (1995), both of which were designed to prevent "viewpoint discrimination." Milford has opened its facilities to a variety of activities, and "we can see no logical difference in kind between the invocation of Christianity by the Club and the invocation of teamwork, loyalty, or patriotism by other associations to provide a foundation for their lessons." "The school has no valid Establishment Clause interest." The meetings were held after school hours, were not school sponsored, and required parental consent. School children are unlikely to view the presence of the meetings in school as a form of endorsement. Opening the school is a sign of "neutrality"; parents decide whether their children can attend; this is not akin to cases where students feel compulsion within a classroom setting; the instructors are not teachers; and exclusion of the Club might be perceived as "hostility" to religion. "We decline to employ Establishment Clause jurisprudence using a modified heckler's veto, in which a group's religious activity can be proscribed on the basis of what the youngest members of the audience might misperceive."

J. Scalia, concurring, observed that this case involved no physical coercion and that any peer pressure "arises from private activities, one of the attendant consequences of a freedom of association that is constitutionally protected." The school had not required "the sterility of speech" from any groups other than the Good News Club.

J. Breyer, concurring in part, stressed the government's need for "neutrality." However, he would give greater scrutiny to whether a child would perceive the school's actions as a form of endorsement and argued that denial of summary judgment to one party should be distinguished from granting summary judgment to the other side.

J. Stevens, dissenting, distinguished religious speech "that is simply speech about a particular topic from a religious point of view," "religious speech that amounts to worship," and religious speech "that is aimed principally at proselytizing or inculcating belief in a particular religious faith." He believed the Good News Club could be excluded because its speech fell within the latter category.

J. Souter, dissenting, argued that the activities of the Good News Club went beyond providing religious perspectives and constituted evangelical worship. He was also uncomfortable with the Supreme Court decision to analyze the facts of the case rather than remanding the case for such examination at the trial court level. He distinguished this case from those in which students were older and more mature, and he feared that "[t]he timing and format of Good News's gatherings . . . may well affirmatively suggest the imprimatur of officialdom in the minds of the young children."

Zelman v. Simmons-Harris, 536 U.S. 639; 122 S. Ct. 2460 (2002)

Facts—Ohio adopted a Pilot Project Scholarship Program to enhance educational choice by providing tuition aid for parents in under-performing school districts, like that in Cleveland, which were under court supervision or management. The program distributed tuition aid according to need to nearby private or public schools and tutorial assistance for qualified individuals who stayed in their existing school. Most students who participated in the program went to parochial schools. Ohio taxpayers challenged the law as a violation of the establishment clause of the First Amendment. The U.S. Supreme Court stayed a preliminary injunction issued by the District Court in this case. The District Court, affirmed by a divided vote of the U.S. Sixth Circuit Court of Appeals, subsequently granted summary judgment for the taxpayers on the basis that the law had the "primary effect" of advancing religion.

Question—Does Ohio's Pilot Project Scholarship Program violate the establishment clause of the First Amendment, as applied to the states via the Fourteenth Amendment?

Decision—No.

Reasons—*C.J. Rehnquist* (5–4). Rehnquist argued that the law in question had a valid secular legislative purpose to aid poor children in failing school systems. He upheld the law against challenges that it had the "primary effect" of advancing religion by relying on three cases. *Mueller v. Allen* (1983), *Witters v. Washington Department of Services for the Blind* (1986), and *Zobrest v. Catalina Foothills School District* (1993) have respectively authorized tax deductions for educational expenses to both public and private schools, for vocational tuition aid for a blind student studying to become a pastor, and for money to hire a sign language interpreter for a student in a parochial school. All distinguished between unconstitutional "government programs that provide aid directly to religious schools . . . and programs of true private choice, in which government aid reaches religious schools only as a result of the genuine and independent choices of private individuals." Rehnquist believed this case fell into the latter category, with the state providing no financial incentive to the religious schools that were popular choices under the program. Rehnquist further denied that any "reasonable observer" would confuse such parental choice with "the imprimatur of government endorsement," and he did not believe that the fact that most parents who participated in the program chose alternate religious schools to be constitutionally significant.

    J. O'Connor's concurring opinion emphasized the continuity of this decision with previous ones, whereas *J. Thomas's* concurrence suggested that states might be permitted greater latitude in establishment clause cases than the national government. *J. Souter's* dissent viewed this opinion as a clear and unprecedented departure from *Everson v. Board of Education* (1947) in that it allowed tax monies to go to religious institutions. *J. Souter's* dissent further expressed concern that expenditures of state monies that ended up funding religious activities could lead to discord.

Van Orden v. Perry, 545 U.S. 677, 125 S. Ct. 2854; 162 L. Ed. 2d 607 (2005)

Facts—Thomas Van Orden, a native Texan and once-licensed lawyer, challenged the existence of a monument to the Ten Commandments on the grounds of the state capitol. The District Court and the Court of Appeals regarded the display as a "passive monument" that would not convey the message that the state was attempting to endorse a specific religion.

Question—Does the establishment clause allow the display of a monument inscribed with the Ten Commandments on the Texas State Capitol grounds?

Decision—Yes.

Reasons—*C.J. Rehnquist* (5–4). This monument is one of seventeen monuments and twenty-one historical markers commemorating various phases of Texas identity. It was contributed in 1961 by the Fraternal Order of Eagles as a means of combating juvenile delinquency. Supreme Court cases point "Janus-like . . . in two directions in applying the Establishment Clause." One set of cases points "toward the strong role played by religion and religious traditions throughout our Nation's history," while the other recognizes "that governmental intervention in religious matters can itself endanger religious freedom." "Our institutions presuppose a Supreme Being, yet these institutions must not press religious observances upon their citizens." Although the Court sometimes applies the three-part Lemon test in establishment clause cases, "it is not useful in dealing with the sort of passive monument that Texas has erected on its Capitol grounds. Instead, our analysis is driven both by the nature of the monument and by our Nation's history." This history is filled with references to religion, including the presence of many such monuments in the nation's capitol. Such contexts are different than those involved in *Stone v. Graham* (1980), where the court invalidated a display of the Ten Commandments in school classrooms. The display here is "far more passive" than such daily reminders.

J. Scalia, concurring. It would be better to reach this result by adjusting establishment clause jurisprudence to recognize "that there is nothing unconstitutional in a State's favoring religion generally, honoring God through public prayer and acknowledgment, or, in a nonproselytizing manner, venerating the Ten Commandments."

J. Thomas, concurring. The Court should return to the "original meaning" of the establishment clause, which was designed simply to prevent legal coercion. Nothing compels Van Orden "to do anything." The Court should abandon precedents that permit "even the slightest public recognition of religion to constitute an establishment of religion." Nor should it deny the religious significance of religious symbols.

J. Breyer, concurring. There is "no single mechanical formula that can accurately draw the constitutional line in every case, but "the relation between government and religion is one of separation, but not of mutual hostility and suspicion." This is a "borderline" case, but the physical setting "suggests little or nothing of the sacred," and the case differs from more overt displays as in the companion *McCreary County* case.

J. Stevens, dissenting. "The sole function of the monument on the grounds of Texas's State Capitol is to display the full text of one version of the Ten Commandments." The establishment clause "has created a strong presumption against the display of religious symbols on public property." Such displays lead to "divisiveness and exclusion," and violate the principle of "neutrality." The monument has a religious purpose, and it specifically points to the Judeo-Christian God. Its display on public property implies "official recognition." The words of the Framers cannot answer questions related to a nation that is now religiously more diverse. Indeed, if the establishment clause were interpreted simply by the Framers, it would only limit *federal* establishments. The Court should interpret the First Amendment "with one eye towards our Nation's history and the other fixed on its democratic aspirations." "Fortunately, we are not bound by the Framers' expectations—we are bound by the legal principles they enshrined in our Constitution."

J. O'Connor, dissenting. Precedents require neutrality as a general rule. A monument with the full text of the Ten Commandments differs from most statutes that the court majority has referenced. The setting is not that of a museum, but "a state capitol building" which "is the civic home of every one of the State's citizens." The monument is not constitutional simply because it has been standing for forty years.

McCreary County v. American Civil Liberties Union, 545 U.S. 844; 125 S. Ct. 2722; 162 L. Ed. 2d 729 (2005)

Facts—Two Kentucky counties (McCreary and Pulaski) exhibited the Ten Commandments in their courthouses. After challenges, they subsequently twice posted two new displays in which the Ten Commandments were displayed along with other documents. The U.S. Sixth Circuit Court affirmed a district court judgment that the displays violated the establishment clause.

Question—Do these counties' displays of the Ten Commandments in courthouses constitute an improper establishment of religion?

Decision—Yes.

Reasons—*J. Souter* (5–4). The county's "manifest objective may be dispositive of the constitutional enquiry." *Lemon v. Kurtzman* (1972) established a three-pronged test for establishment clause cases that mandates "government neutrality between religion and religion, and between religion and nonreligion." Given the prior two displays, the first of which featured only the Ten Commandments, the county's religious purpose, as in *Wallace v. Jaffree*, may be ascertained "without any judicial psychoanalysis of a drafter's heart of hearts." A cited secular purpose "has to be genuine, not a sham, and not merely secondary to a religious objective." *Stone v. Graham* had forbidden similar displays in school classrooms. "The importance of neutrality as an interpretive guide is no less true now than it was when the Court broached the principle in *Everson v. Board of Education* (1947)." The dissenters' argument from original intent is highly selective and does not cover the Founders' full views.

 J. O'Connor, concurring. "[T]he Religion Clauses were designed to safeguard . . . freedom of conscience and belief." The history of these displays clearly shows a religious purpose.

 J. Scalia, dissenting. European statesmen envy the ability of American leaders to invoke the Divine. This recognition goes back to the beginning of the American republic and is quite different than that of the secular republics in Western Europe. There is nothing preventing government from favoring religion over irreligion, which the government has consistently done from the beginning. The Court is inconsistent in its application of the establishment clause, largely because it realizes that it must do so if it is to maintain credibility with the American people. No expression of religion in the public square can be completely impartial. *J. Stevens's* criticisms (in the companion case) are unwarranted. Rather than looking to judicial interpretations of the Framers' aspirations, the Court should defer to "the democratically adopted dispositions of current society." The majority's current secular purpose test goes beyond that in *Lemon* both by inferring purpose from prior legislation and by requiring that such a purpose "predominate" over any others. This has converted "what has in the past been a fairly limited inquiry into a rigorous review of the full record." Persons who viewed these displays viewed them on their own and not in the context of prior ones. They are no more offensive than was legislative prayer that the Court approved in *Marsh v. Chambers* (1983) or holiday displays that were approved in other contexts. Acknowledging the role of religion in U.S. society has a long lineage, and there is no indication that this display advanced one religion over another.

FREE EXERCISE CLAUSE

Reynolds v. United States, 98 U.S. 145; 25 L. Ed. 244; 1848 U.S. LEXIS 1374 (1879)

Facts—George Reynolds was convicted in a District Court in the territory of Utah for bigamy. In addition to claiming that a number of procedural irregularities had voided his conviction, Reynolds argued that the judge should have instructed the jury that Reynolds's religious beliefs were a defense for the crime for which he was convicted.

Questions—(a) Did Reynolds's trial violate due process of law? (b) Should the jury have been instructed that Reynolds's religious beliefs could mitigate his crime?

Decisions—(a) No; (b) No.

Reasons—*C.J. Waite* (9–0). Waite upheld a grand jury indictment as consistent with laws governing the territory. Similarly, he ruled that the judge had properly handled challenges for cause while seating jurors and had properly admitted sworn evidence of a witness (one of Reynolds's wives) unavailable at this trial but available in a previous one where she was subject to cross-examination.

Reynolds justified his actions on the basis that they stemmed from his belief as a member of the Church of Jesus Christ of Latter-day Saints, which had approved his second marriage, but the Court decided that religious belief was not an acceptable reason for violating criminal law. Examining the history of the First Amendment religion clauses, the Court cited Jefferson's belief that it created a "wall of separation" between church and state. The Court ruled that the amendment did not deprive Congress of its power "to reach actions which were in violation of social duties subversive of good order." Waite observed that polygamy had long been considered "odious among the northern and western nations of Europe," and that it had been illegal under common law, which regarded marriage not simply as a "sacred obligation" but also as a "civil contract." States had reaffirmed laws against plural marriages not long after adoption of the First Amendment. "Laws are made for the government of actions, and while they cannot interfere with mere religious belief and opinions, they may with practices." Reynolds's criminal intent could be surmised from the fact that the law was in effect when he broke it. The trial judge was within his rights in pointing to the harm that plural marriages brought upon innocent women and children involved.

In concurrence, *J. Field* argued that insufficient evidence had been provided as to the legitimacy of the trial court's use of testimony from the witness in the previous case.

Cantwell v. Connecticut, 310 U.S. 296; 60 S. Ct. 900; 84 L. Ed. 1213 (1940)

Facts—Newton Cantwell and other Jehovah's Witnesses went from house to house in New Haven, Connecticut, selling books. They were equipped with a record player that described the books, and they asked each householder for permission to play the record before doing so. They were convicted under a statute that said that no person could solicit money for alleged religious purposes from someone not of their sect unless they first secured a permit from the secretary of the Public Welfare Council.

Question—Does this statute deprive the appellants of their liberty and freedom of religion in violation of the First Amendment as guaranteed by the Fourteenth Amendment?

Decision—Yes.

Reasons—*J. Roberts* (9–0). The act required an application to the secretary of the Public Welfare Council of the state. He was empowered to determine whether the cause was religious, and the issuance of a certificate depended upon his affirmative action. If he found that the cause was not religious, it then became a crime to solicit for the cause. He did not issue the certificate as a matter of course. He must first appraise the facts, exercise judgment, and formulate an opinion. He was authorized to withhold certification if he believed the cause not to be religious. Such a censorship of religion as the means of determining its right to survive denies liberty protected by the First Amendment as applied to the states by the Fourteenth Amendment.

Note—Cantwell was the first case to apply the religious guarantees of the First Amendment to the states via the Fourteenth Amendment.

Murdock v. Pennsylvania, 319 U.S. 105; 63 S. Ct. 870; 87 L. Ed. 1292 (1943)

Facts—The city of Jeannette, Pennsylvania, had an ordinance requiring all solicitors to get a license from the treasurer of the borough. The petitioners were Jehovah's Witnesses, who were arrested for asking people to purchase certain religious books, as they distributed literature.

Question—Does this ordinance requiring a license for religious solicitors abridge First and Fourteenth Amendment freedoms of religion?

Decision—Yes.

Reasons—*J. Douglas* (5–4). A tax laid specifically on the freedom of the First Amendment would be unconstitutional. Yet the license tax in this case was just that in substance. The custom of hand-distribution of religious literature is old and has the same claim to protection as other conventional exercises of religion. In this case payment of the license tax is a condition for pursuing their religious activities.

"The fact that the ordinance is 'nondiscriminatory' is immaterial. The protection afforded by the First Amendment is not so restricted. A license tax certainly does not acquire constitutional validity because it classifies the privileges protected by the First Amendment along with the wares and mer-chandise of hucksters and peddlers and treats them all alike. Such equality in treatment does not save the ordinance. Freedom of press, freedom of speech, freedom of religion are in a preferred position. . . .

"Jehovah's Witnesses are not 'above the law.' But the present ordinance is not directed to the problems with which the police power of the state is free to deal. It does not cover, and petitioners are not charged with, breaches of the peace. They are pursuing their solicitations peacefully and quietly. . . ."

J. Reed, J. Frankfurter, and *J. Jackson* viewed the taxes in this case to be reasonable and nondiscriminatory.

Note—*Murdock* specifically reversed *Jones v. Opelika* (1942).

Marsh v. Alabama, 326 U.S. 501; 66 S. Ct. 276; 90 L. Ed. 265 (1946)

Facts—Grace Marsh, a Jehovah's Witness, was distributing religious litera-ture on the street of a privately owned town named Chickasaw that was owned by the Gulf Shipbuilding Corporation and that adjoined Mobile, Alabama.

She was warned that she could not distribute literature without a permit and she would not be issued a permit. She refused to obey and was arrested for violating the Alabama Code, which makes it a crime to enter upon or remain on the premises of another after being warned not to do so.

Question—Is the Alabama statute constitutional?

Decision—No.

Reasons—*J. Black* (5–3). A state statute seeking to punish the distribution of religious literature clearly violates the First and Fourteenth Amendments to the Constitution. One may remain on private property against the will of the owner and contrary to the law of the state so long as the only objection to his presence is that he is exercising an asserted right to spread his religious views.

"When we balance the Constitutional rights of owners of property against those of the people to enjoy freedom of press and religion, as we must here, we remain mindful of the fact that the latter occupy a preferred position. As we have stated before, the right to exercise the liberties safeguarded by the First Amendment 'lies at the foundation of free government by free men' and we must in all cases 'weigh the circumstances and . . . appraise . . . reasons in support of the regulation . . . of the rights,' *Schneider v. State*, 308 U.S. 147. In our view the circumstances that the property rights to the premises where the deprivation of liberty, here involved, took place, were held by others than the public, is not sufficient to justify the state's permitting a corporation to govern a community of citizens so as to restrict their fundamental liberties and the enforcement of such restraint by the application of a state statute. In so far as the state has attempted to impose criminal punishment on appellant for undertaking to distribute religious literature in a company town, its action cannot stand."

J. Reed authored a dissent in which he argued that the majority opinion was unwisely extending the right of religious speech from public to private property.

Note—In *Amalgamated Food Employees Union v. Logan Valley Plaza* (1968), the Court held that picketing of a private shopping center was like picketing at a downtown "business block." Four years later in *Lloyd Corporation v. Tanner* (1972), the Court retreated, holding that a private mall may prohibit handbill distribution when it is unrelated to the shopping center. Four years later again in *Hudgens v. National Labor Relations Board* (1976), the Court overruled *Logan Valley*. Finally, in *Pruneyard Shopping Center v. Robins* (1980), the Court returned to the *Marsh* principle by upholding a

California Supreme Court decision on expansive state free speech grounds. Contrast *Board of Airport Commissioners of the City of Los Angeles v. Jews for Jesus* (1987).

ॐ

Welsh v. United States, 398 U.S. 333; 90 S. Ct. 1792; 26 L. Ed. 2d 308 (1970)

Facts—Welsh was convicted in federal court for refusing to submit to induction into the armed forces, after his application for conscientious objector classification had been denied. Under the statute this status is accorded to those persons who by reason of "religious training and belief" are conscientiously opposed to participation in war in any form. Specifically excluded by the statute from such training and belief are "essentially political, sociological, or philosophical views or a merely personal code." Welsh based his claim on his belief that it is wrong to participate in any war but he stated that his views were not religious. He was not a member of any organized religion at that time.

Question—Does federal law exempt inductees from military service when their objection is based on nonreligious views?

Decision—No.

Reasons—*J. Black* (5–3). Even though Welsh's conscientious objection to war was undeniably based in part on his perception of world politics, the statute should not be read to exclude from classification as conscientious objectors those who hold strong beliefs about our domestic and foreign affairs or even those whose conscientious objection to participation in all wars is founded to a substantial extent upon considerations of public policy. The beliefs involved must be held with the strength of more traditional religious convictions.

Note—Originally used only by those claiming a conscientious objector status on religious grounds, in *United States v. Seeger*, 380 U.S. 128 (1965), the exception grounds were expanded to include deeply held moral and philosophical views. When, however, in reaction to the unpopularity of the Vietnam War, a claim was made only for a specific war, the Court refused. In *Gillette v. United States*, 401 U.S. 437 (1971), in dealing with issues growing out of the Vietnam conflict, the Court handed down some important decisions. Thus, in *Oestereich v. Selective Service Board*, 393 U.S. 233 (1962), the Court held a draft board could not withdraw a divinity student's classification because he participated in an antiwar rally, or accelerate an inductee call because he turned in his draft card, as in *Gunecht v. United States*, 396 U.S. 295 (1970), and that a draft board must honor a nonfrivolous request to reexamine a classification, as in *Mulloy v. United States*, 398 U.S. 410 (1970).

꘡

United States v. Lee, 455 U.S. 252; 102 S. Ct. 1051; 71 L. Ed. 2d 127 (1982)

Facts—Lee, a member of the Old Order Amish, is a farmer and carpenter who, between 1970 and 1977, employed other Amish. He paid no Social Security taxes and filed no Social Security tax returns. The Internal Revenue Service assessed Lee in excess of $27,000, of which he only paid $91.00, and then sued for a refund claiming, inter alia, that the imposition of the Social Security tax violated his First Amendment Free Exercise Rights and those of his Amish employees. Congress had previously accommodated self-employed Amish and self-employed members of other religious groups with similar beliefs by providing exemptions from Social Security taxes. The District Court agreed with Lee.

Question—Do the Social Security taxes interfere with the Free Exercise Rights of the Amish?

Decision—No.

Reasons—*C.J. Burger* (9–0). "Not all burdens on religion are unconstitutional. Because the Social Security System is nationwide, the governmental interest is apparent. The design of the system requires support by mandatory contributions from covered employers and employees. This mandatory participation is indispensable to the fiscal vitality of the Social Security System. The government's interest . . . to the Social Security System is very high. The difficulty in attempting to accommodate religious beliefs in the area of taxation is that 'we are a cosmopolitan nation made up of people of almost every conceivable religious preference.' To maintain an organized society that guarantees religious freedom to a great variety of faiths requires that some religious practices yield to the common good. The tax system could not function if denominations were allowed to challenge the tax system because tax payments were spent in a manner that violates their religious belief. When followers of a particular sect enter into commercial activity as a matter of choice, the limits they accept on their own conduct as a matter of conscience and faith are not to be superimposed on the statutory schemes which are binding on others in that activity."

꘡

Goldman v. Weinberger, 475 U.S. 503; 106 S. Ct. 1310; 89 L. Ed. 2d 478 (1986)

Facts—The petitioner was an ordained Orthodox Jew and a commissioned officer in the U.S. Air Force. In uniform and on duty but in violation of Air Force dress regulations, Goldman claimed the regulations prevented him from wearing his yarmulke (skullcap) in violation of his First Amendment right to freedom of religion. Continued violation of the Air Force dress regulations, he was warned, would lead to a court-martial. Goldman brought suit against the secretary of defense and others. The U.S. District Court granted Goldman injunctive relief against the application of dress regulations but the U.S. Circuit Court of Appeals reversed it. The Supreme Court granted certiorari.

Question—Does the free exercise clause of the First Amendment allow a Jewish officer who is also a rabbi to wear a yarmulke in violation of an Air Force dress regulation?

Decision—No.

Reasons—*J. Rehnquist* (5–4). The Court has repeatedly held that "the military is, by necessity, a specialized society separate from civilian society" and "the military must insist upon a respect for duty and discipline without counterpart in civilian life." The military need not encourage debate or tolerate protest to the extent "that such tolerance is required of the civilian state by the First Amendment." To accomplish its mission "the military must foster instinctive obedience, unity, commitment, and an esprit de corps." Courts must give great deference concerning "the relative importance of a particular military interest." Uniforms encourage a sense "of hierarchical unity by tending to eliminate outward individual distinctions except for those of rank. The Air Force considers them as vital during peace time as during war . . . habits of discipline and unity must be developed in advance of trouble." But whether or not expert witnesses "may feel that religious exceptions . . . are desirable is quite beside the point. The desirability of dress regulations in the military is decided by the appropriate military officials, and they are under no constitutional mandate to abandon their considered professional judgment."

Note—Interpreting this case as an example of statutory construction, Congress subsequently adopted legislation permitting members of the armed forces to wear yarmulkes.

Employment Division, Department of Human Resources of Oregon v. Smith, 494 U.S. 872; 110 S. Ct. 1595; 108 L. Ed. 2d 876 (1990)

Facts—Two drug rehabilitation counselors were fired from their jobs for ingesting peyote as part of the rituals of the Native American Church to which they belonged. Oregon denied them unemployment benefits because they were fired from their jobs for criminal wrongdoing. The Oregon Court of Appeals held that this decision interfered with their free exercise rights under the First Amendment. The Oregon Supreme Court affirmed. The U.S. Supreme Court subsequently sent the case back to the Oregon Supreme Court to ascertain whether state law exempted the use of peyote for religious purposes from its criminal statutes. The Oregon Supreme Court found no such exemption but continued to insist that the denial of unemployment benefits was a denial of free exercise rights.

Questions—(a) Are the appellees entitled to unemployment benefits? (b) Does the free exercise clause of the First and Fourteenth Amendments require a state to show a compelling interest when a generally applicable law falls with special force on a particular religion?

Decisions—(a) No; (b) No.

Reasons—*J. Scalia* (6–3). The free exercise clause of the First Amendment, which applies to the states through the Fourteenth Amendment, first and foremost protects "the right to believe and profess whatever religious doctrine one desires." This does not include the right to violate generally applicable laws that happen to fall with particular force on particular religious adherents. Court decisions that seem to imply this are in fact hybrid cases that involve the freedom of religion in conjunction with some other freedom like freedom of speech. The Court has limited the balancing test in *Sherbert v. Verner*, 374 U.S. 398 (1963) to employment situations and has never applied the "compelling state interest" test articulated there to cases where the conduct of individuals puts them in conflict with state criminal laws. Although it sounds familiar, employment of the compelling state interest test in matters related to free exercise is likely to lead to all kinds of problems. Although states are permitted to make exceptions for individuals who ingest peyote as part of their religion, they are not required by the First and Fourteenth Amendments to do so.

J. O'Connor's concurring opinion advocates retaining the compelling state interest test articulated in *Sherbert v. Verner* for cases like this, but agrees that in the case at hand the state met such a compelling state interest in that its law was aimed at suppressing illegal drug use. *J. Blackmun's* dissent argued the majority undermined "a consistent and exacting standard to test the constitutionality of a state statute that burdens the free exercise of religion." He emphasized not the state's broad interest in fighting drugs but its narrow interest in refusing to exempt religious adherents from this policy. He did not believe that labeling peyote as a Schedule I controlled substance is sufficient to uphold Oregon's restrictions, argued that the ritual use of peyote was far from the drug abuse that the state was attempting to combat, and found little illegal trade in peyote. Blackmun further believed that the majority underestimated the negative impact its ruling would have on the free exercise rights of Native Americans.

Church of Lukumi Babalu Aye v. City of Hialeah, 508 U.S. 520; 113 S. Ct. 2217; 124 L. Ed. 2d 472 (1993)

Facts—The Santeria religion, a fusion of Roman Catholicism and native African religion chiefly developed in the Caribbean, practices animal sacrifice as a means of appeasing spirits known as orishas. Animals are killed in church ceremonies by cutting their carotid arteries and usually eaten thereafter. The Church of Lukumi Babalu Aye, Inc. was established in Hialeah, Florida, and met with considerable negative public reaction. The local city council adopted a number of ordinances designed to prevent animal sacrifice within the city. The church argued that it was protected by the free exercise clause of the First Amendment. A U.S. District Court ruled for the city, finding that it had four compelling interests. The U.S. Eleventh Circuit Court of Appeals affirmed.

Question—Did Hialeah's laws against animal sacrifice violate the free exercise clause of the First Amendment as applied to the states through the Fourteenth Amendment?

Decision—Yes.

Reasons—*J. Kennedy* (9–0). *Department of Human Resources of Oregon v. Smith* (1990), established that "a law that is neutral and of general applicability need not be justified by a compelling governmental interest even if the law has the incidental effect of burdening a particular religious practice." In this case, however, the law is not neutral, and stricter scrutiny was needed. The free exercise clause was designed to prevent discrimination "against some or all religious beliefs" and may not regulate or prohibit conduct "because it is undertaken for religious reasons." The law in question was discriminatory on its face, specifically using words like "sacrifice" and "ritual" that targeted Santeria practices. Its discriminatory purpose was further confirmed by the fact that it permitted "hunting, slaughter of animals for food, eradication of insects and pests, and euthanasia as necessary" but specifically singled out religious sacrifices "for discriminatory treatment." If the city was concerned, as it said, with improper disposal of animal remains, it could have done so without a "flat prohibition of all Santeria sacrificial practice." Similarly, if its main concern were preventing cruelty to animals, it would have applied its regulations to hunting and fishing. Equal protection cases are helpful in pointing the Court to the need for "neutrality," and laws of "general applicability: The principle that government, in pursuit of legitimate interests, cannot in a selective manner impose burdens only on conduct motivated by religious beliefs is essential to the protection of the rights guaranteed by the Free Exercise Clause." This law is both under- and over-inclusive. Once a law is found not to be neutral or generally applicable, it falls not under the test announced in Smith but is subjected to strict scrutiny. This law does not meet this heightened standard.

J. Scalia, concurring, opposed inquiry into the "subjective" intent of those who adopted the statute, preferring to focus on the statute's "effects." *J. Souter*, concurring, called for a reexamination of the *Smith* decision, believing that when laws of general applicability affect religious practices, they should be not only formally neutral but substantively so. He specifically disputed the Court's interpretation of precedents in the *Smith* case. *J. Blackmun*, concurring, also believed the decision in this case should extend beyond "those rare occasions on which the government explicitly targets religion (or a particular religion) for disfavored treatment."

Rosenberger v. University of Virginia, 515 U.S. 810; 115 S. Ct. 2510; 132 L. Ed. 2d 700 (1995)

Facts—While providing funding through student activity fees for a variety of student groups, the University of Virginia denied such funding to Wide Awake Productions (WAP) for publication of an evangelical Christian newspaper. WAP appealed the university's decision. The U.S. District Court upheld the denial of funds against charges that it was unconstitutional viewpoint discrimination. The U.S. Fourth Circuit Court of Appeals held that the university's guidelines did discriminate on the basis of content but upheld them because of the state's "compelling interest" in maintaining separation of church and state.

Question—Did the university's denial of student activity funds to an organization publishing a religious newspaper violate the free speech clause of the First Amendment?

Decision—Yes.

Reasons—*J. Kennedy* (5–4). "It is axiomatic that the government may not regulate speech based on its substantive content or the message it conveys." Once the state establishes an open forum, it must make it available to all. Kennedy cited the precedent in *Lamb's Chapel v. Center Moriches Union Free School District*, 508 U.S. 384 (1993). It is not the state's business to examine the ideas expressed in publications like those at issue here. Subsidies for student publications are permissible as long as they are applied neutrally. Here the university had already gone out of its way to indicate that the publications it was supporting were not reflecting the university's viewpoints by paying outside printers for such services and providing such support to a wide variety of points of view. The university's guidelines would, if applied with any consistency, have prevented support for student "contributors named Plato, Spinoza, and Descartes" as well as for "Karl Marx, Bertrand Russell, and Jean-Paul Sartre." The university's denial of funding represented unconstitutional "viewpoint discrimination." The support provided to WAP was "neutral toward religion." That distinguished these fees "from a tax levied for the direct support of a church or group of churches." Rather, "The University provides printing services to a broad spectrum of student newspapers . . . by reason of their officers and membership." Denial of funding would deny "the right of free speech and would risk fostering a pervasive bias or hostility to religion, which could undermine the very neutrality the Establishment Clause requires."

  J. O'Connor, concurring, noted the difficulty the Court encountered "when two bedrock principles [no viewpoint discrimination and no state funding of religious activities] conflict." She observed that in this case, the student organizations remained independent of the university, that assistance was given only for permissible purposes, that support had been given to a variety of publications, including a newspaper that satirized Christianity and one that promoted a better understanding of Islam, and that the support could still be challenged on the basis that students should not have to support views with which they disagreed.

  J. Thomas, concurring, questioned the accuracy of the dissenters' analysis of James Madison's views on state funding of religion. He believed that Madison's position was consistent with that of religious neutrality. He cited what he believed to be the nation's "tradition of allowing religious adherents to participate in evenhanded government programs."

  J. Souter, dissenting, viewed this as the first time the Court had approved "direct funding of core religious activities by an arm of the State." He focused on the openly evangelical content of the newspaper in question and argued that "[u]sing public funds for the direct subsidization of preaching the word is categorically forbidden under the Establishment Clause, and if the Clause was meant to accomplish nothing else, it was meant to bar this use of public money." Souter based much of his analysis on James Madison's opposition to funding of religion. Souter did not find the presence of "neutrality" to be dispositive in establishment clause cases. He distinguished the provision of a forum from funding of such forums and considered the direct state subsidization of religious evangelism to be "a flat violation of the Establishment Clause." He would limit subsidies of advocacy of any religious viewpoints applying "to Muslim and Jewish and Buddhist advocacy as well as to Christian." He further feared the "momentum" that this case might give to constitutional theory in this area.

Board of Regents v. Southworth, 529 U.S. 217; 120 S. Ct. 1346; 146 L. Ed. 2d 193 (2000)

Facts—Students at the University of Wisconsin, Madison, challenge the expenditure of student activities fees in support of organizations that advocate a number of political views to which they object. Both the U.S. District Court and U.S. Seventh Circuit Court of Appeals invalidated the use of such fees for such purposes.

Questions—(a) Do funds charged to students by a public university for extracurricular activities violate the free speech, free association, and/or free exercise clauses of the First Amendment as applied to the states via the Fourteenth Amendment? (b) Can the designation of such fees be made through student referendums?

Decisions—(a) Such fees are constitutional if they are expended in a way that they are "viewpoint neutral." (b) The lower courts need to reexamine the referendum provision.

Reasons—*J. Kennedy* (9–0). The University of Wisconsin collects over $300 per year through nonrefundable activity fees. About 80 percent of this is classified as unallocable and goes to student health, intramural sports, campus upkeep, and the like. The rest is allocated to registered student organizations (RSOs), which are funded from the Student Government Activity Fund (SGAF). Both sides have stipulated that such funds are administered to a variety of student groups in a "viewpoint neutral" fashion, although monies may also be allocated through a student referendum. Most RSO funding is done on a reimbursement basis. Students challenged the mandatory fees on the basis that they violated free speech, free association, and free exercise rights by forcing students to support views with which they disagreed. The lower court applied a three-part test in *Lehnert v. Ferris Faculty Assn.*, 500 U.S. 507 (1991), to find that the program "was not germane to the University's mission, did not further a vital policy of the University, and imposed too much of a burden on respondents' free speech rights." Other courts had come to different conclusions about similar programs. *J. Scalia* concluded that this case was different from those where the government is speaking or where the organization is speaking on its own. In *Abood v. Detroit Board of Education*, 431 U.S. 209 (1977) and *Keller v. State Bar of California*, 496 U.S. 1 (1990), the Court exempted teachers and members of the legal bar from having to contribute to the support of political views with which they disagreed, but in this case, the university is attempting to facilitate a wide variety of speech. A university might choose to exempt students from supporting causes with which they disagree, but it is not required to do so. The central requirement to which university funds are subjected is that of content neutrality. Because it is unclear how the referendum procedure relates to such neutrality, that issue is remanded to the lower courts.

J. Souter, concurring, accepted the Wisconsin program but was unwilling "to impose a cast-iron viewpoint neutrality requirement to uphold it." He also emphasized the university's discretion in shaping its own educational mission.

∽ঌৡৢ

Gonzales v. Centro Espirita, 546 U.S. 418; 126 S. Ct. 1211; 163 L. Ed. 2d 1017 (2006)

Facts—O Centro Espirita Beneficente Uniano do Vegetal (UDV) is a Christian Spiritist sect based in Brazil with about 130 U.S. members. Members take communion by drinking hoasca, a tea from the Amazon Rainforest that contains a hallucinogen regulated under Schedule I of the Controlled Substances Act (CSA). The U.S. District Court found that this law violated the Religious Freedom Restoration Act of 1993 (RFRA), which required the government to show a compelling interest when burdening religious freedoms and issued a preliminary injunction to prevent Attorney General Alberto R. Gonzales from applying it. Both a panel and an en banc sitting of the Tenth Circuit Court agreed.

Question—Does the Religious Freedom Restoration Act prevent enforcement of federal drug laws to prevent the controlled ritualistic use of hoasca tea by Centro Espirita?

Decision—Yes.

Reasons—*C.J. Roberts* (8–0, Alito not participating). Congress crafted the Religious Freedom Restoration Act to respond to the Court's decision in *Employment Division v. Smith* (1990). The law prevented the government from burdening the free exercise of religion, except in furtherance of a compelling governmental interest and through use of the least restrictive means. Under the Controlled Substances Act of 2000, hoasca is a Schedule I substance, and its use is classified as criminal. Lower courts found that "the evidence on health risks was 'in equipoise,' and similarly that the evidence on diversion was 'virtually balanced.'" The government argues that this is an insufficient basis on which to issue a preliminary injunction, but the Court disagrees on the basis that the government has "failed to show a likelihood of success under the compelling interest test." The government contends that hoasca's classification as a Schedule I substance subjects it to judicial exemption, but "RFRA, and the strict scrutiny test it adopted, contemplate an inquiry more focused than the Government's categorical approach." In cases where the Court applied the compelling interest test, it "looked beyond broadly formulated interests justifying the general applicability of government mandates and scrutinized the asserted harm of granting specific exemptions to particular religious claimants." *Wisconsin v. Yoder* (1972), involving education, and *Sherbert v. Verner* (1963), involving unemployment compensation for individuals who lost their jobs for refusing to work on their Sabbath, were illustrative. "Under the more focused inquiry required by RFRA and the compelling interest test, the Government's mere invocation of the general characteristics of Schedule I substances, as set forth in the Controlled Substances Act, cannot carry the day." There is no indication that Congress specifically "considered the harms posed by the particular use at issue here—the circumscribed, sacramental use of *hoasca* by the UDV." The CSA itself contains a provision authorizing the Attorney General to waive registration of some drug manufacturers consistent with public health and safety, and Congress has made an exemption for the Native American Church to use peyote. Although the government explains this as a result of its "unique relationship" with the tribes, "Nothing about the unique political status of the Tribes makes their members immune from the health risks the Government asserts." Nor is there a difference between "a *congressional* exemption" and "*judicially* crafted exceptions." *Cutter v. Wilkinson*, interpreting the Religious Land Use and Institutionalized Persons Act of 2000, further shows "the feasibility of case-by-case consideration of religious exemptions to generally applicable rules." Although the 1971 United Nations Convention on Psychotropic

Substances, to which the United States has agreed, appears to cover the drug, "the fact that hoasca is covered by the Convention . . . does not automatically mean that the Government has demonstrated a compelling interest in applying the Controlled Substances Act." In adopting RFRA, "Congress recognized that "laws 'neutral' toward religion may burden religious exercise as surely as laws intended to interfere with religious exercise,' and legislated 'the compelling interest test' as the means for the courts to 'strike sensible balances between religious liberty and competing prior governmental interests."

Chapter Ten

FIRST AMENDMENT: POLITICAL RIGHTS

In addition to the two guarantees related to freedom of religion, the First Amendment contains protections for a number of political rights. These include guarantees of freedom of speech and of the press, and for peaceable assembly and petition. Such rights are indispensable to representative government. They are treated alphabetically within this chapter.

The rights of assembly and petition are essential to democratic government. Increasingly, the Supreme Court has recognized that these rights include the right of association, without which they would be relatively meaningless (this right was one of the supports used to establish a right to privacy in *Griswold v. Connecticut* [1965]). Cases in this section indicate that organizations sometimes want to restrict their membership in a way that appears to be in tension with equal rights. The Court generally has to decide the degree to which organizations seeking to make such distinctions are public, and thus subject to governmental regulation, or private, and thus not so subject. The decision in *Boy Scouts of America v. Dale* (2000) is an example of such balancing.

Like the rights of assembly and petition, the freedom of the press is essential to accountability in government. Drawing from English history, U.S. Supreme Court decisions have decided that the core of this provision is a strong presumption against "prior restraint" of publication. The purveyors of publications that are obscene or libelous may be subsequently prosecuted, but the government is very unlikely to enjoin their prior publication, considering this to be the very essence of censorship. This doctrine is clearly stated both in *Near v. Minnesota* (1931) and in *New York Times Company v. United States* (1971).

The Court has formulated various tests and doctrines to deal with special areas of press. Although the Court has not completely invalidated laws against libel, it has made it difficult to collect libel judgments against individuals criticizing public officials, lest such restrictions prove to have a "chilling effect" on legitimate speech. The landmark case in this area remains *New York Times v. Sullivan* (1964), in which the Court established a two-part test designed to limit libel against public figures only when they could show "actual malice," that is, that publications were printed with knowledge of their falsity or with reckless disregard for their truth or falsity. The Court has also been wary of gag orders (witness *Nebraska Press Association v. Stuart* [1976]) and of closed criminal proceedings, which would keep the public from observing the criminal justice process.

Freedom of speech is intimately tied to freedom of the press, and it has raised a similar diversity of issues. The Court has had to decide the degree to which limits on campaign contributions and expenditures limit free speech. *Buckley v. Valeo* (1976) remains a leading case in this area, with the Court's most recent decision in *Citizens United v. Federal Election Commission* (2010), appearing to open the door to significantly greater involvement in elections by unions and corporations.

For many years, the Supreme Court treated "commercial speech" as a separate category deserving less protection than speech related to political or philosophical views. In recent years, however, decisions like *44 Liquormart, Inc. v. Rhode Island* (1996) have moved this area closer and closer to standards applied in other areas related to freedom of the press.

The Supreme Court has attempted, not always with success, to identify what speech is obscene, and therefore subject to governmental regulation. The Court has articulated a number of tests in this area. *Miller v. California* (1973), with its articulation of a three-part test for defining obscenity, remains the current standard in this area, although it has subsequently been modified to deal with special problems connected with obscenity and children, who are believed to be especially vulnerable to exploitation in this area.

Many of the Court's most notable cases have treated governmental regulations of subversive speech. The Court has utilized a variety of tests. It has, for example, applied the "clear and present danger test" in *Schenck v. United States* (1919), the "dangerous tendency" test in *Gitlow v. New York* (1925), the "gravity of the evil" test (a variant of "clear and probable danger") in *Dennis v. United States* (1951), and the threat that speech will create a danger of "imminent lawless action" in *Brandenburg v. Ohio* (1969). This latter test gives far more freedom to subversive speech than previous ones, but some observers believe that this freedom could be undermined by recent concerns about terrorism.

It is often difficult to separate speech from conduct. Some justices, for example, Justice Hugo Black, who favored a wide range of freedom of speech, drew the line when it came to symbolic speech, but the Court majority usually links the two. The Supreme Court decision in *Texas v. Johnson* (1989) permitting demonstrators to burn the U.S. flag, proved particularly wrenching as was the Court's more recent decision in *Virginia v. Black* (2003) dealing with cross-burning.

The Supreme Court is particularly wary of governmental regulations that appear to limit speech on the basis of content. The Court is more sympathetic, however, when governments adopt regulations designed to impose time, place, and manner restrictions on the dissemination of speech than it is with regulations designed to prefer certain types of speech over others. This area overlaps, in part, with the line between "pure" speech and "symbolic" speech. Despite the decision in *West Virginia Board of Education v. Barnette* (1943), protecting the rights of students in public schools not to have to salute the U.S. flag when this salute violated their consciences, and *Tinker v. Des Moines* (1969), permitting students to wear black armbands in protest of the war in Vietnam, cases like *Bethel School District No. 503 v. Fraser* (1986), *Hazelwood School District v. Kuhlmeier* (1988), and *Morse v. Frederick* (2007) indicate that the Court still does not believe that speech in a school setting is always equivalent to that in an adult world. *Garcetti v. Ceballas* (2006) rounds out the chapter by further demonstrating that work-related speech might not enjoy the same protection as speech in general.

ASSOCIATION [IMPLIED], ASSEMBLY, AND PETITION

DeJonge v. Oregon, 299 U.S. 353; 57 S. Ct. 255; 81 L. Ed. 278 (1937)

Facts—DeJonge was indicted in Multnomah County, Oregon, for violating the criminal syndicalism law of the state, which criminalized advocacy of crime, physical violence, sabotage, or any unlawful acts as methods of accomplishing industrial change or political revolution. DeJonge was a member of the Communist Party and spoke at an advertised meeting sponsored by the Communist Party.

Question—Did Oregon's criminal syndicalism law deny freedom of assembly and speech as applied to the states by the due process clause of the Fourteenth Amendment?

Decision—Yes.

Reasons—*C.J. Hughes* (8–0). The only offense for which the accused was charged, convicted, and sentenced to imprisonment for seven years was taking part in a meeting held under the auspices of the Communist Party. While states may protect themselves and the privileges of our institutions from abuse, precedents do not permit such a curtailment of the right of free speech as the Oregon statute demanded.

Freedom of speech, press, and peaceful assembly are fundamental rights safeguarded by the due process clause of the Fourteenth Amendment. Holding a peaceful public meeting for lawful discussion cannot be made a crime. The Court was not here upholding the objectives of the Communist Party. The defendant was still entitled to his personal right of free speech, although he was a member of the Communist Party, if the activity was carried on in a lawful manner, without incitement to violence or crime.

Note—*DeJonge* was the first case to apply the First Amendment's freedom of assembly to the states via the due process clause of the Fourteenth Amendment.

❧

Hague v. Congress of Industrial Organizations, 307 U.S. 496; 59 S. Ct. 954; 83 L. Ed. 1423 (1939)

Facts—This case involved the validity of an ordinance of Jersey City that prohibited assemblies "in or upon public streets, highways, public works, or public buildings" without a permit from the director of public safety. In reliance on this ordinance, the officers of the city had enforced a policy against the distribution of circulars, leaflets, and handbills of the CIO, which was then organizing in the city.

Question—Does an ordinance prohibiting public assemblies without permits violate the due process clause of the Fourteenth Amendment?

Decision—Yes.

Reasons—*J. Roberts* (5–2). Although the Court has held that the Fourteenth Amendment created no rights in the citizen of the United States but merely secured existing rights against state abridgment, the right peaceably to assemble and discuss topics and to communicate respecting them, whether orally or in writing, is a privilege inherent in the citizenship of the United States that the amendment protects.

Citizenship of the United States would be little better than a name if it did not carry with it the right to discuss national legislation and the benefits, advantages, and opportunities that inure to citizens. However, the privileges and immunities section of the Fourteenth Amendment is applicable only to natural persons and not to artificial or legal persons.

J. McReynolds and *J. Butler* wrote short dissenting opinions focusing on the rights of municipalities to control their parks and streets and on prior precedents.

⚜

United Public Workers of America v. Mitchell, 330 U.S. 75; 67 S. Ct. 556; 91 L. Ed. 754 (1947)

Facts—The Hatch Act, enacted in 1940, makes it unlawful for federal employees to engage in certain specified political activities. The appellants, with the exception of George Poole, asked for a declaration of the legally permissible limits of regulation. The Court held that this would be an advisory opinion and refused to take jurisdiction. However, Poole was a ward executive committeeman of a political party and was politically active on election day as a worker at the polls and paymaster for other party workers. He had violated the Hatch Act.

Question—Does the Hatch Act violate the political rights reserved to the people under the Ninth and Tenth Amendments?

Decision—No.

Reasons—*J. Reed* (4–3). The practice of excluding classified employees from party offices and personal political activities at the polls is an old one. In *Ex parte Curtis* the decision was confirmed that prohibited employees from giving or receiving money for political purposes to or from other employees of the government because this was not a right protected by the Constitution, but one that was subject to regulation.

The prohibitions under discussion were not dissimilar, since they involved contributions of energy instead of money. Congress and the president are responsible for efficiency in the public service, and if they think prohibiting active political service will best obtain the objective, there is no constitutional objection. If Congress oversteps reasonable limits, the courts will interfere but only when congressional interference passes beyond the general existing conception of government power.

In dissent, *J. Black* argued that the Court majority took too narrow a view of the First Amendment. *J. Douglas* supported a declaratory judgment in cases where a judgment will keep people from having to risk their jobs.

⚜

NAACP v. Alabama, 357 U.S. 449; 78 S. Ct. 1163; 2 L. Ed. 2d 1488 (1958)

Facts—Alabama sought to enjoin the National Association for the Advancement of Colored People (NAACP) from conducting further activities within the state. As a foreign corporation, Alabama courts had found the NAACP in contempt because of its failure to supply its membership list to the state (it had provided other requested records). In addition to fining the organization $100,000, the Circuit Court of Alabama had enjoined the organization from further activities within the state, a decision that the Alabama Supreme Court refused to review.

Question—Does Alabama's order to the NAACP to produce its membership list violate the due process clause of the Fourteenth Amendment?

Decision—Yes, this order interfered with the right of association that is necessary to effective advocacy.

Reasons—*J. Harlan* (9–0). Harlan first established that the Court had jurisdiction, denying that the Alabama Supreme Court's denial of certiorari either rested on "an independent nonfederal ground" or was consistent with its own precedents. Harlan further accepted the right of the NAACP to assert the rights of its members: "To require that it be claimed by the members themselves would result in nullification of the right at the very moment of its assertion." Lawful association is tied to effective advocacy. Court decisions have established "the close nexus between the freedoms of speech and assembly" and "between freedom to associate and privacy in one's association." Past disclosures of NAACP memberships have led to "economic reprisal, loss of employment, threat of physical coercion, and other manifestations of public hostility." Although the state argued that such consequences would be the result of private rather than state action, "the crucial factor is the interplay of governmental and private action, for it is only after the initial exertion of state power represented by the production order that private action takes hold." Alabama has not established a substantial need for such information, and its order to produce the membership list is thus invalid.

Branti v. Finkel, 445 U.S. 507; 100 S. Ct. 1287; 63 L. Ed. 2d 574 (1980)

Facts—Finkel and Tabakman, two Republican assistant public defenders, were about to be discharged by Branti, the newly appointed county public defender, who was a Democrat. Upon his formal appointment, Branti began issuing termination notices for six of the nine assistants then in office. With one possible exception, the nine who were to be appointed or retained were all Democrats and were selected by Democratic legislators and town chairmen. Finkel and Tabakman brought suit to enjoin Branti, contending they had been selected for discharge solely because of their Republican Party status.

Question—Do the First and Fourteenth Amendments to the Constitution protect an assistant public defender who is satisfactorily performing his job from discharge solely because of his political beliefs?

Decision—Yes.

Reasons—*J. Stevens* (6–3). "If the First Amendment protects a public employee from discharge based on what he has said, it must also protect him from discharge on what he believes." Unless the government can demonstrate an overriding interest of vital importance, "requiring that a person's private beliefs conform to those of the hiring authority, his beliefs cannot be the sole basis depriving him of continued public employment." Party affiliation may be an acceptable requirement for some types of government employment. "[I]f an employee's private political beliefs would interfere with the discharge of his public duties, his First Amendment Rights may be required to yield to the State's vital interest in maintaining governmental effectiveness and efficiency. . . . [T]he ultimate inquiry is not whether the label 'policymaker' or 'confidential' fits a particular position; rather, the question is whether the hiring authority can demonstrate that party affiliation is an appropriate requirement for the effective performance of the public office involved. . . . The primary . . . responsibility of an assistant public defender is to represent individual citizens in the controversy with the state. . . . [W]hatever policymaking occurs in the public defender's office must relate to the needs of individual clients and not to any partisan political interests. It would undermine, rather than promote, the effective performance of an assistant public defender's office to make his tenure dependent on his allegiance to the dominant political party."

∽❧

Board of Directors of Rotary International v. Rotary Club of Duarte, 481 U.S. 537; 107 S. Ct. 1940; 95 L. Ed. 2d 474 (1987)

Facts—Each local Rotary Club is a member of Rotary International in which (as of 1982) there were 19,788 clubs worldwide in 157 countries with a total membership of a little more than 900,000 members. Individuals are admitted to membership according to a "classification system" that includes representatives of every worthy and recognized business, professional, or institutional activity in the community. The system permits additional members as associate, senior active, or past service, but does not limit the number of clergymen, journalists, or diplomats. Although each Rotary adopts its own rules, membership is open only to men. Although women are invited to attend various activities and can even form auxiliary units, they cannot be members. When the Duarte Rotary admitted women, the directors revoked their charter. Meanwhile the local Rotary went to court. After a bench trial in favor of Rotary, the California Court of Appeals reversed the decision.

Question—Did the California statute (Unruh Act) that required California Rotary Clubs to admit women members violate the First Amendment?

Decision—No.

Reasons—*J. Powell* (7–0). The California Court of Appeals found that Rotary Clubs—although committed to humanitarian service, high ethical standards in all vocations, and a concern for good will and world peace—are business establishments and therefore subject to the Unruh Act. The trial court erred in holding that Rotary was only incidentally involved in business. The appeals court rejected the view that Rotary does not provide services or facilities to its members. Rotary is not a small intimate club that gives rise to "continuous, personal, and social" relationships of a kind of which the Court is solicitous in protecting. Rotary does not fall in this category. In determining this protection "we consider factors such as size, purpose, selectivity and whether others are excluded. "Many of the Rotary Clubs central activities are carried on in the presence of visitors and strangers. Rather than keep an atmosphere of privacy they "seek to keep their windows and doors open to the whole world." The evidence fails "to demonstrate that admitting women to Rotary Clubs will affect in any significant way the existing members' ability to carry out their various purposes." The Unruh Act does not violate the right of expressive association afforded by the First Amendment.

Note—In July 1984, the Court (7–2) held in *Roberts v. United States Jaycees*, 468 U.S. 609 (1984), that women must be admitted to membership in the Jaycees. The Court asserted that a Minnesota state law compelling Jaycees to accept women as members did not violate freedom of association and could cover the Jaycees since local chapters were not small, intimate, and selective. The Court uses essentially the same reasoning in opening up Rotary International to women. The state had a "compelling interest" in eradicating discrimination. The Court, voting 9–0, made a clean sweep in *New York State*

Club Ass'n v. New York City (487 U.S. 1 (1988) holding that women must be admitted to large social clubs traditionally restricted to men.

Frisby v. Schultz, 487 U.S. 474; 108 S. Ct. 2495; 101 L. Ed. 2d 420 (1988)

Facts—Brookfield, Wisconsin, is a residential suburb of Milwaukee. It has a population of about 5,000. Antiabortionists Sandra Schultz and Robert Braun, along with others, targeted the home of a doctor who allegedly performed abortions. The picketing was orderly and peaceful but generated substantial controversy and numerous complaints. The town board passed an ordinance that held: "It is unlawful for any person to engage in picketing before or about the residence or dwelling of any individual in the town of Brookfield." The federal District Court granted appellees' motion for a preliminary injunction, concluding that the ordinance was not narrowly tailored enough to restrict protected speech in a public forum. The Court of Appeals ultimately affirmed.

Question—Does the Brookfield ordinance that permits picketing "before or about" private residences violate the First Amendment?

Decision—No.

Reasons—*J. O'Connor* (6–3). The ordinance itself recites the primary purpose of the picket ban, as "the protection and preservation of the home." The practice of picketing before or about residences and dwellings causes emotional disturbance and distress to the occupants. The ordinance also evinces a concern for public safety. Speech in a public forum should be uninhibited, and restrictions should be carefully scrutinized. A public street does not lose its status as a traditional public forum simply because it runs through a residential neighborhood. The ordinance is readily subject to a narrow construction for the words "residence" and "dwelling" are singular and suggest "that the ordinance is intended to prohibit only picketing focused on, and taking place in front of, a particular residence." We construe the ban to be a limited one—"only focused picketing taking place solely in front of a particular residence." It does not cover marching through the area or walking in front of an entire block. There are other alternatives. Protesters can visit a neighborhood, singly or in groups, may go from door to door or distribute mail by hand or by delivery. "A statute is narrowly tailored if it targets and eliminates no more than the exact source of the "evil" it seeks to remedy. Largely because of its narrow scope, the facial challenge to the ordinance must fail."

Note—Even the Supreme Court is not immune to litigation. A federal law prohibits the "display of any flag, banner, or device designed or adapted to bring into public notice any party, organization, or movement" in the Supreme Court Building or on its grounds, which include the public sidewalks constituting the outer boundaries of the grounds. The Court held that the sidewalks are public areas under the free speech provision of the First Amendment. *United States v. Grace* (461 U.S. 171, 1983).

◌৯৵

Hurley v. Irish-American Gay, Lesbian and Bisexual Group of Boston, 515 U.S. 557; 115 S. Ct. 2338; 132 L. Ed. 2d 487 (1995)

Facts—Since 1947 an unincorporated group of veterans has sponsored the St. Patrick's Day Parade in Boston. In 1992, it refused a request by the Irish-American Gay, Lesbian and Bisexual Group of Boston for a permit to participate in its parade and was ordered by a state court to let the group take part. Again in 1993, a state trial court ruled that the gay group had a right to participate under the state's public accommodation law, a judgment affirmed by the Supreme Judicial Court of Massachusetts. Hurley and other members of the Veterans Council argued that the state accommodation law violated rights of free expression and association.

Question—Do the First and Fourteenth Amendment protections of speech and association give organizers of a parade the right to exclude groups advocating messages of which they disapprove?

Decision—Yes.

Reasons—*J. Souter* (9–0). Parades are "public drams of social relations" and constitute a form of "expression, not just motion." Such expression can be conveyed through symbols as well as through words. Although the Massachusetts public accommodations law has a "venerable history," it is applied here in a peculiar way in that parade organizers did not attempt to exclude all participants who were gay, lesbian, or bisexual, but simply those marching as members of a group celebrating such lifestyles. The Court argued that "a speaker has the autonomy to choose the content of his own message." The parade organizers act as composers, selecting and rejecting groups on the basis of what they think merits celebration. Unlike cable companies, which might have to transmit programs of which they disapprove, here there is a real chance that parade viewers will associate the parade organizers with the views of the groups they permit to participate. "While the law is free to promote all sorts of conduct in place of harmful behavior, it is not free to interfere with speech for no better reason than promoting an approved message or discouraging a disfavored one, however enlightened either purpose may strike the government." The Court's opinion "rests not on any particular view about the Council's message but on the Nation's commitment to protect freedom of speech. Disapproval of a private speaker's statement does not legitimize use of the Commonwealth's power to compel the speaker to alter the message by including one more acceptable to others."

◦৯𝓵

Boy Scouts of America v. Dale, 530 U.S. 640; 120 S. Ct. 2446; 147 L. Ed. 2d 554 (2000)

Facts—The Monmouth Council of the Boy Scouts of America revoked the adult membership of an assistant scoutmaster, James Dale, a former Eagle Scout, who had announced his homosexuality while in college. Dale had claimed protection of membership under New Jersey's public accommodation law. A New Jersey Superior Court Chancery Division Court decision classified the Boy Scouts as a private group and upheld the Boy Scouts. Both the New Jersey Superior Court's Appellate Division and the New Jersey Supreme Court upheld the application of New Jersey's public accommodation law to the Scouts. The Scouts argued that New Jersey's law interfered with its expressive freedom under the First Amendment.

Question—Did New Jersey's public accommodation law interfere with the Boy Scouts' rights of expressive association under the First Amendment?

Decision—Yes.

Reasons—*C.J. Rehnquist* (5–4). Pointing to *Roberts v. United States Jaycees* (1984), Rehnquist noted that "[t]he forced inclusion of an unwanted person in a group infringes the group's freedom of expressive association if the presence of that person affects in a significant way the group's ability to advocate public or private viewpoints." Rehnquist's review of Boy Scout values, including those of being "morally straight" and "clean" as well as subsequent statements about homosexual conduct by state leaders, convinced him that the Scouts' exclusion of avowed homosexuals was essential to the expression of its views. The New Jersey law attempts to widen the notion of "public accommodations," beyond more physical locations to include regulation of membership in private groups like the Boy Scouts. In so doing, it interferes with the "Scouts' freedom of expressive association." The Court is not concerned about whether the view of the

Boy Scouts regarding homosexuality is right or wrong, but merely decides that in this case, forcing the group to accept homosexual members "would derogate from the organization's expressive message."

J. Stevens and *J. Souter* dissented. Stevens commended the New Jersey law as an attempt "to replace prejudice with principle." His review of Boy Scout policies did not convince him that opposition to homosexuality was one of its central purposes, and he thought that statements to that effect were essentially self-serving. He further rejected the idea that Dale's continuing membership would convey the message that the Scouts endorsed homosexuality. Stevens tied negative views of homosexuals to "atavistic opinions about certain racial groups" and "prejudices." Souter left open the possibility that a group could be so associated with a point of view opposing homosexuality that a public accommodation law would interfere with its legitimate right of expressive speech, but he did not believe that the Boy Scouts had demonstrated that opposition to homosexuality was one of its own key principles.

⌖

Rumsfeld v. Forum, 547 U.S. 47; 126 S. Ct. 1297; 164 L. Ed. 2d 156 (2006)

Facts—The Forum for Academic and Institutional Rights, Inc. (FAIR), an association of law schools and law faculties, challenged the Solomon Amendment, which tied federal funding to colleges and universities (excepting those that were pacifist) to giving military recruiters equal access to their facilities, as violations of the institutions' First Amendment rights of speech and association. A U.S. district court rejected this claim, but the Third Circuit reversed and issued an injunction against enforcement of the Solomon Amendment.

Question—Does enforcement of the Solomon Amendment, conditioning federal aid to schools on their provision of equal access to military recruiters, violate the First Amendment rights of speech and association of colleges and universities?

Decision—No.

Reasons—*C.J. Roberts* (8–0, *J. Alito* not participating). Congress adopted the Solomon Amendment when colleges and universities, who disagreed with the military's exclusion of openly gay recruits, sought to restrict the access of military recruiters. "The Solomon Amendment does not focus on the *content* of a school's recruiting policy. . . . Instead, it looks to the *result* achieved by the policy." The Court generally gives deference to congressional decisions tied to its power to provide for the national defense. Here Congress has exercised this power through its spending clause. Deference should arguably be even greater since "universities are free to decline the federal funds." "The Solomon Amendment neither limits what law schools may say nor requires them to say anything. Law schools remain free under the statute to express whatever views they may have on the military's congressionally mandated employment policy, all the while retaining eligibility for federal funds." "[T]he Solomon Amendment regulates conduct, not speech. It affects what law schools must *do*—afford equal access to military recruiters—not what they may or may not *say*." Just because Congress prevents participating schools from discriminating against military recruiters does not mean that it is telling them what they must say. This is not, therefore, a case of "compelled speech." "In this case, accommodating the military's message does not affect the law schools' speech, because the schools are not speaking when they host interviews and recruiting receptions. Unlike a parade organizer's choice of parade contingents, a law school's decision to allow recruiters on campus is not inherently expressive." Moreover, the burdens on conduct do not violate the test established in *United States v. O'Brien* (1968). "The expressive component of a law school's action is not created by the conduct itself but by the speech that accompanies it." Just as the Solomon Amendment does not violate freedom of speech, so too it does not violate freedom of association. By definition, recruiters are "outsiders who come onto campus for the limited purpose of trying to hire students—not to become members of the school's expressive association." "Students and faculty are free to associate to voice their disapproval of the military's message." In short, "FAIR has attempted to stretch a number of First Amendment doctrines well beyond the sort of activities these doctrines protect."

◈

PRESS

Abrams v. United States, 250 U.S. 616; 40 S. Ct. 17; 63 L. Ed. 1173 (1919)

Facts—Abrams and four other Russians were indicted for conspiring to violate the Espionage Act. They published two leaflets that denounced the efforts of capitalist nations to interfere with the Russian Revolution, criticized the president and the "plutocratic gang in Washington" for sending American troops to Russia, and urged workers producing munitions in the United States not to betray their Russian comrades.

Question—Does the Espionage Act violate the First Amendment?

Decision—No.

Reasons—*J. Clarke* (7–2). The Court reasoned that the plain purpose of their propaganda was to excite, at the supreme crisis of the war, disaffection, sedition, riots, and, as they hoped, revolution, in this country, for the purpose of embarrassing, and if possible defeating, the military plans of the government in Europe.

J. Holmes authored a stinging dissent in which he spoke of the value of "free trade in ideas—that the best test of truth is the power of the thought to get itself accepted in the competition of the market. . . ."

Near v. Minnesota ex rel. Olson, 283 U.S. 697; 51 S. Ct. 625; 75 L. Ed. 1357 (1931)

Facts—A Minnesota statute provided for the abatement, as a public nuisance, of a "malicious, scandalous and defamatory newspaper, magazine, or other periodical." The county attorney of Hennepin County brought action against a publication known as *The Saturday Press*, published by the defendants in the city of Minneapolis. The periodical in various issues charged certain public officers with gross neglect of duty or grave misconduct in office.

Question—Does the closing of a newspaper as a public nuisance infringe the liberty of the press as guaranteed by the Fourteenth Amendment?

Decision—Yes.

Reasons—*C.J. Hughes* (5–4). It is no longer questioned that liberty of the press is one of the personal freedoms protected by the Fourteenth Amendment. However, the police powers of the state must be admitted and the limits determined.

The liberty of the press in the meaning of the Constitution is principally immunity from previous restraint. The statute cannot be justified by giving a publisher an opportunity to present his evidence. It would be only a step to a complete system of censorship. "The fact that the liberty of the press may be abused by miscreant purveyors of scandal does not make any the less necessary the immunity of the press from previous restraint in dealing with official misconduct. Subsequent punishment for such abuses as may exist is the appropriate remedy, consistent with constitutional privilege."

Scandal that tends to disturb the peace is a serious public evil, but the threat to liberty is even more so. The statute, by its operation and effect was unconstitutional.

Note—*Near* was the first case in which the Supreme Court invalidated a state law regarding freedom of the press under the Fourteenth Amendment. Although condemning prior restraint of the press, which he considered to be of the very essence of censorship, the chief justice cited a limited number of occasions (many dealing with information about battle plans during war) where such censorship would be admissible.

⤷❧

Grosjean v. American Press Co., 297 U.S. 233; 56 S. Ct. 444; 80 L. Ed. 660 (1936)

Facts—A group of newspapers in the state of Louisiana brought suit to prevent enforcement of a statute levying a 2 percent gross receipts tax on them. The statute levied a tax only on newspapers having a circulation of 20,000 copies per week, making it applicable to only thirteen newspapers. Only one of these was not openly opposed to Senator Huey P. Long, who had influenced the passage of the law.

Question—Does the Louisiana statute taxing newspapers above a certain circulation abridge the freedom of the press, being contrary to the due process clause of the Fourteenth Amendment?

Decision—Yes.

Reasons—*J. Sutherland* (9–0). Sutherland dealt at length with the various attempts in the history of the British government to tax newspapers. Inevitably such a tax produced two results, a hampering of the circulation, and more or less resistance on the part of citizens. The tax imposed by this statute was not one for the purpose of supporting the government, but a tax to limit the circulation of information to the public, which circulation is necessary for a free people and a free government. Even the form of this tax was suspicious, being based solely upon the amount of circulation.

⤷❧

Bridges v. California (Times-Mirror Co. v. Superior Court of California) 314 U.S. 252; 62 S. Ct. 190; 86 L. Ed. 892 (1941)

Facts—While a motion for a new trial was pending in a case involving a dispute between an AFL and a CIO union of which Bridges was an officer, he either caused to be published or acquiesced in the publication of a telegram which he had sent to the secretary of labor. The telegram referred to the judge's decision as "outrageous," said that its attempted enforcement would tie up the port of Los Angeles and involve the entire Pacific Coast, and concluded with the announcement that the CIO union did "not intend to allow state courts to override the majority vote of members in choosing its officers and representatives and to override the National Labor Relations Board."

Newspaper editorials that commented on pending action before the same court were also involved. "The editorial thus distinguished was entitled 'Probation for Gorillas'?" After vigorously denouncing two members of a labor union who had previously been found guilty of assaulting nonunion truck drivers, it closed with the observation: "Judge A. A. Scott will make a serious mistake if he grants probation to Matthew Shannon and Kennan Holmes. This community needs the example of their assignment to the jute mill."

Both Bridges and the newspaper were cited for contempt and convicted.

Question—Do the convictions violate rights of free speech and due process as guaranteed by the First Amendment made applicable to the States by the Fourteenth Amendment?

Decision—Yes.

Reasons—*J. Black* (5–4). The telegram that Bridges sent to the secretary of labor criticizing the decision of the court was merely a statement of the facts that the secretary of labor was entitled to receive regarding an action that might result in a strike. "Again, we find exaggeration in the conclusion that the utterance even 'tended' to interfere with justice. If there was electricity in the atmosphere, it was generated by the facts; the charge added by the Bridges telegram can be dismissed as negligible."

The influence of the editorials was likewise minimized by the Court: "This editorial, given the most intimidating construction it will bear, did no more than threaten future adverse criticism which was reasonably to be expected anyway in the event of a lenient disposition of the pending case. To regard it, therefore, as in itself of substantial influence upon the course of justice would be to impute to judges a lack of firmness, wisdom, or honor, which we cannot accept as a major premise."

⚜

Martin v. City of Struthers, Ohio, 319 U.S. 141; 63 S. Ct. 862; 87 L. Ed. 1313 (1943)

Facts—An ordinance of the city of Struthers made it unlawful for any person distributing circulars or handbills from door to door to ring the doorbell, sound the knocker, or in any way to summon the inmate of the residence to the door. The appellant, Thelma Martin, challenged this ordinance as violating the right of freedom of the press, and religion as guaranteed by the First and Fourteenth Amendments.

Question—Does the city possess the power so to legislate in the light of the constitutional guarantee of freedom of speech and press?

Decision—No.

Reasons—*J. Black* (6–3). The freedom of the First Amendment embraces the right to distribute literature, and protects the right to receive it. Here is a case in which the civil rights of an individual and the rights of the individual householder to determine his willingness to accept a message conflict with the ordinance of this city protecting the interests of all its citizens, whether they want that protection or not.

Freedom to distribute literature is clearly vital to the preservation of a free society. The city may set reasonable police and health regulations, but must leave the individual householder free to decide for himself whether he will receive or reject the stranger at his door. Stringent prohibition can serve no purpose but that forbidden by the Constitution, the naked restriction of the dissemination of ideas. "We conclude that the ordinance is invalid because in conflict with the freedom of speech and press."

New York Times Company v. Sullivan, 376 U.S. 254; 84 S. Ct. 710; 11 L. Ed. 2d 686 (1964)

Facts—Sullivan, a City Commissioner of Montgomery County, Alabama, brought a civil action for libel against the *New York Times* and various African American signatories of a full-page advertisement in that newspaper that Sullivan deemed to be libelous. A Circuit Court in Montgomery County awarded Sullivan $500,000 in punitive damages, which the Alabama Supreme Court affirmed.

Questions—(a) Is this award for libel in violation of freedom of speech and press as guaranteed by the First and Fourteenth Amendments? (b) What standard should be applied in cases where public officials sue for libel in matters involving acts committed in their public capacities?

Decisions—(a) Yes; (b) To win libel judgments related to their conduct in office, public officials must demonstrate that statements made about them were made with "actual malice," that is with knowledge that the statements were false or with reckless disregard for their truth or falsity.

Reasons—*J. Brennan* (9–0). Brennan's review of the advertisement in question noted that it did not specifically mention Sullivan by name. It did contain a number of factual inaccuracies, although there was no evidence that it resulted in any "actual pecuniary loss" to Sullivan. Brennan rejected Alabama's claim that this case involved private as opposed to public action since the libel judgment clearly affected the rights of speech and press. He similarly distinguished this case from prior cases regulating "commercial" speech that did not convey the same public information as that contained in the advertisement in question. Although the Court has recognized that "libel" is not, per se, protected by the First Amendment, it should be particularly sensitive to awards given to criticism of official conduct. The First and Fourteenth Amendments have expressed a "profound national commitment to the principle that debate on public issues should be uninhibited, robust, and wide-open, and that it may well include vehement, caustic, and sometimes unpleasantly sharp attacks on government and public officials." The test of truth is insufficient in and of itself, because some degree of misstatement is likely in public speech. Although never struck down in court, the attack on the validity of the Sedition Act of 1798 has "carried the day in the court of history." Civil suits can have a similar chilling effect on free speech as do criminal laws. Laws requiring complete truthfulness for all factual assertions would lead to "self-censorship." The constitution "prohibits a public official from recovering damages for a defamatory falsehood relating to his official conduct unless he proves that the statement was made with 'actual malice'—that is, with knowledge that it was false or with reckless disregard of whether it was false or not." Alabama's presumption of actual malice does not meet such a burden. Just as public officials enjoy protection for comments they make in pursuit of their duties, so too criticisms of public officials must remain robust. There is insufficient evidence to show actual malice in this case or to demonstrate that the materials in question referred specifically to Sullivan.

J. Black's concurrence would completely prohibit damages to public officials for criticisms of how they handled their jobs. He feared that the doctrine of "actual malice" would prove to be "an elusive, abstract concept, hard to prove and hard to disprove." *J. Goldberg's* concurrence also advocated "an absolute, unconditional privilege to criticize official conduct despite the harm which may flow from excesses and abuses." He argued, however, that "Purely private defamation has little to do with the political ends of a self-governing society" and that it could thus be regulated.

New York Times Company v. United States, 403 U.S. 713; 91 S. Ct. 2140; 29 L. Ed. 2d 820 (1971)

Facts—The U.S. went to district court to enjoin publication of the Pentagon Papers by the *New York Times* and the *Washington Post*. Daniel Ellsberg, a Pentagon employee who had grown disaffected with the war in Vietnam, had turned these documents, which detailed the history of U.S. involvement in Vietnam, over to the newspapers. One Court of Appeals had affirmed a district denial of an injunction and another had remanded the case for further hearings.

Question—Can the judiciary prevent the publication of material that the government deems harmful to the national interest in the absence of a statute on the matter?

Decision—No.

Reasons—*Per Curiam* (6–3). "The Bill of Rights changed the original Constitution into a new charter under which no branch of government could abridge the freedom of press, speech, religion, and assembly. . . . Both the history and language of the First Amendment support the view that the press must be left free to publish news, whatever the source, without censorship, injunction, or prior restraint. . . . To find that the president has the 'inherent power' to halt the publication of news by resort to the courts would wipe out the First Amendment and destroy the fundamental liberty and security of the very people the government hopes to make 'secure' . . . the word 'security' is a broad, vague generality whose contours should not be invoked to abrogate the fundamental law embodied in the First Amendment."

Dissenters led by *C.J. Burger* and *J. Harlan* noted that the *New York Times* had plenty of time to review the documents (and consult with the government) prior to publication. The dissenters also thought that the president was entitled to greater deference in matters involving foreign affairs.

స్⁀

Branzburg v. Hayes, in re Pappas; United States v. Caldwell, 408 U.S. 205; 92 S. Ct. 2646; 33 L. Ed. 2d 626 (1972)

Facts—On November 15, 1969, the *Louisville Courier-Journal* carried a story under Paul Branzburg's byline describing in detail the drug activities of two persons. He was subpoenaed by the Jefferson County grand jury, but he refused to identify the two hashish makers since he had promised them not to reveal their identity. Branzburg maintained that if forced to reveal confidential sources, reporters would be measurably deterred from furnishing publishable information, and that this would work to the detriment of a free press. This case was combined with similar cases where reporters had been investigating the Black Panther organization.

Question—Must reporters respond to grand jury subpoenas and answer questions relevant to an investigation into the commission of a crime?

Decision—Yes.

Reasons—*J. White* (5–4). The great weight of authority is that newsmen are not exempt from the normal duty of appearing before a grand jury and answering such questions. The First Amendment interest asserted by newsmen is outweighed by the general obligation of citizens to appear before a grand jury or at trial, pursuant to a subpoena, and to give what information they possess. Public interest in law enforcement and in ensuring effective grand jury proceedings outweighs the consequential but uncertain burden on news gathering.

Dissenters led by *J. Stewart* and *J. Douglas* stressed reporters' need for confidentiality and the important role that they play in providing for public access to information that might otherwise be unavailable.

Note—As one consequence of *Branzburg*, some states have passed "shield laws" that extend privileged communication to journalists as it has been open to spouses, doctors, lawyers, and clergy.

৵৶

Nebraska Press Association v. Stuart, 427 U.S. 539; S. Ct. 2791; 49 L. Ed. 2d 683 (1976)

Facts—On October 18, 1975, the police found six members of the Henry Kellie family murdered in their home in Sutherland, Nebraska, a town of about 800 persons. A suspect, Edwin Charles Simants, was arrested. The crime attracted very wide coverage. The county attorney and Simants jointly asked the judge for an order restricting the flow of news so as to guarantee the defendant a fair trial. The judge agreed. His order prohibited everyone in attendance from releasing or authorizing for public dissemination in any form or manner whatsoever any testimony given or evidence deduced. The judge's order prohibited the press from reporting in five areas. The Nebraska Supreme Court affirmed.

Question—Can a judge, in order to ensure a defendant a fair trial under the guarantees of the Sixth Amendment, restrain the news media from reporting information as to pretrial events relating to a murder?

Decision—No.

Reasons—*C.J. Burger* (9–0). The problems presented by this case, said the Court, are as old as the republic itself. From the very first days of the Constitution there was a potential conflict between the First and the Sixth Amendments. These problems have an impact and history outside the Court. "We cannot," said the Court, "resolve all of them, for it is not the function of this Court to write a code. We look instead to this particular case and the legal context in which it arises." Pretrial publicity, however, "does not inevitably lead to an unfair trial." What the judge says and how he acts also sets the tone of the trial and whether or not the defendant receives a fair trial. "A prior restraint, by contrast and by definition, has an immediate and irreversible sanction. If it can be said that a threat of criminal or civil sanctions after publication 'chills' speech, prior restraint 'freezes' it at least for a time." The Court will not assign priorities between the First and Sixth Amendments. "There is no finding that alternative measures," said the Court, "would not have protected the defendant's rights."

❦

Herbert v. Lando, 441 U.S. 153; 99 S. Ct. 1635; 60 L. Ed. 2d 115 (1979)

Facts—In 1969–1970, Anthony Herbert, a retired army officer, received substantial publicity when he accused his superiors of covering up war atrocities. Three years later, a producer of a CBS program, Barry Lando, broadcast a report on Herbert and his accusations and published a related article in *Atlantic Monthly*. Herbert sued for defamation in a federal district court, claiming the television program and the magazine article falsely and maliciously portrayed him as a liar. He conceded he was a "public figure" and the First and Fourteenth Amendments preclude recovery absent proof that Lando had published damaging falsehoods with "actual malice"; that is, with knowledge that the statements were false or with reckless disregard of whether they were false or not. Lando refused to answer questions on First Amendment grounds involving the editorial process and the state of mind of those who edit, produce, or publish. The district court upheld Herbert, but it was reversed in the Court of Appeals.

Question—Can a reporter accused of damaging falsehoods and injury to someone's reputation be required to reveal his "state of mind" when preparing his material?

Decision—Yes.

Reasons—*J. White* (6–3). The Court is "being asked to modify firmly established constitutional doctrine by placing beyond reach a range of direct evidence relevant to proving knowing or reckless falsehood by the publisher of the alleged libel. . . ." The Court rejects this view and "according an absolute privilege to the editorial process of a media defendant in a libel case is not required, authorized or presaged by our prior cases, and would substantially enhance the burden of proving actual malice. . . . Courts have traditionally admitted any direct or indirect evidence relevant to the state of mind . . . without encountering constitutional objections. . . . Spreading false information in and of itself carries no First Amendment credentials."

Gannett Co. v. DePasquale, 443 U.S. 368; 99 S. Ct. 2898; 61 L. Ed. 2d 608 (1979)

Facts—Two men committed murder. At their pretrial hearing their attorneys requested that the public and the press be excluded so as not to jeopardize the defendants' ability to receive a fair trial. The district attorney did not oppose the motion. A reporter who was employed by Gannett Co., the petitioner, was present in the courtroom but made no objection. Judge DePasquale granted the motion. The reporter wrote a letter to the judge the next day and requested access to the transcript, which was denied. DePasquale allowed another hearing, but refused to vacate the order or grant Gannett immediate access to the transcript, ruling that the defendants' right to a fair trial outweighed the interests of the press and the public. The Supreme Court of New York reversed the trial judge's order. Before the case was heard at the Appellate Division, the defendants pleaded guilty to lesser included offenses, and a transcript of the suppression hearing was made available to Gannett. The New York Court of Appeals reversed the lower court and upheld the exclusion of the press and the public from the pretrial proceeding.

Question—Does the state court order for protection of defendants' fair-trial rights in a murder case, agreed to by prosecution and defense, violate the Constitution in barring members of the press and public from the pretrial suppression hearing?

Decision—No.

Reasons—*J. Stewart* (5–4). "To safeguard the due process rights of the accused, a trial judge has an affirmative constitutional duty to minimize the effects of prejudicial pretrial publicity. . . . And because of the Constitution's pervasive concern for these due process rights, a trial judge may surely take protective measures even when they are not strictly and inescapably necessary.

. . . Among the guarantees that the amendment provides to a person charged with the commission of a criminal offense, and to him alone, is the 'right to a speedy and public trial, by an impartial jury.' The Constitution nowhere mentions any right of access to a criminal trial on the part of the public; its guarantee, like the others enumerated, is personal to the accused. . . . Several factors lead to the conclusion that the actions of the trial judge here were consistent with any right of access the petitioner may have had under the First and Fourteenth Amendments. First, none of the spectators present in the courtroom, including the reporter employed by the petitioner, objected when the defendants made the closure notice. . . . Furthermore, any denial of access in this case was not absolute but only temporary. Once the danger of prejudice had dissipated, a transcript of the suppression hearing was made available."

❦

Richmond Newspapers, Inc. v. Commonwealth of Virginia, 448 U.S. 555; 100 S. Ct. 2814; 65 L. Ed. 2d 973 (1980)

Facts—Before the trial of a suspected murderer began, counsel for the defendant moved that the proceedings be closed to the public, thus excluding two Richmond newspaper reporters from the courtroom. There was no objection by the prosecution and the decision to clear the courtroom was left entirely to the discretion of the presiding judge. After the judge ordered that the courtroom be kept clear of all parties except the witnesses when they testified, Richmond Newspapers sought a hearing on a motion to vacate the order. The court denied the motion and ordered the trial to continue with the press and public excluded. The judge then granted a defense motion to strike the prosecution's evidence and found the defendant not guilty of murder, and the court granted the newspaper's motion to intervene in the case. The newspaper petitioned the Virginia Supreme Court for writs of mandamus and prohibition and filed an appeal from the trial court's closure order, but the Virginia Supreme Court dismissed the petitions and denied the appeal.

Question—Is the right of the public and press to attend criminal trials guaranteed under the United States Constitution?

Decision—Yes.

Reasons—*C.J. Burger* (7–1). "The origins of the proceeding, which has become the modern criminal trial in Anglo-American justice can be traced back beyond reliable historical records. . . . [T]hroughout its evolution, the trial has been open to all who cared to observe . . . we are bound to conclude that a presumption of openness inheres in the very nature of a criminal trial under our system of justice. The Bill of Rights was enacted against the backdrop of the long history of trials being presumptively open. Public access to trials was then regarded as an important aspect of the process itself. . . . In guaranteeing freedoms such as those of speech and press, the First Amendment can be read as protecting the right of everyone to attend trials so as to give meaning to those explicit guarantees. . . . [T]he First Amendment guarantees of speech and press, standing alone, prohibit government from summarily closing courtroom doors which had long been open to the public at the time that amendment was adopted. . . . [A] trial courtroom . . . is a public place where the people generally— and representatives of the media—have a right to be present, and where their presence historically has been thought to enhance the integrity and quality of what takes place. We hold that the right to attend criminal trials is implicit in the guarantees of the First Amendment; without the freedom to attend such trials, . . . important aspects of freedom of speech and of the press could be eviscerated."

J. Rehnquist, dissenting, decried the Supreme Court's increased willingness to intervene in matters involving state trials. He favored allowing the state court to strike the ultimate balance between First and Sixth Amendment rights.

⚜

Chandler and Granger v. Florida, 449 U.S. 560; 101 S. Ct. 802; 66 L. Ed. 2d 740 (1981)

Facts—A canon of the Florida Code of Judicial Conduct permitted still photography and electronic media coverage of judicial proceedings subject to the control of the presiding judge. The trial judges were obliged to protect the fundamental right of the accused in a criminal case to a fair trial. A jury in a Florida trial court convicted appellants Chandler and Granger, former Miami Beach policemen, who were charged with a crime that attracted media attention, over objections that the television coverage of parts of their trials denied them a fair and impartial trial.

Question—Does televising a criminal trial deny the accused his fundamental right to a fair trial as is guaranteed by the due process clause of the Fourteenth Amendment?

Decision—No.

Reasons—*C.J. Burger* (8–0). "An absolute constitutional ban on broadcast coverage of trials cannot be justified simply because there is a danger that, in some cases, prejudicial broadcast accounts of pretrial and trial events may impair the ability of jurors to decide the issue of guilt or innocence uninfluenced by extraneous matter. The risk of juror prejudice is present in any publication of a trial, but the appropriate safeguard against such prejudice is the defendant's right to demonstrate that the media's coverage of his case—be it printed or broadcast—compromised the ability of the particular jury that heard the case to adjudicate fairly. . . . The Florida guidelines place on trial judges positive obligations to be on guard to protect the fundamental right of the accused to a fair trial. . . . To demonstrate prejudice in a specific case a defendant must show something more than juror awareness that the trial is such as to attract the attention of broadcasters . . . unless we were to conclude that television coverage under all conditions is prohibited by the Constitution, the states must be free to experiment . . . because this court has no supervisory authority over state courts, our review is confined to whether there is a constitutional violation. We hold that the Constitution does not prohibit a state from experimenting with [its] program."

◇๛

Hustler *Magazine v. Falwell, 485 U.S. 46; 108 S. Ct. 876; 99 L. Ed. 2d 41 (1988)*

Facts—In a district court Jerry Falwell, a nationally known minister, sought to recover damages for libel and intentional infliction of emotional distress arising from an advertisement "parody" that portrayed him in a drunken incestuous tryst with his mother in an outhouse. This "parody" featured in *Hustler* magazine was modeled on an advertisement for Compari Liqueur that played on the double entendre of "first times." Falwell, claiming an invasion of privacy and the intentional infliction of emotional distress, asked for libel damages. The District Court discounted the libel and privacy claims but accepted the argument based on emotional distress, which the United States Court of Appeals upheld

Question—May a public figure recover damages for the intentional infliction of emotional distress as a result of a parody?

Decision—No.

Reasons—*C.J. Rehnquist* (8–0). The state's interest in protecting Falwell from emotional distress was insufficient to deny First Amendment protection. "The First Amendment recognizes no such thing as a 'false' idea." Criticism of public figures will not always be reasoned or moderate. They likely are subject to vehement and caustic attacks. This does not mean all speech is immune. Under the *Sullivan* doctrine we have held that a speaker is liable for reputational damage caused by a defamatory falsehood but only if the statement was made 'with knowledge that it was false or with reckless disregard of whether it was false or not.'" Although falsehoods have little value, they are nevertheless inevitable in free debate even "when a speaker or writer is motivated by hatred or ill-will." To hold otherwise cartoonists would continually be subject to suits—because "the art of the cartoonist is often not reasoned or even handed, but slashing and one sided." Outrageous speech in political and social discourse has an inherent subjectiveness about it, which would allow a jury to impose liability on the basis of the jurors tastes or their dislike of a particular expression.

SPEECH

Campaign-Related

Buckley v. Valeo, 424 U.S. 1; 96 S. Ct. 612; 46 L. Ed. 2d 659 (1976)

Facts—Congress passed in 1971, and in 1974 amended, the Federal Election Campaign Act. This act broadly attempted to limit individual political contributions to $1,000 to any single candidate with an overall annual limitation of $35,000 by any single contributor. It further required reporting and disclosure of contributions and expenditures above certain threshold levels; established a system of public financing of presidential campaigns; and created a Federal Election Commission.

Questions—(a) Does the Federal Election Campaign Act of 1974 violate the First Amendment's freedom of communication and freedom of association? (b) Do its subsidy provisions violate the general welfare clause? (c) Does the Federal Election Commission as constituted violate the doctrine of the separation of powers?

Decisions—(a) No; (b) No; (c) Yes.

Reasons—*Per Curiam.* (Vote varied from one issue to another.) The Court held part of the Federal Election Campaign Act constitutional and part unconstitutional. Held constitutional under Congress's power to regulate elections and prevent corruption, was the part that allowed Congress to set ceilings on political contributions as against the charge that the act violated the speech and associational provisions of the First Amendment and to provide public financing of presidential nominating conventions and primaries against the charge that it violated the general welfare clause (Article I, Section 8, Clause 1). The part that set limits to independent political expenditures by individuals and groups is unconstitutional because it burdens the right of free speech as well as setting limits to the personal expenditures by the candidate himself. The Court also voided the method of nominating the members of the commission as violating the doctrine of separation of powers. "The act's contributions and expenditure limitations," said the Court, "impinge on protected associational freedoms. Making a contribution, like joining a political party, serves to affiliate a person with a candidate." Although Congress can regulate elections it cannot "appoint those who are to administer the regulatory statute" in violation of the appointing clause.

Note—In *McConnell v. Federal Election Commission* 540 U.S. 93 (2003), the Court upheld provisions of the Bipartisan Campaign Finance Reform Act of 2001 (McCain-Feingold Act) that limited indirect "soft-money" contributions to campaigns.

Elrod v. Burns, 427 U.S. 347; 96 S. Ct. 2673; 49 L. Ed. 2d 547 (1976)

Facts—Non–civil service employees of the Cook County Sheriff's Office in Illinois who were Republicans sought an injunction to prevent the newly elected Democrat from firing them. The U.S. Seventh Circuit Court of Appeals overturned the District Court's denial of the injunction.

Question—Do the First and Fourteenth Amendments limit the dismissal of non–civil service employees on the basis of their political party affiliation?

Decision—Yes, it limits the dismissal of employees who are not in policy-making positions.

Reasons—*J. Brennan* (writing for three justices in a 5–4 decision). The case did not present a "political question" unfit for judicial resolution. Although patronage was not new, its "cost" was "the restraint it places on freedom of belief and association," core values protected by the First Amendment. Public debate should be robust and patronage practices made such debate less likely. First Amendment rights are not absolute, but impairments of such rights are subject to "strict scrutiny," and must be by the least restrictive means. The state asserts an interest in insuring "effective government and the efficiency of public employees," but wholesale dismissals are inefficient and should be made on a basis other than that of "mere political association." Moreover, efficiency can be guarded through the accountability of elected officials to the electorate. The state also asserts the need for loyalty among governmental officials, but such a goal can be achieved by "limiting patronage dismissals to policymaking positions." The state's interest in preserving democratic processes is a valid objective but can be achieved through less restrictive alternatives. Brennan concluded that "patronage dismissals severely restrict political belief and association" and upheld the injunction.

J. Stewart concurred, but limited his decision to "whether a non-policymaking, nonconfidential government employee can be discharged or threatened with discharge from a job that he is satisfactorily performing upon the sole ground of his political beliefs."

C.J. Burger dissented on the basis that this decision represented unwarranted intervention into state affairs.

J. Powell focused in dissent on historical practice. He observed that the individuals who brought suit took their positions knowing they were patronage positions. He further argued that patronage contributed to democracy "by stimulating political activity and by strengthening parties," especially at state and local levels. He thus concluded that "patronage hiring practices sufficiently serve important state interests, including some interests sought to be advanced by the First Amendment, to justify a tolerable intrusion on the First Amendment interests of employees or potential employees."

Republican Party of Minnesota v. White, 536 U.S. 765; 122 S. Ct. 2528; 153 L. Ed. 2d 694 (2002)

Facts—The Minnesota Supreme Court issued a rule that prohibited judicial candidates from announcing their view on disputed legal or political issues. Gregory Wersal, running for associate justice of the Minnesota Supreme Court, distributed literature criticizing several of its opinions and had a complaint filed against him with the Office of Lawyers Professional Responsibility. Wersal withdrew from the election but later ran again and sought an advisory opinion as to whether it would enforce its "announce clause"; the Board responded equivocally. Wersal subsequently sought a declaration that the clause violated the First Amendment and sought an injunction against its enforcement. The U.S. District Court and the U.S. Eighth Circuit Court both upheld the provision.

Question—Does the judicially promulgated rule in Minnesota prohibiting judicial candidates from announcing their views on disputed legal or political issues violate the First and Fourteenth Amendments?

Decision—Yes.

Reasons—*J. Scalia* (5–4). Scalia distinguished the "announce" clause from the "pledges or promises" clause that banned specific promises as a condition of election. The announce clause has been broadly construed to cover comments on past decisions; moreover, its exemption for "general discussion" of cases is limited: "the announce clause prohibits a judicial candidate from stating his views on any specific nonfanciful legal question within the province of the court for which he is running, except in the context of discussing past decisions—and in the latter context as well, if he expresses the view that he is not bound by *stare decisis*." Such limitations are suspect both because they are content based and because they deal with speech that is at the very core of the First Amendment. The state justified these limitations as attempts to preserve judicial impartiality and its appearance, but they are not narrowly tailored to these ends. The announce clause was not needed to assure impartiality whether interpreted to assure equal application of the law to litigants, to avoid preconceptions in favor of particular legal views, or to insure open-mindedness. Specifically, the clause did nothing about opinions that judges have expressed either prior to announcing their candidacy or once they are on the bench. The separate clause dealing with "pledges or promises" addresses such issues much more specifically. Judicial elections are similar to others and require the same kinds of free speech. Moreover, "[t]he practice of prohibiting speech by judicial candidates on disputed issues . . . is neither long not universal." Judicial elections did not become widespread until the Jacksonian period and did not initially limit the speech of candidates, and by the end of World War II, judicial canons similar to those in Minnesota applied to such elections in only eleven states. The clause points to "an obvious tension between the article of Minnesota's popularly approved Constitution which provides that judges shall be elected, and the Minnesota Supreme Court's announce clause which places most subjects of interest to the voters off limits."

J. O'Connor, concurring, expressed her concerns about state judicial elections, with the campaigning and fund-raising they require.

J. Kennedy, concurring, argued that the clause at issue should be invalidated on First Amendment grounds, with or without a state showing of a compelling interest.

J. Stevens, dissenting, argued that the Court failed to distinguish the real differences between regular elections and those for judgeships. Judges are different because rather than serving constituents they have "a duty to uphold the law and to follow the dictates of the Constitution." States should not have to make "an all or nothing choice of abandoning judicial elections or having elections in which anything goes."

J. Ginsburg, dissenting, also emphasized that "judges represent the Law." She further argued that "The ability of the judiciary to discharge its unique role rests to a large degree on the manner in which judges are selected." Whereas legislative and executive officers "serve in representative capacities," judges "do not sit as representatives of particular persons, communities, or parties; they serve no faction or constituency." Therefore the rationale that justifies uninhibited speech in one case does not justify it in another. Such speech tends to undermine impartiality and the perception of impartiality. Minnesota should not require that judges "be treated as politicians simply because they are chosen by popular vote."

☙❧

Citizens United v. Federal Election Commission, No. 08-205 (2010)

Facts—The Bipartisan Campaign Reform Act of 2002 (BCRA) prohibited corporations and unions from making independent expenditures for electioneering communications within 30 days of a primary election. *McConnell v. Federal Election Commission* (2003) had rejected a facial challenge to this law. Citizens United challenged the law after becoming concerned that a negative documentary on Hillary Clinton, which it hoped to air on cable television, would be illegal. The case was reargued after the Court specifically asked parties to address whether it should overrule precedents.

Question—(a) Do election laws prohibiting independent corporate and union broadcast of campaign-related materials relative to specific candidates violate the First Amendment? (b) Do related disclaimer and disclosure requirements violate the amendment?

Decision—(a) Yes; (b) no.

Reasons—*J. Kennedy* (5–4). The *McConnell* decision largely rested on *Austin v. Michigan Chamber of Commerce* (1990), which permitted bans on corporate speech. Austin departed from established precedents and should be overturned. Prior law already prohibits direct contributions from unions and corporations to political candidates. The documentary that Citizens United wanted to distribute fell clearly under the prohibition of the law, which prohibited express advocacy. The Court cannot easily distinguish video-on-demand from other media technology, and it should not carve out a special exception for nonprofit corporations like Citizens United. The government has not provided adequate reason for the Court to consider an as-applied as opposed to a facial challenge to the law, without chilling the exercise of free speech in the interim, especially in the case of such core political speech. A speaker facing uncertainty over the constitutionality of speech is just as effectively censured as if this were a form of prior restraint or a licensing law, especially since the law imposes criminal penalties. Although unions and corporations could work through PACS, these can be "burdensome" and "expensive" alternatives that require excessive paperwork. "Speech is an essential mechanism of democracy, for it is the means to hold officials accountable to the people," and laws burdening such speech are subject to "strict scrutiny." The First Amendment is "[p]remised on mistrust of governmental power" and "stands against attempts to disfavor certain subjects or viewpoints." Moreover, First Amendment protection extends to corporations, and especially to political speech. *Buckley v. Valeo* (1976) did not specifically address the ban on corporation and union independent expenditures, but *First National Bank of Boston v. Bellotti* (1978) "reaffirmed the First Amendment principle that the Government cannot restrict political speech based on the speaker's corporate identity." The *Austin* decision identified "an antidistortion interest" in limiting political speech based on an attempt to prevent the effects of accumulated wealth, but these are at odds with prior cases. "If the antidistortion rationale were to be accepted, . . . it would permit Government to ban political speech simply because the speaker is an association that has taken on the corporate form," and would give Congress undue power. Moreover, Congress would have no basis for distinguishing between corporations that are media corporations and those that are not. *Austin* thus "interferes with the 'open marketplace' of ideas protected by the First Amendment." A ban on indirect contributions cannot be justified as a means of prohibiting corruption, since such contributions are not coordinated with campaigns and involve no quid pro quo. The decision in *Caperton v. A.T. Massey Coal Co.* (2009) does not argue to the contrary. Moreover, this decision is unaffected by *McConnell's* opinion regarding "soft money" expenditures. Considerations of antiquity, reliance, and reasoning are inadequate in this case to support *stare decisis*, especially given *Austin's* own abandonment of previous precedents. Disclaimer and disclosure requirements are valid since that did not impose a "ceiling on campaign-related activities." They help make it clear that the advertisements are not funded by the candidates, and Citizens United has not shown that its members feared retaliation. The court should be particularly reluctant to suppress speech "in the public dialogue preceding a real election."

C.J. Roberts wrote a concurring opinion, joined by *J. Alito*, specifically to address issues of judicial restraint and *stare decisis*.

J. Scalia wrote a concurrence (joined by *J. Alito* and *J. Thomas*) attempting to refute *J. Stevens's* analysis of the original intent of the First Amendment, arguing that the Amendment was designed to protect both private and media interests. "The Amendment is written in terms of 'speech,' not speakers."

J. Stevens authored a dissent arguing that "the distinction between cor-porate and human speakers is significant." He noted that restrictions on corporate expenditures dated back to the Tillman Act of 1907. He ques-tioned whether the broad issue that the Court decided was properly before it and whether the Court should have accepted a facial rather than an as-ap-plied challenge. The Court should wait for real issues rather than attempt to "hedge against future judicial error." The Court could have ruled on much narrower grounds than it did, and the principle of stare decisis would indicate that it should do so. The decision in *Austin* has not shown itself to be as flawed as the majority suggests, and the Court has not adequately addressed issues like "the antiquity of the precedent, the workability of its legal rule, and the reliance interests at stake." Because corporations can operate through PACS, the majority's image of an outright "ban" is inaccu-rate. The limits of this law are narrow enough that they may be construed as a reasonable "time, place, and manner restriction." The *Bellotti* precedent is not nearly as broad as the Court has interpreted it, and the court has long ap-proved "the authority of legislatures to enact viewpoint-neutral regulations based on content and identity." The majority's stance would have given "Tokyo Rose" the same protection to speak to U.S. troops during World War II as their commanders. The Framers had a much narrower view of speech, and of the rights of corporations, than the majority, and the original understanding has been substantiated by the history of regulation in this area. "[T]he Constitution does, in fact, permit numerous 'restrictions on the speech of some in order to prevent a few from drowning out the many.'" The laws at issue are legitimate measures to prevent corruption (not all of which fall into the *quid pro quo* category) and to protect shareholders from expenditures they do not support. The Court should, in any event, defer to legislative judgment on such matters. However useful corporations may be, "They are not themselves members of 'We the People' by whom and for whom our Constitution was established." "The Court's blinkered and apho-ristic approach to the First Amendment may well promote corporate power at the cost of the individual and collective self-expression the Amendment was meant to serve."

J. Thomas concurred with the majority's decision to protect corporate speech but dissented from the part of the opinion that upheld disclosure, dis-claimer, and reporting requirements. Citing the "right to anonymous speech" recognized in *McIntyre v. Ohio Elections Commission* (1995), Thomas cited examples of intimidation and retaliation that had arisen after the disclosure of contributors to Proposition 8, dealing with same-sex marriage, in California.

Commercial Speech

Virginia State Board of Pharmacy v. Virginia Citizens Consumer Council, Inc., 425 U.S. 748; 96 S. Ct. 1817; 48 L. Ed. 2d 346 (1976)

Facts—The appellees, a consumer group, challenged a Virginia law that states that a pharmacist is guilty of unprofessional conduct if he "publishes, advertises or promotes, directly or indirectly, in any manner whatsoever, any amount, price, fee, premium, discount, rebate or credit terms . . . for any drugs which may be dispensed by prescription." The Virginia State Board of Pharmacy was the licensing authority, and a pharmacist was subject to a civil monetary penalty, or to revocation or suspension of his license.

Question—Does the Virginia statute making it unprofessional conduct for a pharmacist to advertise prescription drug prices violate the First Amendment rights of drug consumers?

Decision—Yes.

Reasons—*J. Blackmun* (7–1). Freedom of speech, noted the Court, "presupposes a willing speaker. But where a speaker exists, as in the case here, the protection afforded is to the communication, to its source and to the recipients both." If there is a right to advertise, there is a reciprocal right to receive the advertising. The contention that the advertisement of the prescription drug prices is outside the First Amendment because it is "commercial speech" is rejected. The Court said it was not unmindful of the fact that some commercial speech can be regulated by the state, for example, untruthful speech or wholly false, deceptive, or misleading advertising; and some other speech, for example in the electronic broadcast media is outside the confines of its decision. But society has a strong interest in the free flow of commercial information. Virginia argues that it would protect its citizens from fraud and maintain professional standards but its protectiveness, as to competing drug prices, rests in large measure "on the advantages of their being kept in ignorance."

  J. Rehnquist wrote a dissent protesting against the elevation of protection for commerce speech to the same level as political speech.

Note—*Virginia State Board* logically followed from *Bigelow v. Virginia* (1975), involving a newspaper advertisement. It, in turn, led to other commercial speech cases, such as contraception advertising in *Carey v. Population Services*, 431 U.S. 678; legal advertising, in *Bates v. State Bar*, 433 U.S. 350 (1977); and real estate "for sale" and "sold" signs in *Linmark Associates, Inc. v. Willingboro*, 431 U.S. 85 (1977). A novel case involving free speech and advertising occurred in *Posadas de Puerto Rico Associates v. Tourism Company of Puerto Rico* (478 U.S. 328 [1986]) in which the Court upheld a law restricting advertising by a legal gambling casino against the charge of free speech, due process, and equal protection. Puerto Rico intended to appeal to tourists who want to gamble but not to its own citizens. The Court subsequently overturned that decision in *44 Liquormart, Inc. v. Rhode Island* (1996).

First National Bank of Boston v. Bellotti, 435 U.S. 765; 98 S. Ct. 1407; 55 L. Ed. 2d 707 (1978)

Facts—Appellants were national banking associations and business corporations that wanted to publicize their views. They opposed a referendum proposal to amend the Massachusetts Constitution that would allow the legislature to enact a graduated personal income tax. The attorney general of Massachusetts advised the corporation against making contributions or expenditures "for the purpose of influencing . . . or affecting the vote on any question submitted to the voters other than the one materially affecting any of the property, business or assets of the corporation." The Supreme Judicial Court of Massachusetts held that the corporation could not claim First or Fourteenth Amendment protections for its speech or other activities entitling it to communicate its position on that issue to the general public. Although the 1976 referendum had passed, the Court did not believe the question "moot" inasmuch as another referendum proposal was likely to arise.

Question—Does the Massachusetts law that prohibits corporations from spending money to influence a referendum violate the First and Fourteenth Amendments?

Decision—Yes.

Reasons—*J. Powell* (5–4). Freedom of speech and press embrace the liberty to discuss publicly and truthfully all matters of public concern without previous restraint or fear of subsequent punishment. If the speakers were not corporations, no one would suggest that the state could silence their proposed speech. Speech is indispensable to decision making in a democracy "and this is no less true because the speech comes from a corporation rather than an individual." Although the press informs and educates the public and offers criticism and provides a forum for discussion and debate, it "does not have a monopoly on either the First Amendment or the ability to enlighten." If a legislature may direct business corporations to "stick to business" it may also limit other corporations—religious, charitable, or civil—to their respective "business" when addressing the public. "Such power in government to channel the expression of views is unacceptable under the First Amendment."

J. White and *J. Rehnquist* authored dissents in which they would have deferred to state judgments about the extent of corporate speech on issues not tied directly to such businesses.

෧෯

44 Liquormart, Inc. v. Rhode Island, 517 U.S. 484; 116 S. Ct. 1495; 134 L. Ed. 2d 711 (1996)

Facts—Rhode Island has strict laws prohibiting the advertising of the prices of alcoholic products within the state. 44 Liquormart, Inc. (joined by Peoples Super Liquor Stores, Inc.), a retailer of alcoholic beverages, was fined for advertisements that, while not specifically mentioning the prices of its alcoholic beverages, implied that they were low. A U.S. District Court ruled that Rhode Island's regulations of price advertising violated the First Amendment in that they did not advance the state's interest in reducing alcohol consumption and were more extensive than necessary. The U.S. First Circuit Court of Appeals reversed this judgment.

Questions—(a) Did Rhode Island's limitations on advertising of the price of alcohol violate the First and Fourteenth Amendments' protections for freedom of speech? (b) Are the regulations protected by the Twenty-first Amendment?

Decisions—(a) Yes; (b) No.

Reasons—*J. Stevens* (9–0). Supreme Court decisions in *Bigelow v. Virginia*, 421 U.S. 809 (1975) and *Virginia Bd. of Pharmacy v. Virginia Citizens Consumer Council, Inc.*, 425 U.S. 748 (1976) established "the public's interest in receiving accurate commercial information." Bans against such information are based "on the offensive assumption that the public will respond 'irrationally' to the truth." Although the state has a legitimate interest in promoting temperance, it did not show that the advertising ban will significantly advance this interest or that other less drastic means could not be used instead. The Court's decision in *Posadas de Puerto Rico Associates v. Tourism Co. of P.R.*, 478 U.S. 328 (1986), permitting the banning of information in Puerto Rico of a casino located there, marked a "sharp break from our prior precedent," that was no longer valid and that incorrectly assumed that regulation of speech was less drastic than regulation of conduct. Although the Twenty-first Amendment granted states increased authority over commerce in alcohol, it was not designed to limit any other constitutional rights, including freedom of speech.

J. Scalia, J. Thomas, and *J. O'Connor* all filed concurring opinions.

Obscenity

Burstyn v. Wilson, 343 U.S. 495; 72 S. Ct. 777; 96 L. Ed. 1098 (1952)

Facts—A highly controversial film, *The Miracle*, produced in Italy and starring Anna Magnani, had at first been licensed for showing in New York and had been exhibited in the city for approximately eight weeks. Public reaction resulted in the license being withdrawn on the ground that the movie was "sacrilegious." The distributor of the motion picture brought action in the state courts and ultimately in the Supreme Court of the United States to attempt to force Wilson, New York State Commissioner of Education, to grant the license.

Question—Is the New York statute that permits state authorities to ban films on the ground that they are "sacrilegious" contrary to the First and Fourteenth Amendments?

Decision—Yes.

Reasons—*J. Clark* (9–0). Motion pictures are a significant medium for the communication of ideas. This function is not lessened because they are designed to entertain as well as to inform. Also, their production, distribution, and exhibition for profit do not affect the application of the liberty guaranteed by the First Amendment any more than in the case of books, newspapers, and magazines. Expression by means of motion pictures is included within the free speech and free press guarantee of the First and Fourteenth Amendments. A state cannot ban a film on the basis of a censor's view that it is "sacrilegious." Such a standard is too vague. From the standpoint of freedom of speech and press, the state has no legitimate interest in protecting any or all religions from views sufficiently distasteful to them to justify prior restraint upon the expression of those views.

Roth v. United States (Alberts v. California), 354 U.S. 476; 77 S. Ct. 1304; 1 L. Ed. 2d 1498 (1957)

Facts—Samuel Roth conducted a business in New York in the publication and sale of books, photographs, and magazines. He was indicted and convicted of mailing obscene circulars and advertising and an obscene book in violation of the federal obscenity statute. Combined with this case was *Alberts v. California*, in which David Alberts had been convicted of publishing obscene matter in violation of the California penal code.

Question—Do these statutes regulating obscenity violate the provisions of the First Amendment?

Decision—No.

Reasons—*J. Brennan* (6–3 in *Roth*; 7–2 in *Alberts*). The guarantees of freedom of expression give no absolute protection for every utterance. The protection was fashioned to assure unfettered interchange of ideas for bringing about political and social changes by the people. All ideas having the slightest redeeming social importance have the full protection of the guarantees unless excludable because they encroach upon the limited area of more important interests. But obscenity is not within the area of constitutionally protected speech or press. The test of obscenity is "whether to the average person, applying contemporary community standards, the dominant theme of the material taken as a whole appeals to prurient interest." The Court held that these statutes, applied according to the proper standard for judging obscenity, did not offend constitutional safeguards against convictions based upon protected material. Both trial courts in these cases had sufficiently followed the proper standard.

J. Douglas's dissent stated that the law violated the First and Fourteenth Amendments by making "the legality of a publication turn on the purity of thought which a book or tract instills in the mind of the reader."

<hr/>

Ginzburg v. United States, 383 U.S. 463; 86 S. Ct. 942; 16 L. Ed. 2d 31 (1966)

Facts—Ralph Ginzburg was convicted of violating the federal obscenity statute by producing and selling obscene publications. The government charged that Ginzburg's advertising openly appealed to the erotic interest of potential customers. This case involved another application of what has come to be known as "the Roth test." This attempt to define obscenity was first set forth in *Roth v. United States*, 354 U.S. 476 (1957) and has been elaborated in subsequent cases. Under this test three elements must coalesce to constitute obscenity: (1) the dominant theme of the material in question must appeal to a prurient interest in sex, (2) it must affront contemporary community standards, and (3) the material must be utterly without redeeming social value.

Question—Have the standards of "the Roth test" been correctly applied in this case?

Decision—Yes.

Reasons—*J. Brennan* (5–4). Evidence showed that pandering—the business of purveying textual or graphic matter openly advertised to appeal to the erotic interests of persons—was involved. "The fact that each of these publications was created or exploited entirely on the basis of its appeal to prurient interests strengthens the conclusion that the transactions here were sales of illicit merchandise, not sales of constitutionally protected matter." The determination of the opinion is simply that questionable publications are obscene in a context—here the commercial exploitation of erotica solely for the sake of prurient appeal—which "brands them as obscene as the term is defined in Roth—a use inconsistent with any claim to the shelter of the First Amendment."

　　J. Black, *J. Douglas*, *J. Stewart*, and *J. Harlan* all authored dissents questioning whether the Roth standard gave fair notice and/or questioning the relevancy of the fact that Ginzburg was engaged in "pandering" while selling his materials.

Note—Although the standard for obscenity was outlined in *Roth* and carefully altered in *Miller*, the justices treated Ginzburg differently and made their ruling on the basis of "pandering." This concept was reaffirmed in *Splawn v. California*, 431 U.S. 595 (1977).

Miller v. California, 413 U.S.15; 93 S. Ct. 2607; 37 L. Ed. 2d 419 (1973)

Facts—California applied its criminal statutes to sexually explicit materials sent through the mails to persons who did not request them.

Question—May a state enforce obscenity statutes against publications that offend local community standards as to what is prurient?

Decision—Yes.

Reasons—*C.J. Burger* (5–4). States may regulate works that depict or describe sexual conduct, but such legislation must be carefully limited. The basic guidelines must be (a) whether the average person, applying contemporary community standards, would find the work as a whole appealing to the prurient interest; (b) whether the work depicts or describes in a patently offensive way sexual conduct specifically defined by the applicable state law;

and (c) whether the work as a whole lacks serious literary, artistic, political, or scientific value. The Court rejects the "utterly without redeeming social value" test. Local standards rather than a national definition of obscenity may be used.

J. Douglas and *J. Brennan* authored dissents questioning whether there should be an obscenity exception to the First Amendment and arguing that the revised standards adopted by the Court were still overly broad and risked suppressing protected speech. Significantly, J. Brennan, the author of the *Roth* test, was now in the minority.

∂৯ℛ

New York v. Ferber, 458 U.S. 747; 102 S. Ct. 2248; 73 L. Ed. 3d 1113 (1982)

Facts—New York prohibited knowing depiction of sexual performances by children or distribution thereof. Ferber, a proprietor of a Manhattan bookstore, sold two films to undercover agents of young boys masturbating. A jury found him guilty on two counts, and the appellate division of the New York State Supreme Court affirmed, but the New York Court of Appeals reversed on First Amendment grounds, finding the law to be both under-inclusive and overbroad.

Question—Can a state prohibit the distribution of materials showing children engaged in sexual conduct, even if the material is not legally obscene?

Decision—Yes.

Reasons—*J. White* (writing for five justices in a 9–0 decision). Precedents have established that the First Amendment does not protect obscenity. Although *Miller v. California* (1973) established guidelines for obscenity, a state has greater leeway in regulating "pornographic depictions of children." First, the state has a compelling interest in safeguarding the well-being of children. Second, the distribution of depictions of child sexual activity is related to child abuse both by preserving a permanent record of such abuse and by contributing to the "market" that allows the activity to flourish. Third, the sale and adverting of child pornography provides an economic motive that funds the illegal activity. Fourth, the value of such depictions "is exceedingly modest, if not de minimis." Fifth, the decision is compatible with earlier rulings that specifically define prohibited conduct. Ferber is not in a position to challenge the statute for overbreadth, which does not appear substantial.

J. O'Connor, concurring, noted that the Court was not holding that it would make an exception for child pornography deemed to have serious literary, scientific, or educational value.

J. Brennan's concurrence would, however, limit the law to cases where materials depicting children in sexual activity lacked serious value.

J. Stevens, in concurrence, stated the need to postpone decisions about possible exceptions to the Court's ruling until such time as these decisions actually come to the Court.

∽◦✄

Reno v. American Civil Liberties Union, 521 U.S. 844; 117 S. Ct. 2329; 138 L. Ed. 2d 874 (1997)

Facts—The Communications Decency Act of 1996 (CDA) contained provisions designed to protect minors from "indecent" and "patently offensive" communications via the Internet. A three-judge U.S. District Court decided that these provisions conflicted with the freedom of speech guaranteed by the First Amendment.

Question—Did provisions of the Communications Decency Act of 1996 designed to protect juveniles from adult materials on the Internet violate the First Amendment?

Decision—Yes.

Reasons—*J. Stevens* (7–2). Stevens began by reviewing the extraordinary growth of the Internet. Although the Internet contains a great deal of explicit sexual material, Stevens argued that "almost all sexually explicit images are preceded by warnings as to the content," and "the 'odds are slim' that a user would enter a sexually explicit site by accident." Technology exists whereby individuals could be denied access to websites unless they had a credit card or an adult password, but "credit card verification is only feasible . . . either in connection with a commercial transaction in which the card is used, or by payment to a verification agency." The Communications Decency Act prohibited "the knowing transmission of obscene or indecent messages to any recipient under 18" or "the knowing sending or displaying of patently offensive messages in a manner that is available to a person under 18 years of age." The terms "patently offensive" and "indecent" in the legislation at issue are "inherently vague." Such vagueness and overbreadth pose special problems to free speech. Stevens observed that "the Internet is not as 'invasive' as radio or television and that, quoting the lower court, "Users seldom encounter content 'by accident.'" The uncertainty of the meaning of terms in the statute is troubling both because they constitute "a content-based regulation of speech" and because the CDA is a criminal statute: "In order to deny minors access to potentially harmful speech, the CDA effectively suppresses a large amount of speech that adults have a constitutional right to receive and to address to one another." The statute is not narrowly tailored to achieve its objectives.

J. O'Connor, concurring and dissenting, viewed the CDA as a way to create "adult zones" on the Internet. She would uphold the provisions related to the "knowing transmission" of indecent materials to specific juveniles but agreed that all individuals in a chat room should not have to be reduced to the level of discourse that would be appropriate for the youngest among them.

National Endowment for the Arts v. Finley, 524 U.S. 569; 118 S. Ct. 2168; 141 L. Ed. 2d 500 (1998)

Facts—Stung by outcries over federal funding of art that was considered to be obscene or blasphemous, Congress amended the National Foundation on the Arts and Humanities Act of 1990 to require the National Endowment for the Arts (NEA) to assure that "artistic excellence and artistic merit are the criteria by which |grant| applications are judged, taking into consideration general standards of decency and respect for the diverse beliefs and values of the American public." After a number of performance artists, including Finley, questioned this provision, the U.S. District Court and the U.S. Ninth Circuit invalidated this provision as improper viewpoint discrimination and for being void for vagueness.

Question—Does the provision of the National Foundation on the Arts and Humanities Act of 1990 calling for the NEA to take account of standards of decency and respect for diverse viewpoints violate the First Amendment?

Decision—No.

Reasons—*J. O'Connor* (6 1/2–1 1/2) O'Connor, like the NEA, reads the congressional regulation at issue as "merely hortatory." It "imposes no categorical requirement" and "stands in sharp contrast to congressional efforts to prohibit the funding of certain classes of speech." The NEA interpreted the congressional provision as a call for creating panels that reflected diverse viewpoints. The requirement for the NEA to fund works that are "artistic" already calls for subjective judgments, and considerations of "decency" are appropriate where works are judged in part for their "educational suitability." There is no evidence that the NEA has exercised its power to prohibit funding of disfavored viewpoints. Questions as to whether laws are void for vagueness have primary weight when addressing matters of criminal law, "But when the Government is acting as patron rather than as sovereign, the consequences of imprecision are not constitutionally severe." Congress has merely added "some imprecise considerations to an already subjective selection process."

J. Scalia, concurring, argued that the majority decision is equivalent to saying that "The operation was a success, but the patient died." Scalia believed that Congress was quite clear in expecting that decency and respect were to be taken into account, and he saw no problem with such requirements for "viewpoint discrimination" in cases where government is not restricting speech but deciding which speech it will fund. Those who want to create "indecent and disrespectful art are as unconstrained now as they were before the enactment of this statute." This law was simply designed to limit the funding of such speech. Scalia does not think that the void for vagueness requirement applies to cases involving government funding.

J. Souter, dissenting, viewed the congressional requirement as a clear case of unconstitutional viewpoint discrimination: "a statute disfavoring speech that fails to respect America's 'diverse beliefs and values' is the very model of viewpoint discrimination; it penalizes any view disrespectful to any belief or value espoused by someone in the American populace." He did not think that the NEA had interpreted the statute plausibly. He argued that the decision in *Rosenberger v. Rector and Visitors of University of Virginia*, 515 U.S. 819 (1995) should govern here, in that, once the government creates a forum, it should not discriminate among the viewpoints aired in this forum. Souter was further concerned that the statute was overly broad and vague and "carries with it a significant power to chill artistic production and display."

***

Ashcroft v. The Free Speech Coalition, 535 U.S. 234; 122 S. Ct. 1389; 152 L. Ed. 2d 403; 2002 U.S. LEXIS 1789 (2002)

Facts—In the Child Pornography Prevention Act (CCPA) of 1996, Congress expanded its ban on child pornography to include depictions that appear to involve minors in sexual conduct, including that in which adult actors are portrayed as children and "virtual child pornography" using computer images to simulate such conduct. A U.S. District Court upheld the act, which the U.S. Ninth Circuit Court of Appeals reversed. Four other circuits had sustained the law in other cases.

Question—Does the Child Pornography Prevention Act violate the First and Fourteenth Amendments in banning computer simulations of explicit images that appear to be of actual children engaged in sexual activities but are not?

Decision—Yes.

Reasons—*J. Kennedy* (6–3). The provisions of the CCPA outlaw speech that was not identified as obscene in *Miller v. California* (1973) or in *New York v. Ferber* (1982). Child pornography has been recognized as a category that is not protected by the First Amendment, and Ferber upheld regulations of pornography involving the use of real juveniles, in which children could be harmed during the production process. This law attempts to go further in banning depictions of the very idea of juveniles engaged in sexual behavior. This subject has been the theme of many great works of literature, including some portrayals of Shakespeare's Romeo and Juliet. Although the government argues that materials produced without using real children could be used to seduce children, the same could be said for other innocent things, including "cartoons, video games, and candy." Moreover, the "mere tendency" that such materials might have in whetting the appetites of pedophiles fails to distinguish between "words and deeds, between ideas and conduct." Although prosecution of real pornography might be made more difficult by the task of distinguishing it from simulated pornography, "The Government may not suppress lawful speech as the means to suppress unlawful speech." Similarly, the government's ban on advertising that conveys the impression that it deals with child pornography is "overbroad and unconstitutional."

J. Thomas's concurrence argued for leaving the door open to prosecution of computer-simulated pornography involving children if technological advances make it impossible to distinguish between pornography involving children and that which does not. *C.J. Rehnquist*, in dissent, argued that the Court should save the law simply by interpreting it, not to involve any hint of juvenile sex, but only that which is "hard core" in nature and which is knowingly possessed. *J. O'Connor's* dissent would strike down the prohibition of pornography involving adults that merely appear to be juveniles, but she would uphold the ban on virtual child pornography. She argued that the Government "has a compelling interest in protecting our Nation's children," and that Congress should not have to wait until such children are harmed to adopt legislation. She would interpret the law to allow for regulation of computer-simulated child pornography when such pornography was "virtually indistinguishable from" the real thing.

❧

Ashcroft v. American Civil Liberties Union, 542 U.S. 656; 124 S. Ct. 2783; 159 L. Ed. 2d 690 (2004)

Facts—The Child Online Protection Act (COPA) required commercial Internet postings of sexual material to limit access to minors by requiring use of a credit card, digital certificate, or other reasonable measures. The U.S. Third Circuit affirmed a preliminary injunction against the law. The U.S. Supreme Court decided that the "community standards" language in the statute did not per se make the law invalid, but, on remand, the Third Circuit still concluded that the law was not narrowly tailored to serve a compelling governmental interest, was overbroad, and did not use the least-restrictive means available.

Question—Is there sufficient evidence to sustain the preliminary injunction against enforcement of the Child Online Protection Act?

Decision—Yes.

Reasons—*J. Kennedy* (5–4). COPA is Congress's second attempt to regulate pornography on the Internet, the Court having invalidated the Communications Decency Act of 1996. The Court will uphold injunctions that are not abuses of discretion. The lower court issued the preliminary injunction because it thought the government could apply less restrictive means. Filters constitute such a means: "They impose selective restrictions on speech at the receiving end, not universal restrictions at the source." Filters might also be more effective since they apply to the 40 percent of pornography that is produced abroad. The Commission on Child Online Protection so concluded. "[T]he potential harms from reversing the injunction outweigh those of leaving it in place by mistake since the government has yet to launch any prosecutions under the law." Moreover, "there are substantial factual disputes remaining in the case." Finally, technology continues to change and has already changed significantly since the law was first adopted.

J. Stevens, concurring, believed that the law's use of "contemporary community standards" was defective. He further questioned the value of criminal prosecutions in such cases.

J. Scalia, dissenting. Although agreeing with J. Breyer that the law is constitutional, he did not agree that a law dealing with commercial pornography needed to be subjected to strict scrutiny.

J. Breyer, dissenting. The law at issue only seeks to regulate material that is legally defined as pornography, and the law should be so interpreted. The law "does not censor the material it covers. Rather, it requires providers of the 'harmful to minors' material to restrict minors' access to it by verifying age," which is a relatively modest burden. The least restrictive means test is inappropriate in this case since filtering was the status quo, which Congress found to be unsatisfactory. "It is always true, by definition, that the status quo is less restrictive than a new regulatory law. It is always less restrictive to do *nothing* than to do *something*. But 'doing nothing' does not address the problem Congress sought to address—namely, that, despite the availability of filtering software, children were still being exposed to harmful material on the Internet." Filtering is faulty, allowing some pornography to get through; filtering is costly; filtering depends on parental enforcement; and filtering is so imprecise that it blocks some valuable material. There is no guarantee that filtering will work, and decriminalizing the law "would make the statute less effective." The Court has given lower courts inadequate guidelines as to how to proceed next. It would do better to construe the statute narrowly and seek to enforce it.

Subversive Speech

Schenck v. United States, 249 U.S. 47; 39 S. Ct. 247; 63 L. Ed. 470 (1919)

Facts — Schenck, the general secretary of the Socialist Party, sent out about 15,000 leaflets to men who had been called to military service, urging them to oppose the Conscription Act. He was indicted on three counts under the Espionage Act of 1917 for (1) conspiracy to cause insubordination in the military service of the United States, (2) using the mails for the transmission of matter declared to be nonmailable by the Espionage Act, and (3) the unlawful use of the mails for the transmission of the same matter as mentioned above.

Question — Does the Espionage Act of 1917 violate the freedom of speech and the press guaranteed by the First Amendment?

Decision — No, not when applied to the suppression of speech that constitutes a "clear and present danger" of evils that Congress has a right to prevent.

Reasons — *J. Holmes* (9–0). The defendants claimed that the tendency of the circular to obstruct the draft was protected by the First Amendment. That would be true in normal circumstances, but the character of every act must be judged according to the circumstances in which it was done. What must be ascertained is whether the words are used in such circumstances as "to create a clear and present danger" that would have brought about substantive evils that Congress had a right to prevent. It is a question of proximity and degree. Many things that may be of no consequence in time of peace may not be said when a nation is at war. "The most stringent protection of free speech would not protect a man in falsely shouting fire in a theatre and causing a panic." The statute punishes conspiracies to obstruct as well as actual obstruction. There are no grounds for saying that success alone makes the action a crime.

American Communications Association v. Douds, 339 U.S. 382; 70 S. Ct. 674; 94 L. Ed. 925 (1950)

Facts—Section 9 (h) of the Taft-Hartley Act, the Labor-Management Relations Act of 1947, provides that the National Labor Relations Board shall not investigate any question unless all officers of a labor organization concerned in the dispute sign an affidavit that they are not members of the Communist Party and that they do not advocate overthrowing the U.S. government by force or by illegal means.

Question—Is Section 9 (h) of the Taft-Hartley Act contrary to the First Amendment of the Constitution?

Decision—No.

Reasons—*C.J. Vinson* (5–1). The freedoms of speech, press, or assembly, established in the First Amendment, depend on the power of constitutional government to survive. If it is to survive it must have power to protect itself against unlawful conduct. Thus freedom of speech does not comprehend the right to speak on any subject at any time. Also, this is not merely a matter of speech. The government's interest "is in protecting the free flow of commerce from what Congress considers to be substantial evils of conduct that are not the products of speech at all. Section 9 (h) . . . regulates harmful conduct which Congress has determined is carried on by persons who may be identified by their political affiliations and beliefs. . . . Section 9 (h) is designed to protect the public not against what Communists and others identified therein advocate or believe but against what Congress has concluded they have done and are likely to do again." Because the law was intended to prevent future action rather than to punish past action, it did not violate the ex post facto provision.

In dissent, *J. Black* argued that the law in question was an unconstitutional attempt to interfere with legitimate rights of belief and association.

⌀⋟

Dennis v. United States, 341 U.S. 494; 71 S. Ct. 857; 95 L. Ed. 1137 (1951)

Facts—Eleven leaders of the Communist Party were convicted of violating the 1940 Smith Act. The defendants were convicted of conspiring to organize the Communist Party for the purpose of having it teach and advocate the overthrow and destruction of the U.S. government by force and violence. They claimed Articles Two and Three of the act violated the First Amendment and other provisions of the Bill of Rights and the First and Fifth Amendments because of indefiniteness.

Question—Did the Smith Act violate the right of free speech, or due process?

Decision— No.

Reasons—*C.J. Vinson* (6–2). The Congress has the power to protect the U.S. government from armed rebellion, and the defendants were advocating the violent overthrow of the government. This law was not directed at discussion but against the advocacy of violence. These persons intended to overthrow the U.S. government as soon as conditions would permit. This represented a clear and present danger to the government. It was the existence of the highly organized conspiracy that created the danger. "Whatever theoretical merit there may be to the argument that there is a 'right' to rebellion against dictatorial government is without force where the existing structure of the government provides for peaceful and orderly change. We reject any principle of governmental helplessness in the face of preparation for revolution, which principle, carried to its logical conclusion, must lead to anarchy." Vinson utilized the language of a lower court decision to say that "In each case [courts] must ask whether the gravity of the 'evil,' discounted by its improbability, justifies such invasion of free speech as is necessary to avoid the danger."

J. Black and *J. Douglas* both wrote dissents claiming that these prosecutions were aimed at the belief in, and advocacy of unpopular beliefs, rather than at conduct.

Keyishian v. Board of Regents, 385 U.S. 589; 87 S. Ct. 675; 17 L. Ed. 2d 629 (1967)

Facts—Faculty members of the State University of New York at Buffalo refused to sign a required certificate that they were not, and had never been, Communists. Each was notified that his failure to sign the certificate would require his dismissal. Faculty members brought action for declaratory and injunctive relief.

Question—Does this state program violate the First Amendment as applied to the states by the due process provision of the Fourteenth Amendment?

Decision—Yes.

Reasons—*J. Brennan* (5–4). There can be no doubt of the legitimacy of New York's interest in protecting its education system from subversion. Nevertheless, First Amendment freedoms need breathing space to survive, and therefore government may regulate in the area only with narrow specificity. New York's complicated and intricate scheme plainly violates that standard. Vagueness of wording is aggravated by prolixity; by a profusion of statutes, regulations, and administrative machinery; and by manifold cross-references to interrelated enactments and rules. The Court noted that there was "extraordinary ambiguity" in terms used in the regulations and that the whole was unconstitutionally vague. Such regulations have a chilling effect on the exercise of First Amendment rights.

The Court overruled its holding in *Adler v. Board of Education*, 342 U.S. 485 (1952), noting that "constitutional doctrine which has emerged since that decision has rejected its major premise. That premise was that public employment, including academic employment, may be conditioned upon the surrender of constitutional rights which could not be abridged by direct government action."

The Court concluded that mere membership without a specific intent to further the unlawful aims of an organization is not a constitutionally adequate basis for exclusion from such positions as were here involved. Thus, these regulations infringed on the freedom of association.

J. Clark, dissenting, argued that the issues posed in this case were largely hypothetical in light of changes that had occurred in board policies.

Brandenburg v. Ohio, 395 U.S. 444; 89 S. Ct. 1827; 23 L. Ed. 2d 430 (1969)

Facts—Brandenburg, a Ku Klux Klan leader, was convicted under Ohio's criminal syndicalism statute for remarks that he had been taped making at a Klan rally where he had used racially derogatory terms and mentioned the possibility of taking "revengeance." Ohio's intermediate court of appeals and the state supreme court had both dismissed Brandenburg's appeal.

Question—Does Ohio's criminal syndicalism law violate freedom of speech as guaranteed by the First and Fourteenth Amendments?

Decision—Yes.

Reasons—*Per Curiam* (8–0). The Court argued that later decisions had undermined *Whitney v. California*, 174 U.S. 357 (1927), which had upheld state criminal syndicalism laws. California's syndicalism law was infirm because it defined criminal activity in terms "of mere advocacy not distinguished from incitement to imminent lawless action."

J. Black and *J. Douglas* both authored concurring opinions claiming that the Court should abandon the "clear and present danger test."

Symbolic Speech or Speech and Conduct

Cox v. New Hampshire, 312 U.S. 569; 61 S. Ct. 762; 85 L. Ed. 1049 (1941)

Facts—Cox, a member of the Jehovah's Witnesses, was convicted of violating a city ordinance of the city of Manchester, New Hampshire, that forbade any parade or procession upon a public street unless a license had been obtained from the selectmen of the town. Cox said that he and the defendants did not have a permit, but they also claimed that this ordinance was invalid under the Fourteenth Amendment of the federal Constitution in that it deprived the appellants of their right of freedom of worship, freedom of speech and press, and freedom of assembly, vested unreasonable and unlimited arbitrary and discriminatory powers in the licensing authority, and was vague and indefinite. Each of the defendants claimed to be a minister ordained to preach the gospel in accordance with his belief.

Question—Is this ordinance a valid exercise of the police power of the state and not in conflict with the Constitution?

Decision—Yes.

Reasons—*C.J. Hughes* (9–0). This ordinance is not designed to deprive Cox of freedom of worship but to govern the use of public streets. Cox and the demonstrators were not prosecuted for anything other than that. Civil liberties, as guaranteed by the Constitution, imply the existence of an organized society maintaining public order, without which liberty itself would be lost in the excess of unrestrained abuses. The use of the power of the local authorities is not inconsistent with civil liberties but a means of safeguarding them. Licensing was necessary to afford opportunity for proper policing. "One would not be justified in ignoring the familiar red traffic light because he thought it his religious duty to disobey the municipal command or sought by that means to direct public attention to an announcement of his opinion. . . . We find it impossible to say that the limited authority conferred by the licensing provisions of the statute in question as thus construed by the state court contravened any constitutional right."

West Virginia State Board of Education v. Barnette, 319 U.S. 624; 63 S. Ct. 1178, 87 L. Ed. 1628 (1943)

Facts—Following the decision of the Supreme Court in *Minersville School District v. Gobitis*, 310 U.S. 586 (1940), permitting school boards to require compulsory flag salutes, even for those, like Jehovah's Witnesses, who believed the practice to be a form of idolatry, the West Virginia legislature amended its statutes to require all schools to conduct courses in history, civics, and the Constitution. The Board of Education went further and required a salute and a pledge of allegiance to the flag. Failure to conform was insubordination, dealt with by expulsion. Readmission was denied by statute until compliance. Meanwhile the expelled child was unlawfully absent and the parents were subject to a fine. The appellees, who were Jehovah's Witnesses, sought to restrain the enforcement of this statute.

Question—Does West Virginia's statute requiring compulsory flag salutes in public schools violate the First and Fourteenth Amendments?

Decision—Yes.

Reasons—*J. Jackson* (6–3). Denial of the freedoms guaranteed by the Constitution can only be due to present grave and immediate danger to interests that the state can lawfully protect. The limitations of the Constitution are applied with no fear that freedom to be intellectually and spiritually diverse or even contrary will disintegrate social organization. Freedom of religion and expression cannot be hampered when the expressions and the religious practices dealt with are harmless to others and to the state: "If there is any fixed star in our constitutional constellation, it is that no official, high or petty, can prescribe what shall be orthodox in politics, nationalism, religion, or other matters of opinion or force citizens to confess by word or act their faith therein. If there are any circumstances which permit an exception, they do not now occur to us."

The action of the local authorities in compelling the flag salute and pledge transcended constitutional limitations on their power and invaded the sphere of intellect and spirit that the First Amendment reserves from all official control. Therefore, the Court overruled *Minersville School District v. Gobitis* and affirmed the order restraining the West Virginia regulations.

J. Frankfurter, who was deeply conscious of his own minority status as a Jew, nonetheless authored a passionate dissent distinguishing between the wisdom and the constitutionality of legislation and arguing for judicial restraint and deference to decisions by local school boards as to whether flag salutes did or did not promote patriotism.

Tinker v. Des Moines, 393 U.S. 503; 89 S. Ct. 733; 21 L. Ed. 2d 731 (1969)

Facts—Three students, two in high school and one in junior high, were suspended from school after they wore black armbands to class in protest of the Vietnam War. Principals had previously announced that this form of protest would result in suspension. The U.S. District Court dismissed the complaint brought by the petitioners through their fathers, and the U.S. Eighth Circuit, sitting en banc, equally divided, left the lower court decision in place.

Question—Does the First Amendment (as applied to the states through the Fourteenth) protect the rights of public school students to wear black armbands to school in protest of the Vietnam War?

Decision—Yes.

Reasons—*J. Fortas* (7–2). The wearing of black armbands in silent protest "was closely akin to 'pure speech' which, we have repeatedly held, is entitled to comprehensive protection under the First Amendment." Moreover, "It can hardly be argued that either students or teachers shed their constitutional rights to freedom of speech or expression at the schoolhouse gate." The schools' policy was based on fear of disturbance, but "undifferentiated fear or apprehension of disturbance is not enough to overcome the right to freedom of expression." Here there was no finding that the student speech was disruptive. Moreover, the schools had previously allowed the wearing of other political symbols including the iron cross. "In our system, state-operated schools may not be enclaves of totalitarianism." Student rights embrace school-related as well as classroom activities.

J. Stewart concurred, but said that he did not believe that student rights were coextensive with those of adults.

J. White, concurring, continued to recognize a distinction "between communicating by words and communicating by acts or conduct which sufficiently impinges on some valid state interest."

J. Black, dissenting, did not think that schools were an appropriate forum for such speech. He feared that this decision could signal "the beginning of a new revolutionary era of permissiveness in this country fostered by the judiciary." Black believed the evidence indicated that the student protest had disrupted classes. He did not believe the Court should be in the business of examining the "reasonableness" of speech any more than it once looked into the reasonableness of economic legislation, and he feared that the decision would undermine school discipline.

J. Harlan, dissenting, would have deferred to the judgments of school officials that wearing armbands was disruptive, absent a showing of lack of good faith by such officials.

Lynch v. Donnelly, 465 U.S. 668; 104 S. Ct. 1355; 79 L. Ed. 2d 604 (1984)

Facts—Residents of Pawtucket, Rhode Island, and members of the American Civil Liberties Union challenged the city's display of a nativity scene, or crèche, as part of a much larger display of Christmas symbols designed to enhance the holiday mood. They believed this violated the establishment clause of the First Amendment as applied to states and localities by the Fourteenth Amendment. The U.S. District Court permanently enjoined exclusion of the crèche, and the First U.S. Circuit Court of Appeals affirmed.

Question—Does Pawtucket's inclusion of a nativity scene in a Christmas holiday display violate the establishment clause?

Decision—No.

Reasons—*C.J. Burger* (5–4). *Lemon v. Kurtzman*, 503 U.S. 602 (1971) indicated that the purpose of the religion clauses of the First Amendment is "to prevent, as far as possible, the intrusion of either [the church or the state] into the precincts of the other." Although the metaphor of a "wall" of separation can be useful, "No significant segment of our society and no institution within it can exist in a vacuum or in total or absolute isolation from all the other parts, much less from government." The Court has permitted paid chaplains and has recognized the religious nature of the American people: "Our history is replete with official references to the value and invocation of Divine guidance in deliberations and pronouncements of the Founding Fathers and contemporary leaders." Burger cites the phrase "In God We Trust" on U.S. coins and the words "One nation under God," in the Pledge of Allegiance to the flag. The nativity scene must be judged in context. The scene has the valid secular purpose of celebrating and depicting the origin of the holiday, and this is no greater aid to religion than the provision of secular textbooks to religious schools and other practices that have been permitted. In this case administrative entanglement has been minimal, and, apart from this lawsuit, "there is no evidence of political friction or divisiveness over the crèche." The crèche is a "passive symbol" that can hardly be understood as state endorsement of any religious beliefs.

J. O'Connor, concurring, did not believe the crèche at issue signaled "government endorsement or disapproval of religion." Such endorsement would be wrong because it would send "a message to nonadherents that they are outsiders, not full members of the political community, and an accompanying message to adherents that they are insiders, favored members of the political community." Here the display is much like the presence of religious paintings in a museum of art.

J. Brennan, dissenting, believes the decision is contrary to *Lemon v. Kurtzman*. The purpose was not secular but that announced by the mayor, of "[keeping] Christ in Christmas." The display placed "the government's imprimatur of approval on the particular religious beliefs exemplified by the crèche, and could lead to requests by other religious groups for inclusion of their symbols. The crèche's placement in a much larger Christmas display cannot explain away its religious significance or its centrality within the display as a whole. This is different than simply recognizing a holiday in which individuals may be with their families. Brennan distinguished this display from examples of "ceremonial deism" like the words "In God We Trust" or the words "under God" in the flag salute. He further noted that Christmas was not widely celebrated at the time the Constitution was written and that public celebrations did not emerge until well into the nineteenth century. Religion is too personal and holy to be undertaken by public authorities.

J. Blackmun, dissenting, also argued that the central purpose of the display was the impermissible one of endorsing the Christian view of Christmas.

Texas v. Johnson, 491 U.S. 397; 109 S. Ct. 2533; 105 L. Ed. 2d 342 (1989)

Facts—After he publicly burned a U.S. flag at a protest at the 1984 Republican National Convention in Dallas, Texas, the state sentenced Johnson to jail and fined him under a Texas law prohibiting the desecration of a venerated object. The Court of Appeals for the Fifth District of Texas affirmed the conviction, but the Texas Court of Criminal Appeals overturned the conviction on the basis that burning the flag was a form of protected symbolic speech.

Question—Was Johnson's action in publicly burning a U.S. flag a form of protected expression that the First and Fourteenth Amendments protected?

Decision—Yes.

Reasons—*J. Brennan* (5–4). Burning the flag was a form of "expressive conduct," as other cases dealing with flags have recognized. Although a state has a freer hand in regulating expressive conduct than pure speech, it may not "proscribe particular conduct because it has expressive elements." Texas asserts two interests in this case—preventing breaches of the peace and preserving the flag as a symbol of national unity. The evidence in this case did not indicate that Johnson's actions actually threatened a breach of the peace, nor was his action a form of prohibited "fighting words," in that Johnson did not direct his action to any particular onlooker in particular. Texas's attempt to preserve the flag as a symbol of national unity indicates that its regulation was designed to control "the content of the message he [Johnson] conveyed." "If there is a bedrock principle underlying the First Amendment, it is that the government may not prohibit the expression of an idea simply because society finds the idea itself offensive or disagreeable." It would be difficult to distinguish the U.S. flag from other venerated symbols, and there is no constitutional basis for doing so. A state has the right to make "precatory [recommendatory] regulations" to protect the flag, but it must attempt to persuade rather than punish those who disagree with it.

J. Kennedy's concurrence affirmed that justices sometimes had to make decisions they did not like but that Johnson's "acts were [protected] speech." Arguing that "a page of history is [worth] a volume of logic," *C.J. Rehnquist's* dissent cited numerous historical writings and incidents to indicate that the U.S. flag occupied a unique place, and affirming that Johnson was not punished for what he said but for what he did. He likened Johnson's action to "an inarticulate grunt or roar that . . . is most likely to be indulged in not to express any particular idea, but to antagonize others." He further accused the Court of assuming the "role as a Platonic guardian." *J. Stevens's* dissent likewise argued for the uniqueness of the U.S. flag and argued that the state prosecuted Johnson not for his point of view but "because of the method he chose to express his dissatisfaction with those policies."

Note—In reaction to this decision, Congress quickly adopted a Flag Protection Act, but, using logic similar to that in *Texas v. Johnson*, the Court struck this law down in *United States v. Eichman*, 496 U.S. 310 (1990).

Erie v. Pap's A.M., 529 U.S. 277; 120 S. Ct. 1382; 146 L. Ed. 2d 165 (2000)

Facts—Erie, Pennsylvania, adopted a law prohibiting public nudity and therefore requiring that exotic dancers wear, at a minimum, "pasties" and a "G-string." The owners of "Kandyland" challenged the statute as an interference with freedom of expression protected by the First and Fourteenth Amendments. The Court of Common Pleas struck the law down, the Commonwealth Court reversed, and the Pennsylvania Supreme Court reversed the Commonwealth Court, thus holding that nude dancing was a form of protected expression.

Question—Does the Erie, Pennsylvania, ordinance requiring dancers to wear pasties and a G-string violate the freedom of expression protected by the First and Fourteenth Amendments?

Decision—No.

Reasons—*J. O'Connor* (6–3). Even though Kandyland had closed, it had the potential to reopen, and Erie was faced with a judgment invalidating its ordinance in the meantime. The case was not therefore moot. Nude dancing is a form of "expressive conduct," but it falls "within the outer ambit of the First Amendment's protection." The city's interest in banning total nudity is based on its desire to combat harmful "secondary effects" of such nudity on "public health, safety, and welfare." The city's requirement that dancers wear pasties and a G-string constitute a "de minimus" restriction on freedom of speech "unrelated to the suppression of the erotic message conveyed by nude dancing." In such circumstances, the Court applies the four-part test developed in *U.S. v. O'Brien* [involving the burning of draft cards] (1968). The government's regulation fell within its constitutional powers to regulate health and safety. These are important governmental interests. On its face, the ordinance applies to all nudity and is not therefore aimed only at expressive dancing. Similarly, its impact on conduct is minimal. O'Connor thus reaffirms the Supreme Court's earlier decision in *Barnes v. Glen Theater, Inc.*, 501 U.S. 560 (1991), providing for pasties and G-strings in such circumstances.

J. Scalia's concurrence argued that the Court should consider the case moot, but, if the law were to be considered, it should be considered as a law regulating conduct rather than speech. It fell under "the traditional power of government to foster good morals (*bonos mores*), and the acceptability of the traditional judgment that nude dancing itself is immoral." *J. Stevens's* dissent argued that the Court was widening earlier precedents permitting zoning restrictions so as to "justify the total suppression of protected speech." He disputed the likelihood that pasties and G-strings would do much to control the secondary effects that the city feared and argued that the city was suppressing nude dancing precisely because of its communicative effect. *J. Souter* argued that the city had provided insufficient information for the Court to come to a reasonable conclusion in the case and thought that Erie should develop its case further before the Court rendered its opinion.

Virginia v. Black, 538 U.S. 343; 123 S. Ct. 1536; 155 L. Ed. 2d 535 (2003)

Facts—Virginia law provided criminal penalties for individuals who burned crosses with the intent of intimidating others and treated cross burning as prima facie evidence of such intent. Under this law, Barry Black was convicted of burning a cross at a Ku Klux Klan rally in Carroll County, Virginia. The Court of Appeals of Virginia upheld his conviction for this offense. Similarly, Richard Elliott and Jonathan O'Mara of Virginia Beach were convicted of attempting to burn a cross in the yard of an African American neighbor who had inquired about shots fired in their back yard. The Court of Appeals of Virginia also upheld these convictions. The Supreme Court of Virginia consolidated the cases and, in a divided opinion, struck down the Virginia law as unconstitutional on its face.

Questions—(a) Is the part of the Virginia law making it illegal to burn a cross for the purpose of intimidating individuals constitutional? (b) Is the part of the Virginia law requiring that cross burning be considered prima facie evidence of an intent to intimidate constitutional?

Decisions—(a) Yes; (b) No.

Reasons—*J. O'Connor* (6–3 on issue a; 5–4 on issue b). O'Connor traced the practice of cross burning back to the fourteenth century, when Scottish tribes used the practice to signal one another. In the United States the practice became tied to the Ku Klux Klan, initially born in 1866, and revived in 1915. The Klan has used the cross both to intimidate others and to express group solidarity and support for white supremacy. The First Amendment is designed to allow for the "free trade in ideas," but "the protections afforded by the First Amendment . . . are not absolute." Speech may be limited if it leads to "immediate breach of the peace," if it constitutes "fighting words," or if it involves "True threats." The Virginia Supreme Court relied on the decision in *R.A.V. v. City of St. Paul*, 505 U.S. 377 (1992), to void the Virginia law as impermissible "content discrimination," but not all content discrimination is unconstitutional. Cross burning is definitely a form of symbolic expression, but such expression is not unlimited when it involves an "intent to discriminate." Just as a state may regulate only the worst obscenity or threats against a president, so too, "The First Amendment permits Virginia to outlaw cross burnings done with the intent to intimidate because burning a cross is a particularly virulent form of intimidation." However, instructing the jury that a cross burning is per se a form of intimidation makes this part of the law overly broad, increasing "an unacceptable risk of the suppression of ideas." O'Connor noted that "a burning cross is not always intended to intimidate. Rather, sometimes the cross burning is a statement of ideology, a symbol of group solidarity." O'Connor observed that "It may be true that a cross burning, even at a political rally, arouses a sense of anger or hatred among the vast majority of citizens who see a burning cross. But this sense of anger or hatred is not sufficient to ban all cross burnings." O'Connor thus voided Barry Black's conviction and remanded the cases against Elliott and O'Mara for further proceedings.

J. Stevens, concurring, agreed that the First Amendment is not designed to protect speech designed to intimidate.

J. Thomas, concurring in question a and dissenting in question b, argued that the part of the decision invalidating restrictions against all cross burning ignores "reality." Like Holmes, Thomas believed that "a page of history is worth a volume of logic." Historically, the Klan has been a terrorist organization, abetting lawlessness and instilling fear. The fact that Virginia adopted this law in 1952, when segregation was still in effect, reveals that the law was not designed to squelch Klan speech favoring segregation but only conduct that led to intimidation. The Virginia law rationally draws the inference that cross burning is designed to intimidate and should be upheld.

J. Scalia, concurring in part and dissenting in part, did not believe that the prima facie evidence requirement is void on its face since it is rebuttable.

J. Souter concurred with the majority that the Court makes a content-based distinction but believes the law is therefore unconstitutional. He relied chiefly on *R.A.V. v. St. Paul* to say that a state cannot single out a particular form of expression for special treatment. He denies the parallels between this law and laws designed to regulate obscenity or threats against the life of the president. Instruction to juries under Virginia's law "skews the statute toward suppressing ideas." Virginia should seek to accomplish its objectives though "a content-neutral statute banning intimidation."

Time, Place, and Manner Restrictions on Speech

Kovacs v. Cooper, 336 U.S. 77; 69 S. Ct. 448; 93 L. Ed. 513 (1949)

Facts—An ordinance of Trenton, New Jersey, makes it unlawful to play, use, or operate for advertising or any other purpose on public streets, alleys, or thoroughfares, sound trucks, loud speakers, sound amplifiers, calliopes, or any instrument that emits "loud and raucous noises."

Question—Does this ordinance limiting sound trucks violate the right of freedom of speech and assembly, and the freedom to communicate information and opinions to others?

Decision—No.

Reasons—*J. Reed* (5–4). Freedom of speech is not beyond control. The Court held that the legislation against "loud and raucous noises" is a permissible exercise of municipal authority. The citizen in his home or on the street is not in the position of the passerby who can refuse a pamphlet. He is helpless to escape this interference with his privacy except through the protection of the municipality.

"The preferred position of freedom of speech in a society that cherishes liberty for all does not require legislators to be insensible to claims by citizens to comfort and convenience. To enforce freedom of speech in disregard of the rights of others would be harsh and arbitrary in itself." This is not a restriction upon communication of ideas, but a reasonable protection from distraction.

J. Black and *J. Rutledge*, dissenting, challenged the contention that there was proof in the record indicating that Kovacs had as a matter of fact operated his truck in a manner so as to emit "loud and raucous noises."

❧

Feiner v. New York, 340 U.S. 315; 71 S. Ct. 303; 95 L. Ed. 295 (1951)

Facts—Irving Feiner, a student at Syracuse University, addressed a street meeting of about seventy-five people, urging them to attend a meeting that night on the subject of civil rights. He made derogatory remarks about President Truman, the American Legion, the mayor of Syracuse, and other local political officials. The police arrived and noted the restlessness of the crowd. Feiner was asked several times to stop talking and was then arrested. He was convicted of creating a breach of the peace. Three lower courts in New York upheld his conviction.

Question—Do police violate the right of free speech as guaranteed by the First and Fourteenth Amendments when they stop a lawful assembly when it passes the limits of persuasion and undertakes incitement to riot?

Decision—No.

Reasons—*C.J. Vinson* (6–3). The officers making the arrest were concerned only with the preservation of law and order and not with the suppression of Feiner's views and opinions. The deliberate defiance of Feiner and the imminent danger of reaction in the crowd constituted sufficient reason for state police action. The guarantee of free speech does not license incitement to riot. Moreover, the state courts' approval of the action of the local police was entitled to the utmost consideration.

J. Black, *J. Douglas*, and *J. Minton* did not believe that this speech actually constituted a breach of the peace. They thought lower courts had been too willing to accept the prosecution's point of view.

Federal Communications Commission v. Pacifica Foundation, 438 U.S. 726; 98 S. Ct. 3026; 57 L. Ed. 2d 1073 (1978)

Facts—A satiric humorist, George Carlin, recorded a twelve-minute monologue entitled "Filthy words" before a live audience in a California theater. He noted that these were the sorts of words one could not repeat on the airwaves. He repeated these words in a variety of colloquialisms. In October 1973, a New York radio station broadcast the monologue at 2 p.m., which a father and son heard while in a car. The father complained to the FCC and following some correspondence between the FCC and the Pacifica Foundation, the monologue was judged "patently offensive" though not necessarily "obscene" and, because the broadcast was at a time when children are an audience, the FCC banned the monologue. A three-judge panel of the Court of Appeals reversed.

Question—Does the Federal Communications Commission have power to regulate a radio broadcast that is indecent but not obscene?

Decision—Yes.

Reasons—*J. Stevens* (5–4). Although the commission held the monologue "patently offensive" and not "obscene," it was not its intention to "censor" material but to "channel" it beyond the exposure of children who constitute a daytime audience. Broadcasting requires special treatment because children have access to radios and are often unsupervised by parents, radios are in homes and people's privacy is "entitled to extra deference," and unconsenting adults can tune in without any warning that offensive language is being broadcast. Because there is a scarcity of spectrum space, the government can license in the public interest. Although the FCC cannot edit broadcasts, it cannot be denied its statutory power "to review the content of completed broadcasts in the performance of its regulatory duties." The FCC's ruling covers "patently offensive references to excretory and sexual organs and activities" and will not restrict serious communication by the use of less offensive language. "We simply hold that when the commission finds that a pig has entered the parlor, the exercise of its regulatory power does not depend on the proof that the pig is obscene."

J. Marshall and *J. Stewart*, dissenting, focused both on the right of media to broadcast freely and on the ability of parents to turn a radio off when they found programming to be offensive.

Note—In an earlier case involving zoning, *Village of Euclid, Ohio v. Ambler Realty Co.*, 272 U.S. 365 (1926), the Court said, "a nuisance may merely be a right thing in the wrong place, like a pig in the parlor instead of the barnyard."

∽§⅄

Snepp v. United States, 444 U.S. 507; 100 S. Ct. 763; 62 L. Ed. 2d 704 (1980)

Facts—As a condition of his employment with the CIA in 1968, Frank Snepp executed an agreement promising that he would "not . . . publish . . . any information relating to the agency, its activities or intelligence activities either during or after the term of (his) employment . . . without specific prior approval of the agency." Though Snepp had pledged not to divulge classified information and not to publish any information without prepublication review, he published a book concerning certain CIA activities in South Vietnam without submitting it to the agency for approval.

Questions—(a) Did Snepp breach his fiduciary obligation owed to the CIA by publishing the book without obtaining prepublication review? (b) Could a constructive trust be created allowing the U.S. government to benefit on all profits that Snepp might earn from publishing the book?

Decisions—(a) Yes; (b) Yes.

Reasons—*Per Curiam* (6–3). "Snepp's employment with the CIA involved an extremely high degree of trust. He deliberately and surreptitiously violated his obligation to submit all material for prepublication review. Thus, he exposed the classified information with which he had been entrusted to the risk of disclosure. Whether Snepp violated his trust does not depend upon whether his book actually contained classified information. . . . The government simply claims that, in light of the special trust reposed in him and the agreement that he signed, Snepp should have given the CIA an opportunity to determine whether the material he proposed to publish would compromise classified information or sources. . . . [A] CIA agent's violation of his obligation to submit writings about the agency for prepublication review impairs the CIA's ability to perform its statutory duties. . . .

"A constructive trust . . . protects both the Government and the former agent from unwarranted risks. . . . It deals fairly with both parties by conforming relief to the dimensions of the wrong. If the agent secures prepublication clearance, he can publish with no fear of liability. If the agent publishes unreviewed material in violation of his fiduciary and contractual obligation, the trust remedy simply requires him to disgorge the benefits of his faithlessness."

❧

Bethel School District No. 403 v. Fraser, 478 U.S. 675; 106 S. Ct. 3159; 92 L. Ed. 2d 549 (1986)

Facts—Fraser, a student at Bethel High School in Pierce County, Washington, delivered a sexually suggestive speech in nominating a fellow student for an office. Fraser was subsequently suspended from school and removed from the list of those giving graduation speeches. The U.S. District Court ruled in Fraser's favor, and the U.S. Ninth Circuit Court of Appeals affirmed.

Questions—(a) Did the First Amendment protect Fraser's suggestive speech to a school-age audience? (b) Did the school deny Fraser due process in punishing him?

Decisions—(a) No; (b) No.

Reasons—*J. Rehnquist* (7–2). In *Tinker v. Des Moines* (1969), the Supreme Court recognized that "students do not 'shed their constitutional rights to freedom of speech or expression at the schoolhouse gate.'" Still, schools are designed to prepare students for citizenship, and offensive words that adults might be permitted to utter elsewhere are not necessarily acceptable in a school setting. Fraser's speech was directed to an audience consisting of younger students, and led to some confusion and disorder. Although they did not tell him the specific consequences, teachers had warned Fraser beforehand that his speech was inappropriate. Schools need flexibility in meting out punishments, and "Two days' suspension from school does not rise to the level of a penal sanction calling for the full panoply of procedural due process protections applicable to a criminal prosecution."

J. Brennan's concurrence stressed that the decision was limited to restricting speech in high school settings that school officials considered to be disruptive; Brennan saw no evidence that the school authorities penalized Fraser "because they disagreed with the views he sought to express." *J. Marshall* argued in dissent that the school had "failed to demonstrate that respondent's remarks were indeed disruptive." *J. Stevens* further argued in dissent that the school had not given Fraser "fair notice of the scope of the prohibition and the consequences of its violation," and that courts closer to the situation were better judges of the appropriateness of the speech than was the U.S. Supreme Court.

☙

Hazelwood School District v. Kuhlmeier, 484 U.S. 260; 108 S. Ct. 562; 98 L. Ed. 2d 592 (1988)

Facts—Staff members of *Spectrum*, a high school newspaper, filed a suit against the school district and school officials alleging that the principal had violated their First Amendment rights when he deleted two pages, which dealt with pregnancy and divorce, that he found to be offensive. The principal thought that the article on pregnancy did not adequately protect the anonymity of the pregnant students, friends, and parents, and noted that the article on divorce included comments by a student identified by name (later deleted) who was critical of her father's culpability in the divorce, and who did not have an opportunity to respond. The principal also objected to sexual references as inappropriate for some younger children in the school. The U.S. District Court held that the school authorities were wrong in censoring *Spectrum*, the Court of Appeals reversed, and the Supreme Court granted certiorari.

Question—Did the high school principal have the right to censor a high school newspaper?

Decision—Yes.

Reasons—*J. White* (5–3). "The public schools do not possess all of the attributes of streets, parks, and other traditional public forums." School facilities are considered public forums if, by policy or practice, they were open "for indiscriminate use by the general public." The government does not create a public forum "by inaction or by permitting limited discourse, but only by intentionally opening a nontraditional forum." Student editors felt that *Spectrum* could publish "practically anything" but school officials retained ultimate control over what constituted responsible journalism in a school-sponsored newspaper. "A decision to teach leadership skills in the context of a classroom activity hardly implies a decision to relinquish school control over that activity."

J. Brennan authored a dissent arguing that the principal's action was an unconstitutional and overly broad exercise of censorship over materials that were not disruptive.

☙

Morse v. Frederick, 551 U.S. 393; 127 S. Ct. 2618; 168 L. Ed. 2d 290 (2007)

Facts—Joseph Frederick, a high school senior, was suspended after displaying a fourteen-foot banner saying "BONG HITS 4 JESUS" at an Olympic Torch Relay that passed by his school. The District Court upheld the principal's action, but the Ninth Circuit found that it violated the First Amendment.

Question—Did Frederick have a First Amendment right to display his banner? If so, was the principal liable for damages?

Decision—Answering the first question in the negative, the Court did not address the second.

Reasons—*C.J. Roberts* (5 ½ to 3 ½). This case clearly involves school speech, but the message on Frederick's banner is cryptic. The principal could reasonably suppress the banner on the basis that it advocated illegal drug use. *Tinker v. Des Moines* established that students and teachers do not lose all First Amendment rights, but subsequent cases establish that these rights are not coextensive with those of adults, and *Tinker's* focus on "substantial disruption" is not the exclusive consideration, as *Bethel v. Fraser* (1986) and *Hazelwood School District v. Kuhlmeier* (1988) established. Drug abuse is especially rampant and dangerous among school students and is furthered by peer pressure, which school authorities have the right to resist.

    J. Thomas, concurring. *Tinker* was "without basis in the Constitution" and should be abandoned. *Tinker* did not reflect the original understanding that schools were designed to promote discipline and to serve in place of parents (*in loco parentis*). *Tinker* further "conflicted with the traditional understanding of the judiciary's [limited] role in relation to public schooling." *Tinker* created "a new and malleable standard" that simply creates confusion.

    J. Alito, concurring. The decision means no more than that a school may regulate advocacy of illegal drug use but should not restrict speech questioning the war on drugs.

    J. Breyer, concurring. The Court should simply decide that the principal has qualified immunity from suit under the circumstances of this case and say no more.

    J. Stevens, dissenting. The principal should be given qualified immunity, but "the First Amendment protects student speech if the message itself neither violates a permissible rule nor expressly advocates conduct that is illegal and harmful to students." The banner was simply nonsensical, and attempts to carve out an exception limiting speech advocating drug use is a form of prohibited viewpoint discrimination. "Although this case began with a silly, nonsensical banner, it ends with the Court inventing out of whole cloth a special First Amendment rule permitting the censorship of any student speech that mentions drugs, at least so long as someone could perceive that speech to contain a latent pro-drug message."

Garcetti v. Ceballos, 547 U.S. 410; 126 S. Ct. 1951; 164 L. Ed. 2d 689 (2006)

Facts—Richard Ceballos, a deputy district attorney for Los Angeles County who served as a calendar deputy, concluded that an affidavit contained serious misrepresentations, and recommended dismissing the case. His superiors continued with the case, and Ceballos claims that his employers subsequently retaliated against him for expressing his opinion in a speech (and testifying on behalf of the individual being prosecuted). A U.S. District Court concluded that Cebellos was not entitled to First Amendment protection for a memorandum he wrote in connection with his job, and that, even if he was, his employer had immunity. The U.S. Ninth Circuit Court reversed and held that Ceballos's speech was protected by the First Amendment.

Question—Is Ceballos's workplace speech protected from retaliation by the First Amendment?

Decision—No, protection of speech in the workplace is more limited than that of private citizens.

Reasons—*J. Kennedy* (5–4). The Court has qualified earlier rulings prohibiting employees from objections to conditions placed on employment, including speech. In *Pickering v. Board of Education* (1968), the Court focused on whether an "employee spoke as a citizen on a matter of public concern" and, if so, whether the "government entity had an adequate justification for treating the employee differently from any other member of the general public." Public employees are subject to conditions that members of the general public are not. Ceballos expressed his opinions "pursuant to his duties as a calendar deputy," and "when public employees make statements pursuant to their official duties, the employees are not speaking as citizens for First Amendment purposes, and the Constitution does not insulate their communications from employer discipline." The Court is not in a position to displace "managerial discretion by judicial supervision," and it does not decide what the ramifications are in the context of "scholarship or teaching." Whistle blower laws and labor codes are available to protect employees from abusing their supervisory discretion.

　　J. Stevens, dissenting. Public employees remain citizens at the office and while they can be disciplined for "inflammatory or misguided" speech, they should be protected when their speech is simply unwelcome "because it reveals facts that the supervisor would rather not have anyone else discover."

J. Souter, dissenting. Although employers retain interests in "demanding competence, honesty, and judgment from employees who speak for it in doing their work," employees should be protected by the First Amendment when addressing possible official wrongdoing. "[T]he very idea of categorically separating the citizen's interest from the employee's interest" is untenable. This is not a case where Ceballos's own speech would be mistaken for that of the government itself, and laws protecting whistle-blowers are a "patchwork" that are inadequate to the task.

J. Breyer, dissenting. The Court should protect Ceballos's speech under the *Pickering* precedent: "Where professional and special constitutional obligations are both present, the need to protect the employee's speech is augmented, the need for broad government authority to control that speech is likely diminished, and administrable standards are quite likely available." "I conclude that the First Amendment sometimes does authorize judicial actions based upon a government employee's speech that both (1) involves a matter of public concern and also (2) takes place in the course of ordinary job-related duties."

Chapter Eleven

SECOND, THIRD, AND FOURTH AMENDMENTS

Few Supreme Court decisions directly address either the Second or Third Amendment, and many casebooks do not contain a single case on either amendment. In regard to the Third Amendment, the primary explanation is that, in contrast to British practice prior to the American Revolution, there were relatively few occasions where the U.S. government attempted to billet troops in private houses without the household's consent and thus little opportunity for the development of case law.

The case of the Second Amendment is more complex. With high levels of gun ownership and violence reported almost daily in the United States, the debates over the scope of this amendment are some of the most intense in the nation. Some interpreters believe that the right to bear arms is as antiquated as, and limited by, the opening section of the amendment that refers to state militia. Others argue that, like most other rights within the first ten amendments, the right to bear arms is a personal right. Although Justice Thomas had suggested in *United States v. Lopez* (1995), that the Supreme Court should address the issue directly, it did not do so until *District of Columbia v. Heller* (2008), where a narrow majority of the Supreme Court sided with those who argued that the Second Amendment protected personal rights and accordingly struck down the District's strict gun-control laws. Because this case came from an area of federal jurisdiction, it left future cases to decide whether this provision also applies to state jurisdictions through the due process clause of the Fourteenth Amendment.

The Fourth Amendment presents quite a contrast. It is frequently brought before federal courts and remains rife with interpretative ambiguities. Consistent with the language of the amendment, the recurring question the Court has to answer is what kinds of governmental searches and seizures are "unreasonable."

The amendment outlines a specific procedure to obtain a search warrant designated to locate particular "persons, papers, and affects," a procedure largely designed to prevent the issuance of general warrants, or writs of assistance, that were rife under British rule. The amendment does not, however, specifically state that all warrantless searches are illegal. The Supreme Court has devoted much attention to distinguishing reasonable warrantless searches (such as those involved in "stop and frisk" searches by police officers fearful for their safety, searches made in pursuit of fleeing felons, searches of objects in plain view, and the like) from unreasonable ones.

The Framers of the U.S. Constitution were obviously unfamiliar with electronic eavesdropping and wiretapping, but this has been an area the modern Court has had to face. Initially convinced in *Olmstead v. United States* (1928) that the Fourth Amendment did not prohibit surveillance where no trespass or physical penetration of private residences occurred, it subsequently reversed course in *Katz v. United States* (1967) and decided that such cases should be subject to Fourth Amendment warrant requirements.

The Fourth Amendment does not specify what shall happen in cases where the government conducts illegal searches and seizures, but the Supreme Court has developed the exclusionary rule largely in an attempt to deter illegal police conduct in such cases. Originally applied only to the national government in *Weeks v. United States* (1914), the Court extended this rule to the states in *Mapp v. Ohio* (1961). Largely because this rule often results in the loss of probative evidence, since then the Court has carved out a number of exceptions, as when governmental officials act in reasonable good faith, *United States v. Leon* (1984), or when courts believe that information obtained in a search would otherwise have been the result of "inevitable discovery," *Nix v. Williams* (1984).

The reasonableness of searches often depends on context. *New Jersey v. T.L.O.* (1985) is an example of the relaxed standards applied in school settings. Similarly, a number of recent cases have addressed, and largely upheld, drug testing, both in school settings and in cases where such tests might be needed to either deter or detect drug use among those in sensitive positions that could jeopardize the public safety. Note, however, that *Safford Unified School District # 1 v. Redding* (2009), indicates that there are limits to searches and seizures even within schools.

Fourth Amendment law is riddled with special circumstances and exceptions. Although they are not examined extensively here, the Court has been far less strict about searches of automobiles than of homes, in part because vehicles can be easily moved. There are literally enough contemporary cases regarding the Fourth Amendment to compose a separate casebook.

GUN CONTROL

District of Columbia v. Heller, 128 S. Ct. 2783; 171 L. Ed. 2d 637; 2008 U.S. LEXIS 5268 (2008)

Facts—The District of Columbia banned the possession of handguns in the home and required that any other weapon be made inoperable for immediate use. The District denied Dick Heller, a special policeman authorized to carry a gun at work, a permit to register a handgun for use at home. The District Court dismissed his complaint, but the Court of Appeals for the District of Columbia held that the Second Amendment protects an individual right to possess firearms.

Questions—Does the Second Amendment protect the right of individuals to possess firearms? Has the District of Columbia ordinance denied that right?

Decisions—Yes; Yes.

Reasons—*J. Scalia* (5–4). The words of the Constitution, including the Second Amendment, are to be interpreted by "their normal and ordinary as distinguished from technical meaning." The Second Amendment is divided into a prefatory clause and an operative clause. There must be a link between the two, but "apart from that clarifying function, a prefatory clause does not limit or expand the scope of the operative clause." The Second Amendment refers to the "right of the people"; similar clauses in the First and Fourth Amendments refer to "individual" rights. This phrase is broader than the term "militia" within the prefatory clause. The phrase to "keep and bear arms" was commonly used for possessing weapons, whether an individual was a member of the militia or not. To "bear" meant to be able to "carry." Putting these terms together, the Amendment was designed to codify "a *pre-existing* right," which grew in part from earlier English opposition to game laws that the king had used to deny weapons to those who opposed him. The right was a "natural right" that encompassed that of protecting oneself against "both public and private violence." The prefatory clause's reference to a "well-regulated" militia, "implies nothing more than the imposition of proper discipline and training." The "security of a free state" referred to the nation as a whole. The Second Amendment was developed in reaction to fears that the government would disarm the people. It was patterned on state provisions that were designed to protect individual rights. This interpretation was evident in post-ratification commentaries by St. George Tucker, William Rawle, Joseph Story, and anti-slavery advocates. It was further confirmed by pre–Civil War case law, by post–Civil War legislation, by post–Civil War commentators, and by the Court's own precedents. The Second Amendment was designed to protect weapons "in common use at the time." "Like most rights, the right secured by the Second Amendment is not unlimited." Governments could limit concealed weapons, restrict ownership by felons or the mentally ill, limit guns in "sensitive places," qualify their commercial sale, and limit those that are particularly dangerous. Americans have overwhelmingly chosen handguns to protect themselves. Contrary to *J. Stevens*, the United States Supreme Court decision in *United States v. Miller*, 307 U.S. 174 (1939), did not examine the history of the Second Amendment. *J. Breyer's* approach to balancing interests would eviscerate the Second Amendment: "A constitutional guarantee subject to future judges' assessments of its usefulness is no constitutional guarantee at all." This decision cannot settle all issues relative to guns, but can invalidate the District's complete ban on handguns.

J. Stevens, dissenting, put greater reliance on the Court's decision in *United States v. Miller*. The primary purpose of the Second Amendment was to underscore the Founders' fear of standing armies. The amendment makes no mention of hunting or self-defense. "The preamble [of the amendment] thus both sets forth the object of the Amendment and informs the meaning of the remainder of the text" and is not "mere surplusage." The term "bear arms" was an idiom designed to refer to those who served in militias. "To keep" arms further described "the requirement that militia members store their arms at their homes, ready to be used for service when necessary." "When each word in the text is given full effect, the Amendment is most naturally read to secure to the people a right to use and possess arms in conjunction with service in a well-regulated militia." The Second Amendment was designed to prevent Congress from disarming state militias. Stevens proceeded to dispute each of the precedents that Scalia had cited. He did not think the American Framers had the same concerns as those that motivated the 1689 English Bill of Rights; he thought the reliance on Blackstone was misplaced. He disputed the post-enactment commentary, the post–Civil War legislative history, and judicial precedents.

J. Breyer's dissent argued that the Second Amendment was designed to protect "militia-related, not self-defense-related, interests." He also thought that "the District's regulations, which focused upon the presence of handguns in high-crime urban areas, represents a permissible legislative response to a serious, indeed life-threatening, problem." He proposed that the Court adopt "an interest-balancing inquiry," which would in this case defer to the District judgment that restricting hand-gun possession was a way of combating gun-related deaths. Breyer also disputed the majority's interpretation limiting the scope of the amendment to those "typically possessed by law-abiding citizens for lawful purposes," as well as its list of exceptions that governments could impose. He regarded the District's measure as "a proportionate, not a disproportionate, response to the compelling concerns that led the District to adopt it.

Note—Because it dealt with the District of Columbia, this case did not address whether the right to bear arms was protected by the due process clause of the Fourteenth Amendment against state denial.

ELECTRONIC SURVEILLANCE

Olmstead v. United States, 277 U.S. 438; 48 S. Ct. 564; 72 L. Ed. 944 (1928)

Facts—Olmstead, who was the general manager of a business, was convicted of a conspiracy to violate the National Prohibition Act by unlawfully possessing, transporting, and importing intoxicating liquors and maintaining nuisances, and by selling intoxicating liquors. The information that led to the discovery of the conspiracy and its nature and intent was largely obtained by intercepting messages on the telephones of the conspirators by four federal prohibition officers. However, the wiretapping was done outside the residence, and not in the offices but in the basement of the building housing the offices. All conversations were recorded, and the evidence of the wiretapping was used in court against the conspirators.

Question—Does the use of evidence of private telephone conversations between the defendants and others, intercepted by means of wiretapping, violate the Fourth and Fifth Amendments?

Decision—No.

Reasons—*C.J. Taft* (5–4). There is no room for applying the Fifth Amendment unless the Fourth Amendment was first violated. Therefore, the Court limited its consideration to the Fourth Amendment. The amendment does not forbid what was done in this case. There was no searching. There was no seizure. The evidence was secured by the use of the sense of hearing and that only. There was no entry of the houses or offices of the defendants. By invention of the telephone and its application for the purpose of extending communications, one can talk with another at a far distant place. The language of the amendment cannot be extended and expanded to include telephone wires, reaching to the whole world from the defendant's house or office any more than to the highways along which they are stretched.

"A standard which would forbid the reception of evidence if obtained by other than nice ethical conduct by government officials would make society suffer and give criminals greater immunity than has been known heretofore. In the absence of controlling legislation by Congress, those who realize the difficulties in bringing offenders to justice may well deem it wise that the exclusion of evidence should be confined to cases where rights under the Constitution would be violated by admitting it."

J. Holmes authored a dissent that described governmental participation in wiretapping as "dirty business." *J. Brandeis's* dissent focused on broader dangers to privacy rights.

ॐ

Katz v. United States, 389 U.S. 347; 88 S. Ct. 507; 19 L. Ed. 2d 576 (1967)

Facts—A federal District Court in California convicted Charles Katz of violating federal communication statutes by transmitting wagering information by telephone from Los Angeles to Miami and Boston. At the trial, evidence was introduced of Katz's telephone conversations at his end overheard by FBI agents who had attached an electronic listening and recording device to the outside of the public telephone booth from which Katz had placed his calls. Consistent with precedents, the Court of Appeals had rejected the contention that the recordings had been obtained in violation of the Fourth Amendment because there was "no physical entrance into the area occupied" by the accused.

Question—Are police required to obtain warrants for wiretaps?

Decision—Yes.

Reasons—*J. Stewart* (7–1). The Fourth Amendment protects people and not simply "areas" against unreasonable searches and seizures. The reach of that amendment cannot turn upon the presence or absence of a physical intrusion into any given enclosure. The protection does not extend only to tangible property and to incidents where there has been trespass. What a person seeks to preserve as private, even in an area accessible to the public, may be constitutionally protected. The defendant's presence in a glass phone booth was irrelevant since his intention was not to exclude "the intruding eye" but "the uninvited ear."

The surveillance was so narrowly circumscribed that a judge could have authorized the search and seizure. Omission of this authorization bypassed the safeguards provided by an objective predetermination of probable cause and substituted instead the far less reliable procedure of an after-the-event justification. This sort of bypassing leaves individuals secure from Fourth Amendment violations only in the discretion of the police.

J. Black argued in dissent that eavesdropping was not a search and seizure since there was nothing tangible to be seized. Black noted that the Framers of the Fourth Amendment had not included prohibitions against purposely and surreptitiously overhearing conversations.

Note—*Katz* overruled *Olmstead* and *Goldman v. United States*, 316 U.S. 129 (1942). The Court distinguished between domestic and foreign wiretapping in *United States v. United States District Court*, 407 U.S. 297 (1972).

☙

United States v. United States District Court, 407 U.S. 297; 92 S. Ct. 2125; 32 L. Ed. 2d 752 (1972)

Facts—The U.S. District Court for the Eastern District of Michigan ordered the government fully to disclose to defendants information gathered in wiretaps authorized by the attorney general without judicial warrant. The government was investigating the dynamite bombing of a CIA office, and the defendants thought they may have improperly gathered information for this investigation through an illegal wiretap. The U.S. Sixth Circuit Court of Appeals refused to vacate this order, which the government appealed.

Question—Must the government obtain prior judicial approval for wiretaps in domestic security cases?

Decision—Yes.

Reasons—*J. Powell* (8–0, *J. Rehnquist* not participating). Title III of the Omnibus Crime Control and Safe Streets Act authorized the use of wiretaps when obtained through a court order. The act specified that it was not designed to limit or expand presidential powers. This language was not intended to allow the president or attorney general to evade this requirement in domestic security cases, especially in those where "[t]here is no evidence of any involvement, directly or indirectly, of a foreign power." *Katz v. United States* established both the need for prior judicial approval of wiretaps and the standard of "reasonableness." Reasonableness can vary from one case to another, but there is no warrant for the court to carve out a "national security" exception to this requirement. The concept of national security can be inherently vague, courts should not find the issues surrounding such wiretaps to be "too subtle and complex for judicial evaluation," and judges are used to maintaining secrecy in similar cases. Congress may wish to consider special legislation for national security matters, but warrants will still require probable cause.

J. Douglas, concurring, viewed any national security exception as an invitation to "gross invasions of privacy." He traced the desire to make such an exception to the fact that the nation was "in the throes of another national seizure of paranoia." Douglas was especially concerned about the government's use of wiretaps to keep track of possible political enemies.

J. White, concurring, would base the decision on the interpretation of congressional statute rather than on constitutional grounds.

≈✑

OTHER SEARCH AND SEIZURE

Weeks v. United States, 232 U.S. 383; 34 S. Ct. 341 (1914)

Facts—Weeks was indicted in a federal court in Missouri for nine counts including use of the mail for transporting illegal lottery tickets. After a police officer arrested Weeks at work, a U.S. marshal and police officers twice entered Weeks's house without a search warrant and removed certain possessions and papers, which Weeks asked to be returned. The lower court ordered the return of the items not needed for trial, but allowed the prosecutor to use the incriminating papers. Weeks filed another petition before his trial, but it was denied and he was convicted. Weeks subsequently appealed his conviction on the basis that evidence had been improperly gathered in violation of the Fourth Amendment.

Question—Can evidence gathered illegally without the use of a warrant be used in a criminal federal trial?

Decision—No.

Reasons—*J. Day* (8–0). Citing *Boyd v. United States*, 116 U.S. 616 (1886), Day observed that the Fourth Amendment was intended to embody the idea "that a man's house was his castle and not to be invaded by any general authority to search and seize his goods and papers." This idea had deep roots in English law. This does not preclude the government from searching the person of an accused who is legally arrested but does preclude the use by the United States of incriminating materials gathered by a marshal without a search warrant describing with particularity the goods to be so seized: "If letters and private documents can thus be seized and held and used in evidence against a citizen accused of an offense, the protection of the Fourth Amendment declaring his right to be secure against such searches and seizures is of no value, and, so far as those thus placed are concerned, might as well be stricken from the Constitution." Day distinguished this decision from prior cases in which materials had been gathered in the execution of a legal search warrant or other processes. The use of papers seized from Weeks resulted in prejudicial error, and the Court consequently reversed Weeks's conviction.

Note—This case was the first to apply the so-called exclusionary rule to the national government. Although the Court ruled in *Wolf v. Colorado*, 338 U.S. 25 (1949), that the Fourteenth Amendment applied the Fourth Amendment to the states, it did not apply this same rule to state law enforcement authorities until *Mapp v. Ohio* (1961).

Mapp v. Ohio, 367 U.S. 643; 81 S. Ct. 1684; 6 L. Ed. 2d 1081 (1961)

Facts—Cleveland police officers requested admission to a home to seek a fugitive who was reportedly hiding there. They had also received information that a large amount of policy paraphernalia was hidden in the house. Without a warrant, the police forced their way into the house. They found obscene materials, which they used to convict Ms. Mapp in the state courts.

Question—Is evidence obtained in violation of the search and seizure provision of the Fourth Amendment admissible in a state court?

Decision—No.

Reasons—*J. Clark* (6–3). Precedents have held that the security of one's privacy against arbitrary intrusion of the police is implicit in the concept of ordered liberty and is enforceable against the states through the due process clause. However, the Court has previously refused to exclude evidence thus secured from state courts as "an essential ingredient of the right." Since the Fourth Amendment's right of privacy has been declared enforceable against the states through the due process clause of the Fourteenth Amendment, it is enforceable against them by the same sanction of exclusion as is used against the federal government. All evidence obtained by searches and seizures in violation of the Constitution is, by that same authority, inadmissible in a state court.

J. Black based a concurrence on combining the guarantees in the Fourth and Fifth Amendments as applied to the states by the Fourteenth Amendment.

J. Harlan argued in dissent that the Court was not exercising appropriate self-restraint and that early precedents were sounder.

Terry v. Ohio, 392 U.S. 1; 88 S. Ct. 1868; 20 L. Ed. 2d 889 (1968)

Facts—A seasoned police officer named McFadden observed Terry and two other men repeatedly walking in front of a store as though they were attempting to case it. After he approached and they mumbled in response to a question, he patted down Terry and found one gun in his overcoat and another in his companion's coat pocket. The trial court, the Ohio Court of Appeals, and the Ohio Supreme Court all failed to exclude this evidence, which had led to a sentence for carrying a concealed weapon.

Questions—(a) Did the officer's actions constitute a stop and frisk? (b) Was such a stop and frisk reasonable under provisions of the Fourth and Fourteenth Amendments?

Decisions—(a) Yes; (b) Yes.

Reasons—*C.J. Warren* (8–1). The Court needs to be mindful of both the purpose and limitations of the exclusionary rule and of the demands of police work. Any time an officer "accosts an individual and restrains his freedom to walk away, he has 'seized' that person." Similarly, the officer's pat-down of the defendant's outer clothing and his removal of revolvers constituted a "search." The Fourth Amendment does not outlaw all searches and seizures but only those that are "unreasonable." In this case, the search and seizure were reasonable. The officer was experienced and had reason to believe that a crime was about to be committed. He could not be expected to take "unnecessary risks" with his own life or with that of others in the vicinity. Officers did not need "probable cause" to conduct a pat-down search. The officer acted as "a reasonably prudent man" would act.

J. Black, *J. Harlan*, and *J. White* wrote concurring opinions. Black distanced himself from any reliance on the decision in *Katz v. United States*; Harlan argued that for any police pat-down to be reasonable it should be "immediate and automatic"; and White distanced himself from some comments on the exclusionary rule. In dissent, *J. Douglas* agreed that a search and seizure had occurred and thought that such a search and seizure could only be justified by "probable cause," which he did not believe had been established in this case.

Chimel v. California, 395 U.S. 752; 89 S. Ct. 2034; 23 L. Ed. 2d 685 (1969)

Facts—Three police officers searched the entire home of Chimel in Santa Ana, California. The officers had a warrant authorizing his arrest for the burglary of a coin shop, but no search warrant. Chimel's wife admitted the officers to the house. Some items taken from the house at this time were admitted into Chimel's trial at which he was convicted.

Question—Can the warrantless search of an entire house be justified under the Fourth Amendment as incident to lawful arrest?

Decision—No.

Reasons—*J. Stewart* (7–2). Such a search is unreasonable and thus contrary to the Fourth Amendment. An arresting officer may search the person arrested in order to remove any weapons the prisoner might seek to use and to seize any evidence on the arrestee's person in order to prevent its concealment or destruction. Included here is the area from within which the prisoner might gain possession of a weapon or destructible evidence, the area under his immediate control.

J. White argued in dissent that such searches should be accepted as long as they were incident to lawful arrests.

Note—*Chimel* overruled *Harris v. United States*, 331 U.S. 145 (1947) and *United States v. Rabinowitz*, 339 U.S. 56 (1950).

☙

Zurcher v. The Stanford Daily, *436 U.S. 547; 98 S. Ct. 1920; 56 L. Ed. 2d 525 (1978)*

Facts—On April 9, 1971, officers from the Palo Alto Police Department and the Santa Clara County Sheriff's Department were called to the Stanford University Hospital to remove demonstrators occupying administrative offices. They refused to leave peacefully, and when nine policemen tried to force their way beyond the barricades, demonstrators attacked them with clubs. All nine police were injured. The police could only identify two rioters, but the student newspaper, the *Stanford Daily*, on April 11 carried photos of the riot. The Santa Clara County prosecutor got a warrant to search the offices of the *Stanford Daily* for negatives. The warrant contained no accusation against the newspaper, and the search revealed only the photographs that had appeared. The District Court held that since the newspaper was the innocent object of a search, the prosecutor should have sought a subpoena duces tecum rather than a search warrant. The Court of Appeals affirmed the decision.

Question—Did a warrant, based on probable cause to search a newspaper office for evidence of crimes by third parties, violate the First and Fourth Amendments?

Decision—No.

Reasons—*J. White* (5–3). A valid warrant may be "issued to search any property, whether or not occupied by a third party, at which there is probable cause to believe that fruits, instrumentalities, or evidence of a crime will be found." The Fourth Amendment speaks of search warrants issued on "probable cause" and particularly describing the place to be searched and the persons or things to be seized. As a ". . . constitutional matter they need not even name the person from whom the things will be seized." The critical element in a reasonable search is not that the owner of the property is suspected of crime, but that there is a reasonable cause that the "things" to be searched for are there. The issue is one of reasonableness and the Fourth Amendment does not forbid warrants where the press is involved. Properly administered the preconditions of a proper search warrant afford the press protection against alleged hazards—such as press confidentiality.

 J. Stewart and *J. Stevens* authored dissents in which they argued that this search violated freedom of the press.

Note—The criticism and legislative fallout after *Zurcher* was quick and widespread. A number of states have restricted police searches of newsrooms and require subpoenas, the issuance of which can be challenged in courts, and Congress itself has prohibited courts from issuing warrants to search "the products of news organizations and others engaged in First Amendment activities."

Marshall v. Barlow's, Inc., 436 U.S. 307; 98 S. Ct. 1816; 56 L. Ed. 2d 305 (1978)

Facts—On September 11, 1975, an inspector under the Occupational Safety and Health Act of 1970 (OSHA) entered Barlow's, Inc., an electrical and plumbing installation business in Pocatello, Idaho. No complaint had been made against Barlow (Barlow's, Inc. had simply turned up in the agency's selection process), and the inspector demanded to conduct a search of the working areas without a search warrant. Barlow refused on the basis of the

Fourth Amendment. Despite a federal District Court order, Barlow still refused to admit an inspector without a warrant. A three-judge court agreed with Barlow and the secretary of labor appealed.

Question—Is the statutory authorization for warrantless inspection under OSHA constitutional?

Decision—No.

Reasons—*J. White* (5–3). "The warrant clause of the Fourth Amendment protects commercial buildings as well as private homes" and to hold otherwise would deny American colonial experience. The Fourth Amendment grew out of the experience with the writs of assistance. The Court has already held "that warrantless searches are generally unreasonable. . . ." The businessman, like the occupant of a residence, has a "constitutional right to go about his business free from unreasonable official entries upon his private commercial property." There are recognizable exceptions involving "pervasively regulated businesses," but they have a "history of government oversight that no reasonable expectation of privacy . . . could exist for a proprietor over the stock of such an enterprise," that is, liquor and firearms. The authority to make warrantless searches settles unbridled discretion on administrative and field officers.

   J. Stevens authored a dissent distinguishing routine administrative searches, like the one at issue here, from criminal searches.

Note—Only this provision of OSHA (Occupational Safety and Health Act of 1970) was declared unconstitutional; the Court upheld the act itself in *Atlas Roofing, Inc. v. Occupational Safety and Health Review Commission*, 430 U.S. 442 (1977).

United States v. Ross, 456 U.S. 798; 102 S. Ct. 2157; 72 L. Ed. 2d 572 (1982)

Facts—Acting on information supplied by a reliable informant, the police stopped a described automobile and individual, opened the car's trunk, and discovered heroin. The police then drove the car to the police station where a warrantless search revealed a zippered leather pouch containing over $3,000 in cash. Ross was charged with possession with intent to distribute. He was convicted in the District Court, but the verdict was reversed by a Court of Appeals.

Question—Can the police, who have legitimately stopped an automobile with probable cause to believe that contraband is concealed somewhere within it, conduct a probing search of compartments and containers within the vehicle whose contents are not in plain view?

Decision—Yes.

Reasons—*J. Stevens* (6–3). Since its earliest days, Congress recognized the impracticability of securing a warrant in cases involving the transportation of contraband goods, and in *Carroll v. United States*, 267 U.S. 132 (1925), the Court emphasized the importance of the requirement that officers have probable cause to believe that the vehicle contains contraband.

"Probable cause . . . must be based on objective facts that could justify the issuance of a warrant by a magistrate and not merely on the subjective good faith of the police officers." A lawful search of a fixed premise generally extends to the entire area in which the object of the search may be found and is not limited by the possibility that separate acts of entry or opening may be required to complete the search.

"A warrant to search a vehicle would support a search of every part of the vehicle that might contain the object of the search. When a legitimate search is under way, and when its purpose and its limits have been precisely defined, nice distinctions between closets, drawers, and containers, in the case of a home, or between glove compartments, upholstered seats, trunks, and wrapped packages, in the case of a vehicle, must give way to the interest in the prompt and efficient completion of the task at hand. . . . We hold that the scope of the warrantless search authorized . . . is no broader and no narrower than a magistrate could legitimately authorize by warrant. If probable cause justifies the search of a lawfully stopped vehicle, it justifies the search of every part of the vehicle and its contents that may conceal the object of the search."

J. Marshall argued in dissent that "The majority not only repeals all realistic limits on warrantless automobile searches, it repeals the Fourth Amendment warrant requirement itself. By equating a police officer's estimation of probable cause with a magistrate's, the Court utterly disregards the value of a neutral and detached magistrate."

༄༅

United States v. Leon, 468 U.S. 897; 104 S. Ct. 3405; 82 L. Ed. 2d 677 (1984)

Facts—Police obtained a facially valid search warrant to conduct a search from which they gained evidence that resulted in an indictment for possessing and distributing cocaine. This evidence was suppressed in the U.S. District

Court on the basis that the affidavit had been inadequate to sustain probable cause. The U.S. Ninth Circuit affirmed this judgment.

Question—Should the exclusionary rule apply where law enforcement officials obtained evidence in reasonable, good faith reliance on a search warrant?

Decision—No, there is a good faith exception to the exclusionary rule.

Reasons—*J. White* (6–3). Although some decisions have implied that the exclusionary rule "is a necessary corollary of the Fourth Amendment," this is not the case. As the Court stated in *United States v. Calandra*, 414 U.S. 338 (1974), the rule is "a judicially created remedy designed to safeguard Fourth Amendment rights generally through its deterrent effect, rather than a personal constitutional right of the party aggrieved." The rule exacts "substantial social costs," and has accordingly undergone some modifications, especially where its deterrent effect is attenuated. Deference to magistrates should not apply when officers knowingly provide false information, when the magistrate acts as a mere rubber stamp, or where an affidavit does not give a substantial basis for establishing probable cause. However, the exclusionary rule has particularly limited scope in regard to magistrates for three reasons. First, it "is designed to deter police misconduct rather than to punish the errors of judges." Second, there is no evidence that judges have tried to subvert the Fourth Amendment. Third, there is no basis for believing that such exclusion would deter illegal conduct. In cases where officers are acting in good faith reliance on a search warrant, "the marginal or nonexistent benefits produced by suppressing evidence obtained . . . cannot justify the substantial costs of exclusion."

J. Blackmun, concurring, indicated that any "empirical judgment about the effect of the exclusionary rule in a particular class of cases necessarily is a provisional one."

J. Brennan, dissenting, viewed this as the last of a number of cases that erode the Fourth Amendment. He saw the purpose of the Fourth Amendment as being broader than that of mere deterrence. Members of the judiciary are as duty-bound by the provisions of the Fourth Amendment as are law enforcement officials. The judiciary is not in a position effectively to assess costs and benefits. This decision "will tend to put a premium on police ignorance of the law."

J. Stevens, dissenting, believed this decision departed from settled precedents. The Fourth Amendment represents values higher than expediency.

Nix v. Williams, 467 U.S. 431; 104 S. Ct. 2501; 81 L. Ed. 2d 377 (1984)

Facts—On Christmas Eve in 1968 ten-year-old Pamela Powers disappeared from a YMCA building in Des Moines, Iowa. A fourteen-year-old boy subsequently saw Williams carrying a bundle containing two legs wrapped in a blanket to his car. Williams's car was found in Davenport, Iowa; articles of clothing led police to believe that Williams had dumped the body somewhere along this 160-mile trip. Williams, who was arrested in Davenport, requested his Des Moines attorney, and police agreed to transport him back without questioning him. Police began a search of the area where they thought the girl's body might be. During the trip, a police officer asked Williams to think about the family of the girl who would not have a Christian burial. Williams subsequently led officers to the girl's dead body. In *Brewer v. Williams*, 423 U.S. 1031 (1975), a divided Court ruled that the Sixth Amendment right of counsel precluded police from using evidence that they had secured during the trip to Des Moines. The state subsequently retried Williams excluding his confession but using evidence gathered from the body. The Iowa Supreme Court upheld the conviction of the trial court. The U.S. District Court rejected a federal habeas corpus appeal, but the Eighth U.S. Circuit Court of Appeals reversed on the basis that police had acted in bad faith.

Question—Is there an inevitable discovery exception to the exclusionary rule?

Decision—Yes.

Reasons—*C.J. Burger* (7–2). Past decisions have suppressed evidence regarded as "fruit of the poisonous tree." *Silverthorne Lumber Co. v. United States*, 251 U.S. 385 (1920). However, this doctrine has not applied when police have gathered evidence from an independent source, therefore assuring "that the prosecution is not put in a worse position simply because of some earlier police error or misconduct." Burger decided that "Exclusion of physical evidence that would inevitably have been discovered adds nothing to either the integrity or fairness of a criminal trial." In the case at hand, searchers were within two and one-half miles of where Williams led police to the body, and it was estimated that they would have been at the site within three to five hours. Because it was cold and snowing, the body would have been found in essentially the same condition. It would be pushing the exclusionary rule to the outer limits to apply it to the evidence in this case.

J. White, concurring, took issue with J. Stevens's negative characterization of the police's conduct, noting that the Court had split 5–4 in *Brewer v. Williams*.

J. Stevens, concurring, reiterated his view that police had acted improperly in questioning Williams during his trip to Des Moines.

J. Brennan, dissenting, argued that the standard for ascertaining whether evidence would have been inevitably discovered should not simply be the preponderance of the evidence but clear and convincing evidence.

New Jersey v. T.L.O., 469 U.S. 325; 105 S. Ct. 733; 83 L. Ed. 2d 720 (1985)

Facts—A fourteen-year-old high school freshman in New Jersey (and a companion) were discovered smoking in the school lavatory in violation of school rules. In addition, her purse (which she was made to open) contained cigarette paper commonly used with marijuana, a substantial amount of money, and a list of students who owed T.L.O. money. The lower court found the student delinquent and sentenced her to one year's probation. The Appellate Division affirmed but the Supreme Court of New Jersey reversed the decision.

Question—Is the reasonableness standard a proper standard for determining the legality of searches by school officials?

Decision—Yes.

Reasons—*J. White* (5–3). The Fourteenth Amendment prohibits unreasonable searches and seizures by state officers and protects the rights of students against encroachment by public school officials. Moreover, the Fourth Amendment applies to the activities of civil as well as criminal authorities. The Fourth Amendment requires searches be reasonable and requires balancing the need to search against the invasion that the search entails. The Fourth Amendment "does not protect subjective expectations of privacy that are unreasonable or otherwise illegitimate." Factors against the right to privacy are the substantial interest of school authorities to maintain order and discipline. This requires a certain degree of flexibility and school disciplinary procedures. In striking a balance between expectations of privacy and maintaining a learning environment, there is an easing of restrictions to which public authorities are ordinarily subject. "The warrant requirement, in particular, is unsuited." Nor is "probable cause" an irreducible requirement for the Fourth Amendment demands that searches and seizures be "reasonable." Evidence to be relevant need not conclusively prove the ultimate fact in issue. Reasonable suspicion is not a requirement of absolute certainty. "Sufficient probability, not certainty, is the touchstone of reasonableness. . . . The judgment of the Supreme Court of New Jersey is reversed."

J. Brennan and *J. Marshall* authored partial dissents in which they argued that the Court should require a higher standard than mere reasonableness in cases such as this.

~~~

California v. Ciraolo, 476 U.S. 207; 106 S. Ct. 1809; 90 L. Ed. 2d 210 (1986)

Facts—Policemen acted on a tip that Ciraolo was growing marijuana in his backyard. Because of an inner and outer high fence it was difficult to see anything. The police secured a private plane and at an altitude of 1,000 feet flew over the marijuana patch, made naked-eye observations, and on this basis got a search warrant. The defendant pleaded guilty, the California Court of Appeals reversed and on certiorari the Supreme Court heard the case.

Question—Does a warrantless aerial observation of a marijuana patch violate the Fourth Amendment?

Decision—No.

Reasons—*C.J. Burger* (5–4). The touchstone of the Fourth Amendment analysis is whether a person has a "constitutionally protected reasonable expectation of privacy." The Fourth Amendment protection of the home "has never been extended to require law enforcement officers to shield their eyes when passing by a home on public thoroughfares." The police observations "took place within public navigable airspace . . . any member of the public flying in this airspace who glanced down could have seen everything that these officers observed." *J. Harlan* noted that one who enters a telephone booth is entitled to assume that his conversation is not being intercepted; but this does not translate into "a rule of constitutional dimensions that one who grows illicit drugs in his backyard is entitled to assume his unlawful conduct will not be observed by a passing aircraft or by a power company repair mechanic on a pole overlooking the yard." The Fourth Amendment does not require police flying in public space to obtain a warrant in order to observe what is visible to the naked eye. Reversed.

J. Powell authored a dissent arguing that the Court was reverting to its stance, used prior to *Katz v. United States* (1967), focusing unduly on whether a physical trespass had occurred.

~~~

California v. Greenwood, 486 U.S. 35; 108 S. Ct. 1625; 100 L. Ed. 2d 30 (1988)

Facts—Acting on information that Greenwood might be in the narcotics trade, the Laguna Beach Police Department asked the neighborhood's regular trash collector to pick up the plastic garbage bags at the curb in front of Greenwood's home. Before doing so the trash collector cleaned his truck bin of other refuse, picked up the plastic bags, and turned them over to the police. Searching through the bags, an officer found evidence of narcotic use, which was used for a warrant to search Greenwood's home, where the police discovered quantities of cocaine and hashish.

Question—Does the Fourth Amendment prohibit the warrantless search and seizure of garbage left for collection outside the curtilage of a home?

Decision—No.

Reasons—*J. White* (6–2). "The warrantless search and seizure of the garbage bags left at the curb outside the Greenwood house would violate the Fourth Amendment only if respondents manifested a subjective expectation of privacy in their garbage that society accepts as objectively reasonable." In exposing their garbage to the public, the defendants helped defeat their claim to Fourth Amendment protection. It is common knowledge that garbage in plastic bags left on or at the site of a public street is readily accessible to animals, children, scavengers, snoops, and others of the public. Respondents ". . . could have had no reasonable expectation of privacy in the culpatory items that they discarded." The police, furthermore, ". . . cannot reasonably be expected to avert their eyes from evidence of criminal activity that could have been observed by any member of the public. In *Smith v. Maryland* (1979) the police did not violate the Fourth Amendment by causing a pen register to be installed at the telephone company's office to record the telephone numbers dialed by a criminal suspect, and in *California v. Ciraolo* (1986) the police were not "required by the Fourth Amendment to obtain a warrant before conducting surveillance of the respondent's fenced backyard from a private plane flying at an altitude of 1,000 feet."

J. Brennan argued in dissent that "Scrutiny of another's trash is contrary to commonly accepted notions of civilized behavior."

Knowles v. Iowa, 525 U.S. 113; 119 S. Ct. 484; 142 L. Ed. 2d 492 (1998)

Facts—An officer stopped Knowles for speeding. He issued Knowles a citation but did not arrest him. He did, however, perform a full search of the car, for which he had neither Knowles's consent nor probable cause, and discovered marijuana and a "pot pipe" in the process. The trial court and the Iowa Supreme Court rejected Knowles's request to suppress this evidence, and he was convicted.

Question—Does a speeding citation, issued without an arrest, justify a search of an entire vehicle?

Decision—No, the arrest was unjustified and the products thereof must be excluded.

Reasons—*C.J. Rehnquist* (9–0). In *United States v. Robinson*, 414 U.S. 218 (1973), the Supreme Court permitted the search of a vehicle incident to an arrest. That decision was based on the possible need to disarm a suspect being taken into custody and the need to preserve evidence for later use at a trial. Neither rationale was present here. The officer could have provided for his safety without a full search of the car. Moreover, a search of the car would not lead to any further evidence needed to prosecute the speeding violation.

⌖

Board of Education of Independent School District No. 92 of Pottawatomie County v. Earls, 536 U.S. 822; 122 S. Ct. 2559; 153 L. Ed. 2d 73 (2002)

Facts—Pottawatomie County School District in Oklahoma instituted a Student Activities Drug Testing Policy requiring students participating in extracurricular activities to be subject to random urine tests. Samples were given in closed stalls with faculty members listening. Earls, a member of a number of nonathletic extracurricular activities challenged this regulation as a violation of the Fourth and Fourteenth Amendments. The District Court granted summary judgment for the school district, but the U.S. Tenth Circuit Court of Appeals reversed.

Question—Is the Pottawatomie District's random drug testing of students in extracurricular activities reasonable given Fourth and Fourteenth Amendment requirements?

Decision—Yes.

Reasons—*J. Thomas* (5–4). "Reasonableness" is "the touchstone of the constitutionality of a governmental search." In the "criminal context," this requires "probable cause." Respondents believe that drug testing in the school context requires "individualized suspicion," but Thomas disagrees. In *Veronia School District 47J v. Acton*, 515 U.S. 646 (1995), the Supreme Court upheld drug testing for student athletes. Although such athletes were more routinely subject to deprivation of privacy by situations of collective undress, that issue was not dispositive. What is critical is that both cases involve "a school environment where the State is responsible for maintaining discipline, health, and safety." Like athletes, students in extracurricular activities are subject to faculty supervision on trips. The testing here is even less intrusive than that in Veronia, students found to have been taking drugs are given chances to enter drug counseling, and information is not shared with law enforcement authorities. The school faced evidence of drug use, including observations by teachers of students who appeared to be on drugs and overheard conversations on the subject, and such use is part of a "nationwide epidemic." A requirement that tests be administered only in cases of individual suspicion could unfairly target minorities. Although Thomas believed the policy to be constitutional, he expressed no opinion as to the policy's wisdom.

J. Breyer, concurring, emphasized the seriousness of the national drug problem. He also placed significance on the fact that a "conscientious objector" could "refuse testing while paying a price (nonparticipation) that is serious, but less severe than expulsion from the school."

J. O'Connor's dissent stated her continuing disagreement with the *Veronia* decision.

J. Ginsburg's dissent called the majority decision unreasonable, "capricious," and even "perverse." She saw no more reason to test students in extracurricular activities than to test others since all are subject to similar health risks. Students in nonathletic extracurricular activities that do not involve undressing and showering together have not forfeited as much privacy as others and do not pose as great a threat to others as those playing sports. Students in extracurricular activities are less likely than others to be on drugs. This policy thus "invades the privacy of students who need deterrence least, and risks steering students at greatest risk for substance abuse away from extracurricular involvement that potentially may palliate drug problems." Schools, like governments, teach by example, and the Pottawatomie County schools set a bad example by diminishing students' constitutional protections.

∽◌ℒ

Thornton v. United States, 541 U.S. 615; 124 S. Ct. 2127; 158 L. Ed. 2d 905 (2004)

Facts—After Marcus Thornton exited his car, Officer Deion Nichols of the Norfolk, Virginia, Police Department stopped him for having improper license tags. After discovering drugs on his person from a consensual pat-down search, the officer arrested Thornton and searched the vehicle from which he had exited and discovered a handgun under the driver's seat. Both the U.S. District Court and the U.S. Fourth Circuit Court refused to exclude the evidence.

Question—When police arrest an individual who has recently exited a vehicle, may they search the passenger compartment for evidence?

Decision—Yes, at least in cases where there is reason to believe that the search might provide evidence connected to the cause of the arrest.

Reasons—*C.J. Rehnquist* (7–2 on judgment). In *New York v. Belton* (1981), the Court upheld the contemporaneous search of the passenger compartment of a car when police made a custodial arrest of an individual who had been speeding. It largely did so on the basis of *Chimel v. California* (1969), which had allowed a search of the area within reach of an individual arrested within his home. Such a search was justified to remove any weapons or prevent the concealment or destruction of evidence. *Belton* did not depend for its force on whether the individual was in or out of the car. Both types of individuals pose similar risks. Police should not have to risk arresting individuals in their cars simply in order to have a better chance of getting evidence. *Belton* provides a good "bright-line" rule which is better than having to determine in each case whether an individual was still in control of his vehicle.

   J. O'Connor concurred in all but one footnote. She was sympathetic to *J. Scalia's* dissent but reluctant to adopt it without further arguments.

   J. Scalia, concurring. *Chimel* was based on preserving officer safety or the concealment or destruction of evidence. Its extension has been argued on the basis of three unpersuasive arguments. One is that an arrestee in handcuffs poses a continuing threat. The second avoids trying to penalize an officer who waited to make an arrest but seems to assume that such searches are "the Government's right" rather than an "exception." The third defense is that a bright-line rule is best. "If Belton searches are justifiable, it is not because the arrestee might grab a weapon or evidentiary item from his car, but simply because the car might contain evidence relevant to the crime for which he was arrested." *United States v. Rabinowitz* (1950) is among the cases that would provide precedent for such evidence gathering. "The fact of prior lawful arrest distinguishes the arrestee from society at large, and distinguishes a search for evidence of *his* crime from general rummaging. Moreover, it is not illogical to assume that evidence of a crime is most likely to be found where the suspect was apprehended." The Court should discard the rationale in *Chimel* for "a return to the broader sort of search incident to arrest that we allowed before *Chimel*—limited, of course, to searches of motor vehicles, a category of 'effects' which give rise to a reduced expectation of privacy." Such searches should be limited "to cases where it is reasonable to believe evidence relevant to the crime of arrest might be found in the vehicle."

J. Stevens, dissenting. *New York v. Belton* (1981) attempted to settle prior conflicts by allowing a broader search of automobiles than *Chimel* permitted and was even extended to closed containers within vehicles. *Belton* was not concerned with cases like the one at issue but with the arrests of suspects who were "seated in or driving an automobile at the time the law enforcement official approached." By contrast the majority opinion applies a "swollen rule" that does not give adequate guidance as to "how recent is recent, or how close is close." Just because an officer has authority to search an individual doesn't mean an officer also has cause to search a vehicle.

$\otimes\mkern-6mu\raise2pt\hbox{$\mathscr{P}$}$

Safford Unified School District # 1 v. Redding, 129 S. Ct. 2633; 174 L. Ed. 2d. 354; 009 U.S. LEXIS 4735 (2009)

Facts—An assistant principal escorted thirteen-year-old Savana Redding from her middle school classroom to his office where he confronted her with contraband in a day planner she had lent to another student and asked whether she had been giving pills to other students. After finding no contraband in her backpack, a school nurse seeking evidence of prescription-strength but over-the-counter pain relief pills, took her to her office and had her remove her outer clothing and shake her underwear, somewhat exposing her breasts and pelvic area. The Ninth Circuit Court, sitting en banc, reversed earlier summary judgments dismissing Redding's suit.

Questions—1) Did this warrantless search violate the Fourth and Fourteenth Amendments? 2) Were school authorities liable for this search?

Decisions—1) Yes; 2) No.

Reasons—*J. Souter*. The Fourth Amendment generally requires law enforcement officials to have probable cause, but *New Jersey v. T. L. O.*, 469 U.S. 325 (1969), had reduced this requirement to reasonable suspicion in school settings. In this case, allegations by another student that she had gotten pills from Redding constituted reasonable suspicion sufficient to justify a search of her backpack and outer clothing. Such suspicion could not justify the more "embarrassing, frightening, and humiliating" strip search; "the content of the suspicion failed to match the degree of intrusion," especially given the nature of the pills in question and the unlikelihood that a student would be hiding painkillers in her underwear. School officials are entitled to qualified immunity when established law is unclear, and the fact that lower courts split shows such ambiguity in this case adequate to provide the immunity to school officials. Lower courts would resolve whether the school district was liable.

J. Stevens wrote an opinion agreeing that the search violated the Fourth Amendment but arguing that the conduct was so outrageous that officials should have no qualified immunity. *J. Ginsburg* agreed.

J. Thomas concurred in the immunity ruling but thought the Court had inappropriately second-guessed the search. Officials needed broad authority to address issues involving drug use. He thought officials had appropriately limited the search to areas capable of concealing the contraband. Schools had the right to prohibit unauthorized prescription drugs. "By deciding that it is better equipped to decide what behavior should be permitted in schools, the Court has undercut student safety and undermined the authority of school administrators and local officials."

Chapter Twelve

FIFTH, SIXTH, SEVENTH, AND EIGHTH AMENDMENTS

The provisions in these amendments of the Bill of Rights deal with the rights of individuals accused of crimes, on trial for them, or (in the case of the Eighth Amendment) convicted of them. Solicitude for the rights of criminal defendants might seem to be unusual were it not for the fact that anyone could be falsely accused of such offenses. The U.S. Constitution is based on the unstated premise that individuals are presumed innocent until proven guilty. Proponents of these amendments have further argued that it is better for several guilty individuals to go free than for a single innocent individual to suffer. Moreover, even individuals convicted of criminal offenses are not considered to have forfeited their humanity.

The Fifth Amendment contains the most numerous set of guarantees for individuals accused of crimes. These include a provision for indictment in capital cases, or those involving the death penalty, by a grand jury; a guarantee against twice being tried for the same offense (the provision against "double jeopardy"); a provision against self-incrimination in criminal cases; a guarantee against deprivation of "life, liberty, or property, without due process of law"; and a provision against governmental takings of property without just compensation, which is treated in this book in chapter 7 on property rights.

The Fifth Amendment provision against double jeopardy is designed to prevent prosecutors from wearing down by multiple prosecutions individuals who have been acquitted, but in a federal system, this provision does not always protect individuals from prosecutions at both state and federal levels. Trials conducted after split, or hung, juries (as opposed to acquittals) are also not considered to be violations of the clause.

The due process clause is probably the best-known provision of the Fifth Amendment; a similar clause is found in the Fourteenth Amendment. This clause indicates that judicial processes might occasionally be found flawed simply because of considerations of general unfairness rather than for violating another specific prohibition in the Fifth or surrounding amendments. It is largely through the corresponding due process clause of the Fourteenth Amendment that the Supreme Court has ruled that most provisions within the Bill of Rights are applicable to the states. Most questions involving the due process clause involve what is known as procedural due process—that is, concerns about processes. From time to time, however, the Court has ruled that the very substance of some laws can be so flawed as to deny due process. This idea, known as substantive due process, was particularly prominent in nineteenth-century decisions related to economic matters, and is treated in the chapter on property rights.

The Fifth Amendment provision for a grand jury is for an independent body of citizens that decides whether or not a prosecutor has sufficient evidence to indict an individual, and bring a matter to trial. This provision has not been applied to the states, many of which continue to indict through the use of "information," that is, presentation by a prosecutor of information directly to a judge.

The right to petit juries (guaranteed by the Fifth Amendment in criminal cases and by the Seventh Amendment in civil cases) is a right to a jury of one's peers. The Supreme Court has applied the Fifth Amendment, but not the Seventh Amendment, requirement to the states. Recent cases have given states some leeway in regard to jury size and unanimity (neither of which is specifically designated by this amendment). Cases have also been concerned with the manner in which peremptory challenges are used to exclude individuals from jury service; the Court is especially concerned that such challenges not be exercised on the basis of race or sex.

The right to counsel has assumed increasing importance as the judicial system has become more complex. Over time, the Court has extended this right to police interrogations as well as to court procedures. The Court has further ruled that the government has an obligation to appoint counsel to individuals too poor to afford representation. In its controversial and wide-ranging decision in *Miranda v. Arizona* (1966), the Supreme Court required police officers to warn individuals of their rights. In *Argersinger v. Hamlin* (1972), the Court further decided that counsel should be offered in any case involving a sentence involving incarceration.

The provision against self-incrimination is one of the most controversial in the Fifth Amendment. It is designed to assure that the government does not extract testimony by force or fraud. It has increasingly been applied as well to see that the government does not exert undue psychological pressure on suspects. In this respect, this right overlaps with the provisions for guarantee of counsel.

The Sixth Amendment proceeds to guarantee "a speedy and public trial, by an impartial jury of the state and district wherein the crime shall have been committed," the right of defendants "to be informed of the nature and cause of the accusation," the right to confront witnesses against them, to have "compulsory process" for obtaining witnesses, and the right to "the assistance of counsel." The confrontation clause is the subject of continuing dispute between those on the Court who view it as guaranteeing a face-to-face confrontation between an accuser and the accused, and those who view it as primarily guaranteeing the right to cross-examination.

The Eighth Amendment prohibits excessive bail or fines and prohibits cruel and unusual punishment. The prohibition against cruel and unusual punishment has most frequently been adjudicated in relation to the death penalty, a penalty of unusual severity and finality. In *Furman v. Georgia* (1973), the Supreme Court decided that the penalty as then administered was so arbitrary as to be unconstitutional, but subsequent decisions have allowed for the imposition of the death penalty in cases where the trial and penalty phases of the proceedings are bifurcated and where the penalty phase considers aggravating and mitigating factors that might distinguish one murder from another. Recent cases have been particularly concerned about the imposition of the penalty on individuals who were mentally challenged or who were young. A number of justices, always falling short of a majority, have argued that the death penalty is per se unconstitutional, a violation of evolving standards of justice.

A number of recent cases, most notably those involving the "three-strikes-and-you're-out" laws, have addressed the issue of proportionality of penalties other than capital punishment. Whereas some justices believe the notion of proportionality is implicit in the command against cruel and unusual punishments, other believe that had the authors of the amendment intended to disallow disproportionate punishments, they would specifically have said so.

DOUBLE JEOPARDY AND RIGHT TO CONFRONTATION

United States v. Lanza, 260 U.S. 377; 43 S. Ct. 141; 7 L. Ed. 314 (1922)

Facts—The state of Washington passed a prohibition law before the passage of the National Prohibition Act. Lanza was charged in the federal court of Washington and in the supreme court of Whatcom County, Washington, for the violation of each of the respective acts. He was accused of making, selling, and transporting liquor and of having a still and material for the manufacture of liquor. He brought suit in the federal court to dismiss the suit of the United States on the grounds that he was placed in double jeopardy.

Question—Can the United States punish someone for an act for which the state has already punished him?

Decision—Yes.

Reasons—*C.J. Taft* (9–0). We have two sovereignties, deriving power from different sources, capable of dealing with the same subject matter within the same territory. Each may, without interference from the other, enact laws determining what shall be an offense against its peace and dignity. In doing this, each is exercising its own sovereignty, not that of the other.

It follows that an act denounced as a crime by both national and state sovereignties is an offense against the peace and dignity of both and may be punished by each. The Fifth Amendment applies only to proceedings of the federal government, and the double jeopardy covered therein forbids a second prosecution under the authority of the federal government after a first trial for the same offense under the same authority. Here the same act was an offense against the state of Washington because of a violation of its laws and also an offense against the United States under the National Prohibition Act. The defendant thus committed two different offenses by the same act and a conviction by a court of Washington together with conviction in the federal court was not double jeopardy.

Note—Although often criticized, *Lanza* is still good law and reaffirmed in *Abbate v. United States*, 359 U.S. 187 (1959) and *Bartkus v. Illinois*, 359 U.S. 121 (1959), which maintains the "double-prosecution-is-not-double-jeopardy" rule. Again in *Heath v. Alabama*, 474 U.S. 82 (1985), the Court reinforced it.

Coy v. Iowa, 487 U.S. 1012; 108 S. Ct. 2798; 101 L. Ed. 2d 857 (1988)

Facts—Iowa law provided for a screen to be employed when juveniles testified against their accusers in sexual cases. In the case at hand, two thirteen-year-old girls who were witnesses against Coy (convicted of sexually molesting them as they slept in a tent in the yard next to his) were separated from the defendant by a curtain through which he could see them but they could not see him.

Question—Did the use of a curtain between the accusers and the defendant violate the defendant's (a) Sixth Amendment right of confrontation or (b) his Fifth Amendment right of due process?

Decision—The Court focused on part a in the question and answered yes.

Reasons—*J. Scalia* (6–2, with *J. Kennedy* not participating). Scalia associated the Sixth Amendment right to confrontation with the right of "face-to-face confrontation." He traced this right to the Latin root of the word confront, which "ultimately derives from the prefix 'con-' (from 'contra' meaning 'against' or 'opposed') and the noun 'frons' (forehead)." He further examined usage in Shakespeare and other sources to conclude that "there is something deep in human nature that regards face-to-face confrontation between accused and accuser as "essential to a fair trial in a criminal prosecution." "That face-to-face presence may, unfortunately, upset the truthful rape victim or abused child; but by the same token it may confound and undo the false accuser, or reveal the child coached by a malevolent adult. It is a truism that constitutional protections have costs." Although the confrontation clause is not absolute, "something more than the type of generalized finding underlying such a statute is needed when the exception is not 'firmly . . . rooted in our jurisprudence.'"

J. O'Connor, concurring, stressed that the right to face-to-face confrontation is not absolute and noted that many states have authorized the use of one- or two-way cameras. She "would permit use of a particular trial procedure that called for something other than face-to-face confrontation if that procedure was necessary to further an important public policy," especially when case-specific findings of necessity are made.

J. Blackmun, dissenting, tied the confrontation clause not to face-to-face meetings but to the right to have testimony given under oath and subject to cross-examination. He cited the legal commentator Wigmore to show that this was the essence of the Sixth Amendment right. The Court's acceptance of some hearsay evidence indicates that the preference for face-to-face confrontation is not absolute. In this case, the absolute interpretation of the clause should give way to the public interest in combating child abuse. Blackmun further denied that the presence of the screen was "inherently prejudicial," especially in light of the judge's instructions that jurors were to draw no inferences of guilt from its presence.

Sattazahn v. Pennsylvania, 123 S. Ct. 732; 2003 U.S. LEXIS 748; 71 U.S.L.W. 4023 (2003)

Facts—Pennsylvania law requires that a jury must consider aggravating and mitigating factors in the verdict phase of a capital crime. If the jury does not unanimously agree on the penalty, the judge must enter a life sentence. After a jury deadlocked 9–3 for life in prison, a judge imposed a life sentence on Sattazahn, who had been convicted of participating in a murder in the course of an armed robbery. Sattazahn appealed his conviction for first-degree murder, and, ruling that the trial judge's instructions to the jury had been improper, the Pennsylvania Supreme Court reversed Sattazahn's conviction and ordered a new trial. In this trial, in which an additional aggravating factor was introduced, the jury approved the death sentence, and the Pennsylvania Supreme Court affirmed.

Question—Does the imposition of the death penalty in the second trial violate the double jeopardy provision of the Fifth Amendment or the due process clause of the Fourteenth Amendment?

Decision—No.

Reasons—*J. Scalia* (5–4). When a defendant initiates an appeal of his conviction, double jeopardy is not implicated. *Bullington v. Missouri* (1981) decided that the double jeopardy provision applies only when sentencing proceedings "have the hallmarks of the trial on guilt or innocence." Furthermore, "an 'acquittal' at a trial-like sentencing phase, rather than the mere imposition of a life sentence, is required to give rise to double jeopardy protections." Scalia noted that "normally, 'a retrial following a "hung jury" does not violate the Double Jeopardy Clause.'" Double jeopardy only applies where there has been an acquittal, and there had been none here. The judge's imposition of a sentence in the first case was a "default judgment." Other capital cases have entrusted such determinations to a jury. Here neither the judge nor the jury "acquitted" the defendant. The judgment against Sattazahn does not present a case of "an all-powerful state relentlessly pursuing a defendant who had either been found not guilty or who had at least insisted on having the issue of guilt submitted to the first trier of fact." Similarly, the defendant was given due process so there was no independent violation of the Fourteenth Amendment.

  J. O'Connor concurred while questioning the decisions in *Apprendi v. New Jersey* (2000) and *Ring v. Arizona* (2002).

  J. Ginsburg's dissent, although acknowledging that the issue was close and "genuinely debatable," argued that this case constituted double jeopardy both because it "confronts defendants with a perilous choice," of either not appealing their convictions or risking their lives in so doing and because the death penalty is "unique in both its severity and finality."

✍

DUE PROCESS
(ALSO SEE CHAPTER 14, FOURTEENTH AMENDMENT)

Tumey v. Ohio, 273 U.S. 510; 47 S. Ct. 437; 71 L. Ed. 749 (1927)

Facts—Tumey was arrested and brought before Mayor Pugh of North College Hill, Ohio, on the charge of unlawfully possessing intoxicating liquor.

The mayor, under statutes of Ohio, had the authority to hear a case of one charged with violating this prohibition act. Tumey moved to disqualify the mayor. The mayor denied the motion, proceeded to the trial, convicted Tumey of unlawfully possessing intoxicating liquor within Hamilton County, Ohio, fined him $100, and ordered that he be imprisoned until the fine and costs were paid. As a result of the conviction the mayor received a $12 fee from Tumey that he would not have received if the accused had not been convicted.

Question—Do certain Ohio statutes that provide for a trial by the mayor of a village of one accused of violating the prohibition act of the state deprive the accused of due process of law and violate the Fourteenth Amendment because of the pecuniary and other interests that those statutes give the mayor in the result of the trial?

Decision—Yes.

Reasons—*C.J. Taft* (9–0). "All questions of judicial qualification may not involve constitutional validity. Thus matters of kinship, personal bias, state policy, remoteness of interest would seem generally to be matters of legislative discretion. . . . But it certainly violates the Fourteenth Amendment and deprives a defendant in a criminal case of due process of law to subject his liberty or property to the judgment of a court, the judge of which has a direct, personal, substantial pecuniary interest in reaching a conclusion against him in his case." No matter what the evidence against him, the defendant has the right to have an impartial judge.

∽✦

Bolling v. Sharpe, 347 U.S. 497; 74 S. Ct. 693; 98 L. Ed. 884 (1954)

Facts—This companion case to *Brown v. Board of Education* arose out of the District of Columbia, where, because it is controlled by the national government, the equal protection clause of the Fourteenth Amendment (which limits illegal state actions) does not apply.

Question—Does racial segregation in schools in the District of Columbia violate of the due process clause of the Fifth Amendment?

Decision—Yes.

Reasons—*C.J. Warren* (9–0). Although the Fifth Amendment "does not contain an equal protection clause," the concepts of due process and equal protection "are not mutually exclusive." Thus, "discrimination may be so unjustifiable as to be violative of due process." Liberty denotes more than "freedom from bodily restraint." Racial segregation in schools in the District of Columbia "is not reasonably related to any proper governmental objective" and thus "constitutes an arbitrary deprivation of . . . liberty in violation of the Due Process Clause."

O'Connor v. Donaldson, 422 U.S. 563; 95 S. Ct. 2486; 45 L. Ed. 2d 396 (1975)

Facts—For almost fifteen years, the Florida State Hospital at Chattahoochee confined Kenneth Donaldson as a mental patient "for care, maintenance and treatment." He had made frequent requests for release; responsible persons had agreed to care for him if necessary; he was not dangerous to himself or others; and he had not received treatment for any mental illness at the hospital. Dr. O'Connor, the hospital superintendent during most of the period of confinement, cited a state law that authorized indefinite custodial confinement of the "sick."

Question—Was the state law authorizing indefinite custodial confinement for mentally ill individuals who were not dangerous to others valid under the Fourteenth Amendment?

Decision—No.

Reasons—*J. Stewart* (9–0). A state cannot constitutionally confine without consent a nondangerous individual who is capable of surviving safely in freedom by himself or with the help of willing and responsible family members or friends. This violates a person's right to liberty. "A finding of 'mental illness' alone cannot justify a state's locking a person up against his will and keeping him indefinitely in simple custodial confinement. Assuming that term can be given a reasonably precise content and that the 'mentally ill' can be identified with reasonable accuracy, there is still no constitutional basis for confining such persons involuntarily if they are dangerous to no one and can live safely in freedom."

Note—In *Addington v. Texas*, 439 U.S. 908 (1979), the Court held that a state needed clear and convincing evidence that a person constituted a danger to society before it could confine him or her.

Bordenkircher v. Hayes, 434 U.S. 357; 98 S. Ct. 663; 54 L. Ed. 2d 604 (1978)

Facts—Kentucky charged Hayes with uttering a forged instrument of just over $88. The district attorney offered him five years if he pled guilty but threatened to charge him under Kentucky's Habitual Criminal Act if he did not (Hayes had previously been convicted of illegally detaining a female—the original charge had been rape—and of robbery). Hayes rejected the plea bargain and was subsequently convicted and sentenced to life in prison under the Habitual Criminal Act. The Court of Appeals in Kentucky and a U.S. District Court upheld the sentence, which the Sixth U.S. Court of Appeals subsequently reversed.

Question—Was Hayes's conviction under Kentucky's Habitual Criminal Act in violation of his rights to due process under the Fourteenth Amendment?

Decision—No.

Reasons—*J. Stewart* (5–4). The prosecutor fully informed Hayes of his intentions in this case. Plea bargains when properly administered and guarded can benefit all concerned. They need to be struck in the presence of counsel; to be knowingly made; and, when made, kept. The prosecutor could have initially indicted Hayes under the Habitual Criminal Act, and there is no real difference in prosecutorial discretion in deciding to make such an indictment after Hayes's refusal to accept the plea bargain rather than before.

J. Blackmun, dissenting, saw this case as an impermissible example of prosecutorial vindictiveness, brought against Hayes simply for exercising his constitutional right to a trial. Similarly, *J. Powell* argued that the fact that the prosecutor failed to indict Hayes under the Habitual Criminal Act in the first place indicated that he used this act both to discourage and to penalize Hayes's legitimate exercise of his constitutional rights.

✧

DeShaney v. Winnebago Social Services, 489 U.S. 189; 1095 S. Ct. 998; 103 L. Ed. 2d 249 (1989)

Facts—Four-year-old Joshua DeShaney was the victim of continuing physical abuse by his father that eventually left him with permanent injuries leaving him in need of confinement in an institution for the profoundly retarded. He and his mother brought suit against the state, which had several times intervened on his behalf, asking that the Department of Social Services be held liable for his injuries under the due process clause of the Fourteenth Amendment. The District Court granted summary judgment on behalf of the respondents, a judgment affirmed by the U.S. Seventh Circuit Court of Appeals.

Question—Does the due process clause of the Fourteenth Amendment make the state liable for injuries that a child suffered at the hands of his father?

Decision—No.

Reasons—*C.J. Rehnquist* (6–3). The DeShaneys are attempting to read a substantive component into the due process clause, but this clause was designed "to protect the people from the State, not to ensure that the State protected them from each other." The due process clause does not guarantee affirmative rights. Petitioners claim that such rights can arise out of "certain 'special relationships' created or assumed by the State with respect to particular individuals," but precedents have limited such cases to those like confinement in a prison or mental institution where the state "takes a person in custody and holds him there against his will." The fact that the state at times took temporary custody of Joshua did not make the state his personal guardian after it released him. If the state has a financial obligation to Joshua, it must be democratically ascertained through protection of state tort (personal injury) law rather than through the due process clause.

J. Brennan's dissent focused on the fact that the state had assumed liability by extending protection to him on previous occasions and therefore assuming responsibility for him.

J. Blackmun's dissent accused the majority of engaging in "sterile formalism." He argued that the case before the Court was an "open" question that should be given "a 'sympathetic' reading," which "comports with dictates of fundamental justice and recognizes that compassion need not be exiled from the province of judging."

☙

Scheidler v. National Organization for Women, 537 U.S. 393; 123 S. Ct. 1057; 154 L. Ed. 2d 991 (2003)

Facts—Scheidler and other members of the Pro-Life Action Network (PLAN) were sued in 1986 for violating the Racketeer Influenced and Corrupt Organization Act (RICO). The district and circuit courts both dismissed the charge on the basis that the protestor's actions were not economically motivated, but the U.S. Supreme Court decided that this motivation was not required and sent the case back to the District Court. That court decided that abortion protestors were in violation of the Hobbs Act and state extortion laws and issued a nationwide injunction prohibiting obstructing access to abortion clinics. The Seventh U.S. Circuit Court of Appeals affirmed.

Question—Did attempts to block access to abortion clinics violate the provisions of the Hobbs Act, which prohibited extortion?

Decision—No.

Reasons—*C.J. Rehnquist* (8–1). Absent congressional language to the contrary, the Court presumes "that a statutory term has its common-law meaning." Under common law, extortion was tied to taking something of value. It also required the "acquisition" of such property. Although the protestors in this case interfered with the exercise of property rights, committing "coercion," they did not appropriate such property in an act of "extortion." Criminal statutes must be "strictly construed" so that any ambiguity is resolved in favor of leniency. Since petitioners "did not obtain or attempt to obtain property from respondents, we conclude that there was no basis upon which to find that they committed extortion under the Hobbs Act."

J. Ginsburg, concurring, argued that the Seventh Circuit Court decision interpreted RICO statutes too broadly.

J. Stevens, dissenting, argued that the Court had interpreted RICO too narrowly and cited a number of cases as proof.

Caperton v. A.T. Massey Coal Co., Inc, 129 S. Ct. 2252 (2009)

Facts—A West Virginia jury found Massey Coal liable for $50 million in compensatory and punitive damages. West Virginia held an election for the State Supreme Court of Appeals, which would hear the case on appeal. Massey's chairman, Don Blankenship, funneled $3 million to the campaign of Brent Benjamin, who was challenging an incumbent on that court. After Benjamin won, he refused to disqualify himself from the *Massey* case, and the court reversed the judgment by a 3 to 2 vote.

Question—Did Justice Benjamin's refusal to recuse himself violate due process?

Decision—Yes.

Reasons—*J. Kennedy* (5–4). Blankenship's contributions constituted more than that of all of Benjamin's other supporters combined, and two-thirds of West Virginians doubted his impartiality. Due process requires a "fair trial in a fair tribunal." *Tumey v. Ohio*, 273 U.S. 510 (1927), ruled that a judge must recuse himself when he has "a direct, personal, substantial, pecuniary interest" in a case, and decided that a mayor-judge could not decide on a case in which he would only get paid in the event of a guilty verdict. *Ward v. Monroeville*, 409 U.S. 57 (1972), made a similar decision in a case where fines went to a town's general fisc. *Aetna Life Ins. Co. v. Lavoie*, 475 U.S. 813 (1986), further disqualified a judge from participating in a case involving a punitive damage case almost identical to one he had filed. *Lavoie* stressed the need for an objective component in the recusal decision. Other decisions had disqualified judges who had participated in earlier proceedings. In deciding to recuse himself, Benjamin had looked into his own subjective feelings and found no actual bias, but objective standards "do not require proof of actual bias." The question is whether "'under a realistic appraisal of psychological tendencies and human weakness,' the interest 'poses such a risk of actual bias or prejudgment that the practice must be forbidden if the guarantee of due process is to be adequately implemented.'" Not every campaign contribution will carry such a risk, but the donations involved in this case are extraordinary. Moreover, Blankenship could have reasonably foreseen that the new justice would hear this case. The Court must be especially wary when "a man chooses the judge in his own case." Recusal was necessary in order to preserve "the integrity of the judiciary and the rule of law."

C.J. Roberts, dissenting. Past cases have focused on cases where judges have had "a financial interest in the outcome of the case" or when a judge is trying a defendant for certain criminal contempts. The Court's "probability of bias" standard in this case "cannot be defined in any limited way." Roberts cites forty unanswered questions that the case raises and suggests that "the Court's inability to formulate a 'judicially discernible and manageable standard' strongly counsels against the recognition of a novel constitutional right." The majority's focus on the extreme nature of this case is "so much whistling past the graveyard." The amount of Blankenship's direct contribution to the campaign was minimal, and there is no way to know whether his contributions made the difference. In any case, the majority's "cure is worse than the disease."

J. Scalia, dissenting, argues that the decision will create "vast uncertainty," and will further erode public confidence in the law. The Court is on a misdirected and "quixotic quest to right all wrongs and repair all imperfections through the Constitution."

❦

JURIES

Hurtado v. California, 110 U.S. 516; 4 S. Ct. 111; 28 L. Ed. 232 (1884)

Facts—The plaintiff was charged by the district attorney with murder, by means of an information, in a California county court. The plaintiff was tried, the jury rendered a verdict of murder in the first degree, and the court sentenced him to death. The supreme court of California upheld the judgment. The plaintiff contended that under the due process clause of the Fourteenth Amendment he was entitled to a proper indictment by a grand jury before trial.

Question—In felony cases is an indictment by a grand jury a necessary part of "due process of law" guaranteed by the Fourteenth Amendment?

Decision—No.

Reasons—*J. Matthews* (7–1). The use of indictment by a grand jury was merely one process of the common law handed down to us from the courts of England. It is not a necessary part of the law but merely the way the law has been used. To hold that such a characteristic is essential to due process of law would be to render it incapable of progress or improvement. The information "is merely a preliminary proceeding, and can result in no final judgment, except as a consequence of a regular judicial trial, conducted precisely as in cases of indictments." Therefore the Court reasoned that mere usage of the law at the time the due process clause was added to the Constitution does not imply that that usage is the only means of due process of law.

New procedure does not deny due process. Due process of law must mean more than the actual existing law of the land. "It follows that any legal proceedings enforced by public authority, whether sanctioned by age and custom, or newly devised in the discretion of the legislative power, in furtherance of the general public good, which regards and preserves these principles of liberty and justice, must be held to be due process of law."

In dissent, *J. Harlan*, the first justice to advocate "total incorporation" of the provisions of the Bill of Rights into the Fourteenth Amendment, argued that the right of due process included ancient rights and that the right to a grand jury was among them.

Note—The grand jury provision remains one of the few provisions of the Bill of Rights that has not been incorporated into the Fourteenth Amendment and applied to the states. The grand jury is not widely used in the states although, of course, it is used in the federal courts.

ﻌﻬ

Norris v. Alabama, 294 U.S. 587; 55 S. Ct. 579; 79 L. Ed. 1074 (1935)

Facts—Norris was one of nine African American youths, known as "the Scottsboro boys," who were indicted in 1931 in Jackson County, Alabama, for the crime of rape. They were tried and convicted in Morgan County, Alabama, on change of venue. Norris claimed that his rights guaranteed to him by the Fourteenth Amendment had been violated because the juries that indicted and tried him were chosen to the exclusion of members of his race. The state contended that even if it were assumed that there was no name of an African American on the jury roll, it was not established that race or color caused the omission. They said in this case the commission drawing up the jury did not take into consideration race or color, and that no one had been excluded because of race or color.

Question—Was the exclusion of African Americans from the jury pool constitute a violation of the Fourteenth Amendment?

Decision—Yes.

Reasons—*C.J. Hughes* (8–0). The evidence produced disclosed that African Americans (to whom, consistent with terminology then in use, the Court referred as Negroes) had never been called for jury duty in the two counties involved in this case. Furthermore, it was disclosed that there were some qualified African Americans in these counties. The Court reasoned that this was prima facie evidence that African Americans were denied jury duty because of their race or color, and this was therefore contrary to the Constitution.

Note—*Norris* is the second "Scottsboro case." The first was *Powell v. Alabama*, 287 U.S. 45 (1932), which applied to the states the guarantee of counsel provision of the Sixth Amendment if certain circumstances were present.

᠊ᢀᡒ

Duncan v. Louisiana, 391 U.S. 145; 88 S. Ct. 1444; 20 L. Ed. 491 (1968)

Facts—Duncan, a black youth, was convicted of simple battery, a misdemeanor punishable by two years' imprisonment and a $300 fine. He had slapped a white youth and was sentenced in a Louisiana parish court to sixty days and $150 fine. The Court denied Duncan's request for a jury trial because the Louisiana Constitution granted such trials only in capital punishment cases or in cases of imprisonment at hard labor. Duncan contended that in sentences of two years or more, the Sixth and Fourteenth Amendments secured citizens the right of a jury trial.

Question—Must Louisiana grant criminal defendants a jury trial, under the Sixth and Fourteenth Amendments?

Decision—Yes.

Reasons—*J. White* (7–2). The Fourteenth Amendment denies the states the power to "deprive any person of life, liberty, or property, without due process of law," and in determining the meaning of this language the Court looks for guidance to the Bill of Rights. The Court has already held that many of these rights are protected against state action by the due process clause of the Fourteenth Amendment. "We believe that trial by jury in criminal cases is fundamental to the American scheme of justice. We hold that the Fourteenth Amendment guarantees a right of jury trial in all criminal cases which—were they to be tried in a federal court—would come within the Sixth Amendment's guarantee. Since we consider the appeal before us to be such a case, we hold that the Constitution was violated when Duncan's demand for jury trial was refused. The nation has a deep commitment to the right of jury trial and is reluctant to entrust plenary powers over the life and liberty of the citizen to one judge or to a group of judges."

J. Harlan argued in dissent that the majority did not give due deference to state rules of criminal procedure.

Note—This decision reversed *Jordan v. Massachusetts*, 225 U.S. 167 (1912) and *Maxwell v. Dow*, 176 U.S. 581 (1900).

Burch v. Louisiana, 441 U.S. 130; 99 S. Ct. 1623; 60 L. Ed. 2d 96 (1979)

Facts—Burch and a corporation were both found guilty under the Louisiana criminal code of a nonpetty criminal offense (obscenity) and convicted by a five-person vote of a six-person jury. Although acknowledging that the issue was "close," the Louisiana Supreme Court upheld the conviction.

Question—Does conviction by a nonunanimous six-person jury for a nonpetty offense violate the right to a jury trial guaranteed by the Sixth Amendment and applied to states by the Fourteenth?

Decision—Yes.

Reasons—*C.J. Rehnquist* (9–0 as regards the specific issue). Since *Duncan v. Louisiana* (1968), the Supreme Court has held that the right to a jury trial is so fundamental that it binds the states. In *Williams v. Florida* (1970), the Court upheld the use of a six-person jury, in *Apodaca v. Oregon* (1972), it upheld the conviction by a vote of ten of twelve jurors in noncapital cases, and in *Ballew v. Georgia* (1978) it ruled that a trial by a five-person jury for a nonpetty offense was unconstitutional. This case mixes questions of jury size and unanimity. Admitting that the Court had "already departed from the strictly historical requirements of jury trial," Rehnquist argued "that lines must be drawn somewhere if the substance of the jury trial right is to be preserved." In 1979, only two states other than Louisiana allowed nonunanimous verdicts in jury trials of six people. The state's interest in saving time and reducing the number of hung juries was insufficient to justify a nonunanimous verdict in this case: "when a State has reduced the size of its juries to the minimum number of jurors permitted by the Constitution, the additional authorization of nonunanimous verdicts by such juries sufficiently threatens the constitutional principles that led to the establishment of the size threshold that any countervailing interest of the State should yield."

J. Stevens limited his concurrence to the specific question at issue in the case. *J. Brennan* (joined by *J. Stewart* and *J. Marshall*) agreed that nonunanimous juries in nonpetty cases were unconstitutional but would have struck down the obscenity law at issue in this case as "overbroad and therefore facially unconstitutional."

◦৶৶

Duren v. Missouri, 439 U.S. 357; 99 S. Ct. 664; 58 L. Ed. 2d 579 (1979)

Facts—A Circuit Court of Jackson County, Missouri, indicted Duren for first-degree murder and first-degree robbery. He contended that a provision of the Missouri law that granted women who requested it an automatic exemption from jury service denied him his right to trial by jury from a cross section of the community. The jury selection process in Jackson County randomly selected from the voter registration list. In addition to several exempted categories, the one on women stated: "Any woman who elects not to serve will fill out this paragraph and mail this questionnaire to the jury commissioner at once."

Even those women who do not return the summons were treated as having claimed exemption if they failed to appear for jury service on the appointed day. Under this system only about 15 percent of jurors were women.

Question—Did a system exempting women from grand jury service deny Duren an impartial jury under the Sixth Amendment?

Decision—Yes.

Reasons—*J. White* (8–1). Petitioner Duren proved that the Jackson County, Missouri, community has an adult population of whom over half are women and that the jury venires containing approximately 15 percent women are not reasonably representative of the community. This "gross discrepancy" requires "the conclusion that women were not fairly representative in the source from which petit juries were drawn. . . ." Petitioner demonstrated that the under-representation of women was due to "the operation of Missouri's exemption criteria—whether for the automatic exemption for women or other statutory exemptions. . . ." States remain free to prescribe relevant qualifications for their jurors and provide reasonable exemptions "so long as it may fairly be said that the jury lists or panels are representative of the community." But exempting all women because of "the preclusive domestic responsibilities of some women is insufficient justification for their disproportionate exclusion on jury venires." The constitutional guarantee to a jury drawn from a fair cross section of the community "requires that states exercise proper caution."

J. Rehnquist argued in dissent that the Court was putting too much emphasis on obtaining a fair cross section of the community on juries and too little on convicting the guilty.

ঔৼ

Batson v. Kentucky, 476 U.S. 79; 106 S. Ct. 1712; 90 L. Ed. 2d 69 (1986)

Facts—A Circuit Court in Jefferson County, Kentucky, refused to discharge a jury where the prosecutor had used peremptory challenges to strike African American jurors in the trial of a black defendant. The Kentucky Supreme Court affirmed.

Question—Are peremptory challenges exercised to exclude individuals on the basis of race subject to equal protection review?

Decision—Yes.

Reasons—*J. Powell* (7–2). Powell decided that this case called for a review of *Swain v. Alabama*, 380 U.S. 202 (1965). In *Strauder v. West Virginia*, 100 U.S. 303 (1880), the Court had rejected schemes that excluded racial minorities from the jury pool. The harm of such exclusion extends into the entire community by undermining "public confidence in the fairness of our system of justice." Although *Swain* permitted blacks to show purposeful discrimination in the use of peremptory challenges, it placed "a crippling burden of proof" on the defendants. Powell altered this burden. In cases where a defendant can show he or she is "a member of a racial group capable of being singled out for differential treatment," the defendant may then require the state "to come forward with a neutral explanation for challenging black jurors." "The core guarantee of equal protection, ensuring citizens that their State will not discriminate on account of race, would be meaningless were we to approve the exclusion of jurors on the basis of such assumptions, which arise solely from the jurors' race." This decision will not eviscerate peremptory challenges but will simply require "trial courts to be sensitive to the racially discriminatory use of peremptory challenges."

J. White, concurring, agreed that *Swain v. Alabama* should be overturned to the extent that it required a defendant to offer proof of discrimination that extended beyond the defendant's own case. White did not believe this decision should be applied retroactively.

J. Marshall, concurring, called for the complete elimination of peremptory challenges, which he believed have the "inherent potential . . . to distort the jury process by permitting the exclusion of jurors on racial grounds."

J. Stevens, concurring, defended himself against charges of inconsistency raised in the dissenting opinions.

C.J. Burger, dissenting, accused the Court of ignoring "settled principles." He noted that the defendant had argued before the Court on the basis of the Sixth Amendment rather than the equal protection clause; he did not think the Court should decide the latter issue without full argument. Burger further distinguished the exclusion of African Americans from the jury pool and their exclusion from individual juries through peremptory challenges. By definition, peremptory challenges do not require counsel to supply reasons. The majority decision is likely to inject racial considerations back into the jury selection process.

J. Rehnquist, dissenting, argued that the Court was rejecting long-established practices and precedents on the basis of too little argument. He believed it was often necessary to use "group affiliations, such as age, race, or occupation, as a 'proxy' for potential juror partiality, based on the assumption or belief that members of one group are more likely to favor defendants who belong to the same group."

RIGHT TO COUNSEL

Powell v. Alabama, 287 U.S. 45; 53 S. Ct. 55; 77 L. Ed. 158 (1932)

Facts—Petitioners, nine African American youths, were indicted for the rape of two white girls. A jury tried them six days after the day they were arrested, amidst an atmosphere of tense, hostile public sentiment. They were not represented by counsel or asked if they desired counsel; the judge simply appointed "all members of the bar" to defend them. The jury returned the death penalty. This was affirmed on appeal although the chief justice of the state supreme court strongly dissented, claiming an unfair trial.

Questions—(a) Did the state deny petitioners the right of counsel? (b) If so, did such denial infringe the due process clause of the Fourteenth Amendment?

Decisions—(a) Yes; (b) Yes.

Reasons—*J. Sutherland* (7–2). The basic elements comprising due process of law according to the Constitution are notice and hearing (preliminary steps) together with a legally competent tribunal having jurisdiction of the case. A hearing includes the right and aid of counsel when so desired. The ordinary layman, even the intelligent and educated layman, is not skilled in the science of law and needs the advice and direction of competent counsel. These youths were in effect denied the right to counsel. They were transients and all lived in other states, yet were given no chance to communicate with members of their families to obtain counsel. Further, the trial was carried out with such dispatch that they were accorded no time to prepare a defense employing a counsel of their own choice.

"In the light of . . . the ignorance and illiteracy of the defendants, their youth, the circumstances of public hostility, the imprisonment, and the close surveillance of the defendants by the military forces, the fact that their friends and families were all in other states and communications with them necessarily difficult, and above all that they stood in deadly peril of their lives—we think the failure of the trial courts to give them reasonable time and opportunity to secure counsel was a clear denial of due process."

J. Butler, dissenting, argued that the record in this case did not substantiate claims that the right to counsel had been denied.

❧

Chambers v. Florida, 309 U.S. 227; 60 S. Ct. 472; 84 L. Ed. 716 (1940)

Facts—On May 13, 1933, Robert Darcy was robbed and murdered in Pompano, Florida. The petitioners in this case were among the suspects rounded up for investigation. They were later removed to Dade County Jail at Miami to protect them against mob violence. For a week's period the petitioners were continually questioned, and on the night of Saturday, May 20, the questioning routine became an all-night vigil. On Sunday, May 21, Woodward confessed. After one week of constant denial, all the petitioners "broke." The state utilized these confessions to obtain judgment. The petitioners were not, either in jail or in court, wholly removed from the constant observation, influence, custody, and control of those whose persistent pressure brought about the "sunrise" confessions.

Question—Did the extended interrogation of the defendants violate the due process of law guaranteed by the Fourteenth Amendment?

Decision—Yes.

Reasons—*J. Black* (8–0). The due process clause was intended to guarantee adequate and appropriate procedural standards and to protect, at all times, people charged with or suspected of crime. The rights and liberties of people suspected of crime cannot safely be left to secret processes. Those who have suffered most from these secret and dictatorial processes have always been the poor, the ignorant, the weak, and the powerless.

The Fourteenth Amendment required states to conform to fundamental standards of procedure. The law enforcement methods such as those described in this case are not necessary to uphold our laws. The Constitution prohibits such lawless means regardless of the end in view.

Note—The Court went beyond physical coercion to hold that psychological coercion also violates the due process clause, which binds the states.

$\otimes\vartheta\!\!\!\!\int$

Gideon v. Wainwright, 372 U.S. 335; 83 S. Ct. 792; 9 L. Ed. 2d 799 (1963)

Facts—Clarence E. Gideon was charged in a Florida state court with having broken into and entered a poolroom with intent to commit a misdemeanor. Under Florida law such an offense is a noncapital felony. Gideon appeared in court without funds and without a lawyer. He asked the court to appoint counsel for him. The court refused because Florida law permitted the appointment of counsel for indigent defendants in capital cases only. Gideon appealed his conviction claiming violation of the constitutional guarantee of counsel.

Question—Must states provide counsel to an indigent defendant in noncapital cases?

Decision—Yes.

Reasons—*J. Black* (9–0). The Fourteenth Amendment makes a provision of the Bill of Rights that is "fundamental and essential to a fair trial" obligatory upon the states. The Court noted that "reason and reflection require us to recognize that in our adversary system of criminal justice, any person haled into court, who is too poor to hire a lawyer, cannot be assured a fair trial unless counsel is provided for him. This seems to be an obvious truth. . . . The right of one charged with crime to counsel may not be deemed fundamental and essential to fair trials in some countries, but it is in ours." Thus was the guarantee of counsel in the Sixth Amendment applied to all cases in the state courts, capital and noncapital. In so holding, the Court overruled *Betts v. Brady*, 316 U.S. 455 (1942).

Escobedo v. Illinois, 378 U.S. 478; 84 S. Ct. 1758; 12 L. Ed. 2d 977 (1964)

Facts—Danny Escobedo was convicted of fatally shooting his brother-in-law in Chicago. During the police questioning following his arrest, he was not permitted to consult with the attorney he had retained and who was at police headquarters. In the course of this questioning the police did not advise Escobedo of his constitutional right to remain silent, and he made some incriminating statements.

Question—Was the refusal by the police under the circumstances to honor the request of the accused to consult with his lawyer a violation of the Sixth Amendment?

Decision—Yes.

Reasons—*J. Goldberg* (5–4). When an investigation is no longer a general inquiry into an unsolved crime but has begun to focus on a particular suspect who has been taken into custody, is being interrogated, has requested and been denied counsel, and has not been advised of his constitutional rights, as was the case here, the accused has been denied "the assistance of counsel" guaranteed by the Sixth Amendment. This guarantee was held to be obligatory on the states under the terms of the Fourteenth Amendment in *Gideon v. Wainwright*, 372 U.S. 335 (1963). When the investigatory process becomes accusatory then our adversary system begins to operate and the accused must be permitted to consult with his attorney.

J. Harlan, J. Stewart, and *J. White* authored dissents advocating adherence to earlier precedents and expressing concern over the effect of this decision on law enforcement.

Miranda v. Arizona, 384 U.S. 436; 86 S. Ct. 1602; 16 L. Ed. 2d 694 (1966)

Facts—This decision consolidated four cases that came from Arizona, New York, California, and the federal courts. In each the law enforcement officials had taken the defendant into custody and had interrogated him for the purpose of obtaining a confession. At no time did the police effectively advise a defendant of his right to remain silent or of his right to consult with his attorney. In the lead case, police had arrested Ernesto Miranda at his home and then taken him to a Phoenix police station where two police officers questioned him. After two hours he made a written confession. He was subsequently convicted of kidnapping and rape. In the New York case the charge was first-degree robbery, in the California case it was robbery and first-degree murder, and in the federal case robbery of a savings and loan association and a bank in California.

Question—May police use and elicit statements they obtain from custodial interrogation without first informing suspects of their rights?

Decision—No.

Reasons—*C.J. Warren* (5–4). An individual held for interrogation must be clearly informed that he has the right to consult counsel and to have his lawyer with him during interrogation. Financial inability of an accused person to furnish counsel is no excuse for the absence of counsel since in such an instance a lawyer must be appointed to represent the accused. If he answers some questions and gives some information on his own prior to invoking his right to remain silent this is not to warrant an assumption that the privilege has been waived.

The Court noted that "the prosecution may not use statements, whether exculpatory or inculpatory, stemming from custodial interrogation of the defendant unless it demonstrates the use of procedural safeguards effective to secure the privilege against self-incrimination. By custodial interrogation, we mean questioning initiated by law enforcement officers after a person has been taken into custody or otherwise deprived of his freedom of action in any significant way."

J. Clark, J. Harlan, and *J. White* authored dissents, questioning whether police were in fact engaging in the kind of "third degree" tactics with which the majority had charged them and arguing that the Court was imposing a utopian view of voluntary confessions that was likely to undermine law enforcement efforts.

Argersinger v. Hamlin, 407 U.S. 25; 92 S. Ct. 2006; 32 L. Ed. 2d 530 (1972)

Facts—A Florida court convicted Argersinger of carrying a concealed weapon. He was indigent and was unable to afford a lawyer. The offense was punishable by up to six months in jail and a $1,000 fine. Argersinger was sentenced to ninety days in jail. The Florida Supreme Court rejected his plea that he should have been entitled to court-appointed representation.

Question—Did the state's failure to appoint counsel in a nonpetty offense involving a possible jail term violate the Sixth and Fourteenth Amendments?

Decision—Yes.

Reasons—*J. Douglas* (9–0). In *Duncan v. Louisiana* (1968) the Court held that the right to a jury trial applied to "non-petty offenses punishable by more than six months imprisonment." The right to a jury trial, however, "has a different genealogy" than the right to counsel. "The assistance of counsel is often a requisite to the very existence of a fair trial." The reasoning in *Gideon v. Wainwright* and previous cases applies to any cases, including misdemeanors, involving possible jail time. Time in jail often has serious consequences. Thus, counsel needs to be provided in all such cases other than those involving "a knowing and intelligent waiver."

J. Brennan, concurring, pointed out that in some misdemeanor cases, law students might be able to provide assistance. *J. Burger*, concurring, agreed that any case involving imprisonment should entitle an individual to counsel but argued that judges will be capable of making such predictions beforehand. *J. Powell's* concurrence focused on the issue of "fundamental fairness," and feared that this decision might actually advantage indigent defendants over others. He favored a three-part test that would look at "the complexity of the offense charged," "the probable sentence that will follow," and "the individual factors peculiar to each case."

❧

Dickerson v. United States, 530 U.S. 428; 120 S. Ct. 2326; 147 L. Ed. 2d 405 (2000)

Facts—In 1968 Congress adopted legislation designed to modify *Miranda v. Arizona* (1966) so as to accept voluntary confessions even in cases where police officers had not read defendants their rights. On the basis of *Miranda*, a U.S. District Court suppressed voluntary statements Dickerson made to the FBI in the absence of law enforcement warnings, but the U.S. Fourth Circuit Court decided that the 1968 law had been met and that *Miranda* was not a constitutional rule.

Questions—(a) Are solicited voluntary confessions admissible in the absence of *Miranda* warnings? (b) Was *Miranda* a constitutional ruling?

Decisions—(a) No; (b) Yes.

Reasons—*C.J. Rehnquist* (7–2). Prior to *Miranda*, the Court used the voluntariness test for confessions, relying chiefly on the Fifth and Fourteenth Amendments, but *Miranda* added more "concrete constitutional guidelines," which the 1968 legislation attempted to circumvent. The Supreme Court exercises supervisory authority over other federal courts, which Congress can alter through legislation, but "Congress may not legislatively supersede our decisions interpreting and applying the Constitution." *Miranda* was more than an exercise of the Supreme Court's supervisory power as witnessed by the fact that the decision has also been applied to state court proceedings over which the Court does not have such supervisory authority. The *Miranda* decision "is replete with statements indicating that the majority thought it was a constitutional rule." The Court has subsequently made some exceptions to the *Miranda* decision, but that does not establish that *Miranda* "is not a constitutional rule" but "that no constitutional rule is immutable." Stare decisis weighs heavily against overruling *Miranda*. The rules prescribed in that case have "become embedded in routine police practice to the point where the warnings have become part of our national culture." The Court thus reaffirmed *Miranda* as a constitutional rule that may not be evaded through congressional legislation.

J. Scalia argued that *Miranda* and its progeny did not merely "apply the Constitution" but sought "to expand it," and he believed such an expansion was unwise and undemocratic. He thought it "preposterous" to read *Miranda* as a standard of what the Constitution required. It was not aimed, like the Fifth Amendment, at "compelled" confessions but at "foolish" ones. It was a prophylactic rule that went far beyond constitutional requirements. The subsequent exceptions to *Miranda* did undermine its alleged constitutional foundation. Because *Miranda* required the invalidation of legislation that did not violate the Constitution, it should be abandoned. The "supposed workability" of the *Miranda* rules are not as clear as they seem; they create as many questions as they resolve. The Court's continuing adherence to *Miranda* is a sign of "judicial arrogance."

SELF-INCRIMINATION AND IMMUNITY

Ullmann v. United States, 350 U.S. 422; 76 S. Ct. 497; 100 L. Ed. 511 (1956)

Facts—Congress in 1954 passed the Immunity Act providing that whenever, in the judgment of a U.S. attorney, the testimony of any witness, or the production of books, papers, or other evidence by any witness, in any case or proceeding before any grand jury or court of the United States involving any interference with or endangering of national security (including certain specified federal statutes) is necessary to the public interest, the U.S. attorney, upon the approval of the attorney general, shall make application to the court for an order to the witness to testify. However, the witness cannot subsequently be prosecuted in any court on the basis of the testimony he then gives.

William L. Ullmann refused to answer questions regarding espionage activity before a grand jury of the Southern District of New York despite the statutory provision of immunity, and he was convicted of contempt.

Question—Is the protection Congress provided in the Immunity Act of 1954 sufficiently broad to displace the protection afforded by the constitutional privilege against self-incrimination?

Decision—Yes.

Reasons—*J. Frankfurter* (7–2). The Immunity Act protects a witness who is compelled to answer to the extent of his constitutional immunity, that is, giving testimony that might possibly expose him to a criminal charge. The immunity thus granted by the statute is also effective as against state action. "We cannot say that Congress's paramount authority in safeguarding national security does not justify the restriction it has placed on the exercise of state power for the more effective exercise of conceded federal power." The Court noted that the sole concern of the privilege against self-incrimination "is, as its name indicates, with the danger to a witness forced to give testimony leading to the infliction of 'penalties affixed to the criminal acts. . . .' Immunity displaces the danger. Once the reason for the privilege ceases, the privilege ceases."

The Court also noted that the act does not impose a nonjudicial function on the District Court since this court has no discretion to deny an application for an order requiring a witness to answer, assuming that the statutory requirements have been met.

In dissent, *J. Douglas* argued for a wider view of the Fifth Amendment as a protection for the rights of conscience and dignity and as protection against testimony that might lead to "infamy and disgrace."

Note—In *Kastigar v. United States*, 406 U.S. 441 (1972) the Court distinguished between "use immunity," coextensive with the guarantee of the Fifth Amendment, and "transactional immunity," wider than the Fifth Amendment. The Court has said only the former immunity is required.

Murphy v. Waterfront Commission of New York Harbor, 378 U.S. 52; 84 S. Ct. 1594; 12 L. Ed. 2d 678 (1964)

Facts—A number of persons had been subpoenaed to testify at a hearing conducted by the Waterfront Commission concerning a work stoppage at the Hoboken, New Jersey, piers. Even though they were granted immunity from prosecution under the laws of New Jersey and New York, they refused to testify on the ground that the answers might tend to incriminate them "under federal law, to which the grant of immunity did not purport to extend."

Question—May a state compel a witness, whom it has immunized from prosecution under its laws, to give testimony that might then be used to convict him of a crime against the federal government?

Decision—No.

Reasons—*J. Goldberg* (9–0). There is no continuing legal vitality to or historical justification for the rule that one jurisdiction within our federal structure may compel a witness to give testimony that could be used to convict him of a crime in another jurisdiction. "We hold that the constitutional privilege against self-incrimination protects a state witness against incrimination under federal as well as state law and a federal witness against incrimination under state as well as federal law . . . we hold the constitutional rule to be that a state witness may not be compelled to give testimony which may be incriminating under federal law unless the compelled testimony and its fruits cannot be used in any manner by federal officials in connection with a criminal prosecution against him."

Note—*Murphy* overruled *United States v. Murdock*, 284 U.S. 141 (1931) and *Feldman v. United States*, 332 U.S. 487 (1944).

Malloy v. Hogan, 378 U.S. 1; 84 S. Ct. 1489; 12 L. Ed. 2d 653 (1964)

Facts—William Malloy was arrested during a gambling raid in 1959 by police in Hartford, Connecticut. He was convicted and given a suspended sentence. Later a state court held him in contempt for refusing to answer questions on the basis of possible self-incrimination. The state court held that the Fifth Amendment did not apply to state proceedings.

Question—Does the Fourteenth Amendment safeguard the Fifth Amendment privilege against self-incrimination?

Decision—Yes.

Reasons—*J. Brennan* (5–4). The same standards must determine whether the silence of an accused person in either a federal or a state proceeding is justified. "It would be incongruous to have different standards determine the validity of a claim of privilege based on the same feared prosecution, depending on whether the claim was asserted in a state or federal court."

J. Harlan and *J. White* argued in dissent that this decision made substantial inroads into the idea of federalism and did not give due deference to decisions by judges as to when an answer might prove to be self-incriminatory.

Note—This decision reversed *Twining v. New Jersey*, 211 U.S. 78 (1908) and *Adamson v. California*, 332 U.S. 46 (1947). The due process clause of the Fourteenth Amendment extends the Fifth Amendment protection against self-incrimination to a state offender, as in *Murphy v. Waterfront Commission of New York Harbor*, 378 U.S. 52 (1964), and protects a state witness against self-incrimination under federal as well as state law.

Schmerber v. California, 384 U.S. 757; 86 S. Ct. 1826; 16 L. Ed. 2d 908 (1966)

Facts—Armando Schmerber had been convicted of driving an automobile while under the influence of intoxicating liquor. He had been arrested at a hospital while receiving treatment for injuries suffered in an accident involving the automobile he had apparently been driving. Under police direction a physician at the hospital took a blood sample from Schmerber over his protests. Analysis of the sample of blood indicated intoxication, and the trial court admitted this analysis in evidence.

Questions—Does taking a blood sample under these circumstances (a) deny the accused due process of law, (b) abridge the privilege against self-incrimination, (c) deny the right to counsel, and (d) constitute unreasonable search and seizure?

Decisions—(a) No; (b) No; (c) No; (d) No.

Reasons—*J. Brennan* (5–4). (a) The case of *Breithaupt v. Abram* (352 U.S. 432, 1957) is controlling here. There a similar blood sample was taken while the individual was unconscious. This did not constitute offense against a "sense of justice" and thus there was no denial of due process. (b) *Breithaupt* also controls the self-incrimination aspect of the case. The privilege protects an accused person only from being compelled to testify against himself or otherwise provide the state with evidence of a testimonial or communicative nature. The taking and use of the blood sample did not involve compulsion to these ends. (c) Here there was no issue presented of counsel's ability to assist Schmerber in respect of any rights he did possess. (d) As to the search and seizure claim, there was plainly probable cause for the officer to arrest the accused. Further, the officer "might reasonably have believed that he was confronted with an emergency, in which the delay necessary to obtain a warrant, under the circumstances, threatened 'the destruction of the evidence'. . . . We are told that the percentage of alcohol in the blood begins to diminish shortly after drinking stops, as the body functions to eliminate it from the system."

Finally, the Court noted that the test was performed in a reasonable manner in a hospital environment according to accepted medical practices and emphasized that the judgment was only on the basis of the facts of the present case.

J. Black argued in dissent that the Court was giving too narrow a reading to the Fifth Amendment provision against self-incrimination and its application to the states.

Note—*Schmerber* (conscious) must be contrasted with *Breithaupt v. Abram* (unconscious) and *Rochin v. California* (protesting and "shock the conscience"). Can a robbery suspect be forced to undergo surgery in order to extract a bullet but in doing so run the risk of incriminating himself? The Court said "No" in *Winston v. Lee*, 470 U.S. 653 (1985).

❧

Marchetti v. United States, 390 U.S. 39; 88 S. Ct. 697; 19 L. Ed. 2d 889 (1968)

Facts—A federal District Court in Connecticut (where there were numerous criminal penalties for gambling) convicted James Marchetti for violating federal statutes requiring the payment of an annual gambling occupational stamp tax and for failing to register before accepting wagers. These requirements were part of an intricate system of federal taxation applying to wagering, and the registration requirement was designed to aid the collection of the taxes. The arrangement was challenged as being unconstitutional.

Question—Are the methods employed by Congress in the federal wagering tax statutes consistent with the guarantee against self-incrimination contained in the Fifth Amendment?

Decision—No.

Reasons—*J. Harlan* (7–1). The federal Internal Revenue Service makes available to state law enforcement agencies the names and addresses of those who have paid the wagering tax. This creates a real and appreciable hazard of self-incrimination. The likelihood that any past or present gambling offenses will be discovered is increased. The tax provisions oblige even a prospective gambler to accuse himself of conspiracy to violate laws. Further, the premise that the self-incrimination guarantee is entirely inapplicable to prospective acts is too narrow an application of the privilege. Not merely time or a chronological formula must be considered but also the substantiality of the risks of incrimination. Those persons who properly assert the constitutional privilege as to these wagering tax provisions may not be criminally punished for failure to comply with their requirements.

Note—*Marchetti* overruled *United States v. Kahriger*, 345 U.S. 22 (1953) and *Lewis v. United States*, 348 U.S. 419 (1955).

CRUEL AND UNUSUAL PUNISHMENT

State of Louisiana ex rel. Francis v. Resweber, 329 U.S. 459; 67 S. Ct. 374; 91 L. Ed. 422 (1947)

Facts—Louisiana convicted Willie Francis, an African American citizen, of murder in September 1945 and sentenced him to be electrocuted for the crime. Upon a proper death warrant, Francis was prepared for execution on May 3, 1946, and was placed in the electric chair of the state of Louisiana in the presence of the authorized witnesses. The executioner pulled the switch, but, because of mechanical difficulty, death did not result. The governor of Louisiana issued a new death warrant fixing the execution for May 9, 1946. Because of this, an appeal was made and execution of the sentence was delayed.

Question—Did issuing a new death warrant after a failed electrocution constitute double jeopardy and cruel and unusual punishment?

Decision—No.

Reasons—*J. Reed* (5–4). First, there was no case of double jeopardy: "We see no difference from a constitutional point of view between a new trial for error of law at the instance of the state that results in a death sentence instead of imprisonment for life and an execution that follows a failure of equipment." Second, there was no unusual and cruel punishment involved in this case. The petitioner claimed that the psychological strain was cruel and unusual punishment. The cruelty against which the Constitution protects a convicted man is cruelty inherent in the method of punishment, not the necessary suffering involved in any method employed to extinguish life humanely. Mechanical failure did not constitute unusual or cruel punishment. Third, there was no denial of equal protection of the laws. The state of Louisiana did not single out Francis for special treatment. Equal protection does not extend to accidents. There was no evidence in any of the papers to show any violation of petitioner's constitutional rights.

J. Butler argued in dissent that the Court had given inadequate attention to the degree to which the application of electrical current to the appellee had already inflicted punishment upon him

Note—Although voting against Francis, the Court virtually incorporated the cruel and unusual punishment provisions of the Eighth Amendment into the due process clause of the Fourteenth. The incorporation was definitely accomplished in *Robinson v. California,* (370 U.S. 660 (1962). The Court ruled that it is cruel and unusual punishment to put a convicted criminal to death while he is insane, *Ford v. Wainwright,* 477 U.S. 399 (1986) or to impose a mandatory death penalty on a prison inmate convicted of murder while serving a life sentence without chance of parole, *Sumner v. Shuman,* 483 U.S. 66 (1987).

❧

Gregg v. Georgia, 428 U.S. 153; 96 S. Ct. 2909; 49 L. Ed. 2d 859 (1976)

Facts—Troy Gregg was convicted in a Georgia trial court of robbery and murder. The trial was in two stages, a guilt stage and a sentencing stage. Fred Simons and Bob Moore gave two hitchhikers (Troy Gregg and Floyd Allen) a lift in their car. A short while later they offered a third hitchhiker, Dennis Weaver, a ride. He left the car in Atlanta. Subsequently, the remaining four stopped for a rest, and Allen testified that Gregg ambushed and killed the original occupants, Simons and Moore, at that point. Gregg claimed the killings were in self-defense.

Question—Do the Georgia death penalty statutes violate the cruel and unusual punishment provisions under the Eighth and Fourteenth Amendments?

Decision—No.

Reasons—*J. Stewart* (7–2). "The punishment of death for the crime of murder does not," said the Court, "under all circumstances, violate the Eighth and Fourteenth Amendments." Although the legislature may not impose excessive punishment, it is not required to select the least severe penalty possible. Capital punishment is not invalid per se and was accepted by the Framers of the Constitution. "Legislative measures adopted by the people's chosen representatives weigh heavily in ascertaining contemporary standards of decency," and in this connection the Court noted that, since *Furman v. Georgia* (1972) was struck down, thirty-five states have enacted new statutes providing for the death penalty. Moreover "retribution" and "deterrence" are not "impermissible considerations for a legislature to weigh in determining whether the death penalty should be imposed." The bifurcated proceedings in Georgia have met the concerns of arbitrariness and capriciousness condemned in Furman.

J. Brennan and *J. Marshall* wrote dissents emphasizing that the concept of cruel and unusual punishment needs to evolve with societal understandings. Acknowledging that many states had reenacted capital punishment since *Furman v. Georgia*, Marshall argued that those most knowledgeable about the penalty continued to oppose it.

Note—The Court has outlawed jury sentences "wantonly and . . . freakishly imposed" in *Furman v. Georgia* (1972), as well as mandatory death sentences in *Woodson v. North Carolina* (1977), but not, as in *Gregg*, a two-part proceedings: one for determining guilt and the other for determining the sentence.

McCleskey v. Kemp, 481 U.S. 279; 107 S. Ct. 1756; 95 L. Ed. 2d 262 (1987)

Facts—McCleskey, a black man, was convicted in a Georgia court for armed robbery and the murder of a police officer. The jury recommended the death penalty. After unsuccessfully seeking relief in state courts, he sought a writ of habeas corpus in the federal District Court on the grounds, inter alia, that the sentencing process was administered in a radically biased manner. He offered a statistical study (the Baldus Study) of some two thousand murder cases that occurred in Georgia during the 1970s that "indicates that black defendants who killed white victims have the greatest likelihood of receiving the death penalty." The District Court dismissed the petition, which was affirmed by the Court of Appeals. The Supreme Court granted certiorari.

Question—Does a complex statistical study that indicates that racial discrimination affects capital sentencing determination invalidate McCleskey's capital sentence under the Eighth and Fourteenth Amendments?

Decision—No.

Reasons—*J. Powell* (5–4). The lower courts found the Baldus Study flawed: data were incomplete; it did not take into account the full degree of the aggravating or mitigating circumstances; researchers could not discover whether penalty trials were held in many of the cases; there was no preponderance of evidence that the study data were trustworthy; the methodology was infirm; the various models were unstable; and correlations between race and nonracial variables were unpersuasive. The basic principle is not only that the defendant has to prove the existence of purposeful discrimination but that the decision makers in his case acted with discriminatory purpose. "He offers no evidence specific to his own case that would support an inference that racial considerations played a part in his sentence." The Court has accepted statistics showing a violation of equal protection (as in selection of a jury) and to prove statutory violations. The Baldus Study is insufficient to support an inference of discrimination. We find, in fact, that the "Georgia capital sentencing system could operate in a fair and neutral manner." On this issue objective indicia which reflects the public attitude toward this sanction is firm.

   J. Brennan, J. Blackmun, and *J. Stevens* authored dissents arguing that the Baldus Study did indeed show that irrelevant racial considerations were in fact influencing death-penalty decisions.

Note—In addition to the majority rationale, a factor very much in the mind of the Court is the uneasiness, except in carefully defined areas such as racial discrimination in the public schools, work place, or racial exclusion on juries, of imperiling the criminal justice system mired in social science statistics. Thus, through a "process of regressive analysis" statistics could be utilized in disparities among races, attorneys, judges, gender, geography, social classes, and the like.

❧

Thompson v. Oklahoma, 487 U.S. 815; 108 S. Ct. 2687; 101 L. Ed. 2d 702 (1988)

Facts—William Wayne Thompson was tried and found guilty of murder and sentenced to death. At the time of the offense he was fifteen years old. Under Oklahoma law a boy of that age is a "child." Under the law the "child" can be tried as an adult if the prosecution shows the prosecutive merit of the case and there are no reasonable prospects for rehabilitation within the juvenile system. The Supreme Court granted certiorari.

Question—Is it cruel and unusual punishment to execute a convicted murderer who was fifteen years old at the time of the crime?

Decision—Yes.

Reasons—*J. Stevens* (5–3). Contemporary standards of decency "confirm our judgment that such a young person is not capable of acting with the degree of culpability that can justify the ultimate penalty." Human experience and U.S. history recognize "that there are differences which must be accommodated in determining the rights and duties of children as compared with those of adults." Other than the special certification procedure (used in this instance by the prosecution) "apparently there are no Oklahoma statutes either civil or criminal that treat a person under 16 years of age as anything but a 'child' . . . there is . . . complete or near unanimity among all 50 states and the District of Columbia in treating a person under 16 as a minor for several important purposes." The conclusion that it would "offend civilized standards of decency to execute a person who was less than 16 years old at the time of his or her offense" is consistent with the views expressed by respected professional organizations. A societal factor, moreover, involves American sensibility to jury behavior. The haphazard handing out of death sentences by capital juries was a prime factor in *Furman v. Georgia* (1972). Punishment should be related to culpability and "adolescents as a class are less mature and responsible than adults . . . [they] lack the experience, perspective, and judgment expected of adults. We conclude that the Eighth and Fourteenth Amendments prohibit the execution of a person who was under 16 years of age at the time of his or her offense."

J. O'Connor's concurrence questioned the evidence for a national consensus against using capital punishment for individuals who committed their crimes when under the age of 16, but was unwilling to apply the penalty in such cases unless the law specifically gave consideration to such a minimum age.

J. Scalia, in dissent, would permit the imposition of such a penalty in such circumstances as long as the Court used individualized sentencing.

J. Kennedy did not participate in this decision.

Note—The Supreme Court often draws fine lines. In *Stanford v. Kentucky*, 492 U.S. 361 (1989), the Court decided that juries could impose the death penalty on individuals who were sixteen years or older at the time that they committed their crimes, but it reversed course in *Roper v. Simmons*, 543 U.S. 551 (2005), and drew the line at eighteen.

Payne v. Tennessee, 501 U.S. 808; 111 S. Ct. 2597; 115 L. Ed. 2d 760 (1991)

Facts—In *Booth v. Maryland*, 482 U.S. 496 (1987) and *South Carolina v. Gathers*, 490 U.S. 804 (1989), the Supreme Court barred the use of victim-impact evidence during the penalty phase of a capital trial. Nonetheless, in this case, a Tennessee trial court, affirmed by the Tennessee Supreme Court, upheld the use of a grandmother's testimony as to the effect that the murder of her twenty-eight-year-old daughter and her two-year-old granddaughter had on her three-year-old grandson who survived the brutal stabbings that took the lives of his mother and sister.

Question—Do the Eighth and Fourteenth Amendments prohibit all use of victim-impact statements at the sentencing phases of capital offenses?

Decision—No.

Reasons—*C.J. Rehnquist* (6–3). The Court viewed the use of the grandmother's statements in this case as essentially balancing the positive testimony about Payne and his character that was introduced in Court when it was considering the death penalty. Rehnquist contended that the Court's earlier decisions essentially excluding any evidence other than the "blameworthiness" of the offender unduly limited information that should be available to the jury. The Court had continually widened considerations of mitigating evidence in such cases, and consideration of such evidence without also weighing the impact of the crime "unfairly weighted the scales in a capital trial; while virtually no limits are placed on the relevant mitigating evidence a capital defendant may introduce concerning his own circumstances, the State is barred from either offering 'a quick glimpse of the life' which a defendant 'chose to extinguish,' . . . or demonstrating the loss to the victim's family and to society which has resulted from the defendant's homicide." In this case, Payne's family and friends testified to his good character, and the victim's grandmother made a single statement as to the harm her grandson had suffered. Although adherence to precedent is important, it has less force in matters involving "procedural and evidentiary rules" than in cases "involving property and contract rights, where reliance interests are involved."

In concurrence, *J. O'Connor* noted that, while allowing the use of victim-impact statements, this decision did not require or even recommend that states utilize them. *J. Scalia's* concurrence cited a precedent to argue that stare decisis should not lead to "an imprisonment of reason." *J. Souter* viewed the information in the victim-impact statement as "revealing the individuality of the victim and the impact of the crime on the victim's survivors."

J. Marshall's dissent claimed that "Power, not reason, is the new currency of this Court's decision making" and feared that this overturning of precedent portended still others. *J. Stevens's* dissent expressed the fear that the decision opened the door to irrelevant appeals "to the sympathies or emotions of the jurors" that would lead to inconsistent sentencing.

Atkins v. Virginia, 536 U.S. 304; 122 S. Ct. 2242; 153 L. Ed. 2d 335 (2002)

Facts—Daryl Atkins was convicted of a number of crimes including capital murder for the robbery and shooting of Eric Nesbitt. The jury found aggravating circumstances and sentenced Atkins to death despite testimony at his penalty hearing indicating that he was "mildly mentally retarded" with an IQ of fifty-nine, putting him in the 1 to 3 percent of the population with an IQ of seventy to seventy-five or lower. The supreme court of Virginia issued a divided opinion upholding Atkins's capital sentence.

Question—Does it violate the Eighth ("cruel and unusual punishment") and Fourteenth Amendments to execute an individual who is mildly retarded?

Decision—Yes.

Reasons—*J. Stevens* (6–3). The Eighth Amendment "prohibits 'excessive' sanctions." Sanctions must be judged not according to the time when the amendment was adopted but according to contemporary developments. Since states began considering executions of the mentally retarded in 1986, eighteen states with the death penalty have limited such executions. The "consistency of the direction of [this] change" indicates that "a national consensus has developed against it." The state has the responsibility to decide who should be so classified and how the prohibition on such executions should be enforced. The mentally retarded "have diminished capacities to understand and process information." This makes the rationales of "retribution" and "deterrence" problematic with respect to them and increases the possibility of false confessions that might lead to wrongful executions.

In dissent, *C.J. Rehnquist* noted that although eighteen states with the death penalty prohibited the execution of mentally retarded individuals, nineteen states still permitted it. He also objected to the weight the majority appeared to give to foreign laws and to public opinion polls.

J. Scalia's dissent argued that the Court's decision had "no support in the text or history of the Eighth Amendment" but simply reflected the policy preferences of the majority. He observed that Atkins's retardation had been considered in the sentencing phase of his trial and that under standards in force when the Eighth Amendment was adopted only those who were severely or profoundly retarded (an IQ of twenty-five or below) were given special treatment. The practice of eighteen of thirty-eight states with the death penalty did not establish a contemporary consensus, and legislation in all the states was still in its infancy. Scalia thought a system in which the sentencer weighed the circumstances in individual cases was more consistent with the Eighth Amendment than was a categorical rule against such sentences.

Ring v. Arizona, 536 U.S. 584; 122 S. Ct. 2428; 153 L. Ed. 2d 556; 2002 U.S. LEXIS 4651 (2002)

Facts—A jury that deadlocked on the charge of premeditated murder convicted Ring of a felony murder committed during an armed robbery. By itself this penalty did not carry a death sentence, but a judge subsequently found the presence of aggravating circumstances that resulted in such a penalty. Although the Arizona Supreme Court indicated that U.S. Supreme Court decisions permitting such judicial decisions were in conflict, it upheld the sentence.

Question—Does the requirement of a jury trial as granted by the Sixth and Fourteenth Amendments require a jury rather than a judge to conduct fact-finding as to aggravating factors that could lead to a death penalty determination?

Decision—Yes.

Reasons—*J. Ginsburg* (7–2). In *Walton v. Arizona*, 497 U.S. 639 (1990), the Supreme Court had upheld Arizona's death penalty statute on the basis that the judge's determination of aggravating and mitigating factors "qualified as sentencing considerations, not 'as elements of the offense of capital murder.'" *Apprendi v. New Jersey*, a noncapital case, 530 U.S. 466 (2000), subsequently ruled that the Sixth Amendment prohibited a defendant from receiving a harsher sentence than the defendant would have received in a jury trial. Under the jury verdict in this case, Ring's maximum penalty was life imprisonment; the judge's finding of aggravating circumstances resulted in a death penalty. Although *Walton* had declared that specific factual findings of aggravating circumstances did not need to be made by a jury, juries served as vital fact-finders in English capital cases. Moreover, *Apprendi* ruled that a judge's decision on aggravating factors in a noncapital case amounted to bypassing the requirement that a jury find an individual guilty beyond a reasonable doubt. Such a rule cannot be applied to noncapital cases without also being applied to capital ones. *Walton* and *Apprendi* are "irreconcilable" and *Walton* is therefore overruled.

J. Scalia's concurrence, while lamenting judicial intervening in capital cases, believed the decision in *Ring* was essential to preserving the right of trial by jury. *J. Breyer's* concurrence raised questions about the value of the death penalty but suggested that juries were better guides to contemporary sentiments than judges. *J. O'Connor's* dissent argued that the Court should overrule *Apprendi* rather than *Walton* and pointed to the increased number of appeals and the "destabilizing effect" that the Court's capital punishment decisions were having on the criminal justice system.

Ewing v. California, 538 U.S. 11; 123 S. Ct. 1179; 155 L. Ed. 2d 108 (2003)

Facts—Largely influenced by the kidnapping and murder of twelve-year-old Polly Klaas by a kidnapper who had been released from prison, California adopted a "Three Strikes and You're Out" law designed to increase punishments for prior serious offenders. Under this law, Ewing, who had been previously convicted of four serious or violent felonies, was sentenced to life in prison after a conviction for shoplifting three golf clubs valued at about $1,200. In deciding whether to convict under the recidivist statute, California allowed a judge to determine whether to classify some crimes, called "wobblers," as misdemeanors or felonies and to vacate allegations of prior "serious" or "violent" felony convictions. After reviewing Ewing's prior offenses, the court sentenced him to a term of twenty-five years to life. The state Court of Appeals affirmed, and the California Supreme Court denied review.

Question—Does the sentence of twenty-five years to life violate the Eighth Amendment provision against cruel and unusual punishment as applied to the states by the Fourteenth Amendment?

Decision—No.

Reasons—*J. O'Connor* (for three justices in a 5–4 decision). In sentencing Ewing, the Court reviewed Ewing's complete criminal history, including the fact that he committed his last crime while on parole. *Harmelin v. Michigan*, 501 U.S. 957 (1991), a case upholding the sentence of a first-time offender for possession of drugs, established that the Eighth Amendment contained only a "'narrow proportionality principle' that 'applies to noncapital sentences.'" *Rummel v. Estelle*, 445 U.S. 263 (1980) upheld a state recidivist statute although *Solem v. Helm*, 463 U.S. 277 (1983) prohibited a life sentence without the possibility of parole for a seventh nonviolent felony. *Harmelin* established four principles of proportionality review—"the primacy of the legislature, the variety of legitimate penological schemes, the nature of our federal system, and the requirement that proportionality review be guided by objective factors." The California legislature decided "that individuals who have repeatedly engaged in serious or violent criminal behavior, and whose conduct has not been deterred by more conventional approaches to punishment, must be isolated from society in order to protect the public safety." Although its particular solution is new, judicial deference to state legislative policy decisions is not. The California law specifically addressed the problem of recidivism and attempted to deter crimes. The Court does not sit "as a 'superlegislature' to second-guess these policy choices. It is enough that the State of California has a reasonable basis for believing that dramatically enhanced sentences for habitual felons 'advances the goals of [its] criminal justice system in any substantial way.'" Ewing's sentence is long, but it must be measured against his long record of prior crimes. "The gravity of his offense was not merely 'shoplifting three golf clubs.' Rather, Ewing was convicted of felony grand theft for stealing nearly $1,200 worth of merchandise after previously having been convicted of at least two 'violent' or 'serious' felonies."

J. Scalia, concurring, repeated his view, expressed in *Harmelin v. Michigan*, that, with the possible exception of capital cases, the Eighth Amendment prohibits only certain modes of punishment rather than disproportionate sentences per se.

J. Thomas, concurring, believed that the proportionality test announced in *Solem v. Helm* was "incapable of judicial application."

J. Stevens, dissenting, argued that "proportionality review is not only capable of judicial application but also required by the Eighth Amendment."

J. Breyer, dissenting, argued that the sentence in this case violated the "gross disproportionality" standard, which he sought to illustrate by comparing the sentence that had been upheld in this case with other cases where similar sentences for similar offenses had been struck down. He found that California's sentence was disproportionate to those meted out in California prior to the law at issue as well as to sentences it meted out for other crimes. He also argued that the law was disproportional to punishments in other states and at the federal level. He further traced the "wobbler" classifications to a number of anomalies, and, while acknowledging that the Eighth Amendment created no "bright line" rule, argued that courts need to continue to patrol the outer boundaries of state-imposed punishments.

Baze v. Rees, 128 S. Ct. 1520; 170 L. Ed. 2d 420 (2008)

Facts—Ralph Baze and Thomas C. Bowling were each convicted of two counts of capital murder and sentenced to death by lethal injection in Kentucky. They sued John D. Rees, the commissioner of Kentucky's Department of Corrections and other state officials to have its protocol of injecting three successive drugs declared to be cruel and unusual punishment because of the possibility that it might inflict unnecessary pain.

Question—Does Kentucky's procedure for injecting three successive drugs in performing lethal injections violate the cruel and unusual prohibition of the Eighth and Fourteenth Amendments?

Decision—No.

Reasons—*C.J. Roberts* (7–2). Thirty-five other states and the federal government impose capital punishment for some crimes. Each uses lethal injection. Although the Court had previously upheld hanging and electrocution, lethal injection represents progress toward greater humaneness. Kentucky uses three drugs, sodium thiopental, which produces unconsciousness, pancuronium bromide, a paralytic agent, and potassium chloride, which leads to cardiac arrest. Kentucky requires that a certified phlebotomist and an emergency medical technician be on hand. All forms of capital punishment contain some risk of pain, and the Court has never invalidated a particular procedure for inducing death. In this case petitioners are not as concerned about the proper application of the drugs as about the possibility that the state may apply them improperly, but "Simply because an execution method may result in pain, either by accident or as an inescapable consequence of death, does not establish the sort of 'objectively intolerable risk of harm' that qualifies as cruel and unusual." Moreover the suggested one-drug protocol has its own problems and is not used in other states. Thus, "it is difficult to regard a practice as 'objectively intolerable' when it is in fact widely tolerated." The state court found that laypersons could properly mix the chemicals required and "the asserted problems related to the IV lines do not establish a sufficiently substantial risk of harm to meet the requirements of the Eighth Amendment." Although there are questions about the three-drug protocol, states have generally considered the advantages to outweigh the disadvantages. The court will not intervene absent "a demonstrated risk of severe pain" that has not been established here.

J. Alito, concurring. This case does not involve the constitutionality of capital punishment per se, and objections to current protocols must take into account that the medical profession has rules against participating in executions. The evidence questioning the current protocols is subject to dispute, but the current consensus appears to favor three drugs over one.

J. Stevens, concurring in judgment. Current decisions to retain the death penalty are largely "the product of habit in inattention rather than an acceptable deliberative process that weighs the costs and risks of administering that penalty against its identifiable benefits, and rest in part on a faulty assumption about the retributive force of the death penalty." Traditional justifications of incapacitation, deterrence, and retribution are anachronistic. As the Court once stated in *Furman*, "'[A] penalty may be cruel and unusual because it is excessive and serves no valid legislative purpose.'" Death-qualified juries, the risk of error, the "risk of discriminatory application of the death penalty," and the "irrevocable nature of the consequences" of the penalty all need to be reconsidered.

J. Scalia, concurring. Stevens's interpretation is unacceptable because it attempts to assert judicial opinion for that of democratically-elected bodies and explicit language within the Constitution permitting the death penalty. Nor are Stevens's assertions supported by the evidence. *J. Stevens's* opinion is not relevant unless one is to elevate "rule by judicial fiat" over the will of the people.

J. Thomas, concurring. The Court should get back to the "original understanding" of the Eighth Amendment, which was designed to permit the penalty but forbid needless cruelty. The Court is not in a position to apply "comparative-risk standards."

J. Breyer, concurring. The arguments against the current procedures are outweighed by other scholarship.

J. Ginsburg, dissenting. The second and third drugs administered by Kentucky can cause "a conscious inmate to suffer excruciating pain." It is therefore important for the state to be sure the first drug sufficiently anesthetizes them. The Court should remand to see if further protocols other than the current visual observation are needed to assure this.

Chapter Thirteen

NINTH AMENDMENT, RIGHT TO PRIVACY, AND OTHER UNENUMERATED RIGHTS

When Anti-Federalists first proposed the idea of a bill of rights, some Federalists responded that such a bill was not only unnecessary but also could prove dangerous. Such Federalists feared that if a right was omitted, the government might therefore be able to claim that the right was unprotected by the U.S. Constitution. As a result Congress proposed and the states ratified the Ninth Amendment. It provided that "The enumeration in the Constitution of certain rights shall not be construed to deny or disparage others retained by the people."

Although the Ninth Amendment has rarely been invoked directly, the Supreme Court has recognized the existence of certain unenumerated rights. Although some cases have recognized a right to travel, most cases involving unenumerated rights have centered on matters related to the family or the raising of children. Thus, in *Meyer v. Nebraska* (1923) the Court struck down a state law prohibiting the teaching of German in school. Similarly, in *Pierce v. Society of Sisters* (1925), the Court accepted the rights of parents to educate their children in parochial schools.

The most important case involving the right to privacy was *Griswold v. Connecticut* (1965), in which the Supreme Court invalidated a Connecticut law prohibiting birth control. Although Justice Goldberg relied specifically on the Ninth Amendment in a concurring opinion, Justice William O. Douglas's lead opinion relied on the idea that individual rights had penumbras, or shadows, that implicated broader rights. In formulating a constitutional right to privacy, Douglas specifically cited the First, Third, Fourth, Fifth, Ninth, and Fourteenth Amendments.

The Supreme Court later extended the right to privacy to abortion in *Roe v. Wade* (1973), at least in the first two trimesters, or six months, of pregnancy. The Court has had to resolve numerous controversies that have arisen in the aftermath of this decision including the role of the husband in an abortion decision (the Court has refused to give husbands a veto), the rights of parents of a minor (states may provide that at least one parent may be informed absent the exercise of a judicial bypass proceeding), the government's obligation to fund abortion (not generally required), and the constitutionality of a growing host of restrictions on abortion such as provision of a twenty-four- to forty-eight-hour waiting period, providing information to patients about fetal development, and the like (most of which have been upheld). *Planned Parenthood of Southeastern Pennsylvania v. Casey* (1992) is also frequently cited to explicate the doctrine of stare decisis, or leaving existing precedents in place. In *Gonzales v. Carhart* (2007), the majority cited this case in upholding a congressional law against partial birth abortion despite having invalidated a similar state law in *Stenberg v. Carhart* in 2000.

The Supreme Court attempted to draw the line on privacy in *Bowers v. Hardwick* (1986) when it upheld a state law making homosexual sodomy illegal. This decision was in tension with *Romer v. Evans* (1996), a case treated under the Fourteenth Amendment. In *Romer*, the Supreme Court invalidated a Colorado constitutional provision designed to prevent the enactment of laws preventing discrimination against, or giving special protections to, homosexuals. *Lawrence v. Texas* (2003) has since overturned *Bowers*.

In cases like *Vacco v. Quill* and *Washington v. Glucksberg* (1997), the Court has refused to recognize a constitutional "right to die" or a constitutional right to physician-assisted suicide. The continuing development of technology with its ability to prolong human life, the possibility of human cloning, genetic testing, and similar developments are likely to continue to push privacy issues to the forefront in the near future.

THE RIGHT TO PRIVACY AND
OTHER UNENUMERATED RIGHTS

Meyer v. Nebraska, 262 U.S. 390; 43 S. Ct. 625; 67 L. Ed. 1042 (1923)

Facts—In 1919 Nebraska passed a statute that prohibited the teaching of any subject in any other language than English. Languages could be taught only after the child had successfully passed the eighth grade. Meyer taught in a parochial school and used a German bible history as a text for reading. The use of the text served a double purpose, teaching the German language and religious instruction.

Question—Does a state law prohibiting the teaching of a foreign language violate the "liberty" protected by the Fourteenth Amendment?

Decision—Yes.

Reasons—*J. McReynolds* (7–2). The Court has never attempted to define, with exactness, the liberty guaranteed by the Fourteenth Amendment. Certainly education and the pursuit of knowledge should be encouraged. Mere knowledge of the German language cannot be looked upon as harmful. Meyer's right to teach and the right of parents to hire him so to teach were within the liberty of this amendment.

The statute also forbade the teaching below the eighth grade of any other language except English. The state supreme court had ruled that "ancient or dead languages" did not come within the meaning of this statute. This law interfered with modern language teachers, with the opportunities of children to acquire knowledge, and with the power of parents to control the education of their children.

The state may seek to improve the quality of its citizens, but it must respect certain fundamental rights of the individual, since the protection of the Constitution also extends to those who speak a language other than English. There are advantages to a ready knowledge of ordinary speech, but "a desirable end cannot be promoted by prohibited means."

No emergency has arisen to render knowledge of another language so harmful as to justify its prohibition. Nor is this prohibition justified to protect mental health, since it is well known that a foreign language is more easily acquired at an early age. This statute is arbitrary and without a reasonable relation to any end within the competency of the state.

In a companion case, *Bartels v. Iowa*, 262 U.S. 404, *J. Holmes* authored a dissent highlighting the value of having all Americans "speak a common tongue" and upholding the law in question as a reasonable measure toward this end.

Pierce v. Society of Sisters of the Holy Names of Jesus and Mary, 268 U.S. 510; 45 S. Ct. 571; 69 L. Ed. 1070 (1925)

Facts—In November 1922, the state of Oregon passed a Compulsory Education Act requiring every child from the ages of eight to sixteen to attend public school. Parents or guardians who refused would be guilty of a misdemeanor. The plaintiff corporation conducted a group of private schools, according to the tenets of the Roman Catholic Church. They brought suit challenging that the statute conflicted with the right of parents to choose schools where their children would receive appropriate moral and religious training, and the right of schools and teachers to engage in a useful business or profession.

Question—Can a state require children to attend public schools?

Decision—No.

Reasons—*J. McReynolds* (9–0). Rights guaranteed by the Constitution may not be abridged by state legislation that has no reasonable relation to some purpose within the competency of the state. The liberty of the Constitution forbids the standardization of children by compelling them to attend public school instruction only. "The child is not the mere creature of the state; those who nurture him and direct his destiny have the right, coupled with the high duty, to recognize and prepare him for additional obligations.

"We think it entirely plain that the act of 1922 unreasonably interferes with the liberty of parents and guardians to direct the upbringing and education of children under their control."

Also, the corporations or schools involved had business and property for which they had a claim to protection under the Fourteenth Amendment. These rights, the Court held, were threatened with destruction through this unwarranted compulsion.

ॐ

Buck v. Bell, 274 U.S. 200; 47 S. Ct. 584; 71 L. Ed. 1000 (1927)

Facts—The superintendent of the State Colony for Epileptics and Feeble Minded in the state of Virginia ordered an operation upon Carrie Buck, the plaintiff in error, for the purpose of sterilizing her. She contended that the Virginia statute authorizing the operation was void under the Fourteenth Amendment as denying to her due process of law and the equal protection of the laws. The evidence in this case showed that Carrie Buck's mother was feeble-minded, that Carrie Buck was feeble-minded, and that she had a child that was feeble-minded. All of them were committed to the State Colony. Under the procedure of the law, the rights of the patient were most carefully considered, and every step, as in this case, was taken in scrupulous compliance with the statute and after months of observation.

Question—Does the Virginia law permitting the sterilization of individuals believed to be feeble-minded violate the due process or equal protection clauses of the Fourteenth Amendment?

Decision—No.

Reasons—*J. Holmes* (8–1). The Court reasoned that more than once the public welfare may call upon the best citizens for their lives. The Court said that it would be strange if it could not call upon those who already sap the strength of the state for these lesser sacrifices, in order to prevent the nation from being swamped with incompetence. "But, it is said, however it might be if this reasoning were applied generally, it fails when it is confined to the small number who are in the institutions named and is not applied to the multitudes outside. It is the usual last resort of constitutional arguments to point out shortcomings of the sort." The Court answered that "the law does all that is needed when it does all that it can, indicates a policy, applies it to all within the lines, and seeks to bring within the lines all similarly situated so far and so fast as its means allow." So far as the operations enable those who otherwise must be kept confined to be returned to the world, and thus open the asylum to others, the equality aimed at will be more nearly reached.

    J. Butler dissented without writing an opinion.

Note—*Buck* sanctioned a form of eugenics. *Skinner v. Oklahoma* (1942), as well as more decisions related to reproductive privacy, have deprived *Buck* of any constitutional strength.

Griswold v. Connecticut, 381 U.S. 479; 85 S. Ct. 1678; 14 L. Ed. 2d 510 (1965)

Facts—This case involved the constitutionality of Connecticut's birth control law. The statute provided that "any person who uses any drug, medical article or instrument for the purpose of preventing conception" was to be subject to fine or imprisonment or both. The statute further specified that a person who assisted another in committing any offense could be prosecuted and punished as if he were the principal offender. Estelle Griswold, executive director of the Planned Parenthood League of Connecticut, was convicted of being an accessory.

Question—Is the Connecticut statute proscribing birth control valid under the Constitution?

Decision—No.

Reasons—*J. Douglas* (7–2). First, the appellants were held to have standing to raise the constitutional issue because they were accessories to violation of the criminal statute inasmuch as they were advising married persons as to the means of preventing conception. The decision established a new constitutional "right of privacy" citing penumbras, or shadows, of provisions in the First, Third, Fourth, Fifth, Ninth, and Fourteenth Amendments. The Court noted that "specific guarantees in the Bill of Rights have penumbras, formed by emanations from those guarantees that help give them life and substance . . . the right of privacy which presses for recognition here is a legitimate one. The present case, then, concerns a relationship lying within the zone of privacy created by several constitutional guarantees. . . . We deal with a right of privacy older than the Bill of Rights." In the course of the opinion the Court referred favorably to the Ninth Amendment's provision that "The enumeration in the Constitution, of certain rights, shall not be construed to deny or disparage others retained by the people."

J. Goldberg's concurring opinion emphasized the Ninth Amendment.

J. Black and *J. Stewart* authored dissents distinguishing between the wisdom (or unwisdom) of a law and its constitutionality. Neither could find specific constitutional authority for the Court's discovery of a right to privacy within the Constitution.

Note—The right to privacy that this decision recognized became the cornerstone of the abortion decision in *Roe v. Wade*, 410 U.S. 113 (1973).

❦

Shapiro v. Thompson, 394 U.S. 618; 89 S. Ct. 1322; 22 L. Ed. 2d 600 (1969)

Facts—Statutory provisions in Connecticut, Pennsylvania, and the District of Columbia denied welfare assistance to persons who were residents and met all other eligibility requirements except that they had not resided within the jurisdiction for at least a year immediately preceding their applications for assistance.

Question—Does this law limiting welfare payments create a classification that constitutes discrimination involving denial of equal protection of the laws?

Decision—Yes.

Reasons—*J. Brennan* (6–3). The purpose of inhibiting migration into a state by needy persons is constitutionally impermissible. Our constitutional concepts of personal liberty require that all citizens be free to travel throughout the country without unreasonable restrictions. Where the right of interstate movement is involved, the constitutionality of a statute must be judged by the stricter standard of whether the statute promotes a compelling state interest. In the current instance the waiting period requirement was held clearly to violate the equal protection clause. In the matter of the District of Columbia, since only states are bound by the equal protection clause, the one-year requirement was held to violate the due process clause of the Fifth Amendment.

C.J. Warren and *J. Stewart* both wrote dissents arguing that Congress had approved residency requirements for welfare applicants and questioning the application of the "compelling state interest" doctrine to such an issue.

Roe v. Wade, 410 U.S. 113; 93 S. Ct. 705; 35 L. Ed. 2d 147 (1973)

Facts—Texas statutes prohibited abortions except by medical advice for the purpose of saving the life of the mother. A woman proceeding under the pseudonym of Jane Roe instituted a federal class action against the district attorney of Dallas County challenging the validity of the statutes. Because the pregnancy did not threaten her life, she could not obtain a legal abortion in Texas.

Questions—(a) Does the term "person" as used in the Fourteenth Amendment include the unborn? (b) Does the right of privacy include a woman's decision on an abortion?

Decisions—(a) No; (b) Yes, at least through the second trimester of pregnancy.

Reasons—*J. Blackmun* (7–2). (a) The Constitution does not define "person" as such. However, the use of the word in the various instances where it is used in the Constitution is such that the word has application only postnatally. The unborn have never been recognized in the law as persons in the whole sense. "We need not resolve the difficult question of when life begins. When those trained in the respective disciplines of medicine, philosophy, and theology are unable to arrive at any consensus, the judiciary, at this point in the development of man's knowledge, is not in a position to speculate as to the answer." Abortion laws largely developed in the nineteenth century. They have been explained as attempts: to discourage illicit sex (Texas has not advanced this argument in this case); to protect the health of women at a time when the procedure often posed health risks that were greater than carrying a pregnancy to term; and to protect prenatal life.

(b) The Constitution does not explicitly recognize any right of privacy. However, for years the Court has recognized that a right of personal privacy does exist under the Constitution. This has been primarily based upon the Fourteenth Amendment's concept of personal liberty and the Ninth Amendment's reservation of rights to the people. This right is not unqualified and is subject to state regulation when important interests intervene. The right of privacy is broad enough to cover the decision as to an abortion. The right is not absolute and is subject to state interests as to protection of health, medical standards, and prenatal life.

Pregnancy can be divided into three-month periods—trimesters. During the first period there is no agreement as to the fetus being a person and risks to women from abortion are not greater than the risks of childbirth, so the discretion rests with the woman and her physician. During the second trimester, the health risks to women from abortion increase sufficiently to justify state regulations of the procedure to protect such health. During the final trimester, when the fetus is viable and can sustain life outside the womb, the state may even proscribe abortions, except when necessary to preserve the life or health of the mother.

J. White and *J. Rehnquist* authored dissents questioning federal intervention in this area previously left to the states and further questioning the application of the Fourteenth Amendment to an issue so far removed from its original purpose.

Zablocki v. Redhail, 434 U.S. 374; 98 S. Ct. 673; 54 L. Ed. 2d 618 (1978)

Facts—Redhail was a Wisconsin resident who, under a paternity statute, was unable to marry in Wisconsin or elsewhere as long as he maintained a Wisconsin residence. In January 1972, when Redhail was a minor and a high school student, he was subject to a paternity suit and a court order, in May 1972, requiring him to pay $109.00 monthly as support for the child until she reached 18 years of age. In September 1974, Redhail applied for a marriage license and Zablocki, the clerk of Milwaukee County, refused on the sole ground that Redhail had not obtained a court order granting him permission. Redhail had not satisfied his support obligations of his illegitimate child—in excess of $3,700—who had been a public charge since birth.

Question—Can Wisconsin prevent members of a certain class of residents from marrying in the state or elsewhere without first obtaining a court order?

Decision—No.

Reasons—*J. Marshall* (8–1). The Court has continuously confirmed the right to marry. The right to marry is of "fundamental importance for all individuals." The freedom of personal choice in matters of marriage and family life is one of the liberties protected by the due process clause of the Fourteenth Amendment. Not every statute that relates to marriage must be subject to rigorous scrutiny. On the contrary, reasonable regulations that do not significantly interfere with the decision to marry may legitimately be imposed. But the statutory classification here clearly does interfere directly and substantially with the right to marry. "When a statutory classification significantly interferes with the exercise of a fundamental right, it cannot be upheld unless it is supported by sufficiently important state interests and is closely tailored to effect only those interests." The Wisconsin statute is both "grossly underinclusive" and "substantially overinclusive."

J. Rehnquist, dissenting, would have applied the "rational basis test" providing for minimal scrutiny of such legislation and would have upheld it as "a permissible exercise of the State's power to regulate family life and to assure the support of minor children."

☙

Harris v. McRae, 448 U.S. 297; 100 S. Ct. 2671; 6S L. Ed. 2d 784 (1980)

Facts—Title XIX of the Social Security Act established the Medicaid program in 1965 to provide federal financial assistance to states that choose to reimburse certain costs of medical treatment for needy persons. Since 1976, versions of the so-called Hyde Amendment have severely limited the use of any federal funds to reimburse the cost of abortions under the Medicaid program. The Hyde Amendment, named after Illinois Congressman Henry Hyde, was attached on the grounds, inter alia, that it violates the due process clause of the Fifth Amendment and the religion clauses of the First Amendment and that, despite the Hyde Amendment, a participating state remains obligated under Title XIX to fund all medically necessary abortions. The District Court agreed that the state was free from obligation to pay for elective abortions but ruled that the Hyde Amendment violated the First, Fifth, and Fourteenth Amendments.

Questions—(a) Must a state pay for elective abortions when, under the Hyde Amendment, Congress has withdrawn its support? (b) Does the Hyde Amendment violate constitutional guarantees?

Decisions—(a) No; (b) No.

Reasons—*J. Stewart* (6–3). Nothing in Title XIX as originally enacted, or in its legislative history, suggests that Congress intended to require a participating state "to assume the full costs of providing any health services in its Medicaid plan . . . if Congress chooses to withdraw federal funding for a particular service, a state is not obliged to continue to pay for that service as a condition of continued federal financial support of other services." The state, *Maher v. Roe*, 432 U.S. 464 (1977), can make a value judgment favoring childbirth over abortion "but it has imposed no restriction on access to abortions that was not already there. . . . [I]t simply does not follow that a woman's freedom of choice carries with it a constitutional entitlement to the financial resources to avail herself of the full range of protected choices." To require this funding as a due process entitlement would mean that Congress was mandated "to subsidize the medically necessary abortion of an indigent woman even if Congress had not enacted a Medicaid program to subsidize other medically necessary services." The parties lack standing under the free exercise clause, and the Fifth Amendment is not a source of substantive rights or liberties, but rather a right to be free from invidious governmental discrimination.

J. Brennan, J. Marshall, J. Blackmun, and *J. Stevens* all authored dissents arguing that this decision permitted discrimination against women unable to afford abortions.

ে৺

Bowers v. Hardwick, 478 U.S. 186; 106 S. Ct. 2841; 92 L. Ed. 2d 140 (1986)

Facts—In August 1982 respondent was charged with violating a Georgia statute that had criminalized sodomy. He had committed this act with another male in the bedroom of his home, where they had been discovered by a police officer serving a warrant. Respondent Hardwick brought suit in the District Court challenging the constitutionality of the statute insofar as it criminalized consensual sodomy. The District Court affirmed; the Court of Appeals reversed.

Question—Does the Fourteenth Amendment confer a fundamental right to engage in sodomy and hence invalidate state laws that criminalize such conduct and have done so for a long time?

Decision—No.

Reasons—*J. White* (5–4). "We . . . register our disagreement with the Court of Appeals and with respondent that the Court's prior cases have construed the Constitution to confer a right of privacy that extends to homosexual sodomy." The cases enumerated by the Court of Appeals bear no resemblance "to the claimed constitutional right of homosexuals to engage in acts of sodomy." Moreover, the claim made by this listing of cases "insulated from state proscription is unsupportable." The Court is "quite unwilling" to announce that homosexuals have a fundamental right of sodomy. Neither in the doctrines implicit in the concept of ordered liberty" nor "deeply rooted in this nation's history and tradition" is sodomy protected. Sodomy was a criminal offense at common law, forbidden by the original thirteen colonies, and with the adoption of the Fourteenth Amendment in 1868, all but five of the thirty-seven states in the Union had criminal sodomy laws. Today, twenty-four states plus the District of Columbia have criminalized sodomy. Such claims of freedom to engage in sodomy are "facetious." Finally, the Court is not inclined to take a more "expansive view" of its "authority to discover new fundamental rights embedded in the due process clause."

J. Blackmun's dissent argued that this case was not about the right to sodomy but about the right to privacy, which he thought should be extended to homosexuals as well as to others.

⇛

Planned Parenthood of Southeastern Pennsylvania v. Casey, 505 U.S. 833; 112 S. Ct. 2791; 120 L. Ed. 2d 674 (1992)

Facts—Pennsylvania adopted restrictions on abortions. These required informed consent and a twenty-four-hour waiting period, either the consent of at least one parent or the exercise of a judicial bypass mechanism in cases where minors sought abortions, a requirement that a married woman sign a statement indicating that she had informed her husband of her decision, compliance with all of the above requirements except in cases of "medical emergencies" threatening a woman's life or health, and record-keeping and reporting provisions. The U.S. District Court struck down all these requirements whereas the U.S. Third Circuit Court of Appeals upheld all but the spousal notification requirement. The Bush administration asked the Supreme Court to overrule *Roe v. Wade* in this case.

Questions—(a) Are the regulations regarding abortions adopted by Pennsylvania constitutional? (b) Should *Roe v. Wade* be overturned?

Decisions—(a) Yes, all are constitutional except for the spousal notification decision; (b) No, the central holding of *Roe v. Wade* should be reaffirmed.

Reasons—*J. O'Connor, J. Kennedy, J. Souter* (5–4). These three justices, joined in part by *J. Blackmun* and *J. Stevens*, affirmed that "the essential holding of *Roe v. Wade* should be retained and once again reaffirmed." This holding consisted of the recognition of the woman's right to have an abortion without "undue interference from the State" prior to viability, the state's right to restrict abortions after viability, and the recognition of a state's interest in pregnancy during the entire process. The three justices writing for the Court traced the right of abortion to the "liberty" interest of the Fourteenth Amendment, going back through a long series of privacy precedents. The articulation of this liberty requires the judicial exercise of "reasoned judgment." The three justices expressed great concern for the doctrine of stare decisis (adherence to precedents). The decision in *Roe* had not proved to be "unworkable," but after two decades, it had created a strong "reliance interest" among women who have built careers around their power to control pregnancies. The Court contrasted the decision in *Roe v. Wade* to those in *Lochner v. New York* (1905), recognizing economic due process, and *Plessy v. Ferguson* (1896), providing for racial segregation. Unlike those cases, they did not believe that *Roe* was based on disproven theories. The Court's legitimacy depends on appearing principled, and caving in to popular pressure against *Roe* would undermine the Court's power. Unlike the central holding, the trimester formula outlined in *Roe* could be discarded. The three justices instead outlined an "undue burden" test (introduced in a previous case by O'Connor) that did not recognize the right to an abortion as a fundamental absolute right but one in which the state also had an interest. The majority believed the only provision of the Pennsylvania abortion law that created an undue burden was that of spousal notification, citing numerous studies showing that most wives already notify their husbands and arguing that, for others, such notification might lead to either physical or psychological spousal abuse.

J. Stevens agreed with the Court's emphasis on stare decisis but feared that the state's interest in abortion was not truly secular in nature. He believed that requiring women to be told certain information or requiring that they wait 24 hours for an abortion did impose an undue burden on them. *J. Blackmun* (the author of *Roe v. Wade*), also in partial concurrence and partial dissent, praised the courage of the three authors of the Court's opinion but would subject all abortion restrictions to strict scrutiny and thought that the regulations at issue were all attempts by the state to conscript "women's bodies into its service, forcing women to continue their pregnancies, suffer the pains of childbirth, and in most instances, provide years of maternal care." He defended the trimester formula and faulted the chief justice's dissent for its "stunted conception of individual liberty."

C.J. Rehnquist accused the majority of retaining the "outer shell" of *Roe* but of beating "a wholesale retreat from the substance of that case." He would overrule *Roe*, leaving the issue to individual states. He argued that this case did not present a real "reliance interest." He did not think that the Court should rule with a view toward public opinion and faulted the "undue burden" test as being even less precise than the previous "strict scrutiny" formula. Rehnquist favored upholding all parts of the Pennsylvania law.

J. Scalia's dissent attempted to answer one-by-one the arguments of the Court for adhering to stare decisis in this case and viewed the plurality opinion as an indication that "The Imperial Judiciary lives." Like Rehnquist, Scalia believed public opinion was irrelevant to judicial decision-making but believed that the Court's original decision in *Roe v. Wade* to declare abortion a guaranteed national liberty, rather than leaving the matter at the state level, had largely led to the unrest that the Court was attempting to ignore.

Vacco v. Quill, Washington v. Glucksberg, 521 U.S. 702; 117 S. Ct. 2258; 138 L. Ed. 2d 772 (1997)

Facts—The state of Washington prohibited individuals from aiding suicides (the law does not prohibit the withholding of "life-sustaining treatment"). Physicians who sometimes treated terminally ill individuals challenged the law as an undue burden on the "liberty interest" protected by the due process clause of the Fourteenth Amendment. The U.S. District Court agreed. Although the Ninth Circuit originally voted to reverse, it affirmed the District Court after a rehearing en banc.

Issue—Is a law prohibiting physician-assisted suicide a violation of the "liberty interest" protected by the due process clause of the Fourteenth Amendment?

Decision—No.

Reasons—*C.J. Rehnquist* (9–0). Rehnquist noted that bans against suicide and assisted suicide dated back hundreds of years in the Anglo-American legal tradition and were incorporated into state statues as early as 1828. A number of states had recently reconsidered and reaffirmed these laws. The "liberty" protected by the due process clause has been recognized to include such rights as the right to marry, the right to raise and educate children, and the right to privacy. Such rights have been limited, however, to those regarded as "fundamental" and "deeply rooted in this Nation's history and tradition." The "right to die" asserted by the lower courts fits neither criterion. The Washington law serves a number of important interests. It was designed to reflect an "unqualified interest in the preservation of human life"; as a means of "protecting the integrity and ethics of the medical profession"; as a way of "protecting vulnerable groups—including the poor, the elderly, and disabled persons—from abuse, neglect, and mistakes"; and as a way of setting the state down the path of voluntary or even involuntary euthanasia.

J. O'Connor's concurrence distinguished the right of assisted suicide from allowing physicians to alleviate suffering, even when such palliative care could hasten death. *J. Stevens's* concurrence pointed to room for "further debate about the limits that the Constitution places on the power of the States to punish the practice." Rejecting an "absolute right to physician-assisted suicide," he thought there might be a more limited one.

J. Souter's concurrence stressed the need for careful deliberation on such matters that weighed respective interests without issuing blanket rulings. *J. Ginsburg* agreed with O'Connor's concurrence.

J. Breyer did not think the right at issue was adequately characterized as a "right to commit suicide" and believed that a law (unlike the one at issue here) prohibiting palliative care that might incidentally shorten life could be unconstitutional.

Note—In a companion case, *Vacco v. Quill*, 521 U.S. 793 (1997) the Court also overturned a decision by the U.S. Second Court of Appeals. The Appeals Court had ruled that a New York law allowing doctors to terminate care but prohibiting them from administering drugs to end life violated the equal protection clause of the Fourteenth Amendment.

Lawrence v. Texas, 539 U.S. 558; 123 S. Ct. 2472; 156 L. Ed. 2d 508 (2003)

Facts—Responding to a report of a weapons disturbance, Houston police legally entered Lawrence's apartment and discovered another man and him engaged in an intimate sexual act. Both were arrested and convicted by a justice of the peace under a Texas law defining sexual intercourse between individuals of the same sex as deviate. The Harris County Criminal Court and the Texas Fourteenth District Court both upheld these convictions, the latter court relying specifically on the decision in *Bowers v. Hardwick*, 478 U.S. 186 (1986), in which the U.S. Supreme Court had upheld a Georgia statute prohibiting sodomy.

Questions—(a) Does the Texas statute violate the liberty guaranteed by the due process clause of the Fourteenth Amendment? (b) Is *Bowers v. Hardwick* still good law?

Decisions—(a) Yes; (b) No.

Reasons—*J. Kennedy* (6–3). Liberty is designed to protect individuals against undue governmental intrusion. Such liberty has been related to privacy interests going back to decisions in *Pierce v. Society of Sisters*, 268 U.S. 510 (1925), *Meyer v. Nebraska*, 262 U.S. 390 (1923), and *Griswold v. Connecticut*, 381 U.S. 479 (1965). Cases since *Griswold* have further indicated that privacy interests are personal in nature. In *Bowers*, the Georgia statute that was sustained technically differed from the case at hand in ostensibly applying to both homosexual and heterosexual sodomy, but the cases are otherwise similar. The majority's decision in *Bowers*, linking the decision as to whether individuals had the right to engage in sodomy failed "to appreciate the extent of the liberty at stake." *Bowers's* assertion that laws against sodomy had a long history failed to note that such laws were directed against both homosexual and heterosexual sodomy and that they were rarely enforced in cases of private conduct, other than in the case of "predatory" or nonconsensual acts. Although laws against homosexual sodomy may reflect popular opinions, "The issue is whether the majority may use the power of the State to enforce these views on the whole society through operation of the criminal law." Trends throughout the Western world as well as in the United States have eroded prohibitions against private homosexual conduct. Laws prohibiting homosexual consensual conduct demean the lives of homosexuals and, in addition to criminal conviction, can result in stigma against them. Stare decisis is not "an inexorable command," and Kennedy accordingly overruled not only this law but the decision in *Bowers v. Hardwick* that supported it. Kennedy noted that the decision did not involve minors, individuals who might be injured or coerced, public conduct, or prostitution. He also observed that "It does not involve whether the government must give formal recognition to any relationship that homosexual persons seek to enter." In this case, however, he found "no legitimate state interest which can justify its intrusion into the personal and private life of the individual."

J. O'Connor, concurring, rested her opinion on the equal protection clause of the Fourteenth Amendment and would have struck down the Texas law on the basis that it was not "rationally related to a legitimate state interest." Unlike the law at issue in *Bowers*, which she would leave untouched until that issue was specifically raised in Court, the law in question "makes homosexuals unequal in the eyes of the law" by specifically outlawing homosexual but not heterosexual sodomy.

J. Scalia's dissent pointed to what he believed to be the contradiction between this case and the decision upholding the core of the abortion decision in *Planned Parenthood of Southeastern Pennsylvania v. Casey*, 505 U.S. 833 (1992) on the basis of stare decisis. Scalia believed the decision in *Lawrence* was a return to the discredited idea of "substantive due process," and he cited a long history of laws against sodomy to demonstrate that the right could not be fundamental. He feared that this decision could have implications for "criminal laws against fornication, bigamy, adultery, adult incest, bestiality, and obscenity." He further argued that "This reasoning leaves on pretty shaky grounds state laws limiting marriage to opposite-sex couples." He accused the majority of having "signed on to the so-called homosexual agenda." By contrast, he would permit states through democratic decision-making either to permit or to outlaw sodomy.

J. Thomas's dissent characterized the law as "uncommonly silly" but found no constitutional basis on which to invalidate it.

❦

Gonzales v. Carhart, 550 U.S. 124; 127 S. Ct. 1610; 167 L. Ed. 2d 480 (2007)

Facts: After the Court invalidated Nebraska's regulation of "partial birth abortions," in *Stenberg v. Carhart*, 530 U.S. 914 (2000), Congress adopted the Partial-Birth Abortion Ban Act of 2003, which sought to limit dilation and extraction (D&X) abortion procedures, in which fetuses were purposely killed when part of their bodies had been delivered and part was actually in the birth canal. Congress designed the law to be more specific in its application and coverage, but the lower courts that reviewed the legislation struck it down on the authority of *Stenberg*.

Question—Do the regulations on abortion in the Partial-Birth Abortion Ban Act of 2003 constitute an undue burden on a woman's right to get an abortion?

Decision—No.

Reasons—*J. Kennedy* (5–4). After reviewing the procedures used in abortion, Kennedy described how testimony about the procedure had led to public revulsion and the eventual passage of the law at issue. Congressional hearings had found that "[a] moral, medical, and ethical consensus exists that the practice of performing a partial-birth abortion . . . is a gruesome and inhumane procedure that is never medically necessary and should be prohibited." Moreover, the language of the congressional law differed from the state law in *Stenberg*. This law should be measured under the standards of *Planned Parenthood of Southeastern Pa. v. Casey*, 505 U.S. 833 (1992). It permitted women to obtain abortions prior to fetal viability, allowed for state regulation after viability with exceptions for women's life and health, and affirmed the state's legitimate interest throughout pregnancy in protecting the health of women and fetuses. This third interest is especially relevant. The new law "is not void for vagueness, does not impose an undue burden from any overbreadth, and is not invalid on its face." The law specifically applies only to vaginal deliveries in which individuals knowingly attempt to kill fetuses after certain "anatomical 'land-marks'" have been crossed. Doctors of reasonable intelligence will know what the law prohibits. It is not designed to prohibit dilation and evacuation (D&E) procedures in which the fetus is removed in parts but only intact D&E procedures. Moreover, it does not punish accidental intact D&E procedures. In examining whether the law poses an "undue burden" on women seeking abortions, Kennedy notes that Congress thought that killing a fetus "just inches before completion of the birth process" would "coarsen society to the humanity of not only newborns, but all vulnerable and innocent human life, making it increasingly difficult to protect such life." The government has additional interests in "protecting the integrity and ethics of the medical profession." Congress determined that "the abortion methods it proscribed had a 'disturbing similarity to the killing of a newborn infant,'" that might, in turn lead women into "depression and loss of esteem." The regulation would be unconstitutional if it "subject[ed] [women] to significant health risks," but there is significant medical disagreement on this point, and "The Court has given state and federal legislatures wide discretion to pass legislation in areas where there is medical and scientific uncertainty." Moreover, "If the intact D&E procedure is truly necessary in some circumstances, it appears likely an injection that kills the fetus is an alternative under the Act that allows the doctor to perform the procedure." If the safety of non D&X alternatives arises in individual cases, "the proper means to consider [such] exceptions is by as-applied [rather than facial] challenges."

J. Thomas and *J. Scalia*, concurring, note that they do not believe any of the Court's jurisprudence relative to abortion is grounded in the Constitution.

J. Ginsburg, dissenting, argues that this decision departs from *Planned Parenthood of Southeastern Pa. v. Casey*. She feared that it "blurs the line, firmly drawn in *Casey*, between previability and postviability abortions. And, for the first time since *Roe*, the Court blesses a prohibition with no exception safeguarding a woman's health." Abortion restrictions affect a woman's control over her destiny and compromise their health. Lower courts called into question "facts" that Congress sought to establish through its investigations, including arguments that there were alternatives that were equally safe for maternal health. The law seems to prefer one arguably "brutal" method of abortion over another, but "Our obligation is to define the liberty of all, not to mandate our own moral code." Majority reflections on women's regret over abortion simply repeat antiabortion shibboleths. The lack of a health exception for the procedure "burdens *all* women for whom it is relevant." The law thus departs from the respect for precedent that *Casey* recognized. The only "redemptive" element of the decision is its willingness to consider future as-applied challenges.

Chapter Fourteen

THIRTEENTH AND FOURTEENTH AMENDMENTS

The Constitution of 1787 accepted but did not glorify slavery, an institution it never directly named. Under that Constitution, however, slaves were counted as three-fifths of a person for purposes of taxation and representation in the U.S. House of Representatives. Similarly, Congress was prohibited from laying more than a minimal tax on the importation of slaves for twenty years, and states were obligated to return fugitives to states from which they had fled. This latter obligation became a particularly contentious issue between free and slave states prior to the Civil War, as did the issue of slavery in the territories.

The Republican Party that nominated Abraham Lincoln for the presidency in 1860 formed largely in opposition to the expansion of slavery in the territories. Although he acknowledged the right of the Supreme Court to determine Dred Scott's fate, Lincoln adamantly opposed this decision that denied that blacks like Scott could become U.S. citizens and that declared the Missouri Compromise, which had prohibited slavery in northern U.S. territories, to have been illegal.

When Lincoln was elected in 1860, southern states sought to secede while Lincoln sought to preserve the Union he had sworn an oath to defend. Lincoln and others increasingly recognized that the division of the nation in slave and free sections would lead to continuing turmoil, and, as a war measure, he issued the Emancipation Proclamation freeing slaves behind enemy lines. This Proclamation was expanded and made permanent with the ratification of the Thirteenth Amendment in 1865, which prohibited involuntary servitude except as a punishment for a crime. It was followed by ratification of the Fourteenth Amendment in 1868 and the Fifteenth Amendment, treated in chapter 15 on voting rights, in 1870.

The Fourteenth Amendment is one of the most important in U.S. history. Overturning the *Dred Scott* decision (1857), Section 1 of the Fourteenth Amendment extended citizenship to "all persons born or naturalized in the

United States, and subject to the jurisdiction thereof." Section 1 further provided to all U.S. citizens guarantees that states would not deny them of their "privileges and immunities" of U.S. citizenship, of "life, liberty, or property, without due process of law" (a provision echoing a guarantee in the Fifth Amendment that had previously been applied only to the national government), or of "equal protection of the laws" (all topics treated later in this chapter).

Sections 2 through 4 of the Fourteenth Amendment are largely historic curiosities. Section 2, unsuccessfully designed to reduce representation of states that discriminated on the basis of race, offended advocates of women's suffrage (many of whom had worked for African American emancipation) by its exclusive concern with the deprivation of the rights of males twenty-one years and older. Section 3 limited officeholding by members of the Confederacy until such time, not long in coming, when Congress lifted this ban by a two-thirds vote. Section 4 reaffirmed the debt of the United States while renouncing that of the Confederate states and while rejecting any monetary claims for slave emancipation.

Section 5 of the Fourteenth Amendment is an enforcement clause. This clause is receiving increased attention. In cases like *Katzenbach v. Morgan* (1965) the Supreme Court ruled that Congress had power under this provision to enact civil rights legislation that it would not otherwise be able to enact. At the time, some justices worried that if the Congress could use its power to expand rights, it might later seek to restrict them; this led some scholars to speculate that perhaps this provision created a "one-way ratchet" where rights could be expanded but not diminished. In recent cases the Supreme Court has become increasingly wary of congressional "interpretations" that effectively "rewrite" or "reinterpret" the amendment. This issue is at the cutting edge of arguments as to the degree to which constitutional interpretation is vested chiefly in the judiciary and the degree to which the responsibility for such interpretation should be shared with the other branches.

Much of what gives potency to the Fourteenth Amendment is that its due process clause has been the vehicle through which courts have applied most, but not all, guarantees in the Bill of Rights to the states. This development, which has largely been accomplished through a process known as "selective incorporation," although vital to an understanding of the Fourteenth Amendment, was treated in chapter 8 on the Bill of Rights.

When it comes to protecting individuals against racial discrimination, the equal protection clause has ultimately proven to be the most important. In part this is a result of historical accident. Although many had anticipated that the privileges and immunities clause would be the most important clause in protecting the rights of racial minorities, the Supreme Court narrowly interpreted that clause in the *Slaughterhouse Cases* (1883), defining the rights of U.S. citizens. As chapter 7 on property rights reveals, courts applied the due process clause largely to corporations and used it to limit governmental regulation of industries. The scope of the Fourteenth Amendment was further limited in the *Civil Rights Cases* of 1883 when the Court distinguished illegal state actions, prohibited by the Fourteenth Amendment, from private acts of discrimination, that were not so prohibited.

Even this line appeared to fade in *Plessy v. Ferguson* (1896) when the Supreme Court sanctioned discriminatory "Jim Crow" legislation using the doctrine of "separate but equal." That is, separation of the races did not imply inequality as long as both races were treated equally. This experiment failed miserably. Initially, groups like the National Association for the Advancement of Colored People (NAACP) attempted to work within this doctrine by demonstrating that states were not treating citizens of different races equally and by insisting that they do so. Eventually, however, the NAACP challenged the doctrine directly, and in a case involving public education in *Brown v. Board of Education* (1954), the Supreme Court decided that separate educational facilities were inherently unequal. Since then, the Court has generally looked with strict scrutiny (its most intensive level of review) for classifications based on race. The Court has permitted the use of busing as a means of promoting desegregation, and it has delivered a number of decisions on the question as to whether racial classifications that were once used to disadvantage the minority race can now be used to their advantage. *Ricci v. DeStefano* (2009) is the most recent of these decisions that is treated in this book.

The Court has generally also given exacting scrutiny to classifications based on alienage. Like race, individuals do not control where they are born, and this fact generally has very little do to with their personal merit. In some cases, however, the Court has ruled that a state may reserve the exercise of certain important governmental functions to citizens.

As in the case of their race and nation of ancestry, individuals do not choose their sex. As is true of racial minorities, women in the United States were long subject to discrimination, not attaining protections for the right to vote until the ratification of the Nineteenth Amendment in 1920. Increasingly, the Court has looked with suspicion on classifications based on sex, particularly in cases where they appear based on stereotypes about male and female roles. Sex is often subject to what is referred to as "intermediate scrutiny," that is, to closer attention than most classifications but not quite the scrutiny to which the Court generally subjects race.

The Court has had to apply equal protection analysis to a variety of other classifications. These include age, illegitimacy, wealth, mental retardation, and the like. Although the Court has struck down a number of classifications based on illegitimacy, it has generally been more deferential to governmental classifications based on these other factors.

More than 140 years after its adoption, the Fourteenth Amendment remains at the cutting edge of constitutional thought. Its provisions have shown themselves to be extremely adaptable over time, and they are likely to continue to be so in the future.

DUE PROCESS (ECONOMIC) AND FREEDOM OF CONTRACT

Enforcement Powers

Katzenbach v. Morgan, 384 U.S. 641; 86 S. Ct. 1717; 16 L. Ed. 2d 828 (1966)

Facts—Section 4(E) of the Voting Rights Act of 1965 provided that individuals who had successfully completed six or more grades in Puerto Rican schools where a language of instruction other than English was used could not be denied the right to vote on the basis of English literacy tests. A three-judge District Court decided that the law exceeded congressional powers and violated state powers under the Tenth Amendment. In *Lassiter v. Northampton County Board of Elections* (1959) the Court had previously upheld state use of literacy tests.

Question—Does Congress have power under Section 5 of the Fourteenth Amendment (the enforcement clause) to prohibit state literacy tests that would otherwise be constitutional?

Decision—Yes.

Reasons—*J. Brennan* (7–2). Section 5 of the Fourteenth Amendment enlarged congressional powers by granting Congress power to enforce equal protection provisions of the Fourteenth Amendment. The issue is whether this law is an appropriate means of enforcing such legislation. Section 5 intended to give Congress broad powers similar to those it exercised under the necessary and proper clause and is similar to the enforcement clause (Section 2) of the Fifteenth Amendment. Congress had reasons to believe that its legislation limiting literacy tests furthered equal protection. Legislation designed for such purposes should not be subject to strict judicial scrutiny.

J. Harlan, dissenting, argued that voting rights were a state concern and that the Court should avoid establishing a double standard for cases involving what it considered to be "fundamental liberties" like voting rights. Harlan believed this legislation went beyond legislative remediation and effectively undermined earlier judicial constructions of the Constitution. He feared that if Congress could expand protections under its Section 5 powers, it might just as easily restrict them.

South Carolina v. Katzenbach, 383 U.S. 301; 86 S. Ct. 803; 15 L. Ed. 2d 769 (1966)

Facts—Congress enacted the Voting Rights Act of 1965 to combat systematic discrimination against African American voters in a number of states. In certain areas, where voting had been suppressed, the law provided for the suspension of literacy tests, for the assignment of federal voting registrars, and for the suspension of all new voting regulations without prior federal approval. Because this case involved a dispute between a state and a citizen of another state, it was a case of original jurisdiction that went directly to the U.S. Supreme Court.

Question—Are the provisions of the Voting Rights Act of 1965 legitimate exercises of congressional powers to enforce the Fifteenth Amendment?

Decision—Yes.

Reasons—*C.J. Warren* (8–1). The purpose of the Voting Rights Act of 1965 was "to banish the blight of racial discrimination in voting, which has infected the electoral process in parts of our country for nearly a century." Congress adopted the law after extensive hearings and by wide margins. There has been a long history of discrimination in voting against African Americans, and individual suits had proved to be costly and not particularly effective. The Fifteenth Amendment was designed to prohibit discrimination on the basis of race, and the enforcement clause of the amendment (Section 2) allows Congress to adopt any rational means to effectuate the aims of the amendment. Congress had the right to tailor its legislation to those areas where it found direct evidence of voting discrimination. Although the U.S. Supreme Court upheld the constitutionality of literacy tests in *Lassiter v. Northampton County Board of Elections*, 360 U.S. 45 (1959), it decided in this same case that a test that appeared to be "fair on its face" might "be employed to perpetuate that discrimination which the Fifteenth Amendment was designed to uproot." Allowing such tests to remain in place where they had been applied in a discriminatory fashion, "would freeze the effect of past discrimination in favor or unqualified white registrants." Although the suspension of new voting requirements might be considered "an uncommon exercise of congressional power . . . the Court has recognized that exceptional conditions can justify legislative measures not otherwise appropriate."

In a partial concurrence and a partial dissent, *J. Black* opposed Section 5 of the Voting Rights Act, which required states to get prior approval for changes in their voting regulations. He viewed this requirement as inconsistent with the idea of federalism and argued that it treated the states as though they "are little more than conquered provinces."

ℝ₧

City of Boerne v. Flores, 521 U.S. 507; 117 S. Ct. 2157; 138 L. Ed. 2d 614 (1997)

Facts—After the Supreme Court's decision in *Employment Division v. Smith*, 494 U.S. 872 (1990), Congress held hearings and adopted the Religious Freedom Restoration Act of 1995 (RFRA). The law mandated that governments should not adopt laws of general applicability that substantially burden individual religious freedoms unless they could show that such laws furthered "a compelling governmental interest" and were "the least restrictive means of furthering that compelling governmental interest." In the case at hand, the City Council of Boerne, Texas, attempted to limit the expansion of a Catholic Church in a historic district under its historic landmarks ordinance. The local archbishop claimed protection under RFRA.

The U.S. District Court argued that the RFRA exceeded congressional powers, but the Fifth Circuit Court upheld the law's constitutionality.

Question—Are the provisions of the Religious Freedom Restoration Act of 1995 a proper exercise of congressional authority under Section 5 of the Fourteenth Amendment to enforce its provisions?

Decision—No, the law is not an attempt to "enforce" the amendment but to interpret and redefine its terms.

Reasons—*J. Kennedy* (6–3). Kennedy noted that in *Employment Division v. Smith* (1990), the Court had abandoned the balancing test it had established in *Sherbert v. Verner* (1963), deciding in *Smith* that, when states adopted laws of general applicability, lawmakers did not need to show that they met a "compelling state interest." RFRA had attempted to overturn this decision. The national government is one of "enumerated powers." Although Section 5 of the Fourteenth Amendment is a positive grant of power to Congress, this power is not unlimited. The power is a "remedial" power, extending "only to 'enforcing' the provisions of the Fourteenth Amendment." The means that

Congress adopts to enforce the amendment must show "a congruence and proportionality between the injury to be prevented or remedied and the means adopted to that end." When Congress debated the Fourteenth Amendment, it modified its language to give itself "remedial" rather than "substantive" powers. "The power to interpret the Constitution in a case or controversy remains in the Judiciary." The best interpretation of cases such as *Katzenbach v. Morgan* (1966) is that Congress can fully enforce, but cannot expand existing constitutional powers. If it were permitted to do so, the Constitution would cease to be paramount law and "Shifting legislative majorities could change the Constitution and effectively circumvent the difficult and detailed amendment process." In judging the constitutionality of congressional enforcement efforts, the Court examines the "congruence" and the "proportionality" of its legislation. In adopting the RFRA, the Congress rested chiefly upon anecdotal evidence to require states to adopt a heavy burden that imposes "substantial costs." In so doing, Congress exceeded its enforcement powers.

J. Stevens's concurrence stressed that the RFRA gave an undue preference to religion, which was forbidden by the First Amendment. *J. Scalia's* concurrence attempted to refute historical evidence that the dissenters had cited to prove that the First Amendment was initially understood to require exemptions of religious individuals from laws of general applicability that were not specifically aimed at them. *J. O'Connor's* dissent focused on what she considered to be the Court's earlier misstep in the *Smith* case (abandoning the "compelling state interest test"), which she thought was inconsistent with history and judicial precedent and which she believed further undermined the protection of religious liberty. *J. Souter's* dissent also raised questions about the *Smith* case and argued that a decision should await resolution of the historical questions raised there. *J. Breyer's* dissent also questioned whether *Smith* was correctly decided and would set that case for reargument.

❧

EQUAL PROTECTION AND PRIVILEGES AND IMMUNITIES

African Americans and Racial Classifications

Scott v. Sandford, 19 Howard (60 U.S.) 393; 15 L. Ed. 691 (1857)

Facts—In 1834, Dr. Emerson, a surgeon in the U.S. Army, took Dred Scott, a black slave, to Rock Island, Illinois, where slavery was prohibited by statute. In 1836, Emerson took Scott to Fort Snelling, in the territory of Louisiana, which was north of the line of (36°30'), and consequently an area in which the Missouri Compromise had forbidden slavery. In 1838, Scott was brought back to Missouri, and in 1847 he brought suit in the Missouri Circuit Court to recover his freedom, basing his action on previous decisions that residence in free territory conferred freedom. Before the commencement of this suit, Scott was sold to Sanford, incorrectly spelled Sandford, a citizen of New York, thus giving the Court jurisdiction under its diversity of citizenship requirements.

Questions—(a) Can a black slave become a rights-bearing member of the political community formed and brought into existence by the Constitution of the United States? (b) Was the Missouri Compromise constitutional?

Decisions—(a) No; (b) No.

Reasons—*C.J. Taney* (7–2). Blacks were neither included nor intended to be included under the word "citizen" in the Constitution, and therefore could claim none of the rights and privileges secured to citizens of the United States.

A state could bestow the right of state citizenship upon any person it thought proper. However, no state could by its own laws make a person a member of the United States by making him a member in its own territory. Nor could a state clothe an individual with the rights and privileges of the United States, or of any other state.

The history of our country and the language of the Declaration of Independence, as well as the legislation of the colonies, point to the fact that blacks had no rights that the white man was bound to respect, and that he might justly and lawfully be reduced to slavery. The Constitution shows that public opinion had undergone no change, and pledged the states to maintain the property of the master by returning any escaped slaves.

The next question involved asked whether Scott, together with his family, was free in Missouri by reason of the stay in the territory of the United States? The plaintiff here relied on the act of Congress prohibiting involuntary servitude north of Missouri (36°30'). The difficulty here was whether Congress was authorized to pass such a law, according to the Constitution.

The power of Congress over the person or property of an individual can never be a mere discretionary power, but must be regulated by the Constitution. Rights of property are identified with the rights of a person who may not be deprived of them without due process of law. An act of Congress that deprives a man of his property because he came into a particular territory can hardly be called the process of law. Therefore the Court held that the act of Congress (the Missouri Compromise) that prohibited a citizen from holding slave property of this kind north of the line mentioned was not warranted in the Constitution and was therefore void. Dred Scott and his family were not free by reason of being taken there.

The plaintiff also contended that he was free by reason of being taken to the state of Illinois, and that, being free, he was not again reduced to a state of slavery when brought back to Missouri. *Strader v. Graham* established that the status of the slaves depended on the law of the state of residence. Therefore, Scott's status, free or slave, depended on the law of Missouri, not of Illinois.

In the light of these considerations, the plaintiff was not a citizen in the sense of the Constitution, and the courts had no jurisdiction in this case.

All nine justices wrote opinions in Scott. *J. McLean* and *J. Curtis* authored dissents claiming that blacks had been citizens when the United States was formed and that the national government had power to regulate slavery within the territories.

Note—*Scott* marked only the second time in United States history—the first occurred in *Marbury v. Madison* (1803)—that the Supreme Court invalidated an act passed by Congress on the basis that it was unconstitutional. *Dred Scott* inflamed attitudes on slavery rather than assuaged them, and was reversed by Section 1 of the Fourteenth Amendment, which reads: "All persons born or naturalized in the United States, and subject to the jurisdiction thereof, are citizens of the United States and of the state wherein they reside."

The Civil Rights Cases, 109 U.S. 3; 3 S. Ct. 18; 27 L. Ed. 835 (1883)

Facts—Various hotels, theaters, and railway companies had denied to African Americans the full enjoyment of the accommodations thereof, contrary to the act of Congress requiring no discrimination. Those proprietors had been indicted or sued for the penalty prescribed by the act.

Question—Does the Fourteenth Amendment compel a private citizen to refrain from the practice of discrimination?

Decision—No.

Reasons—*J. Bradley* (8–1). The law was founded on the Fourteenth Amendment. This amendment was concerned only with states practicing discrimination. It makes no mention of individual persons infringing on individual rights. If the state does not assist the discrimination of an individual against another individual, it is purely a matter between the two individuals. "In fine, the legislation which Congress is authorized to adopt in this behalf is not general legislation upon the rights of the citizen, but corrective legislation; that is, such as may be necessary and proper for counteracting such laws as the states may adopt or enforce, and which by the amendment they are prohibited from making or enforcing."

In dissent, *J. Harlan* argued that the Thirteenth and Fourteenth Amendments were broad in scope and intended not simply to eliminate slavery but also the "badges and incidents" thereof. Harlan further focused on the "public" character of the institutions and accommodations in question.

Note—Largely because of this decision, Congress has justified most modern legislation prohibiting racial discrimination in public accommodations through the exercise of its power under the commerce clause rather than under the Fourteenth Amendment. The Court accepted this justification of the Civil Rights Act of 1964 in *Heart of Atlanta Motel v. United States*, 379 U.S. 241 (1964).

Plessy v. Ferguson, 163 U.S. 537; 16 S. Ct. 1138; 41 L. Ed. 256 (1896)

Facts—In 1892, Plessy, a citizen of Louisiana, having seven-eighths Caucasian and one-eighth African blood, boarded a train from New Orleans to Covington in the same state. The conductor ordered him to sit in the car for black passengers. When Plessy refused to obey the order, he was forcibly jailed by a policeman and charged with violating a state statute (contemporaneously called a "Jim Crow" law) of July 10, 1890, which required separate accommodations for white and black passengers. Plessy was convicted of violating the law, and he filed a demurrer against Ferguson, judge of the Criminal District Court. Plessy appealed when the state court denied relief.

Question—Does the Louisiana statute providing "equal but separate" railway carriages for white and black passengers violate the Thirteenth and Fourteenth Amendments?

Decision—No.

Reasons—*J. Brown* (7–1). The object of the law is to ensure absolute equality of both races before the law. However, this is a political equality, not a social equality. The case hinges on whether or not this is a reasonable regulation. Established usages, customs, and traditions, as well as the preservation of public peace and good order, must be considered. Gauged by this standard, separate public conveyances are neither unreasonable nor contrary to the Fourteenth Amendment.

If blacks assume that this separation makes them inferior, it is not by reason of the act. If the civil and political rights of both races be equal, that is sufficient. The Constitution cannot put them on the same plane socially.

J. Harlan argued in dissent that "our Constitution is color-blind, and neither knows nor tolerates classes among citizens," and that, rather than relieving social tensions between the races, compulsory segregation laws would aggravate them.

Note—The Supreme Court upheld the doctrine of "separate but equal" articulated in *Plessy* until it reversed the decision in *Brown v. Board of Education of Topeka*, 347 U.S. 483 (1954).

Missouri ex rel. Gaines v. Canada, 305 U.S. 337; 59 S. Ct. 232; 83 L. Ed. 208 (1938)

Facts—The Law School of the University of Missouri refused Lloyd Gaines, an African American, admittance because of his race. He had completed his undergraduate training at Lincoln University, an all-black school. Missouri had separated the white students from the black students all through the school system, but as yet the state had not added a law school to the course of study at Lincoln University. If an African American student wanted to go to law school, Missouri would pay his tuition in an out-of-state school that accepted blacks.

Question—Did a state's refusal to accept an African American student into an in-state school violate the equal protection guarantee of the Fourteenth Amendment?

Decision—Yes.

Reasons—*J. Roberts* (7–2). The actions of the curators of the university are equivalent to the official actions of the state itself. State policy is that blacks attend Lincoln University while whites attend the University of Missouri. Meanwhile blacks are granted the opportunity of studying, tuition paid, at any nearby state university pending the full development of Lincoln University to the level of the University of Missouri. Although such an arrangement is praiseworthy, the fact that Lincoln University actually does not have a law school at present is a deprivation of equal privileges, since Gaines is denied an advantage extended to white students. The advantages of an alternate program allowing study in a nearby state and the relative excellence of that program with that offered by Missouri are beside the point since the whole consideration is whether or not Missouri had given equal privileges to both white and black students within the state. This has not been done; therefore the state statute violates the Fourteenth Amendment by discrimination.

As an individual Gaines was entitled to the equal protection of the laws, and the state was bound to furnish him within its borders facilities for a legal education substantially equal to those that the state afforded for persons of the white race.

J. McReynolds argued in dissent for deference to state decisions regarding education while pointing to the special difficulties in accommodating Gaines.

Note—This was one of the early cases in which the Supreme Court began to stress the "equal" component of the "separate but equal" standard that it had articulated in *Plessy v. Ferguson*, 163 U.S. 537 (1896).

☙

Screws v. United States, 325 U.S. 91; 65 S. Ct. 1031; 89 L. Ed. 1495 (1945)

Facts—Screws was a county sheriff who enlisted the assistance of a policeman and a deputy in an arrest. They arrested an African American late at night on a warrant charging him with the theft of a tire. They placed handcuffs on the individual. When they arrived at the courthouse square, the petitioners immediately started to beat him. They claimed he had reached for a gun. The police beat the African American into unconsciousness, and he died at a hospital within an hour. An indictment returned against the petitioners charged violation of Section 20 of the federal Criminal Code. This section makes it a criminal offense willfully to deprive one under color of law, of rights, privileges, or immunities secured to him by the Constitution and laws of the United States.

Question—Can Congress apply the Fourteenth Amendment to individual state officers when they act "under color of law"?

Decision—Yes.

Reasons—*J. Douglas* (5–4). Here the officers had deprived the accused of various rights guaranteed by the Fourteenth Amendment, "the right not to be deprived of life without due process of law; the right to be tried upon the charge on which he was arrested, by due process of law and if found guilty to be punished in accordance with the laws of Georgia." The Court stated that history shows that the word "willfully" was not added to the act until 1909. The Court reasoned that the word "willfully" makes the act less severe by requiring proof of purposeful discriminatory action. The Court therefore required a specific intent to deprive a person of a federal right, leaving no possibility for charging the act unconstitutional on grounds of vagueness.

The Court held that the petitioners acted "under color of law" in making the arrest since they were officers of the law. By their own admissions they assaulted the African American in order to protect themselves. It was their duty under Georgia law to make the arrest effective. Therefore, their conduct came within the statute.

The Court further reasoned that the problem is not whether state law has been violated, but whether someone acting under "color of any law" has deprived an inhabitant of the state of a federal right. The fact that it is also a violation of state law does not make it any the less a federal offense punishable as such. Nor does its punishment by federal authority encroach on state authority or relieve the state from its responsibility for punishing state offenses.

J. Murphy's dissent emphasized the vagueness of the federal statute at issue. *J. Roberts's* dissent emphasized that this prosecution should have proceeded under state rather than under federal laws.

Note—*Screws* and *Benanti v. United States*, 355 U.S. 96 (1957), which held that illegal wiretapping by state officers would not be permitted in federal courts, and *United States v. Classic*, 313 U.S. 299 (1941), involving primaries selecting candidates for federal office, are examples of the application to state officials of federal law. The Court has made "under color of law" and "under pretense of" state law mutually interchangeable.

Shelley v. Kraemer, 334 U.S. 1; 68 S. Ct. 836; 92 L. Ed. 1161 (1948)

Facts—This case involved two instances of enforcement by state courts of private agreements, known as restrictive covenants, which barred African Americans from holding real property in certain sections of St. Louis and Detroit. Shelley, a black, purchased some property in a section of St. Louis covered by a restrictive covenant that barred such ownership. Other owners of property in the same area requested relief, but a Missouri trial court refused it. However, the supreme court of Missouri reversed the ruling of the lower court and ordered the African Americans to vacate their newly occupied property. The Detroit case was similar. Blacks acquired property in a privately restricted zone and were ordered out by a state court. The supreme court of Michigan upheld the lower court.

Question—Do orders by state courts enforcing private restrictive covenants based on race and color violate the equal protection clause of the Fourteenth Amendment?

Decision—Yes.

Reasons—*C.J. Vinson* (6–0). Restrictive covenants drawn up by private individuals do not in themselves violate the Fourteenth Amendment. As long as they are completely private and voluntary, they are within the law. Here, however, there was more. Through their courts, the states aided in the enforcement of the covenants. Indeed, if it were not for the courts, the purpose of the agreements would not be fulfilled. The fact that the state merely carries out something started by private individuals does not free the state from a part in the original intent; nor does the fact that it is the judicial branch of the government that carries out the discrimination. The judicial branch of the government is subject to the Constitution as much as are the executive and legislative branches. The states here involved were playing, through their judiciaries, an integral part in a policy of discrimination in clear violation of the Fourteenth Amendment, which prohibits the states from denying equal protection of the laws.

Note—*Shelley* did not invalidate private restrictive covenants but only state enforcement. *Jones v. Alfred H. Mayer Co.*, 392 U.S. 409 (1968), however, ruled that the Civil Rights Act of 1866, enacted by Congress to enforce the Thirteenth Amendment, bars all racial discrimination, private as well as public, in the sale or rental of property.

Sweatt v. Painter, 339 U.S. 629; 70 S. Ct. 848; 94 L. Ed. 1114 (1950)

Facts—The University of Texas Law School denied admission to Sweatt solely because he was black, and state law prohibited African Americans from admission to the school. The state of Texas then established a law school for blacks that was not on an academic par with the law school of the University of Texas.

Question—Did Sweatt's denial of admission to the University of Texas Law School constitute a denial of equal protection?

Decision—Yes.

Reasons—*C.J. Vinson* (9–0). As an individual Sweatt was entitled to the equal protection of the laws, and the state was bound to furnish facilities for legal education substantially equal to those the state afforded to persons of the white race. Such education was not available to him in a separate law school as offered by the state. In assessing equality, the Court must examine not only tangible factors capable of measurement but also intangible factors like the prestige of the school, the reputation of alumni, and so forth.

McLaurin v. Oklahoma State Regents, 339 U.S. 637; 70 S. Ct. 851; 96 L. Ed. 1149 (1950)

Facts—Mr. G. W. McLaurin, an African American, applied to the University of Oklahoma to pursue studies leading to a doctorate in education. After a three-judge District Court held that the state had a constitutional duty to provide him with the education he sought, the Oklahoma legislature required that he be educated on a segregated basis. McLaurin was required to sit at a desk in an anteroom adjoining the classroom, to sit at a designated desk on the mezzanine floor of the library, not to use the desks in the regular reading room, and to eat at a different time in the school cafeteria. McLaurin filed a motion to have these conditions removed, which the lower court rejected.

Question—Can a state university, after admitting a student to graduate instruction, afford him different treatment from the other students solely because of his race?

Decision—No.

Reasons—*C.J. Vinson* (9–0). By setting McLaurin apart from the other students, the state hindered his pursuit of effective graduate study. "There is a vast difference—a Constitutional difference—between restrictions imposed by the state which prohibit the intellectual commingling of students and the refusal of individuals to commingle where the state presents no such bar." The conditions under which this appellant was forced to study deprived him of his personal and present right to equal protection of the laws.

Note—*McLaurin* and *Sweatt v. Painter*, 339 U.S. 629 (1950) were handed down the same day. Both cases helped erode the "separate but equal" doctrine of *Plessy v. Ferguson*.

❧

Brown v. Board of Education of Topeka, 347 U.S. 483; 74 S. Ct. 686; 98 L. Ed. 873 (1954)

Facts—A series of cases went to the Supreme Court from the states of Kansas, South Carolina, Virginia, and Delaware. Since all of the cases involved the same basic problem—African American minors, through their legal representatives, seeking the aid of the courts in obtaining admission to the public schools of their respective communities on a non-segregated basis—all were determined by one decision of the Court. The Kansas case became the nominal leading case. In the various states, the black children were of elementary or high school age or both. Segregation requirements were on a statutory and state constitutional basis except in Kansas where only statutory provisions were involved.

Question—Does segregation of children in public schools solely on the basis of race, even though the physical facilities and other "tangible" factors may be equal, deprive the children of the minority group of equal educational opportunities?

Decision—Yes.

Reasons—*C.J. Warren* (9–0). Although the intentions of the authors of the Fourteenth Amendment regarding segregation were not altogether clear, the issue of segregation in schools needed to be decided not in the light of the nineteenth century but in light of the modern world in which education had significantly expanded and was generally considered essential for success in life.

Intangible factors involved in the separation of students of similar age and qualifications solely because of their race need very serious consideration. Such segregation of white and black children in public schools has a detrimental effect upon the black children, an impact that is greater when it has the sanction of law. It "generates a feeling of inferiority as to their status in the community that may affect their hearts and minds in a way unlikely ever to be undone. . . . We conclude that in the field of public education the doctrine of 'separate but equal' has no place. Separate educational facilities are inherently unequal. Therefore, we hold that the plaintiffs and others similarly situated for whom the actions have been brought are, by reason of the segregation complained of, deprived of the equal protection of the laws guaranteed by the Fourteenth Amendment."

Note—This was the historic school desegregation case that reversed the "separate but equal" doctrine of *Plessy v. Ferguson*, 163 U.S. 537 (1896). In a companion case, *Bolling v. Sharpe*, the Court decided that desegregation would also apply in the District of Columbia.

❧

Brown v. Board of Education II, 349 U.S. 294; 75 S. Ct. 753; 99 L. Ed. 1083 (1955)

Facts—After the Supreme Court's historic decision in *Brown v. Board of Education* (1954), the Court ordered rearguments on how this ruling should be implemented. The U.S. attorney general as well as attorneys general of several states participated in oral arguments.

Question—How should the racial desegregation in *Brown v. Board of Education* be implemented?

Decision—The Court would place primary responsibility with local school officials, as overseen by courts of original jurisdiction, exercising equitable remedies. Schools should make good faith efforts to progress toward desegregation "with all deliberate speed."

Reasons—*C.J. Warren* (9–0). Noting that substantial steps had already been taken to advance school desegregation, Warren said that "School authorities have the primary responsibility for elucidating, assessing, and solving these problems; courts will have to consider whether the action of school authorities constitutes good faith implementation of the governing constitutional principles." Warren decided that the courts that originally heard the desegregation cases would have primary responsibility for overseeing them. Such oversight would be governed by "equitable principles," which Warren characterized as having "a practical flexibility in shaping its remedies and by a facility for adjusting and reconciling public and private needs." School districts should "make a prompt and reasonable start toward full compliance with our May 17, 1954, ruling" but may then be given extra time. District Courts should act to see that such compliance takes place "with all deliberate speed."

Note—*Brown v. Board of Education* faced a policy of "massive resistance" throughout the South. Some scholars have argued that the phrase "with all deliberate speed" (added at the suggestion of Justice Felix Frankfurter) encouraged states to resist, but, given the volatility of the desegregation issue, such resistance would likely have occurred with or without this particular phrase.

❧

Loving v. Virginia, 388 U.S. 1; 87 S. Ct. 1817; 18 L. Ed. 2d 1010 (1967)

Facts—Two residents of Virginia, a black woman and a white man, Richard Loving, were married in the District of Columbia. They then returned to Caroline County, Virginia, where they were indicted for violation of Virginia's ban on interracial marriages. The Supreme Court of Appeals of Virginia upheld their conviction. The central provision of the state's Racial Integrity Act was the absolute prohibition of a "white person" marrying other than another "white person."

Question—Does the Virginia law that prevents marriages between persons solely on the basis of racial classification violate the Fourteenth Amendment?

Decision—Yes.

Reasons—*C.J. Warren* (9–0). The statutes violate both the equal protection and due process clauses of the Fourteenth Amendment. "Virginia's miscegenation statutes rest solely upon distinctions drawn according to race. . . . There can be no doubt that restricting the freedom to marry solely because of racial classifications violates the central meaning of the equal protection clause. . . . The freedom to marry has long been recognized as one of the vital personal rights essential to the orderly pursuit of happiness by free men. Marriage is one of the 'basic civil rights of man,' fundamental to our very existence and survival. . . . Under our Constitution, the freedom to marry, or not marry, a person of another race resides with the individual and cannot be infringed by the State."

Note—This decision had the effect of invalidating antimiscegenation laws not only in Virginia but also in some fifteen states.

❦

Jones v. Alfred H. Mayer Co., 392 U.S. 409; 88 S. Ct. 2186; 20 L. Ed. 2d 1189 (1968)

Facts—Jones claimed that the Mayer Company refused to sell him a house in a particular section of St. Louis County solely because he was African American. A federal statute that Congress enacted in 1866 under its power to enforce the Thirteenth Amendment places all citizens on the same level as white citizens to receive, hold, and dispose of real and personal property.

Question—Does the federal statute of 1866 apply to private as well as public sale or rental of property?

Decision—Yes.

Reasons—*J. Stewart* (7–2). Congress has power under the Thirteenth Amendment to determine what are the "badges and the incidents of slavery" and the authority to translate that determination into legislation. Such badges of slavery include restraints on the right to inherit, purchase, lease, sell, and convey property. The statute prohibits all discrimination against blacks in matters of property by private owners as well as by public authorities.

   J. Harlan, dissenting, questioned both the Court's construction of the Thirteenth Amendment and the wisdom of addressing the issue using a nineteenth-century law just as Congress had adopted the Civil Rights Act of 1968 to remedy racial discrimination in housing.

Swann v. Charlotte-Mecklenburg Board of Education, 402 U.S. 1; 91 S. Ct. 1267; 28 L. Ed. 2d 554 (1971)

Facts—The Charlotte-Mecklenburg school system encompasses the city of Charlotte and surrounding Mecklenburg County, North Carolina. Two-thirds of the African American students in the system attended schools that were either totally black or more than 99 percent black. The federal District Court ordered the school authorities to carry out a plan for desegregation of the schools that involved bus transportation of pupils in order to bring about integration.

Question—Does the District Court have the power to order a county-wide school busing plan to promote racial desegregation?

Decision—Yes.

Reasons—*C.J. Burger* (9–0). The Court had previously held that school authorities have the duty to take affirmative action to bring about desegregation. When the school authorities do not carry out this obligation to remedy violations of the equal protection guarantee, the District Court has broad equitable power to fashion a remedy that will assure a unitary school system. School authorities may be required to employ bus transportation as one tool of school desegregation. There is no requirement that every school in every community reflect the racial composition of the school system as a whole, but a District Court, again as part of its equitable remedial discretion, may make use of mathematical ratios. The burden is on the school authorities to satisfy the Court that their racial composition is not the result of present or past discriminatory action.

Moose Lodge No. 107 v. Irvis, 407 U.S. 163; 92 S. Ct. 1965; 32 L. Ed. 2d 627 (1972)

Facts—The Moose Lodge of Harrisburg, Pennsylvania, refused service to Leroy Irvis, an African American who was present as the guest of a member. Irvis claimed that since the state liquor board had issued the lodge a private club liquor license, the refusal of service to him was a "state action" in violation of the equal protection clause of the Fourteenth Amendment.

Question—Does discrimination by a lodge constitute state action if the state had granted it a liquor license?

Decision—No.

Reasons—*C.J. Rehnquist* (6–3). The Moose Lodge is a private club in the ordinary meaning of that term. It is not publicly funded. Only members and guests are permitted in any lodge of the order. The Court has never held that a private entity that discriminates involves the state because of some benefit or service furnished by the state. Since state-furnished services include all manner of things, such as police and fire protection, such a holding would utterly emasculate the distinction between private as distinguished from state conduct. The state must have significantly involved itself with invidious discriminations in order for the discriminatory action to fall within the ambit of the constitutional prohibition.

In dissent, *J. Douglas* and *J. Marshall* emphasized the scarcity of liquor licenses, therefore arguing that conferral of such a license converted the actions of the lodge into unconstitutional state action.

⊸৩ঞ়

Milliken v. Bradley, 418 U.S. 717; 94 S. Ct. 3112; 41 L. Ed. 2d 1069 (1974)

Facts—Both the federal District Court and the Court of Appeals had held that inter-district busing was needed to bring about the desegregation of the Detroit city and adjacent or nearby school districts, specially to Wayne, Oakland, and Macomb Counties.

Question—Does the equal protection clause require busing between independent school districts to bring about desegregation?

Decision—No.

Reasons—*C.J. Warren* (5–4). School district lines cannot be casually ignored or treated as a mere administrative convenience. Such would be contrary to the history and tradition of public education. In this country local autonomy for school districts has long been thought essential. However, school district lines are not sacrosanct if they conflict with the Fourteenth Amendment. Here the Court held that there was no inter-district violation and so no basis for an inter-district remedy. Even if the state might be derivatively responsible for Detroit's segregated conditions, there was no constitutional justification for an inter-district remedy since there was no evidence of activity by the state or outlying districts that had a cross-district effect. The constitutional right of African Americans residing in Detroit is to attend a unitary school system in that district. Cross-district busing would involve an expansion of that right without any support in either constitutional principle or precedent.

J. Douglas, *J. White*, and *J. Marshall* all authored dissents emphasizing past state actions that had led to residential segregation, the need to eliminate all vestiges of such segregation, and the inadequacy of the majority ruling to achieve such an objection.

Regents of the University of California v. Bakke, 438 U.S. 265; 98 S. Ct. 2733; 57 L. Ed. 2d 750 (1978)

Facts—Allan Bakke, a white male, twice applied (1973–1974) to the Medical School of the University of California at Davis. Despite strong "bench marks" (interviewers' summaries, overall grade point average, science courses grade point, MCAT scores, letters of recommendation, extracurricular activities, and other biographical data), he was rejected. Davis had two admissions programs for its entering class of one hundred students, the regular and the special admissions program. The special admissions program set aside sixteen seats in each class for various racial minority groups who did not compete with the eighty-four other applicants (who competed against one another) and who were not required to meet the grade point average of regular nonminority applicants. Bakke's overall scores were significantly higher than the special applicants. He claimed that the Davis "quota system" violated the California Constitution, the equal protection clause of the Fourteenth Amendment, and Title VI of the Civil Rights Act of 1964. The Supreme Court of California agreed.

Questions—(a) Is the admissions program of the University of California at Davis that set aside sixteen class positions for minority students unlawful? (b) Are considerations of race in admissions programs always unlawful?

Decisions—(a) Yes; (b) No. Note: *J. Powell* voted with one majority on question a and voted again with another majority on question b.

Reasons—*J. Powell* (5–4). "When a classification denies an individual opportunities or benefits enjoyed by others solely because of his race or ethnic background, it must be regarded as suspect. The Davis admissions program of explicit racial classification has never been countenanced by this court." It tells applicants who are not "minorities" that no matter how superior or strong their qualifications, they will never be allowed the chance to compete for admission with all the other applicants. Racial and ethnic classifications are inherently suspect and call for exacting judicial scrutiny. The Davis program operated as a racial quota and is invalidated. But Title VI of the Civil Rights Act of 1964 prescribes only those racial classifications that would violate the equal protection clause if employed by a state or its agencies. The California Supreme Court erred in holding that race can never be considered in evaluating an applicant, for the "state has a substantial interest that legitimately may be served by a properly devised admissions program involving the competitive consideration of race and ethnic origin." Powell stressed that race, like considerations of other individual characteristics, could serve as a "plus" in diversifying campuses.

J. Brennan led the justices who would have permitted not only considerations of race but the use of quotas to achieve diversity. The use of race in this case did not stigmatize those like Bakke who were rejected and did serve the worthy purpose of providing representation in the medical profession for racial minorities.

J. Stevens led those justices who thought that Title VI of the Civil Rights Act of 1964 made it clear that Congress did not intend to approve considerations of race.

United Steel Workers of America v. Weber, Kaiser Aluminum v. Weber, United States v. Weber, 443 U.S. 193; 99 S. Ct. 2721; 61 L. Ed. 2d 480 (1979)

Facts—In 1974 the United Steel Workers of America (USWA) and Kaiser Aluminum and Chemical Corporation (Kaiser) entered into a master collective-bargaining agreement covering terms and conditions of employment. It included an affirmative action plan designed to eliminate racial imbalances in Kaiser's then almost exclusively white craftwork forces by reserving for black employees 50 percent of the openings in in-plant craft-training programs until the percentage of black craft workers equaled the percentage of blacks in the local labor force. Craft trainees was selected on the basis of seniority. At the Kaiser plant in Gramercy, Louisiana, a black was selected with less seniority than several white production workers whose bids were rejected. Thereafter, Brian Weber, a white man, instituted a class action in the U.S. District Court alleging that the manner of filling craft trainee positions discriminated against him in violation of Title VII of the Civil Rights Act of 1964.

Question—Does Title VII prohibit all private, voluntary race-conscious affirmative action plans?

Decision—No.

Reasons—*J. Brennan* (5–2). "Given . . . legislative history, we cannot agree
with respondent that Congress intended to prohibit the private sector from taking effective steps to accomplish the goal that Congress designed Title VII to
achieve . . . in view of Congress's desire to avoid undue federal regulation of
private businesses, use of the word 'require' rather than the phrase 'require or
permit' (in Sec. 703 j) fortifies the conclusion that Congress did not intend to
limit traditional business freedom to such a degree as to prohibit all voluntary,
race-conscious affirmative action. We need not today define in detail the line of
demarcation between permissible and impermissible affirmative action plans. It
suffices to hold that the challenged Kaiser-USWA affirmative action plan falls
on the permissible side of the line. The purposes of the plan mirror those of the
statute. Both were designed to break down old patterns of racial segregation
and hierarchy. Both were structured to 'open employment opportunities for
Negroes in occupations which have been traditionally closed to them.' At the
same time the plan does not unnecessarily trammel the interests of the white
employees. The plan does not require the discharge of white workers and their
replacement with new black hires. Nor does the plan create an absolute bar to
the advance of white employees; half of those trained in the program will be
white. Moreover, the plan is a temporary measure; it is not intended to maintain
racial balance, but simply to eliminate a manifest racial imbalance. We conclude, therefore, that the adoption of the Kaiser-USWA plan for the Gramercy
plant falls within the area of discretion left by Title VII to the private sector
voluntarily to adopt affirmative action plans designed to eliminate conspicuous
racial imbalance in traditionally segregated job categories."

    C.J. Burger and *J. Rehnquist* authored dissents claiming that this opinion con-
tradicted clear congressional language designed to prohibit racial preferences.
Rehnquist said that the decision was a "tour de force reminiscent not of jurists
such as Hale, Holmes and Hughes, but of escape artists such as Houdini."

☙

Fullilove v. Klutznick, 448 U.S. 448; 100 S. Ct. 2758; 65 L. Ed. 2d 902 (1980)

Facts—In 1977 Congress passed the Public Works Employment Act, which
provides that "at least 10 percent of federal funds for local public works projects must be used by the state or local grantee to procure services or supplies
from businesses owned by minority group members, defined as United States
citizens," who are Blacks, Spanish-speaking, Orientals, Indians, Eskimos, and
Aleuts. The "minority business enterprise" (MBE) section of the act also requires the government to seek out all available, qualified MBEs, lower or waive

bonding requirements where feasible, help in getting working capital, and award contracts to MBEs even though they are not the lowest bidders. Several associations of construction contractors and subcontractors filed suit alleging they suffered economic injury under MBE requirements, which on its face violated the equal protection clause of the Fourteenth Amendment. The District Court upheld the MBE program and the Court of Appeals affirmed.

Question—Does the "minority business enterprise" (MBE) requirement of the Public Works Employment Act of 1977 violate the equal protection clause of the Fourteenth Amendment?

Decision—No.

Reasons—*C.J. Burger* (6–3). "This Court has recognized that the power to provide for the . . . general welfare" is an independent grant of legislative authority distinct from other broad congressional powers. ". . . Congress has frequently employed the spending power to further broad policy objectives by conditioning receipt of federal monies upon compliance by the recipient with federal statutory and administrative directives. . . . The reach of the spending power, within its sphere, is at least as broad as the regulatory powers of Congress. If, pursuant to its regulatory powers, Congress could have achieved the objectives of the MBE program, then it may do so under the spending power." Congress ". . . could have drawn on the Commerce clause to regulate the practices of prime contractors on federally funded public works projects." Moreover a ". . . review of our cases persuades us that the objectives of the MBE program are within the power of Congress under (Section) 5 'to enforce by appropriate legislation' the equal protection guarantees of the Fourteenth Amendment. . . . We reject the contention that in the remedial context the Congress must act in a wholly 'color-blind' fashion. Where federal anti-discrimination laws have been violated, an equitable remedy may in the appropriate case include a racial or ethnic factor. . . . Congress, not the Courts, has the heavy burden of dealing with a host of intractable economic and social problems."

    J. Stewart and *J. Stevens* authored dissents calling for a color-blind constitution and associating set-asides both with shoddy work and with "animosity and discontent."

∽❦

Adarand Constructors, Inc. v. Pena, 515 U.S. 200; 115 S. Ct. 2097; 132 L. Ed. 2d 158 (1995)

Facts—A division of the U.S. Department of Transportation awarded a contract for highway construction in Colorado to Mountain Gravel and Construction Company, which solicited bids for subcontracts for guardrails. It awarded the contract to Gonzalez Construction Company over Adarand Constructors because, although Adarand submitted a lower bid, government financial incentives—up to 10 percent of the subcontract—for subcontracting "socially and economically disadvantaged individuals" (largely determined by race) made the Gonzalez bid more profitable. Adarand filed suit challenging the federal incentives. The U.S. District Court granted summary judgment for the government, which the U.S. Tenth Circuit Court of Appeals affirmed. In so doing it applied an "intermediate standard" for reviewing racial classifications, largely based on the Supreme Court decisions in *Fullilove v. Klutznick*, 448 U.S. 448 (1980), dealing with a 10 percent set-aside for minority contractors, and *Metro Broadcasting, Inc. v. FCC*, 497 U.S. 547 (1990), allowing the federal government to consider race in granting broadcast licenses.

Question—What level of scrutiny should courts apply when reviewing federal racial classifications designed to benefit minority groups?

Decision—Such classifications should be subject, like corresponding state classifications, to "strict scrutiny," the Court's highest such level.

Reasons—*J. O'Connor* (5–4). Since *Bolling v. Sharpe* (1954), the Supreme Court has recognized that denials of equal protection can be so severe as to constitute denial of due process. Although *Fullilove* and *Metro Broadcasting* permitted greater deference to federal racial classifications than to those at the state level, the decision in *Richmond v. J. A. Croson Company* 488 U.S. 469 (1989), voiding a 30 percent set-aside requirement for contractors established by the Richmond City Council, indicated that all racial classifications needed to be subject to "strict scrutiny." This case established the principles of skepticism, consistence, and congruence. Skepticism requires that "Any preference based on racial or ethnic criteria must necessarily receive a most searching examination." Consistency requires that the level of review does not vary by the race of the individuals burdened by a particular racial classification. Congruence requires that equal protection claims under the Fifth Amendment be treated similarly to those under the Fourteenth Amendment. These principles are based on the idea "that the Fifth and Fourteenth Amendments to the Constitution protect *persons, not groups*," and that constitutional rights are personal in nature. In thus overturning the intermediate scrutiny standard that the Court applied in *Metro Broadcasting*, the Court was not departing from but restoring "the fabric of the law." Since the Court of Appeals relied on *Metro Broadcasting* and *Fullilove* in applying "intermediate" scrutiny to this case, the majority remanded it to that court for further consideration.

    J. Scalia's concurrence emphasized that "government can never have a 'compelling interest' in discriminating on the basis of race in order to 'make up' for past racial discrimination in the opposite direction." He also argued that the Constitution did not recognize "either a creditor or debtor race." *J. Thomas's* concurrence suggested that so-called "benign" racial classifications were a form of "racial paternalism."

J. Stevens's dissent agreed with the majority's "skepticism" but not with its other two standards. He thought there was "a significant difference between a decision by the majority to impose a special burden on the members of a minority race and a decision by the majority to provide a benefit to certain members of that minority notwithstanding its incidental burden on some members of the majority." The principles of "consistency" would "disregard the difference between a 'No Trespassing' sign and a welcome mat." The principle is further inconsistent with the Court's past use of gender classifications, which were subject to intermediate scrutiny. Similarly, the principle of "congruence" ignored documented differences between state and federal action recognized in previous cases, which should be given greater deference. *J. Souter's* dissent focused on what he believed to be the belated introduction in pleadings of the issue the Court was being called upon to decide as well as on his belief that the Court should give greater consideration to the doctrine of stare decisis. *J. Ginsburg's* dissent focused on the "persistence of racial inequality and a majority's acknowledgment of Congress' authority to act affirmatively, not only to end discrimination, but also to counteract discrimination's lingering effects." She feared that the Court's "strict scrutiny" standard would prove to be "'fatal' for classifications burdening groups that have suffered discrimination in our society."

Gratz v. Bollinger, 539 U.S. 244; 123 S. Ct. 2411; 155 L. Ed. 2d 510 (2003)

Facts—Gratz and another petitioner, Hamacher, both white, applied to the University of Michigan's undergraduate college in 1995 and 1997. Although "well qualified," both were rejected. The university used a system of points, 100 (out of 150) of which were needed to guarantee admission. The school automatically gave members of racial minorities twenty such points in order to promote diversity. Gratz and Hamacher subsequently filed a class action suit arguing that the university admission program violated the equal protection clause of the Fourteenth Amendment and Title VI of the Civil Rights Act of 1964. The U.S. District Court accepted the petitioners' class action status and ruled that race could serve as a compelling state interest but found this program was not narrowly tailored to this interest. The U.S. Supreme Court consolidated this case with *Grutter v. Bollinger*, a decision in which the Circuit Court had upheld use of racial considerations in law school admissions at the University of Michigan, prior to a Circuit Court decision.

Question—Does a public university's admission system that automatically awards twenty of a needed one hundred points required for undergraduate admission to underrepresented racial minorities violate the equal protection clause of the Fourteenth Amendment and federal statutes?

Decision—Yes.

Reasons—*C.J. Rehnquist* (6–3). The admissions system at the University of Michigan had undergone a number of significant changes, but it included a system whereby underrepresented racial minorities were awarded twenty points not available to others. After reviewing the similarities between this case and *Grutter v. Bollinger*, Rehnquist concluded that the petitioners had standing. Rehnquist further reasoned that all racial classifications are subject to strict scrutiny under the equal protection clause. This, in turn, requires that programs utilizing such classifications must be "narrowly tailored" to "further compelling governmental interests." Citing the *Bakke* decision (1978), Rehnquist argued that such narrow tailoring required "individualized consideration" of applicants that the Michigan undergraduate program did not provide when it automatically awarded underrepresented racial minorities 20 out of 150 total points. The program therefore violates both the Constitution and federal statutes.

J. O'Connor, concurring, agreed that the Michigan system did not provide adequate individualized review. *J. Thomas*, concurring in striking the program, would have held "that a State's use of racial discrimination in higher education admissions is categorically prohibited by the Equal Protection Clause." *J. Breyer's* concurrence largely agreed with that of O'Connor.

J. Stevens's dissent denied that the petitioners had standing. *J. Souter's* dissent also argued that standing was lacking. Souter went on to argue that there was nothing unique about awarding points on the basis of race, since other factors, like athletic ability and socioeconomic disadvantage, also qualified individuals for points. Souter argued that racial diversity was important, and he did not believe that the twenty points that Michigan had awarded transformed race into a decisive factor. Indeed, he thought it was "especially unfair to treat the candor of the admissions plan as an Achilles' heel." *J. Ginsburg's* dissent further argued that "government decision makers may properly distinguish between policies of exclusion and inclusion." In this case, there was no evidence that the university was attempting to discriminate against a race or to reserve seats simply on the basis of color.

Grutter v. Bollinger, 539 U.S. 306; 123 S. Ct. 2235; 156 L. Ed. 2d 304 (2003)

Facts—Grutter, a white Michigan resident who had applied to and been rejected by the law school at the University of Michigan, argued that the school had discriminated against her on the basis of race in violation of the Fourteenth Amendment and federal statutes. The District Court struck down the school's use of race, but the U.S. Sixth Circuit Court of Appeals found that the school's consideration of race was narrowly tailored toward the permissible goal of increasing diversity, much like the program that Justice Lewis Powell had commended at Harvard, when he had struck down the quota system at the University of California at Davis in the *Bakke* decision of 1978.

Questions—(a) Does diversity constitute a compelling state interest for taking race into account in university admissions? (b) Did the admissions policies of the University of Michigan Law School violate the Fourteenth Amendment or federal statutes?

Decisions—(a) Yes; (b) No.

Reasons—*J. O'Connor* (5–4). The admissions program at the University of Michigan Law School was designed both to "focus on academic ability" and to provide "a flexible assessment of applicants' talents, experiences, and potential 'to contribute to the learning of those around them.'" The school included "soft" variables, including considerations of race in meeting its goals and attempting to get a "critical mass" of minority students so that such minorities would not feel isolated, but the university had not specified this mass "in terms of numbers or percentages." Referring to the *Bakke* case, 438 U.S. 265 (1978), O'Connor endorsed Powell's view in that decision "that student body diversity is a compelling state interest that can justify the use of race in university admissions." Racial classifications require strict scrutiny, but this scrutiny need not be "strict in theory, but fatal in fact." O'Connor believed that the university's judgment that diversity was essential to its educational mission was due judicial deference, and she cited evidence that American businesses consider skills in dealing with people from diverse backgrounds to be important. Governmental programs using racial classifications should be narrowly tailored to their objectives, thus invalidating quota systems and providing for individualized consideration of applicants. Michigan did not focus exclusively on race but used it as one factor among many. O'Connor noted that the university did not intend for the program to be permanent and expected that such programs would be unnecessary in another twenty-five years. In the meantime, the program was not precluded either by the U.S. Constitution or by federal law.

J. Ginsburg's concurring opinion expressed reservations about setting a twenty-five-year deadline for such programs.

C.J. Rehnquist's dissent argued that the majority's standard had been too deferential to constitute strict scrutiny. He found little relationship between the law school program and its goal of achieving a "critical mass," observing that this mass varied significantly from one racial group to another and correlated too closely with racial percentages in the population to have arisen randomly. He further argued that Michigan had not established a precise enough termination date for its programs.

J. Kennedy's dissent focused on what he believed was undue deference by the majority to Michigan's use of race. Like Rehnquist, he believed the percentages of minorities accepted each year implied that the university was giving too much consideration to race.

J. Scalia in dissent noted that "today's Grutter-Gratz split double header seems perversely designed to prolong the controversy and the litigation."

J. Thomas's dissent began with a quotation from Frederick Douglass, indicating that American blacks "can achieve in every avenue of American life without the meddling of university administrators." He embraced the idea that discrimination should end in twenty-five years but saw no need to wait that long. Thomas did not believe that the university had established a compelling state interest for its policies and especially rejected any goal of remedying past racial discrimination as too "amorphous." Thomas saw no "pressing public necessity in maintaining a public law school at all and, it follows, certainly not an elite law school." Thomas did not believe that the First Amendment interest of the university was sufficient to allow it to violate the Fourteenth Amendment, and he compared this decision to the Court's decision in *United States v. Virginia*, 518 U.S. 515 (1996), outlawing discrimination based on sex at the Virginia Military Academy. By focusing on race, the Fourteenth Amendment distinguished the preference at issue in this case from the "legacy" and other preferences that universities sometimes used. Thomas found nothing hallowed about the idea of "selective" admissions and expressed some concern about possible racial biases in the Law School Admission Test (LSAT). He further argued that the attempt to decide whether racial preferences helped or hurt a minority group was "benighted." Beyond hurting those whom it rejected, discrimination "engenders attitudes of superiority or, alternatively, provokes resentment among those who believe that they have been wronged by the government's use of race," and cited the decision as "yet another example of judicial selection of a theory of political representation based on skin color."

Note—This decision affirmed Justice Powell's argument in *Bakke* (1978) that diversity could constitute a "compelling state interest," but suggested, in conjunction with *Gratz v. Bollinger*, that the Court would oppose strict racial preferences or considerations of race that were based on stereotypes rather than on individualized consideration of applications.

❧

Ricci v. DeStefano, 129 S. Ct. 2658; 174 L. Ed. 2d 490 (2009)

Facts—New Haven, Connecticut, used objective examinations to determine eligibility for promotion for firefighters, but it threw out results of its last test after whites outperformed African Americans. White and Hispanic firefighters who had done well sued the city, which had acted to avoid liability under Title VII of the Civil Rights Act of 1964, which prohibited both intentional acts of employment discrimination on the basis of race and policies that had a disparate impact on the races. Both the District and U.S. Second Circuit Courts granted summary judgments for the city.

Issue—When New Haven discarded its examinations, did it discriminate against white and Hispanic firefighters in violation of the Civil Rights Act of 1964 and the equal protection clause of the Fourteenth Amendment?

Decision—Because the law violated the Civil Rights Act, the Court did not address whether it also violated the equal protection clause.

Reasons—*J. Kennedy* (5–4) concluded that race-based action was impermissible unless the city could prove that it would have been liable under disparate-impact statutes, which burden it had not met. Since the law violated the Civil Right Act, the Court would not reach the equal protection issue. Kennedy reviewed the manner in which the test had been developed. He noted that one firefighter who had done well had spent more than $1,000 to prepare for the test and had to overcome learning disabilities, including dyslexia. The city abandoned the test because "too many whites and not enough minorities would be promoted were the lists to be certified." This violated the law's prohibition against making adverse employment actions because of an individual's race. Past cases, like *Richmond v. J. A. Croson Co.*, 488 U.S. 469 (1989), had limited remedial actions absent a "strong basis in evidence" that such actions were necessary. The city had ignored evidence that pointed to the exam's validity and pointed to no evidence that it was not job-related.

    J. Scalia, concurring, noted that the Court had merely postponed deciding whether such actions violated the equal protection clause. *J. Alito*, concurring, pointed to evidence that city politicians had sabotaged the test to curry favor with minority groups. The city's primary concern was not about "violating the disparate-impact provision of Title VII but a simple desire to please a politically important racial constituency."

J. Ginsburg, dissenting, denied that the white firefighters had any "vested right to promotion." The firefighting profession has a legacy of racial discrimination, which the city was attempting to remedy. Individuals did raise questions about the test even before results came back. An intent to remedy the disparate impact of an exam differs from an intent to discriminate against majority-race applicants. *Griggs v. Duke Power Co.*, 401 U.S. 424 (1971), indicated that the Court prohibits "not only overt discrimination but also practices that are fair in form, but discriminatory in operation." New Haven had "ample cause to believe its selection process was flawed and not justified by business necessity." *J. Alito* was wrong to equate "political considerations with unlawful discrimination." New Haven did not engage in "race-based discrimination in violation of Title VII."

Protection, Privileges, and Immunities: Aliens

United States v. Wong Kim Ark, 169 U.S. 649; 18 S. Ct. 456; 42 L. Ed. 890 (1898)

Facts—The collector of the port of San Francisco denied admission into the United States to Wong Kim Ark, a Chinese person who had been born in California and was returning from a temporary visit to China. His parents were subjects of the emperor of China, but had a permanent domicile and residence in the United States and were carrying on business here. They were not employed in any official diplomatic capacity for the emperor of China.

Question—Does a child born in the United States of parents who were subject to a foreign power but not serving in a diplomatic capacity become a citizen of the United States at birth?

Decision—Yes.

Reasons—*J. Gray* (7–2). Wong Kim Ark became a citizen at birth by virtue of the first clause of the Fourteenth Amendment, "All persons born or naturalized in the United States, and subject to the jurisdiction thereof, are citizens of the United States and of the state wherein they reside." The Constitution nowhere defines the meaning of the word "citizen" or "natural-born citizen." The meaning of the phrase must therefore be interpreted in the light of the common law.

The fundamental principle of the common law was birth within the allegiance of the king. Children of aliens born in England were natural-born subjects, as were children of ambassadors representing England, although born on foreign soil. Children of foreign ambassadors or diplomats or of alien enemies were not natural-born subjects since they were born outside the obedience of the king. This was the rule in all the English colonies up to the Declaration of Independence.

Roman law, which considered the citizenship of the child to be that of the parents, was not a principle of international law since there was no settled and definite rule at the time the Fourteenth Amendment was adopted.

C.J. Fuller's dissent disputed the validity of English common law precedents and argued that Ark was not a U.S. citizen because, even though born in the United State, he had not, as the Fourteenth Amendment required, been "subject to the jurisdiction" of the United States at birth.

Note—*Wong Kim Ark* is the first instance in which the Court interpreted the citizens clause of the Fourteenth Amendment. The two rules of citizenship used universally are *jus soli* (law of the soil) and *jus sanguinis* (rule of the blood). The U.S. recognizes both rules.

❦

Truax v. Raich, 239 U.S. 33; 36 S. Ct. 7; 60 L. Ed. 131 (1915)

Facts—Arizona passed a law providing that when any company, corporation, partnership, association, or individual employs more than five workers at any one time, not less than 80 percent must be qualified electors or native-born citizens of the United States or some subdivision thereof. Raich, a native of Austria living in Arizona, lost his job as a result of this legislation since his employer feared the penalty that might be incurred. Raich filed his suit, asserting that the act denied equal protection of the laws to him.

Question—Is the Arizona act repugnant to the Fourteenth Amendment of the Constitution?

Decision—Yes.

Reasons—*J. Hughes* (8–1). Raich had been admitted to the United States under federal law. He was thus admitted with the privilege of entering and living anywhere in the United States. Being lawfully an inhabitant of Arizona, the complainant was entitled under the Fourteenth Amendment to the equal protection of its laws. The Fourteenth Amendment states that all persons within the territorial jurisdiction of the United States are entitled to the due process and equal protection clauses of the amendment. This includes aliens. Although this law did not totally exclude aliens from equal rights by setting down a percentage, it did give the state power to exclude aliens totally from equal protection within their borders. Thus the Arizona act was against aliens as such in competition with citizens of a defined category and clearly fell under the condemnation of the Constitution. The use of the state's police power does not permit the state to deny to lawful inhabitants the ordinary means of earning a livelihood.

J. McReynolds argued in dissent that this suit against Arizona was precluded under the terms of the Eleventh Amendment.

Note—In an earlier case, *Yick Wo v. Hopkins*, 118 U.S. 356 (1886), the Court held that the Fourteenth Amendment protected persons, not just citizens. *Truax* amplified this decision. In *Graham v. Richardson*, 403 U.S. 365 (1971), the Court ruled that classifications based on alienage, like those based on nationality and race, are inherently suspect.

Girouard v. United States, 328 U.S. 61; 66 S. Ct. 826; 90 L. Ed. 1084 (1946)

Facts—In 1943 Girouard filed a petition for naturalization in the District Court of Massachusetts. He stated in his application that he understood the principles of the U.S. government and that he was willing to take the oath of allegiance required of all citizens-to-be. However, he said that he would not bear arms in the defense of the country, but that he would serve as a noncombatant. He was a Seventh Day Adventist and his religious views did not permit him to bear arms. He was admitted to citizenship by the District Court, but this decision was reversed by the Court of Appeals.

Question—Does the fact that an alien refuses to bear arms deny him citizenship?

Decision—No.

Reasons—*J. Douglas* (5–3). The oath required of aliens does not in terms require that they promise to bear arms, nor has Congress expressly made any such finding a prerequisite to citizenship. To hold that it is required is to read it into the act by unreasonable implication. The Court could not assume that Congress intended to make such an abrupt and radical departure from our traditions unless it spoke in unequivocal terms.

Religious scruples against bearing arms have been recognized by Congress in the various draft laws. This is evidence that one can support and defend our government even though his religious convictions prevent him from bearing arms. "We cannot believe that the oath was designed to exact something more from one person than from another."

J. Stone authored a dissent arguing that the majority decision conflicted with precedents, which Congress had not changed, despite having had the opportunity to do so.

Note—*Girouard* reversed *U.S. v. Schwimmer*, 279 U.S. 644 (1929) and *United States v. Macintosh*, 283 U.S. 605 (1931).

Oyama v. California, 332 U.S. 633; 68 S. Ct. 269; 92 L. Ed. 249 (1948)

Facts—The California Alien Land Law forbade aliens ineligible for citizenship to acquire, own, occupy, lease, or transfer agricultural land. The father, Kajiro Oyama, was a Japanese citizen ineligible for citizenship. He bought six acres of land in 1934, and the seller executed the deed to Fred Oyama, then six years old, and an American citizen. Some six months later, the father petitioned the court to be Fred's guardian, which was ordered, and the father posted the necessary bond. In 1937, two adjoining acres were acquired. In 1942, Fred and his family were evacuated from the Pacific Coast. In 1944 when he was sixteen and still forbidden to return home, the state filed a petition to escheat the two parcels of land, contending that there was an intent to violate and evade the Alien Land Law.

Question—Does a statute making aliens ineligible to own land deprive Fred Oyama of equal protection of the laws and of his privileges as an American citizen?

Decision—Yes.

Reasons—*C.J. Vinson* (6–3). The state of California had discriminated against Fred Oyama based solely on his parents' country of origin. By the Fourteenth Amendment, and a federal statute, all states must accord to all citizens the right to take and hold real property. Under California law, infancy does not incapacitate a minor from holding real property. A minor citizen holding such property may have his father appointed his guardian, whether he be a citizen, an eligible alien, or an ineligible alien. At this point, the laws differ, pointing in one direction for minors whose parents cannot be naturalized, and in another direction for all other children.

Only the most exceptional circumstances can excuse such discrimination in the face of the equal protection clause and a federal statute giving all citizens the right to own land. In this case, the conflict was between a state's right to form a policy of landholding within its boundaries, and the right of American citizens to own land anywhere in the United States. When these two rights clash, the country of the father's origin may not be used as a pretense for subordinating the rights of the citizen.

J. Reed and *J. Jackson* authored dissents, arguing that Oyama's actions were designed to evade a law, the constitutionality of which the Court still recognized.

Takahashi v. Fish & Game Commission, 334 U.S. 410; 68 S. Ct. 1138; 92 L. Ed. 1478 (1948)

Facts—Takahashi, a Japanese alien ineligible for citizenship, brought suit for mandamus in the California Superior Court to compel issuance to him of a commercial fishing license. The commission denied him the license on the ground that a California law forbade giving a commercial fishing license to a person ineligible for citizenship. Holding this provision violative of the equal protection clause of the federal Constitution, the Superior Court granted the petition. The California Supreme Court reversed. The Fish and Game Commission contended that the California law was a conservation measure and that the fishing waters belonged to the state. Takahashi contended that the law was the outgrowth of racial antagonism.

Question—Can California use the federally created racial ineligibility to citizenship as a basis to bar Takahashi from a commercial fishing license?

Decision—No.

Reasons—*J. Black* (7–2). The Constitution grants the power to regulate immigration and naturalization to the federal government. Furthermore, the Fourteenth Amendment embodies the "general policy that all persons lawfully in this country shall abide 'in any state' on an equality of legal privilege with all citizens under non-discriminatory laws."

Whatever special public interests there may be, due to ownership of fish by California citizens, are inadequate to justify this legislation. The barring of aliens from landownership rests solely upon the power of the states to control the devolution and ownership of land within their borders, but cannot be extended to cover this case.

J. Reed's dissent emphasized the view that California's action was a legitimate attempt by a sovereign state to preserve its resources.

Foley v. Connelie, 435 U.S. 291; 98 S. Ct. 1067; 55 L. Ed. 2d 287 (1978)

Facts—New York State has a law prohibiting aliens from serving as state troopers. Foley, an alien planning to become a naturalized citizen, applied to take the Civil Service examination to become a trooper but was denied the opportunity. A three-judge U.S. District Court affirmed this denial, which was then appealed to the U.S. Supreme Court.

Question—Did the New York law limiting state trooper positions to citizens violate the equal protection clause of the Fourteenth Amendment?

Decision—No.

Reasons—*C.J. Burger* (6–3). State troopers are part of "a law enforcement body which exercises broad police authority throughout the State." Classifications involving aliens require "heightened judicial solicitude," but such classifications are neither all illegal nor do they require "strict scrutiny." Although police do "not formulate policy, *per se*, . . . they are clothed with authority to exercise an almost infinite variety of discretionary powers." An arrest is a serious matter involving "a very high degree of judgment and discretion." Such implementation of broad public policies may legitimately be confined to U.S. citizens.

J. Stewart's concurrence questions whether this decision can be reconciled with others, but he doubts their validity. *J. Blackmun's* concurrence stressed that classifications based on alienage should be "inherently suspect." *J. Marshall's* dissent sees "a vast difference between the formulation and execution of broad public policy and the application of that policy to specific factual settings." *J. Stevens* sees nothing that would suggest that "aliens as a class lack the intelligence or the courage to serve the public as police officers," and argues that this case should be governed by a previous decision allowing alien attorneys to practice law.

Plyler v. Doe, 457 U.S. 202; 102 S. Ct. 2382; 72 L. Ed. 2d 786 (1982)

Facts—In May 1975, the Texas legislature revised its educational laws to withhold from school districts any state funds for the education of children who were not "legally admitted" into the United States and authorized local school districts to deny enrollment to such children. A class action was filed in the District Court on behalf of certain school-age children of Mexican origin. The District Court enjoined the school corporations from excluding the undocumented children, holding that the Texas law violated the equal protection clause. The Court of Appeals affirmed.

Question—May Texas deny to undocumented school-age children the free public education that it provides to children who are citizens of the United States or legally admitted aliens?

Decision—No.

Reasons—*J. Brennan* (5–4). "Whatever his status under the immigration laws, an alien is surely a 'person' in any ordinary sense of that term. Aliens, whose presence in this country is unlawful, have long been recognized as 'persons' guaranteed due process of law by the Fifth and Fourteenth Amendments. We have clearly held that the Fifth Amendment protects aliens whose presence in this country is unlawful from invidious discrimination by the federal government. . . . Neither our cases nor the logic of the Fourteenth Amendment supports the construction of the phrase 'within its jurisdiction' to mean that illegal aliens are not within a state's jurisdiction. . . . The Equal Protection Clause was intended to work nothing less than the abolition of all caste and invidious class based legislation. . . . Use of the phrase 'within its jurisdiction' thus does not detract from, but rather confirms, the understanding that the protection of the Fourteenth Amendment extends to anyone, citizen or stranger, who is subject to the laws of a state, and reaches into every corner of a state's territory. That a person's initial entry into a state, or into the United States, was unlawful, and that he may for that reason be expelled, cannot negate the simple fact of his presence within the state's territorial perimeter. Given such presence, he is subject to the full range of obligations imposed by the state's civil and criminal laws. And until he leaves the jurisdiction—either voluntarily, or involuntarily in accordance with the Constitution and laws of the United States—he is entitled to the equal protection of the laws that a state may choose to establish."

  C.J. Burger's dissent begins: "Were it our business to set the nation's social policy . . ." and continues: "However, the constitution does not constitute us as 'platonic guardians' nor does it vest in this Court the authority to strike down laws because they do not meet our standards of desirable social policy, 'wisdom,' or 'common sense.'"

Protection, Privileges, and Immunities: Sexual Classifications

Reed v. Reed, 404 U.S. 71; 92 S. Ct. 251; 30 L. Ed. 2d 225 (1971)

Facts—Sally, a mother, separated from her husband and on the death of her adopted son filed a petition in the Probate Court of Ada County, Idaho. She sought to be named administratrix of her son Richard's estate. Meanwhile the father, Cecil, similarly wanted to be named administrator. Although the Idaho Probate Code favored neither one nor the other, the Probate Court appointed the father as administrator exclusively on the basis of his sex. The separated wife appealed.

Question—In selecting an administrator or administratrix of the estate of a deceased adopted minor son, can the state base its decision on gender?

Decision—No.

Reasons—*C.J. Burger* (9–0). "We have concluded that the arbitrary preference established in favor of males by . . . the Idaho code cannot stand in the face of the Fourteenth Amendment's command that no state deny the equal protection of the laws to any person within its jurisdiction." The Fourteenth Amendment does not deny to states the power to treat different classes of persons in different ways. "The equal protection clause of that amendment does, however, deny to States the power to legislate that different treatment be accorded to persons placed by a statute into different classes on the basis of criteria wholly unrelated to the objective of that statute." The equal protection clause cannot be abridged merely for administrative convenience as suggested by Idaho or to avoid family controversy. ". . . [T]he choice in this context may not lawfully be mandated solely on the basis of sex."

Note—The Burger Court's first opinion declared a state law invalid because it discriminated against women. Although sex is not in the "suspect classification," as decided in *Michael M. v. Superior Court of Sonoma County*, 450 U.S. 464 (1981), the Supreme Court generally subjects classifications on the basis of sex to heightened levels of scrutiny.

Frontiero v. Richardson, 411 U.S. 677; 93 S. Ct. 1764; 36 L. Ed. 2d 582 (1973)

Facts—Sharon Frontiero, a lieutenant in the U.S. Air Force, sought dependency allowances for her husband. Dependency would have been assumed for a man in her position, but women were required to show that men depended upon them for one-half or more of their support. Because she made no such showing, Frontiero's request was denied. A three-judge District Court upheld this denial.

Question—Did differing requirements for establishing dependency on males and females violate the due process clause of the Fifth Amendment of the U.S. Constitution?

Decision—Yes.

Reasons—*J. Brennan* (8–1; Brennan's decision represents that of a plurality, 4 justices, on the Court). The differential requirements for establishing male and female dependency rest on the idea that men are typically the "breadwinners" in households. Classifications based on sex, like those based on race, alienage, and national origin "are inherently suspect and must therefore be subjected to close judicial scrutiny." This decision is consistent with the Court's decision in *Reed v. Reed*, 404 U.S. 71 (1971), striking down an Idaho statute requiring that a male should be automatically preferred to a female in administering an estate. Brennan observed that "our Nation has had a long and unfortunate history of sex discrimination. Traditionally, such discrimination was rationalized by an attitude of 'romantic paternalism' which, in practice, put women, not on a pedestal, but in a cage." Although such stereotypes have been reduced, "women still face pervasive, although at times more subtle, discrimination in our educational institutions, in the job market and, perhaps most conspicuously, in the political arena." Sex, "like race and national origin, is an immutable characteristic determined solely by the accident of birth" and it "frequently bears no relation to ability to perform or contribute to society." Congress has "manifested an increasing sensitivity to sex-based classifications," including the Civil Rights Act of 1964, the Equal Pay Act of 1963, and the proposal of the Equal Rights Amendment. The classification in this case is based solely on sex and the armed forces' desire for "administrative convenience." The government has not actually demonstrated, however, that it is cheaper to grant dependency allowances to all men than to make individualized determinations of need. In any event, mere administrative efficiency is insufficient to meet the Court's close scrutiny.

J. Powell, concurring, would await state action on the proposed Equal Rights Amendment before deciding whether sex should be considered to be a suspect category.

J. Stewart concurs in the opinion on the basis of *Reed v. Reed*, while *J. Rehnquist* dissents for reasons stated in the opinion of the lower court.

Note—Because this case involves the U.S. government, it is brought under the Fifth Amendment rather than under the Fourteenth. Only four justices agreed to treat sex as a "suspect category" requiring a "compelling state interest."

❦

Michael M. v. Superior Court of Sonoma County, 450 U.S. 464; 101 S. Ct. 1200; 67 L. Ed. 2d 437 (1981)

Facts—Michael M., a seventeen-year-old male, was charged with violating California's statutory rape law. The complaint, filed on behalf of the victim by her older sister, stated that on June 3, 1978, petitioner and Sharon, the alleged sixteen-year-old victim, met at a bus stop and soon moved away from their friends and began to kiss. Petitioner then made more sexual advances for which he was rebuffed. After being struck in the face, Sharon submitted to sexual intercourse. California's statutory rape law defines unlawful sexual intercourse as "an act of sexual intercourse accomplished with a female not the wife of the perpetrator, where the female is under the age of 18 years."

Question—Does California's gender-based statutory rape law violate the equal protection clause of the Fourteenth Amendment?

Decision—No.

Reasons—*C.J. Rehnquist* (5–4). "We hold that the Equal Protection Clause does not demand that a statute necessarily apply equally to all persons or . . . things which are different in fact . . . to be treated as though they were the same. . . . We need not be medical doctors to discern that young men and women are not similarly situated with respect to the problems and risks of sexual intercourse. . . . All of the significant harmful and inescapably identifiable consequences of teenage pregnancy fall on the young female . . . pregnancy itself constitutes a substantial deterrence to young females. . . . A criminal sanction imposed solely on males thus serves roughly to equalize the deterrents on the sexes."

J. Brennan and *J. Stevens* authored dissents. They argued that gender-neutral laws prohibiting sex with minors could be just as effective as gender-specific laws and might even prove to be a greater deterrent to undesired sexual conduct.

❦

Hishon v. King & Spalding, 467 U.S. 69; 104 S. Ct. 2299; 81 L. Ed. 2d 59 (1984)

Facts—Petitioner, a female lawyer, was employed in 1972 as an associate in a large law firm in Atlanta. Respondent law firm was a general partnership and in 1980 consisted of fifty partners and approximately fifty lawyers employed as associates. Hishon alleged that her initial decision to join the firm was based on the possibility of ultimately becoming a partner "as a matter of course" after five or six years for associates who receive satisfactory evaluations. In May 1978 the firm considered and rejected Hishon for admission to partnership. She filed a charge with the Equal Employment Opportunity Commission that she was discriminated against because of her sex under Title VII of the Civil Rights Act of 1964. The District Court dismissed the complaint, and a U.S. Court of Appeals affirmed the decision.

Question—Did the respondent law firm deny petitioner a partnership on grounds of sex and did respondent's promise to consider her on a "fair and equal basis" create a binding employment contract?

Decision—Yes.

Reasons—*C.J. Burger* (9–0). Title VII of the Civil Rights Act of 1964 defines an unlawful practice for an employer to fail, refuse to hire, or discharge an individual or discriminate against an individual, because of race, color, religion, sex, or national origin. Petitioner alleges that the law firm is an employer. "A benefit that is part and parcel of the employment relationship may not be doled out in a discriminatory fashion. . . ." The benefit of partnership consideration "was allegedly linked directly with an associate's status as an employee, and this linkage was far more than coincidental. . . ." Once a contractual employment relationship is established, the provisions of Title VII attach, forbidding unlawful discrimination as to the "terms, conditions, or privileges of employment," which clearly include "benefits that are part of the employment contract." The benefit a plaintiff is denied need not be employment "to fall within Title VII's protection; it need only be a term, condition, or privilege of employment." The statute or its legislative history does not support an exemption of partnership decisions from scrutiny. Respondent has not shown that "the application of Title VII in this case would infringe its constitutional rights of expression or association."

United States v. Virginia, 518 U.S. 515; 116 S. Ct. 2264; 135 L. Ed. 2d 735 (1996)

Facts—The Virginia Military Institute (VMI), a state-supported institution, offered an education to men but not to women. Women seeking admission under the equal protection clause of the Fourteenth Amendment initially lost in a U.S. District Court, which found that the education at VMI had "substantial benefits," including adding diversity to the Virginia state system of higher education. The U.S. Fourth Circuit Court subsequently mandated that VMI should accept women, that the state should establish a parallel institution, or that VMI should become private. VMI subsequently set up a parallel program at Mary Baldwin College, with less emphasis on the "adversative system" and other military components of education at VMI. The District Court and a divided Circuit Court upheld this plan.

Question—Does VMI's continuing exclusion of women constitute a denial of equal protection under the Fourteenth Amendment of the U.S. Constitution?

Decision—Yes.

Reasons—*J. Ginsburg* (7–1; Thomas [whose son attended VMI] not participating). Ginsburg argued that individuals seeking to maintain gender classifications "must demonstrate an 'exceedingly persuasive justification' for that action" and must show that the means it employs are "substantially related" to such action. Physical differences between men and women are enduring, but are not the cause for reinforcing stereotypes. Although Virginia argues that single-sex education affords pedagogical benefits, its arguments in this case appear to be mere rationalizations for keeping things as they are. Arguments that women will not fit into VMI's program, or would not, for the most part, want to attend, tend to be self-fulfilling. Virginia's establishment of a program at Mary Baldwin College is significantly different and is neither tangibly or intangibly equal to that provided at VMI. This program does not provide equal protection for Virginia's sons and daughters.

C.J. Rehnquist's concurrence objected to the majority's requirement that Virginia must show an "exceedingly persuasive justification" for its education practices. He agrees, however, that the system at Mary Baldwin fell short of equality and thus of the equal protection standard articulated in the Fourteenth Amendment. *J. Scalia's* dissent focused on the majority's deprecation of history and tradition. Because the Constitution was silent as to the best method of education, he thought that the Court should be as well. He associated the majority decision with "smug assurances" of the age rather than with constitutional mandates.

Protection, Privileges, and Immunities: Various Other Classifications

San Antonio Independent School District v. Rodriguez, 411 U.S. 1; 93 S. Ct. 1278; 36 L. Ed. 2d 16 (1973)

Facts—Mexican American parents whose children attended elementary and secondary schools in a school district in San Antonio that had a low property-tax base challenged the Texas system of financing public education. The growing disparities between districts in population and taxable property were responsible in part for the increasingly notable differences in levels of local expenditure for education.

Question—Does the state's system of financing public education infringe on a fundamental right explicitly or implicitly protected by the Constitution?

Decision—No.

Reasons—*J. Powell* (5–4). There is no real evidence that the financing system discriminates against any definable category of "poor" people or that it results in the absolute deprivation of education. As a result, the disadvantaged class is not susceptible to identification in traditional terms. At least where wealth is involved, the equal protection clause does not require absolute equality or precisely equal advantages. "Education, of course, is not among the rights afforded explicit protection under our federal Constitution. Nor do we find any basis for saying it is implicitly so protected." Insofar as the system of financing schools results in disparities, it cannot be said that the arrangement is so irrational as to be individually discriminatory. There is need for reform in tax systems, but the challenged state action certainly furthers a legitimate state purpose or interest. The ultimate solutions must come from the lawmakers and from the democratic pressures of those who elect them.

   J. Brennan, J. White, and *J. Marshall* all authored dissents claiming that the Texas scheme served no rational interest and discriminated against individuals from poorer educational districts.

∽⥊

Cleburne v. Cleburne Living Center, 473 U.S. 432; 105 S. Ct. 3249; 87 L. Ed. 2d 313 (1985)

Facts—The city of Cleburne, Texas, denied a permit for a group home for the mentally retarded. The U.S. District Court upheld the ordinance and its application, arguing that no fundamental right or suspect class was at issue. By contrast, the U.S. Fifth Circuit Court of Appeals decided that mental retardation was a "quasi-suspect classification" that should be subject to "intermediate-level scrutiny," and that the evidence was "invalid on its face because it did not substantially further any important governmental interests."

Questions—(a) Is mental retardation a suspect or quasi-suspect category? (b) Is the application of the Cleburne city ordinance rational and legal?

Decisions—(a) No; (b) No.

Reasons—*J. White* (6–3 on [a]; 9–0 on [b]). There are three levels of review under the equal protection clause of the Fourteenth Amendment. Minimal or "rational basis" review, most commonly applied to general economic and social legislation, presumes legislation to be valid as long as it is "rationally related to a legitimate state interest." The Court applies "strict scrutiny" requiring the showing of "a compelling state interest" to classifications based on "race, alienage, or national origin." Gender classifications fall in between, requiring "a heightened standard of review" and also requiring that such classifications be "substantially related to a sufficiently important governmental interest." The Court, however, has not applied heightened scrutiny to classifications based on age.

White thought the Circuit Court was wrong to classify mental retardation as a quasi-suspect category. Individuals who are retarded do have a "reduced ability to cope and function in the everyday world." Moreover, Congress and state legislatures have demonstrated concern for the retarded "in a manner that belies a continuing antipathy or prejudice and a corresponding need for more intrusive oversight by the judiciary." Such laws show that the retarded are not "politically powerless." If the retarded were classified as a suspect or quasi-suspect category, the Court would need to consider similar classifications for "the aging, the disabled, the mentally ill, and the infirm."

Still, legislation dealing with the retarded "must be rationally related to a legitimate governmental purpose" that was not present in this case, which rested on biases and unfounded community perceptions. The Cleburne City Council had not applied its objections to group homes for the retarded to other dwellings (fraternity houses, apartments, hospitals, etc.) of similar size and capacity, and they are therefore invalid.

J. Stevens's concurrence eschewed the Court's three-tier system of review for "a continuum of judgmental responses to differing classifications which have been explained in opinions by terms ranging from 'strict scrutiny' at one extreme to 'rational basis' at the other."

J. Marshall's partial dissent argued that the Court should invalidate the statute itself, and not simply its specific application in this case. He argued that the Court had in fact applied the heightened scrutiny it renounced. Marshall would apply heightened scrutiny to this case because of both the importance of the interest at stake (a group home for the retarded) and the invidiousness of the classification. He further described a "lengthy and tragic history" of discrimination against the retarded (including the eugenics movement), which he thought the majority decision underplayed. Noting the ordinance's archaic reference to the "feeble-minded," Marshall would have invalidated the ordinance in question.

◦ঌৢ

Meritor Savings Bank v. Vinson, 477 U.S. 57; 106 S. Ct. 2399; 91 L. Ed. 2d 49 (1986)

Facts—Vinson, a former employee, claimed that during her employment at the bank she had been subjected to sexual harassment. She worked at the bank for four years, was discharged in November 1978, and sued in the District Court, claiming that her supervisor had constantly subjected her to sexual harassment in violation of Title VII. The bank denied knowledge of any sexual harassment. The District Court denied relief. The Court of Appeals for the District of Columbia reversed. It also denied that the bank was without liability merely because it did not know of the harassment. The Supreme Court granted certiorari.

Question—Does sexual harassment without economic loss creating a hostile or abusive work environment violate Title VII of the 1964 Civil Rights Act?

Decision—Yes.

Reasons—*J. Rehnquist* (9–0). Unwelcome sexual advances create an offensive or hostile working environment in violation of Title VII. The Court rejects petitioner's view that Title VII is concerned only with "economic" or "tangible" discrimination. Not all workplace conduct—such as "mere utterance of an ethnic or racial epithet"—affects the term, condition, or privilege of employment. But actions that are severe or persuasive enough to alter the conditions of the victim's employment create an abusive working environment. That conduct was "voluntary" in the sense that the complainant was not forced against her will "is not a defense to a sexual harassment suit under Title VII." We refuse to accept the Court of Appeals' view that petitioner Taylor was covered by his employer, the Bank, even though the employer neither knew nor reasonably could have known of the alleged misconduct. We hold that a claim of "hostile environment" sex discrimination is actionable under Title VII. We reject petitioner's view that the existence of a grievance, a policy against discrimination "coupled with respondent's failure to invoke that procedure, must insulate petitioner from liability."

Note—Courts have identified two types of sexual harassment—that based on a quid pro quo, in which sex is expected in exchange for a benefit, and that, like this case, based on a hostile environment.

✑✐

Gregory v. Ashcroft, 501 U.S. 452; 111 S. Ct. 2395; 115 L. Ed. 2d 440 (1991)

Facts—The Age Discrimination in Employment Act of 1967 (ADEA) applied to state employees except for elected officials or those appointed to policy-making positions. Two Missouri state judges, who were required by state law to retire at the age of 70, argued that as officials appointed by the governor and subject to retention elections they were exempt from the law and that, in any event, the law requiring their retirement did not have a "rational basis" as would be required by the equal protection clause of the Fourteenth Amendment. The District Court and the U.S. Eighth Circuit Court of Appeals both rejected the judges' arguments.

Questions—(a) Did the ADEA apply to state judges appointed by the governor and subject to retention elections? If not, (b) did the forced retirement of state judges at the age of 70 violate the equal protection clause of the Fourteenth Amendment?

Decisions—(a) No; (b) No.

Reasons—*J. O'Connor* (6–3 on central issue; more split on others). O'Connor focused on "the system of dual sovereignty between the State and the Federal Government." She extolled this system and its intention (along with separation of powers among the three branches of the national government) of forming a "double security" to protect liberty. The supremacy clause grants Congress power to impose its will when operating under delegated powers, but states have special powers under the Tenth Amendment, especially when they are legislating in regard to their own "political function." When it attempts to regulate state policy choices, the national government must state this intention plainly. This law does not do so. When it comes to interpreting the Fourteenth Amendment, the Court recognizes that, unlike the commerce clause, this amendment was specifically designed as an "interference with state authority." Earlier cases, however, have established that "the Fourteenth Amendment does not override all principles of federalism." Congress should not be assumed to be exercising its enforcement powers under Section 5 of the Fourteenth Amendment unless it specifically states its intention to do so. All that a state needs to show when making a distinction based on age is a "rational basis," since such a classification affects "neither a suspect group nor a fundamental interest." "It is an unfortunate fact of life that physical and mental capacity sometimes diminish with age." Voluntary retirement and public oversight may not be adequate remedies. Although forced retirement is "founded on a generalization," it is not an irrational one.

J. White argued that the ADEA was not intended to apply to judges, but he did not accept O'Connor's "plain statement" rule in this context. He further argued that O'Connor overemphasized Tenth Amendment concerns and understated congressional powers under Section 5 of the Fourteenth Amendment.

J. Blackmun in dissent did not believe that state judges were exempt from the ADEA, and he examined the deliberations on the legislation to bolster his case. He believed that the Missouri retirement provision did violate the ADEA, which he clearly believed to be within congressional authority to enact.

Romer v. Evans, 517 U.S. 620; 116 S. Ct. 1620; 134 L. Ed. 2d 884 (1996)

Facts—Colorado voters adopted an amendment to the state's constitution (Amendment 2) that prohibited all state and local legislation designed to protect homosexuals. The trial court issued a preliminary injunction against enforcement of the amendment; the Colorado Supreme Court decided that the amendment should be subject to strict scrutiny and remanded the case to the trial court. It enjoined enforcement of the law, and the Colorado Supreme Court affirmed.

Question—Does a state constitutional provision prohibiting legislation designed to aid homosexuals conflict with the equal protection clause of the Fourteenth Amendment?

Decision—Yes.

Reasons—J. *Kennedy* (6–3). The state view that this amendment was designed to do no more than deny special rights to homosexuals was "implausible." Instead, he argued that "Homosexuals, by state decree, are put in a solitary class with respect to transactions and relations in both private and governmental spheres." Laws designed to prohibit discrimination typically enumerate the specific groups they are designed to protect, and Amendment 2 would prohibit such enumeration on behalf of homosexuals. The amendment thus "imposes a special disability upon those persons alone." Typically, the Court will uphold laws that neither burden fundamental rights nor target a suspect class if such laws bear "a rational relation to some legitimate end" but both the "broad and undifferentiated disability" that this law imposes on a single class and its broad breadth seem "inexplicable by anything but animus toward the class it affects" and therefore "lacks a rational relationship to legitimate state interests." Kennedy argued that "the resulting disqualification of a class of persons from the right to seek specific protections from the law is unprecedented in our jurisprudence." Kennedy further described the amendment as "a status-based enactment divorced from any factual context from which we could discern a relationship to legitimate state interests; it is a classifications of persons undertaken for its own sake, something the Equal Protection Clause does not permit."

J. Scalia, dissenting, said that "The Court has mistaken a Kulturkampf [cultural-war] for a fit of spite." Because the Constitution is silent on the issue, it should be left to democratic majorities. He also argued that the decision in this case contradicted *Bowers v. Hardwick*. If, as *Bowers* suggested, homosexual conduct could be criminalized, then "it is constitutionally permissible for a State to enact other laws merely *disfavoring* homosexual conduct." The only "animus" that Colorado has adopted is "moral disapproval of homosexual conduct," which it registered by reasonable means. The amendment no more disadvantages homosexuals than the establishment clause of the First Amendment disadvantages "theocrats" or the republican form of government clause disadvantages "monarchists." If this amendment is invalid, then so should be long-stating constitutional provisions, recognized in *Davis v. Beason*, 133 U.S. 333 (1890) designed to prohibit polygamy. The Court's decision rested less on the Constitution than on "the views and values of the lawyer class from which the Court's Members are drawn."

꙰

Miller v. Albright, 523 U.S. 420; 118 S. Ct. 1428; 140 L. Ed. 2d 475 (1998)

Facts—Lorelyn Miller was born to a Filipino-national mother in 1970, filed an application for U.S. citizenship in 1991, and was rejected. The next year a U.S. citizen named Charlie Miller who had served in the U.S. Armed Forces in the Philippines entered a "voluntary paternity agreement" specifying his paternity. The daughter's reapplication was still denied on the basis that it failed to meet statutory criteria. Both father and daughter then filed suit against the secretary of state in a U.S. District Court in Texas, but the Court rejected the father's standing, and the daughter's case was moved to the U.S. District Court for the District of Columbia. It decided that federal courts had no power to grant citizenship. The U.S. Court of Appeals for the District of Columbia accepted the daughter's right to sue but upheld the differential requirements for children of citizen fathers and mothers on the basis that they fostered ties between such children and the United States.

Question—Do congressional rules distinguishing between the ways that illegitimate children of a U.S. citizen mother and a U.S. citizen father become citizens violate the Fifth Amendment? (Note, the Fifth Amendment, rather than the Fourteenth, is at issue here because the case involves the national government.)

Decision—No.

Reasons—*J. Stevens* (6–3. Denied relief to Miller; severely fractured on other parts of the decision). Under provisions of the Fourteenth Amendment, an individual can become a citizen through birth or naturalization. Congress has distinguished between "citizen fathers and citizen mothers of children born out of wedlock." Whereas those born abroad of citizen mothers need only show that such mothers resided continuously in the United States for a year or more, those claiming to be born of citizen fathers must show a blood relationship "by clear and convincing evidence," must show that the father was a U.S. citizen at the time of the person's birth; must show that the father provided financial support to the age of eighteen and, before the child reaches eighteen, must legitimize the child, acknowledging paternity "in writing under oath" or establishing such paternity "by adjudication of a competent court." Stevens agreed that Lorelyn Miller has standing in this case since the decision affects her claims of citizenship. He rejected the idea that the differential standards for men rested on simple stereotypes—"There is no doubt that ensuring reliable proof of a biological relationship between the potential citizen and its citizen parent is an important governmental objective." Mothers and fathers are "differentially situated"—"The blood relationship to the birth mother is immediately obvious and is typically established by hospital records and birth certificates; the relationship to the unmarried father may often be undisclosed and unrecorded in any contemporary public record." Congress has compensated by allowing fathers to establish their paternity over an eighteen-year period. The congressional law also serves "the interest in encouraging the development of a healthy relationship between the citizen parent and the child while the child is a minor; and the related interest in fostering ties between the foreign-born child and the United States." This is not a case of stereotyping but a product of genuine biological differences.

J. O'Connor's concurring opinion expressed the view that the rules against third-party suits did not give the daughter the right to bring a case on behalf of her father's claim. As to her own claim, it triggered only minimal "rational basis" scrutiny, which the government met.

J. Scalia's concurrence accepted the daughter's right to sue but argued that only Congress, not the courts, could confer citizenship.

J. Ginsburg's and *J. Breyer's* dissents accepted the daughter's standing and argued that the law did rest on stereotypes and that such stereotypes were subject to higher judicial scrutiny that they failed to pass.

Connecticut Department of Public Safety v. John Doe, 538 U.S. 1; 123 S. Ct. 1160; 155 L. Ed. 2d 93 (2003)

Facts—Connecticut's "Megan's Law" requires individuals convicted of sexual offenses to register with the Department of Public Safety (DPS) upon their release. The department makes an Internet registry available in which individuals can find the names and addresses of such individuals within their communities. The respondent, a convicted sex offender subject to the law, obtained a summary judgment from a District Court enjoining this posting on the basis that it violated his "liberty interest" and on the basis that it violated the due process clause of the Fourteenth Amendment by not affording him a pre-deprivation hearing to determine his current dangerousness. The U.S. Second Circuit Court of Appeals affirmed the lower court injunction.

Question—Does a state law requiring the posting of the names of sexual offenders on the Internet violate the liberty interest or the due process clause of the Fourteenth Amendment?

Decision—No.

Reasons—*C.J. Rehnquist* (9–0). Rehnquist cited a precedent indicating that "Sex offenders are a serious threat in this Nation." Megan's Law was a response to this threat. The DPS posting was accompanied by a warning that use of the directory for injury or harassment was illegal and indicating that it had made no individualized determination that individuals listed were currently dangerous. Although the respondent contends that having his name listed on the registry damages his reputation, the Court ruled in *Paul v. Davis*, 424 U.S. 693 (1976) that "mere injury to reputation, even if defamatory, does not constitute the deprivation of a liberty interest." However, even if he were entitled to such a hearing, "due process did not entitle him to a hearing to establish a fact that was not material under the Connecticut statute." Megan's Law applied whether or not an individual was considered to be currently dangerous or not, so an individualized determination of this fact would not remove his name from the list. The respondent disavowed "any reliance on the substantive component of the Fourteenth Amendment's protections." He therefore has no case.

   J. Scalia, concurring, noted that even if the law violates a liberty interest, he has received "due process" because this interest has been abridged by a validly adopted law.

   J. Souter, concurring, noted that the decision "does not foreclose a claim that Connecticut's dissemination of registry information is actionable on a substantive due process principle." Moreover, the fact that Connecticut allows certain sexual offenders to avoid the registration and reporting obligations also raises the possibility of an equal protection challenge.

Chapter Fifteen

VOTING RIGHTS

Article I, and the Twelfth, Fourteenth, Fifteenth,
Nineteenth, Twenty-Third, Twenty-Fourth,
and Twenty-Sixth Amendments

The right to vote is so important that the U.S. Supreme Court has declared it to be "fundamental," but it is not specifically guaranteed in the Constitution. At the time the Constitution was written, voting rights varied significantly from one state to another. Most states initially limited the vote to white males who owned property. Rather than set an independent standard, the Constitution simply specified in Article I that states would apply the same standards to national elections that they applied to their own.

The Electoral College mechanism for selecting the president in the United States provides for an indirect method of electing a president that keeps the president relatively independent of the other two branches of government. States are accorded electoral votes according to their total number of U.S. representatives and senators. The Twelfth Amendment modified this complex mechanism by specifying that presidential electors now cast separate votes for president and vice president, and the Twenty-third Amendment further extended some electoral votes to individuals in the District of Columbia who were previously denied such representation. The presidential election of 2000 was brought to its dramatic conclusion (in which George W. Bush, who was behind in the popular vote, nonetheless got a majority of the electoral votes) through the Supreme Court decision *in Bush v. Gore* (2000). This was the first case in which a judicial decision helped determine the outcome of a presidential election, although a judicial commission that consisted in part of Supreme Court justices had a significant influence on the election of 1876.

A number of constitutional amendments now prohibit discrimination in voting based on certain forbidden characteristics. Although it faced numerous modes of evasion and was not effectively enforced until the 1960s, the Fifteenth Amendment (1870) prohibited discrimination in voting on the basis of race. In *Guinn v. United States* (1915), the Court used this amendment to eliminate so-called grandfather clauses, which effectively discriminated against African American voters. Because in many states the winners of Democratic primaries were virtually guaranteed to win the general election, the Court took an important step in facilitating voting by African Americans when it later decided that such elections were not considered to be private actions but state actions subject to the restraints of the Fourteenth and Fifteenth Amendments.

The Nineteenth Amendment prohibited discrimination in voting on the basis of sex. States ratified the Nineteenth Amendment in 1920, almost seventy-five years since the Seneca Falls Convention meeting in New York had first called for such rights. Prior to ratification, an increasing number of states had extended voting rights to women, but the Nineteenth Amendment assured that such rights would now be exercised throughout the nation.

The Twenty-fourth Amendment (1964) eliminated the poll tax in national elections, thus terminating a mechanism that had long deterred indigent individuals from voting. The Twenty-sixth Amendment (1971) prohibited denial or abridgement of the right to vote for individuals age eighteen or older—most states had previously set the age at twenty-one. The more youthful age reflected increasing educational levels among youth and was ratified at a time when many individuals under the age of twenty-one were serving in the military.

Until *Baker v. Carr* (1962), treated under the political questions doctrine in chapter 3 on Article III, the Supreme Court considered most matters involving voting rights to be nonjusticiable political questions, but after *Baker*, the Court wandered into areas involving districting of congressional elections as well as of state electoral districts. Since then, the Court has fairly consistently applied a "one-person/one-vote" standard, basically calling for equal representation within districts with similar numbers of members. Gerrymandering of districts (drawing them for partisan advantage) has long been an accepted part of political life, but recent cases have raised questions as to whether such gerrymandering, which was used to disadvantage racial minorities, can now be designed to increase their representation.

VOTING RIGHTS

Ex parte Yarbrough, 110 U.S. 651; 4 S. Ct. 152; 28 L. Ed. 274 (1884)

Facts—Yarbrough and others were convicted in a federal court for having conspired to intimidate a black person from voting for a member of Congress, in violation of the federal statutes.

Question—May Congress punish violations of election laws under the Constitution?

Decision—Yes.

Reasons—*J. Miller* (9–0). "That a government whose essential character is republican, whose executive head and legislative body are both elective, whose most numerous and powerful branch of the legislature is elected by the people directly, has no power to appropriate laws to secure this election from the influence of violence, of corruption, and of fraud, is a proposition so startling as to arrest attention and demand the gravest consideration." If this government "is anything more than a mere aggregation of delegated agents of other states and governments, each of which is superior to the general government, it must have the power to protect the elections on which its existence depends from violence and corruption." The Court has never adhered to the proposition that every power of Congress must be expressly granted. The right to vote in a congressional election is not dependent upon each state . . . for the office is one "created by the Constitution and by that alone. It also declares how it shall be filled, namely: by elections. . . . If the Government of the United States has within its constitutional domain no authority to provide against these evils . . . it will be at the mercy of the combinations of those who respect no right but brute force, on the one hand, and unprincipled corruptionists on the other."

Guinn v. United States, 238 U.S. 347; 35 S. Ct. 926; 59 L. Ed. 1340 (1915)

Facts—In 1910 Oklahoma amended its constitution with a "grandfather" clause that prohibited individuals who could not read or write from voting unless they were descendants of individuals who had been so entitled. African American citizens of Oklahoma charged that the amendment violated the Fifteenth Amendment.

Question—Does Oklahoma's grandfather clause violate the Fifteenth Amendment?

Decision—Yes.

Reasons—*C.J. White* (8–0). The Court reasoned that the Oklahoma amendment was designed to bypass the provisions of the Fifteenth Amendment by setting the date of voting eligibility for those that could not read or write prior to the adoption of the Fifteenth Amendment. Since African Americans had no eligibility before that date, the Court reasoned that this amendment was an attempt to deny voting because of color or race.

"We say this because we are unable to discover how, unless the prohibitions of the Fifteenth Amendment were considered, the slightest reason was afforded for basing the classification upon a period of time prior to the Fifteenth Amendment. Certainly it cannot be said that there was any peculiar necromancy in the time named which engendered attributes affecting the qualification to vote which would not exist at another and different period unless the Fifteenth Amendment was in view."

❧

Nixon v. Condon, 286 U.S. 73; 52 S. Ct. 484; 76 L. Ed. 984 (1932)

Facts—The African American petitioner brought this action against judges of a primary election in Texas for their refusal to allow him to vote by reason of his race or color. This was the second time Nixon had been denied the opportunity to vote. The first time the Supreme Court ruled a Texas statute denying the right of an African American to vote in a party primary was void. (See *Nixon v. Herndon*, 273 U.S. 536 [1927].) Texas then passed a new statute stating that the state executive committee of each party should determine who can vote in primaries. Under this statute, the Democratic Party executive committee adopted a resolution allowing only white persons to vote in its party primary.

Question—Does the Texas statute vesting the state executive committee of each party with the power to determine who can vote in its primaries violate the Fourteenth Amendment?

Decision—Yes.

Reasons—*J. Cardozo* (5–4). "The test is not whether the members of the executive committee are the representatives of the state in the strict sense in which an agent is the representative of his principal. The test is whether they are to be classified as representatives of the state to such an extent and in such a sense that the great restraints of the Constitution set limits to their action." The new statute placed the power in an executive committee, and thus the action was really state action and not private action, and was therefore subject to the limitations of the Fourteenth Amendment.

J. McReynolds's dissent portrayed the Texas Democratic Committee as a private organization and therefore not covered by provisions in the Fourteenth and Fifteenth Amendments covering discriminatory state actions.

❧

United States v. Classic, 313 U.S. 299; 61 S. Ct. 1031; 85 L. Ed. 1368 (1941)

Facts—In Louisiana, a primary election to nominate a party candidate for representative in Congress was conducted at public expense and regulated by state statute. Candidates to be voted on in the general election were restricted to primary nominees, to persons, not candidates in the primary, who filed nomination papers with the requisite number of signatures, and to persons whose names might lawfully be written on the ballot by the electors. Some of the votes of qualified voters were deliberately changed for the benefit of a different candidate. Classic, a commissioner of elections, was convicted under the Federal Criminal Code, which prohibits interference with constitutional rights.

Question—Are primary elections subject to congressional regulation?

Decision—Yes.

Reasons—*J. Stone* (5–3). Although the state government has the power to regulate these primary elections, Congress still has the duty to see that the integrity of these elections is maintained. The state had made these primary elections an integral part of the act of choosing one's representative. Thus it would fall under the meaning of elections of Article I, Sections 2 and 4 of the Constitution. "The right to participate in the choice of representatives for Congress includes, as we have said, the right to cast a ballot and to have it counted at the general election whether for the successful candidate or not. Where the state law has made the primary an integral part of the procedure of choice or where in fact the primary effectively controls the choice, the right of the elector to have his ballot counted at the primary, is likewise included in the right protected by Article I, Section 2."

    J. Douglas's dissent viewed the government's attempt to regulate primary elections as an attempt to enforce federal common law principles.

Note—This decision overruled *Newberry v. United States* (1921) and *Grovey v. Townsend* (1935) and led to *Smith v. Allwright* (1944).

❦

Smith v. Allwright, 321 U.S. 649; 64 S. Ct. 757; 88 L. Ed. 987 (1944)

Facts—Lonnie E. Smith, an African American citizen of Texas, sued for damages for the refusal of election and associate election judges to give him a ballot to vote in the primary election of July 27, 1940, for the nomination of Democratic candidates for the U.S. Senate and House of Representatives, and other state offices. This refusal was based solely on race and color. He fulfilled all other requirements for voting. Election officials were acting under a state of Texas Democratic Party convention resolution that limited membership in the Democratic Party to white persons.

Question—Does the action of the Democratic convention limiting the right to vote in primary elections constitute state action?

Decision—Yes.

Reasons—*J. Reed* (8–1). The privilege of membership in a political party is of no concern to the state. However, when the privilege of membership in the party is an essential qualification for voting in the primary and selecting candidates for a general election, the action of the party is the action of the state. "When primaries become a part of the machinery for choosing officials, state and national, as they have here, the same tests to determine the character of discrimination or abridgement should be applied to the primary as are applied to the general election. If the state requires a certain electoral procedure, prescribes a general election ballot made up of party nominees so chosen and limits the choice of the electorate in general elections for state officers, practically speaking, to those whose names appear on such a ballot, it endorses, adopts and enforces the discrimination against Negroes practiced by a party entrusted by Texas law with the determination of the qualifications of participants in the primary. This is state action within the meaning of the Fifteenth Amendment."

In dissent, *J. Roberts* emphasized what he believed to be the Court's cavalier treatment of earlier precedents.

Note—In *Newberry v. United States*, 256 U.S. 232 (1921) the Court said that Congress could not regulate primaries; in *Nixon v. Herndon*, 273 U.S. 536 (1927) that the state Democratic Party could not exclude African Americans from voting; and in *Nixon v. Condon*, 286 U.S. 73 (1932) that the state Democratic Party committee could not discriminate. In *Grovey v. Townsend*, 295 U.S. 45 (1935), however, the Court held a state convention to be a private organization and its discrimination licit. When *United States v. Classic*, 313 U.S. 299 (1941) overruled Grovey, saying that a primary was an integral part of the election process, it was a short step for *Smith v. Allwright* to declare the party's discrimination to be state action.

Gomillion v. Lightfoot, 364 U.S. 339; 81 S. Ct. 125; 5 L. Ed. 2d 110 (1960)

Facts—In 1957, the Alabama state legislature passed Local Act No. 140 changing the boundaries of Tuskegee from a square to a twenty-eight-sided figure. This virtually excluded African Americans from being able to vote in city elections. A number of blacks challenged this law as a violation of the Fourteenth and Fifteenth Amendments. The District Court dismissed for failure to state a cognizable claim, and a divided Fifth Circuit Court of Appeals affirmed.

Question—Did the Alabama law altering the boundaries of Tuskegee violate the Fifteenth Amendment?

Decision—Yes.

Reasons—*J. Frankfurter* (9–0). Alabama's action "was not an ordinary geographic redistricting measure even within familiar abuses of gerrymandering." Precedents have established that "The [Fifteenth] Amendment nullifies sophisticated as well as simple-minded modes of discrimination." Against the charge of racial discrimination, Alabama has not offered "any countervailing municipal function which Act 140 is designed to serve." State apportionment actions are subject to constitutional restraints. Other cases in which the Court has refused to intervene did not "sanction a differential of racial lines." An issue does not become "political" simply because it involves adjustment of municipal boundaries.

J. Douglas reiterated his dissent in *Colegrove v. Green*, 328 U.S. 549 (1946), where the Court had declared other voting issues to be political questions.

J. Whittaker would have relied on the equal protection clause of the Fourteenth Amendment rather than on the Fifteenth Amendment.

Wesberry v. Sanders, 376 U.S. 1; 84 S. Ct. 526; 11 L. Ed. 2d 481 (1964)

Facts—Qualified voters of Georgia's Fifth Congressional District brought action to set aside a Georgia statute establishing congressional districts. The population of the Fifth District was two to three times greater than that of some other congressional districts in the state. Since there is only one congressman for each district, it was claimed that there resulted a debasement of the people's right to vote because their congressman represented two to three times as many people as did congressmen from some other Georgia districts.

Question—Does Georgia's districting statute abridge the requirement of Article I, Section 2 of the Constitution of the United States?

Decision—Yes.

Reasons—*J. Black* (6–3). The statute contracts the value of some votes and expands the value of others. In its historical context the command of Article I, Section 2 that representatives be chosen "by the people of the several states" means that as nearly as practicable one person's vote in a congressional election is to be worth as much as another's. "While it may not be possible to draw congressional districts with mathematical precision, that is no excuse for ignoring our Constitution's plain objective of making equal representation for equal numbers of people with the fundamental goal for the House of Representatives. That is the high standard of justice and common sense which the founders set for us."

In a partial dissent, *J. Clark* argued that the case should be remanded to the District Court to rule on its merits.

J. Harlan's dissent questioned the one-person/one-vote standard, and *J. Stewart*, although believing the issue at hand was justiciable, did not think the Constitution required equality of representation among districts.

❧

Reynolds v. Sims, 377 U.S. 533; 84 S. Ct. 1362; 11 L. Ed. 2d 506 (1964)

Facts—Taxpayers and voters of Jefferson County, Alabama, challenged the apportionment of the Alabama legislature, the most recent of which was based on the 1900 federal census despite the requirement of the state constitution that the legislature be apportioned decennially. As a result of population growth, Jefferson County and others were alleged to have suffered serious discrimination with respect to the allocation of legislative representation.

Also, there were two plans for apportionment pending. One was a proposed amendment to the state constitution. The other was a statute enacted as standby legislation to take effect if the proposed constitutional amendment should fail of adoption or be declared void by the courts. Neither plan provided for apportionment of either of the houses of the Alabama legislature on a population basis.

Question—Does Alabama's law basing state legislative apportionment on factors other than population violate the equal protection clause of the Fourteenth Amendment?

Decision—Yes.

Reasons—*C.J. Warren* (8–1). "A predominant consideration in determining whether a state legislative apportionment scheme constitutes an invidious discrimination violative of rights asserted under the equal protection clause is that the rights allegedly impaired are individual and personal in nature. . . . Legislators represent people, not trees or acres. . . . The right to elect legislators in a free and unimpaired fashion is a bedrock of our political system. . . . Overweighting and overvaluing the votes of persons living in one place has the certain effect of dilution and undervaluing the votes of those living elsewhere. Full and effective participation by all citizens in state government requires that each citizen have an equally effective voice in the election of members of his state legislature."

As a basic constitutional standard the equal protection clause requires that the seats in both houses of a bicameral state legislature must be apportioned by population. An individual's right to vote for state legislators is unconstitutionally impaired when its weight is in a substantial fashion diluted when compared with the votes of citizens living in other parts of the state. This applies to both houses of the legislature.

Attempted reliance on the federal analogy to state legislative apportionment arrangements "appears often to be little more than an after-the-fact rationalization offered in defense of maladjusted state apportionment arrangements." Apportionment on a population basis requires an honest and good faith effort to set up districts on a practical basis. Mathematical exactness or precision is hardly a workable constitutional requirement.

In a concurring opinion, *J. Clark* argued that the Court should simply declare that the apportionment scheme in question was an indefensible "crazy quilt," while *J. Stewart* pointed to sixty years of legislative inactivity as a cause for action.

In dissent, *J. Harlan* reiterated his views, expressed in earlier cases, that the Court had gone far beyond the mandate of the Fourteenth Amendment.

Oregon v. Mitchell, 400 U.S. 112; 91 S. Ct. 260; 27 L. Ed. 2d 272 (1970)

Facts—Oregon, Arizona, Texas, and Idaho resisted compliance with the Voting Rights Act Amendments of 1970. Original actions were brought to question the validity of the statute. The Voting Rights Act Amendments provided for three things: (1) the reduction of the minimum age of voters in both state and federal elections from twenty-one to eighteen, (2) prohibition of the use of literacy tests in all elections, state and federal, and (3) prohibitions disqualifying voters in presidential elections because of failure to meet state residency requirements.

Question—Does the Voting Rights Amendment of 1970 lowering the voting age to eighteen infringe on powers reserved to the states under the Constitution to control their own elections?

Decision—Yes, when applied to state and local elections but not otherwise.

Reasons—*J. Black* (5–4). The Constitution reserved to the states the power to regulate the election of their own officials, but Congress has ultimate supervisory power over congressional and presidential elections. Congress has the authority under the original Constitution to permit eighteen-year-old citizens to vote in national elections and to prohibit states disqualifying voters in presidential elections because of failure to meet residence requirements. This comes under Article I, Section 4 and Article II, Section 1 of the Constitution, the former dealing with congressional elections and the latter with presidential elections. Beyond the original Constitution the enforcement provisions of the Fourteenth and Fifteenth Amendments allow for the literacy test ban.

Black's opinion split the difference between four justices on the Court who believed that Congress could establish the voting age in both state and federal elections and those who thought it could only establish such limits in federal elections.

Note—The Twenty-sixth Amendment overturned that part of this decision that would have limited the lowered voting age only to federal elections.

⤜✒

Dunn v. Blumstein, 405 U.S. 330; 92 S. Ct. 995; 31 L. Ed. 2d 274 (1972)

Facts—James Blumstein moved to Tennessee on June 12, 1970, to assume his duties to teach law at Vanderbilt University in Nashville. He attempted to register to vote on July 1, 1970. Tennessee law authorized the registration only of persons who, at the time of the next election, will have been residents of the state for a year and of the county for three months. The county registrar therefore refused to register Blumstein.

Question—Does a state law requiring residency in a state for a year and in the county for three months violate the equal protection clause of the Fourteenth Amendment?

Decision—Yes.

Reasons—*J. Marshall* (6–1). Such laws must be measured by a strict equal protection test. They are unconstitutional unless the state can demonstrate that such laws are "necessary to promote a compelling governmental interest." A preelection waiting period may aid in preventing fraud, but the Court felt that thirty days should be an ample period of time for the state to complete whatever administrative tasks are necessary to prevent fraud, while a year or three months would be too much. As to residence requirements limiting the franchise to voters who are minimally knowledgeable about the issues, such requirements exclude too many people who should not and need not be excluded. "They represent a requirement of knowledge unfairly imposed on only some citizens." The Court also noted that, in addition to depriving citizens of the right to vote, such laws also directly impinge on the exercise of the right to travel.

C.J. Burger argued in dissent that a durational residency requirement was just as valid as setting a minimum voting age.

Shaw v. Reno, 509 U.S. 630; 113 S. Ct. 2816; 125 L. Ed. 2d 511 (1993)

Facts—After the 1990 census, North Carolina became entitled to a twelfth seat in the U.S. House of Representatives. After the U.S. attorney general objected to a plan that included only one predominately black district, the state created a second with irregularly shaped boundaries that snaked for much of its length along Interstate 85. A three-judge U.S. District Court rejected claims that the district violated Article I and the Fourteenth Amendment.

Question—Do voters have the right to challenge state officials over apportionment of a congressional district on the basis that the district constitutes a racial gerrymander?

Decision—Yes.

Reasons—*J. O'Connor* (5–4). *Reynolds v. Sims* (1964) indicated that "The right to vote freely for the candidate of one's choice is the essence of a democratic society." The North Carolina plan in this case closely "resembles the most egregious racial gerrymanders of the past." The Court has not required a completely color-blind Constitution, but it has insisted on giving strict scrutiny to racial classifications. The Fourteenth Amendment was designed to prevent discrimination on the basis of race, and racial classifications are "presumptively invalid." O'Connor argued that "reapportionment is one area in which appearances do matter." The district in question "bears an uncomfortable resemblance to political apartheid." Such districting is likely to send the message that the primary obligation of representatives "is to represent the members of the group, rather than their constituency as a whole." It is also likely to reinforce racial stereotypes and to "balkanize us into competing voting factions."

J. White's dissent argued that the Court sidestepped its decision in *United Jewish Organizations of Williamsburgh, Inc. v. Carey* (1977), where it had upheld a gerrymander that benefited Hasidic Jews. White did not believe that North Carolina's action had deprived anyone of the right to vote so he believed that there were no parties with a real injury. He argued that the Court was too concerned with the appearances of the district. If the majority were seeking a "compelling interest," it would have to look no further than North Carolina's desire to comply with provisions of the Voting Rights Act. In his dissent, *J. Blackmun* argued that "the conscious use of race in redistricting does not violate the Equal Protection Clause unless the redistricting plan denied a particular group equal access to the political process or to minimize its voting strength unduly." *J. Stevens's* dissent questioned the majority's assumption that the Constitution imposed "contiguity or compactness" requirements on state configurations of district lines. He did not believe that unusually shaped districts were unconstitutional when they were designed to facilitate rather than to hinder minority race power. *J. Souter's* dissent also saw no reason to give strict scrutiny to such districts. He argued that past cases had not prevented others from taking racial considerations into account as long as such considerations did not adversely affect others: "the mere placement of an individual in one district instead of another denies no one a right or benefit provided to others."

Bush v. Vera, 517 U.S. 952; 116 S. Ct. 1941; 135 L. Ed. 2d 248 (1996)

Facts—After being entitled to three more U.S. representatives after the 1990 census, Texas, in an attempt to comply with the Voting Rights Act of 1965, created and reconfigured three districts to ensure a majority of African Americans and Hispanics. After voters challenged state officials, including then Governor George W. Bush, about these districts, a three-judge U.S. District Court ruled that they violated the equal protection clause of the Fourteenth Amendment.

Question—Did the Texas redistricting violate the equal protection clause of the Fourteenth Amendment?

Decision—Yes, redistricting that resulted in oddly shaped districts was subject to "strict scrutiny" and was "not narrowly tailored to serve a compelling state interest."

Reasons—*J. O'Connor* (5–4). According to precedents, the Court should apply strict scrutiny "where 'redistricting legislation . . . is so extremely irregular on its face that it rationally can be viewed only as an effort to segregate the races for purposes of voting, without regard for traditional districting principles.'" Such strict scrutiny is triggered whenever race is the "predominate factor" used in districting. Although there is evidence that the redistricting here involved "mixed motives," and especially the desire to protect incumbents, the computer programs used analyzed block-by-block racial data and resulted in oddly shaped districts without attention to traditional concerns of "principles of compactness and regularity." Anytime the use of race is this apparent, the Court has to apply strict scrutiny and to see that any remedies are "narrowly tailored" to their objectives. Neither the state's interest in avoiding liability under the "results" test of the Voting Rights Act, nor its interest in remedying past discrimination, nor the "nonretrogression principle" of the Voting Rights Act (designed to prevent racial minorities from losing ground as a result of redistricting provisions), were compelling enough to justify what Texas has done in this case.

In a separate concurring opinion, O'Connor expressed the view that compliance with the results test of the Voting Rights Act can be a compelling state interest that can coexist with the decision in *Shaw v. Reno* (1993), albeit not by designing oddly shaped districts that ignore "traditional districting principles and deviate substantially from the hypothetical court-drawn district, *for predominantly racial reasons*." In his concurring opinion, *J. Kennedy* argued that the part of the majority decision relating to strict scrutiny was unnecessary to its decision.

J. Stevens argued in dissent that "the Court has misapplied its own tests for racial gerrymandering, both by applying strict scrutiny to all three of these districts, and then by concluding that none can meet that scrutiny." He further argued that in *Shaw v. Reno*, the Court had "struck out into a jurisprudential wilderness that lacks a definable constitutional core and threatens to create harms more significant than any suffered by the individual plaintiffs." In his dissent, *J. Souter* further argued that the majority decision failed "to identify an injury distinguishable from the consequences of concededly constitutional conduct" and further pointed to what he believed to be the arbitrariness of the *Shaw* decision and its progeny.

Bush v. Gore, 531 U.S. 98; 121 S. Ct. 525; 148 L. Ed. 2d 388 (2000)

Facts—After the initial vote count in the Florida presidential election of 2000, electors pledged to Republican candidates George Bush and Dick Cheney led

Democrats Al Gore and Joe Lieberman by a mere 1,784 votes out of more than 4.8 million cast. Because the margin was so close, state law tripped an automatic machine recount, which further reduced Bush's lead. Gore sought manual recounts in selected Florida districts where he thought there may be "undervotes" because of "hanging chads," caused when voting machines did not completely punch through computer cards, leaving open the possibility that counting machines did not record all votes (these were sometimes designated as "undervotes"). The Florida Supreme Court subsequently waived a statutorily imposed deadline of November 14, which the Florida Secretary of State Kathryn Harris attempted to enforce, with the state court initially extending the date to November 26, after which the secretary of state declared Bush and Cheney to be the winners. Gore contested this certification, and the Florida Supreme Court accepted this challenge with respect to Miami-Dade County, ordered that vote counting there be continued, and awarded Gore votes that had been submitted in Palm Beach and Miami Counties after November 26. Because the 2000 presidential electoral vote was so close, the decision in Florida would determine the outcome for the entire nation. This is the second time that the U.S. Supreme Court dealt with this issue; it had previously vacated a November 21 Florida Supreme Court order backing hand counts in selected counties and remanded the case to that court for further consideration.

Question—Did the recounts ordered by the Florida Supreme Court violate the equal protection clause of the Fourteenth Amendment?

Decision—Yes.

Reasons—*Per Curiam* (7–2 on equal protection issue; 5–4 on the issue of stopping the recounts). There is no fundamental right to vote for presidential electors absent state investiture of such action in the people, but once such a right is vested, the right is regarded as fundamental and "equal weight" and "equal dignity" need to be accorded to each vote. Voting rights can be effectively denied by "debasement or dilution" as well as by outright denial. Although Florida's desire to ascertain "the intent of the voter" is "unobjectionable as an abstract proposition," the Florida Court did not set forth "specific standards to ensure its equal application." Different standards were being used to count votes by hand not only among different counties but even within them. For Florida to reach the "safe harbor" prescribed by congressional law (the time before which such votes were considered presumptively valid), the selection of electors must be certified by December 12. This was the date of the U.S. Supreme Court's decision, and further remedies were therefore impossible. Extending the deadlines still further would violate Florida law. The Court majority noted that "when contending parties invoke the process of courts . . . it becomes our unsought responsibility to resolve the federal and constitutional issues the judicial system has been forced to confront."

J. Rehnquist (joined by *J. Scalia* and *J. Thomas*) argued that while in ordinary cases, "comity and respect for federalism" would compel deference to state court decisions, this case involved the election of a U.S. president. Article II, Section 2, clause 2 provided for appointment of state electors according to state legislative direction. The legislature had vested the secretary of state with the power to certify an election. Although the U.S. Supreme Court generally defers to state court interpretations of its laws, here respect for the state legislature required federal intervention. State law distinguished between election protests and electoral contests. The Florida Supreme Court's interpretation of a "legal vote" departed from the legislative scheme for recognizing only ballots that were clearly marked. The court-ordered recount could not be properly carried out and judicially reviewed as ordered by the Florida Supreme Court so that order must be invalidated.

J. Stevens's (joined by *J. Ginsburg* and *J. Breyer*) dissent argued that precedents dictated acceptance of the opinions of state supreme courts in regard to interpretations of state law. The majority opinion elevated the interest in finality over the interest in seeing that all votes were counted. That decision undermined "the Nation's confidence in the judge as the impartial guardian of the rule of law."

J. Souter (with *J. Breyer* and partial votes of *J. Stevens* and *J. Ginsburg*) also dissented. The U.S. Supreme Court should not have issued a stay of the Florida Supreme Court's decision. Although the federal rule sets a "safe harbor" date for a state's certification of votes, it did not require a state to meet it. The Florida Supreme Court had not changed state legislative provisions for voting because those laws also provided for ascertaining voter intent. The Florida court's interpretation of occasions for recounts, while not mandated by state law, was a permissible interpretation of that law. The case should have been remanded to that court with instructions to establish "uniform standards" for counting votes.

J. Ginsburg (with *J. Stevens* and partial agreement by *J. Souter* and *J. Breyer*). If she were interpreting Florida law independently, she might side with the chief justice, but the U.S. Supreme Court had no such obligation to oversee a state supreme court's interpretation of state law. "The Chief Justice contradicts the basic principle that a State may organize itself as it sees fit." Ginsburg did not find a violation of the equal protection clause, and she rejected the court's concern with the December 12th deadline. In a much noted move, Ginsburg left off the traditional "respectfully" in her statement, "I dissent."

J. Breyer (with partial agreement of *J. Stevens, J. Ginsburg,* and *J. Souter*) argued that "The Court was wrong to take this case. It was wrong to grant a stay." Whatever the equal protection concerns, the majority was unwarranted in halting the vote count. The court had no business turning that "presumption that legislatures would want to take advantage of [Sec.] 5's 'safe harbor' provision into a mandate that trumps other statutory provisions and overrides the intent that the legislature did express." The decision in this case was political rather than legal and should be decided by the political branches and according to the guidelines Congress established after the presidential election of 1876. Judicial intervention risked "a self-inflicted wound."

৩৯

Crawford v. Marion County, 128 S. Ct. 1610; 170 L. Ed. 2d 574 (2008)

Facts—William Crawford and other petitioners (including the Indiana Democratic Party) challenged the constitutionality of Indiana's Voter ID Law (SEA 483) that requires citizens voting in person on election day to present photo identification issued by the government or cast a provisional ballot contingent on bringing such identification within 10 days (the state offers free identification to those who can establish their residence and identity). An extensive opinion by a District Court upheld the law as did a divided panel of the Seventh U.S. Court of Appeals.

Question—Does Indiana's Voter ID Law violate the equal protection clause of the Fourteenth Amendment?

Decision—No.

Reasons—*J. Stevens* (6–3). *Harper v. Virginia Bd. of Elections* (1966) established that a state cannot condition voting on payment of a tax, but evenhanded restrictions to protect balloting have been accepted under a balancing test. In the case at hand, Indiana supports its restrictions as measures designed to promote election modernization, avoid voting fraud, and safeguard voter confidence. In establishing the National Voter Registration Act of 1993, Congress attempted both "to increase the number of registered voters and protect the integrity of the electoral process." In some counties, Indiana's voter rolls have been inflated by as much as 41.4 percent. While the federal law did not require voter identification, it was consistent with such a requirement. Although there are no reported examples of voter impersonation in Indiana, there "is no question about the legitimacy or importance of the State's interest in counting only the votes of eligible voters." Safeguarding voter confidence is also a legitimate state objective. Although Indiana's requirement for photo identification is burdensome, it is "mitigated by the fact that, if eligible, voters without photo identification may cast provisional ballots that will ultimately be counted." In balancing the law against its attackers, the Court notes that petitioners have not established the number of voters without photo identification and fails to quantify how many poor or elderly voters are affected. The fact that the law was overwhelmingly supported by Republicans over Democrats is irrelevant as long as the state's interests are "both neutral and sufficiently strong."

J. Scalia, concurring, would prefer to settle the case "on the grounds that petitioners' premise [that the law burdens some voters more than others] is irrelevant and that the burden at issue is minimal and justified." Although the law might have different impacts, it is applied uniformly to all voters and provides state-issued photos for those who lack them. Any "disparate impact" is irrelevant absent "proof of discriminatory intent." An "individual-focused" or "case-by-case approach" encourages undue litigation.

J. Souter, dissenting. The law imposes "nontrivial burdens on the voting rights of tens of thousands of the State's citizens" and is unconstitutionally applying prior balancing standards. Travel costs, fees needed to secure identification, and the like will especially impact "poor, old, and disabled voters who do not drive a car." The state's justifications are unpersuasive and do not reach problems of absentee ballots. The fraud the state is attempting to detect is unlikely to be significant, and while the state claims to be following recommendations of the Carter-Baker Commission, it rejected its phase-in recommendation. "The State's asserted interest in modernizing elections and combating fraud are decidedly modest; at best, they fail to offset the clear inference that thousands of Indiana citizens will be discouraged from voting."

J. Breyer, dissenting. The state's interests must be balanced against the "disproportionate burden upon those eligible voters who lack a driver's license or other statutorily valid form of photo ID." Indiana's requirements go beyond less restrictive photo identification systems adopted by Florida and Georgia, which accept a wider range of identification.

❦

Northwest Austin Municipal Utility District Number One v. Holder, 129 S. Ct. 2504; 174 L. Ed. 2d 140; 2009 U.S. LEXIS 4539 (2009)

Facts—A small utility district with an elected board in Texas was required by Section 5 of the Voting Rights Act of 1965 to get federal preclearance before it could change its elections. A U.S. District Court rejected claims that the utility should be eligible to bypass this provision under the "bailout" provision in Section 4(a) of the Act or that Section 5 was unconstitutional. The district sued Attorney General Holder.

Questions—a) Is the utility district eligible for the bailout provision? b) Is the preclearance provision of the Voting Rights Act justified under Section 2 (the enforcement provision) of the Fifteenth Amendment?

Decisions—a) Yes; b) Issue avoided.

Reasons—*C.J. Roberts* (8 ½ to ½). Roberts largely confines his opinion to statutory construction. Deciding that the district is eligible to pursue the bailout option, he decided not to reach the constitutional question. Roberts did observe that Section 5 of the Voting Rights Act was intended to be temporary, and that the original act of 1965 had been extended to the year 2031. Many of the problems it sought to address had been so addressed. Section 5 had gone beyond the prohibitions of the Fifteenth Amendment, and the data on which it had been based was now dated. Both the "Act's preclearance requirements and its coverage formula raise serious constitutional questions." Although the Court should not "shrink" from its duty, it is proper to decide a case on statutory grounds where the Court can avoid constitutional issues, and past definitions of "political subdivisions" allowed the utility district, and other state subdivisions, to apply for an exemption.

J. Thomas concurred in the judgment but, absent assurance that the utility district would actually receive a bailout, would have held that Section 5 exceeded congressional authority to enforce the Fifteenth Amendment. States had primary authority to structure their electoral systems. The exceptional circumstances that gave rise to Section 5 no longer existed and cannot be justified where evidence of intentional discrimination is lacking. "Punishment for long past sins is not a legitimate basis for imposing a forward-looking preventative measure that has already served its purpose."

MEMBERS OF THE SUPREME COURT
OF THE UNITED STATES, 1789–2010

Chief Justices	State	Dates Served	Appointed by	Born/Died
John Jay	NY	1789–1795	Washington	1745–1829
John Rutledge	SC	1795	Washington	1739–1800
Oliver Ellsworth	CT	1796–1800	Washington	1745–1807
John Marshall	VA	1801–1835	J. Adams	1755–1835
Roger B. Taney	MD	1836–1864	Jackson	1777–1864
Salmon P. Chase	OH	1864–1873	Lincoln	1808–1873
Morrison R. Waite	OH	1874–1888	Grant	1816–1888
Melville W. Fuller	IL	1888–1910	Cleveland	1833–1910
Edward D. White	LA	1910–1921	Taft	1845–1921
William H. Taft	OH	1921–1930	Harding	1857–1930
Charles E. Hughes	NY	1930–1941	Hoover	1862–1948
Harlan F. Stone	NY	1941–1946	F. D. Roosevelt	1872–1946
Fred M. Vinson	KY	1946–1953	Truman	1890–1953
Earl Warren	CA	1953–1969	Eisenhower	1891–1974
Warren Earl Burger	MN	1969–1986	Nixon	1907–1995
William H. Rehnquist	AZ	1986–2005	Reagan	1924–2005
John R. Roberts, Jr.	IN	2005–	G. W. Bush	1955–

Associate Justices	State	Dates Served	Appointed by	Born/Died
John Rutledge	SC	1789–1791	Washington	1739–1800
William Cushing	MA	1789–1810	Washington	1732–1810
James Wilson	PA	1789–1798	Washington	1742–1798
John Blair Jr.	VA	1789–1796	Washington	1732–1800
James Iredell	NC	1790–1799	Washington	1751–1799
Thomas Johnson	MD	1791–1793	Washington	1732–1819
William Paterson	NJ	1793–1806	Washington	1745–1806
Samuel Chase	MD	1796–1811	Washington	1741–1811

Associate Justices	State	Dates Served	Appointed by	Born/Died
Bushrod Washington	VA	1798–1829	J. Adams	1762–1829
Alfred Moore	NC	1799–1804	J. Adams	1755–1810
William Johnson	SC	1804–1834	Jefferson	1771–1834
Henry B. Livingston	NY	1806–1823	Jefferson	1757–1823
Thomas Dodd	KY	1807–1826	Jefferson	1765–1826
Joseph Story	MA	1811–1845	Madison	1779–1845
Gabriel Duval	MD	1812–1835	Madison	1752–1844
Smith Thompson	NY	1823–1843	Monroe	1768–1843
Robert Trimble	KY	1826–1828	J. Q. Adams	1777–1828
John McLean	OH	1829–1861	Jackson	1785–1861
Henry Baldwin	PA	1830–1844	Jackson	1780–1844
James M. Wayne	GA	1835–1867	Jackson	1790–1867
Philip P. Barbour	VA	1836–1841	Jackson	1783–1841
John Catron	TN	1837–1865	Jackson	1786–1865
John McKinley	AL	1837–1852	Van Buren	1780–1852
Peter V. Daniel	VA	1841–1860	Van Buren	1784–1860
Samuel Nelson	NY	1845–1872	Tyler	1792–1873
Levi Woodbury	NH	1846–1851	Polk	1789–1851
Robert C. Grier	PA	1846–1870	Polk	1794–1870
Benjamin R. Curtis	MA	1851–1857	Fillmore	1809–1874
John A. Campbell	AL	1853–1861	Pierce	1811–1889
Nathan Clifford	ME	1858–1881	Buchanan	1803–1881
Noah H. Swayne	OH	1862–1881	Lincoln	1804–1884
Samuel F. Miller	IA	1862–1890	Lincoln	1816–1890
David Davis	IL	1862–1877	Lincoln	1815–1886
Stephen J. Field	CA	1863–1897	Lincoln	1816–1899
William Strong	PA	1870–1880	Grant	1808–1895
Joseph R. Bradley	NJ	1870–1892	Grant	1813–1892
Ward Hunt	NY	1872–1882	Grant	1810–1886
John M. Harlan	KY	1877–1911	Hayes	1833–1911
William B. Woods	GA	1880–1887	Hayes	1824–1887
Stanley Matthews	OH	1881–1889	Garfield	1824–1889
Horace Gray	MA	1881–1902	Arthur	1828–1902
Samuel Blatchford	NY	1882–1893	Arthur	1820–1893
Lucius Q. C. Lamar	MS	1888–1893	Cleveland	1825–1893
David J. Brewer	KS	1889–1910	Harrison	1837–1910
Henry B. Brown	MI	1890–1906	Harrison	1836–1913
George Shiras Jr.	PA	1892–1903	Harrison	1832–1924
Howell E. Jackson	TN	1893–1895	Harrison	1832–1895
Edward D. White*	LA	1894–1910	Cleveland	1845–1921
Rufus W. Peckham	NY	1895–1909	Cleveland	1838–1909
Joseph McKenna	CA	1898–1925	McKinley	1843–1926
Oliver W. Holmes Jr.	MA	1902–1932	T. Roosevelt	1841–1935

Associate Justices	State	Dates Served	Appointed by	Born/Died
William R. Day	OH	1903–1922	T. Roosevelt	1849–1923
William H. Moody	MA	1906–1910	T. Roosevelt	1853–1917
Horace H. Lurton	TN	1909–1914	Taft	1844–1914
Charles E. Hughes*	NY	1910–1916	Taft	1862–1948
Willis Van Devanter	WY	1910–1937	Taft	1859–1941
Joseph R. Lamar	GA	1910–1916	Taft	1857–1916
Mahlon Pitney	NJ	1912–1922	Taft	1858–1924
James C. McReynolds	TN	1914–1941	Wilson	1862–1946
Louis D. Brandeis	MA	1916–1939	Wilson	1856–1941
John H. Clarke	OH	1916–1922	Wilson	1857–1945
George Sutherland	UT	1922–1938	Harding	1862–1942
Pierce Butler	MN	1922–1939	Harding	1866–1939
Edward Sanford	TN	1923–1930	Harding	1865–1930
Harlan F. Stone*	NY	1925–1941	Coolidge	1872–1946
Owen J. Roberts	PA	1930–1945	Hoover	1875–1955
Benjamin N. Cardozo	NY	1932–1938	Hoover	1870–1938
Hugo L. Black	AL	1937–1971	F. D. Roosevelt	1886–1971
Stanley F. Reed	KY	1938–1957	F. D. Roosevelt	1884–1980
Felix Frankfurter	MA	1939–1962	F. D. Roosevelt	1882–1965
William O. Douglas	CT	1939–1975	F. D. Roosevelt	1898–1980
Frank Murphy	MI	1940–1949	F. D. Roosevelt	1890–1949
James F. Byrnes	SC	1941–1942	F. D. Roosevelt	1879–1972
Robert H. Jackson	NY	1941–1954	F. D. Roosevelt	1892–1954
Wiley B. Rutledge Jr.	IA	1943–1949	F. D. Roosevelt	1894–1949
Harold H. Burton	OH	1945–1958	Truman	1888–1964
Tom C. Clark	TX	1949–1967	Truman	1890–1977
Sherman Minton	IN	1949–1956	Truman	1890–1965
John M. Harlan	NY	1955–1971	Eisenhower	1899–1971
William J. Brennan Jr.	NJ	1956–1990	Eisenhower	1906–1997
Charles E. Whittaker	MO	1957–1962	Eisenhower	1901–1972
Potter Stewart	OH	1958–1981	Eisenhower	1915–1985
Byron R. White	CO	1962–1993	Kennedy	1917–2002
Arthur J. Goldberg	IL	1962–1965	Kennedy	1908–1990
Abe Fortas	TN	1965–1969	Johnson	1910–1982
Thurgood Marshall	MD	1967–1991	Johnson	1908–1993
Harry A. Blackmun	MN	1970–1994	Nixon	1908–1999
Lewis F. Powell Jr.	VA	1972–1987	Nixon	1907–1998
William H. Rehnquist*	AZ	1972–1986	Nixon	1924–2005
John Paul Stevens**	IL	1975–2010	Ford	1920–
Sandra Day O'Connor	AZ	1981–2006	Reagan	1930–
Antonin Scalia	VA	1986–	Reagan	1936–
Anthony Kennedy	CA	1987–	Reagan	1936–

Associate Justices	State	Dates Served	Appointed by	Born/Died
David Souter	NH	1990–2009	G. H. W. Bush	1939–
Clarence Thomas	VA	1991–	G. H. W. Bush	1948–
Ruth Bader Ginsburg	DC	1993–	Clinton	1933–
Steven G. Breyer	MA	1994–	Clinton	1938–
Samuel A. Alito, Jr.	NJ	2006–	G. W. Bush	1950–
Sonia Sotomayor	NY	2009–	Obama	1954–

*After serving as Associate Justice was appointed Chief Justice.

**At the time of publication of this book, Justice Stevens had announced that he would be stepping down from the Court as of the 2010 summer recess.

The Constitution of the United States

Signed September 17, 1787
Effective March 4, 1789

We the people of the United States, in order to form a more perfect union, establish justice, insure domestic tranquility, provide for the common defense, promote the general welfare, and secure the blessings of liberty to ourselves and our posterity, do ordain and establish this Constitution for the United States of America.

ARTICLE I

Section 1. All legislative powers herein granted shall be vested in a Congress of the United States, which shall consist of a Senate and House of Representatives.

Section 2. 1. The House of Representatives shall be composed of members chosen every second year by the people of the several states, and the electors in each state shall have the qualifications requisite for electors of the most numerous branch of the state legislature.

2. No person shall be a representative who shall not have attained to the age of twenty-five years, and been seven years a citizen of the United States, and who shall not, when elected, be an inhabitant of that state in which he shall be chosen.

3. [*Representatives and direct taxes shall be apportioned among the several states which may be included within this union, according to their respective numbers, which shall be determined by adding to the whole number of free persons, including those bound to service for a term of years, and excluding Indians not taxed, three-fifths of all other persons.*]* The actual

---

* Changed by Sec. 2 of the Fourteenth Amendment.

enumeration shall be made within three years after the first meeting of the Congress of the United States, and within every subsequent term of ten years, in such manner as they shall by law direct. The number of representatives shall not exceed one for every thirty thousand, but each state shall have at least one representative; and until such enumeration shall be made, the state of New Hampshire shall be entitled to choose three, Massachusetts eight, Rhode Island and Providence plantations one, Connecticut five, New York six, New Jersey four, Pennsylvania eight, Delaware one, Maryland six, Virginia ten, North Carolina five, South Carolina five, and Georgia three.

4. When vacancies happen in the representation from any state, the executive authority thereof shall issue writs of election to fill such vacancies.

5. The House of Representatives shall choose their speaker and other officers; and shall have the sole power of impeachment.

Section 3. 1. The Senate of the United States shall be composed of two senators from each state, [*chosen by the legislature thereof*]* for six years; and each senator shall have one vote.

2. Immediately after they shall be assembled in consequence of the first election, they shall be divided as equally as may be into three classes. The seats of the senators of the first class shall be vacated at the expiration of the second year, of the second class at the expiration of the fourth year, and of the third class at the expiration of the sixth year, so that one third may be chosen every second year; [*and if vacancies happen by resignation, or otherwise, during the recess of the legislature of any state, the executive thereof may make temporary appointments until the next meeting of the legislature, which shall then fill such vacancies.*]**

3. No person shall be a senator who shall not have attained to the age of thirty years, and been nine years a citizen of the United States, and who shall not, when elected, be an inhabitant of that state for which he shall be chosen.

4. The vice-president of the United States shall be president of the Senate, but shall have no vote, unless they be equally divided.

5. The Senate shall choose their other officers, and also a president pro tempore, in the absence of the vice-president, or when he shall exercise the office of the president of the United States.

6. The Senate shall have the sole power to try all impeachments. When sitting for that purpose, they shall be on oath or affirmation. When the president of the United States is tried, the chief justice shall preside: and no person shall be convicted without the concurrence of two thirds of the members present.

7. Judgment in cases of impeachment shall not extend further than to removal from office, and disqualifications to hold and enjoy any office of

* Changed by the Seventeenth Amendment.
** Changed by the Seventeenth Amendment.

honor, trust or profit under the United States: but the party convicted shall nevertheless be liable and subject to indictment, trial, judgment and punishment, according to law.

Section 4. 1. The times, places, and manner of holding elections for senators and representatives, shall be prescribed in each state by the legislature thereof; but the Congress may at any time by law make or alter such regulations, except as to the places of choosing senators.

2. The Congress shall assemble at least once in every year, and such meeting shall be [*on the first Monday in December*],* unless they shall by law appoint a different day.

Section 5. 1. Each House shall be the judge of the elections, returns and qualifications of its own members, and a majority of each shall constitute a quorum to do business; but a smaller number may adjourn from day to day, and may be authorized to compel the attendance of absent members, in such manner, and under such penalties as each House may provide.

2. Each House may determine the rules of its proceedings, punish its members for disorderly behavior, and, with the concurrence of two thirds, expel a member.

3. Each House shall keep a journal of its proceedings, and from time to time publish the same, excepting such parts as may in their judgment require secrecy; and the yeas and nays of the members of either House on any question shall, at the desire of one fifth of those present, be entered on the journal.

4. Neither House, during the session of Congress, shall, without the consent of the other, adjourn for more than three days, nor to any other place than that in which the two Houses shall be sitting.

Section 6. 1. The senators and representatives shall receive a compensation for their services, to be ascertained by law, and paid out of the treasury of the United States. They shall in all cases, except treason, felony, and breach of the peace, be privileged from arrest during their attendance at the session of their respective Houses, and in going to and returning from the same; and for any speech or debate in either House, they shall not be questioned in any other place.

2. No senator or representative shall, during the time for which he was elected, be appointed to any civil office under the authority of the United States, which shall have been created, or the emoluments whereof shall have been increased during such time; and no person holding any office under the United States shall be a member of either House during his continuance in office.

Section 7. 1. All bills for raising revenue shall originate in the House of Representatives; but the Senate may propose or concur with amendments as on other bills.

---

* Changed by Sec. 2 of the Twentieth Amendment.

2. Every bill which shall have passed the House of Representatives and the Senate, shall, before it becomes a law, be presented to the president of the United States; if he approves he shall sign it, but if not he shall return it, with his objections to that House in which it shall have originated, who shall enter the objections at large on their journal, and proceed to reconsider it. If after such reconsideration two thirds of that House shall agree to pass the bill, it shall be sent, together with the objections, to the other House, by which it shall likewise be reconsidered, and if approved by two thirds of that House, it shall become a law. But in all such cases the votes of both Houses shall be determined by yeas and nays, and the names of the persons voting for and against the bill shall be entered on the journal of each House respectively. If any bill shall not be returned by the president within ten days (Sundays excepted) after it shall have been presented to him, the same shall be a law, in like manner as if he had signed it, unless the Congress by their adjournment prevent its return, in which case it shall not be a law.

3. Every order, resolution, or vote to which the concurrence of the Senate and the House of Representatives may be necessary (except on a question of adjournment) shall be presented to the president of the United States; and before the same shall take effect, shall be approved by him, or being disapproved by him, shall be repassed by two thirds of the Senate and House of Representatives, according to the rules and limitations prescribed in the case of a bill.

Section 8. The Congress shall have the power:

1. To lay and collect taxes, duties, imposts, and excises, to pay the debts and provide for the common defense and general welfare of the United States; but all duties, imposts, and excises shall be uniform throughout the United States;

2. To borrow money on the credit of the United States;

3. To regulate commerce with foreign nations, and among the several States, and with the Indian tribes;

4. To establish a uniform rule of naturalization, and uniform laws on the subject of bankruptcies throughout the United States;

5. To coin money, regulate the value thereof, and of foreign coin, and fix the standard of weights and measures;

6. To provide for the punishment of counterfeiting the securities and current coin of the United States;

7. To establish post offices and post roads;

8. To promote the progress of science and useful arts, by securing for limited times to authors and inventors the exclusive right to their respective writings and discoveries;

9. To constitute tribunals inferior to the Supreme Court;

10. To define and punish piracies and felonies committed on the high seas, and offenses against the law of nations;

11. To declare war, grant letters of marque and reprisal, and make rules concerning captures on land and water;

12. To raise and support armies, but no appropriation of money to that use shall be for a longer term than two years;

13. To provide and maintain a navy;

14. To make rules for the government and regulation of the land and naval forces;

15. To provide for calling forth the militia to execute the laws of the Union, suppress insurrections and repel invasions;

16. To provide for organizing, arming, and disciplining the militia, and for governing such part of them as may be employed in the service of the United States, reserving to the States respectively, the appointment of the officers, and the authority of training the militia according to the discipline prescribed by Congress.

17. To exercise exclusive legislation in all cases whatsoever, over such district (not exceeding ten miles square) as may, by cession of particular states, and the acceptance of Congress, become the seat of the government of the United States, and to exercise like authority over all places purchased by the consent of the legislature of the state in which the same shall be, for the erection of forts, magazines, arsenals, dockyards, and other needful buildings; and

18. To make all laws which shall be necessary and proper for carrying into execution the foregoing powers, and all other powers vested by this Constitution in the government of the United States, or in any department or officer thereof.

Section 9. 1. The migration or importation of such persons as any of the states now existing shall think proper to admit, shall not be prohibited by the Congress prior to the year one thousand eight hundred and eight, but a tax or duty may be imposed on such importation, not exceeding ten dollars for each person.

2. The privilege of the writ of habeas corpus shall not be suspended, unless when in cases of rebellion or invasion the public safety may require it.

3. No bill of attainder or ex post facto law shall be passed.

4. [*No capitation, or other direct, tax shall be laid, unless in proportion to the census or enumeration herein before directed to be taken.*]*

5. No tax or duty shall be laid on articles exported from any State.

6. No preference shall be given by any regulation of commerce or revenue to the ports of one state over those of another: nor shall vessels bound to, or from, one state be obliged to enter, clear, or pay duties in another.

7. No money shall be drawn from the treasury, but in consequence of appropriations made by law; and a regular statement and account of the receipts and expenditures of all public money shall be published from time to time.

---

* Changed by the Sixteenth Amendment.

8. No title of nobility shall be granted by the United States: and no person holding any office of profit or trust under them, shall, without the consent of the Congress, accept of any present, emolument, office, or title, of any kind whatever, from any king, prince, or foreign state.

Section 10. 1. No state shall enter into any treaty, alliance, or confederation; grant letters of marque and reprisal; coin money; emit bills of credit; make anything but gold and silver coin a tender in payment of debts; pass any bill of attainder, ex post facto law, or law impairing the obligation of contracts, or grant any title of nobility.

2. No state shall, without the consent of the Congress, lay any imposts or duties on imports or exports, except what may be absolutely necessary for executing its inspection laws: and the net produce of all duties and imposts laid by any state on imports or exports, shall be for the use of the treasury of the United States; and all such laws shall be subject to the revision and control of the Congress.

3. No state shall, without the consent of the Congress, lay any duty of tonnage, keep troops, or ships of war in time of peace, enter into any agreement or compact with another state, or with a foreign power, or engage in war, unless actually invaded, or in such imminent danger as will not admit of delay.

ARTICLE II

Section 1. 1. The executive power shall be vested in a president of the United States of America. He shall hold his office during the term of four years, and, together with the vice-president, chosen for the same term, be elected as follows:

2. Each state shall appoint, in such manner as the legislature thereof may direct, a number of electors, equal to the whole number of senators and representatives to which the state may be entitled in the Congress: but no senator or representative, or person holding an office of trust or profit under the United States, shall be appointed an elector.

3. [*The electors shall meet in their respective states, and vote by ballot for two persons, of whom one at least shall not be an inhabitant of the same state with themselves. And they shall make a list of all the persons voted for, and of the number of votes for each; which list they shall sign and certify, and transmit sealed to the seat of the government of the United States, directed to the president of the Senate. The president of the Senate shall, in the presence of the Senate and House of Representatives, open all the certificates, and the votes shall then be counted. The person having the greatest number of votes shall be the president, if such number be a majority of the whole number of electors appointed; and*

if there be more than one who have such majority, and have an equal number of votes, then the House of Representatives shall immediately choose by ballot one of them for president; and if no person have a majority, then from the five highest on the list the said House shall in like manner choose the president. But in choosing the president, the votes shall be taken by states, the representation from each state having one vote; a quorum for this purpose shall consist of a member or members from two thirds of the states, and a majority of all the states shall be necessary to a choice. In every case, after the choice of the president, the person having the greatest number of votes of the electors shall be the vice-president. But if there should remain two or more who have equal votes, the Senate shall choose from them by ballot the vice president.]*

3. The Congress may determine the time of choosing the electors, and the day on which they shall give their votes; which day shall be the same throughout the United States.

4. No person except a natural born citizen, or a citizen of the United States, at the time of the adoption of this Constitution, shall be eligible to the office of president; neither shall any person be eligible to that office who shall not have attained to the age of thirty-five years, and been fourteen years a resident within the United States.

5. [*In case of the removal of the president from office, or of his death, resignation, or inability to discharge the powers and duties of the said office, the same shall devolve on the vice president, and the Congress may by law provide for the case of removal, death, resignation, or inability, both of the president and vice-president, declaring what officer shall then act as president, and such officer shall act accordingly, until the disability be removed, or a president shall be elected.*]**

6. The president shall, at stated times, receive for his services a compensation, which shall neither be increased nor diminished during the period for which he shall have been elected, and he shall not receive within that period any other emolument from the United States, or any of them.

7. Before he enter on the execution of his office, he shall take the following oath or affirmation:—"I do solemnly swear (or affirm) that I will faithfully execute the office of president of the United States, and will to the best of my ability, preserve, protect and defend the Constitution of the United States."

Section 2. 1. The president shall be commander in chief of the army and navy of the United States, and of the militia of the several states, when called into the actual service of the United States; he may require the opinion, in writing, of the principal officer in each of the executive departments, upon

---

* Changed by the Twelfth Amendment.
** Changed by the Twenty-fifth Amendment.

any subject relating to the duties of their respective offices,* and he shall have power to grant reprieves and pardons for offenses against the United States, except in cases of impeachment.

2. He shall have power, by and with the advice and consent of the Senate, to make treaties, provided two thirds of the senators present concur; and he shall nominate, and by and with the advice and consent of the Senate, shall appoint ambassadors, other public ministers and consuls, judges of the Supreme Court, and all other officers of the United States, whose appointments are not herein otherwise provided for, and which shall be established by law: but the Congress may by law vest the appointment of such inferior officers, as they think proper, in the president alone, in the courts of law, or in the heads of departments.

3. The president shall have power to fill up all vacancies that may happen during the recess of the Senate, by granting commissions which shall expire at the end of their next session.

Section 3. He shall from time to time give to the Congress information of the state of the Union, and recommend to their consideration such measures as he shall judge necessary and expedient; he may, on extraordinary occasions, convene both Houses, or either of them, and in case of disagreement between them with respect to the time of adjournment, he may adjourn them to such time as he shall think proper; he shall receive ambassadors and other public ministers; he shall take care that the laws be faithfully executed, and shall commission all the officers of the United States.

Section 4. The president, vice-president, and all civil officers of the United States, shall be removed from office on impeachment for, and conviction of, treason, bribery, or other high crimes and misdemeanors.

ARTICLE III

Section 1. The judicial power of the United States shall be vested in one Supreme Court, and in such inferior courts as the Congress may from time to time ordain and establish. The judges, both of the Supreme and inferior courts, shall hold their offices during good behavior, and shall, at stated times, receive for their services, a compensation, which, shall not be diminished during their continuance in office.

Section 2. 1. The judicial power shall extend to all cases, in law and equity, arising under this Constitution, the laws of the United States, and treaties made, or which shall be made, under their authority;—to all cases affecting ambassadors, other public ministers and consuls;—to all cases of admiralty and maritime jurisdiction;—to controversies to which the United States shall

---

* Superseded by the Twelfth Amendment.

be a party;—to controversies between two or more states; [*between a state and citizens of another state;—*]* between citizens of different states;—between citizens of the same state claiming lands under grants of different states, and between a state, or the citizens thereof, and foreign states, citizens or subjects.

2. In all cases affecting ambassadors, other public ministers and consuls, and those in which a state shall be party, the Supreme Court shall have original jurisdiction. In all the other cases before mentioned, the Supreme Court shall have appellate jurisdiction, both as to law and to fact, with such exceptions, and under such regulations as the Congress shall make.

3. The trial of all crimes, except in cases of impeachment, shall be by jury; and such trial shall be held in the state where the said crimes shall have been committed; but when not committed within any state, the trial shall be at such place or places as the Congress may by law have directed.

Section 3. 1. Treason against the United States shall consist only in levying war against them, or in adhering to their enemies, giving them aid and comfort. No person shall be convicted of treason unless on the testimony of two witnesses to the same overt act, or on confession in open court.

2. The Congress shall have power to declare the punishment of treason, but no attainder of treason shall work corruption of blood, or forfeiture except during the life of the person attainted.**

ARTICLE IV

Section 1. Full faith and credit shall be given in each state to the public acts, records, and judicial proceedings of every other state. And the Congress may by general laws prescribe the manner in which such acts, records and proceedings shall be proved, and the effect thereof.

Section 2. 1. The citizens of each state shall be entitled to all privileges and immunities of citizens in the several states.***

2. A person charged in any state with treason, felony, or other crime, who shall flee from justice, and be found in another state, shall on demand of the executive attorney of the state from which he fled, be delivered up, to be removed to the state having jurisdiction of the crime.

3. [*No person held to service or labor in one state under the laws thereof, escaping into another, shall in consequence of any law or regulation therein, be discharged from such service or labor, but shall be delivered up on claim of the party to whom such service or labor may be due.*]****

---

* Changed by the Eleventh Amendment.
** See the Eleventh Amendment.
*** See the Fourteenth Amendment, Sec. 1.
**** Changed by the Thirteenth Amendment.

Section 3. 1. New states may be admitted by the Congress into this Union; but no new state shall be formed or erected within the jurisdiction of any other state, nor any state be formed by the junction of two or more states, or parts of states, without the consent of the legislatures of the states concerned as well as of the Congress.

2. The Congress shall have power to dispose of and make all needful rules and regulations respecting the territory or other property belonging to the United States; and nothing in this Constitution shall be so construed as to prejudice any claims of the United States, or of any particular state.

Section 4. The United States shall guarantee to every state in this Union a republican form of government, and shall protect each of them against invasion; and on application of the legislature, or of the executive (when the legislature cannot be convened) against domestic violence.

ARTICLE V

The Congress, whenever two thirds of both Houses shall deem it necessary, shall propose amendments to this Constitution, or, on the application of the legislatures of two thirds of the several states, shall call a convention for proposing amendments, which in either case, shall be valid to all intents and purposes, as part of this Constitution when ratified by the legislatures of three fourths of the several states, or by conventions in three fourths thereof, as the one or the other mode of ratification may be proposed by the Congress; Provided that no amendment which may be made prior to the year one thousand eight hundred and eight shall in any manner affect the first and fourth clauses in the ninth section of the first article; and that no state, without its consent, shall be deprived of its equal suffrage in the Senate.

ARTICLE VI

1. All debts contracted and engagements entered into, before the adoption of this Constitution, shall be as valid against the United States under this Constitution, as under the Confederation.*

2. This Constitution, and the laws of the United States which shall be made in pursuance thereof; and all treaties made, or which shall be made, under the authority of the United States, shall be the supreme law of the land; and the Judges in every state shall be bound thereby, anything in the Constitution or laws of any state to the contrary notwithstanding.

---

* See the Fourteenth Amendment, Sec. 4.

3. The senators and representatives before mentioned, and the members of the several state legislatures, and all executive and judicial officers, both of the United States and of the several states, shall be bound by oath or affirmation to support this Constitution; but no religious test shall ever be required as a qualification to any office or public trust under the United States.

ARTICLE VII

The ratification of the conventions of nine states shall be sufficient for the establishment of this Constitution between the states so ratifying the same.

Done in Convention by the unanimous consent of the States present the seventeenth day of September in the year of our Lord one thousand seven hundred and eighty-seven, and of the independence of the United States of America the twelfth. In witness whereof we have hereunto subscribed our names. [Names omitted]

Articles in addition to, and amendment of, the Constitution of the United States of America, proposed by Congress, and ratified by the legislatures of the several states pursuant to the fifth article of the original Constitution.

AMENDMENTS
First Ten Amendments proposed by Congress Sept. 25, 1789.
Ratified by three-fourths of the States December 15, 1791.

ARTICLE I

Congress shall make no law respecting an establishment of religion, or prohibiting the free exercise thereof; or abridging the freedom of speech, or of the press; or the right of the people peaceably to assemble, and to petition the government for a redress of grievances.

ARTICLE II

A well regulated militia, being necessary to the security of a free state, the right of the people to keep and bear arms, shall not be infringed.

ARTICLE III

No soldier shall, in time of peace be quartered in any house, without the consent of the owner, nor in time of war, but in a manner to be prescribed by law.

ARTICLE IV

The right of the people to be secure in their persons, houses, papers, and effects, against unreasonable searches and seizures, shall not be violated, and no warrants shall issue, but upon probable cause, supported by oath or affirmation, and particularly describing the place to be searched, and the persons or things to be seized.

ARTICLE V

No person shall be held to answer for a capital, or otherwise infamous crime, unless on a presentment or indictment of a grand jury, except in cases arising in the land or naval forces, or in the militia, when in actual service in time of war or public danger; nor shall any person be subject for the same offense to be twice put in jeopardy of life or limb; nor shall be compelled in any criminal case to be a witness against himself, nor be deprived of life, liberty, or property, without due process of law: nor shall private property be taken for public use without just compensation.

ARTICLE VI

In all criminal prosecutions, the accused shall enjoy the right to a speedy and public trial, by an impartial jury of the state and district wherein the crime shall have been committed, which district shall have been previously ascertained by law, and to be informed of the nature and cause of the accusation; to be confronted with the witnesses against him; to have compulsory process for obtaining witnesses in his favor, and to have the assistance of counsel for his defense.

ARTICLE VII

In suits at common law, where the value in controversy shall exceed twenty dollars, the right of trial by jury shall be preserved, and no fact tried by a jury shall be otherwise reexamined in any court of the United States, than according to the rules of the common law.

ARTICLE VIII

Excessive bail shall not be required, nor excessive fines imposed, nor cruel and unusual punishments inflicted.

ARTICLE IX

The enumeration in the Constitution of certain rights shall not be construed to deny or disparage others retained by the people.

ARTICLE X

The powers not delegated to the United States by the Constitution, nor prohibited by it to the states, are reserved to the states respectively, or to the people.

ARTICLE XI

Proposed by Congress March 5, 1794. Ratified January 8, 1798.

The judicial power of the United States shall not be construed to extend to any suit in law or equity, commenced or prosecuted against one of the United States by citizens of another state, or by citizens or subjects of any foreign state.

ARTICLE XII

Proposed by Congress December 12, 1803. Ratified September 25, 1804.

The electors shall meet in their respective states, and vote by ballot for president and vice-president, one of whom, at least, shall not be an inhabitant of the same state with themselves; they shall name in their ballots the person voted for as president, and in distinct ballots, the person voted for as vice-president, and they shall make distinct lists of all persons voted for as president and of all persons voted for as vice-president, and of the number of votes for each, which lists they shall sign and certify, and transmit sealed to the seat of the government of the United States, directed to the president of the Senate;—The president of the Senate shall, in the presence of the Senate and House of Representatives, open all the certificates and the votes shall then be counted;—The person having the greatest number of votes for president, shall be the president, if such number be a majority of the whole number of electors appointed; and if no person have such majority, then from the persons having the highest numbers not exceeding three on the list of those voted for as president, the House of Representatives shall choose immediately, by ballot, the president. But in choosing the president, the votes shall be taken by states, the representation from each state having one vote; a quorum for this purpose shall consist of a member or members from two thirds of the states, and a majority of all the states shall be necessary to a choice. [*And if the House of Representatives shall not choose a president whenever the right of choice shall devolve upon them, before the fourth day of March next following, then the vice-president shall act as president, as in the case of the death or other constitutional disability of the president.*]* The person having the greatest number of votes as vice-president shall be the vice-president, if such number be a majority of the whole number of electors appointed, and if no person have a majority, then from the two highest numbers on the list, the Senate shall choose the vice-president; a quorum for the purpose shall consist of two thirds of the whole number of Senators, and a majority of the whole number shall be necessary to a choice. But no person constitutionally ineligible to the office of president shall be eligible to that of vice-president of the United States.

ARTICLE XIII

Proposed by Congress February 1, 1865. Ratified December 18, 1865.

Section 1. Neither slavery nor involuntary servitude, except as punishment for crime whereof the party shall have been duly convicted, shall exist within the United States, or any place subject to their jurisdiction.

Section 2. Congress shall have power to enforce this article by appropriate legislation.

ARTICLE XIV

Proposed by Congress June 16, 1866. Ratified July 23, 1868.

Section 1. All persons born or naturalized in the United States, and subject to the jurisdiction thereof, are citizens of the United States and of the state wherein they reside. No state shall make or enforce any law which shall abridge the privileges or immunities of citizens of the United States; nor shall any state deprive any person of life, liberty, or property, without due process

---

* Superseded by Sec. 3 of the Twentieth Amendment.

of law; nor deny to any person within its jurisdiction the equal protection of the laws.

Section 2. Representatives shall be apportioned among the several states according to their respective numbers, counting the whole number of persons in each state, excluding Indians not taxed. But when the right to vote at any election for the choice of electors for president and vice-president of the United States, representatives in Congress, the executive and judicial officers of a state, or the members of the legislature thereof, is denied to any of the male inhabitants of such state, being twenty-one years of age, and citizens of the United States, or in any way abridged, except for participation in rebellion, or other crime, the basis of representation therein shall be reduced in the proportion which the number of such male citizens shall bear to the whole number of male citizens twenty-one years of age in such state.·

Section 3. No person shall be a senator or representative in Congress, or elector of president and vice president, or hold any office, civil or military, under the United States, or under any state, who having previously taken an oath, as a member of Congress, or as an officer of the United States, or as a member of any state legislature, or as an executive or judicial officer of any state, to support the Constitution of the United States, shall have engaged in insurrection or rebellion against the same, or given aid or comfort to the enemies thereof. But Congress may by a vote of two thirds of each House, remove such disability.

Section 4. The validity of the public debt of the United States, authorized by law, including debts incurred for payment of pensions and bounties for services in suppressing insurrection or rebellion, shall not be questioned. But neither the United States nor any state shall assume or pay any debt or obligation incurred in aid of insurrection or rebellion against the United States, or any claim for the loss or emancipation of any slave; but all such debts, obligations, and claims shall be held illegal and void.

Section 5. The Congress shall have power to enforce, by appropriate legislation, the provisions of this article.

ARTICLE XV

Proposed by Congress February 27, 1869. Ratified March 30, 1870.

Section 1. The right of citizens of the United States to vote shall not be denied or abridged by the United States or by any state on account of race, color, or previous condition of servitude.

Section 2. The Congress shall have power to enforce this article by appropriate legislation.

ARTICLE XVI

Proposed by Congress July 12, 1909. Ratified February 25, 1913.

The Congress shall have power to lay and collect taxes on incomes, from whatever source derived, without apportionment among the several states, and without regard to any census or enumeration.

ARTICLE XVII

Proposed by Congress May 16, 1912. Ratified May 31, 1913.

The Senate of the United States shall be composed of two senators from each state, elected by the people thereof, for six years; and each senator shall have one vote. The electors in each state shall have the qualifications requisite for electors of the most numerous branch of the state legislature.

When vacancies happen in the representation of any state in the Senate, the executive authority of such state shall issue writs of election to fill such vacancies: Provided, That the legislature of any state may empower the executive thereof to make temporary appointments until the people fill the vacancies by election as the legislature may direct.

This amendment shall not be so construed as to affect the election or term of any senator chosen before it becomes valid as part of the Constitution.

ARTICLE XVIII

Proposed by Congress December 17, 1917. Ratified January 29, 1919.

Section 1. [*After one year from the ratification of this article, the manufacture, sale, or transportation of intoxicating liquors within, the importation thereof into, or the exportation thereof from the United States and all territory subject to the jurisdiction thereof for beverage purposes is hereby prohibited.*]

Section 2. [*The Congress and the several states shall have concurrent power to enforce this article by appropriate legislation.*]

Section 3. [*This article shall be inoperative unless it shall have been ratified as an amendment to the Constitution by the legislatures of the several states, as provided in the Constitution, within seven years from the date of the submission hereof to the states by Congress.*][*]

---

* Repealed by the Twenty-first Amendment.

ARTICLE XIX

Proposed by Congress June 5, 1919. Ratified August 26, 1920.

The right of citizens of the United States to vote shall not be denied or abridged by the United States or by any state on account of sex.

The Congress shall have power by appropriate legislation to enforce the provisions of this article.

ARTICLE XX

Proposed by Congress March 3, 1932. Ratified January 23, 1933.

Section 1. The terms of the president and vice-president shall end at noon on the 20th day of January, and the terms of Senators and Representatives at noon on the 3d day of January, of the years in which such terms would have ended if this article had not been ratified; and the terms of their successors shall then begin.

Section 2. The Congress shall assemble at least once in every year, and such meeting shall begin at noon on the 3d day of January, unless they shall by law appoint a different day.

Section 3. If, at the time fixed for the beginning of the term of the president, the president-elect shall have died, the vice-president-elect shall become president. If a president shall not have been chosen before the time fixed for the beginning of his term, or if the president-elect shall have failed to qualify, then the vice-president-elect shall act as president until a president shall have qualified; and the Congress may by law provide for the case wherein neither a president-elect nor a vice-president-elect shall have qualified, declaring who shall then act as president, or the manner in which one who is to act shall be selected, and such person shall act accordingly until a president or vice-president shall have qualified.

Section 4. The Congress may by law provide for the case of the death of any of the persons from whom the House of Representatives may choose a president whenever the right of choice shall have devolved upon them, and for the case of the death of any of the persons from whom the Senate may choose a vice-president whenever the right of choice shall have devolved upon them.

Section 5. Sections 1 and 2 shall take effect on the 15th day of October following the ratification of this article.

Section 6. This article shall be inoperative unless it shall have been ratified as an amendment to the Constitution by the legislatures of three-fourths of the several states within seven years from the date of its submission.

ARTICLE XXI

Proposed by Congress February 20, 1933. Ratified December 5, 1933.

Section 1. The Eighteenth Article of amendment to the Constitution of the United States is hereby repealed.

Section 2. The transportation or importation into any state, territory, or possession of the United States for delivery or use therein of intoxicating liquors in violation of the laws thereof, is hereby prohibited.

Section 3. This article shall be inoperative unless it shall have been ratified as an amendment to the Constitution by conventions in the several states, as provided in the Constitution, within seven years from the date of the submission thereof to the states by the Congress.

ARTICLE XXII

Proposed by Congress March 24, 1947. Ratified February 26, 1951.

Section 1. No person shall be elected to the office of the president more than twice, and no person who has held the office of president, or acted as president, for more than two years of a term to which some other person was elected president shall be elected to the office of the president more than once. But this article shall not apply to any person holding the office of president when this article was proposed by the Congress, and shall not prevent any person who may be holding the office of president, or acting as president, during the term within which this article becomes operative from holding the office of president or acting as president during the remainder of such term.

Section 2. This article shall be inoperative unless it shall have been ratified as an amendment to the Constitution by the legislatures of three-fourths of the several states within seven years from the date of its submission to the states by the Congress.

ARTICLE XXIII

Proposed by Congress June 16, 1960. Ratified March 29, 1961.

Section 1. The district constituting the seat of government of the United States shall appoint such manner as the Congress may direct:

A number of electors of president and vice-president equal to the whole number of Senators and Representatives in Congress to which the district would be entitled if it were a state, but in no event more than the least populous state; they shall be in addition to those appointed by the states, but they shall be considered, for the purposes of election of president and vice-president, to be electors appointed by a state; and they shall meet in the district and perform such duties as provided by the twelfth article of amendment.

Section 2. The Congress shall have the power to enforce this article by appropriate legislation.

ARTICLE XXIV

Proposed by Congress August 27, 1962. Ratified January 23, 1964.

Section 1. The right of citizens of the United States to vote in any primary or other election for president or vice-president, for electors for president or vice-president, or for Senator or Representative in Congress, shall not be denied or abridged by the United States or any state by failure to pay any poll tax or other tax.

Section 2. The Congress shall have the power to enforce this article by appropriate legislation.

ARTICLE XXV

Proposed by Congress July 6, 1965. Ratified February 10, 1967.

Section 1. In case of the removal of the president from office or of his death or resignation, the vice-president shall become president.

Section 2. Whenever there is a vacancy in the office of the vice-president, the president shall nominate a vice-president who shall take office upon confirmation by a majority vote of both Houses of Congress.

Section 3. Whenever the president transmits to the president pro tempore of the Senate and the Speaker of the House of Representatives his written declaration that he is unable to discharge the powers and duties of his office, and until he transmits to them a written declaration to the contrary, such powers and duties shall be discharged by the vice-president as acting president.

Section 4. Whenever the vice-president and a majority of either the principal officers of the executive departments or of such other body as Congress may by law provide, transmit to the president pro tempore of the Senate and the Speaker of the House of Representatives their written declaration that the president is unable to discharge the powers and duties of his office, the vice-president shall immediately assume the powers and duties of the office as acting president.

Thereafter, when the president transmits to the president pro tempore of the Senate and the Speaker of the House of Representatives his written declaration that no inability exists, he shall resume the powers and duties of his office unless the vice-president and a majority of either the principal officers of the executive department or of such other body as Congress may by law provide, transmit within four days to the president pro tempore of the Senate and the Speaker of the House of Representatives their written declaration that the president is unable to discharge the powers and duties of his office. Thereupon Congress shall decide the issue, assembling within forty-eight hours for that purpose if not in session. If the Congress, within twenty-one days after receipt of the latter written declaration, or, if Congress is not in session, within twenty-one days after Congress is required to assemble, determines by two-thirds vote of both Houses that the president is unable to discharge the powers and duties of his office, the vice-president shall continue to discharge the same as acting president; otherwise, the president shall resume the powers and duties of his office.

ARTICLE XXVI

Proposed by Congress March 23, 1971. Ratified June 30, 1971.

Section 1. The right of citizens of the United States, who are eighteen years of age or older, to vote shall not be denied or abridged by the United States or by any State on account of age.

Section 2. The Congress shall have power to enforce this article by appropriate legislation.

ARTICLE XXVII

Proposed by Congress September 25, 1789. Ratified May 8, 1992.

No law, varying the compensation for the services of the Senators and Representatives, shall take effect, until an election of Representatives shall have intervened.

GLOSSARY OF LEGAL TERMS

Administrative law   Branch of law that creates administrative agencies, establishes their methods of procedure and the scope of judicial review of agency practices.

Adversary system   Legal proceeding with opposing parties who contest an issue or issues.

A fortiori   With stronger reason. Logical argument that because one fact exists, another that is included within it, must also exist.

Amicus curiae   Friend of the court. Person or organization who has no right to appear in court and is not a party to the suit, but who is allowed to introduce arguments, authority, or evidence to protect their interest.

Amnesty   An act of "forgetfulness" by a sovereign state for a crime committed. A pardon is "forgiveness." Amnesty is usually granted for political offenses while pardon is for criminal acts. Amnesty is usually a group action whereas pardons are individual in their application.

Appellant   Party who appeals an adverse decision from one court or jurisdiction to another.

Appellee   Party in a suit against whom an appeal is taken. One who opposes an appellant.

Attainder   Legislative act directed against a specific person charged with a crime, pronouncing him guilty without a judicial trial. Usually without following recognized rules of procedure.

Bail   Freedom given accused person who posts an appearance bond.

Bankruptcy   Insolvency or the inability to pay one's debts. A legal process in which assets are sold to pay creditors and allow the debtor to start anew.

Beyond a reasonable doubt   Proof required for conviction in a criminal trial necessary to overcome a presumption of accused's innocence. Proof must be more than skepticism and less than absolutely no possibility of error.

Bicameralism   The division of a legislative branch into two houses. The U.S. Congress is divided into a House of Representatives and a Senate.

Bill of Rights   First ten amendments to the U.S. Constitution and also those enumerated in state constitutions which list rights a person enjoys that cannot be infringed by governments.

Brief   Written notes citing issues, legal points, precedents, and arguments that constitute the essentials of a case.

Capital crime   One for which the death penalty may be, but not necessarily must be, inflicted.

Case or controversy   Facts that furnish an occasion for the exercise of the jurisdiction of a court. Terms are distinguishable because multiple controversies may exist within a single case. Issues must be real and parties must be clearly identifiable and time for judicial determination "ripe."

Certiorari   To be informed of; to be made certain. Proceeding for reexamination of a lower tribunal's decision in order for an appellate court to ascertain whether an error has occurred in the original trial. Writ is directed at the lower tribunal to send a record of the proceedings to the appellate court.

Change of venue   Venue designates the place where a court of competent jurisdiction may hear and decide a case. A transfer to a different trial place may be permitted if unfairness or other difficulties make desirable a change of the site of the trial at the request of the defendant.

Civil liberties   Immunities from governmental interference or limitations on governmental actions that reserve and preserve individual rights. This concept is negative in its nature.

Civil rights   A positive concept of rights possessed, defined, and circumscribed by laws for use and protection of citizens. Thus rights are claimed, asserted, and protected whereas liberties inhibit the actions of officials.

Closed shop   Labor bargaining unit whereby only union members may be employed. (See Open shop and Union shop.)

Code   Complete system of positive law, scientifically arranged, and promulgated by legislative authority. Compilation of existing laws into a logical and understandable whole relative to subjects to which they relate.

Collusion   Secret agreement between two or more persons with apparently conflicting interests to deceive a court and obtain an unlawful and unfair advantage over a third party.

Comity   Principle that one state or jurisdiction will give effect to the laws and judicial decisions of another as a matter of courtesy and deference. Also called "full faith and credit."

Common law   Body of law and theory, developed in England from custom and ancient usages, that has provided a base for most states' judicial systems. This base is one that modifies or complements law created by legislative enactments termed statutory law. Also called "case law."

Commutation   An executive act that changes a punishment from greater to less. It differs from a pardon because there is no "forgiveness" of the crime. A reprieve is a "postponement" of the penalty.

Compact   An agreement or convention between two or more sovereign nations or states that creates obligations between their independent parts. Mutual consent resulting in binding law is the basis on which such relationship exists.

Contempt of court   Act calculated to embarrass or obstruct a court or lessen its authority or dignity.

Contract   Legally enforceable promise between two or more persons that creates or modifies a legal relationship. Legal consideration is necessary as a valid "offer" and "acceptance."

Court of record   Those whose proceedings are permanently recorded and which have authority to fine or imprison for contempt.

Declaratory judgment   Decision by a court to establish rights of the parties or express an opinion of the court on a question of law without ordering anything to be done. It stands by itself and no executory process follows.

De facto   In fact; actually; in reality. Often used to qualify a legal term and is contrasted with "de jure." Office, position, and/or status exist under some color of right and are successfully maintained until overturned by legal process.

De jure   By right; by justice; lawful; legitimate. Term connotes "as a matter of law" while de facto connotes "as a matter of conduct or practice not founded upon law."

Delegated powers   Powers granted to the national government under the Constitution. The first three articles enumerate them relative to the legislative, executive, and judicial branches. Such powers may be specific or implied. Power, which results from several read in combination, is termed "resulting powers."

Directed verdict   Jury verdict in either a civil or criminal case by order of the trial judge when the opposing party fails to present a prima facie case or an adequate defense.

Domicile   Place where individual has permanent home and if absent has intention to return. Law presumes every person possesses one.

Double jeopardy   Provision in Fifth Amendment that prohibits double punishment and double prosecution in criminal suits for the same offense.

Duces tecum   Bring with you. Writ (subpoena is most commonly used with this term) requiring party summoned to appear at hearing with certain documents or evidence.

Due process   Consists of two types: procedural and substantive. Daniel Webster defined the first as that "which hears before it condemns, which proceeds upon inquiry, and renders judgment only after trial." Substantive due process is denied if any part of the trial or result "shocks the conscience of the court." (See Fair trial.)

Elastic clause   Final paragraph of Article I, Section 8 of the U.S. Constitution, which delegates powers to Congress authorizing all laws "necessary and proper" to carry out enumerated powers. Clause allows Congress to choose "means" by which it will execute its authority. It has enabled national government to adjust to needs of the times and reduce need for amendments. (See Necessary and proper clause.)

Eminent domain   Right of sovereign to take private property for public use or public purpose on payment of just compensation.

Enabling act   Act of Congress authorizing people of a territory to take the necessary steps to prepare for statehood. Includes calling a convention to draft a constitution and preparing to conduct elections.

En banc   In the bench; by full court. Many appellate courts sit with three or more judges from among a larger number, but sometimes either by their own motion or that of the litigant the court will consider the matter by the full court. A notation to this effect generally heads or precedes the opinion.

Equal protection   Requirement of Fourteenth Amendment that state laws not arbitrarily discriminate against persons. Identical treatment is not required nor is classification forbidden so long as either bears a reasonable relationship to the end sought. Three areas exist: (a) where any discrimination is clearly illegal, (b) suspect areas that will be carefully scrutinized by courts, and (c) no public involvement can be found and no protection will be afforded.

Establishment clause   Basic principle of American government set forth in First Amendment that forbids governmental sponsorship of religion. Position of neutrality must be maintained by state and it may neither advance nor retard religion. No public funds may be extended on behalf of any church, nor shall any public school be used for sectarian religious observances. Courts have attempted to distinguish between services that are primarily of benefit to pupils and those that advance religious tenets. (See Separation of church and state.)

Estoppel   Person's own act, which precludes him from making a contrary claim.

Exclusionary rule   Rule of law that otherwise admissible evidence may not be used in a criminal trial if it was obtained by police conduct that was illegal.

Ex parte   On one side only; by or for one party. Name following this type of case is that of the party upon whose application the case is heard. Process is nonadversarial and usually deals with an injunction, bankruptcy, or other single-party court orders. For example, *Ex parte Milligan*, 4 Wallace 2 (1866).

Ex post facto   After the fact. Law passed after the occurrence of a fact or commission of an act, which retrospectively changes the legal consequences of such a fact or deed. In the United States, the term is limited to those laws that may impose punishment, penalties, or forfeitures.

Ex rel.   From *ex relatione*, meaning "on relation." In such cases an attorney general or other such individual institutes a suit on the basis of information provided by a private individual.

Extradition   Return by a state of a fugitive from justice upon the demand of the executive authority of the state in which the crime was committed. This is an obligation imposed by Article IV of the U.S. Constitution. The term extradition is properly used when the return of the fugitive is sought between two nations pursuant to a treaty.

Fair trial   Hearing by an impartial court that usually utilizes a properly selected jury, an impartial judge, an atmosphere of calm, available witnesses testifying without fear or favor, a defendant represented by competent attorneys who assert their client's rights forcefully and fully, and all ascertainable, relevant truths sought to be considered. The test should not be observance only of proper rules of procedure, but the subjective question was "Was it fair?" (See Due process.)

Felony   Serious crime distinguished from those minor or lesser-termed misdemeanors. Usually, the distinction is based on whether or not the maximum penalty that could be imposed is one year or more imprisonment. If so, the crime is a felony.

Full faith and credit   Article 4, Section 1 requires that court judgments, records, public acts, and court decisions of one state be treated as equally binding in the courts of all the other states. (See Comity.)

General welfare   Article I, Section 8 of the U.S. Constitution authorizes Congress to lay and collect taxes, provide for the common defense and general welfare of the United States. Liberals and strict constructionists argue about whether this is an unlimited grant of power or whether it is a grant limited to only those authorized by other sections of the Constitution. A liberal view has prevailed and the spending power of Congress has not been successfully challenged.

Gerrymander   Drawing of legislative district boundary lines in order to obtain a partisan or a factional advantage.

Government corporation   Agency of government that administers a business enterprise. Activity is usually commercial, produces revenue, and needs greater flexibility than regular departments. State-level equivalents are normally called "Authorities."

Grandfather clause   Exempting existing persons or businesses from restrictive provisions of a civil law which would be retroactive in application. Such a clause protects an already established business from meeting newly created criteria. Also name for a provision by which states used to limit voting rights to those whose grandfathers had voted, thus excluding African Americans.

Grand jury   Investigative body that is part of court system whose duty it is to accuse persons (indict) when sufficient evidence has been presented or discovered to justify holding a person for trial.

Guardian-ad-litem   Person lawfully empowered and charged with the duty of prosecuting or defending a minor in any suit to which he is a party. Generally used when suit on behalf of a minor is termed by "next friend" of plaintiff.

Habeas corpus   You have the body. Object of writ is to bring a party in custody into open court before a judge; not to determine the person's guilt or innocence, but only to ascertain whether the prisoner is restrained of his liberty without due process.

Harmless error   One not sufficiently prejudicial to an appellant or does not affect his substantive rights so as to justify a reviewing court from overturning or modifying the lower court decision. (See Reversible error.)

Hatch Acts   Two corrupt practice acts passed in 1939 and 1940 that forbade civil service employees from being pressured to make political contributions or to participate actively in partisan political activities. The first act applied to federal employees and the second to state and local political appointees.

High crimes and misdemeanors   Listed along with treason and bribery as grounds for impeachment, the term has never been precisely defined. Discretion is vested completely in Congress to define term. In practice the phrase is usually restricted to unethical conduct and criminal offenses; not incompetence or political disagreement.

Hung jury   Trial jury that is unable to reach any agreement on the guilt or innocence of the defendant.

Immunity   Legal exemption from a duty which would otherwise be imposed, such as testifying in a criminal trial. (See Judicial immunity.)

Impeach   To question the truthfulness of a witness's testimony or for a legislative body to charge a public official with a crime which, if convicted of, would cause his removal from office.

Implied powers   Inferred powers possessed by the national government from those specifically enumerated in the U.S. Constitution. Concept is derived from the "necessary and proper" clause in Article I, Section 8. (See Necessary and proper clause and Elastic clause.)

In camera   In the chambers. Judicial act performed by a judge who is not acting in an open court. If the court is not in session or the act occurs elsewhere, the term "in chambers" may be used to indicate the act was official but not public.

Indictment   Criminal accusation by a grand jury. Must be written and of sufficient clarity to inform the accused of the nature of his crime. (See Information and Grand jury.)

Information   Criminal accusation by a competent public official and not by a grand jury. Must be written and sworn to before a proper magistrate. (See Indictment.)

Inherent powers   Authority vested in the national government, particularly in the area of foreign affairs, that does not depend on a specific grant of power. They are derived from the fact that the United States is a sovereign power.

Injunction   Order issued by a court in an equity proceeding to compel or restrain an act. Mandatory ones compel the performance of an act and prohibitory ones restrain.

In loco parentis   In the place of a parent. If used in a judicial proceeding the relationship is nonadversarial. If used to identify a personal or institutional relationship the claimant to the status may assume parental rights and must assume parental duties and responsibilities.

In re   In the matter of; concerning. Proceeding in a nonadversary matter in which there is some material thing involved. It is sometimes used in a manner similar to an *ex parte* proceeding where one party makes an application on his own behalf.

Inter alia   Among other things.

Interlocutory   Order or court decree that is not final.

Interstate commerce   Buying and selling; transportation of goods and persons, navigable waters, commercial intercourse, electronic communication, and all the necessary facilities are subject to national regulation and control if they affect more than one state.

Intestate   Deceased who does not leave a will.

Involuntary servitude   Persons compelled by force, coercion, imprisonment, or against their will to labor for another. (See Servitude.)

Judicial activist   Person who believes the court system should determine desirable social policy when legislatures or Congress fail to do so.

Judicial immunity   Legal exception from duty to testify on a claim of self-incrimination whereupon court absolves witness from any criminal penalty, thereby coercing witness to testify.

Judicial notice   Court takes note of certain facts known to most people and thereby eliminating need for producing evidence necessary to prove their existence.

Judicial power   Authority exercised by that branch of government charged with declaring what law is and its construction or meaning.

Judicial review   Power of courts to declare invalid acts of legislatures and executive agencies, as well as subordinate courts.

Jurisdiction   Authority vested in a court to hear and decide a case.

Jury (grand)   See Grand jury.

Jury (trial)   Sometimes called petit jury. An impartial body that sits in judgment of facts in either civil or criminal cases. Under federal law (which is not followed in all state proceedings) a trial jury must consist of twelve persons and reach a unanimous verdict.

Jus sanguinis   Right of blood; law of the blood. Legal principle by which citizenship is determined by parentage rather than by place of birth.

Jus soli   Law of the soil. Basic rule under which American citizenship is determined by place of birth rather than by parentage.

Justiciable question   Dispute that can be settled through exercise of judicial power. Controversy must actually exist, plaintiff must have a substantial interest and standing to sue, case must be "ripe" for adjudication, other remedies must have been exhausted, and court hearing case must possess jurisdiction. Question may be ruled "political" if court believes other branches of government could better handle the matter.

Kentucky and Virginia Resolutions   (1799) Written by Thomas Jefferson and James Madison opposing the Alien and Sedition Acts of 1798. Expressed the concept that held that a state may place itself between national government and one of its citizens. Each state was judge of constitutionality of actions of national government. Developed by others into the doctrines of "interposition" or "nullification," these theories contradicted Article VI, Section 2 of the U.S. Constitution. (See Nullification.)

Libel   Defamatory written expression or oral expression on tape, radio, or TV that is untrue.

Malfeasance   Commission of an illegal act.

Mandamus   We command. Writ issued by a court to compel performance of an act. It may be issued to an individual or corporation as well as to a public official if the act is to compel the performance of a ministerial duty which the official must perform. A discretionary act will not be mandated. Failure to obey the court order is contempt of court.

Mandate   Judicial command usually directed by an appellate court to a lower court. Also means popular support for a political program.

Martial law   Military government established over civilian population during emergency in which military decrees supersede civilian law and military tribunals replace civil courts.

Master-in-chancery   Judicial officer appointed by courts of equity to hear testimony and make reports which, when approved by the presiding judge, become the decision of the court.

Military law   Law enacted by Congress that governs the members of the armed forces and also established procedures for trial by courts-martial for alleged infractions. Authority: Article I, Section 8, Paragraph 14.

Ministerial act   Act performed by explicit directions, usually by statute, by a subordinate official. Such acts must involve no discretion nor be quasijudicial in character. Ministerial acts may be compelled to be performed through mandamus, while discretionary acts may not be so ordered unless a clear abuse of discretion can be demonstrated. (See Mandamus.)

Miranda rule   Prior to any questioning in a criminal proceeding, the person must be warned that he has a right to remain silent, and that any statement he does make may be used against him, and that he has the right to the presence of an attorney, either one of his own or court appointed. If these rights are waived the act must be done "knowingly" and "intelligently."

Misfeasance   Improper performance of a legal act.

Mitigation   Does not constitute a justification or excuse of the offense, but facts which, in fairness and mercy, may be considered as extenuating or decreasing the degree of moral culpability. Such circumstances may reduce or lessen the penalty imposed.

Moot case   One that a court refused to hear because the issue or issues are no longer in dispute.

Moratorium   Suspension of all or certain legal remedies.

Naturalization   Adoption by an alien of the rights and privileges of citizenship. Legal procedure whereby an alien becomes a citizen.

Navigable waters   Encompass all waters within the boundaries of the United States, which are, can be made to be, or contribute to the use as waterways for interstate or foreign commerce, such as rivers, streams, lakes, and inlets. The flow of any such waters cannot be impeded without the consent of the national government.

Necessary and proper clause   Found in final paragraph of Article I, Section 8 of the U.S. Constitution. Congress being limited to its delegated powers is permitted to choose the means by which it executes its authority. Broad construction of this clause permits great flexibility of interpretation and reduces need for amendments. (See Elastic clause and Implied powers.)

Nullification   Declaration by a state that a national law is null and void and therefore not binding on its citizens. Formulated by John C. Calhoun, who argued that the Union was a compact between sovereign states, and the national government was not the final judge of its own powers. Developed into the doctrine of secession, the invalidity of which was determined by the Civil War. Rejection of concept based on Article VI, Section 2; the supremacy clause of the U.S. Constitution. (See Kentucky and Virginia Resolutions.)

Nunc pro tunc   Now for then. Acts allowed to be done after the time when they should have been with the same effect as if performed at the proper time. Purpose is not to supply omitted action but to supply omission in record of action really performed but omitted through inadvertence or mistake.

Obiter dictum   Otherwise said. Passing or incidental statements made in a judicial opinion which are unnecessary to the disposition of the case. Many are generalities with no actual bearing on issues involved.

Obligation of contract   Civil obligation to perform the terms of a legal contract but in the absence of specific performance as a remedy, then the party breaking the promise must pay damages.

Obscenity   Defined in *Miller v. California* (1973) as conduct or material appealing to prurient (lustful) interests, violating contemporary community standards, and lacking serious literary, artistic, political, or scientific value. Anything so found is not protected by the free speech guarantee of the First Amendment.

Omnibus bill   Legislative act that incorporates various separate and distinct matters that necessitates the executive accepting some provision that he does not approve, or defeat the whole enactment; this because he does not have an "item" veto.

Open court   One open to spectators who attend in an orderly and decent manner. This is in contradistinction to one closed to the public because of confidentiality as a recognized interest.

Open primary   Direct voting system that permits voters to choose the party primary in which they wish to vote without disclosing their party affiliation, if any.

Open shop   Industry that may or may not employ nonunion workers. (See Closed shop and Union Shop.)

Opinion (advisory)   Formal opinion by a court on question of law submitted by a legislative body or government official, but which has not yet become an actual case.

Opinion (concurring)   Separate opinion in which one or more judges agree with the result reached by the majority, but disagree with the reasoning or arguments.

Opinion (court)   Decision reached in a case by the court expounding the law and detailing the reasons upon which the decision is based.

Opinion (dissenting)   Separate opinion in which particular members of court disagree with the majority position and expound their own view.

Opinion (per curiam)   Concurred in by the entire court but without disclosing which judge was the author.

Original jurisdiction   Authority of a court to hear a case for the first time. This jurisdiction is to be distinguished from "appellate," which hears cases on appeal from other courts or regulatory agencies.

Original package   Legal doctrine that package prepared for interstate or foreign shipment becomes subject to state taxes and/or police power regulation after it is opened, divided, or has reached its final destination.

Pandering   To pimp or cater to the lust of another or the promotion of obscenity.

Peonage   Condition of enforced servitude. One condemned to labor for another against his will. (See Servitude.)

Per curiam   By the court. An opinion by the whole court as distinguished from one written by one judge. Sometimes it denotes an opinion written by the chief justice or presiding judge.

Perjury   In criminal law the willful lying under oath or affirmation by a witness in a judicial proceeding.

Petit jury   See Jury.

Plea bargaining   Process whereby the prosecutor and the accused in a criminal proceeding negotiate a settlement of the case by a plea of "guilty" by the accused to a lesser charge.

Plebiscite   Vote on an issue by the entire people entitled to franchise. Act is closely akin to a referendum.

Police power   Attribute of states and their subdivisions to impose restrictions upon private rights reasonably related to matters of health, safety, morals, and general welfare of the public.

Political question   Supreme Court doctrine that certain constitutional issues cannot be settled by the judicial branch. Generally invoked when question could be better resolved by either the executive or legislative branches.

Posse comitatus   Power or force of the county. The population of a county which the sheriff may summon and mobilize to keep the peace or make an arrest for a felony. Mode is immaterial so long as the object is to require assistance.

Preemption   Federal doctrine relating to state legislation based upon the supremacy clause of the federal Constitution, which deprives a state of jurisdiction where a federal act supersedes (Article VI, Section 2).

Presentment clause   Constitution clause that provides that all legislation be presented to the president for the president's signature or veto, the latter of which two-thirds majorities in both houses of Congress can override.

Prima facie   At first sight; on the first appearance; on the face of it; so far as can be judged by the first disclosure; presumably; a fact presumed to be true unless disproved by some evidence to the contrary.

Privileges and immunities   U.S. Constitution uses this clause in Article IV, Section 2 and in the Fourteenth Amendment. The first refers to uniform nonpolitical treatment of all citizens regardless of which state they are in; whereas the second use in the Fourteenth Amendment has not been completely defined. It is basically a limitation placed upon each state in matters of civil liberties in their relationship to U.S. citizens.

Probable cause   Necessary preliminary element in issuance of search, seizure, or arrest warrants that consists of existence of facts and circumstances within official's knowledge or trustworthy information that creates a reasonable belief that a crime is involved, to the satisfaction of an unbiased and objective magistrate, or later to be so determined by such a judge if the act has already occurred.

Procedural due process   Quoting Daniel Webster as procedure "which hears before it condemns, which proceeds upon inquiry, and renders judgment only after trial." The Supreme Court considers that there has been a denial if any procedure is shocking to the conscience or makes impossible a fair and enlightened system of justice. (See Substantive due process.)

Quartering of soldiers   Prohibition found in Third Amendment against housing soldiers in private homes during times of peace without the consent of the owner. In wartime quartering may be done under conditions prescribed by law.

Quid pro quo   What for what. The giving or exchange of one valuable thing for another. In a contract the concept is essential for its enforceability; i.e., consideration.

Quo warranto   By what authority. Civil writ which tests the legal right of a company to operate a business or of a public official to discharge duties of the office that may or may not have been usurped.

Rationale   Reasoning of the court as the explanation for the decision it reached.

Reapportionment   New allocation of legislative seats based on census statistics. In the national House of Representatives there are 435 seats to be distributed among the 50 states. As population shifts so does an individual state's allocation.

Recess   Temporary adjournment of a trial or a legislative session after it has started. If the delay is substantial, it is called a continuance. If a terminal time has been reached, it is termed an adjournment, and if no date has been set for a reopening, it is "sine die."

Recidivist A habitual criminal or sometimes called an incorrigible criminal. One who is frequently occupied with crime.

Released time The practice by which public school children can be dismissed from classes during the school day to attend some religious exercise.

Replevin An action whereby an owner recovers goods from someone who has illegal possession of them.

Res judicata A matter adjudged; a thing judicially decided; a matter settled by a court of competent jurisdiction; with adherence to due process and without error; finally decided. Term is synonymous with res adjudicata.

Resulting powers Powers of the national government derived from combination of delegated or implied powers; thus, powers that result from a number of other powers, rather than inferred from a single delegated or implied power.

Retroactive law Includes both retrospective and ex post facto, the former technically applying only to civil law and the latter to criminal or penal law. The former may be valid but the latter (ex post facto) is constitutionally prohibited under the U.S. Constitution.

Reversible error One substantially affecting appellant's legal rights and, if uncorrected, would result in an injustice occurring that justifies the reversing of a judgment handed down by a lower court. This term is synonymous with that of "prejudicial error" and is distinguishable from "harmless error."

Rider (bill) Provision that is unlikely to pass on its own merits is added to an important bill so that it will "ride" through the legislative process and become the law if the legislation to which it is attached passes. It should be noted that the president does not have "item" veto. (See Omnibus bill.)

Rule of reason Supreme Court holding (1910 in Standard Oil case) that not every combination in restraint of trade is illegal but only those unreasonably so.

Scienter Guilty knowledge used in pleadings and signifies that a crime or tort was done knowingly, understandably, and designedly. Term is synonymous with criminal plea of premeditation.

Search and seizure Must be reasonable and based on "probable cause." Usually based on warrant, but some exceptions may occur.

Search warrant Order issued by a judge to law enforcement officers to conduct a search of specified places for specified things and bring them before the court. Issuance order is based upon "probable cause" supported by sworn allegations and things searched for and seized must be particularly described.

Sedition Illegal action that tends to cause the disruption and overthrow of the government. An insurrectionary movement tending toward treason but lacking an overt act or direct and open violence.

Self-incrimination The Fifth Amendment provides that no person shall be compelled in any criminal case to be a witness against himself. This guarantee has been extended to legislative committees and executive agencies. It has not been extended to protect another person or to save oneself from shame or disgrace. Persons who are beyond criminal prosecution by reason of a grant of immunity or pardon may not refuse to testify.

Separate but equal doctrine   From 1896 to 1954 the Supreme Court upheld racial segregation if each race was provided with equal facilities. In the latter year the Court, after a series of weakening decisions, finally declared that "separate educational facilities are inherently unequal." For all practical purposes this separate but equal doctrine is now repudiated and constitutes a denial of "equal protection of the law" as guaranteed in the Fourteenth Amendment.

Separation of church and state   Basic principle declaring that government must be neutral and neither advance nor retard religion. Two facets of this issue, both articulated in the First Amendment, are involved: (a) no establishment of religion, and (b) no prohibition of the free exercise of religion. The permissible limitations of these issues are highly controversial and unresolved. (See Establishment clause.)

Separation of powers   Major principle of U.S. government in which power is divided into three branches: (a) legislative, (b) executive, and (c) judicial. Each is independent of the others but the separation is not complete. Legislative and executive are political, but the judicial is less so. Thus, no single branch can make, interpret, and enforce the law.

Seriatim   In due order; successively; in order; in succession; individually; one by one; separately; severally. Court determination in which each judge or justice writes a separate opinion which may or may not agree in whole or in part with his brethren's opinions.

Servitude   Peonage or slavery. The Thirteenth Amendment prohibits its existence in the United States except as punishment for a crime. Forcing the fulfillment of a contract, to support a child, military or jury service, or to pay alimony is not totally banned nor are laws that force service where public safety is jeopardized. Imprisonment or forced labor to pay a debt is, however. (See Involuntary servitude and Peonage.)

Solicitor general   Official in the U.S. Department of Justice who conducts and argues cases on behalf of the government before the Supreme Court. His approval is required before any appeal may be taken on behalf of the federal government to any appellate court.

Standing to sue   Legal rights of a person or group to challenge a judicial decision or conduct of another in a court, especially in regard to government conduct. Their status as litigants is essential to the necessary requirement that a controversy exists. Thus, standing to sue is dependent on the existence and the degree of the interest affected by the adverse relationships and the outcome of the trial.

Stare decisis   To abide by, or adhere to, decided cases. A policy in which the court decides to stand by precedent and not to disturb a settled point of law. Doctrine that when a court has once laid down a principle of law as applicable to a certain state of facts, it will adhere to that principle and apply it to all future cases where facts are substantially the same.

Subpoena   Two types: (a) to compel attendance at a judicial hearing, some administrative agency hearing, or legislative inquiry, and (b) *duces tecum*, to bring relevant papers to such a meeting. Failure to respond to such a command may result in a contempt charge.

Substantive rights   Those essential for personal liberty. Generally includes those listed in First and Fourteenth Amendments to the U.S. Constitution. Those usually listed are freedoms of speech, press, religion, assembly, petition, and equal protection of the law. These rights are to be distinguished from procedural, which are protected by due process and fair trial concepts and are concerned with the manner by which the substantive rights are protected. (See Procedural due process.)

Suffrage   Right or privilege of casting a vote at public election—or participating meaningfully in the political process.

Summons   Writ directed to the sheriff or other proper officer requiring that official to notify the person named that an action has been commenced against him/her in the court whence the writ issues, and that he/she is required to appear, on the day named, and answer the complaint in such an action.

Taft-Hartley (Labor-Management Relations Act of 1947)   Major revision of Wagner Act (1935), which places some limitations on internal union activities and enhances the power of individual workers. Passage of this law gave impetus to AFL-CIO merger in 1955.

Taxation (intergovernmental immunity)   Exemption of state and national governmental agencies and property from taxation by each other. This principle is subject to national supremacy, Article VI, clause 2.

Tort   Any private or civil wrong or injury, except for breach of contract, resulting from a failure to perform a legal duty, which causes an injury to another.

Trial   May be either civil or criminal, held in accordance with the law of the land before a judge who has jurisdiction. Trial must be public, conducted fairly before an impartial magistrate, and, in the case of criminal trials, started without an unreasonable delay.

True bill   Accusation returned by a grand jury indicting (accusing) the individual investigated. The Fifth Amendment of the U.S. Constitution requires that this be done for any capital or infamous crime. Many states have replaced this procedure by substituting an information that permits a prosecutor alone to bring charges.

Uniform Code of Military Justice   Law enacted by Congress in 1950 that governs the conduct of enlisted men and officers of the U.S. Armed Forces.

Union shop   Labor bargaining unit in which nonunion members must join union within a prescribed period after employment. (See Closed shop and Open shop.)

United States Code   Compilation of U.S. laws in force and classified by subject matter. Annual supplements are made and entire code is revised every six years. Resolutions adopted by Congress are not considered statutes and are therefore not included.

Voir dire   To speak the truth. Prospective examination by the court or attorneys of prospective jurors to determine their qualification for jury service. Term also used where initial hearing on some issue of law or fact is held out of the presence and hearing of the jury.

Waiver   Intentional and voluntary giving up of some known right. It may be either express or inferred from circumstances but courts must use every reasonable presumption against the loss of any constitutional right. Abandonment of any right must be an intelligent one and a hearing should be held with explicit findings of fact supporting the waiver recorded.

War Powers   Authority either expressly, impliedly, or inherently found in the national government to protect our nation from its enemies. Such power is vested in Congress and the president but the exercise by them is always subject to judicial scrutiny. Control over the domestic economy has now been accepted as a necessary part of these War Powers.

Warrant   Written order directing the arrest of a person involved in a crime or the search of specified property for either contraband or evidence. Both warrants are based upon a showing of probable cause before an impartial magistrate.

White primaries   Attempts by several states to exclude African Americans from voting by leaving determination of primary qualifications to political party acting as a private organization. This objective to be attained was based on the argument that political parties were private clubs and therefore discrimination was permissible. Such attempts have all been found to be unconstitutional.

Wiretapping   Use of listening devices to intercept and record private messages electronically. Improper interception would involve the exclusionary rule in a criminal trial and a suit for the invasion of privacy in a civil suit. Federal law and state law are not in agreement and the entire area is highly controversial and in a state of flux. Permissible "wire tapping" includes issuance of a warrant by a qualified judge.

Writs   Orders issued by a court either ordering the performance of an act or prohibiting the act. Orderly progress of judicial functions is largely dependent on writs and essential to the enforcement of their decisions. (See Injunctions.)

Alphabetical List of Cases Briefed

Abington School District v. Schempp, 374 U.S. 203 (1963)   213
Ableman v. Booth, 21 Howard (62 U.S.) 506 (1859)   109
Abrams v. United States, 250 U.S. 616 (1919)   259
Adamson v. California, 332 U.S. 46 (1947)   204
Adarand Constructors, Inc. v. Pena, 515 U.S. 200 (1995)   418
Adkins v. Children's Hospital, 261 U.S. 525 (1923)   184
Agostini v. Felton, 521 U.S. 203 (1997)   224
Alden v. Maine, 527 U.S. 706 (1999)   128
American Communications Association v. Douds, 339 U.S. 382 (1950)   292
Argersinger v. Hamlin, 407 U.S. 25 (1972)   359
Ashcroft v. American Civil Liberties Union, 542 U.S. 656 (2004)   289
Ashcroft v. The Free Speech Coalition, 535 U.S. 234 (2002)   288
Ashwander v. Tennessee Valley Authority, 297 U.S. 288 (1936)   11
Atkins v. Virginia, 536 U.S. 304 (2002)   371
Bailey v. Drexel Furniture Co., 259 U.S. 20 (1922)   41
Baker v. Carr, 369 U.S. 186 (1962)   121
Barenblatt v. United States, 360 U.S. 109 (1959)   30
Barron v. Baltimore, 7 Peters (32 U.S.) 243 (1833)   200
Batson v. Kentucky, 476 U.S. 79 (1986)   353
Baze v. Rees, 128 S. Ct. 1520 (2008)   374
Bethel School District No. 403 v. Fraser, 478 U.S. 675 (1986)   307
BMW of North America, Inc. v. Gore, 517 U.S. 559 (1996)   189
Board of Directors of Rotary International v. Rotary Club of Duarte,
   481 U.S. 537 (1987)   253
*Board of Education of Independent School District No. 92 of
   Pottawatomie County v. Earls*, 536 U.S. 822 (2002)   332
Board of Regents v. Southworth, 529 U.S. 217 (2000)   243
Bolling v. Sharpe, 347 U.S. 497 (1954)   343

Bordenkircher v. Hayes, 435 U.S. 357 (1978)　　345
Boudmediene v. Bush (2008)　　100
Bowers v. Hardwick, 478 U.S. 186 (1986)　　386
Bowsher v. Snyar, 478 U.S. 714 (1986)　　77
Boy Scouts of America v. Dale, 530 U.S. 640 (2000)　　257
Brandenburg v. Ohio, 395 U.S. 444 (1969)　　294
Branti v. Finkel, 445 U.S. 507 (1980)　　252
Branzburg v. Hayes, 408 U.S. 205 (1972)　　265
Bridges v. California, 314 U.S. 252 (1941)　　261
Brown v. Board of Education of Topeka, 347 U.S. 483 (1954)　　409
Brown v. Board of Education II, 349 U.S. 294 (1955)　　410
Brown v. Maryland, 12 Wheaton (25 U.S.) 419 (1827)　　3
Buck v. Bell, 274 U.S. 200 (1927)　　380
Buckley v. Valeo, 424 U.S. 1 (1976)　　272
Bunting v. Oregon, 243 U.S. 426 (1917)　　183
Burch v. Louisiana, 441 U.S. 130 (1979)　　351
Burstyn v. Wilson, 343 U.S. 495 (1952)　　282
Bush v. Gore, 531 U.S. 98 (2000)　　457
Bush v. Vera, 517 U.S. 952 (1996)　　456
Calder v. Bull, 3 Dallas (3 U.S.) 386 (1798)　　171
California v. Ciraolo, 476 U.S. 207 (1986)　　330
California v. Greenwood, 486 U.S. 35 (1988)　　331
Camps Newfound/Owatonna, v. Town of Harrison, 520 U.S. 564 (1997)　　143
Cantwell v. Connecticut, 310 U.S. 296 (1940)　　233
Caperton v. A.T. Massey Coal Co., Inc., 129 S. Ct. 2252 (2009)　　347
Chambers v. Florida, 309 U.S. 227 (1940)　　355
Champion v. Ames, 188 U.S. 321 (1903)　　7
Chandler and Granger v. Florida, 449 U.S. 560 (1981)　　270
Charles River Bridge Co. v. Warren River Bridge, 11 Peters (36 U.S.)
　　420 (1837)　　173
Cherokee Nation v. Georgia, 30 U.S. 1 (1831)　　138
Chimel v. California, 395 U.S. 752 (1969)　　323
Chisholm v. Georgia, 2 Dallas (2 U.S.) 419 (1793)　　137
Church of Lukumi Babalu Aye v. City of Hialeah, 508 U.S. 520 (1993)　　240
Citizens United v. Federal Election Commission, No. 08-205 (2010)　　276
City of Boerne v. Flores, 521 U.S. 507 (1997)　　400
The Civil Rights Cases, 109 U.S. 3 (1883)　　403
Cleburne v. Cleburne Living Center, 473 U.S. 432 (1985)　　437
Clinton v. City of New York, 524 U.S. 417 (1998)　　79
Clinton v. Jones, 520 U.S. 681 (1997)　　70
Cohens v. Virginia, 6 Wheaton (19 U.S.) 264 (1821)　　107
Coleman v. Miller, 307 U.S. 433 (1939)　　166
Collector v. Day, 11 Wallace (78 U.S.) 113 (1871)　　33
Commonwealth of Massachusetts v. Mellon, 262 U.S. 447 (1923)　　111
Connecticut Department of Public Safety v. John Doe,
　　538 U.S. 1 1160 (2003)　　444

Cook v. Gralike, 531 U.S. 510 (2001)   146
Cooley v. The Board of Wardens of the Port of Philadelphia,
    12 Howard (53 U.S.) 299 (1851)   4
Cooper v. Aaron, 358 U.S. 1 (1958)   113
Cox v. New Hampshire, 312 U.S. 569 (1941)   295
Coy v. Iowa, 487 U.S. 1012 (1988)   340
Coyle v. Smith, 221 U.S. 559 (1911)   154
Crawford v. Marion County, 128 S. Ct. 1610 (2008)   460
Crosby v. National Foreign Trade Council, 530 U.S. 363 (2000)   145
Dames and Moore v. Regan, 453 U.S. 654 (1981)   66
In re Debs, 158 U.S. 564 (1895)   6
DeJonge v. Oregon, 299 U.S. 353 (1937)   249
Dennis v. United States, 341 U.S. 494 (1951)   292
DeShaney v. Winnebago Social Services, 489 U.S. 189 (1989)   345
Dickerson v. United States, 530 U.S. 428 (2000)   359
Dillon v. Gloss, 256 U.S. 368 (1921)   165
District of Columbia v. Heller, 128 S. Ct. 2783 (2008)   315
Dolan v. City of Tigard, 512 U.S. 374 (1994)   193
Duncan v. Kahanamoku, 327 U.S. 304 (1946)   90
Duncan v. Louisiana, 391 U.S. 145 (1968)   350
Dunn v. Blumstein, 405 U.S. 330 (1972)   454
Duren v. Missouri, 439 U.S. 357 (1979)   352
Eakin v. Raub, 12 Serg. & Rawle 330 (Pa. S. Ct.) (1825)   108
Edwards v. Aguillard, 482 U.S. 578 (1987)   221
Edwards v. California, 314 U.S. 160 (1941)   143
Eldred v. Ashcroft, 537 U.S. 186 (2003)   50
Elk Grove v. Newdow, 542 U.S. 1 (2004)   118
Elrod v. Burns, 427 U.S. 347 (1976)   273
Employment Division, Department of Human Resources of Oregon v.
    Smith, 494 U.S. 872 (1990)   239
Engel et al. v. Vitale et al., 370 U.S. 421 (1962)   212
Equal Employment Opportunity Commission v. Wyoming,
    460 U.S. 226 (1983)   158
Erie v. Pap's A.M., 529 U.S. 277 (2000)   300
Erie Railroad Co. v. Tompkins, 304 U.S. 64 (1938)   112
Escobedo v. Illinois, 378 U.S. 478 (1964)   357
Everson v. Board of Education of Ewing Township, 330 U.S. 1 (1947)   209
Ewing v. California, 123 S. Ct. 1179 (2003)   373
Federal Communications Commission v. Pacifica Foundation,
    438 U.S. 726 (1978)   305
Federal Maritime Commission v. South Carolina State Ports Authority,
    535 U.S. 743 (2002)   133
Feiner v. New York, 340 U.S. 315 (1951)   304
First National Bank of Boston v. Bellotti, 435 U.S. 765 (1978)   280
Flast v. Cohen, 392 U.S. 83 (1968)   114
Fletcher v. Peck, 6 Cranch (10 U.S.) 87 (1810)   171

Foley v. Connelie, 435 U.S. 291 (1978)   430
44 Liquormart, Inc. v. Rhode Island, 517 U.S. 484 (1996)   281
Frisby v. Schultz, 487 U.S. 474 (1988)   255
Frontiero v. Richardson, 411 U.S. 677 (1973)   432
Fullilove v. Klutznick, 448 U.S. 448 (1980)   417
Gannett Co. v. DePasquale, 443 U.S. 368 (1979)   268
Garcetti v. Ceballos, 547 U.S. 410 (2006)   310
Garcia v. San Antonio Metropolitan Transit Authority,
    469 U.S. 528 (1985)   159
Gibbons v. Ogden, 9 Wheaton (22 U.S.) 1 (1824)   2
Giboney v. Empire Storage & Ice Co., 336 U.S. 490 (1949)   188
Gideon v. Wainwright, 372 U.S. 335 (1963)   356
Ginzburg v. United States, 383 U.S. 463 (1966)   283
Girouard v. United States, 328 U.S. 61 (1946)   427
Gitlow v. New York, 268 U.S. 652 (1925)   200
Goldman v. Weinberger, 475 U.S. 503 (1986)   238
Goldwater v. Carter, 444 U.S. 996 (1979)   83
Gomillion v. Lightfoot, 364 U.S. 339 (1960)   451
Gonzales v. Carhart, 550 U.S. 124 (2007)   392
Gonzales v. Centro Espirita, 546 U.S. 418 (2006)   244
Gonzales v. Raich, 545 U.S. 1 (2005)   19
Good News Club v. Milford Central School, 533 U.S. 98 (2001)   226
Gratz v. Bollinger, 539 U.S. 244 (2003)   420
Gravel v. United States, 408 U.S. 606 (1972)   52
Graves v. New York ex rel. O'Keefe, 306 U.S. 466 (1939)   45
Gregg v. Georgia, 428 U.S. 153 (1976)   366
Gregory v. Ashcroft, 501 U.S. 452 (1991)   440
Griswold v. Connecticut, 381 U.S. 479 (1965)   381
Grosjean v. American Press Co., 297 U.S. 233 (1936)   261
Ex parte Grossman, 267 U.S. 87 (1925)   63
Grutter v. Bollinger, 539 U.S. 306 (2003)   422
Guinn v. United States, 238 U.S. 347 (1915)   447
Hague v. Congress of Industrial Organizations, 307 U.S. 496 (1939)   250
Haig v. Agee, 453 U.S. 280 (1981)   67
Hamdan v. Rumsfeld, 548 U.S. 557 (2006)   97
Hamdi v. Rumsfeld, 542 U.S. 507 (2004)   93
Hamilton v. Kentucky Distilleries & Warehouse Co.,
    251 U.S. 146 (1919)   87
Hammer v. Dagenhart, 247 U.S. 251 (1918)   9
J. W. Hampton, Jr. & Co. v. United States, 276 U.S. 394 (1928)   21
Hans v. Louisiana, 134 U.S. 1 (1890)   127
Harris v. McRae, 448 U.S. 297 (1980)   385
Hawaii Housing Authority v. Midkiff, 467 U.S. 229 (1984)   192
Hawke v. Smith, 253 U.S. 221 (1920)   164
Hazelwood School District v. Kuhlmeier, 484 U.S. 260 (1988)   308

Head Money Cases (Edye v. Robertson), 112 U.S. 580 (1884)   80
Heart of Atlanta Motel, Inc. v. United States, 379 U.S. 241 (1964)   16
Helvering v. Davis, 301 U.S. 619 (1937)   45
Herbert v. Lando, 441 U.S. 153 (1979)   267
Hishon v. King & Spalding, 467 U.S. 69 (1984)   435
Holden v. Hardy, 169 U.S. 366 (1898)   180
Hollingsworth v. Virginia, 3 Dallas (3 U.S.) 378 (1798)   162
Home Building and Loan Association v. Blaisdell, 290 U.S. 398 (1934)   175
Houston, E. & W. Texas Ry. Co. v. United States, 234 U.S. 342 (1914)   8
Hurley v. Irish-American Gay, Lesbian and Bisexual Group of Boston,
   515 U.S. 557 (1995)   256
Hurtado v. California, 110 U.S. 516 (1884)   348
Hustler *Magazine v. Falwell*, 485 U.S. 46 (1988)   271
Hylton v. United States, 3 Dallas (3 U.S.) 171 (1796)   31
Illinois ex rel. McCollum v. Board of Education, Champaign County,
   Illinois, 333 U.S. 203 (1948)   210
Immigration and Naturalization Service v. Chadha, 462 U.S. 919 (1983)   75
Johnson v. Eisentrager, 339 U.S. 763 (1950)   91
Jones v. Alfred H. Mayer Co., 392 U.S. 409 (1968)   412
Jones v. United States, 529 U.S. 848 (2000)   18
Katz v. United States, 389 U.S. 347 (1967)   318
Katzenbach v. Morgan, 384 U.S. 641 (1966)   398
Kelo v. City of New London, 545 U.S. 469 (2005)   194
Kentucky Whip and Collar Co. v. Illinois Central R.R. Co.,
   299 U.S. 334 (1937)   12
Keyishian v. Board of Regents, 385 U.S. 589 (1967)   293
Kimel v. Florida Board of Regents, 528 U.S. 62 (2000)   130
Knowles v. Iowa, 525 U.S. 113 (1998)   332
Korematsu v. United States, 323 U.S. 214 (1944)   89
Kovacs v. Cooper, 336 U.S. 77 (1949)   303
Lapides v. Board of Regents of University of Georgia,
   535 U.S. 613 (2002)   132
Lawrence v. Texas, 539 U.S. 558 (2003)   390
Lee v. Weisman, 505 U.S. 577 (1992)   222
Legal Tender Cases, 12 Wallace (78 U.S.) 457 (1871)   34
Leisy v. Hardin, 135 U.S. 100 (1890)   141
Lemon v. Kurtzman, 403 U.S. 602 (1971)   214
Lincoln Federal Labor Union No. 19129 v. Northwestern Iron and
   Metal Co., 335 U.S. 525 (1949)   187
Lochner v. New York, 198 U.S. 45 (1905)   181
Loving v. Virginia, 388 U.S. 1 (1967)   411
Luther v. Borden, 7 Howard (48 U.S.) 1 (1849)   119
Lynch v. Donnelly, 465 U.S. 668 (1984)   298
Malloy v. Hogan, 378 U.S. 1 (1964)   362
Mapp v. Ohio, 367 U.S. 643 (1961)   321

Marbury v. Madison, 1 Cranch (5 U.S.) 137 (1803)   105
Marchetti v. United States, 390 U.S. 39 (1968)   364
Marsh v. Alabama, 326 U.S. 501 (1946)   234
Marsh v. Chambers, 463 U.S. 783 (1983)   219
Marshall v. Barlow's Inc., 436 U.S. 307 (1978)   324
Martin v. City of Struthers, Ohio, 319 U.S. 141 (1943)   262
Martin v. Hunter's Lessee, 1 Wheaton (14 U.S.) 304 (1816)   106
Martin v. Mott, 12 Wheaton (25 U.S.) 19 (1827)   58
Ex parte McCardle, 7 Wallace (74 U.S.) 506 (1869)   110
McCleskey v. Kemp, 481 U.S. 279 (1987)   367
McCray v. United States, 195 U.S. 27 (1904)   38
McCreary County v. American Civil Liberties Union, 545 U.S. 844 (2005)   230
McCulloch v. Maryland, 4 Wheaton (17 U.S.) 316 (1819)   28
McGrain v. Daugherty, 273 U.S. 135 (1927)   29
McLaurin v. Oklahoma State Regents, 339 U.S. 637 (1950)   409
Meritor Savings Bank v. Vinson, 477 U.S. 57 (1986)   439
Ex parte Merryman, 17 Fed. Cas. 9487 (1861)   59
Meyer v. Nebraska, 262 U.S. 390 (1923)   378
Michael M. v. Superior Court of Sonoma County,
    450 U.S. 464 (1981)   434
Miller v. Albright, 523 U.S. 420 (1998)   442
Miller v. California, 413 U.S. 15 (1973)   284
Ex parte Milligan, 4 Wallace (71 U.S.) 2 (1866)   85
Milliken v. Bradley, 418 U.S. 717 (1974)   414
Miranda v. Arizona, 384 U.S. 436 (1966)   358
Mississippi v. Johnson, 4 Wallace (71 U.S.) 475 (1867)   60
Missouri ex rel. Gaines v. Canada, 305 U.S. 337 (1938)   405
Missouri v. Holland, 252 U.S. 416 (1920)   81
Missouri v. Jenkins, 495 U.S. 33 (1990)   116
Mistretta v. United States, 488 U.S. 361 (1989)   26
Monaco v. Mississippi, 292 U.S. 313 (1934)   128
Moose Lodge No. 107 v. Irvis, 407 U.S. 163 (1972)   413
Morehead v. New York ex rel. Tipaldo, 298 U.S. 587 (1936)   186
Morrison v. Olson, 487 U.S. 654 (1988)   78
Morse v. Frederick, 551 U.S. 393 (2007)   309
Mulford v. Smith, 307 U.S. 38 (1939)   47
Muller v. Oregon, 208 U.S. 412 (1908)   182
Munn v. Illinois, 94 U.S. 113 (1877)   178
Murdock v. Pennsylvania, 319 U.S. 105 (1943)   234
Murphy v. Waterfront Commission of New York Harbor,
    378 U.S. 52 (1964)   362
Muskrat v. United States, 219 U.S. 346 (1911)   120
Myers v. United States, 272 U.S. 52 (1926)   62
NAACP v. Alabama, 357 U.S. 449 (1958)   252
National Endowment for the Arts v. Finley, 524 U.S. 569 (1998)   287

National Labor Relations Board v. Jones & Laughlin Steel Corporation,
   301 U.S. 1 (1937)   43
National Labor Relations Board v. Yeshiva University,
   444 U.S. 672 (1980)   48
National League of Cities v. Usery, 426 U.S. 833 (1976)   157
National Prohibition Cases (Rhode Island v. Palmer),253 U.S. 350 (1920)   163
NCAA v. Board of Regents of University of Oklahoma, 468 U.S. 85 (1984)   48
In re Neagle, 135 U.S. 1 (1890)   61
Near v. Minnesota ex rel. Olson, 283 U.S. 697 (1931)   260
Nebbia v. New York, 291 U.S. 502 (1934)   185
Nebraska Press Association v. Stuart, 427 U.S. 539 (1976)   266
New Jersey v. T.L.O., 469 U.S. 325 (1985)   329
New York v. Ferber, 458 U.S. 747 (1982)   285
New York v. United States, 505 U.S. 144 (1992)   148
New York Times Company v. Sullivan, 376 U.S. 254 (1964)   263
New York Times Company v. United States, 403 U.S. 713 (1971)   265
Nix v. Williams, 467 U.S. 431 (1984)   328
Nixon v. Condon, 286 U.S. 73 (1932)   448
Nixon v. Fitzgerald, 457 U.S. 731 (1982)   69
Nixon v. United States, 506 U.S. 224 (1993)   123
Norris v. Alabama, 294 U.S. 587 (1935)   349
Northern Securities Co. v. United States, 193 U.S. 197 (1904)   37
Northwest Austin Municipal Utility District Number One v. Holder,
   129 S. Ct. 2504 (2009)   461
O'Connor v. Donaldson, 422 U.S. 563 (1975)   344
Olmstead v. United States, 277 U.S. 438 (1928)   317
Oregon v. Mitchell, 400 U.S. 112 (1970)   453
Oyama v. California, 332 U.S. 633 (1948)   428
Palko v. Connecticut, 302 U.S. 319 (1937)   201
Panama Refining Co. v. Ryan, 293 U.S. 388 (1935)   22
Payne v. Tennessee, 501 U.S. 808 (1991)   370
Pennsylvania v. Nelson, 350 U.S. 497 (1956)   135
Pierce v. Society of Sisters of the Holy Names of Jesus and Mary,
   268 U.S. 510 (1925)   379
Planned Parenthood of Southeastern Pennsylvania v. Casey,
   505 U.S. 833 (1992)   387
Plessy v. Ferguson, 163 U.S. 537 (1896)   404
Plyler v. Doe, 457 U.S. 202 (1982)   430
Pollock v. Farmers' Loan and Trust Co., 158 U.S. 601 (1895)   35
Powell v. Alabama, 287 U.S. 45 (1932)   354
Powell v. McCormack, 395 U.S. 486 (1969)   51
Printz v. United States, Mack v. United States, 521 U.S. 898 (1997)   150
The Prize Cases, 2 Black (67 U.S.) 635 (1863)   84
Puerto Rico v. Branstad, 483 U.S. 219 (1987)   140
Ex parte Quirin, 317 U.S. 1 (1942)   88

Rasul v. Bush, 542 U.S. 466 (2004)   95

Rathbun, Humphrey's Executor v. United States, 295 U.S. 602 (1935)   64

Reed v. Reed, 404 U.S. 71 (1971)   432

Regents of the University of California v. Bakke, 438 U.S. 265 (1978)   415

Reno v. American Civil Liberties Union, 521 U.S. 844 (1997)   286

Republican Party of Minnesota v. White, 536 U.S. 765 (2002)   274

Reynolds v. Sims, 377 U.S. 533 (1964)   452

Reynolds v. United States, 98 U.S. 145 (1879)   232

Ricci v. DeStefano (2009)   424

Richmond Newspapers, Inc. v. Commonwealth of Virginia,
    448 U.S. 555 (1980)   269

Ring v. Arizona, 536 U.S. 584 (2002)   372

Rochin v. California, 342 U.S. 165 (1952)   205

Roe v. Wade, 410 U.S. 113 (1973)   383

Romer v. Evans, 517 U.S. 620 (1996)   441

Rosenberger v. University of Virginia, 515 U.S. 810 (1995)   241

Rostker v. Goldberg, 453 U.S. 57 (1981)   93

Roth v. United States, 354 U.S. 476 (1957)   282

Rumsfeld v. Forum, 547 U.S. 47(2006)   258

Safford Unified School District # 1 v. Redding, S. Ct. 2633 (2009)   335

San Antonio Independent School District v. Rodriguez, 411 U.S. 1 (1973)   437

Santa Clara County v. Southern Pacific Railroad Company,
    118 U.S. 394 (1886)   180

Santa Fe School District v. Doe, 530 U.S. 290 (2000)   225

Sattazahn v. Pennsylvania, 123 S. Ct. 732 (2003)   341

Schechter Poultry Corp. v. United States, 295 U.S. 495 (1935)   23

Scheidler v. National Organization for Women, 537 U.S. 393 (2003)   346

Schenck v. United States, 249 U.S. 47 (1919)   291

Schmerber v. California, 384 U.S. 757 (1966)   363

Scott v. Sandford, 19 Howard (60 U.S.) 393 (1857)   401

Screws v. United States, 325 U.S. 91 (1945)   406

Selective Draft Law Cases (Arver v. United States), 245 U.S. 366 (1918)   86

Shapiro v. Thompson, 394 U.S. 618 (1969)   382

Shaw v. Reno, 509 U.S. 630 (1993)   455

Shelley v. Kraemer, 334 U.S. 1 (1948)   407

The Shreveport Case, 234 U.S. 342 (1914)   8

Slaughterhouse Case, 16 Wallace (83 U.S.) 36 (1873)   177

Smith v. Allwright, 321 U.S. 649 (1944)   449

Smith v. Doe, 123 S. Ct. 1140 (2003)   147

Snepp v. United States, 444 U.S. 507 (1980)   306

South Carolina v. Katzenbach, 383 U.S. 301 (1966)   399

South Carolina v. United States, 199 U.S. 437 (1905)   38

South Dakota v. Dole, 483 U.S. 203 (1987)   49

Southern Pacific Co. v. Arizona, 325 U.S. 761 (1945)   134

Sprietsman v. Mercury Marine, 537 U.S. 51 (2002)   136

Stafford v. Wallace, 258 U.S. 495 (1922) — 10

Standard Oil Co. of New Jersey v. United States, 221 U.S. 1 (1910) — 40

State Farm Mutual Auto Insurance Company v. Campbell, 123 S. Ct. 1513 (2003) — 190

State of Louisiana ex rel. Francis v. Resweber, 329 U.S. 459 (1947) — 365

Steward Machine Co. v. Davis, 301 U.S. 548 (1937) — 42

Stone v. Graham, 449 U.S. 39 (1980) — 217

Stone v. Mississippi, 101 U.S. 814 (1880) — 174

Stone v. Powell, 428 U.S. 465 (1976) — 115

Swann v. Charlotte-Mecklenburg Board of Education, 402 U.S. 1 (1971) — 413

Sweatt v. Painter, 339 U.S. 629 (1950) — 408

Swift and Co. v. United States, 196 U.S. 375 (1905) — 39

Takahashi v. Fish & Game Commission, 334 U.S. 410 (1948) — 429

Terry v. Ohio, 392 U.S. 1 (1968) — 322

Texas v. Johnson, 491 U.S. 397 (1989) — 299

Texas v. White, 1 Wallace (74 U.S.) 700 (1869) — 153

Thompson v. Oklahoma, 487 U.S. 815 (1988) — 368

Thornton v. United States, 541 U.S. 615 (2004) — 333

Tinker v. Des Moines, 393 U.S. 503 (1969) — 297

Truax v. Raich, 239 U.S. 33 (1915) — 426

Trustees of Dartmouth College v. Woodward, 4 Wheaton (17 U.S.) 518 (1819) — 172

Tumey v. Ohio, 273 U.S. 510 (1927) — 342

Ullmann v. United States, 350 U.S. 422 (1956) — 360

United Public Workers of America v. Mitchell, 330 U.S. 75 (1947) — 251

United States v. Belmont, 301 U.S. 324 (1937) — 82

United States v. Butler, 297 U.S. 1 (1936) — 42

United States v. Carolene Products Co., 304 U.S. 144 (1938) — 202

United States v. Classic, 313 U.S. 299 (1941) — 449

United States v. Curtiss-Wright Export Corp., 299 U.S. 304 (1936) — 24

United States v. F. W. Darby Lumber Co., 312 U.S. 100 (1941) — 156

United States v. E. C. Knight Co., 156 U.S. 1 (1895) — 5

United States v. Lanza, 260 U.S. 377 (1922) — 339

United States v. Lee, 455 U.S. 252 (1982) — 237

United States v. Leon, 468 U.S. 897 (1984) — 326

United States v. Lopez, 514 U.S. 549 (1995) — 17

United States v. Lovett, 328 U.S. 303 (1946) — 74

United States v. Morrison, 529 U.S. 598 (2000) — 151

United States v. Nixon, 418 U.S. 683 (1974) — 68

United States v. Ross, 456 U.S. 798 (1982) — 325

United States v. Southeastern Underwriters Association, 332 U.S. 533 (1944) — 15

United States v. United States District Court, 407 U.S. 297 (1972) — 319

United States v. Virginia, 518 U.S. 515 (1996) — 436

United States v. Wong Kim Ark, 169 U.S. 649 (1898) — 425

United States Trust Co. v. New Jersey, 431 U.S. 1 (1977) — 176

United Steel Workers of America v. Weber, Kaiser Aluminum v. Weber,
    United Staes v. Weber, 443 U.S. 193 (1979)   416
University of Alabama Board of Trustees v. Garrett, 531 U.S. 356 (2001)   131
U.S. Term Limits, Inc. v. Thornton, 514 U.S. 779 (1995)   53
Vacco v. Quill, Washington v. Glucksberg, 521 U.S. 702 (1997)   389
Van Orden v. Perry, 545 U.S. 677 (2005)   229
Veazie Bank v. Fenno, 8 Wallace (75 U.S.) 533 (1869)   32
Village of Euclid, Ohio v. Ambler Realty Co., 272 U.S. 365 (1926)   192
Virginia v. Black, 538 U.S. 343 (2003)   302
Virginia v. Tennessee, 148 U.S. 503 (1893)   142
Virginia State Board of Pharmacy v. Virginia Citizens Consumer
    Council, Inc., 425 U.S. 748 (1976)   279
Wallace v. Jaffree, 472 U.S. 38 (1985)   220
Watkins v. United States, 354 U.S. 178 (1957)   29
Weeks v. United States, 232 U.S. 383 (1914)   320
Welsh v. United States, 398 U.S. 333 (1970)   236
Wesberry v. Sanders, 376 U.S. 1 (1964)   451
West Coast Hotel Co. v. Parrish, 300 U.S. 379 (1937)   13
West Virginia State Board of Education v. Barnette, 319 U.S. 624 (1943)   296
Wickard v. Filburn, 317 U.S. 111 (1942)   14
Widmar v. Vincent, 454 U.S. 263 (1981)   217
Wisconsin v. Yoder, 406 U.S. 205 (1972)   216
Woods v. Cloyd W. Miller Co., 333 U.S. 138 (1948)   90
Worcester v. Georgia, 31 U.S. 515 (1832)   139
Yakus v. United States, 321 U.S. 414 (1944)   25
Ex parte Yarbrough, 110 U.S. 651 (1884)   446
Youngstown Sheet & Tube Co. v. Sawyer, 343 U.S. 579 (1952)   65
Zablocki v. Redhail, 434 U.S. 374 (1978)   384
Zelman v. Simmons-Harris, 536 U.S. 639 (2002)   228
Ziffrin v. Reeves, 308 U.S. 132 (1939)   155
Zobrest v. Catalina Foothills School District, 509 U.S. 1 (1993)   223
Zorach v. Clauson, 343 U.S. 306 (1952)   211
Zurcher v. The Stanford Daily, 436 U.S. 547 (1978)   323

Chronological List of Cases by Chief Justice

CHIEF JUSTICES JOHN JAY, JOHN RUTLEDGE, OLIVER ELLSWORTH
(1789–1801)
Chisholm v. Georgia (1793)   137
Hylton v. United States (1796)   31
Calder v. Bull (1798)   171
Hollingsworth v. Virginia (1798)   162

CHIEF JUSTICE JOHN MARSHALL (1801–1835)
Marbury v. Madison (1803)   105
Fletcher v. Peck (1810)   171
Martin v. Hunter's Lessee (1816)   106
Trustees of Dartmouth College v. Woodward (1819)   172
McCulloch v. Maryland (1819)   28
Cohens v. Virginia (1821)   107
Gibbons v. Ogden (1824)   2
Eakin v. Raub (1825)   108
Brown v. Maryland (1827)   3
Martin v. Mott (1827)   58
Cherokee Nation v. Georgia (1831)   138
Worcester v. Georgia (1832)   139
Barron v. Baltimore (1833)   200

CHIEF JUSTICE ROGER B. TANEY (1836–1864)
Charles River Bridge Co. v. Warren River Bridge (1837)   173
Luther v. Borden (1849)   119
Cooley v. The Board of Wardens of the Port of Philadelphia (1851)   4
Scott v. Sandford (1857)   401
Ableman v. Booth (1859)   109
Ex parte Merryman (1861)   59
The Prize Cases (1863)   84

511

CHIEF JUSTICE SALMON P. CHASE (1864–1873)

Ex parte Milligan (1866)	85
Mississippi v. Johnson (1867)	60
Ex parte McCardle (1869)	110
Texas v. White (1869)	153
Veazie Bank v. Fenno (1869)	32
Collector v. Day (1871)	33
Legal Tender Cases (1871)	34
Slaughterhouse Cases (1873)	177

CHIEF JUSTICE MORRISON R. WAITE (1874–1888)

Munn v. Illinois (1877)	178
Reynolds v. United States (1879)	232
Stone v. Mississippi (1880)	174
The Civil Rights Cases (1883)	403
Head Money Cases (1884)	80
Hurtado v. California (1884)	348
Ex parte Yarbrough (1884)	446
Santa Clara County v. Southern Pacific Railroad Co. (1886)	180

CHIEF JUSTICE MELVILLE W. FULLER (1888–1910)

Hans v. Louisiana (1890)	127
Leisy v. Hardin (1890)	141
In re Neagle (1890)	61
Virginia v. Tennessee (1893)	142
In re Debs (1895)	6
Pollock v. Farmers' Loan and Trust Co. (1895)	35
United States v. E. C. Knight (1895)	5
Plessy v. Ferguson (1896)	404
Holden v. Hardy (1898)	180
United States v. Wong Kim Ark (1898)	425
Champion v. Ames (1903)	7
McCray v. United States (1904)	38
Northern Securities Co. v. United States (1904)	37
Lochner v. New York (1905)	181
South Carolina v. United States (1905)	38
Swift and Co. v. United States (1905)	39
Muller v. Oregon (1908)	182
Standard Oil Co. of New Jersey v. United States (1910)	40

CHIEF JUSTICE EDWARD D. WHITE (1910–1921)

Coyle v. Smith (1911)	154
Muskrat v. United States (1911)	120
The Shreveport Case (1914)	8
Weeks v. United States (1914)	320

Guinn v. United States (1915) — 447
Truax v. Raich (1915) — 426
Bunting v. Oregon (1917) — 183
Selective Draft Law Cases (1918) — 86
Hammer v. Dagenhart (1918) — 9
Abrams v. United States (1919) — 259
Hamilton v. Kentucky Distilleries & Warehouse Co. (1919) — 87
Schenck v. United States (1919) — 291
Hawke v. Smith (1920) — 164
Missouri v. Holland (1920) — 81
National Prohibition Cases (1920) — 163

CHIEF JUSTICE WILLIAM HOWARD TAFT (1921–1930)
Dillon v. Gloss (1921) — 165
Bailey v. Drexel Furniture Co. (1922) — 41
Stafford v. Wallace (1922) — 10
United States v. Lanza (1922) — 339
Adkins v. Children's Hospital (1923) — 184
Commonwealth of Massachusetts v. Mellon (1923) — 111
Meyer v. Nebraska (1923) — 378
Gitlow v. New York (1925) — 200
Ex parte Grossman (1925) — 63
Pierce v. Society of Sisters of the Holy Names of Jesus and Mary (1925) — 379
Myers v. United States (1926) — 62
Village of Euclid, Ohio v. Ambler Realty Co. (1926) — 192
Buck v. Bell (1927) — 380
McGrain v. Daugherty (1927) — 29
Tumey v. Ohio (1927) — 342
J.W. Hampton, Jr. and Co. v. United States (1928) — 21
Olmstead v. United States (1928) — 317

CHIEF JUSTICE CHARLES EVANS HUGHES (1930–1941)
Near v. Minnesota ex rel. Olson (1931) — 260
Nixon v. Condon (1932) — 448
Powell v. Alabama (1932) — 354
Home Building and Loan Association v. Blaisdell (1934) — 175
Monaco v. Mississippi (1934) — 128
Nebbia v. New York (1934) — 185
Norris v. Alabama (1935) — 349
Panama Refining Co. v. Ryan (1935) — 22
Rathbun, Humphrey's Executor v. United States (1935) — 64
Schechter Poultry Corp v. United States (1935) — 23
Ashwander v. Tennessee Valley Authority (1936) — 11
Grosjean v. American Press Co. (1936) — 261

Morehead v. New York ex rel. Tipaldo (1936)	186
United States v. Butler (1936)	42
United States v. Curtiss-Wright Export Corp. (1936)	24
DeJonge v. Oregon (1937)	249
Helvering v. Davis (1937)	45
Kentucky Whip and Collar Co. v. Illinois Central R.R. Co. (1937)	12
National Labor Relations Board v. Jones & Laughlin Steel Corp. (1937)	43
Palko v. Connecticut (1937)	201
Steward Machine Co. v. Davis (1937)	42
United States v. Belmont (1937)	82
West Coast Hotel Co. v. Parrish (1937)	13
Erie Railroad Co. v. Tompkins (1938)	112
Missouri ex rel. Gaines v. Canada (1938)	405
United States v. Carolene Products Co. (1938)	202
Coleman v. Miller (1939)	166
Graves v. New York ex rel. O'Keefe (1939)	45
Hague v. Congress of Industrial Organizations (1939)	250
Mulford v. Smith (1939)	47
Ziffrin v. Reeves (1939)	155
Cantwell v. Connecticut (1940)	233
Chambers v. Florida (1940)	355

CHIEF JUSTICE HARLAN FISKE STONE (1941–1946)

Bridges v. California (1941)	261
Cox v. New Hampshire (1941)	295
Edwards v. California (1941)	143
United States v. Classic (1941)	449
United States v. F. W. Darby Lumber Co. (1941)	156
Ex parte Quirin (1942)	88
Wickard v. Filburn (1942)	14
Martin v. City of Struthers, Ohio (1943)	262
Murdock v. Pennsylvania (1943)	234
West Virginia State Board of Education v. Barnette (1943)	296
Korematsu v. United States (1944)	89
Smith v. Allwright (1944)	449
United States v. Southeastern Underwriters Association (1944)	15
Yakus v. United States (1944)	25
Screws v. United States (1945)	406
Southern Pacific Co. v. Arizona (1945)	134
Duncan v. Kahanamoku (1946)	90
Girouard v. United States (1946)	427
Marsh v. Alabama (1946)	234
United States v. Lovett (1946)	74

CHIEF JUSTICE FRED M. VINSON (1946–1953)
Adamson v. California (1947)   204
Everson v. Board of Education of Ewing Township (1947)   209
State of Louisiana ex rel. Francis v. Resweber (1947)   365
United Public Workers of America v. Mitchell (1947)   251
Illinois ex rel. McCollum v. Board of Education, Champaign County,
   Illinois (1948)   210
Oyama v. California (1948)   428
Shelley v. Kraemer (1948)   407
Takahashi v. Fish & Game Commission (1948)   429
Woods v. Cloyd W. Miller Co. (1948)   90
Giboney v. Empire Storage & Ice Co. (1949)   188
Kovacs v. Cooper (1949)   303
Lincoln Federal Labor Union v. Northwestern Iron and Metal Co. (1949)   187
American Communications Association v. Douds (1950)   292
McLaurin v. Oklahoma State Regents (1950)   409
Sweatt v. Painter (1950)   408
Dennis v. United States (1951)   292
Feiner v. New York (1951)   304
Burstyn v. Wilson (1952)   282
Rochin v. California (1952)   205
Youngstown Sheet & Tube Co. v. Sawyer (1952)   65
Zorach v. Clauson (1952)   211

CHIEF JUSTICE EARL WARREN (1953–1969)
Bolling v. Sharpe (1954)   343
Brown v. Board of Education of Topeka (1954)   409
Brown v. Board of Education II (1955)   410
Pennsylvania v. Nelson (1956)   135
Ullmann v. United States (1956)   360
Roth v. United States (1957)   282
Watkins v. United States (1957)   29
Cooper v. Aaron (1958)   113
NAACP v. Alabama (1958)   252
Barenblatt v. United States (1959)   30
Gomillion v. Lightfoot (1960)   451
Mapp v. Ohio (1961)   321
Baker v. Carr (1962)   121
Engel et al. v. Vitale et al. (1962)   212
Abington School District v. Schempp (1963)   213
Gideon v. Wainwright (1963)   356
Escobedo v. Illinois (1964)   357
Malloy v. Hogan (1964)   362
Murphy v. Waterfront Commission of New York Harbor (1964)   362

Heart of Atlanta Motel, Inc. v. United States (1964) — 16
New York Times Company v. Sullivan (1964) — 263
Reynolds v. Sims (1964) — 452
Wesberry v. Sanders (1964) — 451
Griswold v. Connecticut (1965) — 381
Ginzburg v. United States (1966) — 283
Katzenbach v. Morgan (1966) — 398
Miranda v. Arizona (1966) — 358
Schmerber v. California (1966) — 363
South Carolina v. Katzenbach (1966) — 399
Katz v. United States (1967) — 318
Keyishian v. Board of Regents (1967) — 293
Loving v. Virginia (1967) — 411
Duncan v. Louisiana (1968) — 350
Flast v. Cohen (1968) — 114
Jones v. Alfred H. Mayer Co. (1968) — 412
Marchetti v. United States (1968) — 364
Terry v. Ohio (1968) — 322
Brandenburg v. Ohio (1969) — 294
Chimel v. California (1969) — 323
Shapiro v. Thompson (1969) — 382
Powell v. McCormack (1969) — 51
Tinker v. Des Moines (1969) — 297

CHIEF JUSTICE WARREN BURGER (1969–1986)

Oregon v. Mitchell (1970) — 453
Welsh v. United States (1970) — 236
Lemon v. Kurtzman (1971) — 214
New York Times Company v. United States (1971) — 265
Reed v. Reed (1971) — 432
Swann v. Charlotte-Mecklenburg Board of Education (1971) — 413
Argersinger v. Hamlin (1972) — 359
Branzburg v. Hayes (1972) — 265
Dunn v. Blumstein (1972) — 454
Gravel v. United States (1972) — 52
Moose Lodge No. 107 v. Irvis (1972) — 413
United States v. United States District Court (1972) — 319
Wisconsin v. Yoder (1972) — 216
Frontiero v. Richardson (1973) — 432
Miller v. California (1973) — 284
Roe v. Wade (1973) — 383
San Antonio Independent School District v. Rodriguez (1973) — 437
Milliken v. Bradley (1974) — 414
United States v. Nixon (1974) — 68
O'Connor v. Donaldson (1975) — 344

Buckley v. Valeo (1976)	272
Elrod v. Burns (1976)	273
Gregg v. Georgia (1976)	366
National League of Cities v. Usery (1976)	157
Nebraska Press Association v. Stuart (1976)	266
Stone v. Powell (1976)	115
Virginia State Board of Pharmacy v. Virginia Citizens Consumer Council, Inc. (1976)	279
United States Trust Co. v. New Jersey (1977)	176
Regents of the University of California v. Bakke (1978)	415
Bordenkircher v. Hayes (1978)	345
Federal Communications Commission v. Pacifica Foundation (1978)	305
First National Bank of Boston v. Bellotti (1978)	280
Foley v. Connelie (1978)	430
Marshall v. Barlow's, Inc. (1978)	324
Zablocki v. Redhail (1978)	384
Zurcher v. The Stanford Daily (1978)	323
Burch v. Louisiana (1979)	351
Duren v. Missouri (1979)	352
Gannett Co. v. DePasquale (1979)	268
Goldwater v. Carter (1979)	83
Herbert v. Lando (1979)	267
United Steel Workers of America v. Weber, Kaiser Aluminum v. Weber, United States v. Weber (1979)	416
Branti v. Finkel (1980)	252
Fullilove v. Klutznick (1980)	417
Harris v. McRae (1980)	385
National Labor Relations Board v. Yeshiva University (1980)	48
Richmond Newspapers, Inc. v. Commonwealth of Virginia (1980)	269
Snepp v. United States (1980)	306
Stone v. Graham (1980)	217
Chandler and Granger v. Florida (1981)	270
Dames and Moore v. Regan (1981)	66
Haig v. Agee (1981)	67
Michael M. v. Superior Court of Sonoma County (1981)	434
Rostker v. Goldberg (1981)	93
Widmar v. Vincent (1981)	217
New York v. Ferber (1982)	285
Nixon v. Fitzgerald (1982)	69
Plyler v. Doe (1982)	430
United States v. Lee (1982)	237
United States v. Ross (1982)	325
Equal Employment Opportunity Commission v. Wyoming (1983)	158
Immigration and Naturalization Service v. Chadha (1983)	75
Marsh v. Chambers (1983)	219

Hawaii Housing Authority v. Midkiff (1984)   192
Hishon v. King & Spalding (1984)   435
Lynch v. Donnelly (1984)   298
NCAA v. Board of Regents of University of Oklahoma (1984)   48
Nix v. Williams (1984)   328
United States v. Leon (1984)   326
Cleburne v. Cleburne Living Center (1985)   437
Garcia v. San Antonio Metropolitan Transit Authority (1985)   159
New Jersey v. T.L.O. (1985)   329
Wallace v. Jaffree (1985)   220
Batson v. Kentucky (1986)   353
Bethel School District No. 403 v. Fraser (1986)   307
Bowers v. Hardwick (1986)   386
Bowsher v. Snyar (1986)   77
California v. Ciraolo (1986)   330
Goldman v. Weinberger (1986)   238
Meritor Savings Bank v. Vinson (1986)   439

CHIEF JUSTICE WILLIAM REHNQUIST (1986–2005)
Board of Directors of Rotary International v. Rotary Club of Duarte (1987)   253
Edwards v. Aguillard (1987)   221
McCleskey v. Kemp (1987)   367
Puerto Rico v. Branstad (1987)   140
South Dakota v. Dole (1987)   49
California v. Greenwood (1988)   331
Coy v. Iowa (1988)   340
Frisby v. Schultz (1988)   255
Hazelwood School District v. Kuhlmeier (1988)   308
Hustler *Magazine v. Falwell* (1988)   271
Morrison v. Olson (1988)   78
Thompson v. Oklahoma (1988)   368
DeShaney v. Winnebago Social Services (1989)   345
Mistretta v. United States (1989)   26
Texas v. Johnson (1989)   299
*Employment Division, Department of Human Resources of
    Oregon v. Smith* (1990)   239
Missouri v. Jenkins (1990)   116
Gregory v. Ashcroft (1991)   440
Payne v. Tennessee (1991)   370
Lee v. Weisman (1992)   222
New York v. United States (1992)   148
Planned Parenthood of Southeastern Pennsylvania v. Casey (1992)   387
Church of Lukumi Babalu Aye v. City of Hialeah (1993)   240
Nixon v. United States (1993)   123
Shaw v. Reno (1993)   455

Zobrest v. Catalina Foothills School District (1993)   223
Dolan v. City of Tigard (1994)   193
Adarand Constructors, Inc. v. Pena (1995)   418
Hurley v. Irish-American Gay, Lesbian and Bisexual Group of
    Boston (1995)   256
Rosenberger v. University of Virginia (1995)   241
United States v. Lopez (1995)   17
U.S. Term Limits, Inc. v. Thorton (1995)   53
BMW of North America, Inc. v. Gore (1996)   189
Bush v. Vera (1996)   456
44 Liquormart, Inc. v. Rhode Island (1996)   281
Romer v. Evans (1996)   441
United States v. Virginia (1996)   423
Agostini v. Felton (1997)   224
Camps Newfound/Owatonna, v. Town of Harrison (1997)   143
City of Boerne v. Flores (1997)   400
Clinton v. Jones (1997)   70
Printz v. United States, Mach v. United States (1997)   150
Reno v. American Civil Liberties Union (1997)   286
Vacco v. Quill, Washington v. Glucksberg (1997)   389
Clinton v. City of New York (1998)   79
Knowles v. Iowa (1998)   332
Miller v. Albright (1998)   442
National Endowment for the Arts v. Finley (1998)   287
Alden v. Maine (1999)   128
Board of Regents v. Southworth (2000)   243
Boy Scouts of America v. Dale (2000)   257
Bush v. Gore (2000)   457
Crosby v. National Foreign Trade Council (2000)   145
Dickerson v. United States (2000)   359
Erie v. Pap's A.M. (2000)   300
Jones v. United States (2000)   18
Kimel v. Florida Board of Regents (2000)   130
Santa Fe School District v. Doe (2000)   225
United States v. Morrison (2000)   151
Cook v. Gralike (2001)   146
Good News Club v. Milford Central School (2001)   226
University of Alabama Board of Trustees v. Garrett (2001)   131
Atkins v. Virginia (2002)   371
Ashcroft v. The Free Speech Coalition (2002)   288
Board of Education of Independent School District No. 92 of
    Pottawatomie County v. Earls (2002)   332
Federal Maritime Commission v. South Carolina State Ports
    Authority (2002)   133
Lapides v. Board of Regents of University of Georgia (2002)   132

Republican Party of Minnesota v. White (2002)   274
Ring v. Arizona (2002)   372
Sprietsman v. Mercury Marine (2002)   136
Zelman v. Simmons-Harris (2002)   228
Connecticut Department of Public Safety v. John Doe (2003)   444
Eldred v. Ashcroft (2003)   50
Ewing v. California (2003)   373
Gratz v. Bollinger (2003)   420
Grutter v. Bollinger (2003)   422
Lawrence v. Texas (2003)   390
Sattazahn v. Pennsylvania (2003)   341
Scheidler v. National Organization for Women (2003)   346
Smith v. Doe (2003)   147
State Farm Mutual Auto Insurance Company v. Campbell (2003)   190
Virginia v. Black (2003)   302

INDEX

Abbate v. United States, 340
Abood v. Detroit Bd. of Education, 244
abortion, 244, 377, 384–85, 387–89,
    392–94
accommodation of religion, 207
actual malice, 264
Adams, John, 105
Adamson v. California, 199, 363
Addington v. Texas, 344
Adkins v. Children's Hospital, 14, 185
Adler v. Board of Education, 294
advertising alcohol prices, 281–82
advice and consent, 105
aerial search, 330
Aetna Life Ins. Co. v. Lavoie, 348
affirmative action programs, 415–25
African Americans, 401–25
age classifications, 397
Age Discrimination in Employment Act,
    130, 158, 440
aggravating factors, 341
Agostine v. Felton, 223
Agricultural Adjustment Act, 14, 42
Agriculture Act of 1938, 47
Aguilar v. Felton, 224
Ahrens v. Clark, 96
aid to parochial schools, 208, 214–15
Alaska Sex Offender Registration Act,
    147

Alberts v. California, 283
Alden v. Maine, 134
Alien Enemy Act of 1798, 92
aliens, 397, 425–31
Alien Tort Statute, 96
all-white primaries, 446, 448–50
*Amalgamated Food Employees Union v.
    Logan Valley Plaza*, 235
amendments, constitutional, 161–67
Americans with Disabilities Act, 131
Amish, 216, 237
animal sacrifice, 240–41
announce clause, 274–76
Antifederalists, 377
antitrust laws, 37, 39–40
Apodaca v. Oregon, 351
Apprendi v. New Jersey, 342, 372–73
Argersinger v. Hamlin, 338
Arizona Train Limit Law, 134
Arizona v. Evans, 116
armbands and symbolic speech, 249,
    297–98
Articles of Confederation, 1, 125, 161
Ashurst-Sumners Act of 1935, 12–13
Ashwander Rules, 12
assisted suicide, 389
*Atlas Roofing, Inc. v. Occupational
    Safety & Health Review Comm.*,
    325

Authorization for the Use of Military
Force, 94–95
automobile searches, 314, 325–26

Baker v. Carr, 76, 105, 123, 446
Bakke decision, 422
Balanced Budget and Emergency
Deficit Control Act of 1985, 77
Baldus Study, 367–68
Ballew v. Georgia, 351
Bank of U.S. constitutionality, 28–29
Barenblatt v. United States, 30
Barnes v. Glen Theater, Inc., 301
Barron v. Baltimore, 198
Bartkus v. Illinois, 340
Bartles v. Iowa, 379
Bates v. State Bar, 279
Benanti v. United States, 407
Berman v. Parker, 193, 195
*Bethel School District No. 503 v.
Fraser*, 249, 309
Betts v. Brady, 357
Bible reading in public schools, 213–14
bicameralism, 1, 75–76
bigamy, 208, 232–33
Bigelow v. Virginia, 279, 281
bill of attainder, 75
Bill of Rights, 100, 198; incorporation,
200–5
Bipartisan Campaign Finance Reform
Act of 2001, 273, 276–78
birth control law, 381–82
Black, Hugo Lafayette, 199, 248
Black Panthers, 266
Blacks, 401–25
blockade, 84–85
blood sample, 363–64
BMW v. Gore, 170, 191
*Board of Airport Commissioners v. Jews
for Jesus*, 236
*Board of Education of Kiryas Joel
Village School District v. Grumet*, 224
Bolling v. Sharpe, 419
Booth v. Maryland, 370
Bowers v. Hardwick, 378, 390, 442

Bowsher v. Synar, 73
Boyd v. United States, 320
Boy Scouts of America v. Dale, 247
*Braden v. 30th Judicial Circuit Court of
KY*, 96
Brady Handgun Violence Prevention
Act (1992), 150
Brandeis Brief, 183
Brandeis, Louis D., 183
Brandenburg v. Ohio, 248
Braunfeld v. Brown, 216
Breithaupt v. Abram, 363–64
Brewer v. Williams, 328
Bricker Amendment, 82
Brown v. Board of Education, 113–14,
343, 397, 405, 410–11
Brown v. Maryland, 141
Buckley v. Valeo, 248, 277
Bullington v. Missouri, 342
Burma, 145
burning: cross, 249, 302–3; flag, 249,
299–300
Bush v. Gore, 51, 445
bussing to promote desegregation, 413,
414–15
bus transportation to parochial schools,
209–10

Calder v. Bull, 169
California Alien Land Law, 428
California v. Ciraolo, 331
campaign-related speech, 272–78
capital punishment. *See* death penalty
Cardozo, Benjamin, 199
Carey v. Population Services, 279
Carlin, George, 305
Carroll v. United States, 326
Carter v. Carter Coal Co., 44
Carter, Jimmy, 64, 66, 93
case or controversy, 121
Central Intelligence Agency, 67, 306–7
*Charles C. Steward Machine Co. v.
Davis*, 456
*Charles River Bridge Co. v. Warren
River Bridge*, 169

charter, 172
checks and balances, 73
chief justice, 104
chief law enforcement officials, 150
child labor, 9–10, 166
Child Labor Tax Law of 1919, 41
Child Online Protection Act (COPA),
    289–90
Child Pornography Prevention Act
    (CPPA) of 1996, 288
Chisholm v. Georgia, 126, 127–28, 129,
    130, 133, 162
Christmas crèche, 298
citizenship, 296, 402–3
*Citizens United v. Federal Election
    Commission*, 248
City of Boerne v. Flores, 131, 208–9
City of Renton v. Playtime Theatres, 192
Civil Rights Act of 1964, 19, 159, 415–
    16, 424–25, 433, 438
Civil Rights Act of 1968, 413
Civil Rights Cases, 152, 297
Clayton Act, 41
clear and present danger test, 248
*Cleburne v. Cleburne Living Center,
    Inc.*, 132
Clinton v. City of New York, 2
Clinton v. Jones, 58
coerced confessions, 355–56
Colegrove v. Green, 122, 451
Coleman v. Miller, 162
collective bargaining, 48
Collector v. Day, 46
Combatant Status Review Tribunal, 97,
    100–2
commander-in-chief, 58, 73
commerce powers, 2–21
commercial speech, 248, 279–81
common law, federal, 112–13
Communications Decency Act of 1996,
    286, 290
Communications Workers v. Beck, 188
Communist Control Act of 1954, 135
Communist Party, 29, 31, 135, 249,
    292–93, 293–94

community, cross-section of, 352
Compassionate Use Act, 19–29
compelling state interest test, 208
compensatory damages, 189–90, 190–
    91, 347–48
Comprehensive Drug Abuse Prevention
    and Control Act, 19–21
comptroller general, 77
Compulsory Education Act (Oregon), 379
compulsory flag salute, 296
compulsory process, 339
compulsory school attendance laws,
    216, 379–80
concurring opinions, 104
confederal government, 125
Confederate government, 153
confidentiality of new sources, 265
confrontation, right to, 340–41
congressional investigations, 29–31
*Connecticut Department of Public
    Safety v. John Doe*, 148
Controlled Substance Act, 19–21, 245
conscientious objectors, 236–37
Conscription Act, 291
contract clause, 171–77
Controlled Substance Act, 245
Cooper v. Aaron, 7
Copyright Term Extension Act (1998),
    50
corporations, 172, 180, 280
council, right of, 328, 354–59
Court of Appeals for the District of
    Columbia, 103
Coyle v. Smith, 157
creation science, 221
criminal anarchy, 200
criminal syndicalism law, 249, 294
criminal trials: press access to, 269;
    television of, 270
cross burning, 302–3
cross-examination, 339, 341
cruel and unusual punishments, 365–76
Cummings v. Missouri, 75
Curtis, Ex parte, 251
Cutter v. Wilkinson, 245

dancing, nude, 300–1
dangerous tendency test, 248
Dartmouth College v. Woodward, 169
Davis v. Beason, 442
deaf interpreter in parochial schools,
    223–24
death penalty, 365–73, 374–76
delegata potestas non potest delegari,
    23, 25
delegation of powers, 21–27
Dennis v. United States, 248
*Department of Human Resources of
    Oregon v. Smith*, 240
Detainee Treatment Act of 2005, 97,
    100
deterrence function of punishment, 371
dilation and evacuation (D&E), 392
dilation and extraction (D&X), 392–93
Dillon v. Gloss, 162
direct and indirect taxes, 32
dissenting opinions, 104
District of Columbia v. Heller, 313
divided government, 57
Dobbins v. Erie County, 46
domestic dependent nations, 138
dormant commerce clause, 126, 144
double jeopardy, 201–2, 337, 339–40,
    341–42, 365–66
double standard, 200
Douglas, William O., 377
Douglass, Frederick, 423
draft cards, 301
drug testing, 332–33
dual federalism, 42
due process clauses, 177–92
during good behavior, 104
Duncan v. Louisiana, 351, 359
durational residency requirements, 454

education funding, 437
EEOC v. Wyoming, 130, 159
Eighteenth Amendment, 126, 163,
    165–66
Eighth Amendment, 365–76
election of 2000, 445, 457–60

Electoral College, 57, 445
electronic surveillance, 314, 317–20
eleemosynary institution, 172
Elementary and Secondary Education
    Act of 1965, 114
Eleventh Amendment, 126–34, 138
Ellsburg, Daniel, 265
El Paso v. Simmons, 176
Emancipation Proclamation, 395
Emergency Price Control Act of 1942,
    25
enemy combatant, 93–94
Equal Pay Act of 1963, 433
equal protection clause of Fourteenth
    Amendment, 121, 401–25
Equal Rights Amendment, 162, 433
Espionage Act, 162, 259–70, 291
Ethics in Government Act of 1978, 78
*Everson v. Board of Education of Ewing
    Township*, 208, 215, 229, 231
evolution, 221
exclusionary rule, 116, 314, 320–22
executive agreements, 73
executive branch, 57–71
executive order of president, 89
executive powers, 58–68
executive privilege and limitations, 58,
    68–71
ex post facto law, 171
extradition, 140–41

Fairfax's Devisee v. Hunter's Lessee,
    106
Fair Labor Standards Act, 10, 128, 157
fair trial, 268
faith-based initiatives, 208
Faubus, Orval, 113–14
Federal Boat Safety Act, 136
federal coastal license, 2
federal common law, 112–13
Federal Communications Commission,
    305–6
Federal Election Campaign Act of 1974,
    272
Federal Extradition Act, 140

federalism, 103, 125–60, 161
Federalists, 377
Federal Maritime Commission, 133
Federal Motor Carriers Act of 1935, 155
federal preemption, 134–37
Federal Sentencing Commission, 73
Federal Trade Commission, 64
Federal Trade Commission Act, 41
Feldman v. United States, 362
Field v. Clark, 22
Fifteenth Amendment, 178, 447–48
Fifth Amendment: double jeopardy and
    right of confrontation, 337, 339–42;
    due process clause, 93, 342–48;
    grand jury indictment, 337; self-
    incrimination and immunity, 204,
    360–65; takings clause, 192–96, 200
fighting words, 302
Filled Milk Act, 202
First Amendment: association,
    assembly, and petition, 249–58;
    establishment clause, 114–15, 118–
    19, 209–31; freedom of the press,
    259–71; freedom of speech, 272–
    314; free exercise clause, 232–46
First National Bank of Boston v.
    Bellotti, 277–78
flag burning, 299–300
Flag Protection Act, 300
flag salute, 249
Flast v. Cohen, 112
Fletcher v. Peck, 169
Ford, Gerald, 64, 69
Ford v. Wainwright, 366
foreign language, teaching of, 278–79
Forum for Academic and Institutional
    Rights, 258–59
44 Liquormart, Inc. v. Rhode Island,
    248, 280
Fourteenth Amendment, 131, 143, 178,
    395–444
Fourth Amendment, 313–24, 317–36
Frankfurter, Felix, 199
freedom of contract, 13, 177–92
Frothingham v. Mellon, 114

fruit of the poisonous tree, 328
fugitive slave, 109–10
Fullilove v. Klutznick, 419
fundamental fairness, 199, 204
Furman v. Georgia, 339, 367

gag orders, 248, 266–67
gambling, 364–65
garbage, searches of, 331–32
Garcetti v. Ceballas, 249
Garcia v. San Antonio Metropolitan
    Transportation Authority, 130,
    158–59
Garland, Ex parte, 75
gerrymandering, 446, 455–57
Gibson, John Bannister, 109
Gideon v. Wainwright, 357, 359
Gillette v. United States, 236
Gitlow v. New York, 199, 248
Goldman v. United States, 319
Goldwater v. Carter, 73
Gonzales v. Carhart, 378
good-faith exception, 327
Graham v. Richardson, 427
grandfather clauses, 446, 447–48
grand jury, 265–66, 337, 349
Gratz v. Bollinger, 423
Gravel v. United States, 1
Graves et al., Tax Commissioners v.
    New York ex rel. O'Keefe, 34
gravity of the evil test, 248
Griffin v. California, 204–5
Griggs v. Duke Power Co., 425
Griswold v. Connecticut, 247, 377, 390
Grovey v. Townsend, 449, 450
Grutter v. Bollinger, 421
guarantee clause, 111, 121
Guinn v. United States, 445
Gunecht v. United States, 237
Gun-Free School Zones Act of 1990,
    17–18
gun ownership, 313, 315–17

habeas corpus, 59–60, 85–86, 90, 94–
    97, 115–16

Habeas Corpus Act of 1679, 100
Habitual Criminal Act, 345
Hammer v. Dagenhart, 157
handbill distribution, 262
Harlan, John Marshall I, 199
Harmelin v. Michigan, 373
Harper v. Virginia Board of Elections, 460
Harris v. United States, 323
Hatch Act, 251
Hawaiian Organic Act, 90
Hawaii Housing Authority v. Midkiff, 170, 195
Hawaii Land Reform Act of 1967, 192–93
Hazelwood School District v. Kuhlmeier, 249, 309
head of government, 57–58
head of state, 57–58
Heart of Atlanta Motel v. United States, 404
Heath v. Alabama, 340
Hepburn v. Griswold, 35
Hirabayashi v. United States, 89
Hobbs Act, 347
Hollingsworth v. Virginia, 161
Home Building & Loan Association v. Blaisdell, 169, 176
homosexuals, 386, 390, 91, 441–42
hostile environment, 440
House Committee on Unamerican Activities, 29–31
House Judiciary Committee, 69
House of Representatives, 1
Housing and Rent Act of 1947, 90, 91
Hudgens v. National Labor Relations Board, 235
Hyde Amendment, 385

illegitimacy classifications, 442–43
Immigration and Nationality Act, 75
Immigration and Naturalization Service v. Chadha, 73, 77
imminent lawless action threat, 248, 294
Immunity Act, 360

immunity from civil suits, 69–71
impeachment, 123–24
implied powers, 28–31, 197
income tax, 35–36, 45–46
independent counsel, 78–79
Indian tribe, 128, 138–49
inevitable discovery, 314
Inflation Control Act of October 2, 1942, 25
informant, 325
information, indictment by, 338, 348–49
"In God We Trust," 298–99
inherent powers, 35, 61
intentional infliction of emotional distress, 271
intermediate scrutiny, 397, 418
Internal Security Act of 1950, 135
International Economic Powers Act, 66
interposition, 125
Interstate Commerce Commission, 8

Jackson, Andrew, 140
Japanese exclusion, 89
Jaworski, Leon, 68
Jefferson, Thomas, 105, 198, 207
Jehovah's Witnesses, 233–36, 295–96
Jim Crow laws, 397, 404–5
Johnson v. Eisentrager, 95–96, 98, 101
Jones v. Alfred H. Mayer Co., 408
Jones v. Opelika, 234
Jordan v. Massachusetts, 351
judicial branch, 103–24
judicial review, 104
Judiciary Act of 1789, 96, 105
Judiciary Act of 1801, 105
Julliard v. Greenman, 29
jurisdiction, 105–7
jury exemptions, 352–53
jury selection, 349–50, 352–54
jury size, 351–52
jury trial, 350–51
jus sanguinis, 426
jus soli, 426
just compensation clause, 170
justiciability, 104

Kastigar v. United States, 361
Katzenbach v. McClung, 17, 396
Katzenbach v. Morgan, 401
Katz v. United States, 314, 319, 322, 330
Keating-Owen Act, 9
Keller v. State Bar of California, 244
Kelo v. City of New London, 170
Kennedy v. Mendoza-Martinez, 147
Kentucky v. Dennison, 140–41
Klaas, Polly, 373
Knickerbocker Ice Co. v. Stewart, 23
Korematsu v. United States, 74
Ku Klux Klan, 60, 294, 302

*Lamb's Chapel v. Center Moriches
    Union Free School Dist.*, 227, 242
Landrum-Griffin Labor Act, 75
*Lassiter v. Northhampton County Board
    of Elections*, 398–99
Lawrence v. Texas, 378
Law School Admission Test (LSAT),
    423
Lee v. Weisman, 119, 225–26
Legal Tender Cases, 28–29
legislative branch, 1–56; privileges and
    terms of members, 51–55
legislative veto, 73, 76
Lehnert v. Ferris Faculty Assn., 244
Leisy v. Hardin, 4
Lemon Test, 208, 223
Lemon v. Kurtzman, 208, 220, 231, 299
lethal injection, 374–76
Lewinsky, Monica, 71
Lewis v. United States, 263–64
libel, 47–48, 365
liberty of contract, 170
licensing laws, 234, 250–51
Lincoln, Abraham, 74, 395
Line Item Veto Act, 79–80
Linmark Associates, Inc. v. Willingboro,
    279
literacy tests, 453
Lloyd Corporation v. Tanner, 235
Lochner v. New York, 130, 170, 182,
    388

Locke, John, 169
lotteries, 7–8, 107–8, 174–75
Low-Level Radioactive Waste Policy
    Amendments Act of 1985, 148–49
Lyng v. International Union, 188

Madison, James, 73, 105, 198
Magna Carta, 100
Maher v. Roe, 385
Malloy v. Hogan, 204
Mapp v. Ohio, 314, 321
Marbury v. Madison, 104, 109, 403
marriage, right of, 384–85
Marsh v. Chambers, 232
Marshall, John, 104, 157, 169, 174, 198
martial law, 86
Martin v. Hunter's Lessee, 108
Maryland v. Wirtz, 157
massive resistance, 411
Maternity Act of 1921, 111
Maxwell v. Dow, 351
McCarran Act, 16
*McConnell v. Federal Election
    Commission*, 273, 276
McCreary County v. ACLU, 208
McCulloch v. Maryland, 2, 26, 197
McIntyre v. Ohio Elections Commission,
    278
Medicaid, 385
Megan's Law, 148, 444
mental retardation: classification, 397,
    437–39; and death penalty, 371
Metro Broadcasting, Inc. v. FCC, 419
Meyer v. Nebraska, 377, 390
*Michael M. v. Superior Court of
    Sonoma County*, 432
migratory birds, 81–82
military commission, 84–86, 88–89
Military Selective Service Act, 93
militia, 58–59
Miller v. California, 238, 285, 289
Milligan, Ex parte, 74, 94
Minersville School District v. Gobitis,
    296
Minimum Wage Act of 1918, 184

minimum wages, 13–14, 156, 184
Minnesota Mortgage Moratorium Law, 175
minority business enterprises, 417–18
Miracle, The, 282
Miranda v. Arizona, 338, 359–60
miscegenation laws, 412
Missouri Compromise, 401–2
Missouri v. Holland, 25
Missouri v. Jenkins, 118
Mistretta v. United States, 73
moment of silence in school, 220–21
mootness, 105
Morehead v. New York ex rel. Tipaldo, 14
Morrison v. Olson, 73
movies, and First Amendment, 282
Mueller v. Allen, 223, 228
Mulford v. Smith, 42
Muller v. Oregon, 181
Mulloy v. United States, 237
Munn v. Illinois, 170, 181
Murphy v. Ford, 64
Murray v. Curlett, 214
Myers v. United States, 58

National Association for the Advancement of Colored People (NAACP), 152, 297
National Collegiate Athletic Association, 48–49
National Endowment for the Arts, 287
National Foundation on the Arts and Humanities Act of 1990, 287
National Industrial Recovery Act, 22–23, 23–24
National Labor Relations Act, 43, 48
National Labor Review Board v. Jones and Laughlin Steel Corp., 6
National League of Cities v. Usery, 159–60
National Minimum Drinking Age Amendment of 1984, 49–50
National Prohibition Act, 63, 165, 317, 339

Native American Church, 239–40
nativity scene, 298–99
Nazi saboteurs case, 88–89
Neagle, In re, 25, 58
Near v. Minnesota, 247
Nebraska Press Association v. Stuart, 248
necessary and proper clause, 2
neutrality toward religion, 207
Newberry v. United States, 449, 450
New Hampshire v. Maine, 142
New Jersey v. T.L.O., 314, 335
newspapers: criticisms of judges, 261–62; search of offices, 323–24
New London Development Corporation, 194
New York Milk Control Board, 185
New York State Club Association v. New York City, 254–55
New York Times Company v. United States, 247
New York Times v. Sullivan, 248
New York v. Belton, 335
New York v. Ferber, 289
New York v. United States, 151
Nineteenth Amendment, 446
Ninth Amendment, 91, 251, 377–93
Nixon, Richard, 68–70
Nixon v. Condon, 450
Nixon v. Fitzgerald, 58, 71
Nixon v. Herndon, 448, 450
Nix v. Williams, 314
Nollan v. California Coastal Commission, 194
Northern Securities, 41
nude dancing, 300–1
nullification, 125

obscenity, 248, 282–91
Occupational Safety and Health Act of 1970, 324–25
Oestereich v. Selective Service Board, 236
oleomargarine tax, 38
Olmstead v. United States, 314, 319

Omnibus Crime Control and Safe
　　Streets Act, 319
"One nation under God," 298
one person/one vote, 446
open forum, 218, 241–42
Oregon v. Mitchell, 162
original package doctrine, 4
Organized Crime Control Act of 1970,
　　18

Packers and Stockyards Act of 1921, 10
Palko v. Connecticut, 199
pandering, 284
paper money, 34–35
parade permits, 250
parade, right of association, 256
pardon power, 63–64
parliamentary system, 57
parochial schools: aid to, 214–15, 223,
　　228; bus transportation to, 209; deaf
　　interpreter in, 223; voucher programs
　　for, 228
parody of public figures, 271
patronage. *See* political party affiliation
Paul v. Davis, 444
Paul v. Virginia, 16
Pennsylvania Sedition Act, 135
Pentagon Papers, 265
penumbral rights, 381
peremptory challenges, 353
person, definition of, 383
petit jury, 338, 350, 351, 372
peyote, 239–40
pharmacy advertising, 279
physician-assisted suicide, 389
Pickering v. Board of Education,
　　310–11
picketing, 255–56
Pierce v. Society of Sisters, 377, 390
pilotage regulations, state, 4
*Planned Parenthood of Southeastern
　　Pennsylvania v. Casey*, 378, 391
plea bargaining, 345
pledge to the flag, 118

Plessy v. Ferguson, 388, 397, 406, 409,
　　410
political party affiliation, 252, 273–74
political questions, 77, 84, 105, 119–24,
　　162
Pollock v. Farmers' Loan & Trust Co.,
　　32, 162
poll taxes, 446
polygamy. *See* bigamy
*Posadas de Puerto Rico Associates v.
　　Tourism Co. of Puerto Rico*, 280,
　　281
Powell v. Alabama, 350
Powell v. McCormack, 1, 54, 77
prayer: at public school games, 225;
　　at public school graduations, 119,
　　222–23; in public schools, 212–13;
　　in state legislatures, 212–13, 219
presentment clause, 75, 79
presumption of innocence, 337
primary elections, 449–50
Prince v. Massachusetts, 216
prior restraint, 247, 260–61
privacy, right to, 247, 381, 383–84
privileges and immunities clause, 396
Prize Cases, The, 74
property rights, 169–96
Prudential Insurance Co. v. Benjamin, 16
Pruneyard Shopping Center v. Robins,
　　235
public facilities, religious use of, 226–27
public figure, 263–64, 267–68, 271–72
public schools: Bible reading in, 213;
　　prayer in, 212, 222, 225; religious
　　instruction in, 210
Public Works Employment Act, 417
punitive damages, 170, 189–91

qualifications clause (Article I), 146
quid pro quo, 440
Quirin, Ex parte, 92, 94, 97–98

Racketeer Influenced and Corrupt
　　Organization Act (RICO), 346
Rahrer, In re, 141

Rathbun, Humphrey's Executor v.
United States, 63, 75
rational basis review, 437, 440
R.A.V. v. City of St. Paul, 302–3
Reconstruction Acts of 1867, 60
Reed v. Reed, 433
Rehnquist, William, 124
released time programs, 211
reliance interests, 387–88
Religious Freedom Restoration Act,
244–46, 400–1
religious instruction public schools, 210
Religious Land Use and Institutionalized
Persons Act of 2000, 245
religious use of public facilities, 226–27
removal powers of president, 62, 64
Republican Party, 395
residency requirements, 453–55
restrictions of speech: time, place, and
manner, 303–11
restrictive covenants, 407–8
retribution function of punishment, 371
Reynolds v. Sims, 455
Reynolds v. United States, 208, 216
Ricci v. DeStefano, 397
Richmond v. J. A. Croson Co., 419, 424
right to counsel, 338, 354–60
right to die, 378
right to work, 187
Ring v. Arizona, 342
ripeness, 105
Roberts v. United States Jaycees, 254,
257
Robinson v. California, 366
Rochin v. California, 364
Roe v. Wade, 377, 382, 387
Romer v. Evans, 378
Roosevelt, Theodore, 37, 58
Roper v. Simmons, 369
*Rosenberger v. Rector and Visitors of
the University of Virginia*, 209, 227
Rostker v. Goldberg, 74
Roth test, 283–84
Roth v. United States, 283–84
Ruckelshaus v. Monsanto Co., 195

rule of four, 104
rule of reason, 40–41
Rummel v. Estelle, 373

sacrilegious speech, 282
safe harbor provision, 458–59
*Santa Clara County v. Southern Pacific
Railroad Co.*, 170
Santeria religion, 240–41
Schenck v. United States, 248
Schinck v. Reed, 64
Schneider v. State, 235
school attendance laws, 216, 379
School District of Grand Rapids v. Ball,
224
Scottsboro boys, 349–50
Scott v. Sandford, 106, 162, 395
searches, aerial, 336
search incident to arrest, 323, 333–35
Second Amendment, 151, 313, 315–17
Sedition Act of 1798, 264
selective exclusiveness doctrine, 5
selective incorporation, 199, 201–2, 396
selective incorporation plus, 199
selective service, 86–87
self-incrimination, 338, 360–65
Seminole Tribe v. Florida, 128, 130
Senate, 1
Seneca Falls Convention, 446
Sentencing Commission, 26–27
Sentencing Reform Act of 1984, 26–27
"separate but equal," 405, 406, 409, 410
separation of church and state. *See* wall
of separation
separation of powers, 27, 70, 73, 74–80
Seventeenth Amendment, 126
sexual classifications, 432–36
sexual harassment, 132, 439–49
Shaw v. Reno, 457
Sherbert v. Verner, 208, 239, 244, 400
Sherman Anti-Trust Act, 5–6, 15, 40
Sherman, Roger, 198
shield laws, 266
*Silverthorne Lumber Co. v. United
States*, 328

Sirica, John J., 68
Sixteenth Amendment, 36, 162, 170
Sixth Amendment, 116, 266
Skinner v. Oklahoma, 381
Slaughterhouse Cases, 170, 381, 396–97
Smith Act of 1940, 292
Smith v. Allwright, 449
Smith v. Maryland, 331
Social Security Act, 42, 385
Social Security taxes, 216, 237
sodomy, 386–87, 390–91
"soft money" contributions, 273
Solem v. Helm, 373
sound trucks, 303–4
South Carolina Exposition and Protest, 126
sovereign immunity, state, 126–34
special prosecutor, 73
speech: commercial, 279–81; student, 297, 307–9; symbolic, 295–302
speech and debate clause, 52
speedy trial, 338
spending clause, 49–50
Splawn v. California, 284
Springer v. United States, 36
standing, 80, 104, 118–19
Stanford v. Kentucky, 369
stare decisis, 387–88
state action, 413–14
state boundary lines, 142–43
state capitals, 154
State Farm Insurance v. Campbell, 170
state pilotage laws, 4–5
state police powers, 156–60
statutory rape laws, 434
steamboat monopoly, 2–3
sterilization, compulsory, 380–81
Stone, Harlan Fiske, 2, 199, 203
Stone v. Graham, 214, 229–31
stop and frisk, 314, 322–23
Strader v. Graham, 403
Strauder v. West Virginia, 353
stream of commerce, 11
strict scrutiny, 419, 437, 457

student activity fees, 241–43, 243–44
student searches, 329–30, 332–33, 335–36
student speech, 196–98, 307–10
subpoena *duces tecum*, 68
substantive due process, 170, 338
subversive speech, 291–95
sugar refining monopoly, 5–6
Sumner v. Shuman, 366
supremacy clause, 47
surveillance, electronic, 317–19
suspect category, 415, 434, 432
Suspension Clause, 95, 100, 107, 109
Swain v. Alabama, 353–54
Sweatt v. Painter, 409
Swift v. Tyson, 113
"switch in time that saved nine," 170, 186
symbolic speech, 295–303

Taft-Hartley Act, 66, 292
"take title" provision, 148–49
takings clause, 170, 192–96
Taney, Roger, 169, 174
tariffs, 21
tax: on carriages, 31–32; liquor, 38–39; newspapers, 261
taxes, spending and regulatory powers, 31–51
televising trials, 270–71
Ten Commandments: monument to, 229–30; posting of, 214, 217, 230–32
Tennessee Valley Authority, 11–12
Tenth Amendment, 45, 47, 87, 91, 126, 146, 149, 156–60, 251
Tenure of Office Act, 62
term limits, congressional, 53–54
Texas v. Johnson, 248
Texas v. White, 126
Third Amendment, 313
Thirteenth Amendment, 87, 178, 395
three-fifths clause, 1
three-strikes-and-you're-out laws, 339, 373
Tilton v. Richardson, 215

time, place, and manner restrictions on
speech, 303–11
Tinker v. Des Moines, 249, 307, 309
tort remedies, 348
total incorporation, 199, 349
total incorporation plus, 199
Trail of Tears, 140
transactional immunity, 361
treaties and executive agreements,
80–84
trimesters, 384
Truman, Harry S., 74
Tumey v. Ohio, 347
Twelfth Amendment, 445
Twenty-first Amendment, 49–50, 155,
161, 281–82
Twenty-fourth Amendment, 446
Twenty-second Amendment, 57
Twenty-seventh Amendment, 162, 198
Twenty-sixth Amendment, 162, 446,
454
Twenty-third Amendment, 445
Twining v. New Jersey, 205, 363

Uniform Code of Military Justice, 97
unitary executive, 95
unitary government, 125
*United Jewish Organizations of
Williamsburgh, Inc. v. Carey*, 456
*United States Steel Corp. v. Multistate
Tax Commission*, 143
*United States Trust Company v. New
Jersey*, 169, 175
United States v. Brown, 75
United States v. Calandra, 327
United States v. Carolene Products, 199
United States v. Classic, 407, 450
*United States v. Curtiss-Wright Export
Corp.*, 23
United States v. Darby Lumber Co., 6,
10, 126
United States v. Eichman, 300
United States v. Grace, 256
United States v. Kahriger, 365
United States v. Lee, 216

United States v. Leon, 18, 20, 152, 313
United States v. Lopez, 18, 20, 152, 313
United States v. Macintosh, 428
United States v. Miller, 316
United States v. Morrison, 20
United States v. Nixon, 58
United States v. O'Brien, 259, 301
United States v. Rabinowitz, 323
United States v. Schwimmer, 428
United States v. Seeger, 236
*United States v. United States District
Court*, 319
United States v. Virginia, 423
unreasonable searches and seizures,
313–14
Unruh Act, 254
Urgent Deficiency Appropriation Act,
74
U.S. Courts of Appeal, 103
U.S. District Courts, 104
use immunity, 361
U.S. Supreme Court, 103
U.S. Term Limits, Inc. v. Thornton, 1, 146

Vacco v. Quill, 378, 390
Van Orden v. Perry, 208
Veronia School District 47J v. Acton,
333
victim impact statements, 370–71
Vietnam War, 297
*Village of Euclid, Ohio v. Ambler Realty
Co.*, 306
Violence Against Women Act of 1994,
151
Virginia and Kentucky Resolutions, 125
*Virginia Board of Pharmacy v. Virginia
Citizens Consumer Council, Inc.*, 281
Virginia v. Black, 249
Volstead Act, 163–64
vote: right to, 445–62
Voter ID Law, 460
Voting Rights Act Amendments of
1970, 453–54
Voting Rights Act of 1964, 398–400,
456, 461–62

voucher programs for parochial schools, 228–29

Wallace v. Jaffree, 231
wall of separation between church and state, 207, 210
Walton v. Arizona, 372
Walz v. Tax Commission, 215
war-making powers, 84–102
War Powers Resolution of 1973, 25, 74
War-Time Prohibition Act, 87
Washington v. Glucksburg, 378
Watergate break-in, 68–69
Watkins v. United States, 31
wealth classifications, 397, 437
Webb-Kenyon Act, 13
Webster, Daniel, 3, 173
Weeks v. United States, 314
welfare eligibility, 382
West Coast Hotel v. Parrish, 185–86
West Virginia Board of Education v. Barnette, 220, 249
Whitney v. California, 294
Wickard v. Filburn, 19–20
Widmar v. Vincent, 214
Wiener v. United States, 63
Williams, Roger, 207, 210

Williams v. Florida, 351
Wilson Act, 141
Winston v. Lee, 364
Winthrop, William, Col., 98–99
"with all deliberate speed," 410
Withrow v. Williams, 116
Witters v. Washington Dept. of Services for the Blind, 223, 225, 228
wobblers, 374
Wolf v. Colorado, 321
Woodson v. North Carolina, 367
workplace speech, 310–11
writ of certiorari, 104
writ of habeas corpus. *See* habeas corpus
writ of mandamus, 105
writs of assistance, 314

Yamashita, In re, 92
Yick Wo v. Hopkins, 427
Youngstown Sheet and Tube Co. v. Sawyer, 25, 71

Zobrest v. Catalina Foothills School District, 224, 228
zoning, 192
Zorach v. Clausen, 211

ABOUT THE AUTHOR

John R. Vile is a professor of political science and dean of the University Honors College at Middle Tennessee State University. He is the author and editor of numerous books on political science and constitutional law including *A Companion to the United States Constitution and Its Amendments*, 5th ed.; *Constitutional Law in Contemporary America*; *The Encyclopedia of Constitutional Amendments, Proposed Amendments, and Amending Issues*, 3rd ed.; *The Encyclopedia of the First Amendment*; *The Constitutional Convention of 1787: A Comprehensive Encyclopedia of America's Founding*; *Great American Lawyers*; *Great American Judges*, and other works.